Y0-BQX-242

Huck Finn among the Critics:

A Centennial Selection

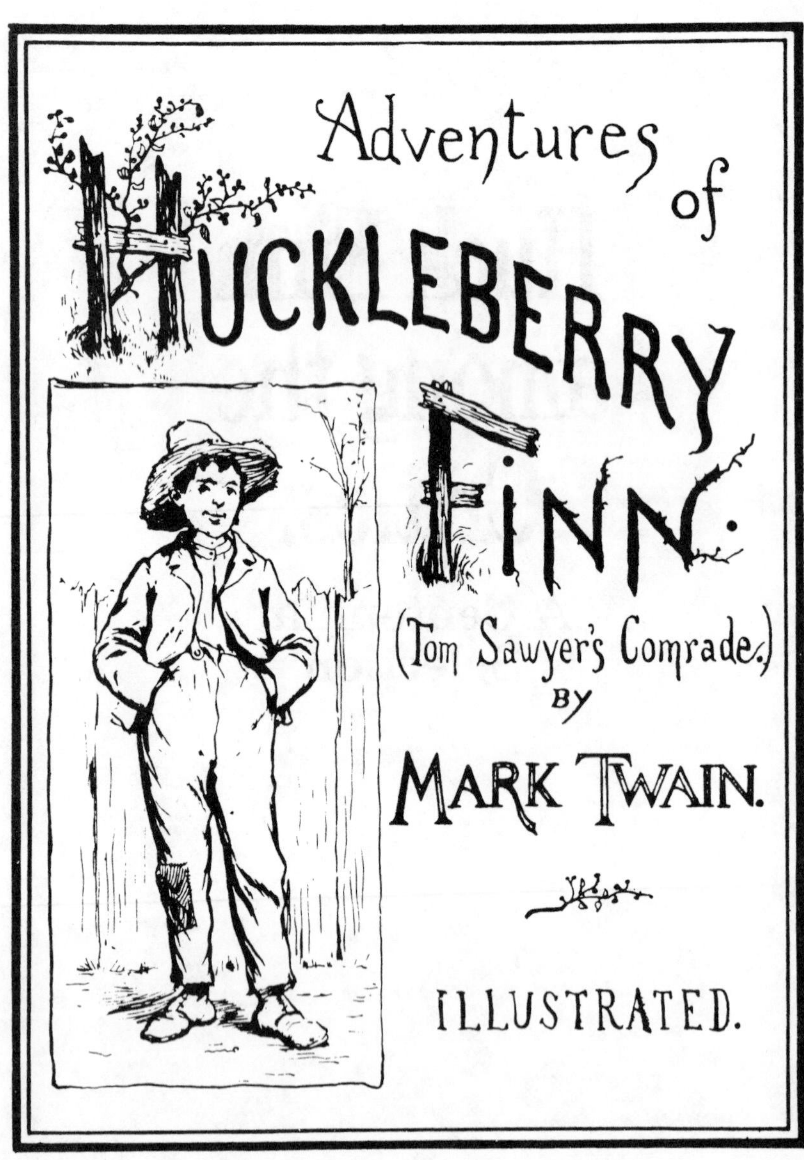

Cover of the first American edition of *Adventures of Huckleberry Finn*, 1885.

Huck Finn among the Critics:

A Centennial Selection

Edited by
M. Thomas Inge

UNIVERSITY PUBLICATIONS OF AMERICA
Frederick, Maryland

University Publications of America, Inc.
44 North Market Street, Frederick, Maryland 21701

Library of Congress Cataloging-in-Publication Data
Main entry under title:

Huck Finn among the critics.

Bibliography: p.
1. Twain, Mark, 1837-1910. Adventures of Huckleberry Finn—Addresses, essays, lectures. I. Inge, M. Thomas.
PS1305.H83 1985 813'.4 85-17776
ISBN 0-89093-747-8
ISBN 0-89093-746-X (pbk.)

Printed in the United States of America

Contents

Appendix

Introduction

Among those novels which would qualify as contenders for the title of the "Great American Novel," surely *Adventures of Huckleberry Finn* by Mark Twain, or Samuel L. Clemens, would be a strong candidate. It is probably the most frequently printed, widely translated, and commonly read novel in American literary history, and Huck himself has passed into folk-knowledge and stands as a living literary legend alongside such universal figures as Falstaff, Hamlet, and Don Quixote. There must be few corners of the world where he is not known.

What is to account for his enviable position? What led Ernest Hemingway in *Green Hills of Africa* (1935) to make his often quoted but seldom explained statement, "All modern American literature comes from one book by Mark Twain called *Huckleberry Finn* ... it's the best book we've had. All American writing comes from that. There was nothing before. There has been nothing as good since"? While Hemingway was engaged in hyperbole to a certain extent, it is true that *Adventures of Huckleberry Finn* stands at the very center of the development of a distinctively American and modern literature.

By allowing an uneducated fourteen-year-old boy to tell his own story in his own language, more directly attuned to the reality of American life than any author before him had dared, Samuel Clemens created an appropriate symbol for the new nation, then a little over one hundred years old, in all its roughness, crudity, and moral uncertainty. Huck's language is purely American in a way no previous author had written it for the printed page; Clemens thereby set aside British English as the only appropriate idiom for serious literature. Henry James had experimented with point of view in his novels, but no one had allowed a character of Huck's station in life to serve as both the central character and consciousness for a novel. In addressing the problems of freedom vs. social responsibility, public character and private vice, and the institutionalization of racism, Clemens was dealing with what would prove to be the central social and political conflicts of twentieth century America.

Without Huckleberry Finn's example, it could be argued, there might have been no Henry Fleming for Stephen Crane, no George Willard for Sherwood Anderson, no Nick Adams for

Hemingway, no Ike McCaslin for William Faulkner, no Eugene Gant for Thomas Wolfe, no Nick Carraway for F. Scott Fitzgerald, no Studs Lonigan for James T. Farrell, no Holden Caulfield for J.D. Salinger, or no Augie March for Saul Bellow—all of whom share in the tradition established by Clemens. If that is to claim too much, at least one can say it would have been more difficult for these adolescent explorers of the nature of American society to have come into being without Huck's precedence. Drawing on the figure of the young picaro in world literature, Clemens thoroughly modernized and Americanized him for effective artistic use in the twentieth century. Thus what Hemingway may have been suggesting was that in language, style, structure, and themes, American literature has not been the same since *Adventures of Huckleberry Finn.*

Yet this same novel, so highly influential and much admired by writer and reader alike, has been one of the most controversial and frequently banned books of American literature. Controversy and censure accompanied its birth. The first British edition appeared on December 10, 1884, and the first American edition on February 18, 1885. Within a month of its American appearance, the Public Library Committee of Concord, Massachusetts, met and decided to ban it from their shelves. The decision was reported in the pages of the Boston *Transcript* for March 17, 1885, as follows:

> The Concord (Mass.) Public Library Committee has decided to exclude Mark Twain's latest book from the library. One member of the committee says that, while he does not wish to call it immoral, he thinks it contains but little humor, and that of a very coarse type. He regards it as the veriest trash. The librarian and the other members of the committee entertain similar views, characterizing it as rough, coarse and inelegant, dealing with a series of experiences not elevating, the whole book being more suited to the slums than to intelligent, respectable people.

A few days later, the Springfield *Republican* came to the support of the committee's action in an editorial:

> The Concord public library committee deserves well of the public by their action in banishing Mark Twain's new book, 'Huckleberry Finn,' on the ground that it is trashy and vicious. It is time that this influential pseudonym should cease to carry into homes and libraries unworthy productions. Mr. Clemens is a genuine and powerful humorist, with a bitter vein of satire on the weaknesses of humanity which is sometimes wholesome, sometimes only grotesque, but in

> certain of his works degenerates into a gross trifling with every fine feeling. The trouble with Mr. Clemens is that he has no reliable sense of propriety. His notorious speech at an *Atlantic* dinner, marshalling Longfellow and Emerson and Whittier in vulgar parodies in a Western miner's cabin, illustrated this, but not in much more relief than the 'Adventures of Tom Sawyer' did, or these Huckleberry Finn stories, do....They are no better in tone than the dime novels which flood the blood-and-thunder reading population. Mr. Clemens has made them smarter, for he has an inexhaustible fund of 'quips and cranks and wanton wiles,' and his literary skill is, of course, superior: but their moral level is low, and their perusal cannot be anything less than harmful.

Louisa May Alcott, author of *Little Women* and prominent citizen of Concord, added her curt opinion: "If Mr. Clemens cannot think of something better to tell our pure-minded lads and lassies, he had best stop writing for them."

The situation was soon compounded by what was for Clemens a delicious irony when the Free Trade Club of the very same community of Concord offered him honorary membership. He could not resist writing a satirical letter of acceptance in which he noted:

> It does look as if Massachusetts were in a fair way to embarrass me with kindnesses this year....a committee of the public library of your town has condemned and excommunicated my last book, and doubled its sale. This generous action of theirs must necessarily benefit me in one of two additional ways. For instance, it will deter other libraries from buying the book; and you are doubtless aware that one book in a public library prevents the sale of a sure ten and a possible hundred of its mates. And secondly it will cause the purchasers of the book to read it, out of curiosity, instead of merely intending to do so after the usual way of the world and library committees; and then they will discover, to my great advantage and their own indignant disappointment, that there is nothing objectionable in the book, after all.

This was but a forewarning of what the novel was to experience throughout its later life. Hardly a year has gone by without some public library, elementary school, or state textbook committee either rejecting the book, restricting its availability, or requiring that passages be deleted in revised texts. Usually this has been done on the basis of perceived racism, antisocial attitudes, or its being a corrupting influence on young readers. To the sensitive reader, such charges are amazing, because the novel remains in American culture one of the works most challenging to racial bigotry, social and political hypocrisy, and moral compromise. There is an integrity at the heart of the novel that cannot help but touch the reader, and if any work of art has the power to exert a positive influence, then surely this one does.

If *Adventures of Huckleberry Finn* has been a center of social and political controversy, it has also been the subject of considerable critical debate. The majority of contemporary reviewers and later commentators on Mark Twain found the novel praiseworthy—among them William Dean Howells; Professors Brander Matthews of Columbia University, Barrett Wendell of Harvard, and William Lyon Phelps of Yale; Andrew Lang and Robert Louis Stevenson of Scotland; Sir Walter Besant and V. S. Pritchett of England. This praise reached a particularly high pitch in 1913 when H. L. Mencken, who usually found more to debunk in American culture than to praise, announced, "I believe that 'Huckleberry Finn' is one of the great masterpieces of the world, that it is the full equal of 'Don Quixote'," and went on to note that it would be read by generation after generation for the sheer love of it, long after most books written in America before it had disappeared.

Then in the late 1940s and early 1950s, a critical argument began when two distinguished critics, Lionel Trilling and T. S. Eliot, both stated their admiration for the novel but also felt obliged to defend the ending. Once Sawyer reentered the narrative and Huck fell under his influence, Huck seemed to forget the moral crisis he had undergone in deciding not to turn Jim in to the authorities, and he allows his new found fellow human being and friend to undergo an elaborate and demeaning game for the sake of frivolous high adventure and romantic play. The presumed flaw had been seen from the start when Thomas Sergeant Perry, reviewing the novel for the May 1885 issue of *Century Magazine*, found this portion "somewhat forced" and out of place in the book. But now nearly every major critic of American literature felt compelled to enter the fray, some finding the ending simply "cheating" as Hemingway put it, and others finding all sorts of thematic, symbolic, and structural patterns to prove the ending inevitable and irreplaceable. The most extreme response was John Seelye's spoof on the whole debate, *The True Adventures of Huckleberry Finn* (1970), a rewriting of the novel to give the critics the version they wanted, in which Huck observes, "And now that they've got *their* book, maybe they'll leave the other one alone." Not likely. The issue is far from settled at the centennial of the book's publication and the debate is likely to continue.

Like many another complex work of literature, there is no single critical approach or method which will yield a definitive analysis of the book's flaws and virtues.

Clemens once said that "a classic is something that everybody wants to have read and nobody wants to read." His own classic, *Adventures of Huckleberry Finn*, puts the lie to this piece of sarcasm, but then this was the same man who wrote in its preface, "Persons attempting to find a motive in this narrative will be prosecuted; persons attempting to find a moral in it will be banished; persons attempting to find a plot in it will be shot."

Critics can't be scared off that easily, particularly by a work so fully in possession of all three characteristics. In a presentation copy of the novel, Clemens wrote, "This is Huck Finn, a child of mine of shady reputation. Be good to him for his parent's sake." Posterity has clearly taken this more sober advice quite seriously.

The present anthology is intended as a tribute to *Adventures of Huckleberry Finn* on the occasion of its centennial. It contains criticism covering the entire span of its lively existence, from early impressionistic reviews and commentary, through the great debate of the mid-twentieth century, down to the present decade. The principles of selection in all cases have been originality of thought and usefulness in gaining new appreciations for the novel, although not every essay with these virtues could be reprinted. Also included are background essays on Mark Twain as a representative American figure and the composition of the novel, and in an appendix discussions of the illustrations for the first edition and the various film adaptations. An annotated checklist of criticism concludes the volume. The whole is meant to serve as an overview of the critical past and a prelude to another hundred years of commentary to come.

M. Thomas Inge
Randolph-Macon College

BACKGROUNDS

Map of the area covered in the novel, drawn by Charles Dibner, *Tom Sawyer and Huckleberry Finn*, 1943. "Everyman's Library." *Courtesy Elsevier-Dutton Publishing Co., Inc.*

Mark Twain and His Times

Arthur G. Pettit

From the vantage point of history, it is easy to discredit Mark Twain's boast that he was the representative man. He was an American original; the country had never seen the like, and doubtless never will again. Yet for all his peculiarities, Mark Twain's self-promotion as the representative American had to be based on a solid list of biographical credentials. Eccentricity and genius were not enough. To qualify as the country's mouthpiece, he had to experience, personally and vividly, the main historical events of his time. He did so in a manner equalled by few of his countrymen and surpassed by none. In part through sheer luck in happening to be in the right place at the right time, in part through shrewd talent in stage-managing his public and private affairs, Mark Twain touched on more celebrated episodes in his country's history than any famous American rival. The list of his personal experiences reads like a table of contents for a textbook in nineteenth-century American history: Slavery in the Border South; Life on the Mississippi; The House Divided; The Civil War; The Frontier West; Reconstruction; The American Innocent Abroad; The Industrial Revolution; The Politics of Business; The Gilded Age. His biographical claim to the title of Representative American began with his birth and childhood in the border South and ended with his "conversion" and death as a Connecticut Yankee. Born to a poor but proud slaveholding family in bor-

From: "Mark Twain and His Times: A Bicentennial Appreciation." *South Atlantic Quarterly*, 76:2 (Spring 1977), 133–46. Reprinted with permission.

der Missouri, young Sam Clemens was raised on the notion that he was a half-southern aristocrat and a half-midwestern democrat. His mother, Jane Lampton Clemens, was a fiery Kentuckian who boasted a wondrously exiguous connection to English feudal lords and Virginia slaveowners, but her corncob-puffing style made her more at home in Hannibal, Missouri, than she would have been in the drawing rooms of Savannah or Charleston. Clemens's father, John Marshall Clemens, was a poverty-stricken storeowner who considered himself an authentic throwback to the ethos of a previous generation—a leftover Whig stranded in the backwater of Missouri who sought to improve his status by owning a few black "household servants." Mark Twain remembered as a boy watching his father "cuff" a slave boy named Lewis who became the model for Aunt Polly's "small colored boy" Jim in *Tom Sawyer*, and flog an "uppity nigger wench" named Jenny who became the model for the rebellious slave woman Roxana in *Pudd'nhead Wilson*. At age nine, standing on Hannibal's main street, Sam Clemens watched an overseer crush a slave's skull with a piece of iron ore. Two years later, while rowing around the foot of the island in the Mississippi that became Jackson's Island in *Tom Sawyer* and *Huckleberry Finn*, he happened upon a black corpse, disembowelled and sunk in the river by slavehunters. When he was fourteen, a slave who was accused of raping a white woman was lynched on the outskirts of Hannibal, before one of the largest crowds ever assembled for a social function in that part of Missouri.

If these boyhood memories of slavery provided Mark Twain with nightmares that lasted a lifetime, they also echoed the memories of a good many Americans raised in the antebellum South. Indeed, to trace Mark Twain's shifting views of slavery, blacks, and race relations over fifty years of writing and lecturing is to plot the evolving attitudes and opinions of a good many Americans, North and South, in the half-century after slavery. We have Sam Clemens's word for it that as a southern teenager he accepted the South's peculiar institution without moral reservations. Later, during his steamboating years on the Mississippi, he favored secession; and when the lower South left the Union, so did Clemens, serving briefly in a Confederate guerilla unit. Through the 1850's and into the 1860's, he ranted against "niggers" and told a long series of popular jokes about "nigger odor," fried "nigger" steaks, black sexual promiscuity, and the evils of miscegenation. Yet from the 1880's to his death, he befriended Frederick Douglass and Booker T. Washington, financed several black students through Yale Law School, wrote blistering essays about atrocities committed against blacks, and created two of the outstanding black characters in American literature: Nigger Jim and Roxana. As a native southerner, Mark Twain began his public career as a segregationist and Negrophobe. As a self-professed "reconstructed" Yankee, he turned himself into a champion of interracial brotherhood in *Huckleberry Finn* and ended his life as a prophet of racial war and the complete extermination of black and white alike.

These experiences as a native southerner, however "reconstructed," placed Mark Twain in the ranks of a sizable minority of Americans. His five and a half years in the Far West, however, greatly enlarged his qualifications as a national rather than a regional spokesman. At a time when Horace Greeley was advising young men to go West, Clemens deserted the Confederacy and travelled to Nevada and California, where his experiences as a miner and a journalist established his early reputation in the East as a wild and wooly westerner, and added "The Jumping Frog of Calaveras County" and *Roughing It* to the list of imperishable tall tales about the Far West. Coming east in 1866 on the laurels of the jumping frog, Mark Twain signed up for the Gilded Age's first elitist charter tour of Europe and the Holy Land. Posing as the Innocent Abroad, he told the folks back home what they wanted to hear: Lake Como was smaller than lake Tahoe; the storied Danube was dirty and lacked the size and charm of the muddy Mississippi; and the Great Masters of Italian art were better off dead. More than any travel book of the age, *The Innocents Abroad; or, The New Pilgrim's Progress,* is an implicit commentary on, and an unmistakable product of, nineteenth-century America.

It was as a spokesman for the Gilded Age that Mark Twain finally transcended his reputation as a native southerner, a sometime westerner, and an adopted Yankee to become the country's foremost national man—a legend in his lifetime, a protagonist of the American experience who was expected to record, and to reflect, certain widely held opinions of his time. Setting out to be both participant and critic in that gilded age that bears the title he gave it, he was pulled in so many directions at once by his enormous energies and diffuse interests that he became, curiously, the country's "united" man only by experiencing the most profound and disquieting sense of personal and philosophical disunity. Part of the problem was brought on by his sudden rise to fame and fortune. Between 1867 and 1874 he married into eastern respectability and a quarter-million dollars, built a lavish mansion in Hartford, Connecticut, and rose spectacularly in financial, social, and literary status—altogether an intoxicating experience that left Mark Twain himself a little giddy, and more than a little uncertain about his permanent status. Though probably the most colorful and conspicuous American of his time, he felt the need to search out a long list of politicians, tycoons, ministers, and men of letters to admire, emulate, or pit himself against: Ulysses S. Grant, Theodore Roosevelt, steel magnate Andrew Carnegie, Standard Oil mogul Henry H. Rogers, clergymen Henry Ward Beecher and Joseph Twichell, Bret Harte, George Washington Cable, William Dean Howells. A man of many faces who never achieved a unified personality, Mark Twain was a great tangle of tensions and dualities. The most vain of men, he acknowledged his vanity with a childlike innocence that became a vital part of his appeal. A self-dramatized misanthrope who ranted tirelessly against the damned human race, he loved a few people with an intensity that was downright discomfiting. A master of invective who spewed forth a great stream of venom and kept a "Hate List" for years which recorded enemies as "eunuchs," "missing links," and "sexless tapeworms," he followed up many of his public and private scurrilities with deep remorse and prolonged self-flagellation. Proud of his reputation as a liar, he was probably the most completely honest man of his time and was surely his own most severe critic, censor, and tormentor.

Much of Mark Twain's charm—and much of his personal agony—was based on the fact that he could be counted upon to support and oppose, attack and defend almost every conceivable subject of his day—and reverse himself within the fortnight. His boast that he was "the whole human race compacted and crammed into a single suit of clothes"—a man housing in his person "every quality and every defect that is findable in the mass of the race"—was not intended altogether as a joke. No man of his time zigzagged more widely across the full spectrum of what foreign critics flattered themselves to be distinctly "American" traits of character. If we are to measure Mark Twain's full importance to his times, we must play his life and personality against the backdrop of the mind and mood of nineteenth-century America. Foreign observers had long charged that Americans were the least philosophical of all people, that they were bothered by theories and speculations, and that they listened to their foremost philosopher, Ralph Waldo Emerson, only when Emerson stopped prattling about the Soul, the Ego, and the "spermatic man" and started talking common sense. That most Americans failed to understand Emerson most of the time disturbed them not at all; the fault, they suspected, was Emerson's and not theirs, and they may have been right. No philosophy that got much beyond common sense commanded the American's interest for long, and he ruthlessly transformed even the most abstract metaphysics into practical ethics. His favorite native philosophies and religions—instrumentalism and pragmatism, Mormonism and Christian Science—were "practical" in theory and in application. And so too with Mark Twain, who detested theories, worshipped "facts," ignored Emerson, and dabbled for years in pragmatism and Christian Science. As a self-acknowledged "philosopher" of sorts, he held protean opinions that offered a little something for everyone. Fancying himself a level-headed thinker in the tradition of Franklin and Jefferson, he usually relied on snap judgments, to be abandoned later if they didn't hold up under criticism or if the initial enthusiasm wore off. Fascinated by pragmatic logic in the mode of William James, he reached most conclusions by impulse, argued in support of self-evident propositions, and showed little patience for sustained inquiry. Untroubled by inconsistencies, he was alternately a determinist or a nondeterminist, a realist or an idealist, a pessimist or an optimist, an eccentric or a conformist, a hard-boiled pragmatist or a starry-eyed romantic. Like those of many of his countrymen, his philosophical sympathies and personal affections oscillated between Europe and America, East and West, North and South, the past and the present, aristocracy and democracy, solitude and society, indolence and industry, the intellect and the heart, dream as reality and reality as dream.

Nowhere was Mark Twain's boast that he housed "every quality and every defect" of the race more embarrassingly accurate than in his energetic participation in the rush and clatter, the chink and heft of Gilded Age moneymaking. Nothing in all history had succeeded like late nineteenth-century America, and Mark Twain joined his countrymen in celebrating the fact. Nowhere on the globe had nature been at once so generous and so hospitable, and her unbounded riches were available to all who had the enterprise to take them and the good fortune to be white. The self-made man was still the hero in Gilded Age America, as he had been in Jacksonian America, and by "made" most Americans meant enriched rather than cultivated or educated. Foreign critics who thought this vulgar had little conception of its connection with the realities of American life. Long accustomed to watching even their most visionary blueprints for expansion outstripped by reality, nineteenth-century Americans showed a collective passion for facts and figures to measure and quantify their country's astounding progress: farm acreage, population statistics, stock market averages, wheat and corn production records, tons of steel, bales of cotton, miles of railroads. Long accustomed to watching their temporary economic setbacks resolved by practical ingenuity, they showed a high regard for technology and for mechanical inventions: the cotton gin, steamboat, harvester, steel-tipped plow, Westinghouse brake, McCormick reaper, hydraulic steam-drill, vulcanized rubber, the telegraph and telephone.

And so too with Mark Twain, the prototypical self-made tinkerer of the Gilded Age. As entrepreneur, impresario, inventor, speculator, and publisher, busily pouring thousands of dollars into schemes and squabbles of all sorts, he was his own Colonel Beriah Sellers, the hapless booster who boasts and bribes his way through the best-selling expose of the era, *The Gilded Age*. The central dilemma of Mark Twain's career as a businessman was that his distress with the era he named and satirized was proportionate to his complicity in it. Like several prominent Americans of the time, he was not entirely pleased with the direction the country was taking: men as philosophically incompatible as Henry Adams, Henry George, Henry James, Carl Schurz, Clarence Darrow, Eugene Debs, Edwin Godkin, and George Curtis decried the materialist cast and financial distemper of the times. The Gilded Age had its prophets of pessimism as well as its preachers of progress—and no man served both camps more feverishly than Mark Twain. Out of patience with the moneymaking phobia of the times, he nonetheless enthusiastically embraced the "sivilization" that Huck Finn lit out from. Given to ranting over Rockefeller's oil monopoly, Carnegie's steel empire, and Vanderbilt's crooked railroads, he tried for thirty years to become a millionaire monopolist himself. Deeply distraught over the shady business ethics of the Gilded Age, he considered several questionable enterprises, including fire extinguishers that worked like hand grenades and a concoction of kerosene and cheap perfume to be marketed as a cure for "Chilblains." Infuriated over the speculative madness of the Era of Get Rich Quick, he invested in an engraving company, a publishing company, an insurance house, a watch factory, a carpet manufacturing firm, a health food called Plasmon, a diaper agency, a scissors manufacturing firm, and the Paige typesetter that bankrupted him. Fascinated by gadgets of all sorts, he was one of the first writers to use (and discard) a newfangled typewriter and a dictating machine, and one of the first Americans to install (and grow to despise) a telephone in his home. Fond of recalling Huck Finn's simple existence on raft and river, he personally had more in common with another character of his creation: Hank Morgan, the showy mechanic of *A Connecticut Yankee in King Arthur's Court* who coins the term, the "New Deal," to characterize his career as developer of machines and attitudes that bring progress and destruction to Arthurian England. To the end of his life, Mark Twain remained torn between the niceties of his wealthy existence and a nostalgic fondness for prewar, agrarian America. He had lofty conceptions about the simple life but no gift for living it.

In matters of education and refinement, no less than philosophy and business, Mark Twain took on the air of a comon cultural property of the country who was expected to act out certain national mannerisms and cultural prejudices. Much of his charisma was based on the same combination of personal eccentricities and folksy mannerisms which made up the appeal of several of the country's second-generation heroes. When Americans heard that Andrew Jackson had spelled poorly and smoked a corncob pipe, or that Lincoln was largely self-educated and told earthy jokes, or that Grant issued monosyllabic war memos and chewed his cigars to shreds, they took these gestures as self-reflecting symbols of democracy in action. And so when Mark Twain, the drawling, corncob-puffing humorist, mussed his hair before a photograph, or played upon his humble origins and lack of education, he was perfecting a plain-folks image that—for all his private flirtings with royalty and aristocracy—placed him squarely in the social mainstream of nineteenth-century America. And when he confessed that he had trouble with "high" culture, he earned the enduring affection of his countrymen. European critics had long criticized Americans for practicing cultural chauvinism; that is, for enjoying Robert Browning, Stephen Foster, and Currier and Ives while pretending to fancy the Continental poets, the Great Masters, and the compositions of Old World musicians long dead. Mark Twain, echoing his country's split-level mood, began his cultural "career" as a brassy young Innocent Abroad who preferred the "shiny" reproductions of famous Old World paintings to the originals and declared that he was glad the Great Masters were no longer alive to make mischief. Later, as a member in precarious standing of the eastern establishment, he faithfully made Old World pilgrimages to moldy cathedrals and dank museums, and he tried for years to listen to opera without visible signs of agony. Finally, with a string of undeleted expletives, he gave it all up, echoing the sentiments of a good many Americans when he confided that he preferred Browning to Shakespeare, "nigger" minstrels to opera, and no art at all to "high" art. But perhaps the most revealing glimpse into Mark Twain's bifocal view of the culture of the Gilded Age is the half-respectable, half-heretical mansion he built outside Hartford, Connecticut, in 1874. For all his grumbling about the garishness of the Gilded Age, Mark Twain's gaudy, polychrome-gingerbread "castle" at Nook Farm is a classic of the era—a bewildering mixture of traditional decor and outlandish trimmings. Old World furniture and Oriental rugs co-habit with a tropical indoor garden and a bright red bedroom. Delicate outdoor towers and turrets clash with a forest of chimneys which, for a brief time, were strapped with lightning rods that gave a dazzling pyrotechnic display during summer thunderstorms—a sis-boom-bah sideshow that might have made Tom Sawyer green with envy.

In matters of political and sexual morality, too, Mark Twain straddled his times—sometimes teetering on the edge of public propriety, sometimes balancing toward the center of acceptable conduct. Despite his fondness for what William Dean Howells tactfully called "Elizabethan parlance," Clemens voluntarily suppressed most of his private jokes and jottings about scatology, masturbation, onanism, and animal intercourse; and he was genuinely stunned when it was rumored that Henry Ward Beecher, the era's foremost man of the cloth and a family friend, had committed adultery. Yet Mark Twain saw nothing wrong with Beecher's accepting several thousand dollars worth of stock from banker Jay Cooke for puffing the Northern Pacific railroad in a sermon. Indeed, while he fired irate broadsides at the era's numerous equivalents of Watergate, he was hardly a consistent champion of political rectitude or of democratic liberalism. At once the idol of the common man and the pet and protégé of the plutocracy, Mark Twain endorsed labor unions and hobnobbed with Standard Oil moguls, supported the Russian Revolution and feared the "mob," denounced Tammany Hall and received several "professional" favors of his own in the publishing world. Fond of championing the common man and denouncing Congress as the only "distinctly native American criminal class," he flirted with royalty and held private sessions in Speaker Czar Reed's chambers to lobby for a more equitable copyright law. An ardent advocate of liberal immigration laws, he privately felt so direly threatened by the wave of new eastern Europeans that he proposed a sweeping (and anonymous) solution to the danger of mob-rule in America. Instead of restricting the suffrage, which would be unconstitutional, why not expand it by giving men of education and property (such as Clemens) five or even ten votes apiece—thus blending meritocracy and oligarchy?

If America refused accommodation to his terms, Mark Twain would prefer to leave it. Between 1872 and 1907 he spent more than eleven years abroad. First England and then Germany stood for the hallowed virtues of thrift and stability that his own country had lost in the frenzied getting and spending of the Gilded Age. The United States was going mad; and if he did not wish to expatriate himself permanently because it was not profitable, the least he could do was to withdraw as much as possible from the stink and corruption of the present by retreating aesthetically into the past. Convinced that his anger was too great to be unleashed into imaginative literature about the American present, Mark Twain increasingly turned to the Old World past and to an earlier America for his literary material—the farther back, the better. Except for *The Gilded Age*, written early in the era, all of Mark Twain's major books were to be tales of yesterday: the frontier West, the South before the War, the England of King Arthur and the Plantagenets, the France of Joan of Arc, the Germany of medieval times, the Austria of the Middle Ages. Indeed the central drama of Mark Twain's life as a man of letters was his discovery of a series of usable pasts which enabled him to escape the day-to-day business and political harassments of the present. More than any other factor, it was the moral and mercenary decadence of the Gilded Age—by whose standards Mark Twain lived and whose values he alternately embraced and loathed—that drove him to seek refuge in the dream world of times and places other than his own.

The last two decades of Mark Twain's life veered into a dead-end despair that he did not hesitate to read as an omen for the entire country and, finally, the world. He was always subject to seizures of remorse and self-recrimination, and his sense of guilt and his paroxysms of rage and bereavement about almost everything—his family, his public life, the books he had censored, the ideas he had suppressed—grew in the 1890's to the point that he began to question his sanity. Beneath the public image of the crotchety old sage, parading in his white suit, walrus mustache, and black cigar, lay a bitter and neurotic cynic who believed, he said, in nothing. Life had no dignity or meaning. The mass of men were cowards, and he was in the front row, carrying a yellow-streaked banner. Man was a slave of circumstance, his mind a mere machine, his body a mangy museum of diseases rotting in the intestine of God. The human race began as dirt, departed as stench, and was useful in between as a breeding place for bacteria, a repository for worms, and a urinal for dogs. The world, "the true one," was odious and horrible. It would have been better if Noah had missed the boat. If sheep had been created first, man would be a plagiarism.

Much of Mark Twain's despair grew out of the crushing financial and family misfortunes that struck him in the last fifteen years of his life. In 1894 his private publishing company was shut down, its capital too quickly siphoned off to feed the Paige typesetting machine, that "baby with a Gargantuan appetite" that devoured most of his earnings and his wife's inheritance for nine long years. The diabolical typesetter finally failed, and Mark Twain declared bankruptcy, with his wife holding the humiliating position of largest legal creditor. The gilded house in Hartford, symbol of the distance he had traveled from Hannibal, Missouri, was sold. The family idyll was destroyed. In 1896, on the last leg of his global debt-paying tour, Mark Twain received word that his favorite daughter Susy, aged twenty-four, had died in delirium at home, slowly and painfully, from meningitis.

His wife Livy declined into invalidism and death in 1904. His youngest daughter Jean, an epileptic, died on Christmas Eve, 1909. Of the six members of the family (a son had died years before as an infant) only one daughter, Clara, married and living in Europe, survived Clemens.

In the midst of personal tragedy there was public triumph. Outwardly, the popular folk figure Mark Twain remained much the same, dictating his memoirs, reading his fan mail, emerging from seclusion to receive the accolades of a doting public, recouping his fortune, and building a less eccentric mansion at Stormfield in Connecticut. Inwardly, however, he changed a good deal. Fearing madness if he became enslaved by family guilt, he worked, as he said, like a madman. Aware that he had reached the age when he could no longer afford to be prodigal, he also found that the literary luck he had always counted on had finally run out. The late piles of skimpy manuscripts, sometimes ending in mid-sentence, reveal a man poisoned with self-loathing and consumed with a well-grounded fear that he was losing his creative powers. When the time seemed ripe to speak what his friend Howells called "the black heart's-truth," to lay his soul bare, to write the final indictment of the damned race that he kept promising the public and himself, it was too late. Like the derelict steamboats he had seen rotting on the great river when he returned to his childhood home in old age, his spark was quenched, his fire out. No sooner would he start a story about the pristine, prewar Mississippi Valley, with the mile-wide river shining in the summer sun, than the currents of his mind would veer toward some dark vortex of horror—toward caves, tombs, red-hot oceans, and Antarctic wastelands in which phantom ships are consumed by sea monsters and the ocean boils down into a molten lunar landscape. Even the cozy, all-white village of St. Petersburg, hugging the ever-summer banks of the Mississippi, failed him. In one of his last, pitiful efforts to recall the magic valley of his youth, Mark Twain reprised Huck, Tom, and Nigger Jim as toothless old men and placed them atop Holliday Hill, there to call the roll of their long-dead boyhood companions before dying themselves. Finally, even the sun-lit river that had flowed through *Tom Sawyer* and *Huckleberry Finn* froze on him.

Whatever the metaphor, these late visions have in common utter despair. Clutched by turn-of-the-century anxiety, Mark Twain felt that time and history were passing him by. The old century—*his* century—was a part of the past, booted into history by rough-riding Teddy Roosevelt ("the Tom Sawyer of the political world"), as he charged up San Juan Hill and promised fresh military "excursions" in the Philippines and the Orient. Enraged over the extraterritorial escapades of new-century imperialism, Mark Twain lent his tired voice to those of a good many of his countrymen who, like himself, had lived through the Mexican War and the Civil War only to see the flag further tarnished in the nation's first overseas engagements. The country was going to hell in a basket; and if the mass of Americans did not follow their foremost "humorist" into deepest despair, Mark Twain nonetheless echoed the feelings of a growing minority of Americans who began to question the purpose and direction of the new century. That he was no longer representative of the majority mind and mood of his countrymen by the time of his death in 1910 actually enhances rather than diminishes his importance. For what Mark Twain viewed as the decline and fall of his country, followed by the entire world, amounts almost to a national cliché in our own time. In the twilight of his life—having enlarged on his role as the representative American by appointing himself Ambassador At Large For the Human Race—Mark Twain saw the history of his country as a parable of man's tragic but richly deserved lot around the globe: America was simply the world in microcosm. To take his last writings and remarks seriously is to hear Mark Twain saying that there had been, after all, no noble New World experiment, no unique American destiny, no fulfilled mission, and no realistic American dream. Furthermore, there was to be no cleansing or catharsis of the American conscience, no purging of national guilt for the sins of the past, and no new chapter in American history: no new deal, no new frontier, no great society. With this message, Mark Twain played the final act in his one-man role as a national stagepiece. Like other writers who followed him a half-century later, he cursed his country; and in doing so he decried a part of himself and remained the quintessential American to the end.

The Composition of Huckleberry Finn

Hamlin Hill and Walter Blair

Samuel Langhorne Clemens began writing and traveling while he was in his teens, and kept up both "occupations" as a reporter in the Far West, the Sandwich Islands, and Europe and the Near East until the late 1860's. Soon after his marriage in 1870 Mark Twain (as he had signed himself since 1863) settled down to do more "serious" literary work than that of a reporter, though continuing to utilize the remembrances of his earlier days in travel books (*The Innocents Abroad*, 1869, and *Roughing It*, 1872), newspaper and magazine articles and a collaborative novel (*The Gilded Age*, 1873). In 1874, returning for the first time in a sustained literary work to the scenes, settings, characters, and incidents of his boyhood in Hannibal, Missouri, he began work on *The Adventures of Tom Sawyer*. In a way, *Tom* was the first mining of appropriated youthful memories that included "Old Times on the Mississippi" and *Adventures of Huckleberry Finn* as the most important yields.

During the summer of 1876, while proofs for *Tom* were still coming to him, Mark Twain began the manuscript of what was to become *Huck*. That summer, he wrote through Chapter XVI of the book, except for the *Walter Scott* episode in Chapter XII and Chapters XIII and XIV. Apparently he was carried on into the second book by the impetus of the first. In subject matter, charac-

From *The Art of Huckleberry Finn*, Second Edition (San Francisco: Chandler Publishing Company, 1969), pp. 2-7. Reprinted with permission.

terization, and tone, the opening chapters of the new book sound more appropriate to *Tom Sawyer* than they do to the middle section of *Huck Finn*.

Somewhere along the way, though, Twain conceived a distinct idea for the second book, and the indication is that he had done so even before he completed *Tom Sawyer* in the summer of 1875. He and William Dean Howells, editor of the *Atlantic Monthly*, conducted a debate about *Tom Sawyer* that centered in the idea of having the boy "drift into manhood." Ultimately Twain decided not to carry Tom "beyond boyhood" but to create another "boy of twelve & run him on through life." In 1874, he had written an outline note in the manuscript of *Tom Sawyer* that has significant overtones: "1, Boyhood & Youth; 2 y & early manh; 3 the Battle of Life in many lands; 4 (age 37 to 40,) return & meet grown babies & toothless old drivelers who were the grandees of his boyhood. The Adored Unknown a faded old maid & full of rasping, puritanical vinegar piety." Three things stand out in this: the main character was to grow to maturity, to be carried "on through life"; he was to travel "in many lands" while he matured; and when he ultimately returned home he was to become disillusioned. Though Huck does not grow up physically in the book and does not travel in many lands, on a long journey he does mature morally, and does reach the point of revolting against the mores of antebellum slaveholding society. The note, though inchoate, sounds as though it is exploring themes and structures which were to become *Huckleberry Finn*. From the beginning of his work on *Tom Sawyer*, therefore, Twain quite possibly had in mind some of the things his novel would do.

Twain composed the 1876 chapters in the comparative seclusion of Quarry Farm in Elmira, New York, an isolated spot in which Theodore and Susan Crane had built him an odd eight-sided study. Here he wrote about 400 pages during a month or so. Relatively undisturbed, then, enjoying a string of best-sellers, his wife in better health than usual, and already basking in the national limelight (no small matter to him), Twain ground out portions of the book which if not completely idyllic at least reflected to some extent the serenity of their author's situation. As little more than a continuation of *Tom*, the first few chapters of the book fail to utilize the preliminary but abandoned *Tom Sawyer* outline, and *Huckleberry Finn* begins with its protagonist little more than the straight man for Tom the rigid rule-follower. But even in this overflow from the earlier volume, there are foreshadowings of some of the most important matter of later parts of the novel. Huck's pragmatic common sense—in conflict with Tom's romanticism, with Widow Douglas's rosy idealism, and with Miss Watson's stern authoritarianism—suggests his character, his methods of combatting force, and his desire to test by practical application the impressive but thin veneer of the culture in which he is living; all of these suggestions will be found repeated on more serious levels further along in the novel.

A basic tendency of Huck's is to act independently and to gauge his relations with others according to the "best way to get along." From the first, his getting along when he can and "lighting out" when he can't are recurrent patterns. Pap Finn, in his tirade against the government and the free Negro, reflects the irrational biases of the Southerner, just as his greed for Huck's share of the treasure foreshadows the avaricious traits of the characters to be encountered later. So although it is quite true that the structure of the novel is to shift and that the tone will change several times, themes which will have significance are introduced in the St. Petersburg chapters written in 1876.

After the high jinks with Tom, as most critics have noted, the basic concern of the section is one of escape down the Mississippi River. As Huck and Jim, two outsiders allied by fear and self-interest, make their way down toward Cairo and freedom from slavery and people who try to "sivilize" Huck, the river not only controls the movement of the two but also determines the idyllic tone, the emotional security, and the most important action. In the 1876 chapters Huck and Jim are important for their relationship to each other; their only contact with the shore is the short encounter with the two slave hunters. This companionship through isolation which the river imposes makes the Mississippi something like a major character. It delivers up a canoe for Huck's initial escape and a raft for Huck's and Jim's downstream trip, guides the two runaways downriver, and providentially offers money and Barlow knives; it provides the fog that sends Jim and Huck past Cairo, and therefore makes necessary Huck's initial verdict concerning slave society, in the scene of the storm that separates Jim and Huck and leads to Huck's perception, after he tricks Jim, that a Negro is a human being worthy of respect. The river in the 1876 chapters, then, is more than a passive setting for an escape on a raft; as Huck comes to understand Jim during the part of their journey when they are sealed off from society, the Mississippi operates as a controlling force.

When Twain put the manuscript aside in 1876, he had used a large share of his memories of the Upper Mississippi and Hannibal. His characters' plan to sail up the Ohio toward free states threatened to carry the story into waters unfamiliar to the author. Also, if the theme of liberation was to be kept, the urge to continue down the Mississippi—the part of the river Twain knew from his piloting years—would give an implausible turn to the action.

For three years Twain left his manuscript; then in 1879-1880 he returned to it to write the Grangerford-Shepherdson feud chapters (XVII and XVIII). Since here Huck and Jim are separated, away from the river, and in a static setting, these chapters postponed this important decision. But these nevertheless are vital chapters. In them, Twain's relatively genial assault on the South of the earliest portion is replaced by a fiercer one. At the Grangerfords', the façade of material gaudiness, sentimentality, and religion is shown covering a brutal, bloodthirsty society. The completely lost origins of the feud, the descriptions of the Grangerfords' house, the account of Emmeline's sentimental creations, the church service with two feuding families listening to a sermon on brotherly love with their guns in easy reach: these are a forceful literary indictment.

Between 1876 and 1882, some disrupting things happened to the mind of Sam Clemens to make the rest of Mark Twain's book differ from the first part. A series of abortive or unsuccessful literary projects and a disheartening trip to Europe increased his cantankerousness. Reading Carlyle, Dickens, Baring-Gould, and others on the French Revolution increased his dissatisfaction with the "damned human race," which he vented in works on "Universal Suffrage," "The Great Revolution in Pitcairn," and *The Prince and the Pauper*. Suspicions aroused by his associates in business dealings made him certain that he was being cheated right and left. His reading in W. E. H. Lecky's *History of European Morals*, which he had discovered some years earlier, led him toward a deterministic philosophy and a predilection for brooding over the value of a conscience. In Presidential election campaigning during 1879, the Republicans (Clemens among them) made much of the alliance of the Democratic Party with the South—the part of the country where, so political propaganda alleged, duels, murders, lynchings, feuds, and brutality to Negroes were everyday happenings. His work on an anthology, eventually to be published as *Mark Twain's Library of Humor* (1888), refamiliarized him with an impressive number of old Southwestern humorists. A trip on the Mississippi in 1882 did more than just revive memories of his youth; it also provided him with ammunition for an attack on the South, material dealing with feuds, duels, and mob rule, some of which he deleted from *Life on the Mississippi* at its publisher's suggestion. In different ways these experiences had effects on the Mark Twain who returned to his manuscript and on the portions of *Huck Finn* he had still to write.

In 1879 or 1880, part way through the feud chapters, Twain paused to take stock of his manuscript, surveying the story so far and projecting it into the future in the jottings that have become known as the "A Notes"* of *Huckleberry Finn*. Some of the pages refer back to manuscript already written, and some contain ideas Twain would use later. Others, which eventually he discarded, suggest he may have thought about keeping Huck and Jim in the vicinity of the Grangerfords, winding up with a murder trial with all the trimmings for a grand finale. (Notations about the village school and fire suggest a stay of some length and others might be interpreted as hinting at the trial.) Even before he finished writing the notes, though, he had hit upon ideas for *Richard III* and the Royal Nonesuch, the circus scene, two tramp printers who fleece the river-town folks, and the identity of one of his tramps—"the King." One note, wherein he tells himself to resurrect the old raft for continued use, reveals that he had made up his mind to continue the downstream drift of Huck and Jim.

When he returned to the book itself again—some time between late 1880 and early 1883—Twain put into action those two "tramp printers," the Duke and the Dauphin. They solved many problems: by appropriating the raft through sheer force, they kept it going on a river Twain himself knew; their shenanigans ashore allowed for continued exploitation of the orneriness of Southern whites; the pair also allowed the author to keep on writing basically anecdotal, episodic material rather than strain-

*The working notes are reproduced in Bernard DeVoto's "Noon and the Dark—*Huckleberry Finn*," pp. 45-104 of *Mark Twain at Work* (Cambridge: Harvard University Press, 1942).

ing to keep his story sustained in one setting and with one cast of characters, often a dangerous thing for him to do. Apparently in this burst of energy, between 1880 and the summer of 1883, he wrote Chapters XIX, XX, and at least part of XXI.

The segment of material on Bricksville—Boggs and Sherburn, the attempted lynching, the circus, the Royal Nonesuch—not only embodies a wealth of source materials; it also continues the raft-shore dichotomy begun in the Grangerford-Shepherdson chapters, in which the serenity and security of the raft contrast with the violence and lawlessness of the shore. More important, Huck, having found that Jim is a fine human being, now in a series of adventures along the Arkansas shore gets a chance to reevaluate the society that insists Jim is merely property. Having had a chance to learn the truth about the Negro, Huck is now given the opportunity on zig-zags between shore and raft to observe the Southern white: a creature characterized by Mark Twain, in the Bricksville segment alone, as sadistic, lazy, stupid, gullible—an unthinking, conforming part of a herd.

The "C Notes" to the book, which Twain wrote some time between the Bricksville chapters and the completion of his manuscript, are centered almost entirely around the plans for the "evasion," the burlesque rescue of Jim from Uncle Silas. Only one of the notes—"Jim cries, to think of his wife & 2 chn"—echoes the Jim of the upper-river chapters, and accounts probably for the insertion of Jim's memories about his deaf daughter in Chapter XXIII. By exploiting the character of the river-townsmen, the whole section builds up to Huck's two vital verdicts: "Human beings *can* be awful cruel to one another," and "All right, then, I'll *go* to hell."

Both of these decisions occur *before* the ten final chapters that drag out Jim's rescue to tedious length. Does *Huck Finn* really end, as Ernest Hemingway once suggested, when Jim is stolen from Huck? The problem has engaged many students of the novel for quite some time, and every once in a while somebody offers a new justification for the last chapters. People have suggested that the burlesque evasion returns to the mood of Hannibal-St. Petersburg, that it returns Huck to anonymity when Tom Sawyer takes front-stage center, that it burlesques "authorities" of the variety that have caused the South's decay, that it amplifies a theme of Huck's search for a family which runs through the novel; but the very fact that this insistence is necessary suggests an uneasiness which the ending causes. Having struggled with his conscience and reached an independent, nonconforming opinion, Huck gives up his freedom to follow Tom's lead in an elaborately absurd scheme to free Jim which, whatever alibis can be offered for it, reduces both Huck and Jim in stature.

In the summer and autumn of 1883, Twain also wrote most of Chapter XII and Chapters XIII and XIV following his suggestion (in Note C-4) to have the pair back on the raft find some books about royalty. Thus the *Walter Scott* episode (one of the rare instances when "shore people" intrude on the river in the first fifteen chapters) and the discussion about Solomon and the French language were crammed into their places in 1883, and the novel was complete.

In spite of its fantastically chaotic composition, halts and flurries when Twain allowed his "tank" of inspiration to fill up, drain, and fill up again, *Huckleberry Finn*, like all literature, has to be evaluated as a complete work of art. Critics therefore pose and try to answer the question, "Did Twain manage to write a unified novel in spite of the conditions under which it was written? Does *Huck Finn* hold together?" A few critics are convinced that Twain failed, because the tone and characterization of the last fifth of the novel are inconsistent. Others suggest that the presence of the river, the indictment of Southern society, the pattern of death and rebirth, the gradual moral awakening of the hero, or the juxtaposition of comic and tragic variations on the same theme operate to give the book a unity that transcends even its burlesque conclusion.

EARLY RESPONSE

Unsigned Review

Attributed to William Ernest Henley

For some time past Mr. Clemens has been carried away by the ambition of seriousness and fine writing. In *Huckleberry Finn* he returns to his right mind, and is again the Mark Twain of old time. It is such a book as he, and he only, could have written. It is meant for boys; but there are few men (we should hope) who, once they take it up, will not delight in it. It forms a companion or sequel, to *Tom Sawyer*. Huckleberry Finn, as everybody knows, is one of Tom's closest friends; and the present volume is a record of the adventures which befell him soon after the event which made him a person of property and brought Tom Sawyer's story to a becoming conclusion. They are of the most surprising and delightful kind imaginable, and in the course of them we fall in with a number of types of characters of singular freshness and novelty, besides being schooled in half a dozen extraordinary dialects—the Pike County dialect in all its forms, the dialect of the Missouri negro, and 'the extremest form of the backwoods South-Western dialect,' to wit. Huckleberry, it may be noted, is stolen by his disreputable father, to escape from whom he contrives an appearance of robbery and murder in the paternal hut, goes off in a canoe, watches from afar the townsfolk hunting for his dead body, and encounters a runaway negro—Miss Watson's Jim—an old particular friend of Tom Sawyer and himself. With Jim he goes south down the river, and is the hero of such scrapes and experiences as make your mouth water (if you have ever been a boy) to read of them. We do not purpose to tell a sin-

From *Athenaeum* (London), No. 2983 (December 27, 1884), 855.

gle one; it would be unfair to author and reader alike. We shall content ourselves with repeating that the book is Mark Twain at his best, and remarking that Jim and Huckleberry are real creations, and the worthy peers of the illustrious Tom Sawyer.

Unsigned Review

Attributed to Brander Matthews

The boy of to-day is fortunate indeed, and, of a truth, he is to be congratulated. While the boy of yesterday had to stay his stomach with the unconscious humour of *Sandford and Merton*, the boy of to-day may get his fill of fun and of romance and of adventure in *Treasure Island* and in *Tom Brown* and in *Tom Sawyer*, and now in a sequel to *Tom Sawyer*, wherein Tom himself appears in the very nick of time, like a young god from the machine. Sequels of stories which have been widely popular are not a little risky. *Huckleberry Finn* is a sharp exception to this general rule. Although it is a sequel, it is quite as worthy of wide popularity as *Tom Sawyer*. An American critic once neatly declared that the late G. P. R. James hit the bull's-eye of success with his first shot, and that for ever thereafter he went on firing through the same hole. Now this is just what Mark Twain has not done. *Huckleberry Finn* is not an attempt to do *Tom Sawyer* over again. It is a story quite as unlike its predecessor as it is like. Although Huck Finn appeared first in the earlier book, and although Tom Sawyer reappears in the later, the scenes and the characters are otherwise wholly different. Above all, the atmosphere of the story is different. *Tom Sawyer* was a tale of boyish adventure in a village in Missouri, on the Mississippi river, and it was told by the author. *Huckleberry Finn* is autobiographic; it is a tale of boyish adventure along the Mississippi river told as it appeared to Huck Finn. There is not in *Huckleberry Finn* any one scene quite as funny as those in which Tom Sawyer gets his friends to whitewash the fence for him, and then uses the spoils thereby acquired to attain the highest situa-

From *Saturday Review* (London), 59 (January 31, 1885), 153-54.

tion of the Sunday school the next morning. Nor is there any distinction quite as thrilling as that awful moment in the cave when the boy and the girl are lost in the darkness, and when Tom Sawyer suddenly sees a human hand bearing a light, and then finds that the hand is the hand of Indian Joe, his one mortal enemy; we have always thought that the vision of the hand in the cave in *Tom Sawyer* is one of the very finest things in the literature of adventure since Robinson Crusoe first saw a single footprint in the sand of the seashore. But though *Huckleberry Finn* may not quite reach these two highest points of *Tom Sawyer*, we incline to the opinion that the general level of the later story is perhaps higher than that of the earlier. For one thing, the skill with which the character of Huck Finn is maintained is marvellous. We see everything through his eyes—and they are his eyes and not a pair of Mark Twain's spectacles. And the comments on what he sees are his comments—the comments of an ignorant, superstitious, sharp, healthy boy, brought up as Huck Finn had been brought up; they are not speeches put into his mouth by the author. One of the most artistic things in the book—and that Mark Twain is a literary artist of a very high order all who have considered his later writings critically cannot but confess—one of the most artistic things in *Huckleberry Finn* is the sober self-restraint with which Mr. Clemens lets Huck Finn set down, without any comment at all, scenes which would have afforded the ordinary writer matter for endless moral and political and sociological disquisition. We refer particularly to the account of the Grangerford-Shepherdson feud, and of the shooting of Boggs by Colonel Sherburn. Here are two incidents of the rough old life of the South-Western States, and of the Mississippi Valley forty or fifty years ago, of the old life which is now rapidly passing away under the influence of advancing civilization and increasing commercial prosperity, but which has not wholly disappeared even yet, although a slow revolution in public sentiment is taking place. The Grangerford-Shepherdson feud is a vendetta as deadly as any Corsican could wish, yet the parties to it were honest, brave, sincere, good Christian people, probably people of deep religious sentiment. Not the less we see them taking their guns to church, and, when occasion serves, joining in what is little better than a general massacre. The killing of Boggs by Colonel Sherburn is told with equal sobriety and truth; and the later scene in which Colonel Sherburn cows and lashes the mob which has set out to lynch him is one of the most vigorous bits of writing Mark Twain has done.

In *Tom Sawyer* we saw Huckleberry Finn from the outside; in the present volume we see him from the inside. He is almost as much a delight to any one who has been a boy as was Tom Sawyer. But only he or she who has been a boy can truly enjoy this record of his adventures, and of his sentiments and of his sayings. Old maids of either sex will wholly fail to understand him or to like him, or to see his significance and his value. Like Tom Sawyer, Huck Finn is a genuine boy; he is neither a girl in boy's clothes like many of the modern heroes of juvenile fiction, nor is he a "little man," a full-grown man cut down; he is a boy, just a boy, only a boy. And his ways and modes of thought are boyish. As Mr. F. Anstey understands the English boy, and especially the English boy of the middle classes, so Mark Twain understands the American boy, and especially the American boy of the Mississippi Valley of forty or fifty years ago. The contrast between Tom Sawyer, who is the child of respectable parents, decently brought up, and Huckleberry Finn, who is the child of the town drunkard, not brought up at all, is made distinct by a hundred artistic touches, not the least natural of which is Huck's constant reference to Tom as his ideal of what a boy should be. When Huck escapes from the cabin where his drunken and worthless father had confined him, carefully manufacturing a mass of very circumstantial evidence to prove his own murder by robbers, he cannot help saying, "I did wish Tom Sawyer was there, I knowed he would take an interest in this kind of business, and throw in the fancy touches. Nobody could spread himself like Tom Sawyer in such thing as that." Both boys have their full share of boyish imagination; and Tom Sawyer, being given to books, lets his imagination run on robbers and pirates and genies, with a perfect understanding with himself that, if you want to get fun out of this life, you must never hesitate to make believe very hard; and, with Tom's youth and health, he never finds it hard to make believe and to be a pirate at will, or to summon an attendant spirit, or to rescue a prisoner from the deepest dungeon 'neath the castle moat. But in Huck this imagination has turned to superstition; he is a walking repository of the juvenile folklore of the Mississippi Valley—a folklore partly traditional among the white settlers, but largely influenced by intimate association with the negroes. When Huck was in his room at night all by himself waiting for the signal Tom Sawyer was to give him at midnight, he felt so lonesome he wished he was dead:—

"The stars was shining and the leaves rustled in the woods ever so mournful; and I heard an owl, away off, who-whooing about somebody that was dead, and a whippowill and a dog crying about somebody that was going to die; and the wind was trying to whisper something to me, and I couldn't make out what it was, and so it made the cold shivers run over me. Then away out in the woods I heard that kind of a sound that a ghost makes when it wants to tell about something that's on its mind and can't make itself understood, and so can't rest easy in its grave, and has to go about that way every night grieving. I got so downhearted and scared I did wish I had some company. Pretty soon a spider went crawling up my shoulders, and I flipped it off and it lit in the candle; and before I could budge it was all shrivelled up. I didn't need anybody to tell me that that was an awful bad sign and would fetch me some bad luck, so I was scared and most shook the clothes off me. I got up and turned around in my tracks three times and crossed my breast every time; and then I tied up a little lock of my hair with a thread to keep witches away. But I hadn't no confidence. You do that when you've lost a horse-shoe that you've found, instead of nailing it up over the door, but I hadn't ever heard anybody say it was any way to keep off bad luck when you'd killed a spider."

And, again, later in the story, not at night this time, but in broad daylight, Huck walks along a road:—

"When I got there it was still and Sunday-like, and hot and sunshiny—the hands was gone to the fields; and there was them kind of faint dronings of bugs and flies in the air that makes it seem so lonesome and like everybody's dead and gone; and if a breeze fans along and quivers the leaves, it makes you feel mournful, because you feel like it's spirits whispering—spirits that's been dead ever so many years—and you always think they're talking about *you*. As a general thing it makes a body wish *he* was dead too, and done with it all."

Now, none of these sentiments are appropriate to Tom Sawyer, who had none of the feeling for nature which Huck Finn had caught during his numberless days and nights in the open air. Nor could Tom Sawyer either have seen or set down this instantaneous photograph of a summer storm:—

"It would get so dark that it looked all blue-black outside, and lovely; and the rain would thrash along by so thick that the trees off a little ways looked dim and spider-webby; and here would come a blast of wind that would bend the trees down and turn up the pale underside of the leaves; and then a perfect ripper of a gust would follow along and set the branches to tossing their arms as if they was just wild; and next, when it was just about the bluest and blackest—fst! it was as bright as glory, and you'd have a little glimpse of tree-tops a-plunging about, away off yonder in the storm, hundreds of yards further than you could see before; dark as sin again in a second, and now you'd hear the thunder let go with an awful crash, and then go rumbling, grumbling, tumbling down the sky towards the underside of the world, like rolling empty barrels down stairs, where it's long stairs and they bounce a good deal, you know."

The romantic side of Tom Sawyer is shown in most delightfully humorous fashion in the account of his difficult devices to aid in the easy escape of Jim, a runaway negro. Jim is an admirably drawn character. There have been not a few fine and firm portraits of negroes in recent American fiction, of which Mr. Cable's Bras-Coupe in the *Grandissimes* is perhaps the most vigorous, and Mr. Harris's Mingo and Uncle Remus and Blue Dave are the most gentle. Jim is worthy to rank with these; and the essential simplicity and kindliness and generosity of the Southern negro have never been better shown than here by Mark Twain. Nor are Tom Sawyer and Huck Finn and Jim the only fresh and original figures in Mr. Clemens's new book; on the contrary, there is scarcely a character of the many introduced who does not impress the reader at once as true to life—and therefore as new, for life is so varied that a portrait from life is sure to be as good as new. That Mr. Clemens draws from life, and yet lifts his work from the domain of the photograph to the region of art, is evident to any one who will give his work the honest attention which it deserves. Mr. John T. Raymond, the American comedian, who performs the character of Colonel Sellers to perfection, is wont to say that there is scarcely a town in the West and South-West where some man did not claim to be the original of the character. And as Mark Twain made Colonel Sellers, so has he made the chief players in the present drama of boyish adventure; they are taken from life, no doubt, but they are so aptly chosen and so broadly drawn that they are quite as typical as they are actual. They have one great charm, all of them—they are not written about and about; they are not described and dissected and analysed; they appear and play their parts and disappear; and yet they leave a sharp impression of indubitable vitality and individuality. No one, we venture to say, who reads this book will readily forget the Duke and the King, a pair of as pleasant "confidence operators" as one may meet in a day's journey, who leave the story in the most appropriate fashion, being clothed in tar and feathers and ridden on a rail. Of the more broadly humorous passages—and they abound—we have not left ourselves space to speak; they are to the full as funny as in any of Mark Twain's other books; and, perhaps, in no other book has the humourist shown so much artistic restraint, for there is in *Huckleberry Finn* no mere "comic copy," no straining after effect; one might almost say that there is no waste word in it....

Review

Thomas Sergeant Perry

Mark Twain's "Tom Sawyer" is an interesting record of boyish adventure; but, amusing as it is, it may yet be fair to ask whether its most marked fault is not too strong adherence to conventional literary models? A glance at the book certainly does not confirm this opinion, but those who recall the precocious affection of Tom Sawyer, at the age when he is losing his first teeth, for a little girl whom he has seen once or twice, will confess that the modern novel exercises a very great influence. What is best in the book, what one remembers, is the light we get into the boy's heart. The romantic devotion to the little girl, the terrible adventures with murderers and in huge caves, have the air of concessions to jaded readers. But when Tom gives the cat Pain-Killer, is restless in church, and is recklessly and eternally deceiving his aunt, we are on firm ground—the author is doing sincere work.

This later book, "Huckleberry Finn," has the great advantage of being written in autobiographical form. This secures a unity in the narration that is most valuable; every scene is given, not described; and the result is a vivid picture of Western life forty or fifty years ago. While "Tom Sawyer" is scarcely more than an apparently fortuitous collection of incidents, and its thread is one that has to do with murders, this story has a more intelligible plot. Huckleberry, its immortal hero, runs away from his worthless father, and floats down the Mississipi on a raft, in company with Jim, a runaway negro. This plot gives great opportunity for varying incidents. The travelers spend some time on an island;

From *Century Magazine*, 30 (May 1885), 171-72.

they outwit every one they meet; they acquire full knowledge of the hideous fringe of civilization that then adorned that valley; and the book is a most valuable record of an important part of our motley American civilization.

What makes it valuable is the evident truthfulness of the narrative, and where this is lacking and its place is taken by ingenious invention, the book suffers. What is inimitable, however, is the reflection of the whole varied series of adventures in the mind of the young scapegrace of a hero. His undying fertility of invention, his courage, his manliness in every trial, are an incarnation of the better side of the ruffianism that is one result of the independence of Americans, just as hypocrisy is one result of the English respect for civilization. The total absence of morbidness in the book—for the *mal du siècle* has not yet reached Arkansas—gives it a genuine charm; and it is interesting to notice the art with which this is brought out. The best instance is perhaps to be found in the account of the feud between the Shepherdsons and the Grangerfords, which is described only as it would appear to a semi-civilized boy of fourteen, without the slightest condemnation or surprise,—either of which would be bad art,—and yet nothing more vivid can be imagined. That is the way that a story is best told, by telling it, and letting it go to the reader unaccompanied by sign-posts or directions how he shall understand it and profit by it. Life teaches its lessons by implication, not by didactic preaching; and literature is at its best when it is an imitation of life and not an excuse for instruction.

As to the humor of Mark Twain, it is scarcely necessary to speak. It lends vividness to every page. The little touch in "Tom Sawyer," where, after the murder of which Tom was an eye-witness, it seemed "that his school-mates would never get done holding inquests on dead cats and thus keeping the trouble present to his mind," and that in the account of the spidery six-armed girl of Emmeline's picture in "Huckleberry Finn," are in the author's happiest vein. Another admirable instance is to be seen in Huckleberry Finn's mixed feelings about rescuing Jim, the negro, from slavery. His perverted views regarding the unholiness of his actions are most instructive and amusing. It is possible to feel, however, that the fun in the long account of Tom Sawyer's artificial imitation of escapes from prison is somewhat forced; everywhere simplicity is a good rule, and while the account of the Southern *vendetta* is a masterpiece, the caricature of books of adventure leaves us cold. In one we have a bit of life; in the other Mark Twain is demolishing something that has no place in the book.

Yet the story is capital reading, and the reason of its great superiority to "Tom Sawyer" is that it is, for the most part, a consistent whole. If Mark Twain would follow his hero through manhood, he would condense a side of American life that, in a few years, will have to be delved out of newapapers, government reports, county histories, and misleading traditions by unsympathetic sociologists.

The Art of Mark Twain

Andrew Lang

The duty of self-examination is frequently urged upon us by moralists. No doubt we should self-examine our minds as well as our conduct now and then, especially when we have passed the age in which we are constantly examined by other people. When I attempt to conduct this delicate inquiry I am puzzled and alarmed at finding that I am losing Culture. I am backsliding, I have not final perseverance, unless indeed it is Culture that is backsliding and getting on to the wrong lines. For I ought to be cultured; it is my own fault if I have not got Culture.

I have been educated till I nearly dropped; I have lived with the earliest Apostles of Culture, in the days when Chippendale was first a name to conjure with, and Japanese art came in like a raging lion, and Ronsard was the favourite poet, and Mr. William Morris was a poet too, and blue and green were the only wear, and the name of Paradise was Camelot. To be sure, I cannot say that I took all this quite seriously, but 'we too have played' at it, and know all about it. Generally speaking, I have kept up with Culture. I can talk (if desired) about Sainte-Beuve, and Mérimée, and Félicien Rops; I could rhyme 'Ballades,' when they were 'in,' and knew what a *pantoom* was. I am acquainted with the scholia on the Venetus A. I have a pretty taste in Greek gems. I have got beyond the stage of thinking Mr. Cobden Sanderson a greater binder than Bauzonnet. With practice I believe I could do an epigram of Meleager's into a bad imitation of a sonnet by Joachim du Bellay, or a sonnet of Bellay's into a bad imitation of a Greek epi-

From *Illustrated London News*, 98 (February 14, 1891), 222.

gram. I could pass an examination in the works of M. Paul Bourget. And yet I have not Culture. My works are but a tinkling brass, because I have not Culture. For Culture has got into new regions where I cannot enter, and, what is perhaps worse, I find myself delighting in a great many things which are under the ban of Culture.

This is a dreadful position, which makes a man feel like one of those Liberal politicians who are always 'sitting on the fence,' and who follow their party, if follow it they do, with the reluctant acquiescence of the prophet's donkey. Not that I *do* follow it. I cannot rave with pleasure over Tolstoi, especially as he admits that 'The Kreutzer Sonata' is not 'only his fun' but a kind of Manifesto. I have tried Hartmann, and I prefer Plato. I don't like poems by young ladies in which the verses neither scan nor rhyme, and the constructions are all linguistically impossible. I am shaky about Blake, though I am stalwart about Mr. Rudyard Kipling.

This is not the worst of it. Culture has hardly a new idol but I long to hurl things at it. Culture can scarcely burn anything, but I am impelled to sacrifice to that same. I am coming to suspect that the majority of Culture's modern disciples are a mere crowd of very slimly educated people, who have no natural taste or impulse; who do not really know the best things in literature; who have a feverish desire to admire the newest thing, to follow the latest artistic fashion; who prate about 'style' without the faintest acquaintance with the ancient examples of style, in Greek, French, or English; who talk about the classics and criticise the classical critics and poets, without being able to read a line of them in the original. Nothing of the natural man is left in these people; their intellectual equipment is made up of ignorant vanity, and eager desire of novelty, and a yearning to be in the fashion.

Take, for example—and we have been a long time in coming to him—Mark Twain. If you praise him among persons of Culture, they cannot believe that you are serious. They call him a Barbarian. They won't hear of him, they hurry from the subject; they pass by on the other side of the way. Now I do not mean to assert that Mark Twain is 'an impeccable artist,' but he is just as far from being a mere coarse buffoon. Like other people, he has his limitations. Even Mr. Gladstone, for instance, does not shine as a Biblical critic, nor Mark Twain as a critic of Italian art nor as a guide to the Holy Land. I have abstained from reading his work on an

American at the Court of King Arthur, because here Mark Twain is not, and cannot be, at the proper point of view. He has not the knowledge which would enable him to be a sound critic of the ideal of the Middle Ages. An Arthurian Knight in New York or in Washington would find as much to blame, and justly, as a Yankee at Camelot. Let it be admitted that Mark Twain often and often sins against good taste, that some of his waggeries are mechanical, that his books are full of passages which were only good enough for the corner of a newspaper. Even so, the man who does not 'let a laugh out of him'—like the Gruagach Gaire—at the story of the Old Ram, or of the Mexican Plug, or of the editing of the country newspaper, or of the Blue Jay, or at the lecture on the German language, can hardly have a laugh in him to let out. Chesterfield very gravely warns his son that it is wrong and vulgar to laugh; but the world has agreed to differ from Chesterfield. To 'Homo Ridens' Mark Twain is a benefactor beyond most modern writers, and the Cultured, who do not laugh, are merely to be pitied. But his art is not only that of a maker of the scarce article—mirth. I have no hesitation in saying that Mark Twain is one among the greatest of contemporary makers of fiction. For some reason, which may perhaps be guessed, he has only twice chosen to exercise his art seriously, in *Tom Sawyer* and in *Huckleberry Finn*. The reason, probably, is that old life on the Mississippi is the only form of life in which Mark Twain finds himself so well versed that he can deal with it in seriousness. Again, perhaps his natural and cultivated tendency to extravagence and caricature is only to be checked by working on the profound and candid seriousness of boyhood. These are unlucky limitations, if they really exist, for they have confined him, as a novelist, to a pair of brief works, masterpieces which a fallacious appearance has confounded with boys' books and facetiae. Of the two, by an unheard-of stroke of luck, the second, the sequel, is by far the better. I can never forget nor be ungrateful for the exquisite pleasure with which I read *Huckleberry Finn* for the first time, years ago. I read it again last night, deserting *Kenilworth* for Huck. I never laid it down till I had finished it. I perused several passages more than once, and rose from it with a higher opinion of its merits than ever.

What is it that we want in a novel? We want a vivid and original picture of life; we want character naturally displayed in action, and if we get the excitement of adventure into the bargain, and that adventure possible and plausible, I so far differ from the newest school of criticism as to think that we have additional cause for gratitude. If, moreover, there is an unstrained sense of humour in the narrator, we have a masterpiece and *Huckleberry Finn* is nothing less. Once more, if the critics are right who think that art should so far imitate nature as to leave things at loose ends, as it were, not pursuing events to their conclusions, even here *Huckleberry Finn* should satisfy them. It is the story of the flight down the Mississippi of a white boy and a runaway slave. The stream takes them through the fringes of life on the riverside; they pass feuds and murders of men, and towns full of homicidal loafers, and are intermingled with the affairs of families, and meet friends whom they would wish to be friends always. But the current carries them on: they leave the murders unavenged, the lovers in full flight; the friends they lose for ever; we do not know, any more than in reality we would know, 'what became of them all.' They do not return, as in novels, and narrate their later adventures.

As to the truth of the life described, the life in little innocent towns, the religion, the Southern lawlessness, the feuds, the lynchings, only persons who have known this changed world can say if it be truly painted, but it looks like the very truth, like an historical document. Already *Huckleberry Finn* is an historical novel, and more valuable, perhaps, to the historian than *Uncle Tom's Cabin*, for it was written without partisanship, and without 'a purpose.' The drawing of character seems to be admirable, unsurpassed in its kind. By putting the tale in the mouth of the chief actor, Huck, Mark Twain was enabled to give it a seriousness not common in his work, and to abstain from comment. Nothing can be more true and more humorous than the narrative of this outcast boy, with a heart naturally good, with a conscience torn between the teachings of his world about slavery and the promptings of his nature. In one point Mark Twain is Homeric, probably without knowing it. In the *Odyssey*, Odysseus frequently tells a false tale about himself, to account for his appearance and position when disguised on his own island. He shows extraordinary fertility and appropriateness of invention, wherein he is equalled by the feigned tales of Huckleberry Finn. The casual characters met on the way are masterly: the woman who detects Huck in a girl's dress; the fighting families of Shepherdson and Grangerford; the homicidal Colonel Sherburne, who cruelly shoots old Boggs, and superbly quells the mob of would-be lynchers; the various old aunts and uncles; the negro Jim; the two wandering impostors; the hateful father of Huck himself. Then Huck's compliment to Miss Mary Jane, whom he thought of afterwards 'a many and a many million times,' how excellent it is! 'In my opinion she had more sand in her than any girl I ever see; in my opinion she was just full of sand. It sounds like flattery, but it ain't no flattery. And when it comes to beauty—and goodness, too—she lays over them all.' No novel has better touches of natural description; the starlit nights on the great river, the storms, the whole landscape, the sketches of little rotting towns, of the woods, of the cotton-fields, are simple, natural, and visible to the mind's eye. The story, to be sure, ends by lapsing into burlesque, when Tom Sawyer insists on freeing the slave whom he knows to be free already, in a manner accordant with 'the best authorities.' But even the burlesque is redeemed by Tom's real unconscious heroism. There are defects of taste, or passages that to us seem deficient in taste, but the book remains a nearly flawless gem of romance and of humour. The world appreciates it, no doubt, but 'cultured critics' are probably unaware of its singular value. A two-shilling novel by Mark Twain, with an ugly picture on the cover, 'has no show,' as Huck might say, and the great American novel has escaped the eyes of those who watch to see this new planet swim into their ken. And will Mark Twain never write such another? One is enough for him to live by, and for our gratitude, but not enough for our desire.

My Favorite Novelist and His Best Book

Sir Walter Besant

I have been invited to write upon my 'Favorite Novel.' Alas, I have so many favorite novels! How can I incur the jealousy of all the others by selecting one as the favorite? Novels are live things; they love admiration; they resent neglect; they hate the preference of others. Like Charles Lamb, who loved every book because it was a book—except the Law List—I love every novel because it is a novel—except those which are not novels, but only shams. I love the novel of adventure; I find the *Three Musketeers* as delightful now as when I sat in a corner, breathless, panting, and followed, all a lifelong holiday, the fortunes of the Immortal Three who were Four. And I love the novel which portrays human life and society, whether it is *Tom Jones* or *Humphrey Clinker*, or *Nicholas Nickleby*. And I love Charlotte Yonge's gentle girls; and Marryat's anything but gentle sailor; and Lever's swaggering soldier; and Jane Austen, and Maria Edgeworth, and Wilkie Collins, and Charles Reade, and Edgar Allan Poe, and Hawthorne, and Oliver Wendell Holmes—not to speak of living men and women by the score whose works I read with joy.

Of a novel I ask but one thing. 'Seize me,' I say—'seize me and hold me with a grip of steel. Make me deaf and blind to all the world so long as I read in thine enchanted pages. Carry me whither thou wilt. Play on me; do with me what thou wilt, at

From *Munsey's Magazine*, 18 (February 1898), 659-64.

thine own sweet will. Make me shriek with pain; fill my eyes with tears and my heart with sorrow; let me laugh aloud, let me bubble over with the joy of silent mirth; let me forget that the earth is full of oppression and wickedness. Only seize me and hold me tight—immovable, rapt, hypnotized; deaf and blind to all the world.'

I confess that unless this condition is fulfilled I cannot read a novel. Many novels I try to read, only to lay them down. A few such I have had to read on occasions—they were rare—when an editor has asked me to review a novel. To me it is more painful than words can tell to read such a book; it is more irksome than any convict's task to write a review of such a book. The only excuse that I will admit from a reviewer who dishonestly pronounces judgment on a book which he has not read is that the novel was one of the kind which cannot be read. If he pleads that excuse, I pity him and pass on. For this reason, also, I am in no hurry to take up any new novel. I like to have it 'tasted' for me first. The tasting enables me to escape the attempt to read a great many new novels. As a rule I buy only those of which other people have already spoken. As a wise man and a philosopher, I take my recommendations not from the critics, but from the other people. Then, if a story possesses the gift of grip, I am ready to forgive all other sins. A novel cannot be really bad, though it may have many faults, if it seizes the reader and holds him spellbound till the last page.

These remarks prepare the way for a selection which is perhaps unexpected. I do not respond to the invitation by taking one of the acknowledged masterpieces; nor shall I worry myself to find something fresh to say about a book which has already been reviewed over and over again. Cervantes, Fielding, Dickens, Thackery—all these I leave to the professors of literature, and to the critic of the big and serious 'appreciation'—to him who estimates influence, finds out blemishes, and explores the sources. I am only a critic in so far as I really do know the points of a good novelist and something about the art of construction of a novel; and I prefer to apply this knowledge on the present occasion to a work of perhaps humbler pretensions, albeit a work of genius, and a work which will live and will belong to the literature of the language. I speak of one of my favorites; not my single favorite. I love the book for a variety of excellent reasons, but not to the exclusion of other books. It is expected of a well regulated mind that it cannot love more than one woman at a time. This galling restriction applies not to the lover of the novels, which, with poetry, are the fair women of literature. One can love them all—yes, all. So catholic is love in literature, so wide is his embrace, so universal; so free from jealousy are his mistresses.

The book which I have selected is Mark Twain's *Huckleberry Finn*. At the outset I observe, and intend to respect, a warning after the title page to the effect that any person who may try to find a motive in the narrative will be prosecuted; that any person who may try to find a moral in it will be banished, and that persons attempting to find a plot will be shot.

Let us repeat this warning. Let us not try to find in *Huckleberry Finn* either motive, moral, or plot.

I lay it down as one of the distinctive characteristics of a good story that it pleases—or rather, seizes—every period of life; that the child, and his elder brother, and his father, and his grandfather, may read it with like enjoyment—not equal enjoyment, because as a man gets older and understands more and more what the world of men and women means, he reads between the lines and sees things which the child cannot see and cannot understand. Very likely, if the painting is true to nature, he sees things which the artist himself could not see or understand. The note of genius is that it suggests so much more than it meant to suggest, and goes so much deeper than the poet himself intended. To discover and to read the superadded letterpress, the invisible part of the printed page, is one of the compensations of age.

The first quality that I claim for this book, then, is that it does appeal to all ages and every age. The boy of twelve reads it with delight beyond his power of words to express; the young man reads it; the old man reads it. The book is a joy to all alike. For my own part, I have read it over and over again, yet always with delight and always finding something new in its pages.

There is no motive in the book; there is no moral; there is no plot. The book is like a panorama in which the characters pass across the stage and do not return. They follow each other with the unexpectedness belonging to a voyage down a river. All happens by chance; the finger of providence—which means the finger of Mark Twain—is nowhere visible. There is no motive; there is no moral; there is no plot. This directing, intervening, meddlesome finger you will find very often in the novel which does not permit itself to be read; it sticks out in the carpenter's novel. You see the thumb—it wants washing—in the novel made by rule. It is nowhere visible in *Huckleberry Finn*.

The book commends itself, to begin with, by the humorous treatment of perfectly serious situations. It is unconsciously humorous, it is humourous because the narrator sees no humor in anything. In some places, when an English boy would have rolled on the floor with laughing, the American boy relates the scene without a smile. Indeed, from beginning to end, there is hardly a smile. Yet, while all the situations lie open for sentiment, for moralizing, or for laughing, the actors are perfectly serious—and perfectly comic.

The reason of the serious nature of the performance is that the narrator is a boy whose experiences of life have not, so far, inclined him to look at things from a humorous point of view. He is the son of a drunken scoundrel, the disgrace and terror of the town.

> He said he'd cowhide me till I was black and blue if I didn't raise some money for him. I borrowed three dollars from Judge Thatcher, and pap took it and got drunk and went a-blowing around and cussing and whooping and carrying on; and he kept it up all over town, with a tin pan, till 'most midnight. Then they jailed him; next day they had him before court and jailed him again for a week.

Even the boys in the town spoke of him as 'a man who used to lay drunk with the hogs in the tan yard.' It is with the gravest face that the boy speaks of his father; relates how he took the pledge in presence of the judge—who 'said it was the holiest time on record'—and broke it the next day; and how he had delirium tremens and tried to murder his son. With such a father; with no education; with no religion; living about in the woods; without respect of persons; untruthful whenever it seemed easier to conceal the truth; yielding when necessary; watchful of opportunities; not immoral, but unmoral—the boy starts off to tell his tale of adventure. Writers of fiction, of whom there are now so many, will understand the difficulty of getting inside the brain of that boy, seeing things as he saw them, writing as he would have written, and acting as he would have acted; and presenting to the world a true, faithful, and living *effigies* of that boy. The feat has been accomplished: there is no character in fiction more fully, more faithfully presented than the character of *Huckleberry Finn*. What that character finally appears, when the book is finished, when the glamour dies away, when the figure stands out plainly before us, I will endeavor to portray after touching on some of the points of *Huckleberry's* pilgrimage.

The earlier chapters, with *Tom Sawyer* and the other boys, are hardly worthy to be taken as an introduction to the book. But they are soon got over. The adventures really begin with the boy's life in the cabin where his father has taken him. The man was always drunk, always abusing and threatening the boy, always falling about in his half drunk moments, and cursing.

Down he went in the dirt and rolled there and held his toes; and the cussing he done there laid over anything he had ever done previous. He said so, his own self, afterwards.

Observe the boy's standard as to cursing considered as fine art.

He escapes; he finds a canoe drifting down the river; he gets on board, takes certain steps which will make his father believe that he has been murdered, and paddles down the river to an island. The river is the mighty Mississippi; and now we are on or beside its waters and hear the swirl and the swish as the current rolls past the reeds and sedges of the island and washes the planks of the craft. We see the huge lumber rafts making their slow way with the stream; we hear, with the boy, the voice of the man on board—'Stern oars! Heave her head to stabboard!'

On his desert island the boy, perfectly happy, caught fish and broiled them; found wild strawberries—the *fraises à quatre saisons* which flourish all over the world; and went about exploring his kingdom. It was a glorious time, only it was difficult to get through the day. Presently he found another resident on the island, the runaway 'nigger' *Jim,* whom he knew very well. The white boy was so wild, so uncivilized, that even in a slave holding State he had imbibed no proper feeling as regards runaway slaves. He chummed with *Jim* immediately. The river rises; the island is under water; they live in a cave on a rock which is above the flood; they paddle about in the canoe, either on the river or among the woods; they pick up things that come floating down—among other things part of a lumber raft.

It was lucky they found the raft, because smoke had been seen on the island, and suspicion had arisen about the runaway 'nigger.' They decided to run away from their island and to make for the first point where a fugitive slave would be free. They loaded the raft with all they had; they carried their canoe on board; and in the dead of night they slipped off the island and so down stream. Where they were going to, whither the river would carry them, they never inquired. The book, you see, has no plot, no motive, no moral.

They ran about seven or eight hours every night, the current making four miles an hour. They fished as they slid down the stream. Sometimes they took a swim to keep off sleepiness.

It was kind of solemn, drifting down the big still river, laying on our backs looking up at the stars, and we didn't feel like talking loud and it wasn't often that we laughed, only a little kind of a low chuckle.

Every night about ten o'clock, the boy went ashore to some village and bought ten or fifteen cents' worth of meal or bacon.

Sometimes I lifted a chicken that wasn't roosting comfortable. Pap always said, 'Take a chicken when you get a chance, because if you don't want him yourself you can easy find somebody that does, and a good deed ain't never forgot.' I never see pap when he didn't want the chicken himself, but that is what he used to say, anyway.

In the same way, the boy went into the fields and borrowed a watermelon or a 'mush melon' or a 'punkin' or some new corn. The book, you observe, has no moral.

They then take on board the immortal pair of rogues and vagabonds—the *King* and the *Duke.* Writes the young philosopher:

It didn't take me long to make up my mind that these liars wasn't no kings and dukes at all, but just low down humbugs and frauds. But I never said nothing, never let on; kept it to myself. It's the best way; then you don't have no quarrels and don't get into no trouble.

The chapters with the *King* and the *Duke* are amazing for the sheer impudence of the two rogues and the remarks of the boy. He makes no remonstrance, he affects no indignation; he falls in with every pretense on which his assistance is required, and he watches all the time—watches for the chance to upset their little plans. And such plans! One sells quack medicines; plays and recites; lectures on mesmerism and phrenology; teaches singing and geography at schools for a change; does anything that comes handy. The other preaches temperance, also religion; gets up camp meetings; is a missionary; lays on hands for curing paralysis and the like. Together they agree to get up scenes from Shakespere, especially the balcony scene in *Romeo and Juliet*; to discover water and treasure by means of the divining rod; to dissipate witch spells; to get subscriptions and advertisements for a bogus paper; to continue the preaching, and so on. The great *coup* was the personation of a man in England, brother of a man just deceased. This, in fact, very nearly came off; it would have come off, with a bag of six thousand dollars, but for the boy, who defeats their villainies. How he does this, how the older of the two rogues sells *Jim* for a runaway, how the two rascals, the *King* and the *Duke,* have to ride on a rail, how *Jim* is recovered, is well known by those who have read the book, and can be easily learned by those who have not. It is a book which, to repeat, has no moral. One does not expect the punishment of villainy; yet it is pleasant to catch this last glimpse of the *King* and the *Duke* thus honored by their grateful fellow citizens. This American custom of riding a rogue on a rail is not, as is generally supposed, an invention or a growth of the American people, though they are eminently inventive. It crossed the Atlantic from the old country, where, under the name of 'Riding the Stang'—a rail for the men, a basket for the women—it flourished in certain parts almost down to the present time.

Also, though the book has no moral, one is pleased to find the 'nigger' receiving his freedom at the end. And, although it has no plot, one is delighted to find that *Huckleberry* remains the same at the end as he began at the beginning. That blessed boy, who has told as many lies as there are pages in the book, is left impenitent.

> I reckon I got to light out for the Territory ahead of the rest, because Aunt Sally she's going to adopt me and civilize me, and I can't stand it. I been there before.

These are his parting words.

It was fifty years ago. Do you know what happened afterwards? I will tell you. *Huckleberry,* of course, remained not civilized; he went to live with *Jim* on Jackson Island. They had a raft and a canoe; they fished and shot and trapped; they built a log hut. *Tom Sawyer* used to visit them till he was taken away and sent to college and became a lawyer. He is now, as everybody knows, the governor of his State, and may possibly become President. Presently *Jim* died. Then *Huckleberry* was left alone. He still lives on Jackson Island in his log hut. He is now an old man; his beard is as white as that of the veteran fraud, the *King;* he is full of wisdom and wise thoughts; long and lonely nights beneath the stars, watching the endless roll of the Mississippi, have made him wise. Of the world he still knows nothing; of his ancient fibs and tricks he is impenitent.

There is another side of the book. It belongs to the fifties, the old time before the civil war, when the 'institution' was flourishing against all the efforts of the Abolitionists. Without intending it—the book has no motive—the boy restores for us that life in the Southern States. It is now so far off that even those who are old enough to remember it think of it as a kind of dream. Consider how far off it is. There is the elderly maiden lady, full of religion, who tries to teach the boy the way to heaven. She herself is living, she says, so as to go there. She has one old 'nigger' who has been with her all her life—a faithful servant, an affectionate creature. This pious woman deliberately proposes to sell the man— to *sell* him— for the sum of eight hundred dollars, or one hundred and sixty pounds sterling. Only forty years ago! Yet how far off! How far off! Is there, anywhere in the Southern States of today, any living lady who could in cold blood sell an old servant into slavery among strangers? Then there is the feud between the families of the *Grangerfords* and the *Shepherdsons.* They have a feud—do families in the South have feuds and go shooting each other now? It seems so far off; so long ago. The *Shepherdsons* and the *Grangerfords* alike are all filled out with family pride; no descendant of all the kingly houses of Europe could be prouder of family than these obscure planters. They have no education; they shoot at each other whenever they meet; they murder even the boys of either family. It is only a glimpse we catch of them as we float down the Mississippi, but it belongs to a time so long ago—so long ago.

There is another glimpse—of a riverside town. It consists of one street, of stores with awnings in front; loafers in wide straw hats and neither coat nor waistcoat lie and sit about. They do nothing; they borrow 'chaws' of tobacco of each other; the street is quite quiet and empty. Presently some wagons come in from the country, and the town is animated. It is a kind of market day. Then a drunken man rides amuck through the town, roaring and threatening. He threatens one prominent citizen so long that, after a while, the man says he has lost patience, and shoots the drunkard dead. It is all so long ago, you see. Or we are at a camp meeting—perhaps those meetings go on still, somewhere. There are a thousand people present. The meeting is provided with sheds for preaching and sheds for selling watermelons and lemonade. The young men go barefooted; the girls have sun-bonnets and linsey woolsey frocks. Some of them listen to the preaching; some sit out and carry on flirtations of the more elementary. People are invited to the mourners' bench; they crowd in, on the invitation, moved by the contagious emotion, weeping, crying, throwing themselves down in the straw. Among them, weeping more bitterly than the rest, is the wicked old *King;* he has got conviction of sin; he is broken down; he is on the mourners' bench. He is so contrite that you may hear his groans above all the rest. He begs permission to speak to the people; he confesses that he has been a pirate all his life; he is now repentant; he will be a pirate no more; he will go among his old friends and convert them. It will be difficult without money, but he will try—he will try. So they take up a collection for him, and he goes back to the raft, after kissing all the girls, with eighty seven dollars and twenty five cents in his purse. He had also found a three gallon keg of whisky, too, under a wagon. The good old man said, 'Take it all around, it laid over any day he'd ever put in, in the missionary line. Heathens,' he said, 'don't amount to shucks, alongside of pirates, to work a camp meeting with.' There are still, perhaps, country villages and places in the Central States, of which we of England know so little, where the people are simple and unsuspicious, and enjoy a red hot religion; but the world has moved, even for them. There are surely no country places left where such a ridiculous old fraud as the *King* could be believed. It may be objected that the characters are extravagant. Not so. They are all exactly and literally true; they are quite possible in a country so remote and so primitive. Every figure in the book is a type; *Huckleberry* has exaggerated none. We see the life—the dull and vacuous life—of a small township upon the Mississippi forty years ago; so far as I know, it is the only place where we can find that phase of life portrayed.

If the scenes and characters of the book are all life-like and true to nature, still more life-like is the figure of the boy as he stands out, at the end, when we close the volume, selfrevealed.

He is, to begin with, shrewd. It is a word which may have a good or a bad meaning; in the former sense, I think that shrewdness is a more common characteristic of the American than of the

Englishman. I mean that he is more ready to question, to doubt, to examine, to understand. He is far more ready to exercise freedom of thought; far less ready to accept authority. His individuality is more intense; he is one against the world; he is more readily on the defensive. *Huckleberry*, therefore, however it may be with his countrymen at large, is shrewd. He questions everything. For instance, he is told to pray for everything. He tries it; he prays for fish hooks. None come; he worries over the matter a while, and then he concludes to let it go. If he has no religion, however, he has plenty of superstition; he believes all the wonderful things the 'nigger' *Jim* tells him: the ghosts and the signs of bad luck and good luck.

He has an immense natural love for the woods and forests; for the open air; for the great river laden with the rafts forever going down the stream; for the night as much as the day; for the dawn as much as the splendor of the noonday.

If he loves the still and solemn night and the woods, he loves also the creatures in the woods—squirrels, turtles, snakes. He is a boy who belongs to the river, which he will never desert. His lies and his thievings and his acquiescence in frauds—to be sure, he was forced—do not affect his nature; he passes through these things and will shake them off and forget them. All his life he will live in the present, which is a part of the nomadic spirit. He will look on without indignation at the things men do around him; but his home will be on Jackson's Island in a log hut, alone, and far from the haunts of men. And he will never grow weary of watching the lumber rafts go by; or of sitting beside the mighty flood; or of watching the day break, and the sun set; or of lying in the shade so long as he can look at the snakes and the turtles or listen while a couple of squirrels 'set on a limb and jabber at him friendly.' Because, you see, there is no moral in this book; and no motive; and no plot.

Mark Twain: An Inquiry

William Dean Howells

...So far as I know, Mr. Clemens is the first writer to use in extended writing the fashion we all use in thinking, and to set down the thing that comes into his mind without fear or favor of the thing that went before or the thing that may be about to follow. I, for instance, in putting this paper together, am anxious to observe some sort of logical order, to discipline such impressions and notions as I have of the subject into a coherent body which shall march columnwise to a conclusion obvious if not inevitable from the start. But Mr. Clemens, if he were writing it, would not be anxious to do any such thing. He would take whatever offered itself to his hand out of that mystical chaos, that divine ragbag, which we call the mind, and leave the reader to look after relevancies and sequences for himself. These there might be, but not of that hard-and-fast sort which I am eager to lay hold of, and the result would at least be satisfactory to the author, who would have shifted the whole responsibility to the reader, with whom it belongs, at least as much as with the author. In other words, Mr. Clemens uses in work on the larger scale the method of the elder essayists, and you know no more where you are going to bring up in *The Innocents Abroad* or *Following the Equator* than in an essay of Montaigne. The end you arrive at is the end of the book, and you reach it amused but edified, and sorry for nothing but to be there. You have noted the author's thoughts, but not his order of thinking; he has not attempted to trace the threads of association

From "Mark Twain: An Inquiry," *North American Review*, 172 (February 1901), 306-21.

not his logic, has convinced you, or, rather, it has persuaded you, for you have not been brought under conviction. It is not certain that this method is of design with Mr. Clemens; that might spoil it; and possibly he will be as much surprised as any one to know that it is his method. It is imaginable that he pursues it from no wish but to have pleasure of his work, and not to fatigue either himself or his reader; and his method may be the secret of his vast popularity, but it cannot be the whole secret of it. Any one may compose a scrapbook, and offer it to the public with nothing of Mark Twain's good-fortune. Everything seems to depend upon the nature of the scraps, after all; his scraps might have been consecutively arranged, in a studied order, and still have immensely pleased; but there is no doubt that people like things that have at least the appearance of not having been drilled into line. Life itself has that sort of appearance as it goes on; it is an essay with moments of drama in it rather than a drama; it is a lesson, with the precepts appearing haphazard, and not precept upon precept; it is a school, but not always a schoolroom; it is a temple, but the priests are not always in their sacerdotal robes; sometimes they are eating the sacrifice behind the altar and pouring the libations for the god through the channels of their dusty old throats. An instinct of something chaotic, ironic, empiric in the order of experience seems to have been the inspiration of our humorist's art, and what finally remains with the reader, after all the joking and laughing, is not merely the feeling of having had a mighty good time, but the conviction that he has got the worth of his money. He has not gone through the six hundred pages of *The Innocents Abroad*, or *Following the Equator*, without having learned more of the world as the writer saw it than any but the rarest traveller is able to show for his travel; and possibly, with his average practical American public, which was his first tribunal, and must always be his court of final appeal, Mark Twain justified himself for being so delightful by being so instructive. If this bold notion is admissible, it seems the moment to say that no writer ever imparted information more inoffensively.

But his great charm is his absolute freedom in a region where most of us are fettered and shackled by immemorial convention. He saunters out into the trim world of letters, and lounges across its neatly kept paths, and walks about on the grass at will, in spite of all the signs that have been put up from the beginning of literature, warning people of dangers and penalties for the slightest trespass.

One of the characteristics I observe in him is his single-minded use of words, which he employs as Grant did to express the plain, straight meaning their common acceptance has given them with no regard to their structural significance or their philological implications. He writes English as if it were a primitive and not a derivative language, without Gothic or Latin or Greek behind it, or German and French beside it. The result is the English in which the most vital works of English literature are cast, rather than the English of Milton and Thackeray and Mr. Henry James. I do not say that the English of the authors last named is less than vital, but only that it is not the most vital. It is scholarly and conscious; it knows who its grandfather was; it has the refinement and subtlety of an old patriciate. You will not have with it the widest suggestion, the largest human feeling, or perhaps the loftiest reach of imagination, but you will have the keen joy that exquisite artistry in words can alone impart, and that you will not have in Mark Twain. What you will have in him is a style which is as personal, as biographical as the style of any one who has written, and expresses a civilization whose courage of the chances, the preferences, the duties, is not the measure of its essential modesty. It has a thing to say, and it says it in the word that may be the first or second or third choice, but will not be the instrument of the most fastidious ear, the most delicate and exacting sense, though it will be the word that surely and strongly conveys intention from the author's mind to the reader's. It is the Abraham Lincolnian word, not the Charles Sumnerian; it is American, Western.

Now that Mark Twain has become a fame so world-wide, we should be in some danger of forgetting, but for his help, how entirely American he is, and we have already forgotten, perhaps, how truly Western he is, though his work, from first to last, is always reminding us of the fact. But here I should like to distinguish. It is not alone in its generous humor, with more honest laughter in it than humor ever had in the world till now, that his work is so Western. Any one who has really known the West (and really to know it one must have lived it) is aware of the profoundly serious, the almost tragical strain which is the fundamental tone in the movement of such music as it has. Up to a certain point, in the presence of the mystery which we call life, it trusts and hopes and laughs; beyond that it doubts and fears, but it does not cry. It is more likely to laugh again, and in the work of Mark Twain there is little of the pathos which is supposed to be the ally of humor, little suffusion of apt tears from the smiling eyes. It is too sincere for that sort of play; and if after the doubting and the fearing it laughs again, it is with a suggestion of that resentment which youth feels when the disillusion from its trust and hope comes, and which is the grim second-mind of the West in the presence of the mystery. It is not so much the race-effect as the region-effect; it is not the Anglo-American finding expression, it is the Westerner, who is not more thoroughly the creature of circumstances, of conditions, but far more dramatically their creature than any prior man. He found himself placed in them and under them, so near to a world in which the natural and primitive was obsolete, that while he could not escape them, neither could he help challenging them. The inventions, the appliances, the improvements of the modern world invaded the hoary eld of his rivers and forests and prairies, and, while he was still a pioneer, a hunter, a trapper, he found himself confronted with the financier, the scholar, the gentleman. They seemed to him, with the world they represented, at first very droll, and he laughed. Then they set him thinking, and, as he never was afraid of anything, he thought over the whole field and demanded explanations of all his prepossessions—of equality, of humanity, of representative government, and revealed religion. When they had not their answers ready, without accepting the conventions of the modern world as solutions or in any manner final, he laughed again, not mockingly, but patiently, compassionately. Such, or somewhat like this, was the genesis and evolution of Mark Twain.

Missouri was Western, but it was also Southern, not only in the institution of slavery, to the custom and acceptance of which Mark Twain was born and bred without any applied doubt of its divinity, but in the peculiar social civilization of the older South from which his native State was settled. It would be reaching too far out to claim that American humor, of the now prevailing Western type, is of Southern origin, but without staying to attempt it I will say that I think the fact could be established; and I think one of the most notably Southern traits of Mark Twain's humor is its power of seeing the fun of Southern seriousness, but this vision did not come to him till after his liberation from neighborhood in the vaster Far West. He was the first, if not the only, man of his section to betray a consciousness of the grotesque absurdities in the Southern inversion of the civilized ideals in behalf of slavery, which must have them upside down in order to walk over them safely. No American of Northern birth or breeding could have imagined the spiritual struggle of Huck Finn in deciding to help the negro Jim to his freedom, even though he should be forever despised as a negro thief in his native town, and perhaps eternally lost through the blackness of his sin. No Northerner could have come so close to the heart of a Kentucky feud, and revealed it so perfectly, with the whimsicality playing through its carnage, or could have so brought us into the presence of the sardonic comi-tragedy of the squalid little river town where the store-keeping magnate shoots down his drunken tormentor in the arms of the drunkard's daughter, and then cows with bitter mockery the mob that comes to lynch him. The strict religiosity compatible in the Southwest with savage precepts of conduct is something that could make itself known in its amusing contrast only to the native Southwesterner, and the revolt against it is as constant in Mark Twain as the enmity to New England orthodoxy is in Doctor Holmes. But he does not take it with such serious resentment as Doctor Holmes is apt to take his inherited Puritanism, and it may be therefore that he is able to do it more perfect justice, and impart it more absolutely. At any rate, there are no more vital passages in his fiction than those which embody character as it is affected for good as well as evil by the severity of the local Sunday-schooling and church-going.

I find myself, in spite of the discipline I intend for this paper, speaking first of the fiction, which by no means came first in Mark Twain's literary development. It is true that his beginnings were in short sketches, more or less inventive, and studies of life in which he let his imagination play freely; but it was not till he had written *Tom Sawyer* that he could be called a novelist. Even now I think he should rather be called a romancer, though such a book as *Huckleberry Finn* takes itself out of the order of romance and places itself with the great things in picaresque fiction. Still, it is more poetic than picaresque, and of a deeper psychology. The probable and credible soul that the author divines in the son of the town-drunkard is one which we might each own brother, and the art which portrays this nature at first hand in the person and language of the hero, without pose or affectation, is fine art.

In the boy's history the author's fancy works realistically to an end as high as it has reached elsewhere, if not higher; and I who like *The Connecticut Yankee in King Arthur's Court* so much have half a mind to give my whole heart to *Huckleberry Finn*.

Both *Huckleberry Finn* and *Tom Sawyer* wander in episodes loosely related to the main story, but they are of a closer and more logical advance from the beginning to the end than the fiction which preceded them, and which I had almost forgotten to name before them. We owe to *The Gilded Age* a type in Colonel Mulberry Sellers which is as likely to endure as any fictitious character of our time. It embodies the sort of Americanism which survived through the Civil War, and characterized in its boundlessly credulous, fearlessly adventurous, unconsciously burlesque excess the period of political and economic expansion which followed the war. Colonel Sellers was, in some rough sort, the American of that day, which already seems so remote, and is best imaginable through him. Yet the story itself was of the fortuitous structure of what may be called the autobiographical books, such as *The Innocents Abroad* and *Roughing It*. Its desultory and accidental character was heightened by the co-operation of Mr. Clemens's fellow-humorist, Charles Dudley Warner, and such coherence as it had was weakened by the diverse qualities of their minds and their irreconcilable ideals in literature. These never combined to a sole effect or to any variety of effects that left the reader very clear what the story was all about; and yet from the cloudy solution was precipitated at least one character which, as I have said, seems of as lasting substance and lasting significance as any which the American imagination has evolved from the American environment.

If Colonel Sellers is Mr. Clemens's supreme invention, as it seems to me, I think that his *Connecticut Yankee* is his highest achievement in the way of a greatly imagined and symmetrically developed romance. Of all the fanciful schemes in fiction, it pleases me most, and I give myself with absolute delight to its notion of a keen East Hartford Yankee finding himself, by a retroactionary spell, at the court of King Arthur of Britain, and becoming part of the sixth century with all the custom and ideas of the nineteenth in him and about him. The field for humanizing satire which this scheme opens is illimitable; but the ultimate achievement, the last poignant touch, the most exquisite triumph of the book, is the return of the Yankee to his own century, with his look across the gulf of the ages at the period of which he had been a part and his vision of the sixth-century woman he had loved holding their child in her arms.

It is a great fancy, transcending in aesthetic beauty the invention in *The Prince and the Pauper*, with all the delightful and affecting implications of that charming fable, and excelling the heart-rending story in which Joan of Arc lives and prophesies and triumphs and suffers. She is, indeed, realized to the modern sense as few figures of the past have been realized in fiction; and is none the less of her time and of all time because her supposititious historian is so recurrently of ours. After Sellers, and Huck Finn, and Tom Sawyer, and the Connecticut Yankee, she is the author's finest creation; and if he had succeeded in portraying no other woman-nature, he would have approved himself its fit interpreter in her. I do not think he succeeds so often with that nature as with the boy-nature or the man-nature, apparently because it does not interest him so much. He will not trouble himself to make women talk like women at all times; oftentimes they talk too much like him, though the simple, homely sort express themselves after their kind; and Mark Twain does not always write men's dialogue so well as he might. He is apt to burlesque the lighter colloquiality, and it is only in the more serious and most tragical junctures that his people utter themselves with veracious simplicity and dignity. That great, burly fancy of his is always tempting him to the exaggeration which is the condition of so much of his personal humor, but which when it invades the drama spoils the illusion. The illusion renews itself in the great moments, but I wish it could be kept intact in the small, and I blame him that he does not rule his fancy better. His imagination is always dramatic in its conceptions, but not always in its expressions; the talk of his people is often inadequate caricature in the ordinary exigencies, and his art contents itself with makeshift in the minor action. Even in *Huck Finn*, so admirably proportioned and honestly studied, you find a piece of lawless extravagance hurled in, like the episode of the two strolling actors in the flatboat; their broad burlesque is redeemed by their final tragedy—a prodigiously real and moving passage—but the friend of the book cannot help wishing the burlesque was not there. One laughs, and then despises one's self for laughing, and this is not what Mark Twain often makes you do. There are things in him that shock, and more things that we think shocking, but this may not be so much because of their nature as because of our want of naturalness; they wound our conventions rather than our convictions. As most women are more the subjects of convention than men, his humor is not for most women; but I have a theory that, when women like it, they like it far beyond men. Its very excess must satisfy that demand of their insatiate nerves for something that there is enough of; but I offer this conjecture with instant readiness to withdraw it under correction. What I feel rather surer of is that there is something finally feminine in the inconsequence of his ratiocination, and his beautiful confidence that we shall be able to follow him to his conclusion in all those turnings and twistings and leaps and bounds by which his mind carries itself to any point but that he seems aiming at. Men, in fact, are born of women, and possibly Mark Twain owes his literary method to the colloquial style of some far ancestress who was more concerned in getting there, and amusing herself on the way, than in ordering her steps.

Possibly, also, it is to this ancestress that he owes the instinct of right and wrong which keeps him clear as to the conditions that formed him, and their injustice. Slavery in a small Missouri River town could not have been the dignified and patriarchal institution which Southerners of the older South are fond of remembering or imagining. In the second generation from Virginia ancestry of this sort, Mark Twain was born to the common necessity of looking out for himself, and, while making himself practically of another order of things, he felt whatever was fine in the old and could regard whatever was ugly and absurd more tolerantly, more humorously than those who bequeathed him their enmity to it. Fortunately for him, and for us who were to enjoy his humor, he came to his intellectual consciousness in a world so large and free and safe that he could be fair to any wrong while seeing the right so unfailingly; and nothing is finer in him than his gentleness with the error which is simply passive and negative. He gets fun out of it, of course, but he deals almost tenderly with it, and hoards his violence for the superstitions and traditions which are arrogant and active. His pictures of that old river-town, Southwestern life, with its faded and tattered aristocratic ideals and its squalid democratic realities, are pathetic, while they are so unsparingly true and so inapologetically and unaffectedly faithful.

The West, when it began to put itself into literature, could do so without the sense, or the apparent sense, of any older or politer world outside of it; whereas the East was always looking fearfully over its shoulder at Europe, and anxious to account for itself as well as represent itself. No such anxiety as this entered Mark Twain's mind, and it is not claiming too much for the Western influence upon American literature to say that the final liberation of the East from this anxiety is due to the West, and to its ignorant courage or its indifference to its difference from the rest of the world. It would not claim to be superior, as the South did, but it could claim to be humanly equal, or, rather, it would make no claim at all, but would simply be, and what it was, show itself without holding itself responsible for not being something else.

The Western boy of forty or fifty years ago grew up so close to the primeval woods or fields that their inarticulate poetry became part of his being, and he was apt to deal simply and uncritically with literature when he turned to it, as he dealt with nature. He took what he wanted, and left what he did not like; he used it for the playground, not the workshop of his spirit. Something like this I find true of Mark Twain in peculiar and uncommon measure. I do not see any proof in his books that he wished at any time to produce literature, or that he wished to reproduce life. When filled up with an experience that deeply interested him, or when provoked by some injustice or absurdity that intensely moved him, he burst forth, and the outbreak might be altogether humorous, but it was more likely to be humorous with a groundswell of seriousness carrying it profoundly forward. In all there is something curiously, not very definably, elemental, which again seems to me Western. He behaves himself as if he were the first man who was ever up against the proposition in hand. He deals as newly, for instance, with the relations of Shelley to his wife, and with as personal and direct an indignation, as if they have never attracted critical attention before; and this is the mind or the mood which he brings to all literature. Life is another affair with him; it is not a discovery, not a surprise; every one else knows how it is; but here is a new world, and he explores it with a ramping joy, and shouts for the reader to come on and see how, in spite of all the lies about it, it is the same old world of men and women, with really nothing in it but their passions and prejudices and hypocrisies. At heart he was always deeply and essentially romantic, and once must have expected life itself to be a fairy dream. When it did not turn out so he found it tremendously amusing still, and his excpectation not the least amusing thing in it, but without rancor, without grudge or bitterness in his disillusion, so that his latest word is as sweet as his first. He is deeply and essentially romantic in his literary conceptions, but when it comes to working them out he is helplessly literal and real; he is the impassioned lover, the helpless slave of the concrete. For this reason, for his wish, his necessity, first to ascertain his facts, his logic is as irresistible as his laugh.

All life seems, when he began to find it out, to have the look of a vast joke, whether the joke was on him or on his fellow-beings, or if it may be expressed without irreverence, on their common creator. But it was never wholly a joke, and it was not long before his literature began to own its pathos. The sense of this is not very apparent in *The Innocents Abroad*, but in *Roughing It* we began to be distinctly aware of it, and in the successive books it is constantly immiment, not as a clutch at the heartstrings, but as a demand of common justice, common sense, the feeling of proportion. It is not sympathy with the under dog merely as under dog that moves Mark Twain; for the under dog is sometimes rightfully under. But the probability is that it is wrongfully under, and has a claim to your inquiry into the case which you cannot ignore without atrocity. Mark Twain never ignores it; I know nothing finer in him than his perception that in this curiously contrived mechanism men suffer for their sorrows rather oftener than they suffer for their sins; and when they suffer for their sorrows they have a right not only to our pity but to our help. He always gives his help, even when he seems to leave the pity to others, and it may be safely said that no writer has dealt with so many phases of life with more unfailing justice. There is no real telling how any one comes to be what he is; all speculation concerning the fact is more or less impudent or futile conjecture; but it is conceivable that Mark Twain took from his early environment the custom of clairvoyance in things in which most humorists are purblind, and that being always in the presence of the under dog, he came to feel for him as under with him. If the knowledge and vision of slavery did not tinge all life with potential tragedy, perhaps it was this which lighted on the future humorist the indignation at injustice which glows in his page. His indignation relieves itself as often as not in a laugh; injustice is the most ridiculous thing in the world, after all, and indignation with it feels its own absurdity.

It is supposable, if not more than supposable, that the ludicrous incongruity of a slaveholding democracy nurtured upon the Declaration of Independence, and the comical spectacle of white labor owning black labor, had something to do in quickening the sense of contrast which is the fountain of humor, or is said to be so. But not to drive too hard a conjecture which must remain conjecture, we may reasonably hope to find in the untrammelled, the almost unconditional life of the later and farther West, with its individualism limited by nothing but individualism, the outside causes of the first overflow of the spring. We are so fond of classification, which we think is somehow interpretation, that one cannot resist the temptation it holds out in the case of the most unclassifiable things; and I must yield so far as to note that the earliest form of Mark Twain's work is characteristic of the greater part of it. The method used in *The Innocents Abroad* and in *Roughing It* is the method used in *Life on the Mississippi*, in *A Tramp Abroad*, and in *Following the Equator*, which constitute in bulk a good half of all his writings, as they express his dominant aesthetics. If he had written the fictions alone, we should have had to recognize a rare inventive talent, a great imagination and dramatic force; but I think it must be allowed that the personal books named overshadow the fictions. They have the qualities that give character to the fictions, and they have advantages that the fictions have not and that no fiction can have. In them, under cover of his pseudonym, we come directly into the presence of the author, which is what the reader is always longing and seeking to do; but unless the novelist is a conscienceless and tasteless recreant to the terms of his art, he cannot admit the reader to his intimacy. The personal books of Mark Twain have not only the charm of the essay's inconsequent and desultory method, in which invention, fact, reflection, and philosophy wander after one another in any following that happens, but they are of an immediate and most informal hospitality which admits you at once to the author's confidence, and makes you frankly welcome not only to his thought but to his way of thinking. He takes no trouble in the matter, and he asks you to take none. All that he requires is that you will have common sense, and be able to tell a joke when you see it. Otherwise the whole furnishing of his mental mansion is at your service, to make such use as you can of it, but he will not be always directing your course, or requiring you to enjoy yourself in this or that order.

In the case of the fictions, he conceives that his first affair is to tell a story, and a story when you are once launched upon it does not admit of deviation without some hurt to itself. In Mark Twain's novels, whether they are for boys or for men, the episodes are only those that illustrate the main narrative or relate to it, though he might have allowed himself somewhat larger latitude in the old-fashioned tradition which he has oftenest observed in them. When it comes to the critical writings, which again are personal, and which, whether they are criticisms of literature or of life, are always so striking, he is quite relentlessly logical and coherent. Here there is no lounging or sauntering, with entertaining or edifying digressions. The object is in view from the first, and the reasoning is straightforwardly to it throughout. This is as notable in the admirable paper on the Jews, or on the Austrian situation, as in that on Harriet Shelley, or that on Cooper's novels. The facts are first ascertained with a conscience uncommon in critical writing of any kind, and then they are handled with vigor and precision till the polemic is over. It does not so much matter whether you agree with the critic or not; what you have to own is that here is a man of strong convictions, clear ideas, and ardent sentiments, based mainly upon common sense of extraordinary depth and breadth.

In fact, what finally appeals to you in Mark Twain, and what may hereafter be his peril with his readers, is his common sense. It is well to eat humble pie when one comes to it at the table d'hote of life, and I wish here to offer my brother literary men a piece of it that I never refuse myself. It is true that other men do not really expect much common sense of us, whether we are poets or novelists or humorists. They may enjoy our company, and they may like us or pity us, but they do not take us very seriously, and they would as soon we were fools as not if we will only divert or comfort or inspire them. Especially if we are humorists do they doubt our practical wisdom; they are apt at first sight to take our sense for a part of the joke, and the humorist who convinces them that he is a man of as much sense as any of them, and possibly more, is in the parlous case of having given them hostages for seriousness which he may not finally be able to redeem.

I should say in the haste to which every inquiry of this sort seems subject, that this was precisely the case with Mark Twain. The exceptional observer must have known from the beginning that he was a thinker of courageous originality and penetrating sagacity, even when he seemed to be joking; but in the process of time it has come to such a pass with him that the wayfaring man can hardly shirk knowledge of the fact. The fact is thrown into sudden and picturesque relief by his return to his country after the lapse of time long enough to let a new generation grow up in knowledge of him. The projection of his reputation against a background of foreign appreciation, more or less luminous, such as no other American author has enjoyed, has little or nothing to do with his acceptance on the new terms. These poor Germans, Austrians, Englishmen, and Frenchmen who have been, from time to time in the last ten years, trying to show their esteem for his peculiar gifts could never come as close to the heart of his humor as we could; we might well doubt if they could fathom all his wisdom, which begins and ends in his humor; and if ever they seemed to chance upon his full significance, we naturally felt a kind of grudge, when we could not call it their luck, and suspected him of being less significant in the given instances than they supposed. The danger which he now runs with us is neither heightened nor lessened by the spread of his fame, but is an effect from intrinsic causes. Possibly it might not have been so great if he had come back comparatively forgotten; it is certain only that in coming back more remembered than ever, he confronts a generation which began to know him not merely by his personal books and his fiction, but by those criticisms of life and literature which have more recently attested his interest in the graver and weightier things.

Graver and weightier, people call them, but whether they are really more important than the lighter things, I am by no means sure. What I am amused with, independently of the final truth, is the possibility that his newer audience will exact this serious mood of Mr. Clemens, whereas we of his older world only suffered it, and were of a high conceit with our liberality in allowing a humorist sometimes to be a philosopher. Some of us indeed, not to be invidiously specific as to whom, were always aware of potentialities in him, which he seemed to hold in check, or to trust doubtfully to his reader as if he thought they might be thought part of the joke. Looking back over his work now, the later reader would probably be able to point out to earlier readers the evidence of a constant growth in the direction of something like recognized authority in matters of public import, especially those that were subject to the action of the public conscience as well as the public interest, until now hardly any man writing upon such matters is heard so willingly by all sorts of men. All of us, for instance, have read somewhat of the conditions in South Africa which have eventuated in the present effort of certain British politicians to destroy two free republics in the interest of certain British speculators; but I doubt if we have found the case anywhere so well stated as in the closing chapters of Mark Twain's *Following the Equator*. His estimate of the military character of the billigerents on either side is of the prophetic cast which can come only from the thorough assimilation of accomplished facts; and in those passages the student of the actual war can spell its anticipative history. It is by such handling of such questions, unpremeditated and almost casual as it seems, that Mark Twain has won his claim to be heard on any public matter, and achieved the odd sort of primacy which he now enjoys.

But it would be rather awful if the general recognition of his prophetic function should implicate the renunciation of the humor that has endeared him to mankind. It would be well for his younger following to beware of reversing the error of the elder, and taking everything in earnest, as these once took nothing, in earnest from him. To reverse that error would not be always to find his true meaning, and perhaps we shall best arrive at this by shunning one another's mistakes. In the light of the more modern appreciation, we elders may be able to see some things seriously that we once thought pure drolling, and from our experience his younger admirers may learn to receive as drolling some things that they might otherwise accept as preaching. What we all should wish to do is keep Mark Twain what he has always been: a comic force unique in the power of charming us out of our cares and troubles, united with as potent an ethic sense of the duties, public and private, which no man denies in himself without being false to other men. I think we may hope for the best he can do to help us deserve our self-respect, without forming Mark Twain societies to read philanthropic meanings into his jokes, or studying the Jumping Frog as the allegory of an imperializing republic. I trust the time may be far distant when the Meditation at the Tomb of Adam shall be memorized and declaimed by ingenuous youth as a mystical appeal for human solidarity.

The Burden of Humor

H. L. Mencken

What is the origin of the prejudice against humor? Why is it so dangerous, if you would keep the public confidence, to make the public laugh?

Is it because humor and sound sense are essentially antagonistic? Has humanity found by experience that the man who sees the fun of life is unfitted to deal sanely with its problems? I think not. No man had more of the comic spirit in him than William Shakespeare, and yet his serious reflections, by the sheer force of their sublime obviousness, have pushed their way into the race's arsenal of immortal platitudes. So, too, with Aesop, and with Lincoln and Johnson, to come down the scale. All of these men were humorists, and yet all of them performed prodigies of indubitable wisdom. And contrariwise, many an undeniable pundit has had his guffaw. Huxley, if he had not been the greatest intellectual duellist of his age, might have been its greatest wit. And Beethoven, after soaring to the heights of tragedy in the first movement of the Fifth Symphony, turned to the divine fooling, the irresistible bull-fiddling of the *scherzo*.

No, there is not the slightest disharmony between sense and humor and respectability, despite the almost universal tendency to assume that there is. But, why, then, that widespread error? What actual fact of life lies behind it, giving it a specious appearance of reasonableness? None other, I am convinced, than the fact that the average man is far too stupid to make a joke.

He may *see* a joke and love a *joke*, particularly when it floors

From *The Smart Set*, 38 (February 1913), 151-54

and flabbergasts some person he dislikes, but the only way he can himself take part in the priming and pointing of a new one is by acting as its target. In brief, his personal contact with humor tends to fill him with an accumulated sense of disadvantage, of pricked complacency, of sudden and crushing defeat; and so, by an easy psychological process, he is led into the idea that the thing itself is incompatible with true dignity of character and intellect. Hence his deep suspicion of jokers, however their thrusts. "What a damphool!"—this same half-pitying tribute he pays to wit and butt alike. He cannot separate the virtuoso of comedy from his general concept of comedy itself, and that concept is inextricably mixed with memories of foul ambuscades and mortifying hurts. And so it is not often that he is willing to admit any wisdom in a humorist, or to condone frivolity in a sage.

In all this, I believe, there is a plausible explanation of the popular, and even of the critical attitude toward the late Samuel Langhorne Clemens (Mark Twain). Unless I am so wholly mistaken that my only expiation lies in suicide, Mark was the noblest literary artist who ever set pen to paper on American soil, and not only the noblest artist, but also one of the most profound and sagacious philosophers. From the beginning of his maturity down to his old age he dealt constantly and earnestly with the deepest problems of life and living, and to his consideration of them he brought a truly amazing instinct for the truth, an almost uncanny talent for ridding the essential thing of its deceptive husks of tradition, prejudice, flubdub and balderdash. No man, not even Nietzsche, ever did greater execution against those puerilities of fancy which so many men mistake for religion, and over which they are so eager to dispute and break heads. No man had a keener eye for that element of pretense which is bound to intrude itself into all human thinking, however serious, however painstaking, however honest in intent. And yet, because the man had humor as well as acumen, because he laughed at human weakness instead of weeping over it, because he turned now and then from the riddle of life to the joy of life—because of this habit of mind it is the custom to regard him lightly and somewhat apologetically, as one debarred from greatness by unfortunate infirmities.

William Dean Howells probably knew him better than any other human being, but in all that Howells has written about him one is conscious of a conditioned admiration, of a subtle fear of allowing him too much merit, of an ineradicable disinclination to take him quite seriously. The Mark that Howells draws is not so much a great artist as a glorious *enfant terrible*. And even William Lyon Phelps, a hospitable and penetrating critic, wholly loose of orthodox shackles—even Phelps hems and haws a bit before putting Mark above Oliver Wendell Holmes, and is still convinced that "The Scarlet Letter" is an incomparably finer work of art than "Huckleberry Finn."

Well, such notions will die hard, but soon or late, I am sure, they will inevitably die. So certain am I, indeed, of their dying that I now formally announce their death in advance, and prepare to wait in patience for the delayed applause. In one of his essays Dr. Phelps shows how critical opinion of Mark has gradually evolved from scorn into indifference, and from indifference into toleration, and from toleration into apologetic praise, and from apologetic praise into hearty praise. The stage of unqualified enthusiasm is coming—it has already cast its lights before England—and I am very glad to join the lodge as a charter member. Let me now set down my faith, for the literary archeologists of day after tomorrow:

I believe that "Huckleberry Finn" is one of the great masterpieces of the world, that it is the full equal of "Don Quixote" and "Robinson Crusoe," that it is vastly better than "Gil Blas," "Tristram Shandy," "Nicholas Nickleby" or "Tom Jones." I believe that it will be read by human beings of all ages, not as a solemn duty but for the honest love of it, and over and over again, long after every book written in America between the years 1800 and 1860, with perhaps three exceptions, has disappeared entirely save as a classroom fossil. I believe that Mark Twain had a clearer vision of life, that he came nearer to its elementals and was less deceived by its false appearances, than any other American who has ever presumed to manufacture generalizations, not excepting Emerson. I believe that, admitting all his defects, he wrote better English, in the sense of cleaner, straighter, vivider, saner English, than either Irving or Hawthorne. I believe that four of his books—"Huck," "Life on the Mississippi," "Captain Stormfield's Visit to Heaven," and "A Connecticut Yankee"—are alone worth more, as works of art and as criticisms of life, than the whole output of Cooper, Irving, Holmes, Mitchell, Stedman, Whittier and Bryant. I believe that he ranks well above Whitman and certainly not below Poe. I believe that he was the true father of our national literature, the first genuinely American artist of the blood royal.

Such is my feeling at the moment, and such has been my feeling for many a moon. If any gentleman in the audience shares it, either wholly or with qualifications, then I advise him to buy and read the biography of Mark lately published by Albert Bigelow Paine (*Harper*), for therein he will find an elaborate, painstaking and immensely interesting portrait of the man, and sundry shrewd observations upon the writer.

Not that I agree with Paine in all his judgments. Far from it, indeed. It seems to me that he gets bogged hopelessly when he tries to prove that "The Innocents Abroad" is a better book than "A Tramp Abroad," that he commits a crime when he puts "Joan of Arc" above "Huck Finn," and that he is too willing to join Howells and other such literary sacristans in frowning down upon Mark's clowning, his weakness for vulgarity, his irrepressible maleness. In brief, Paine is disposed, at times, to yield to current critical opinion against what must be his own good sense. But when you have allowed for all this—and it is not obtrusive—the thing that remains is a vivid and sympathetic biography, a book with sound merit in every chapter of it, a mountain of difficulties triumphantly surmounted, a fluent and excellent piece of writing. Paine tells everything that is worth hearing, whether favorable to Mark or the reverse, and leaves out all that is not worth hearing. One closes the third volume with unbounded admiration for the industry of the biographer, and with no less admiration for his frankness and sagacity. He has given us a rich and colorful book, presenting coherently a wise selection from a perfect chaos of materials. The Mark Twain that emerges from it is almost as real as Huckleberry Finn.

And what a man that Mark Twain was! How he stood above and apart from the world, like Rabelais come to life again, observing the human comedy, chuckling over the eternal fraudulence of man! What a sharp eye he had for the bogus, in religion, politics, art, literature, patriotism, virtue! What contempt he emptied upon shams of all sorts—and what pity! Mr. Paine reveals for us very clearly, by quotation and exposition, his habitual attitude of mind. He regarded all men as humbugs, but as humbugs to be dealt with gently, as humbugs too often taken in and swindled by their own humbuggery. He saw how false reasoning, false assumptions, false gods had entered into the very warp and woof of their thinking; how impossible it was for them to attack honestly the problems of being; how helpless they were in the face of life's emergencies. And seeing all this, he laughed at them, but not often with malice. What genuine indignation he was capable of was leveled at life itself and not at its victims. Through all his later years the riddle of existence was ever before him. He thought about it constantly; he discussed it with everyone he knew; he made copious notes of his speculations. But he never came to any soothing custom-made conclusion. The more he examined life, the more it appeared to him to be without meaning, and even without direction; the more he pondered upon the idea of God, the more a definite idea of God eluded him. In the end, as Mr. Paine tells us, he verged toward a hopeless pessimism. Death seemed to him a glad release, an inestimable boon. When his daughter Jean died, suddenly, tragically, he wrote to her sister: "I am so glad she is out of it and safe—safe!"

It is this reflective, philosophizing Clemens who stands out most clearly in Mr. Paine's book. In his own works, our glimpses of him are all too brief. His wife and his friends opposed his speculations, perhaps wisely, for the artist might have been swallowed up in the sage. But he wrote much to please himself and left a vast mass of unpublished manuscript behind him. Certainly it is to be hoped that these writings will see the light, and before long. One book described by Mr. Paine, "Three Thousand Years Among the Microbes," would appear to be a satire so mordant and so large in scale that his admirers have a plain right to demand its publication. And there should be a new edition, too, of his confession of doubt, "What is Man?" of which a few copies were printed for private distribution in 1905. Yet again we have a right to ask for most if not all of his unpublished stories and sketches, many of which were suppressed at the behest of Mrs. Clemens, for reasons no longer worth considering. There is good ground for believing that his reputation will gain rather than suffer by the publication of these things, and in any case it can withstand the experiment, for "Huck Finn" and "Life on the Mississippi" and the "Connecticut Yankee" will remain, and so long as they remain there can be no question of the man's literary stature. He was one of the great artists of all time. He was the full equal of Cervantes and Molière, Swift and Defoe. He was and is one authentic giant of our national literature.

MODERN CRITICISM

America's First Truly Indigenous Masterpiece

V. S. Pritchett

After reading Hemingway and Faulkner and speculating upon the breach of American with English literature, the mind goes back to the two decisive, indigenous Americans who opened the new vein—Mark Twain and Edgar Allan Poe. Everything really American, really non-English, comes out of that pair of spiritual derelicts, those two scarecrow figures with their half-lynched minds. We have never had the obverse of Puritanism in England, for the political power of Puritanism lasted only a decade. If an Englishman hated Puritanism, he could fall back on the rest of the elaborate English tradition; if an American hated that philosophy (which had become almost totalitarian in the United States), he found himself alone in a wilderness, with nothing but bottomless cynicism and bitterness for his consolation. There has never been in English literature a cynicism to compare with the American; at any rate we have never had the American kind, with its broken chopper edge and its ugly wound. We have also never had its by-product: the humorous practical philosophers, the Josh Billings, Artemus Wards, Will Rogers, the Pudd'nhead Wilsons with their close-fisted proverbs.

"Training is everything. The peach was once a bitter almond: cauliflower is nothing but cabbage with a college education."

Or:

From *New Statesman and Nation*, 22 (August 2, 1941), 113. Title provided by editor.

"Consider well the proportions of things. It is better to be a young June bug than an old bird of Paradise."

Pudd'nhead Wilson was, of course, Twain's invention.

I say we have never had this kind of rumination, but there is one exception to prove the rule and to prove it very well, for he also is an uprooted and, so to speak, colonial writer. The Anglo-Indian Kipling with his "A woman is always a woman, but a good cigar is a smoke," is our first writer in the American school, with a cynicism, a brand of humour and a jungle book of beliefs which, I think, would be characteristic of our literature if we become seriously totalitarian in the future. For English totalitarianism would create the boredom and bitterness of the spiritual wilderness, as surely as Puritanism did in America.

When Mark Twain turned upon the religion of his childhood because it was intolerable, he was unaware that it would destroy him by turning him into a money-grubber of the most disastrously Puritan kind. Fortunately the resources of the imagination are endless even when a fanatical philosophy wrecks human life, genius and happiness. Out of the mess which Twain made of his life, amid the awful pile of tripe which he wrote, there does rise one book which has the serenity of a thing of genius. *Huckleberry Finn* takes the breath away. Knowing Mark Twain's life, knowing the hell of vulgarity from which the book has ascended, one dreads as one turns from page to page the seemingly inevitable flop. How can a low comedian, so tortured and so angry, refrain from blackguarding God, Man and Nature for the narrow boredom of his early life, and ruining the perfect comedy and horror of this story? But imaginative writers appear to get at least one lucky break in their careers; for a moment the conflicts are assimilated, the engine ceases to work against itself. *Huckleberry Finn* does not flop. America gets its first truly indigenous masterpiece. The small boyhood of Huck Finn is the small boyhood of a new culture.

The curious thing about *Huckleberry Finn* is that, although it is one of the funniest books in all literature and really astonishing in the variety of its farce and character, we are even more moved than we are amused by it. Why are we moved? Do we feel the sentiment of sympathy only? Are we sighing with some envy and self-pity? "Alas, Huck Finn is just what I would have been in my boyhood if I had had half a chance?" Are we sorry for the va-gant, or are we moved by his rebellion? These minor feelings may play their part; but they are only sighs on the surface of the main stream of our emotion. Mark Twain has brought to his subject far more than this personal longing; he has become the channel of the generic emotion which floods all really American literature—the emotion of nostalgia. In that absurd, brilliant, hit-or-miss book, *Studies in Classical American Literature*, which is so often dead right, D. H. Lawrence called this feeling the longing of the rebel for a master. It may be simply the longing for a spiritual home, but it is as strong in Mark Twain as it is implicit in Hemingway. One finds this feeling in Anglo-Irish literature which is also colonial and, in a less lasting way, in the work of Kipling. The peculiar power of American nostalgia is that it is not only harking back to something lost in the past, but suggests also the tragedy of a lost future. As Huck Finn and old Jim drift down the Mississippi from one horrifying little town to the next and hear the voices of men quietly swearing at one another across the water; as they pass the time of day with the scroungers, rogues, murderers, the lonely women, the frothing revivalists, the maundering boatmen and fantastic drunks of the river towns, we see the human wastage that is left in the wake of a great effort of the human will, the hopes frustrated, the idealism which has been whittled down to eccentricity and craft. These people are the price paid for building a new country. It is not, once you have faced it—which Dickens did not do in *Martin Chuzzlewit*, obsessed as he was with the negative pathos of the immigrant—it is not a disheartening spectacle; for the value of a native humour like Twain's is that it expresses a profound reality in human nature: the ability of man to adjust himself to circumstance and to live somehow.

Movement is one of the great consolers of human woe; movement, a sense of continual migration, is the history of America. This factor gives Twain's wonderful descriptions of the journey down the Mississippi their haunting overtone. His natural sensibility which is shown nowhere else in his writings and which is indeed vulgarly repressed in them is awakened:

> "...then we set down on the sandy bottom where the water was about knee-deep and watched the daylight come. Not a sound anywhere—perfectly still—just like the whole world was asleep, only sometimes the bullfrogs a-clattering maybe. The first thing to see, looking away over the water, was a kind of dull line—that was the woods on t'other side—-you couldn't make nothing else out;

then a pale place in the sky; then more paleness, spreading around; then the river softened up, away off, and wasn't black any more but grey; you could see little dark spots drifting along, ever so far away—trading scows and such things; and long black streaks—rafts; sometimes you could hear a sweep screaking; or jumbled-up voices, it was so still, and sounds come so far; and by-and-by you could see a streak on the water which you know by the look of the streak that there's a snag in the swift current which breaks on it and that makes that streak look that way; and you see the mist curl up off the water, and the east reddens up, and the river, and you make out a log cabin in the edge of the woods, away on the bank t'other side of the river, being a woodyard likely, and piled by them cheats so you can throw a dog through it anywheres...."

The subject of *Huckleberry Finn* is the comical but also brutal effect of an anarchic rebellion against civilisation and especially its traditions:

"I reckon I got to light out for the Territory ahead of the rest, because Aunt Sally she's going to adopt me and sivilize me and I can't stand it. I been there before."

Huck isn't interested in "Moses and the Bulrushers" because Huck "don't take no stock of dead people." He garbles European history when he is discussing Kings with Jim, the negro. Whether Huck is the kind of boy who will grow up to build a new civilisation is doubtful; Tom Sawyer obviously would do so because he is imaginative. Huck never imagines anything except fears. Huck is "lowdown plain ornery," in trouble because of the way he was brought up with "Pap." He is a natural anarchist and bum. He can live without civilisation, depending on simple affections and workaday loyalties. He is the first of those typical American portraits of the underdog, which have culminated in the "poor white" literature and Charlie Chaplin—an underdog who gets along on horse sense, so to speak. Romanticism, ideas, ideals, are repugnant to Huck.

Mark Twain obliges you to accept the boy as the humorous norm. Without him the violence of the book would be stark reporting of low life. For if this is a great comic book it is also a book of terror and brutality. Think of the scenes: Pap with d.t.'s chasing Huck round the cabin with a knife; Huck sitting up all night with a gun preparing to shoot the old man; Huck's early familiarity with corpses; the pig killing scene; the sight of the frame house (evidently some sort of brothel) floating down the Mississippi with a murdered man in it; the fantastic events at the Southerner's house where two families are shooting each other down in a vendetta; the drunken Boggs who comes into town to pick a quarrel and is eventually coolly shot dead before the eyes of his screaming young daughter by the man he has insulted. The "Duke" and "the King," those cynical rascals whose adventures liven up the second half of the story, are sharpers, twisters and crooks of the lowest kind. Yet a child is relating all this with a child's detachment and with a touch of morbidity. Marvellous as it all is as picaresque episode and as a description of the mess of frontier life, it is strong meat. Sometimes we wonder how Twain's public stomached such illusionless reporting. The sardonic humour and the important fact that in this one book Mark Twain never forced a point nor overwrote—in the Dickens way, for example—are of course the transfiguring and beguiling forces. The corpse and coffin humour is a dry wine which raises his animal spirits. Old Jim not only looked like a dead man after "the King" had painted him blue, but like one "who had been dead a considerable time." Judiciousness is carried to the comic limit.

Is *Huckleberry Finn* one of the great works of picaresque literature? It is, granting the limits of a boy's mind in the hero and the author, a comic masterpiece; but this limitation is important. It is not a book which grows spiritually, if we compare it to *Quixote*, *Dead Souls* or even *Pickwick*; and it is lacking in that civilised quality which you are bound to lose when you throw over civilisation—the quality of pity. One is left with the cruelty of American humour, a cruelty which is softened by the shrewd moralisings of the humorous philosophers—the Josh Billings, the Artemus Wards, the Will Rogers. And once Mark Twain passed this exquisite moment of his maturity, he went to bits in that morass of sentimentality, cynicism, melodrama and vulgarity which have damned him for the adult reader. I advise those who haven't read *Huckleberry Finn* since their school days to read it again.

The Greatness of Huckleberry Finn

Lionel Trilling

In 1876 Mark Twain published *The Adventures of Tom Sawyer* and in the same year he began what he called "another boys' book." He set little store by the new venture and said that he had undertaken it "more to be at work than anything else." His heart was not in it—"I like it only tolerably well as far as I have got," he said, "and may possibly pigeonhole or burn the MS when it is done." He pigeonholed it long before it was done and for as much as four years. In 1880 he took it out and carried it forward a little, only to abandon it again. He had a theory of unconscious composition and believed that a book must write itself; the book which he referred to as "Huck Finn's Autobiography" refused to do the job of its own creation and he would not coerce it.

But then in the summer of 1882 Mark Twain was possessed by a charge of literary energy which, as he wrote to a friend, was more intense than any he had experienced for many years. He worked all day and every day, and periodically he so fatigued himself that he had to recruit his strength by a day or two of smoking and reading in bed. It is impossible not to suppose that this great creative drive was connected with—was perhaps the direct result of—the visit to the Mississippi he had made earlier in the year, the trip which forms the matter of the second part of *Life on the Mississippi*. His boyhood and youth on the river he so profoundly loved had been at once the happiest and most significant part of Mark Twain's life; his return to it in middle age stirred vital memories which revived and refreshed the idea of

Huckleberry Finn. Now at last the book was not only ready but eager to write itself. But it was not to receive much conscious help from its author. He was always full of second-rate literary schemes and now, in the early weeks of the summer, with *Huckleberry Finn* waiting to complete itself, he turned his hot energy upon several of these sorry projects, the completion of which gave him as much sense of satisfying productivity as did his eventual absorption in *Huckleberry Finn*.

When at last *Huckleberry Finn* was completed and published and widely loved, Mark Twain became somewhat aware of what he had accomplished with this book that had been begun as journeywork and depreciated, postponed, threatened with destruction. It is his masterpiece, and perhaps he learned to know that. But he could scarcely have estimated it for what it is, one of the world's great books and one of the central documents of American culture.

2

Wherein does its greatness lie? Primarily in its power of telling the truth. An awareness of this quality as it exists in *Tom Sawyer* once led Mark Twain to say of the earlier work "it is *not* a boys' book at all. It will be read only by adults. It is written only for adults." But this was only a manner of speaking, Mark Twain's way of asserting, with a discernible touch of irritation, the degree of truth he had achieved. It does not represent his usual view either of boys' books or of boys. No one, as he well knew, sets a higher value on truth than a boy. Truth is the whole of a boy's conscious demand upon the world of adults. He is likely to believe that the adult world is in a conspiracy to lie to him, and it is this belief, by no means unfounded, that arouses Tom and Huck and all boys to their moral sensitivity, their everlasting concern with justice, which they call fairness. At the same time it often makes them skillful and profound liars in their own defense, yet they do not tell the ultimate lie of adults: they do not lie to themselves. That is why Mark Twain felt that it was impossible to carry Tom Sawyer beyond boyhood—in maturity "he would lie just like all the other one-horse men of literature and the reader would conceive a hearty contempt for him."

Certainly one element in the greatness of *Huckleberry Finn*—as also in the lesser greatness of *Tom Sawyer*—is that it succeeds first as a boys' book. One can read it at ten and then annually ever after, and each year find that it is as fresh as the year before, that it has changed only in becoming somewhat larger. To read it young is like planting a tree young—each year adds a new growth-ring of meaning, and the book is as little likely as the tree to become dull. So, we may imagine, an Athenian boy grew up together with the *Odyssey*. There are few other books which we can know so young and love so long.

The truth of *Huckleberry Finn* is of a different kind from that of *Tom Sawyer*. It is a more intense truth, fiercer and more complex. *Tom Sawyer* has the truth of honesty—what is says about things and feelings is never false and always both adequate and beautiful. *Huckleberry Finn* has this kind of truth, too, but it has also the truth of moral passion; it deals directly with the virtue and depravity of man's heart.

Perhaps the best clue to the greatness of *Huckleberry Finn* has been given to us by a writer who is as different from Mark Twain as it is possible for one Missourian to be from another. T. S. Eliot's poem, "The Dry Salvages," the third of his *Four Quartets*, begins with a meditation on the Mississippi, which Mr. Eliot knew in his St. Louis boyhood. These are the opening lines:

> I do not know much about gods; but I think that the river
> Is a strong brown god...

And the meditation goes on to speak of the god as

> almost forgotten
> By the dwellers in cities—ever, however, implacable,
> Keeping his seasons and rages, destroyer, reminder of
> What men choose to forget. Unhonoured, unpropitiated
> By worshippers of the machine, but waiting, watching and waiting.[1]

Huckleberry Finn is a great book because it is about a god—about, that is, a power which seems to have a mind and will of its own, and which, to men of moral imagination, appears to embody a great moral idea.

Huck himself is the servant of the river-god, and he comes very close to being aware of the divine nature of the being he serves. The world he inhabits is perfectly equipped to accommodate a deity, for it is full of presences and meanings which it conveys by natural signs and also by preternatural omens and taboos: to look at the moon over the left shoulder, to shake the tablecloth after sundown, to handle a snakeskin, are ways of offending the obscure and prevalent spirits. Huck is at odds, on moral and aesthetic grounds, with the only form of Christianity he knows, and his very intense moral life may be said to derive from his love of the river. He lives in a perpetual adoration of the Mississippi's power and charm. Huck, of course, always expresses himself better than he can know, but nothing draws upon his gift of speech like his response to his deity. After every sally into the social life of the shore, he returns to the river with relief and thanksgiving; and at each return, regular and explicit as a chorus in a Greek tragedy, there is a hymn of praise to the god's beauty, mystery, and strength, and to his noble grandeur in contrast with the pettiness of men.

Generally the god is benign, a being of long sunny days and spacious nights. But, like any god, he is also dangerous and deceptive. He generates fogs which bewilder, and he contrives echoes and false distances which confuse. His sandbars can ground and his hidden snags can mortally wound a great steamboat. He can cut away the solid earth from under a man's feet and take his house with it. The sense of the danger of the river is what saves the book from any touch of the sentimentality and moral ineptitude of most works of the imagination which contrast the life of nature with the life of society.

The river itself is only divine; it is not ethical and good. But its nature seems to foster the goodness of those who love it and try to fit themselves to its ways. And we must observe that we cannot make—that Mark Twain does not make—an absolute opposition between the river and human society. To Huck much of the charm of the river life is human: it is the raft and the wigwam and Jim. He has not run away from Miss Watson and the Widow Douglas and his brutal father to a completely individualistic liberty, for in Jim he finds his true father, very much as Stephen Dedalus in James Joyce's *Ulysses* finds his true father in Leopold Bloom.[2] The boy and the Negro slave form a family, a primitive community—and it is a community of saints.

Huck's intense and even complex moral quality may possibly not appear on a first reading, for one may be caught and convinced by his own estimate of himself, by his brags about his lazy hedonism, his avowed preference for being alone, his dislike of civilization. The fact is, of course, that he is involved in civilization up to his ears. His escape from society is but his way of reaching what society ideally dreams of for itself. Responsibility is the very essence of his character, and it is perhaps to the point that the original of Huck, a boyhood companion of Mark Twain's named Tom Blankenship, did, like Huck, "light out for the Territory," only to become a justice of the peace in Montana, "a good citizen and greatly respected."

Huck does indeed have all the capacities for simple happiness he says he has, but circumstances and his own moral nature make him the least carefree of boys—he is always "in a sweat" over the predicament of someone else. He has a great sense of the sadness of human life, and although he likes to be alone, the words "lonely"and "loneliness" are frequent with him. The note of his special sensibility is struck early in the story: "Well, when Tom and me got to the edge of the hilltop we looked away down into the village and could see three or four lights twinkling where there were sick folks, maybe; and the stars over us was sparkling ever so fine; and down by the village was the river, a whole mile broad, and awful still and grand." The identification of those three of four lonely lights as the lamps of sick-watches defines Huck's character.

His sympathy is quick and immediate. When the circus audience laughs at the supposedly drunken man who tries to ride the horse, Huck is only miserable: "It wasn't funny to me...; I was all of a tremble to see his danger." When he imprisons the intending murderers on the wrecked steamboat, his first thought is of how to get someone to rescue them, for he considers "how dreadful it was, even for murderers, to be in such a fix. I says to myself, there ain't no telling but I might come to be a murderer myself yet, and then how would I like it?" But his sympathy is never sentimental. When at last he knows that the murderers are beyond help, he has no inclination to false pathos. "I felt a little bit heavy-hearted about the gang, but not much, for I reckoned that if they could stand it I could." His will is genuinely good and therefore he has no need to torture himself with guilty second thoughts.

Not the least remarkable thing about Huck's feeling for people is that his tenderness goes along with the assumption that his fellow men are likely to be dangerous and wicked. He travels incognito, never telling the truth about himself and never twice telling the same lie, for he trusts no one and the lie comforts him even when it is not necessary. He instinctively knows that the best way to keep a party of men away from Jim on the raft is to beg them to come aboard to help his family stricken with smallpox. And if he had not already had the knowledge of human weakness and stupidity and cowardice, he would soon have acquired it, for all his encounters forcibly teach it to him—the insensate feud of the Grangerfords and Shepherdsons, the invasion of the raft by the Duke and the King, the murder of Boggs, the lynching party, and the speech of Colonel Sherburn. Yet his profound and bitter knowledge of human depravity never prevents him from being a friend to man.

No personal pride interferes with his well-doing. He knows what status is and on the whole he respects it—he is really a very *respectable* person and inclines to like "quality folks"—but he himself is unaffected by it. He himself has never had status, he has always been the lowest of the low, and the considerable fortune he had acquired in *The Adventures of Tom Sawyer* is never real to him. When the Duke suggests that Huck and Jim render him the personal service that accords with his rank, Huck's only comment is, "Well, that was easy so we done it." He is injured in every possible way by the Duke and the King, used and exploited and manipulated, yet when he hears that they are in danger from a mob, his natural impulse is to warn them. And when he fails of his purpose and the two men are tarred and feathered and ridden on a rail, his only thought is, "Well, it made me sick to see it; and I was sorry for them poor pitiful rascals, it seemed like I couldn't ever feel any hardness against them any more in the world."

And if Huck and Jim on the raft do indeed make a community of saints, it is because they do not have an ounce of pride between them. Yet this is not perfectly true, for the one disagreement they ever have is over a matter of pride. It is on the occasion when Jim and Huck have been separated by the fog. Jim has mourned Huck as dead, and then, exhausted, has fallen asleep. When be awakes and finds that Huck has returned, he is overjoyed; but Huck convinces him that he has only dreamed the incident, that there has been no fog, no separation, no chase, no reunion, and then allows him to make an elaborate "interpretation" of the dream he now believes he has had. Then the joke is sprung, and in the growing light of the dawn Huck points to the debris of leaves on the raft and the broken oar.

"Jim looked at the trash, and then looked at me, and back at the trash again. He had got the dream fixed so strong in his head that he couldn't seem to shake it loose and get the facts back into its place again right away. But when he did get the thing straightened around he looked at me steady without ever smiling, and says:

"'What do dey stan'for? I'se gwyne to tell you. When I got all wore out wid work, en wid de callin' for you, en went to sleep, my heart wuz mos' broke bekase you wuz los', en I didn't k'yer no mo' what became er me en de raf'. En when I wake up en fine you back agin, all safe en soun', de tears come, en I could a got down on my knees en kiss yo' foot, I's so thankful. En all you wuz thinkin' 'bout wuz how you could make a fool uv ole Jim wid a lie. Dat truck dah is *trash;* en trash is what people is dat puts dirt on de head er dey fren's en makes 'em ashamed.'

"Then he got up slow and walked to the wigwam, and went in there without saying anything but that."

The pride of human affection has been touched, one of the few prides that has any true dignity. And at its utterance, Huck's one last dim vestige of pride of status, his sense of his position as a white man, wholly vanishes: "It was fifteen minutes before I could work myself up to go and humble myself to a nigger; but I done it, and I warn't sorry for it afterward, neither."

This incident is the beginning of the moral testing and development which a character so morally sensitive as Huck's must inevitably undergo. And it becomes an heroic character when, on the urging of affection, Huck discards the moral code he has always taken for granted and resolves to help Jim in his escape from slavery. The intensity of his struggle over the act suggests how deeply he is involved in the society which he rejects. The satiric brilliance of the episode lies, of course, in Huck's solving his problem not by doing "right" but by doing "wrong." He has only to consult his conscience, the conscience of a Southern boy in the middle of the last century, to know that he ought to return Jim to slavery. And as soon as he makes the decision according to conscience and decides to inform on Jim, he has all the warmly gratifying emotions of conscious virtue. "Why, it was astonishing, the way I felt as light as a feather right straight off, and my troubles all gone...I felt good and all washed clean of sin for the first time I had ever felt so in my life, and I knowed I could pray now." And when at last he finds that he cannot endure his decision but must change it and help Jim in his escape, it is not because he has acquired any new ideas about slavery—he believes that he detests Abolitionist; he himself answers when he is asked if the explosion of a steamboat boiler had hurt anyone, "No'm, killed a nigger," and of course he finds nothing wrong in the responsive comment, "Well, it's lucky because sometimes people do get hurt." Ideas and ideals can be of no help to him in his moral crisis. He no more condemns slavery than Tristram and Lancelot condemn marriage; he is as consciously *wicked* as any illicit lover of romance and he consents to be damned for a personal devotion, never questioning the justice of the punishment he has incurred.

Huckberry Finn was once barred from certain libraries and schools for its alleged subversion of morality. The authorities had in mind the book's endemic lying, the petty thefts, the denigrations of respectability and religion, the bad language and the bad grammar. We smile at that excessive care, yet in point of fact *Huckleberry Finn* is indeed a subversive book—no one who reads thoughtfully the dialectic of Huck's great moral crisis will ever again be wholly able to accept without some question and some irony the assumptions of the respectable morality by which he lives, nor will ever again be certain that what he considers the clear dictates of moral reason are not merely the engrained customary beliefs of his time and place.

3

We are not likely to miss in *Huckleberry Finn* the subtle, implicit moral meaning of the great river. But we are likely to understand these moral implications as having to do only with personal and individual conduct. And since the sum of individual pettiness is on the whole pretty constant, we are likely to think of the book as applicable to mankind in general and at all times and in all places, and we praise it by calling it "universal." And so it is; but like many books to which that large adjective applies, it is also local and particular. It has a particular moral reference to the United States in the period after the Civil War. It was then when, in Mr. Eliot's phrase, the river was forgotten, and precisely by the "dwellers in cities," by the "worshippers of the machine."

The Civil War and the development of the railroads ended the great days when the river was the central artery of the nation. No contrast could be more moving than that between the hot, turbulent energy of the river life of the first part of *Life on the Mississippi* and the melancholy reminiscence of the second part. And the war that brought the end of the rich Mississippi days also marked a change in the quality of life in America which, to many men, consisted of a deterioration of American moral values. It is of course a human habit to look back on the past and to find it a better and more innocent time than the present. Yet in this instance there seems to be an objective basis for the judgment. We cannot disregard the testimony of men so diverse as Henry Adams, Walt Whitman, William Dean Howells, and Mark Twain himself, to mention but a few of the many who were in agreement on this point. All spoke of something that had gone out of American life after the war, some simplicity, some innocence, some peace. None of them was under any illusion about the amount of ordinary human wickedness that existed in the old days, and Mark Twain certainly was not. The difference was in the public attitude, in the things that were now accepted and made respectable in the national ideal. It was, they all felt, connected with new emotions about money. As Mark Twain said, where formerly "the people had desired money," now they "fall down and worship it." The new gospel was, "Get money. Get it quickly. Get it in abundance. Get it in prodigious abundance. Get it dishonestly if you can, honestly if you must."[3]

With the end of the Civil War capitalism had established itself. The relaxing influence of the frontier was coming to an end. Americans increasingly became "dwellers in cities" and "worshippers of the machine." Mark Twain himself became a notable part of this new dispensation. No one worshipped the machine more than he did, or thought he did—he ruined himself by his devotion to the Paige typesetting machine by which he hoped to make a fortune even greater than he had made by his writing, and he sang the praises of the machine age in *A Connecticut Yankee in King Arthur's Court*. He associated intimately with the dominant figures of American business enterprise. Yet at the same time he hated the new way of life and kept bitter memoranda of his scorn, commenting on the low morality or the bad taste or the smugness and dullness of the men who were shaping the national ideal and directing the destiny of the nation.

Mark Twain said of *Tom Sawyer* that it "is simply a hymn, put into prose form to give it a worldly air." He might have said the same, and with even more reason, of *Huckleberry Finn*, which is a hymn to an older American forever gone, an American which had its great national faults, which was full of violence and even of cruelty, but which still maintained its sense of reality, for it was not yet enthralled by money, the father of ultimate illusion and lies. Against the money-god stands the river-god, whose comments are silent—sunlight, space, uncrowded time, stillness and danger. It was quickly forgotten once its practical usefulness had passed, but, as Mr. Eliot's poem says, "The river is within us...."

4

In form and style *Huckleberry Finn* is an almost perfect work. Only one mistake has ever been charged against it, that it concludes with Tom Sawyer's elaborate, too elaborate, game of Jim's escape. Certainly this episode is too long—in the original draft it was much longer—and certainly it is a falling-off, as almost anything would have to be, from the incidents of the river. Yet it has a certain formal aptness—like, say, that of the Turkish initiation which brings Molière's *Le Bourgeois Gentilhomme* to its close. It is a rather mechanical development of an idea, and yet some device is needed to permit Huck to return to his anonymity, to give up the role of hero, to fall into the background which he prefers, for he is modest in all things and could not well endure the attention and glamour which attend a hero at a book's end. For this purpose nothing could serve better than the mind of Tom Sawyer with its literary furnishings, its conscious romantic desire for experience and the hero's part, and its ingenious schematization of life to achieve that aim.

The form of the book is based on the simplest of all novel-forms, the so-called picaresque novel, or novel of the road, which strings its incidents on the line of the hero's travels. But, as Pascal says, "rivers are roads that move," and the movement of the road in its own mysterious life transmutes the primitive simplicity of the form: the road itself is the greatest character in this novel of the road, and the hero's departures from the river and his returns to it compose a subtle and significant pattern. The linear simplicity of the picaresque novel is further modified by the story's having a clear dramatic organization: it has a beginning, a middle and an end, and a mounting suspense of interest.

As for the style of the book, it is not less than definitive in

American literature. The prose of *Huckleberry Finn* established for written prose the virtues of American colloquial speech. This has nothing to do with pronunciation or grammar. It has something to do with ease and freedom in the use of language. Most of all it has to do with the structure of the sentence, which is simple, direct, and fluent, maintaining the rhythm of the word-groups of speech and the intonations of the speaking voice.

In the matter of language, American literature had a special problem. The young nation was inclined to think that the mark of the truly literary product was a grandiosity and elegance not to be found in the common speech. It therefore encouraged a greater breach between its vernacular and its literary language than, say, English literature of the same period ever allowed. This accounts for the hollow ring one now and then hears even in the work of our best writers in the first half of the last century. English writers of equal stature would never have made the lapses into rhetorical excess that are common in Cooper and Poe and that are to be found even in Melville and Hawthorne.

Yet at the same time that the language of ambitious literature was high and thus always in danger of falseness, the American reader was keenly interested in the actualities of daily speech. No literature, indeed, was ever so taken up with matters of speech as ours was. "Dialect," which attracted even our serious writers, was the accepted common ground of our popular humorous writing. Nothing in social life seemed so remarkable as the different forms which speech could take—the brogue of the immigrant Irish or the mispronunciation of the German, the "affectation" of the English, the reputed precision of the Bostonian, the legendary twang of the Yankee farmer, and the drawl of the Pike County man. Mark Twain, of course, was in the tradition of humor that exploited this interest, and no one could play with it nearly so well. Although today the carefully spelled-out dialects of nineteenth-century American humor are likely to seem dull enough, the subtle variations of speech of *Huckleberry Finn*, of which Mark Twain was justly proud, are still part of the liveliness and flavor of the book.

Out of his knowledge of the actual speech of America Mark Twain forged a classic prose. The adjective may seem a strange one, yet it is apt. Forget the misspellings and the faults of grammar, and the prose will be seen to move with the greatest simplicity, directness, lucidity, and grace. These qualities are by no means accidental. Mark Twain, who read widely, was passionately interested in the problems of style; the mark of the strictest literary sensibility is everywhere to be found in the prose of *Huckleberry Finn.*

It is this prose that Ernest Hemingway had chiefly in mind when he said that "all modern American literature comes from one book by Mark Twain called *Huckleberry Finn.*" Hemingway's own prose stems from it directly and consciously; so does the prose of the two modern writers who most influenced Hemingway's early style, Gertrude Stein and Serwood Anderson (although neither of them could maintain the robust purity of their model); so, too, does the best of William Faulkner's prose, which, like Mark Twain's own, reinforces the colloquial tradition with the literary tradition. Indeed, it may be said that almost every contemporary writer who deals conscientiously with the problems and possibility of prose must feel, directly or indirectly, the influence of Mark Twain. He is the master of the style that escapes the fixity of the printed page, that sounds in our ears with the immediacy of the heard voice, the very voice of unpretentious truth.

Notes

1. Copyright, 1943, by T. S. Eliot, reprinted by permission of Harcourt, Brace and Company.

2. In Joyce's *Finnegans Wake* both Mark Twain and Huckleberry Finn appear frequently. The theme of rivers is, of course, dominant in the book; and Huck's name suits Joyce's purpose, as so many names do, for Finn is one of the many names of his hero. Mark Twain's love of and gift for the spoken language makes another reason for Joyce's interest in him.

3. *Mark Twain in Eruption,* edited by Bernard De Voto (New York: Harper & Brothers, 1940), p. 77.

"Come Back to the Raft Ag'in, Huck Honey"

Leslie Fiedler

It is perhaps to be expected that the Negro and the homosexual should become stock literary themes in a period when the exploration of responsibility and failure has become again a primary concern of our literature. It is the discrepancy they represent that haunts us, that moral discrepancy before which we are helpless, having no resources (no tradition of courtesy, no honored mode of cynicism) for dealing with a conflict of principle and practice. It used once to be fashionable to think of puritanism as a force in our lives encouraging hypocrisy; quite the contrary, its emphasis upon the singleness of belief and action, its turning of the most prosaic areas of life into arenas where one's state of grace is tested, confuse the outer and the inner and make hypocrisy among us, perhaps more strikingly than ever elsewhere, *visible*, visibly detestable, the cardinal sin. It is not without significance that the shrug of the shoulders (the acceptance of circumstance as a sufficient excuse, the sign of self-pardon before the inevitable lapse) seems in America an unfamiliar, an alien gesture.

And yet before the continued existence of physical homosexual love (our crudest epithets notoriously evoke the mechanics of such affairs), before the blatant ghettos in which the Negro conspicuously creates the gaudiness and stench that offend him, the white American must make a choice between coming to terms

From *Partisan Review*, 15 (June 1948), 664-71, and *The Collected Essays of Leslie Fiedler*. Reprinted with permission of Stein & Day Publishers.

with institutionalized discrepancy or formulating radically new ideologies. There are, to be sure, stopgap devices, evasions of that final choice; not the least interesting is the special night club: the "queer" café, the black-and-tan joint, in which fairy or Negro exhibit their fairyness, their Negro-ness as if they were mere divertissements, gags thought up for the laughs and having no reality once the lights go out and the chairs are piled on the tables by the cleaning women. In the earlier minstrel show, a Negro performer was required to put on with grease paint and burnt cork the formalized mask of blackness; while the queer must exaggerate flounce and flutter into the convention of his condition.

The situations of the Negro and the homosexual in our society pose quite opposite problems, or at least problems suggesting quite opposite solutions. Our laws on homosexuality and the context of prejudice they objectify must apparently be changed to accord with a stubborn social fact; whereas it is the social fact, our overt behavior toward the Negro, that must be modified to accord with our laws and the, at least official, morality they objectify. It is not, of course, quite so simple. There is another sense in which the fact of homosexual passion contradicts a national myth of masculine love, just as our real relationship with the Negro contradicts a myth of that relationship; and those two myths with their betrayals are, as we shall see, one.

The existence of overt homosexuality threatens to compromise an essential aspect of American sentimental life: the camaraderie of the locker room and ball park, the good fellowship of the poker game and fishing trip, a kind of passionless passion, at once gross and delicate, homoerotic in the boy's sense, possessing an innocence above suspicion. To doubt for a moment this innocence, which can survive only as *assumed,* would destroy our stubborn belief in a realationship simple, utterly satisfying, yet immune to lust; physical as the handshake is physical, this side of copulation. The nineteenth-century myth of the Immaculate Young Girl has failed to survive in any *felt* way into our time. Rather, in the dirty jokes shared among men in the smoking car, the barracks, or the dormitory, there is a common male revenge against women for having flagrantly betrayed that myth; and under the revenge, the rather smug assumption of the chastity of the revenging group, in so far as it is a purely male society. From what other source could arise that unexpected air of good clean fun which overhangs such sessions? It is this self-congratulatory buddy-buddiness, its astonishing naïveté that breed at once endless opportunities for inversion and the terrible reluctance to admit its existence, to surrender the last believed-in stronghold of love without passion.

It is, after all, what we know from a hundred other sources that is here verified: the regressiveness, in a technical sense, of American life, its implacable nostalgia for the infantile, at once wrongheaded and somehow admirable. The mythic America is boyhood—and who would dare be startled to realize that the two most popular most *absorbed,* I am sure, of the handful of great books in our native heritage are customarily to be found, illustrated, on the shelves of the children's library. I am referring, of course, to *Moby Dick* and *Huckleberry Finn,* so different in technique and language, but alike children's books or, more precisely, *boys'* books.

There are the Leatherstocking Tales of Cooper, too, as well as Dana's *Two Years Before the Mast* and a good deal of Stephen Crane, books whose continuing favor depends more and more on the taste of boys; and one begins to foresee a similar improbable fate for Ernest Hemingway. Among the most distinguished novelists of the American past, only Henry James completely escapes classification as a writer of juvenile classics; even Hawthorne, who did write sometimes for children, must in his most adult novels endure, though not as Mark Twain and Melville submit to, the child's perusal. A child's version of *The Scarlet Letter* would seem a rather farfetched joke if it were not a part of our common experience. Finding in the children's department of the local library what Hawthorne liked to call his "hell-fired book," and remembering that *Moby Dick* itself has as its secret motto *"Ego te baptizo in nomine diaboli,"* one can only bow in awed silence before the mysteries of public morality, the American idea of "innocence." Everything goes except the frank description of adult heterosexual love. After all, boys will be boys!

What, then, do all these books have in common? As boys' books we should expect them shyly, guiltlessly as it were, to proffer a chaste male love as the ultimate emotional experience—and this is spectacularly the case. In Dana, it is the narrator's melancholy love for the *kanaka,* Hope; in Cooper, the lifelong affection of Natty Bumppo and Chingachgook; in Melville, Ishmael's love for Queequeg; in Twain, Huck's feeling for Nigger Jim. At the focus of emotion, where we are accustomed to find in the world's great novels some heterosexual passion, be it "platonic" love or adultery, seduction, rape, or long-drawn-out flirtation, we come instead on the fugitive slave and the no-account boy lying side by side on a raft borne by the endless river toward an impossible escape, or the pariah sailor waking in the tattooed arms of the brown harpooner on the verge of their impossible quest. "*Aloha, aikane, aloha nui,*" Hope cries to the lover who prefers him to all his fellow-whites; and Ishmael in utter frankness tells us: "I found Queequeg's arm thrown over me in the most loving and affectionate manner. You had almost thought I had been his wife ... he still hugged me tightly, as though naught but death should part us twain ... Thus, then, in our heart's honeymoon, lay I and Queequeg—a cosy, loving pair...he pressed his forehead against mine, clasped me around the waist, and said that henceforth we were married."

In Melville, the ambiguous relationship is most explicitly rendered; almost, indeed, openly explained. Not by a chance phrase or camouflaged symbol (the dressing of Jim in a woman's gown in *Huck Finn*, for instance, which can mean anything or nothing at all), but in a step-by-step exposition, the Pure Marriage of Ishmael and Queequeg is set before us: the initial going to bed together and the first shyness overcome, that great hot tomahawk-pipe accepted in a familiarity that dispels fear; next, the wedding ceremony itself (for in this marriage like so many others the ceremonial follows the deflowering), with the ritual touching of foreheads; then, the queasiness and guilt the morning after the *official* First Night, the suspicion that one has joined himself irrevocably to his own worst nightmare; finally, a symbolic portrayal of the continuing state of marriage through the image of the "monkey rope" which binds the lovers fast waist to waist (for the sake of this symbolism, Melville changes a *fact* of whaling practice—the only time in the book), a permanent alliance that provides mutual protection but also threatens mutual death.

Physical it all is, certainly, yet somehow ultimately innocent. There lies between the lovers no naked sword but a childlike ignorance, as if the possibility of a fall to the carnal had not yet been discovered. Even in the *Vita Nuova* of Dante, there is no vision of love less offensively, more unremittingly chaste; that it is not adult seems beside the point. Ishmael's sensations as he wakes under the pressure of Queequeg's arm, the tenderness of Huck's repeated loss and refinding of Jim, the role of almost Edenic helpmate played for Bumppo by the Indian—these shape us from childhood: we have no sense of first discovering them or of having been once without them.

Of the infantile, the homoerotic aspects of these stories we are, though vaguely, aware; but it is only with an effort that we can wake to a consciousness of how, among us who at the level of adulthood find a difference in color sufficient provocation for distrust and hatred, they celebrate, all of them, the mutual love of *a white man and a colored.* So buried at a level of acceptance which does not touch reason, so desperately repressed from overt recognition, so contrary to what is usually thought of as our ultimate level of taboo—the sense of that love can survive only in the obliquity of a symbol, persistent, obsessive, in short, an archetype: the boy's homoerotic crush, the love of the black fused at this level into a single thing.

I hope I have been using here a hopelessly abused word with some precision; by "archetype" I mean a coherent pattern of beliefs and feelings so widely shared at a level beneath consciousness that there exists no abstract vocabulary for representing it, and so "sacred" that unexamined, irrational restraints inhibit any explicit analysis. Such a complex finds a formula or pattern story, which serves both to embody it, and, at first at least, to conceal its full implications. Later, the secret may be revealed, the archetype "analyzed" or "allegorically" interpreted according to the language of the day.

I find the complex we have been examining genuinely mythic; certainly it has the invisible character of the true archetype, eluding the wary pounce of Howells or Mrs. Twain, who excised from *Huckleberry Finn* the cussing as unfit for children, but who left, unperceived, a conventionally abhorrent doctrine of ideal love. Even the writers in whom we find it attained it, in a sense, dreaming. The felt difference between *Huckleberry Finn* and Twain's other books must lie in part in the release from conscious restraint inherent in the author's assumption of the character of Huck; the passage in and out of darkness and river mist, the constant confusion of identities (Huck's ten or twelve names; the question of who is the real uncle, who the true Tom), the sudden intrusions into alien violences without past or future, give the whole work, for all its carefully observed detail, the texture of a dream. For *Moby Dick* such a point need scarcely be made. Even Cooper, despite his insufferable gentlemanliness, his tedium, cannot conceal from the kids who continue to read him the secret behind his overconscious prose: the childish, impossible dream. D. H. Lawrence saw in him clearly the boy's Utopia; the absolute wilderness in which the stuffiness of home yields to wigwam, and "My Wife" to Chingachgook.

I do not recall ever having seen in the commentaries of the social anthropologist or psychologist an awareness of the role of this profound child's dream of love in our relation to the Negro. (I say Negro, though the beloved in the books I have mentioned is variously Indian and Polynesian, because the Negro has become more and more exclusively for us *the* colored man, the colored man *par excellence*.) Trapped in what have by now become shackling clichés—the concept of the white man's sexual envy of the Negro male, the ambivalent horror of miscegenation—they do not sufficiently note the complementary factor of physical attraction, the archetypal love of white male and black. But either the horror or the attraction is meaningless alone; only together do they make sense. Just as the pure love of man and man is in general set off against the ignoble passion of man for woman, so more specifically (and more vividly) the dark desire which leads to miscegenation is contrasted with the ennobling love of a white man and a colored one. James Fenimore Cooper is our first poet of this ambivalence; indeed, miscegenation is the secret theme of the Leatherstocking novels, especially of *The Last of the Mohicans*. Natty Bumppo, the man who boasts always of having "no cross" in *his* blood, flees by nature from the defilement of all women, but never with so absolute a revulsion as he displays toward the squaw with whom at one point he seems at the point of being forced to cohabit; and the threat of the dark-skinned rapist sends pale woman after pale woman skittering through Cooper's imagined wilderness. Even poor Cora, who already has a fatal drop of alien blood that cuts her off from any marriage with a white man, in so far as she is white cannot be mated with Uncas, the noblest of redmen. Only in death can they be joined in an embrace as chaste as that of males. There's no good woman but a dead woman! Yet Chingachgook and the Deerslayer are permitted to sit night after night over their campfire in the purest domestic bliss. So long as there is no mingling of blood, soul may couple with soul in God's undefiled forest.

Nature undefiled—this is the inevitable setting of the Sacred Marriage of males. Ishmael and Queequeg, arm in arm, about to ship out, Huck and Jim swimming beside the raft in the peaceful flux of the Mississippi—here it is the motion of water which completes the syndrome, the American dream of isolation afloat. The notion of the Negro as the unblemished bride blends with the myth of running away to sea, of running the great river down to the sea. The immensity of water defines a loneliness that demands love; its strangeness symbolizes the disavowal of the conventional that makes possible all versions of love. In *Two Years Before the Mast*, in *Moby Dick*, in *Huckleberry Finn* the water is there, is the very texture of the novel; the Leatherstocking Tales propose another symbol for the same meaning: the virgin forest. Notice the adjectives—the virgin forest and the forever inviolable sea. It is well to remember, too, what surely must be more than a coincidence, that Cooper, who could dream this myth, also invented for us the novel of the sea, wrote for the first time in history the sea story proper.

The rude pederasty of the forecastle and the captain's cabin, celebrated in a thousand jokes, is the profanation of a dream; yet Melville, who must have known such blasphemies, refers to them only once and indirectly, for it was *his* dream that they threatened. And still the dream survives; in a recent book by Gore Vidal, an incipient homosexual, not yet aware of the implications of his feelings, indulges in the reverie of running off to sea with his dearest friend. The buggery of sailors is taken for granted everywhere, yet is thought of usually as an inversion forced on men by their isolation from women; though the opposite case may well be true: the isolation sought more or less consciously as an occasion for male encounters. At any rate, there is a context in which the legend of the sea as escape and solace, the fixated sexuality of boys, the myth of the dark beloved, are one. In Melville and Twain at the center of our tradition, in the lesser writers at the periphery, the archetype is at once formalized and perpetuated. Nigger Jim and Queequeg make concrete for us what was without them a vague pressure on the threshold of our consciousness; the proper existence of the archetype is in the realized character, who waits, as it were, only to be asked his secret. Think of Oedipus biding in silence from Sophocles to Freud!

Unwittingly, we are possessed in childhood by these characters and their undiscriminated meaning, and it is difficult for us to dissociate them without a sense of disbelief. What—these household figures clues to our subtlest passions! The foreigner finds it easier to perceive the significances too deep within us to be brought into focus. D. H. Lawrence discovered in our classics a linked mythos of escape and immaculate male love; Lorca in *The Poet in New York* grasped instinctively (he could not even read English) the kinship of Harlem and Walt Whitman, the fairy as bard. But of course we do not have to be conscious of what possesses us; in every generation of our own writers the archetype reappears, refracted, half-understood, but *there*. In the gothic reverie of Capote's *Other Voices, Other Rooms*, both elements of the syndrome are presented though disjunctively: the boy moving between the love of a Negro maidservant and his inverted cousin. In Carson McCullers' *Member of the Wedding*, another variant is invented: a *female* homosexual romance between the boy-girl Frankie and a Negro cook. This time the Father-Slave-Beloved is converted into a figure of a Mother-Sweetheart-Servant, but remains still, of course, satisfactorily black. It is not strange, after all, to find this archetypal complex in latter-day writers of a frankly homosexual sensibility; but it recurs, too, in such resolutely masculine writers as Faulkner, who evokes the myth in the persons of the Negro and the boy of *Intruder in the Dust*.

In the myth, one notes finally, it is typically in the role of outcast, ragged woodsman, or despised sailor ("Call me Ishmael!"), or unregenerate boy (Huck before the prospect of being "sivilized" cries out, "I been there before!") that we turn to the love of a colored man. But how, we cannot help asking, does the vision of the white American as a pariah correspond with our long-held public status: the world's beloved, the success? It is perhaps only the artist's portrayal of *himself*, the notoriously alienated writer in America, at home with such images, child of the town drunk, the hapless survivor. But no, Ishmael is in all of us, our unconfessed universal fear objectified in the writer's status as in the outcast sailor's: that compelling anxiety, which every foreigner notes, that we may not be loved, that we are loved for our possessions and not our selves, that we are really—*alone*. It is that underlying terror which explains our incredulity in the face of adulation or favor, what is called (once more the happy adjective) our "boyish modesty."

Our dark-skinned beloved will take us in, we assure ourselves, when we have been cut off, or have cut ourselves off, from all others, without rancor or the insult of forgiveness. He will fold us in his arms saying, "Honey" or "Aikane"; he will comfort us, as if our offense against him were long ago remitted, were never truly *real*. And yet we cannot ever really forget our guilt; the stories that embody the myth dramatize as if compulsively the role of the colored man as the victim. Dana's Hope is shown dying of the white man's syphilis; Queequeg is portrayed as racked by fever, a pointless episode except in the light of this necessity; Crane's Negro is disfigured to the point of monstrosity; Cooper's Indian smolders to a hopeless old age conscious of the imminent disappearance of his race; Jim is shown loaded down with chains, weakened by the hundred torments dreamed up by Tom in the name of bulliness. The immense gulf of guilt must not be mitigated any more than the disparity of color. (Queequeg is not merely brown but monstrously tattooed; Chingachgook is horrid with paint; Jim is portrayed as the sick A-rab died blue), so that the final reconciliation may seem more unbelievable and tender. The archetype makes no attempt to deny our outrage as fact; it portrays it as meaningless in the face of love.

There would be something insufferable, I think, in that final vision of remission if it were not for the presence of a motivating anxiety, the sense always of a last chance. Behind the white American's nightmare that someday, no longer tourist, inheritor, or liberator, he will be rejected, refused, he dreams of his acceptance at the breast he has most utterly offended. It is a dream so sentimental, so outrageous, so desperate, that it redeems our concept of boyhood from nostalgia to tragedy.

In each generation we *play out* the impossible mythos, and we live to see our children play it: the white boy and the black we can discover wrestling affectionately on any American sidewalk, along which they will walk in adulthood, eyes averted from each other, unwilling to touch even by accident. The dream recedes; the immaculate passion and the astonishing reconciliation become a memory, and less, a regret, at last the unrecognized motifs of a child's book. "It's too good to be true, Honey," Jim says to Huck. "It's too good to be true."

Mark Twain's Masterpiece

T. S. Eliot

The Adventures of Huckleberry Finn is the only one of Mark Twain's various books which can be called a masterpiece. I do not suggest that it is his only book of permanent interest; but it is the only one in which his genius is completely realized, and the only one which creates its own category. There are pages in *Tom Sawyer* and in *Life on the Mississippi* which are, within their limits, as good as anything with which one can compare them in *Huckleberry Finn*; and in other books there are drolleries just as good of their kind. But when we find one book by a prolific author which is very much superior to all the rest, we look for the peculiar accident or concourse of accidents which made that book possible. In the writing of *Huckleberry Finn* Mark Twain had two elements which, when treated with his sensibility and his experience, formed a great book: these two are the Boy and the River.

Huckleberry Finn is, no doubt, a book which boys enjoy. I cannot speak from memory: I suspect that a fear on the part of my parents lest I should acquire a premature taste for tobacco, and perhaps other habits of the hero of the story, kept the book out of my way. But *Huckleberry Finn* does not fall into the category of juvenile fiction. The opinion of my parents that it was a book unsuitable for boys left me, for most of my life, under the impression that it was a book suitable only for boys. Therefore it was only a few years ago that I read for the first time, and in that or-

From an edition of *Adventures of Huckleberry Finn* (London: The Cresset Press /New York: Chanticleer Press, 1950), pp. vii-xvi. Reprinted with permission of Valerie Eliot and Faber & Faber Ltd. Title provided by editor.

der, *Tom Sawyer* and *Huckleberry Finn*.

Tom Sawyer did not prepare me for what I was to find its sequel to be. *Tom Sawyer* seems to me to be a boys' book, and a very good one. The River and *the* Boy make their appearance in it; the narrative is good; and there is also a very good picture of society in a small mid-Western river town (for St. Petersburg is more Western than Southern) a hundred years ago. But the point of view of the narrator is that of an adult observing a boy. And Tom is the ordinary boy, though of quicker wits, and livelier imagination, than most. Tom is, I suppose, very much the boy that Mark Twain had been: he is remembered and described as he seemed to his elders, rather than created. Huck Finn, on the other hand, is the boy that Mark Twain still was, at the time of writing his adventures. We look at Tom as the smiling adult does: Huck we do not look at—we see the world through his eyes. The two boys are not merely different types; they were brought into existence by different processes. Hence in the second book their roles are altered. In the first book Huck is merely the humble friend—almost a variant of the traditional valet of comedy; and we see him as he is seen by the conventional respectable society to which Tom belongs, and of which, we feel sure, Tom will one day become an eminently respectable and conventional member. In the second book their nominal relationship remains the same; but here it is Tom who has the secondary role. The author was probably not conscious of this, when he wrote the first two chapters: *Huckleberry Finn* is not the kind of story in which the author knows, from the beginning, what is going to happen. Tom then disappears from our view; and when he returns, he has only two functions. The first is to provide a foil for Huck. Huck's persisting admiration for Tom only exhibits more clearly to our eyes the unique qualities of the former and the commonplaceness of the latter. Tom has the imagination of a lively boy who has read a good deal of romantic fiction: he might, of course, become a writer—he might become Mark Twain. Or rather, he might become the more commonplace aspect of Mark Twain. Huck has not imagination, in the sense in which Tom has it: he has, instead, vision. He sees the real world; and he does not judge it—he allows it to judge itself.

Tom Sawyer is an orphan. But he has his aunt; he has, as we learn later, other relatives; and he has the environment into which he fits. He is wholly a social being. When there is a secret band to be formed, it is Tom who organizes it and prescribes the rules. Huck Finn is alone: there is no more solitary character in fiction. The fact that he has a father only emphasizes his loneliness; and he views his father with a terrifying detachment. So we come to see Huck himself in the end as one of the permanent symbolic figures of fiction; not unworthy to take a place with Ulysses, Faust, Don Quixote, Don Juan, Hamlet and other great discoveries that man has made about himself.

It would seem that Mark Twain was a man who—perhaps like most of us—never became in all respects mature. We might even say that the adult side of him was boyish, and that only the boy in him, that was Huck Finn, was adult. As Tom Sawyer grown up, he wanted success and applause (Tom himself always needs an audience). He wanted prosperity, a happy domestic life of a conventional kind, universal approval, and fame. All of these things he obtained. As Huck Finn he was indifferent to all these things; and being composite of the two, Mark Twain both strove for them, and resented their violation of his integrity. Hence he became the humorist and even clown: with his gifts, a certain way to success, for everyone could enjoy his writings without the slightest feeling of discomfort, self-consciousness or self-criticism. And hence, on the other hand, his pessimism and misanthropy. To be a misanthrope is to be in some way divided; or it is a sign of an uneasy conscience. The pessimism which Mark Twain discharged into *The Man That Corrupted Hadleyburg* and *What is Man?* springs less from observation of society, than from his hatred of himself for allowing society to tempt and corrupt him and give him what he wanted. There is no wisdom in it. But all this personal problem has been diligently examined by Mr. Van Wyck Brooks; and it is not Mark Twain, but *Huckleberry Finn*, that is the subject of this introduction.

You cannot say that Huck himself is either a humorist or a misanthrope. He is the impassive observer: he does not interfere, and, as I have said, he does not judge. Many of the episodes that occur on the voyage down the river, after he is joined by the Duke and the King (whose fancies about themselves are akin to the kind of fancy that Tom Sawyer enjoys) are in themselves farcical; and if it were not for the presence of Huck as the reporter of them, they would be no more than farce. But, seen through the eyes of Huck, there is a deep human pathos in these scoundrels. On the other hand, the story of the feud between the Grangerfords and the Shepherdsons is a masterpiece in itself: yet Mark Twain could not have written it so, with that economy and restraint, with just the right details and no more, and leaving to the reader to make his own moral reflections, unless he had been writing in the person of Huck. And the *style* of the book, which is the style of Huck, is what makes it a far more convincing indictment of slavery than the sensationalist propaganda of *Uncle Tom's Cabin*. Huck is passive and impassive, apparently always the victim of events; and yet, in his acceptance of his world and of what it does to him and others, he is more powerful than this world, because he is more *aware* than any other person in it.

Repeated readings of the book only confirm and deepen one's admiration of the consistency and perfect adaptation of the writing. This is a style which at the period, whether in America or in England, was an innovation, a new discovery in the English language. Other authors had achieved natural speech in relation to particular characters—Scott with characters talking Lowland Scots, Dickens with cockneys: but no one else had kept it up through the whole of a book. Thackeray's Yellowplush, impressive as he is, is an obvious artifice in comparison. In *Huckleberry Finn* there is no exaggeration of grammar or spelling or speech, there is no sentence or phrase to destroy the illusion that these are Huck's own words. It is not only in the way in which he tells his story, but in the details he remembers, that Huck is true to himself. There is, for instance, the description of the Grangerford interior as Huck sees it on his arrival; there is the list of the objects which Huck and Jim salvaged from the derelict house:

> "We got an old tin lantern, and a butcher-knife without any handle, and a bran-new Barlow knife worth two bits in any store, and a lot of tallow candles, and a tin candlestick, and a gourd, and a tin cup, and a ratty old bedquilt off the bed, and a reticule with needles and pins and beeswax and buttons and thread and all such truck in it, and a hatchet and some nails,and a fish-line as thick as my little finger, with some monstrous hooks on it, and a roll of buckskin, and a leather dog-collar, and a horseshoe, and some vials of medicine that didn't have no label on them; and just as we was leaving I found a tolerable good curry-comb, and Jim he found a ratty old fiddle-bow, and a wooden leg. The straps was broke off of it, but barring that, it was a good enough leg, though it was too long for me and not long enough for Jim, and we couldn't find the other one, though we hunted all round.
>
> "And so, take it all round, we made a good haul."

This is the sort of list that a boy reader should pore over with delight; but the paragraph performs other functions of which the boy reader would be unaware. It provides the right counterpoise to the horror of the wrecked house and the corpse; it has a grim precision which tells the reader all he needs to know about the way of life of the human derelicts who had used the house; and (especially the wooden leg, and the fruitless search for its mate) reminds us at the right moment of the kinship of mind and the sympathy between the boy outcast from society and the negro fugitive from the injustice of society.

Huck in fact would be incomplete without Jim, who is almost as notable a creation as Huck himself. Huck is the passive observer of men and events, Jim the submissive sufferer from them; and they are equal in dignity. There is no passage in which their relationship is brought out more clearly than the conclusion of the chapter in which, after the two have become separated in the fog, Huck in the canoe and Jim on the raft, Huck, in his impulse of boyish mischief, persuades Jim for a time that the latter had dreamt the whole episode.

> "... my heart wuz mos' broke bekase you wuz los', en I didn' k'yer no mo' what become er me en de raf'. En when I wake up en fine you back agin', all safe en soun', de tears come en I could a got down on my knees en kiss' yo' foot, I's so thankful. En all you wuz thinkin' 'bout wuz how you could make a fool uv ole Jim wid a lie. Dat truck dah is *trash*; en trash is what people is dat puts dirt on de head er dey fren's en makes 'em ashamed.'...
>
> "It was fifteen minutes before I could work myself up and humble myself to a nigger—but I done it, and I warn't ever sorry for it afterwards, neither."

This passage has been quoted before; and if I quote it again, it is because I wish to elicit from it one meaning that is, I think, usually overlooked. What is obvious in it is the pathos and dignity of Jim, and this is moving enough; but what I find still more disturbing, and still more unusual in literature, is the pathos and dignity of the boy, when reminded so humbly and humiliatingly, that his position in the world is not that of other boys, entitled from time to time to a practical joke; but that he must bear, and bear alone, the responsibility of a man.

It is Huck who gives the book style. The River gives the book its form. But for the River, the book might be only a sequence of adventures with a happy ending. A river, a very big and powerful river, is the only natural force that can wholly determine the course of human peregrination. At sea, the wanderer may sail or be carried by winds and currents in one direction or another; a change of wind or tide may determine fortune. In the prairie, the direction of movement is more or less at the choice of the caravan; among mountains there will often be an alternative, a guess at the most likely pass. But the river with its strong, swift current is the dictator to the raft or to the steamboat. It is a treacherous and capricious dictator. At one season, it may move sluggishly in a channel so narrow that, encountering it for the first time at that point, one can hardly believe that it has travelled already for hundreds of miles, and has yet many hundreds of miles to go; at another season, it may obliterate the low Illinois shore to a horizon of water, while in its bed it runs with a speed such that no man or beast can survive in it. At such times, it carries down human bodies, cattle and houses. At least twice, at St. Louis, the western and eastern shores have been separated by the fall of bridges, until the designer of the great Eads Bridge devised a structure which could resist the floods. In my own childhood, it was not unusual for the spring freshet to interrupt railway travel; and then the traveller to the East had to take steamboat from the levee up to Alton, at a higher level on the Illinois shore, before he could begin his rail journey. The river is never wholly chartable; it changes its pace, it shifts its channel, unaccountably; it may suddenly efface a sandbar, and throw up another bar where before was navigable water.

It is the River that controls the voyage of Huck and Jim; that will not let them land at Cairo, where Jim could have reached freedom; it is the River that separates them and deposits Huck for a time in the Grangerford household; the River that re-unites them, and then compels upon them the unwelcome company of the King and the Duke. Recurrently we are reminded of its presence and its power.

"When I woke up, I didn't know where I was for a minute. I set up and looked around, a little scared. Then I remembered. The river looked miles and miles across. The moon was so bright I could a counted the drift-logs that went a-slipping along, black and still, hundreds of yards out from shore. Everything was dead quiet, and it looked late, and *smelt* late. You know what I mean—I don't know the words to put it in.

"It was kind of solemn, drifting down the big still river, laying on our backs looking up at the stars, and we didn't ever feel like talking loud, and it warn't often that we laughed, only a little kind of a low chuckle. We had mighty good weather as a general thing, and nothing ever happened to us at all, that night, nor the next, nor the next.

"Every night we passed towns, some of them away up on black hillsides, nothing but just a shiny bed of lights, not a house could you see. The fifth night we passed St. Louis, and it was like the whole world lit up. In St. Petersburg they used to say there was twenty or thirty thousand people in St. Louis, but I never believed it till I see that wonderful spread of lights at two o'clock that still night. There warn't a sound there; everybody was asleep."

We come to understand the River by seeing it through the eyes of the Boy; but the Boy is also the spirit of the River. *Huckleberry Finn*, like other great works of imagination, can give to every reader whatever he is capable of taking from it. On the most superficial level of observation, Huck is convincing as a boy. On the same level, the picture of social life on the shores of the Mississippi a hundred years ago is, I feel sure, accurate. On any level, Mark Twain makes you see the River, as it is and was and always will be, more clearly than the author of any other description of a river known to me. But you do not merely see the River, you do not merely become acquainted with it through the senses: you experience the River. Mark Twain, in his later years of success and fame, referred to his early life as a steamboat pilot as the happiest he had known. With all allowance for the illusions of age, we can agree that those years were the years in which he was most fully alive. Certainly, but for his having practised that calling, earned his living by that profession, he would never have gained the understanding which his genius for expression communicates in this book. In the pilot's daily struggle with the River, in the satisfaction of activity, in the constant attention to the River's unpredictable vagaries, his consciousness was fully occupied, and he absorbed knowledge of which, as an artist, he later made use. There are, perhaps, only two ways in which a writer can acquire the understanding of environment which he can later turn to account: by having spent his childhood in that environment—that is, living in it at a period of life in which one experiences much more than one is aware of; and by having had to struggle for a livelihood in that environment—a livelihood bearing no direct relation to any intention of writing about it, of *using* it as literary material. Most of Joseph Conrad's understanding came to him in the latter way. Mark Twain knew the Mississippi in both ways: he had spent his childhood on its banks, and he had earned his living matching his wits against its currents.

Thus the River makes the book a great book. As with Conrad,

we are continually reminded of the power and terror of Nature, and the isolation and feebleness of Man. Conrad remains always the European observer of the tropics, the white man's eye contemplating the Congo and its black gods. But Mark Twain is a native, and the River God is his God. It is as a native that he accepts the River God, and it is the subjection of Man that gives to Man his dignity. For without some kind of God, Man is not even very interesting.

Readers sometimes deplore the fact that the story descends to the level of *Tom Sawyer* from the moment that Tom himself re-appears. Such readers protest that the escapades invented by Tom, in the attempted "rescue" of Jim, are only a tedious development of themes with which we were already too familiar—even while admitting that the escapades themselves are very amusing, and some of the incidental observations memorable.[1] But it is right that the mood of the end of the book should bring us back to that of the beginning. Or, if this was not the right ending for the book, what ending would have been right?

In *Huckleberry Finn* Mark Twain wrote a much greater book than he could have known he was writing. Perhaps all great works of art mean much more than the author could have been aware of meaning: certainly, *Huckleberry Finn* is the one book of Mark Twain's which, as a whole, has this unconsciousness. So what seems to be the rightness, of reverting at the end of the book to the mood of *Tom Sawyer*, was perhaps unconscious art. For Huckleberry Finn, neither a tragic nor a happy ending would be suitable. No worldly success or social satisfaction, no domestic consummation would be worthy of him; a tragic end also would reduce him to the level of those whom we pity. Huck Finn must come from nowhere and be bound for nowhere. His is not the independence of the typical or symbolic American Pioneer, but the independence of the vagabond. His existence questions the values of America as much as the values of Europe; he is as much an affront to the "pioneer spirit" as he is to "business enterprise"; he is in a state of nature as detached as the state of the saint. In a busy world, he represents the loafer; in an acquisitive and competitive world, he insists on living from hand to mouth. He could not be exhibited in any amorous encounters or engagements, in any of the juvenile affections which are appropriate to Tom Sawyer. He belongs neither to the Sunday School nor to the Reformatory. He has no beginning and no end. Hence, he can only disappear; and his disappearance can only be accomplished by bringing forward another performer to obscure the disappearance in a cloud of whimsicalities.

Like Huckleberry Finn, the River itself has no beginning or end. In its beginning, it is not yet the River; in its end, it is no longer the River. What we call its headwaters is only a selection from among the innumerable sources which flow together to compose it. At what point in its course does the Mississippi become what the Mississippi *means*? It is both one and many; it is the Mississippi of this book only after its union with the Big Muddy—the Missouri; it derives some of its character from the Ohio, the Tennessee and other confluents. And at the end it merely disappears among its deltas: it is no longer there, but it is still where it was, hundreds of miles to the North. The River cannot tolerate any design, to a story which is its story, that might interfere with its dominance. Things must merely happen, here and there, to the people who live along its shores or who commit themselves to its current. And it is as impossible for Huck as for the River to have a beginning or end—a *career*. So the book has the right, the only possible concluding sentence. I do not think that any book ever written ends more certainly with the right words:

> "But I reckon I got to light out for the Territory ahead of the rest, because Aunt Sally she's going to adopt me and civilize me, and I can't stand it. I been there before."

Note

1. *e.g.*, "*Jim* don't know anybody in China."

Mr. Eliot, Mr. Trilling, and Huckleberry Finn

Leo Marx

In the losing battle that the plot fights with the characters, it often takes a cowardly revenge. Nearly all novels are feeble at the end. This is because the plot requires to be wound up. Why is this necessary? Why is there not a convention which allows a novelist to stop as soon as he feels muddled or bored? Alas, he has to round things off, and usually the characters go dead while he is at work, and our final impression of them is through deadness.—E. M. Forster

The *Adventures of Huckleberry Finn* has not always occupied its present high place in the canon of American literature. When it was first published in 1885, the book disturbed and offended many reviewers, particularly spokesmen for the genteel tradition.[1] In fact, a fairly accurate inventory of the narrow standards of such critics might be made simply by listing epithets they applied to Clemens' novel. They called it vulgar, rough, inelegant, irreverent, coarse, semi-obscene, trashy and vicious.[2] So much for them. Today (we like to think) we know the true worth of the book. Everyone now agrees that *Huckleberry Finn* is a masterpiece: it is probably the one book in our literature about which highbrows and lowbrows can agree. Our most serious critics praise it. Nevertheless, a close look at what two of the best among them have recently written will likewise reveal, I believe, serious weaknesses in current criticism. Today the problem of evaluating the book is as much obscured by unqualified praise as

From *American Scholar*, 22 (Autumn 1953), 423-40. Reprinted with permission.

it once was by parochial hostility.

I have in mind essays by Lionel Trilling and T. S. Eliot.[3] Both praise the book, but in praising it both feel obligated to say something in justification of what so many readers have felt to be its great flaw: the disappointing "ending," the episode which begins when Huck arrives at the Phelps place and Tom Sawyer reappears. There are good reasons why Mr. Trilling and Mr. Eliot should feel the need to face this issue. From the point of view of scope alone, more is involved than the mere "ending"; the episode comprises almost one-fifth of the text. The problem, in any case, is unavoidable. I have discussed *Huckleberry Finn* in courses with hundreds of college students, and I have found only a handful who did not confess their dissatisfaction with the extravagant mock rescue of Nigger Jim and the denouement itself. The same question always comes up: "What went wrong with Twain's novel?" Even Bernard De Voto, whose wholehearted commitment to Clemens' genius is well known, has said of the ending that "in the whole reach of the English novel there is no more abrupt or more chilling descent."[4] Mr. Trilling and Mr. Eliot do not agree. They both attempt, and on similar grounds, to explain and defend the conclusion.

Of the two, Mr. Trilling makes the more moderate claim for Clemens' novel. He does admit that there is a "falling off" at the end; nevertheless he supports the episode as having "a certain formal aptness." Mr. Eliot's approval is without serious qualification. He allows no objections, asserts that "it is right that the mood of the end of the book should bring us back to the beginning." I mean later to discuss their views in some detail, but here it is only necessary to note that both critics see the problem as one of form. And so it is. Like many questions of form in literature, however, this one is not finally separable from a question of "content," of value, or, if you will, of moral insight. To bring *Huckleberry Finn* to a satisfactory close, Clemens had to do more than find a neat device for ending a story. His problem, though it may never have occurred to him, was to invent an action capable of placing in focus the meaning of the journey down the Mississippi.

I believe that the ending of *Huckleberry Finn* makes so many readers uneasy because they rightly sense that it jeopardizes the significance of the entire novel. To take seriously what happens at the Phelps farm is to take lightly the entire downstream journey. What is the meaning of the journey? With this question all discussion of *Huckleberry Finn* must begin. It is true that the voyage down the river has many aspects of a boy's idyl. We owe much of its hold upon our imagination to the enchanting image of the raft's unhurried drift with the current. The leisure, the absence of constraint, the beauty of the river—all these things delight us. "It's lovely to live on a raft." And the multitudinous life of the great valley we see through Huck's eyes has a fascination of its own. Then, of course, there is humor—laughter so spontaneous, so free of bitterness present almost everywhere in American humor that readers often forget how grim a spectacle of human existence Huck contemplates. Humor in this novel flows from a bright joy of life as remote from our world as living on a raft.

Yet along with the idyllic and the epical and the funny in *Huckleberry Finn*, there is a coil of meaning which does for the disparate elements of the novel what a spring does for a watch. The meaning is not in the least obscure. It is made explicit again and again. The very words with which Clemens launches Huck and Jim upon their voyage indicate that theirs is not a boy's lark but a quest for freedom. From the electrifying moment when Huck comes back to Jackson's Island and rouses Jim with the news that a search party is on the way, we are meant to believe that Huck is enlisted in the cause of freedom. "Git up and hump yourself, Jim!" he cries. "There ain't a minute to lose. They're after us!" What particularly counts here is the *us*. No one is after Huck; no one but Jim knows he is alive. In that small word Clemens compresses the exhilarating power of Huck's instinctive humanity. His unpremeditated identification with Jim's flight from slavery is an unforgettable moment in American experience, and it may be said at once that any culmination of the journey which detracts from the urgency and dignity with which it begins will necessarily be unsatisfactory. Huck realizes this himself, and says so when, much later, he comes back to the raft after discovering that the Duke and the King have sold Jim:

> "After all this long journey . . . here it was all come to nothing, everything all busted up and ruined, because they could have the heart to serve Jim such a trick as that, and make him a slave again all his life, and amongst strangers, too, for forty dirty dollars."

Huck knows that the journey will have been a failure unless it takes Jim to freedom. It is true that we we do discover, in the end, that Jim is free, but we also find out that the journey was not the means by which he finally reached freedom.

The most obvious thing wrong with the end, then, is the flimsy contrivance by which Clemens frees Jim. In the end we not only discover that Jim has been a free man for two months, but that his freedom has been granted by old Miss Watson. If this were only a mechanical device for terminating the action, it might not call for much comment. But it is more than that: it is a significant clue to the import of the last ten chapters. Remember who Miss Watson is. She is the Widow's sister whom Huck introduces in the first pages of the novel. It is she who keeps "pecking" at Huck, who tries to teach him to spell and to pray and to keep his feet off the furniture. She is an ardent proselytizer for piety and good manners, and her greed provides the occasion for the journey in the first place. She is Jim's owner, and he decides to flee only when he realizes that she is about to break her word (she cannot resist a slave trader's offer of eight hundred dollars) and sell him down the river away from his family.

Miss Watson, in short, is the Enemy. If we except a predilection for physical violence, she exhibits all the outstanding traits of the valley society. She pronounces the polite lies of civilization that suffocate Huck's spirit. The freedom which Jim seeks, and which Huck and Jim temporarily enjoy aboard the raft, is accordingly freedom *from* everything for which Miss Watson stands. Indeed, the very intensity of the novel derives from the discordance between the aspirations of the fugitives and the respectable code for which she is a spokesman. Therefore, her regeneration, of which the deathbed freeing of Jim is the unconvincing sign, hints a resolution of the novel's essential conflict. Perhaps because this device most transparently reveals that shift in point of view which he could not avoid, and which is less easily discerned elsewhere in the concluding chapters, Clemens plays it down. He makes little attempt to account for Miss Watson's change of heart, a change particularly surprising in view of Jim's brazen escape. Had Clemens given this episode dramatic emphasis appropriate to its function, Miss Watson's bestowal of freedom upon Jim would have proclaimed what the rest of the ending actually accomplishes—a vindication of persons and attitudes Huck and Jim had symbolically repudiated when they set forth downstream.

It may be said, and with some justice, that a reading of the ending as a virtual reversal of meanings implicit in the rest of the novel misses the point—that I have taken the final episode too seriously. I agree that Clemens certainly did not intend us to read it so solemnly. The ending, one might contend, is simply a burlesque upon Tom's taste for literary romance. Surely the tone of the episode is familiar to readers of Mark Twain. The preposterous monkey business attendant upon Jim's "rescue," the careless improvisation, the nonchalant disregard for common-sense plausibility—all these things should not surprise readers of Twain or any low comedy in the tradition of "Western humor." However, the trouble is, first, that the ending hardly comes off as burlesque: it is *too* fanciful, *too* extravagant; and it is tedious. For example, to provide a "gaudy" atmosphere for the escape, Huck and Tom catch a couple of dozen snakes. Then the snakes escape.

> "No, there warn't no real scarcity of snakes about the house for a considerable spell. You'd see them dripping from the rafters and places every now and then; and they generly landed in your plate, or down the back of your neck. . . ."

Even if this were *good* burlesque, which it is not, what is it doing here? It is out of keeping; the slapstick tone jars with the underlying seriousness of the voyage.

Huckleberry Finn is a masterpiece because it brings Western humor to perfection and yet transcends the narrow limits of its conventions. But the ending does not. During the final extravaganza we are forced to put aside many of the mature emotions evoked earlier by the vivid rendering of Jim's fear of capture, the tenderness of Huck's and Jim's regard for each other, and Huck's excruciating moments of wavering between honesty and respectability. None of these emotions are called forth by the anticlimactic final sequence. I do not mean to suggest that the inclusion of low comedy per se is a flaw in *Huckleberry Finn*. One does not object to the shananigans of the rogues; there is ample precedent for the place of extravagant humor even in works of high seriousness. But here the case differs from most which come to mind: the major characters themselves are forced to play low comedy roles. Moreover, the most serious motive in the novel, Jim's yearning for freedom, is made the object of nonsense. The conclusion, in short, is farce, but the rest of the novel is not.

That Clemens reverts in the end to the conventional manner of Western low comedy is most evident in what happens to the principals. Huck and Jim become comic characters; that is much more serious ground for dissatisfaction than the unexplained regeneration of Miss Watson. Remember that Huck has grown in stature throughout the journey. By the time he arrives at the Phelps place, he is not the boy who had been playing robbers with Tom's gang in St. Petersburg the summer before. All he has seen and felt since he parted with Tom has deepened his knowledge of human nature and of himself. Clemens makes a point of Huck's development in two scenes which occur just before he meets Tom again. The first describes Huck's final capitulation to his own sense of right and wrong: "All right, then, I'll *go* to Hell." This is the climactic moment in the ripening of his self-knowledge. Shortly afterward, when he comes upon a mob riding the Duke and the King out of town on a rail, we are given his most memorable insight into the nature of man. Although these rogues had subjected Huck to every indignity, what he sees provokes this celebrated comment:

> "Well, it made me sick to see it; and I was sorry for them poor pitiful rascals, it seemed like I couldn't ever feel any hardness against them any more in the world. It was a dreadful thing to see. Human beings can be awful cruel to one another."

The sign of Huck's maturity here is neither the compassion nor the skepticism, for both had been marks of his personality from the first. Rather, the special quality of these reflections is the extraordinary combination of the two, a mature blending of his instinctive suspicion of human motives with his capacity for pity.

But at this point Tom reappears. Soon Huck has fallen almost completely under his sway once more, and we are asked to believe that the boy who felt pity for the rogues is now capable of making Jim's capture the occasion for a game. He becomes Tom's helpless accomplice, submissive and gullible. No wonder that Clemens has Huck remark, when Huck first realizes Aunt Sally has mistaken him for Tom, that "it was like being born again." Exactly. In the end, Huck regresses to the subordinate role in which he had first appeared in *The Adventures of Tom Sawyer*. Most of those traits which made him so appealing a hero now disappear. He had never, for example, found pain or misfortune amusing. At the circus, when a clown disguised as a drunk took a precarious ride on a prancing horse, the crowd loved the excitement and danger; "it warn't funny to me, though," said Huck. But now, in the end, he submits in awe to Tom's notion of what is amusing. To satisfy Tom's hunger for adventure he makes himself a party to sport which aggravates Jim's misery.

It should be added at once that Jim doesn't mind too much. The fact is that he has undergone a similar transformation. On the raft he was an individual, man enough to denounce Huck when Huck made him the victim of a practical joke. In the closing episode, however, we lose sight of Jim in the maze of farcical invention. He ceases to be a man. He allows Huck and "Mars Tom" to fill his hut with rats and snakes, "and every time a rat bit Jim he would get up and write a line in his journal whilst the ink was fresh." This creature who bleeds ink and feels no pain is something less than human. He has been made over in the image of a flat stereotype: the submissive stage-Negro. These antics divest Jim, as will as Huck, of much of his dignity and individuality.[5]

What I have been saying is that the flimsy devices of plot, the discordant farcical tone, and the disintegration of the major characters all betray the failure of the ending. These are not aspects merely of form in a technical sense, but of meaning. For that matter, I would maintain that this book has little or no formal unity independent of the joint purpose of Huck and Jim. What components of the novel, we may ask, provide the continuity which links one adventure with another? The most important is the unifying consciousness of Huck, the narrator, and the fact that we follow the same principals through the entire string of adventures. Events, moreover, occur in a temporal sequence. Then there is the river; after each adventure Huck and Jim return to the raft and the river. Both Mr. Trilling and Mr. Eliot speaks eloquently of the river as a source of unity, and they refer to the river as a god. Mr. Trilling says that Huck is "the servant of the river-god." Mr. Eliot puts it this way: "The River gives the book its form. But for the River, the book might be only a sequence of adventures with a happy ending." This seems to me an extravagant view of the function of the neutral agency of the river. Clemens had a knowledgeable respect for the Mississippi and, without sanctifying it, was able to provide excellent reasons for Huck's and Jim's intense relation with it. It is a source of food and beauty and terror and serenity of mind. But above all, it provides motion; it is the means by which Huck and Jim move away from a menacing civilization. They return to the river to continue their journey. The river cannot, does not, supply purpose. That purpose is a facet of their consciousness, and without the motive of escape from society, *Huckleberry Finn* would indeed "be only a sequence of adventures." Mr. Eliot's remark indicates how lightly he takes the quest for freedom. His somewhat fanciful exaggeration of the river's role is of a piece with his neglect of the theme at the novel's center.

That theme is heightened by the juxtaposition of sharp images of contrasting social orders: the microcosmic community Huck and Jim establish aboard the raft and the actual society which exists along the Mississippi's banks. The two are separated by the river, the road to freedom upon which Huck and Jim must travel. Huck tells us what the river means to them when, after the Wilks episode, he and Jim once again shove their raft into the current: "It *did* seem so good to be free again and all by ourselves on the big river, and nobody to bother us." The river is indifferent. But its sphere is relatively uncontaminated by the civilization they flee, and so the river allows Huck and Jim some measure of freedom at once, the moment they set foot on Jackson's Island or the raft. Only on the island and the raft do they have a chance to practice that idea of brotherhood to which they are devoted. "Other places do seem so cramped and smothery," Huck explains, "but a raft don't. You feel mighty free and easy and comfortable on a raft." The main thing is freedom.

On the raft the escaped slave and the white boy try to practice their code: "What you want, above all things, on a raft, is for everybody to be satisfied, and feel right and kind towards the others." This human credo constitutes the paramount affirmation of *The Adventures of Huckleberry Finn*, and it obliquely aims a devastating criticism at the existing social order. It is a creed which Huck and Jim bring to the river. It neither emanates from nature nor is it addressed to nature. Therefore I do not see that it means much to talk about the river as a god in this novel. The river's connection with this high aspiration for man is that it provides a means of escape, a place where the code can be tested. The truly profound meanings of the novel are generated by the impingement of the actual world of slavery, feuds, lynching, murder, and a spurious Christian morality upon the ideal of the raft. The result is a tension which somehow demands release in the novel's ending.

But Clemens was unable to effect this release and at the same time control the central theme. The unhappy truth about the ending of *Huckleberry Finn* is that the author, having revealed the tawdry nature of the culture of the great valley, yielded to its essential complacency. The general tenor of the closing scences, to which the token regeneration of Miss Watson is merely one superficial clue, amounts to just that. In fact, this entire reading of *Huckleberry Finn* merely confirms the brilliant insight of George Santayana, who many years ago spoke of American humorists, of whom he considered Mark Twain an outstanding representative, as having only "half escaped" the genteel tradition. Santayana meant that men like Clemens were able to "point to what contradicts it in the facts; but not in order to abandon the genteel tradition, for they have nothing solid to put in its place." This seems to me the real key to the failure of *Huckleberry Finn*. Clemens had presented the contrast between the two social orders but could not, or would not, accept the tragic fact that the one he had rejected was an image of solid reality and the other an ecstatic dream. Instead he gives us the cozy reunion with Aunt Polly in a scene fairly bursting with approbation of the entire family, the Phelpses included.

Like Miss Watson, the Phelpses are almost perfect specimens of the dominant culture. They are kind to their friends and relatives; they have no taste for violence; they are people capable of devoting themselves to their spectacular dinners while they keep Jim locked in the little hut down by the ash hopper, with its lone window boarded up. (Of course Aunt Sally visits Jim to see if he is "comfortable," and Uncle Silas comes in "to pray with him.") These people, with their comfortable Sunday-dinner conviviality and the runaway slave padlocked nearby, are reminiscent of those solid German citizens we have heard about in our time who tried to maintain a similarly *gemütlich* way of life within virtual earshot of Buchenwald. I do not mean to imply that Clemens was unaware of the shabby morality of such people. After the abortive escape of Jim, when Tom asks about him, Aunt Sally replies: "Him? ...the runaway nigger? ...They've got him back, safe and sound, and he's in the cabin again, on bread and water, and loaded down with chains, till he's claimed or sold!" Clemens understood people like the Phelpses, but nevertheless he was forced to rely upon them to provide his happy ending. The satisfactory outcome of Jim's quest for freedom must be attributed to the benevolence of the very people whose inhumanity first made it necessary.

But to return to the contention of Mr. Trilling and Mr. Eliot that the ending is more or less satisfactory after all. As I have said, Mr. Trilling approves of the "formal aptness" of the conclusion. He says that "some device is needed to permit Huck to return to his anonymity, to give up the role of hero," and that therefore "nothing could serve better than the mind of Tom Sawyer with its literary furnishings, its conscious romantic desire for experience and the hero's part, and its ingenious schematization of life...." Though more detailed, this is essentially akin to Mr. Eliot's blunt assertion that "it is right that the mood at the end of the book should bring us back to that of the beginning." I submit that it is wrong for the end of the book to bring us back to that mood. The mood of the beginning of *Huckleberry Finn* is the mood of Huck's attempt to accommodate himself to the ways of St. Petersburg. It is the mood of the end of *The Adventures of Tom Sawyer*, when the boys had been acclaimed heroes, and when Huck was accepted as a candidate for respectability. That is the state in which we find him at the beginning of *Huckleberry Finn*. But Huck cannot stand the new way of life, and his mood gradually shifts to the mood of rebellion which dominates the novel until he meets Tom again. At first, in the second chapter, we see him still eager to be accepted by the nice boys of the town. Tom leads the gang in re-enacting adventures he has culled from books, but gradually Huck's pragmatic turn of mind gets him in trouble. He has little tolerance for Tom's brand of make-believe. He irritates Tom. Tom calls him a "numbskull," and finally Huck throws up the whole business:

> "So then I judged that all that stuff was only just one of Tom Sawyer's lies. I reckoned he believed in the A-rabs and the elephants, but as for me I think different. It had all the marks of a Sunday school."

With this statement, which ends the third chapter, Huck parts company with Tom. The fact is that Huck has rejected Tom's romanticizing of experience; moreover, he has rejected it as part of the larger pattern of society's make-believe, typified by Sunday school. But if he cannot accept Tom's harmless fantasies about the A-rabs, how are we to believe that a year later Huck is capable of awestruck submission to the far more extravagant fantasies with which Tom invests the mock rescue of Jim?

After Huck's escape from his "pap," the drift of the action, like that of the Mississippi's current, is *away* from St. Petersburg. Huck leaves Tom and the A-rabs behind, along with the Widow, Miss Watson, and all the pseudo-religious ritual in which nice boys must partake. The return, in the end, to the mood of the beginning therefore means defeat—Huck's defeat; to return to that mood *joyously* is to portray defeat in the guise of victory.

Mr. Eliot and Mr. Trilling deny this. The overriding consideration for them is form—form which seems largely to mean symmetry of structure. It is fitting, Mr. Eliot maintains, that the book should come full circle and bring Huck once more under Tom's sway. Why? Because it begins that way. But it seems to me that such structural unity is *imposed* upon the novel, and therefore is meretricious. It is a jerry-built structure, achieved only by sacrifice of characters and theme. Here the controlling principle of form apparently is unity, but unfortunately a unity much too superficially conceived. Structure, after all, is only one element—indeed, one of the more mechanical elements—of unity. A unified work must surely manifest coherence of meaning and clear development of theme, yet the ending of *Huckleberry Finn* blurs both. The eagerness of Mr. Eliot and Mr. Trilling to justify the ending is symptomatic of that absolutist impulse of our critics to find reasons, once a work has been admitted to the highest canon of literary reputability, for admiring every bit of it.

What is perhaps most striking about these judgments of Mr. Eliot's and Mr. Trilling's is that they are so patently out of harmony with the basic standards of both critics. For one thing, both men hold far more complex ideas of the nature of literary unity than their comments upon *Huckleberry Finn* would suggest. For another, both critics are essentially moralists, yet here we find them turning away from a moral issue in order to praise a dubious structural unity. Their efforts to explain away the flaw in Clemens' novel suffer from a certain narrowness surprising to anyone who knows their work. These facts suggest that we may be in the presence of a tendency in contemporary criticism which the critics themselves do not fully recognize.

Is there an explanation? How does it happen that two of our most respected critics should seem to treat so lightly the glaring lapse of moral imagination in *Huckleberry Finn*? Perhaps—and I stress the conjectural nature of what I am saying—perhaps the kind of moral issue raised by *Huckleberry Finn* is not the kind of moral issue to which today's criticism readily addresses itself. Today our critics, no less than our novelists and poets, are most sensitively attuned to moral problems which arise in the sphere of individual behavior. They are deeply aware of sin, individual infractions of our culture's Christian ethic. But my impression is that they are, possibly because of the strength of the reaction against the mechanical sociological criticism of the thirties, less sensitive to questions of what might be called social or political morality.

By social or political morality I refer to the values implicit in a social system, values which may be quite distinct from the personal morality of any given individual within the society. Now *The Adventures of Huckleberry Finn*, like all novels, deals with the behavior of individuals. But one mark of Clemens' greatness is his deft presentation of the disparity between what people do when they behave as individuals and what they do when forced into roles imposed upon them by society. Take, for example, Aunt Sally and Uncle Silas Phelps, who consider themselves Christians, who are by impulse generous and humane, but who happen also to be staunch upholders of certain degrading and inhuman social institutions. When they are confronted with an escaped slave, the imperatives of social morality outweigh all pious professions.

The conflict between what people think they stand for and what social pressure forces them to do is central to the novel. It is present to the mind of Huck and, indeed, accounts for his most serious inner conflicts. He knows how he feels about Jim, but he also knows what he is expected to do about Jim. This division within his mind corresponds to the division of the novel's moral terrain into the areas represented by the raft on the one hand and society on the other. His victory over his "yaller dog" conscience therefore assumes heroic size: it is a victory over the prevailing morality. But the last fifth of the novel has the effect of diminishing the importance and uniqueness of Huck's victory. We are asked to assume that somehow freedom can be achieved in spite of the crippling power of what I have called the social morality. Consequently the less importance we attach to that force as it operates in the novel, the more acceptable the ending becomes.

Moreover, the idea of freedom, which Mr. Eliot and Mr. Trilling seem to slight, takes on its full significance only when we acknowledge the power which society exerts over the minds of men in the world of *Huckleberry Finn*. For freedom in this book specifically means freedom from society and its imperatives. This is not the traditional Christian conception of freedom. Huck and Jim seek freedom not from a burden of individual guilt and sin, but from social constraint. That is to say, evil in *Huckleberry Finn* is the product of civilization, and if this is indicative of Clemens' rather too simple view of human nature, nevertheless the fact is that Huck, when he can divest himself of the taint of social conditioning (as in the incantatory account of sunrise on the river), is entirely free of anxiety and guilt. The only guilt he actually knows arises from infractions of a social code. (The guilt he feels after playing the prank on Jim stems from his betrayal of the law of the raft.) Huck's and Jim's creed is secular. Its object is harmony among men, and so Huck is not much concerned with his own salvation. He repeatedly renounces prayer in favor of pragmatic solutions to his problems. In other words, the central insights of the novel belong to the tradition of the Enlightenment. The meaning of the quest itself is hardly reconcilable with that conception of human nature embodied in the myth of original sin. In view of the current fashion of reaffirming man's innate depravity, it is perhaps not surprising to find the virtues of *Huckleberry Finn* attributed not to its meaning but to its form.

But "if this was not the right ending for the book," Mr. Eliot asks, "what ending would have been right?" Although this question places the critic in an awkward position (he is not always equipped to rewrite what he criticizes), there are some things which may justifiably be said about the "right" ending of *Huckleberry Finn*. It may be legitimate, even if presumptuous, to indicate certain conditions which a hypothetical ending would have to satisfy if it were to be congruent with the rest of the novel. If the conclusion is not to be something merely tacked on to close the action, then its broad outline must be immanent in the body of the work.

It is surely reasonable to ask that the conclusion provide a plausible outcome to the quest. Yet freedom, in the ecstatic sense that Huck and Jim knew it aboard the raft, was hardly to be had in the Mississippi Valley in the 1840's, or, for that matter, in any other known human society. A satisfactory ending would inevitably cause the reader some frustration. That Clemens felt such disappointment to be inevitable is borne out by an examination of the novel's clear, if unconscious, symbolic pattern. Consider, for instance, the inferences to be drawn from the book's geography. The river, to whose current Huck and Jim entrust themselves, actually carries them to the heart of slave territory. Once the raft passes Cairo, the quest is virtually doomed. Until the steamboat smashes the raft, we are kept in a state of anxiety about Jim's escape. (It may be significant that at this point Clemens found himself unable to continue work on the manuscript, and put it aside for several years.) Beyond Cairo, Clemens allows the intensity of that anxiety to diminish, and it is probably no accident that the fainter it becomes, the more he falls back upon the devices of low comedy. Huck and Jim make no serious effort to turn north, and there are times (during the Wilks episode) when Clemens allows Huck to forget all about Jim. It is as if the author, anticipating the dilemma he had finally to face, instinctively dissipated the power of his major theme.

Consider, too, the circumscribed nature of the raft as a means of moving toward freedom. The raft lacks power and maneuverability. It can only move easily with the current—southward into slave country. Nor can it evade the mechanized power of the steamboat. These impotencies of the raft correspond to the innocent helplessness of its occupants. Unresisted, the rogues invade and take over the raft. Though it is the symbolic locus of the novel's central affirmations, the raft provides an uncertain and indeed precarious mode of traveling toward freedom. This seems another confirmation of Santayana's perception. To say that Clemens only half escaped the genteel tradition is not to say that he failed to note any of the creed's inadequacies, but rather that he had "nothing solid" to put in its place. The raft patently was not capable of carrying the burden of hope Clemens placed upon it.[6] (Whether this is to be attributed to the nature of his vision or to the actual state of American society in the nineteenth century is another interesting question.) In any case, the geography of the novel, the raft's powerlessness, the goodness and vulnerability of Huck and Jim, all prefigure a conclusion quite different in tone from that which Clemens gave us. These facts constitute what Hart Crane might have called the novel's "logic of metaphor," and this logic—probably inadvertent—actually takes us to the underlying meaning of *The Adventures of Huckleberry Finn*. Through the symbols we reach a truth which the ending obscures: the quest cannot succeed.

Fortunately, Clemens broke through to this truth in the novel's last sentences:

> "But I reckon I got to light out for the territory ahead of the rest, because Aunt Sally she's going to adopt me and civilize me, and I can't stand it. I been there before."

Mr. Eliot properly praises this as "the only possible concluding sentence." But one sentence can hardly be advanced, as Mr. Eliot advances this one, to support the rightness of ten chapters. Moreover, if this sentence is right, then the rest of the conclusion is wrong, for its meaning clashes with that of the final burlesque. Huck's decision to go west ahead of the inescapable advance of civilization is a confession of defeat. It means that the raft is to be abandoned. On the other hand, the jubilation of the family reunion and the proclaiming of Jim's freedom create a quite different mood. The tone, except for these last words, is one of unclouded success. I believe this is the source of the almost universal dissatisfaction with the conclusion. One can hardly forget that a bloody civil war did not resolve the issue.

Should Clemens have made Huck a tragic hero? Both Mr. Eliot and Mr. Trilling argue that that would have been a mistake, and they are very probably correct. But between the ending as we have it and tragedy in the fullest sense, there was vast room for invention. Clemens might have contrived an action which left Jim's fate as much in doubt as Huck's. Such an ending would have allowed us to assume that the principals were defeated but alive, and the quest unsuccessful but not abandoned. This, after all, would have been consonant with the symbols, the characters, and the theme as Clemens had created them—and with history.

Clemens did not acknowledge the truth his novel contained. He had taken hold of a situation in which a partial defeat was inevitable, but he was unable to—or unaware of the need to—give imaginative substance to that fact. If an illusion of success was indispensable, where was it to come from? Obviously Huck and Jim could not succeed by their own efforts. At this point Clemens, having only half escaped the genteel tradition, one of whose preeminent characteristics was an optimism undaunted by disheartening truth, returned to it. *Why* he did so is another story, having to do with his parents and his boyhood, with his own personality and his wife's, and especially with the character of his audience. But whatever the explanation, the faint-hearted ending of *The Adventures of Huckleberry Finn* remains an important datum in the record of American thought and imagination. It has been noted before, both by critics and non-professional readers. It should not be forgotten now.

To minimize the seriousness of what must be accounted a major flaw in so great a work is, in a sense, to repeat Clemens' failure of nerve. This is a disservice to criticism. Today we particularly need a criticism alert to lapses of moral vision. A measured appraisal of the failures and successes of our writers, past and present, can show us a great deal about literature and about ourselves. That is the critic's function. But he cannot perform that function if he substitutes considerations of technique for considerations of truth. Not only will such methods lead to errors of literary judgment, but beyond that, they may well encourage comparable evasions in other areas. It seems not unlikely, for instance, that the current preoccupation with matters of form is bound up with a tendency, by no means confined to literary quarters, to shy away from painful answers to complex questions of political morality. The conclusion to *The Adventures of Huckleberry Finn* shielded both Clemens and his audience from such an answer. But we ought not to be as tender-minded. For Huck Finn's besetting problem, the disparity between his best impulses and the behavior the community attempted to impose upon him, is as surely ours as it was Twain's.

Notes

1. I use the term "genteel tradition" as George Santayana characterized it in his famous address "The Genteel Tradition in American Philosophy," first delivered in 1911 and published the following year in his *Winds of Doctrine*. Santayana described the genteel tradition as an "old mentality" inherited from Europe. It consists of the various dilutions of Christian theology and morality, as in transcendentalism—a fastidious and stale philosophy of life no longer relevant to the thought and activities of the United States. "America," he said, "is a young country with an old mentality." (Later references to Santayana also refer to this essay.)

2. For an account of the first reviews, see A. L. Vogelback, "The Publication

and Reception of *Huckleberry Finn* in America," *American Literature*, 11 (November 1939), 260-272.

3. Mr. Eliot's essay is the introduction to the edition of *Huckleberry Finn* Published by Chanticleer Press, New York, 1950. Mr. Trilling's is the introduction to an edition of the novel published by Rinehart, New York, 1948, and later reprinted in his *The Liberal Imagination*, Viking, New York, 1950.

4. *Mark Twain at Work* (Cambridge: Harvard University Press, 1942), p. 92.

5. For these observations on the transformation of Jim in the closing episodes, I am indebted to the excellent unpublished essay by Mr. Chadwick Hansen on the subject of Clemens and Western humor.

6. Gladys Bellamy (*Mark Twain as a Literary Artist*, Norman: University of Oklahoma Press, 1950, p. 221) has noted the insubstantial, dream-like quality of the image of the raft. Clemens thus discusses travel by raft in *A Tramp Abroad*: "the motion of the raft is ... gentle, and gliding, and smooth, and noiseless; it calms down all feverish activities, it soothes to sleep all nervous ... impatience; under its restful influence all the troubles and vexations and sorrows that harass the mind vanish away, and existence becomes a dream ... a deep and tranquil ecstasy."

Huck and Oliver

W. H. Auden

About six months ago I re-read *Huckleberry Finn*, by Mark Twain, for the first time since I was a boy, and I was trying when I read it to put myself back in the position of what it would seem like to re-read the book without knowing the United States very well. Because *Huckleberry Finn* is one of those books which is a key book for understanding the United States; just as I think one could take other books, English books—shall I say *Oliver Twist*?—as corresponding pictures of a British attitude.

• • •

When you read *Huckleberry Finn*, the first thing maybe that strikes somebody who comes from England about it is the difference in nature and in the attitude towards nature. You will find the Mississippi, and nature generally, very big, very formidable, very inhuman. When Oliver goes to stay in the country with Mrs. Maylie, Dickens writes:

> Who can describe the pleasure and delight and peace of mind and tranquillity the sickly boy felt in the balmy air, and among the green hills and rich woods of an inland village.

All very human, very comforting. Huck describes how he gets lost in a fog on the Mississippi, and he writes as follows:

> I was floating along, of course, four or five miles an hour; but you don't ever think of that. No, you *feel* like you are laying dead still on the water; and if a little glimpse of a snag slips by, you don't think to yourself how fast *you're* going, but

From *The Listener*, 50 (October 1, 1953), 540–41. Reprinted with permission of Curtis Brown, Ltd.

you catch your breath and think, my! how that snag's tearing along. If you think it ain't dismal and lonesome out in a fog that way, by yourself, in the night, you try it once—you'll see.

One of the great differences between Europe in general and America is in the attitude towards nature. To us over here, perhaps, nature is always, in a sense, the mother or the wife: something with which you enter into a semi-personal relation. In the United States, nature is something much more savage; it is much more like—shall we say?—St. George and the dragon. Nature is the dragon, against which St. George proves his manhood. The trouble about that, of course, is that if you succeed in conquering the dragon, there is nothing you can do with the dragon except enslave it, so that there is always the danger with a wild and difficult climate of alternating, if you like, between respecting it as an enemy and exploiting it as a slave.

The second thing that will strike any European reader in reading *Huckleberry Finn* is the amazing stoicism of this little boy. Here he is, with a father who is a greater and more horrible monster than almost any I can think of in fiction, who very properly gets murdered later. He runs into every kind of danger; he observes a blood feud in which there is a terrible massacre, and he cannot even bear, as he writes afterwards, to think exactly what happened. Yet, in spite of all these things, which one would expect to reduce a small child either into becoming a criminal or a trembling nervous wreck, Huck takes them as Acts of God which pass away, and yet one side of this stoicism is an attitude towards time in which the immediate present is accepted as the immediate present; there is no reason to suppose that the future will be the same, and therefore it does not, perhaps, have to affect the future in the same kind of way as it does here.

Then, more interestingly, the European reader is puzzled by the nature of the moral decision that Huck takes. Here Huck is with his runaway slave, Jim, and he decides that he is not going to give Jim up, he is going to try to get him into safety. When I first read *Huckleberry Finn* as a boy, I took Huck's decision as being a sudden realization, although he had grown up in a slave-owning community, that slavery was wrong. Therefore I completely failed to understand one of the most wonderful passages in the book, where Huck wrestles with his conscience. Here are two phrases. He says:

> I was trying to make my mouth *say* I would do the right thing and the clean thing, and go and write to that nigger's owner and tell where he was; but deep down inside I knowed it was a lie, and He knowed it. You can't pray a lie—I found that out.

He decides that he will save Jim. He says:

> I will go to work and steal Jim out of slavery again; and if I could think up anything worse, I would do that, too; because as long as I was in, and in for good, I might as well go the whole hog.

When I first read the book I took this to be abolitionist satire on Mark Twain's part. It is not that at all. What Huck does is a pure act of moral improvisation. What he decides tells him nothing about what he should do on other occasions, or what other people should do on other occasions; and here we come to a very profound difference between American and European culture. I believe that all Europeans, whatever their political opinions, whatever their religious creed, do believe in a doctrine of natural law of some kind. That is to say there are certain things about human nature, and about man as a historical creature, not only as a natural creature, which are eternally true. If a man is conservative, he thinks that law has already been discovered. If he is a revolutionary he thinks he has just discovered it; nobody knew anything in the past, but now it is known. If he is a liberal, he thinks we know something about it and we shall gradually know more. But neither the conservative, nor the revolutionary, nor the liberal has really any doubt that a natural law exists.

It is very hard for an American to believe that there is anything in human nature that will not change. Americans are often called, and sometimes even believe themselves to be, liberal optimists who think that the world is gradually getting better and better. I do not really believe that is true, and I think the evidence of their literature is against it. One should say, rather, that deep down inside they think that all things pass: the evils we know will disappear, but so will the goods.

For that very reason you might say that America is a country of amateurs. Here is Huck who makes an essentially amateur moral decision. The distinction between an amateur and a professional, of course, is not necessarily a matter of learning; an amateur might be a very learned person, but his knowledge would be, so to speak, the result of his own choice of reading and chance. *Vice versa*, a professional is not necessarily unoriginal, but he will always tend to check his results against the past and with his colleagues. The word "intellectual" in Europe has always meant, basically, the person who knew what the law was, in whatever sphere, whether it was religion, medicine, or what have you. There has always been a distrust in the States of the person who claimed in advance to know what the law was. Naturally, in any country where people are faced with situations which are really new, the amateur often is right where the professional is wrong; we sometimes use the phrase "professional caution," and that sometimes applies when situations are quite different. On the other hand the amateur tends, necessarily, to think in terms of immediate problems and to demand immediate solutions, because if you believe that everything is going to be completely different the day after tomorrow, it is no good trying to think about that.

A third thing, coupled with that, is that on reading *Huckleberry Finn* most Europeans will find the book emotionally very sad. Oliver Twist has been through all kinds of adventures; he has met people who have become his friends, and you feel they are going to be his friends for life. Huck has had a relationship with Jim much more intense than any that Oliver has known, and yet, at the end of the book, you know that they are going to part and never see each other again. There hangs over the book a kind of sadness, as if freedom and love were incompatible. At the end of the book Oliver the orphan is adopted by Mr. Brownlow, and that is really the summit of his daydream—to be accepted into a loving home. Almost the last paragraph of *Oliver Twist* runs:

> Mr. Brownlow went on, from day to day, filling the mind of his adopted child with stores of knowledge ... becoming attached to him, more and more, as his nature developed itself, and showed the thriving seeds of all he wished him to become....

How does Huck end:

> I reckon I got to light out for the Territory ahead of the rest, because Aunt Sally she's going to adopt me and sivilise me, and I can't stand it. I been there before.

In that way, of course, he is like a character in *Oliver Twist*—the Artful Dodger. But in the case of the Artful Dodger, Dickens shows us this charming young man as nevertheless corrupt, and over him hangs always the shadow of the gallows; he is not the natural hero, as Huck is in *Huckleberry Finn.*

In addition to the attitude towards nature, the attitude towards natural law, there are two more things one might take up briefly; the attitude towards time, and the attitude towards money. Imagine two events in history, *(a)* followed by *(b)*, which in some way are analogous. The danger to the European will be to think of them as identical, so that if I know what to do over *(a)*, I shall know exactly what to do with *(b)*. The danger in America will be to see no relation between these things at all, so that any knowledge I have about *(a)* will not help me to understand *(b)*. The European fails to see the element of novelty; the American fails to see the element of repetition. You may remember that both Oliver and Huck come into some money. In Oliver's case it is money that is his by right of legal inheritance. In Huck's case, it is pure luck. He and Tom Sawyer found a robber's cache. The money came to them only because it could not be restored to its rightful owners. The money, therefore, is not something that you ever think of inheriting by right.

One might put it this way: in Europe, money represents power—that is to say, freedom from having to do what other people want you to do, and freedom to do what you yourself want to do; so that in a sense all Europeans feel they would like to have as much money themselves as possible, and other people to have as little as possible.

In the States, money, which is thought of as something you extract in your battle with the dragon of nature, represents a proof of your manhood. The important thing is not to have money, but to have made it. Once you have made it you can perfectly well give it all away. There are advantages and disadvantages on both sides. The disadvantage in Europe is a tendency towards avarice and meanness; the danger in America is anxiety because, since this quantitative thing of money is regarded as a proof of your manhood, and to make a little more of it would make you even more manly, it becomes difficult to know where to stop. This ties up with something that always annoys me: when I see Europeans accusing Americans of being materialists. The real truth about Americans is they do not care about matter enough. What is shocking is waste; just as what shocks Americans in Europe is avarice.

I have mentioned a few of these things because we live in a time when it has never been so important that America and Great Britain should understand each other. Many misunderstandings arise, not over concrete points, but over a failure to recognize certain presuppositions or attitudes which we all make, according to our upbringing, in such a way that we cannot imagine anybody taking any other one. When those are understood, it is much more possible to help each other's strong points and weaknesses by exchanging them to our mutual profit.

In so far as that can be done, and I am sufficiently much of a liberal optimist to believe it can, the alliance between the States and Great Britain can become a real and genuine and mutually self-critical thing, instead of the rather precarious relationship forced by circumstances which it seems to be at present.

Bad Novels and Great Books

Joseph Wood Krutch

This spring a great many people must have been reading *Huckleberry Finn* at the same moments I was. How many of them, I wonder, were reminded again how conclusively it proves that a great work of fiction does not need to be what is called a "good novel" or, indeed, a merely "good" anything else.

In his recent *A Writer's Notebook* Somerset Maugham commented briefly on the fact that all of the novelists whom he would be willing to call great without reservation—especially Balzac, Dickens, Tolstoy and Dostoevsky—wrote their language rather badly, at least in the limited sense that they did not very often achieve either the polish or the adroitness which constitutes the excellence of many lesser writers. He might have gone on to point out that many of the very greatest novels exhibit also glaring imperfections which go far beyond a mere lack of verbal felicity. Not a few of them, perhaps even most of them, are what a disciple of Flaubert or of Henry James would call "bad novels," no matter how interesting or impressive they may be.

In the case of *Huckleberry Finn* the "badness" is not a matter of carelessly inelegant sentences. In this respect the book is actually extremely "well written" because Mark Twain seems to have polished his style until he achieved precisely that effect of colloquial semi-literacy at which he was aiming. But everybody knows that it is also and unintentionally "a bad novel" in certain

From *New York Times Book Review,* May 23, 1954, p. 2. Reprinted with permission. Title provided by editor.

fundamental respects. Much of it is so improbable as to become at times wholly unconvincing on one level of understanding. It is also episodic, clumsily plotted, and sometimes as crudely melodramatic as a dime novel. One could reasonably argue that, as a whole, it is a botched job just as, in another way, the whole last quarter of *Life on the Mississippi* is botched. But both books are also uniquely delightful and never to be forgotten by anyone who has ever read either.

When Huck explains a mysterious absence by inventing a wonderfully complicated case of the mumps involving symptoms hitherto unknown to medical history, or when he describes the collection of lachrymose crayons and assorted elegiac verses left behind by a departed maiden, the pages are howlingly comic on several different levels from that of pure farce to high intellectual comedy. Obviously Mark had been visited by that same wise counselor who advised Cervantes three hundred years before how he should write so that the simple would be entertained while the wise were finding something which the simple had missed. But the best episodes will not make a "bad novel" into a great book. Some largeness of plan is also necessary.

That largeness of plan *Huckleberry Finn* does have. The whole conception of the journey down the river remains in the mind like the large conception of an epic, and it justifies an interpretation of the book in epic terms which might have surprised the author. The river journey is as unforgettable as the March of the Ten Thousand or as the wanderings of Ulysses. By comparison with that fact the badness of the plotting or the "unconvincing" aspects of the episodes is as irrelevant as the "unconvincing" aspects of the story of the Cyclops.

Once a certain degree of imaginative intensity has been reached we lose all concern with what is ordinarily called "realism." The question whether or not something is "probable" or "convincing" becomes mere fiddle-faddle. One no longer needs to be convinced; one simply knows. Huck floated down the river as indubitably as Hamlet saw a ghost or the Greeks hid in a wooden horse.

Even the intellectual, even the sociological, points are made so much the better because Mark Twain scorns the careful "realism" of the problem novelist. Huck's incredulity in face of the fact that Nigger Jim is as grief-stricken by a personal loss as a white man would have been, his remark that "it doesn't seem natural that he should be," is worth, artistically at least, not only all of *Uncle Tom's Cabin* but also the complete corpus of recent novels about "prejudice." Such a passage is like certain ones in *The Merchant of Venice.* "If a jew is cut does he not bleed?"

Not all the "bad novels" which are also great books are such because they are really not novels at all but epics. There are other good things which "bad novels" may sometimes be—romances, poems, even autobiographies. Perhaps nothing except great energy of some sort is absolutely indispensable. Balzac once declared that "the important point was not to avoid mistakes but to have a quality that sweeps everything in front of it." In the case of *Huckleberry Finn* this quality is essentially epic. And there are ways in which an epic is better than even a "good" novel.

Remarks on the Sad Initiation of Huckleberry Finn

James M. Cox

The Adventures of Huckleberry Finn is one of those rare books which are at once acceptable to the intelligentsia and to that celebrated American phenomenon, the average citizen; it is a book which even anti-literary children read and enjoy. Even if the language of the book should eventually be lost or, worse still, replaced by convenient abridgements, the memory of Huck Finn would still survive among us like some old and indestructible god. In the popular imagination, however, Huck Finn does not exist by himself, but is accompanied by Tom Sawyer, his other half. These two figures are not imagined as individuals; they are conceived as identical twins who roam about the earth stealing jam, beating up sissies, playing hooky, and raising hell in general. Furthermore, the Tom-Huck image exists in terms of Tom Sawyer; the real Huck Finn who floated down the Mississippi with Nigger Jim has been shuffled under the rather trivial aegis of the Bad Boy.

Yet there is a grim logic behind this discomforting shift, for if Huck stands uncomfortably next to Tom Sawyer at least he has been there before. Indeed he even adopted Tom Sawyer's name during those rather flat final chapters of *Huckleberry Finn*. After Huck reached his unknown destination, the Phelps farm, the only terms on which he could exist were Tom's terms, and, driv-

From *Sewanee Review*, 62 (July-September 1954), 389-405. Reprinted with permission.

en to distraction by the hemming forces which threatened to annihilate him, he gave up his freedom to be free. In order to save himself, the fugitive played the part of Tom Sawyer and in playing it he completed his long, arduous, and disillusioning initiation. The characters, the implications, and the art of this initiation can be fully realized by beginning with the work behind *Huckleberry Finn, The Adventures of Tom Sawyer.*

The most striking aspect of *Tom Sawyer* is its almost total lack of plot in the conventional sense of that word. There is little or no transition between episodes; continuity results from appearance and reappearance of the same characters. The most obvious defense of this lack of causal sequence—plot as machinery—is that it reinforces the pervasive determinism of Tom Sawyer's world. Although Tom reacts to the daily occurrences which confront him and although he makes belated attempts to meet his fate, he is quite powerless to initiate the action.

The real unity of Tom Sawyer arises not so much from the underlying determinism as from the insistent rhythm of the novel, a rhythm based upon repetition and variation of central motives. The violence and terror which are just beneath the surface of the boys' world regularly erupt into it. After the pleasures of the schoolroom comes the dark and unknown night, bringing with it fear and death. Even on Jackson's Island, the idyllic innocence of the afternoon is overtaken by a night thunderstorm which almost rips the island apart. Often this repetition is executed in much more subtle terms, providing submerged links between the episodes. Thus in one episode Tom and Joe Harper play Robin Hood in the dark woods, pretending to kill each other. The following night, in another scene, Tom and Huck witness the brutal murder in the graveyard. This effect is repeated when Muff Potter begs Injun Joe to swear secrecy in the matter of the killing, a scene followed by the one in which the boys, who have witnessed the crime, also swear to reveal nothing of what they have seen. They attempt to make their oath "real" by creating careful rituals which they religiously enact. The innocent rituals of the children are performed with grotesque reality by the adults. The chief characters of the book sense the fundamental dangers which confront them after the sun goes down, and they fall back on ritual and superstition to protect themselves from the inscrutable powers which lurk at the edge of the clearing.

The absence of formal transition, the constant rhythm of the action, the double exposure effect arising from the superimposition of one episode upon another all coordinate to give a kind of dream structure to the novel. The presence of characters is often unexplained and their disappearance unaccounted for. Becky Thatcher and Joe Harper fade out of the action toward the end of the novel; the doctor's appearance in the graveyard remains a mystery as does his motive for hiring the grave robbers. Characters slip in and out of their identity by wearing deliberate disguises (disguise and mistaken identity are favorite devices of Mark Twain which he uses brilliantly in *Huckleberry Finn* and interestingly in *A Connecticut Yankee, The Prince and The Pauper, Tom Sawyer, Detective,* and *Pudd'nhead Wilson)*; episodes drift into each other; sometimes, as with the Robin Hood game, an entire episode serves as a mask for another incident. The unity of the novel can be perceived only by looking *through* one scene into another.

Adding to this rhythmic structure and reinforcing the unity is, of course, the central character of Tom. Walter Blair, a Mark Twain specialist who attempted a conventional explanation of the structure of *Tom Sawyer,* contended that the novel deals with a boy's growth, but instead of analyzing the psychology of that growth he wandered away from his fertile suggestion and divided the novel into rather useless structural units. The novel is indeed about growing up. Appearing first merely as a Bad Boy, Tom, as Mr. Blair points out, develops into a character of real interest. His humor has been much discussed, its sources have been thoroughly examined, but the psychology behind it has often been neglected. Tom's repeated death fantasies are nowhere scrutinized by the scholars who have so painstakingly provided a "background" for the novel, yet these very fantasies give Tom's character depth and complexity. Time after time the rhythm of the novel is expressed in terms of his death wish. Tom retires into solitude envisioning the mourning of the village when its inhabitants realize that he is no more. The culmination of the Jackson Island episode is the triumphal return of Tom and his two cronies to witness their own funerals. Even when death closes in on Tom and Becky in the darkness of the cave, Tom awaits it with a certain pleasure.

But there is another death, a death brutal and ghastly, lurking just beyond the boys' world and constantly impinging on it; it is the death in the graveyard and the death of Injun Joe—instead of warmth and protection this death is informed with terror. To see it as a brutal fact waiting in the adult world is to look with wistful eyes at that other death. The cave episode, fantastic from a "realistic" point of view, is oddly appropriate because it embodies the paradox of death and isolation; it is in the cave that Tom, in the very arms of the warm shadow, manages to find the will to force his way to light and safety, but it is also in the cave that Injun Joe meets one of the most violent and horrifying deaths in our literature. The two images of death are united in the cave, and it is hardly pure coincidence that Injun Joe, the demon who has haunted Tom's dreams, lies dead at the sealed doorway of the abyss from which Tom has escaped. Tom has, albeit unconsciously, experienced what Hans Castorp more consciously experienced in the snowstorm; he has glimpsed the sheer terror at the center of his childhood image of death. His immediate return to the cave to seize the treasure suggests his inner triumph.

The discovery of the treasure, significantly hidden under Injun Joe's cross, enables Tom to enter heroically the ranks of the respectable. Of course, he has been slyly respectable all along. Even when he breaks the law he does so with the intimate knowledge that he is expected to break it. His acute dramatic sense enables him to see the part he is to play, and he is therefore constantly aware of his participation in sacred social rites. This awareness results in a kind of compulsive badness in his nature; he achieves the Frommian ideal of wanting to do what society expects him to do. As the curtain drops there is triumphant confirmation of Tom's membership in the cult of the respectable. He is even trying to sell the club to Huck, cautioning him to remain a member of society because if one is to belong to Tom Sawyer's Outlaw Gang one must, paradoxically, obey the law:

> HUCK: Now Tom, hain't you always ben friendly to me? You wouldn't shet me out, would you, Tom? You wouldn't do that, now *would* you, Tom?
>
> TOM: Huck, I wouldn't want to, and I don't want to—but what would people say? Why, they'd say, "Mph! Tom Sawyer's Gang! pretty low characters in it!" They'd mean you, Huck.

The implications of Tom's entrance into society illuminate the differences between Tom and Huck and also throw Mark Twain himself into much sharper focus. Van Wyck Brooks in his *Ordeal of Mark Twain* took the events of Twain's life and tried to see the books as repetitions of his life troubles, attempting to prove that Olivia Langdon and William Dean Howells thwarted Mark Twain's artistic development. Although his contention that Mark Twain never grew up is convincing, his approach is extremely questionable. Bernard De Voto has done much to dispel Brooks' theory that Mark Twain was thwarted, and for all his windiness, De Voto has seen that Twain himself was the prude as much as Olivia Langdon or Howells. A thorough analysis of Mark Twain's work will corroborate De Voto. He actually sought out Olivia Langdon, knowing full well she was a semi-invalid and a puritan. The picture of this "bad boy" coming east to roost is fraught with irony, and certainly his complete trust in Howells' judgment can hardly be blamed on Howells. He was perfectly content with the nickname, "Youth," by which Olivia called him, and he addressed his friend Mrs. Fairbanks as "mother" while his own mother was still very much alive. One scarcely has to be a Freudian to perceive that like Tom Sawyer he sought the authority and protection of respectability. In view of Twain's own quest it is quite remarkable, yet paradoxically inevitable, that *Huckleberry Finn* ever saw the light of day.

The Adventures of Huckleberry Finn is a conscious continuation and extension of *Tom Sawyer*. As he begins his own story, Huck carefully recounts the events of his immediate past. After mentioning the discovery of gold he goes on to say:

> The Widow Douglas she took me for her son, and allowed she would sivilize me; but it was rough living in the house all the time, considering how dismal regular and decent the widow was in all her ways; and so when I couldn't stand it no longer I lit out. I got into my old rags and my sugar-hogshead again, and was free and satisfied. But Tom Sawyer he hunted me up and said he was going to start a band of robbers, and I might join if I would go back to the widow and be respectable. So I went back.

Here is the argument of the entire novel—all that follows revolves around this major theme, Huck's initiation into respectable society. The tragic irony of the novel is Huck's inner awareness that membership in the cult will involve the dissolution of his character and the denial of his values.

Huck is hardly situated comfortably at the Widow Douglas' where Miss Watson plies him with frontier puritanism on the one hand and Tom Sawyer confronts him with bourgeois romanticism on the other, when his ruthless father suddenly appears demanding Huck's money which is happily drawing interest, having been shrewdly invested by Judge Thatcher. Pap's onslaught is momentarily halted by the young judge who, fresh from the East, attempts to reform the outcast drunkard. In a chapter significantly entitled "Pap Starts in on a New Life" the whole initiation and rebirth theme is launched on a tragi-comic note. The beautiful spare room in the judge's home is opened to Pap and great is the celebration by the judge's family as Pap jubilantly begins the new life, but during the night he slips out of the beautiful room, trades his new coat which they have given him for a jug of "forty-rod," and climbs back into the room, gets terribly drunk, finally falls off the porch roof into the yard—"and when they come to look at that spare room they had to take soundings before they could navigate it." After this fearful fall from respectability, Pap seizes Huck, whom he considers as property suddenly become valuable, transports him to a log hut up the river, and imprisons him. He treats Huck so violently that Huck finally stages a mock murder of himself in order to escape. This fake murder is probably the most vital and crucial incident of the entire novel. Having killed himself, Huck is "dead" throughout the entire journey down the river. He is indeed the man without identity who is reborn at almost every river bend, not because he desires a new role, but because he must re-create himself to elude the forces which close in on him from every side. The rebirth theme which began with Pap's reform becomes the driving idea behind the entire action.

Coupled with and inseparable from the theme of rebirth is the central image of death. Huck has hardly assumed the role of outcast when he meets Jim, who is also in frantic flight (interestingly enough, Jim is considered in terms of property too; his motive for escaping was fear of being sold down the river for $800.00), and the two fugitives watch the house of death float by on the swollen Mississippi. When Jim carefully covers up the face of the dead man in the house, the second major image of the novel is forged. These two images, rebirth and death, provide a frame for all succeeding episodes of the arduous initiation. As Huck and Jim move down the river, an oncoming steamboat crashes into their raft, forcing the two outcasts to swim for their lives. From this baptism Huck emerges to enter the new life at the Grangerfords under the name of George Jackson. His final act in that life is to cover the dead face of Buck Grangerford much as Jim had covered Pap's face in the house of death. When the Duke and King come aboard, their unscrupulous schemes force Huck and Jim to appear in new disguises; but the image of death is never absent. It confronts Huck in the little "one-horse town" in Arkansas where Colonel Sherburn shoots the drunken Boggs in cold blood. When the townspeople lift Boggs from the street and take him to the little drug store, Huck peers in through the window to watch him die. The Peter Wilks episode involves the same central images. The Duke and the King disguise themselves as foreign kinsmen of the deceased Wilks and they force Huck to play the role of an English valet. The final scene of the episode takes place in the graveyard where the mob of townsmen has gathered to exhume the buried Wilks in an effort to discover whether the Duke and King are imposters. A flash of lightning reveals the dead man with the gold on his breast where Huck had hidden it. The man who has Huck in charge forgets his prisoner in his zeal to see corpse and gold; Huck takes full advantage of the moment and runs out of that world forever.

Finally, at the Phelps farm the initiation is completed. Huck is reborn as Tom Sawyer and this time no image of death appears. The Duke and the King are far back in his past and the wheel has indeed come full circle. Jim is imprisoned in a cabin much like the one in which pap locked Huck; Tom Sawyer himself comes to the rescue in the role of Sid Sawyer; the entire household, though not the same as the one in which the novel began, is related to it through strong blood ties. The full import of this initiation becomes more clearly evident when the differences between Huck and Tom Sawyer are examined.

All of Tom Sawyer's world has been imported into this novel, but with the addition of Huck as narrator and protagonist and Jim as his companion, Tom's world is seen in sharp perspective. Huck and Jim may have to live in that world but they are not of it, and their very detachment creates a larger and deeper universe of which Tom Sawyer's values are but a part. True, Huck is finally overtaken by the society represented by Tom, but his heroic flight and his inner resistance give dignity to his submission. Huck is, after all, incorruptible and though his body is finally captured by the society which "wants" him so, it has not got his name affixed to it; as the novel ends, the real Huck who cannot die is ready to "light out for the territory," to continue his restless flight from "sivilization." Tom Sawyer's initiation had been routine, had merely confirmed his membership in a society to which he already latently belonged; Tom's whole attitude toward his initiators was, as I pointed out, one of self-consciousness, even affectation. Huck's initiation, on the other hand, is forced upon him; his drama is different in that it is drama, not play; everything is at stake in an elemental conflict where the values of one world are pitted against the values of another. And Huck's humor is deeper and greater because it is underlain by the pathos and tragedy of his situation.

Huck is, in the deepest sense, an outcast. Although Tom is an orphan, he at least has relatives who recognize his credentials and have adopted him. Huck has only Pap, the drunkard, the outcast himself, whose eyes shine through his tangled, greasy hair "like he was behind vines." Pap attains intense symbolic stature in his brief but violent pilgrimage:

> ...There warn't no color in his face where his face showed; it was white; not like another man's white, but a white to make a body's flesh crawl—a tree toad white, a fishbelly white. As for his clothes—just rags, that was all.

There is in this description a supernatural quality which links Pap to Melville's whale. His ways are not so much evil as they are inscrutable; he has somehow gotten consumed by the very nature he set out to conquer and out of the dark union between himself and the River the divine Huck has sprung; Huck certainly belongs more to the river than to the society along its banks, but this in no way makes of him a Rousseauistic child of nature. His lineal descendancy from Pap removes him from the garden of innocence, but if it implies his connection with violence and terror, it also puts him in touch with the deeper human forces which cannot be neatly filed under sociological headings. He has "connections" which, though they do not enable him to get ahead in an acquisitive society, give him a depth and a reality which far surpass anything Tom Sawyer has dreamed of.

Both boys fall back on a world of superstition, but Huck's rituals are naturally inherited while Tom's are appropriated from books. Tom's whole life is an imitation of the romances he has read or heard in the middle class society of which he is a part. The drab and empty life of St. Petersburg forces Tom's mind into an irretrievable past and he pathetically attempts to revive dead chivalry in blighted prairie air. Huck's whole code is, on the contrary, part of him, and he reacts sensitively to life about him. Instead of importing life and law from outside worlds, he invests the objects and people of his world with a life of their own. The difference between Tom Sawyer and Huckleberry Finn is the difference between the primitive and the effete imagination. Tom's drive to dominate his companions, the quality which marks him a devotee at the shrine of William James's bitch goddess, arises from the imitative aspect of his mind. The artificial application of a foreign code demands its strict inflexibility. When Tom organizes his gang at the beginning of the novel he is helpless before the independent machinery of his code; even when the machinery obviously will not work, he insists on its use. In his desire to free Jim according to "the rules," Tom displays utter disregard for him as a human being. The ultimate irony emerges when Huck discovers Tom has known Jim was legally free all the time. This discovery explains the deep mystery to Huck who has been wondering all along why Tom Sawyer would "lower himself" by helping a runaway slave. Through Huck's apparently innocent eyes we get an intimate glimpse into the soul of Tom Sawyer and we see an appalling relationship between Tom and Colonel Sellers, George Babbitt, and, I suppose, Willy Loman.

It is inevitable that Tom should assume Sid Sawyer's role when he reappears at the end of the novel. Sid, Tom's half brother, was the Good Boy of *Tom Sawyer*; he was the eternal prude, the darling of a puritan Sunday School. Yet for all Tom's apparent romantic revolt, his values are Sid's values and though he retains illusions of himself he shows unmistakably that he really is Sid's half brother. In the closing chapters of the novel Tom's very words become "respectable" and "principle," "regular" and "duty."

> ...The thing for us to do is just to do our *duty*, and not worry about whether anybody *sees* us do it or not. Hain't you got no principle at all?

Huck's relationship to Tom is much more distant. True, there are times when he attempts to emulate Tom Sawyer. Even when he stages his own murder he is conscious that Tom Sawyer would think it was "right proud." He sometimes treats Jim the way Tom might treat him. He puts the rattlesnake in Jim's bed and sees the terrifying results. When the two of them board the *Walter Scott*, Huck consciously plays the role of the adventurous Tom much to the dismay of Jim. After Huck and Jim become separated in the fog, Huck attempts to deceive Jim into believing that the separation is a product of Jim's fertile imagination, but Jim humiliates him in the famous passage which ends:

> Dat truck dah is trash; en trash is what people is dat puts dirt on de head er dey frens en makes 'em ashamed.

Most of the time, however, Huck is living on too thin a margin to afford Tom's luxurious romances. His motives, arising from his struggle for survival, allow him to indulge in no impracticalities, but he knows the fugitive must rely on magic and superstition to propitiate the inscrutable powers which confront him. The wedding of the practical and the magical gives Huck's character a mobility in the constricting circumstances which envelop him. But all his mobility is not enough, for the forces which pursue him are as relentless as the Mississippi's current. They appear in the forms of the Duke and King, the Grangerfords and Shepherdsons and their feud, Judith Loftus, even Jim. Every living thing becomes a source of danger to the lost boy without a name. Huck's remarkable observation upon first seeing the Duke and King coming toward him at a run reveals the terror of his plight:

> ...Just as I was passing a place where a kind of a cowpath crossed the crick, here comes a couple of men tearing up the path as tight as they could foot it. I thought I was a goner, for whenever anybody was after anybody I judged it was *me*—or maybe Jim.

Because Huck completely lives his rituals, because he participates to the tips of his fingers in a struggle for survival, and because his whole world and all its values are at stake, he transcends the empty rituals of Tom Sawyer's universe and achieves mythic significance.

When he wearily walks into the Phelps yard and is once more faced with the inevitable proposition of creating himself, he feels his string playing out. At Judith Loftus', at the Grangerfords', before the King and Duke, Huck, the man without identity, had been able to choose his disguise from a vast store of verbal masks which he kept ready at hand; but at the Phelps home even his name has been chosen and he bewilderingly attempts to discover who he is. As he stands before Aunt Sally trying to solve the riddle of his identity, he feels so tight and uncomfortable that he almost wishes he were dead:

> ...Well, I see I was up a stump—and up it good. Providence had stood by me this fur all right, but I was hard and tight aground now. I see it warn't a bit of use to try to go ahead—I'd got to throw up my hand. So I says to myself, here's another place where I got to resk the truth.

The swirl of events never allows him to "resk the truth" (the phrase itself suggests the ironic plight of Huck's position throughout the novel): Uncle Silas Phelps arrives at this precise moment and Huck finds to his delight and amazement that he is supposed to be Tom Sawyer. The very language Huck uses at this point suggests the myth behind the humor:

> By jings, I almost slumped through the floor! But there warn't no time to swap knives; the old man grabbed me by the hand and shook, and kept on shaking.... But if they was joyful, it warn't nothing to what I was; for it was like being born again, I was so glad to find out who I was.

There is bitter irony in Huck's assumption of Tom's name because the values of Tom Sawyer are so antithetical to the values of Huck Finn; in the final analysis, the two boys cannot exist in the same world. When Huck regains his own identity at the very end of the novel he immediately feels the compulsion to "light out for the territory" because he knows that to be Huck Finn is to be the outcast beyond the paling fences. From Mark Twain's point of view in this novel, Tom Sawyer civilization involves obedience, imitation, and is directly opposed to a dynamic and creative frontier imagination. In Tom Sawyer's triumph, the hard core of Mark Twain's later disillusion and pessimism is already evident. Although Huck Finn may escape to the territory, the whole outline of the frontier is receding westward before the surge of a small town culture, and it is indeed doomed country into which Huck must retreat.

Huck Finn cannot be reduced to historical proportions, however, even though there is much in the novel for the historian. The territory to which Huck refers is more than a diminishing area in nineteenth century America. It is a metaphorical equivalent of the broader and deeper vision which Huck and Jim represent. To be in the "territory" is not to be in heaven, for the wilderness and waste places have their perils for the sojourner, as Pap's presence fearfully testifies, but it is to escape the dehumanizing forces of the little towns; it is to be stripped of the pride encouraged by a sterile respectability and to feel absolute humility in the face of the awful unseen powers. Huck and Jim are the only real human beings in the novel—they are human because they can still feel and because they possess a heightened sensitivity to the promises and terrors of life. The characters whom they encounter, with the exception of the young and innocent, have an angularity and rigidity which mark them as grosteques. The blind spots of the eminently respectable become proving grounds for the avaricious; the pretentious righteousness of one group merely encourages the brutal sensationalism of another. Only Huck and Jim possess wholeness of spirit among the horde of fragmentary personalities which parade through the novel. The society which hotly pursues Huck and Jim knows that they possess the real secrets—that is why it so desperately wants to "own" them.

And if Tom has taken Sid's role and Huck has been forced to take Tom's in this rather discouraging progression, who is left to take Huck's place? Fifteen years later Mark Twain could not answer the question, for his imagination had been consumed by what Bernard De Voto calls the symbols of despair. There is someone, however, to take Huck's place in this novel; he is, of course, that primitive of primitives, Jim. He stands in relation to Huck in this novel much as Huck stood in relation to Tom in *Tom Sawyer*, and is in many ways the central figure in the book. It is to Jim that Huck retreats as if to a savior; he it is who mothers Huck as they travel down the big river; and he it is who, knowing secretly that Huck's Pap is dead forever, takes Huck to his own bosom to nourish him through the ordeal of being lost. Acting as Huck's foster father, Jim brings to that role a warmth and gentleness which Huck had never known under the brutal masculinity of his real father. Near the end of the novel, after Jim has accompanied and protected Huck on their perilous journey, how appropriate it is that he should be led back to the Phelps plantation, following his temporary escape with Tom, arrayed in the dress which the boys had stolen from Aunt Sally. The incident points up the ambivalent nature of Jim, emphasizing his role of motherly father to Huck. Leslie Fiedler, looking at the novel as an American myth of love, has searchingly explored this ambivalent relationship.

Jim is also one of the two great human forces in the book. By means of his truth and sincerity, the fraud and hoax of the world along the river banks are thrown into sharp relief. Probably the finest example of Jim's function as a moral norm occurs on the raft just before the King and Duke meet the country boy who unwittingly directs them into the Peter Wilks exploit. Huck awakens at daybreak one morning to see Jim grieving to himself. Jim finally tells him that a whacking sound he heard on shore reminded him of the time he disciplined his little daughter for not obeying a command. Upon repeating his command to no avail, Jim finally struck the child down, only to find that her recent attack of scarlet fever had left her deaf and dumb:

> Oh, Huck, I burst out a-crying en grab her up in my arms, en say, "Oh, de po' little thing! De Lord God Almighty forgive po' ole Jim, kaze he never gwyne to fogive hisself as long's he live!" Oh, she was plumb deef en dumb, Huck, plumb deef en dumb—en I'd ben-a-treat'n her so!

Immediately after this burst of genuine remorse, the Duke and the King launch their expedition to rob the Wilks daughters of their inheritance by pretending to be Peter Wilks' foreign kinsmen. The Duke poses as a deaf mute. By employing the same device he used so successfully in *Tom Sawyer*, Twain establishes a subtle and exquisite relationship between the two episodes. Through Jim's sensitivity the entire Wilks episode is thrown into much more precise focus. Indeed, Jim is the conscience of the novel, the spiritual yardstick by which all men are measured. As the two fugitives move down the river, Huck's whole moral sense grows out of and revolves around the presence of Jim, and his ability to measure up signifies his worth. Huck's whole sense of wrong, his feeling of guilt are products of his intimate association with Jim—his companionship with the runaway slave makes possible his moral growth.

Many critics, intent on seeing Jim as a symbol of the tragic consequences of slavery, have failed to see that he is much more than this. He is that great residue of primitive, fertile force turned free at the end of the novel at the very moment Huck is captured. That Mark Twain recognized in the Negro a new American protagonist is evident not only in his creation of Jim, but in his interesting return to the whole problem of slavery in *Pudd'nhead Wilson*. Certainly Jim and Thomas à Becket Driscoll stand solidly behind Faulkner, Robert Penn Warren, and Richard Wright. Having been thrown from his secure place within the social structure, Jim will be the new fugitive which the bourgeoisie will, with a great deal of hesitation, wish to make respectable.

There is an inexorable and crushing logic inherent in the ending of *Huckleberry Finn*. T. S. Eliot, in his remarkable introductory essay to the Cressett Library edition of the novel, remarked the inevitability of the final chapters, but failed to enlarge upon the generalization. Most critics agree that the ending is much weaker than the rest of the book, as indeed it is, but often they mistakenly gauge that weakness. Certainly Tom's reappearance itself does not weaken the ending. Any comprehensive vision of the book will, it seems to me, consider Tom's presence at the end not only vital but inevitable. The flatness of the ending results from Tom's domination of the action and the style. As soon as he appears, his whole aggressive spirit bids for position, and although Mark Twain attempts to use Huck to exploit the ironies of the situation, Tom's seizure of the style damages the tenor of the novel. It is a stylistic rather than a structural flaw, a failure in taste rather than in conception.

Mark Twain's failure in taste at this particular juncture bears further consideration. *Huckleberry Finn* is without question his greatest work, and diametric opposition of Tom and Huck is eminently clear. The substitution of Tom's humor for Huck's vision indicates that Mark Twain, though aware of the two sets of values, could not keep a proper balance between them because of his fascination with Tom Sawyer. In turning over the narration to Huck Finn he had turned to the incorruptible part of himself which was not for sale and could not be bought. The opening paragraph of the novel indicates that he was not entirely unaware of what he was about:

> You don't know about me without you have read a book by the name of *The Adventures of Tom Sawyer*; but that ain't no matter. That book was made by Mr. Mark Twain, and he told the truth, mainly. There was things which he stretched, but mainly he told the truth.

"Mainly he told the truth." In his novel Mark Twain tried to tell the whole truth through Huckleberry Finn. Although Tom Sawyer makes his presence too much felt at the end of the novel, Mark Twain saw his whole truth with supreme vision. Because of the deeply human values which are at stake, neither the satire nor the humor is tainted by the scoffing disillusion and the adolescent cynicism in which he finally foundered. The unobtrusive formal perfection allows the novel to retain the primitive power and immediacy of the myth which it recreates; its impact strikes us in the profoundest areas of our consciousness, and we are reminded of the darkness and the terror and the violence which stalk the virgin forest where the American dream lies waiting, aware and unaware.

Why Huckleberry Finn *Is a Great World Novel*

By Lauriat Lane, Jr.

Of all forms of literature, the novel is in many ways the hardest to describe with any precision. Its relative newness as a form and its varied and complex nature combine to make this so. Whenever we try to view such a full and living book as *The Adventures of Huckleberry Finn,* some of it always escapes our gaze. In fact, apart from its mere physical presence, paper, ink, glue, covers, and so forth, it is often easiest to assume that the novel does not exist at all, but only the experience of reading it. Each time we read *Huckleberry Finn* we read a certain book, and each time we read it we read a different book. No one of these books is the real *Huckleberry Finn*; in a sense, they all are.

At the heart of *Huckleberry Finn* lies a story about real human figures with genuine moral and ethical problems and decisions, figures placed in a society which we recognize as having everywhere in it the flavor of authenticity—the whole combination treated, for the most part, as directly and realistically as possible. I would like to move beyond this primary description or definition of *Huckleberry Finn,* however, and suggest that the novel may contain other elements equally important to a full appreciation. I would like to extend the novel in three directions, in space, in time, and in degree: in space, by considering some of the ways in which the book extends beyond its position as one of the masterworks of American fiction and becomes, if the term be allowed, a world novel; in time, by considering how much *Huckleberry Finn* resembles a literary form much older than the novel,

From *College English*, 17 (October 1955), 1–5. Reprinted with the permission of the National Council of Teachers of English.

the epic poem; and in degree, by considering just how much *Huckleberry Finn* transcends its position as a realistic novel and takes on the forms and qualities of allegory.

I

A world novel may be defined as that kind of novel whose importance in its own literature is so great, and whose impact on its readers is so profound and far-reaching, that it has achieved worldwide distinction. In the total picture of world literature, such a novel stands out as a work always to be reckoned with. The world novel, however, achieves its position not only through its importance but also because of its essential nature. And in discussing *Huckleberry Finn* as a world novel I shall deal not so much with this importance, as measured by permanent popularity and influence, as with the special qualities *Huckleberry Finn* has in common with certain other world novels.

The first real novel and the first world novel is, by almost universal consent, Cervantes' *The Adventures of Don Quixote*. The most important thing which *Don Quixote* has bequeathed to the novels after it (apart of course from the all-important fact of there being such a thing as a novel at all) is the theme which is central to *Don Quixote* and to almost every great novel since, the theme of appearance versus reality. This theme is also central to *Huckleberry Finn*.

Even on the simplest plot level the world of *Huckleberry Finn* is one of deception. The very existence of Huck at all is a continual deception—he is supposed to be dead. This falseness in his relations with the world at large merely reflects the difference between his standards and those of the outside world. Huck's truth and the truth of the world are diametrically opposed. Throughout the novel his truth is always cutting through the surfaces of the world's appearance and learning the contrary reality beneath. At the climax Huck tells himself, "You can't pray a lie—I found that out." That is to say, the lie of appearance is always far different from the truth of reality, and to the truly heroic and individual conscience no amount of self-delusion can ever bridge the gap lying between.

In the final section of the book, the theme of appearance versus reality reaches almost philosophical proportions. Both because of the way in which Jim's escape is carried out and because of the underlying fact of there being no need for him to escape at all, the situation is one of total dramatic and moral irony. At the end, however, Twain relaxes the tone, straightens out the plot complications, and lets the moral issue fade away. He avoids, in fact, the logical conclusion to the kind of disorder he has introduced into his world-in-fiction, a world in which the distinction between appearance and reality has, from the reader's point of view, been lost forever. For if we cannot tell appearance from reality, if the two do become totally confused and impossible to distinguish, the only answer can be the one Twain eventually came to in his most pessimistic work, *The Mysterious Stranger*; that all is illusion, and nothing really exists. In *Huckleberry Finn*, Twain does not yet reach this point of despair. By centering his action within the essentially balanced mind of the boy, Huck, he keeps his hold on reality and manages to convey this hold on the reader. But the main issue of the novel, between the way things seem and the way they are, is nevertheless one that trembles in the balance almost up to the final page.

Huckleberry Finn also gains its place as a world novel by its treatment of one of the most important events of life, the passage from youth into maturity. The novel is a novel of education. Its school is the school of life rather than of books, but Huck's education is all the more complete for that reason. Huck, like so many other great heroes of fiction—Candide, Tom Jones, Stephen Dedalus, to mention only a few—goes forth into life that he may learn. One of the central patterns of the novel is the progress of his learning.

Yet another theme which *Huckleberry Finn* shares with most of the world's great novels is that of man's obsession with the symbols of material wealth. The book opens with an account of the six thousand dollars Huck got from the robbers' hoard and ends on the same note. Throughout the intervening pages gold is shown to be not only the mainspring of most human action, but usually the only remedy mankind can offer to atone for the many hurts they are forever inflicting on one another. And as Mr. Lionel Trilling has remarked, in a certain sense all fiction is ultimately about money.

The world novel may also convey a total vision of the nation or people from which it takes its origin. It not only addresses the world in a language which is uniquely the language of that nation or people, but it brings before the view of the world at large many character types which are especially national. In *Huckleberry Finn* we recognize in Jim, in the Duke and the Dauphin, in Aunt Sally, and in Huck himself, typically American figures whom Twain has presented for inspection by the world's eye. *Huckleberry Finn* gains much of its justification as a world novel from the fact that it is an intensely American novel as well.

II

In his essay on "The Poetic Principle" Poe remarks that "no very long poem will ever be popular again." In part, no doubt, Poe bases this remark on his own special definition of poetry. But he is also recognizing that during the eighteenth and nineteenth centuries the epic poem was gradually dying out as a literary form. Or, to be more precise, it was gradually merging with another form, the novel. Much of the poetic form of the epic came from the requirements of oral rendition; with the invention of printing, these requirements vanished. More and more writers gradually turned to prose fiction as the appropriate form to accomplish what had once been accomplished in the epic poem. Some novelists, such as Fielding or Scott, drew quite consciously on epic tradition; other novelists and novels, by a more indirect drawing on tradition, took over some of the qualities originally associated with epic poetry.

One quality of the epic poem is simply scope. Some novels confine themselves to treating exhaustively and analytically a limited segment of life. But others seem to be constantly trying to gather all life into their pages and to say, within a single story, all the important things that need to be said. Such novels derive much of their strength from the epic tradition, and *Huckleberry Finn* is such a novel. It has geographical scope. It ranges down the length of the great river and cuts through the center of a whole nation. As it does so, it gains further scope by embracing all levels of society, from the lowest to the highest. And it has the added scope of its own varying qualities, ranging from high comedy to low farce, from the poetic tranquility of life on the raft to the mob violence and human depravity always waiting on the shore.

Epic poetry gives literary form to the national destiny of the people for whom it is written. *Huckleberry Finn* gives literary form to many aspects of the national destiny of the American people. The theme of travel and adventure is characteristically American, and in Twain's day it was still a reality of everyday life. The country was still very much on the move, and during the novel Huck is moving with it. Huck's movements also embody a desire to escape from the constrictions of civilized society. Such a desire is of course not uniquely American, but during the nineteenth century Americans took it and made it their own. The American of that time could always say, as did Huck at the very end of the story, "I reckon I got to light out for the territory ahead of the rest, because Aunt Sally she's going to adopt me and sivilize me, and I can't stand it. I been there before." Another specially American theme is that of the Negro, and Huck is faced with this problem throughout the story. Starting with the typically American prejudices and easy generalizations about Jim, he is gradually shocked into an increasingly complex awareness of Jim as a human being. And although Huck's relations with Jim do not so much embody a national attitude as suggest how the nation may purge itself of one, the theme of the Negro is still one which achieves epic stature in *Huckleberry Finn*.

The epic hero is usually an embodiment of some virtue or virtues valued highly by the society from which he has sprung. Huck has many such virtues. He holds a vast store of practical knowledge which makes itself felt everywhere in the story. He knows the river and how to deal with it; and he knows mankind and how to deal with it. And he has the supreme American virtue of never being at a loss for words. In fact Huck, though he still keeps some of the innocence and naïveté of youth, has much in common with one of the greatest epic heroes, Odysseus, the practical man. Jim also has some of the qualities of an epic hero. He has strength and courage, and he possesses the supreme virtue of epic poetry, loyalty. It is part of Twain's irony that in Huck and Jim we have, in one sense, the two halves of an epic hero. In Huck, the skill and canniness; in Jim, the strength and simple loyalty.

In the society along the shore we see traces of other epic values, values which have survived from a more primitive world. The Grangerford-Shepherdson feud strikes the modern reader as a senseless mess, but as Huck says, "There ain't a coward amongst them Shepherdsons—not a one. And there ain't no cowards amongst the Grangerfords either." Huck sees the essential folly behind this courage, but the reader, one degree further removed from the harsh reality, is allowed the luxury of a double vision. Similarly, Colonel Sherburn, destroying a lynching mob merely by the courage of his presence, illustrates another epic theme, the bravery of one against many.

One final quality which *Huckleberry Finn* derives from its epic ancestry is its poetry. The novel is full of poetry. Not just the passages of lyric description, which mark a pause between the main actions and give a heightened and more literary tone just as they often did in the traditional epic, but also the many similes and turns of speech Huck uses, which, if they are not quite Homeric, are certainly unforgettable. And much of the exaggerated language of the frontier world, one not far removed in kind from that of the primitive migrations, is also a natural part of the epic style.

III

Allegory may be defined simply as the representation of one thing in the form of another. A second definition, more germane to literature, is that allegory is a process by which the spiritual is embodied in the physical. To go one step further, the main purpose of allegory is somehow to embody a spiritual action in a physical action. By making a suitable physical object stand for some metaphysical one, or at least for one which cannot be contained in the terms of normal, everyday life, the writer carries out one of the main purposes of all art, which is to bring to its audience, through the representation of real objects, an awareness and knowledge which transcend the limitations of such reality. Allegory, that is, deals primarily with matters of the spirit.

This assumption helps to explain why the greatest allegories deal either with a physical journey or a physical conflict or both. For a spiritual change, when embodied allegorically, will take the form of a meaningful physical journey through symbolic space. And a spiritual conflict, when embodied allegorically, will take the form of a real physical conflict between significant forces, each of them representing some metaphysical quality.

Although all novels are in a certain sense descended from *Don Quixote*, it is also true that in another sense all novels, and especially English ones, are descended from Bunyan's *Pilgrim's Progress.* The main difference between the allegorical novel as we know it today and Bunyan's narrative of the human soul is that whereas in *Pilgrim's Progress* we have an allegory that tends to turn into a novel, in most modern instances we have a novel that tends to turn into an allegory. As the author, whether he be Melville or Mann or Twain, develops and elaborates his original materials, he may become aware of certain meaningful connections which are tending to establish themselves between the physical objects and the physical narrative he is describing and the related spiritual values and conflicts. Drawing on a tradition which has existed for a long time in literature and which is a natural part of the artistic process in any form, the author finds himself writing allegory. And this is what happened to Mark Twain. Writing as he was a great novel, his masterpiece in fact, he organized and related certain physical materials to certain metaphysical conditions so that their relationship became meaningful in a special way—became, in short, allegory.

Huckleberry Finn is the story of a journey, a real journey. If we are to find any meaning in Huck's journey beyond the literal level, we must seek it first in the medium through which Huck journeys, in the great river down which he drifts during much of the story. And Huck's movements take on at least the external form of a basic symbolic pattern, one seen in such poems as Shelley's *Alastor*, Arnold's *The Future*, and Rimbaud's *Bateau Ivre*, a pattern stated most directly in *Prometheus Unbound*, "My soul is an enchanted boat." Implicit in this pattern is the suggestion that the river journey can have a distinctly metaphysical quality, that it can be, in fact, a journey of the soul as well as of the body. This suggestion is not at all arbitrary. Of all forms of physical progression, that of drifting downstream in a boat, or on a raft, is the most passive one possible. The mind under such conditions is lulled, as Huck's mind is, into the illusion that it has lost all contact with reality and is drifting bodilessly through a world of sleep and of dreams. Thus the nakedness of Huck and Jim when they are alone on the raft becomes a symbol of how they have shucked off the excrescences of the real world, their clothes, and have come as close as possible to the world of the spirit.

All journeys, even allegorical ones, must have a goal. What is the goal of Huck's journey? We find the answer in what happens while Huck and Jim float down the river. The pattern is, very simply, one of an ever-increasing engagement of the world of the raft, of the spirit, with the world of the shore, of reality. As the book progresses, more and more Huck tells about events that take place on the banks, and less and less he tells about those that take place out on the river. No matter how hard Huck and Jim try to escape, the real world is always drawing them back into it. Finally, in the Duke and the Dauphin, themselves fleeing for the moment from the harsh reality of the river's shores, the real world invades the world of the raft, and the latter loses forever the dreamlike and idyllic quality it has often had for the two voyagers. The climax of Huck's lyric praise of the river comes signficantly just before this mood is shattered forever by the arrival of the Duke and the Dauphin.

Parallel to this pattern of the ever-increasing engagement of the world of the shore with that of the raft is a pattern which begins with Huck's pretended death, a death which is actual to all the world but Huck and Jim. The symbolic fact of his death accomplished, Huck must find an identity with which he can face the real world. His assumption of various such identities forms a signficant pattern. The various masks he assumes, starting with that of a girl, as far removed from the reality as possible, gradually draw back nearer the truth. Huck's final disguise, as Tom Sawyer, is only slightly removed from his real self. When he is about to reveal this real self and is instead taken for Tom, Huck almost recognizes the meaning of his journey. For he says to himself, "But if they was joyful, it warn't nothing to what I was; for it was like being born again, I was so glad to find out who I was."

This, then, is the allegory of *Huckleberry Finn*. Dying symbolically almost at the opening of the novel, Huck journeys through the world of the spirit, ever working out a pattern of increasing involvement with the world of reality and with his own self, both cast aside at the beginning of the journey. Only when he is finally forced to assume this real self in the eyes of the world, through the sudden arrival of Aunt Polly, is he allowed to learn the all-important truth Jim has kept from him throughout the novel, that his Pap "ain't comin' back no mo'." We cannot say that Huck has undergone a total initiation and is now fully prepared to take on adulthood, but neither can we doubt that he has undergone a knowledgeful and maturing experience. And at the end of the story he is about to undertake another journey, this time to the west, in search of further experience and further knowledge.

The Structure of Huckleberry Finn

Frank Baldanza

The much-vexed question of the struture of *Huckleberry Finn* has received both distinguished and penetrating attention; T. S. Eliot and Lionel Trilling have defended the plot as a whole in their introductions to editions of the novel, and Leo Marx has ably replied to both.[1] James Cox and Philip Young have attempted symbolic and psychological interpretations which make passing comments on structure.[2] I should like to suggest, however, that both groups of critics, although they have made valuable exploratory searches, have neglected the one aspect of the structure which is perhaps the most rewarding to investigate.

In the first place, as Edgar Goold points out in regard to Twain's theory of the novel:

> Concerning plot construction and related matters Clemens's contribution is of somewhat lesser significance for the writer of fiction than the uninitiated might expect....His own temperament and training did not tend to develop in him the ability to plan carefully and practice the sustained concentration necessary for tight and well-developed plots.[3]

That this failure in planning out his plots had a temperamental basis is corroborated, perhaps, by Twain's virulent antipathy to the total work of such a careful planner as Jane Austen. But many other critics, of whom I choose James Cox as representative, argue that the structure of *Huckleberry Finn* is determined by the in-

From *American Literature*, 27 (November 1955), 347–55. Reprinted with permission.

terplay of sets of symbols—civilization and the frontier, gentility and barbarism, freedom and bondage, and the like. These ideas certainly play a major part in the development of the book because they are, in a certain sense, what the book is about; but the question ought to be in what way Twain uses these ideas. Bernard De Voto, who assures us that "Mark Twain was not a systematic thinker," finds him "as feeble a novice as ever ventured into [metaphysics]."[4] He goes on to say that

> ...there is a type of mind, and the lovers of *Huckleberry Finn* belong to it, which prefers experience to metaphysical abstractions and the thing to its symbol. Such minds think of *Huckleberry Finn* as the greatest work of nineteenth century fiction in America precisely because it is not a voyage in pursuit of a white whale but a voyage among feudists, mobbers, thieves, rogues, nigger-hunters, and murderers, precisely because Huck never encounters a symbol but always some actual human being working out an actual destiny.[5]

But even if we overlook Twain's antisymbolic cast of mind (in which we should hardly be justified), we find that his own ambivalence blurs the neatness of whatever categories we set up. Even though we interpret the book as a "sad initiation" into society, we are baffled by the final sentence in which Huck lights out for the territory; if he has adamantly resisted the culture of the towns, then he is not in any sense "initiated." And if we try to see the book as a progression toward Jim's liberation, we must ask why the Boggs episode, the Shepherdson-Grangerford feud, and the Wilks interlude, which compose the bulk of the central portion, are so remarkably irrelevant to the thesis. Even toward the close of the book, Huck is scandalized by Tom's easy acquiescence in the escape plot, and invokes the wrath of society on such behavior. The resolution of these dilemmas is perhaps to be found in Twain's own ambivalences, but an analysis of these leads us into biography or psychology and inevitably away from *Huckleberry Finn*. Nevertheless, if we hold to any aesthetic standards at all, we hardly have the right to make extravagant claims for a book which we must admit in the same breath is negligible as a work of art.

Let us for a moment abandon the search for any plotted or symbolic or psychological unity in the novel and return to what we know about Mark Twain's temperament and about his habits of composition; in this way we can more easily make an inductive study of the kind of structure he put into the novel, rather than impose from the outside some preconceived pattern. Bernard De Voto, who gave an entire book to Twain's work habits, tells us that

> He wrote on impulse, and when impulse was in circuit with the deeper levels of his phantasy things went well, but when the circuit was broken he could only improvise. Improvisation was responsible for the worst and commonest blemishes in his books—and, because he could not long sustain it, for the breaking-off of many manuscripts. He had little ability to impose structure on his material; he could not think and feel it through to its own implicit form. He got "ideas" for books, stories, or sketches and jotted them down in his notebooks where they survive by the hundred, promising or feeble but almost always undeveloped. He caught fire easily and when an "idea" inflamed him, he attacked it with verve and enthusiasm, trusting to luck, providence, or his demon to make it good.[6]

We might say, as many have said, that the picaresque form would certainly be the ideal genre for such a talent, and that in the kind of episodic, spurting movement of such tales Twain would find his best vehicle; however, at the best, such an "explanation" of the structure of the book consists simply in the substitution of one word for another.

Let us rather try to see whether the very *élan* of his improvisation did not often carry him forward through a form which is implicit in his method. In Chapter VIII of his suggestive *Aspects of the Novel*, E. M. Forster remarks the same method as the fundamental source for the structure of Marcel Proust's *A la Recherche du Temps Perdu*. Like Twain's great river novel, "the book is chaotic, ill constructed, it has and will have no external shape...." But Forster finds that "it hangs together because it is stitched internally, because it contains rhythms."[7] The parallel is enforced by what Forster tells us of Proust's work habits, because he attributes the quality of rhythm in the novel to a type of temperament that accords precisely with what we have already found in Goold's and De Voto's descriptions of Mark Twain: "I doubt that it can be achieved by the writers who plan their books beforehand, it has to depend on a local impulse when the right interval is reached."[8] Local impulse and lack of planning, the two prime characteristics of Twain's genius, then, ought to produce in his novel effects parallel to those rhythmic stitchings that Forster finds so exquisite in the work of the great French novelist.

But before we turn to *Huckleberry Finn* itself, we ought to have a clearer idea of what Forster means by rhythm in the French novel. He selects as his example the "little phrase" from the sonata by Vinteuil, later incorporated into a sextet: Proust employs this musical phrase, which recurs innumerable times in the course of his narrative, in such a manner, says Forster, that in itself it has a "musical" function in the novel. Although most critics are rightly chary about any such metaphorical applications of music to literature, we can see that Forster has a clear definition of what he means by a "musical" function. The use of "repetition plus variation" is the key to this kind of rhythm.[9] Simple repetition of a theme, such as Forster finds in Meredith, is dead patterning; but repetition with variation and development, and especially with varying degrees of emphasis, is rhythm:

> ...the little phrase has a life of its own, unconnected with the lives of its auditors, as with the life of the man who composed it. It is almost an actor, but not quite, and that "not quite" means that its power has gone towards stitching Proust's book together from the inside, and towards the establishment of beauty and the ravishing of the reader's memory. There are times when the little phrase—from its gloomy inception, through the sonata into the sextet—means everything to the reader. There are times when it means nothing and is forgotten, and this seems to me the function of rhythm in fiction; not to be there all the time like a pattern, but by its lovely waxing and waning to fill us with surprise and freshness and hope.[10]

I propose to show that without advanced planning, and spurred by momentary impulses, Mark Twain—in all probability unconsciously—constructed whole passages of *Huckleberry Finn* on an aesthetic principle of repetition and variation. Because the process was unconscious, it does not attain the regularity of Proust's employment of the Vinteuil theme, and we must also remember that Twain was working on a much smaller scale than the seemingly inexhaustible French analyst. But to take one simple example, we remember how Huck early in the book saws his way out of his father's cabin undetected because he works behind a blanket that is stretched over the wall; toward the end of the book, Jim's escape is managed through a hole dug beneath the cabin, again disguised by a hanging blanket. Regardless of how we justify the correspondence on other grounds, it remains as a repetition of an earlier incident with a variation: it is, as Forster remarks, the variation which gives a sense of freshness and surprise, but it is the repetition that ravishes the memory, and, in its implicit assumption of order, it perhaps gives hope too.[11]

If we survey the total bulk of such correspondences in the novel, we find that they bear out our earlier assumption that they occur as unplanned, impulsive repetitions, sometimes seemingly enforcing a moral lesson, and other times existing simply as abstract aesthetic flourishes. An example of the latter is Tom's gratuitous insistence on having a rattlesnake to keep Jim company in the Phelpses' cabin, which recalls, solely for the aesthetic pleasure involved, the great to-do earlier in the book over the rattlesnake skin and over Jim's being bitten in the heel.

The largest group of repetitions centers about the situations in which Huck encounters rogues on his side trips. Here we might distinguish several themes, all of which are involved with the self-defeating nature of evil, as exemplified in Chaucer's "Pardoner's Tale." We need not assume that Twain chose such material for its profound moral significance however; probably it was simply what came to hand and what he knew would please his readers. For the first of these themes, we might use one of Twain's chapter headings, "Better let blame' well alone": if Huck and Jim had not boarded the *Walter Scott* they would have been better off. In the same way, Bill and Packard would have made a clean get-away if they had not returned for Turner's share of the money, thus giving Huck and Jim the chance to take their boat, and consequently abandoning them ironically to the fate they had reserved for Turner. This greedy lingering at the scene of the crime in order to squeeze out every last cent is repeated subtly, and with a variation, when the Duke and the Dauphin, not content with the huge sum of gold, remain at the Wilks home in order to auction the goods and clean up the small change; it is repeated even more subtly, and with even wider variation, when Tom refuses to free Jim the easy way, but lingers in order to fulfil all the conditions of his rigorous code, and suffers a bullet wound because of his greed for glory. This last example, too, shows how the aesthetic requirements of the novel dovetail with the meaning: most critics have been content with explaining the final passages of the novel solely in terms of Tom's romanticism, but with the need for rhythm in mind, we can see that Twain chose—again, probably unconsciously—to manage the incident so that it echoed the previous patterns of "better let blame' well alone."

A second major repetitive theme is that of desertion. Just as Bill and Packard lack even the honor of thieves in their plan to abandon Turner, so, on the third night of the "Royal Nonesuch" performance, Huck and the Duke flee the theater before the performance; Huck thinks that they are abandoning the Dauphin to an angry crowd but to his immense surprise, he finds the Dauphin asleep in the wigwam on the raft. Later in the book, when another angry mob has the three of them in tow in the graveyard at the end of the Wilks episode, Huck flees when he has the chance, and when the Duke and the Dauphin catch up with him at the opening of Chapter XXX, they make the same accusation that Turner might have made to his companions, and that the Dauphin might have made to Huck and the Duke after the Nonesuch flight. "Tryin' to give us the slip, was ye, you pup! Tired of our company, hey?" The elaborate argument on who has a right to desert whom is a kind of climactic repetition of the whole theme in the book, although Twain reserves one more repetition, as a kind of coda, for the splitting up of Tom and Jim and Huck after their flight from the Phelpses.

To these two themes of lingering for spoils and abandoning companions we might add a third, which perhaps approaches patterning more nearly than any of the others—that of the crowd. But again, I think we can see that each invididual treatment of a crowd incident was impulsive on Twain's part, and that any pattern we find in the repetitions is either unconsciously or accidentally ordained. The first large crowd is that on the boat searching for Huck's body, a "good" crowd of friends (with the exception of Pap) bent on a mission of mercy: "Pap, and Judge Thatcher, and Bessie Thatcher, and Joe Harper, and Tom Sawyer, and his old Aunt Polly, and Sid and Mary, and plenty more." Then the first nuance of possibly evil motivations on the part of a crowd is indicated in Mr. Loftus's proposed search of the island to get the reward for Jim's capture. Later we descend to the cowardly violence of the Sherburn lynching manqué, of the odoriferous Nonesuch mob, and of the stupid avengers of the Wilks family; after the tarring and feathering of the royal impostors, we return to the "good" crowd in the final chapters where the farmers and their garrulous wives congregate to help Mr. Phelps. The variation in this employment of crowds is rich and inexhaustible; they are all foiled, regardless of the quality of their motives, except the mob that metes out justice to the Duke and the Dauphin; they are all impressionable and stupid, and their little ruses, like the plan of the first Nonesuch crowd, are all pitifully inadequate. The two "good" crowds which appear at the opening and the closing of the book, do attain their ends, but in so indirect a fashion that they are rendered ridiculous: in the first case, Huck muses that the bread filled with quicksilver *did* reach him, and that the widow's and the parson's prayers *were* answered after a fashion; and in the latter case the crowd *did* finally solve the mystery, but only by pure accident. At the center of the problem, though, is the example of the Shepherdson-Grangerford "crowd"; whether Twain intended it or not, this central incident in the book embodies all the paradoxes of motivation that impelled the other crowds, because it is by a code of honor that these two groups defeat themselves, even as the rogues defeated themselves by lack of a code.

And, in speaking of the gullibility of the crowd and the roguery of the tricksters, we are reminded that before any of these examples of man's baseness occur in the book, Huck, in Chapter XV, gulls Jim himself, and in Huck's conscience-stricken reaction to Jim's eloquent rebuke, Twain sets the pattern for our reaction to the complicated roguery of the vagabonds.

These examples are perhaps sufficient to suggest the kind of rhythm that pulses through the novel by repetition and variation; it remains to indicate that just as such repetitions were conceived unconsciously or accidentally on the author's part, so their influence on the reader may be largely without his conscious attention to the means by which he is beguiled into finding the book somehow ordered within his recollection, but by an order he cannot explain very clearly in terms of conventional plotting or symbols.

Thus it is necessary to survey in detail the abundantly burgeoning variations on change of identity, on superstition and prophecy, and on lying which stitch one chapter to another in the reader's memory. One could nearly make a parlor game of searching out minor correspondences like Huck's dressing as a girl when he visits Mrs. Loftus, and Tom's later insistence on Huck's assumption of the "yaller wench's frock" when he delivers the note to the Phelpses. The very proliferation of such repetitions, in fact, proves that Twain had no control over them and that they simply flowed from his pen as exuberant impulse. What is more, it seems to me that this principle of repetition, as in the preceding example, gives some dignity and power to what had heretofore been excused as the blemishes of a feverishly melodramatic imagination.

It remains to note that in at least one case the principle of repetition rays out to include unconscious recollection of culture tales as well as incidents treated earlier in the novel; this should not surprise us, because Blair and De Voto have shown how the Royal Nonesuch incident was derived from an obscene frontier tale.[12] In the present case, we remember that the critics who emphasize the symbolic structure of the book are quick to point out that Huck is "dead" throughout the book as far as the rest of his friends know. When Jim sees him for the first time, he falls to his knees and entreats the ghost to leave him. The same reaction, with a significant variation, occurs to Tom when he sees Huck toward the end of the book in Chapter XXXIII:

> I says:
>
> "I hain't come back—I hain't been *gone*."
>
> When he heard my voice it righted him up some, but he warn't quite satisfied yet. He says:
>
> "Don't you play nothing on me, because I wouldn't on you. Honest injun, you ain't a ghost?"
>
> "Honest injun, I ain't," I says.[13]
>
> "Well—I—I—well, that ought to settle it, of course; but I can't somehow seem to understand it no way. Looky here, warn't you ever murdered *at all*?"
>
> "No. I warn't ever murdered at all—I played it on them. You come in here and feel of me if you don't believe me."
>
> So he done it; and it satisfied him; and he was that glad to see me again he didn't know what to do.

Tom's doubts on the corporeality of Huck, besides recalling those of Jim, obviously parallel those of his biblical namesake, and this Doubting Thomas satisfies himself in the same way as his predecessor, by feeling of his body. This is, too, an oblique recall of the previous references to Moses and Solomon and the biblical kings. There is no real need to see Huck as a Christ figure, especially since he is Tom's disciple, rather than the reverse; we need only note the fact of Twain's repeating a situation already familiar to his readers simply out of the exuberance of his aesthetic faculty.

If this explanation of the structure of *Huckleberry Finn* has any further recommendation, it is that in accepting it we completely exonerate ourselves—as few other critics can claim to do—from the ominous threats that open the novel.

> "Persons attempting to find a motive in this narrative will be prosecuted; per-

sons attempting to find a moral in it will be banished; persons attempting to find a plot in it will be shot."

Notes

1. Leo Marx, "Mr. Eliot, Mr. Trilling, and *Huckleberry Finn*," *American Scholar*, 22 (Autumn 1953), 423-440.

2. James M. Cox, "Remarks on the Sad Initiation of *Huckleberry Finn*," *Sewanee Review*, 62 (Summer 1954), 389-405; Philip Young, *Ernest Hemingway* (New York: Rinehart & Company, 1952), pp. 181-212.

3. "Mark Twain on the Writing of Fiction," *American Literature*, 26 (May 1954), 148-149.

4. *Mark Twain at Work* (Cambridge, Mass.: Harvard University Press, 1942), p. 99.

5. *Ibid.*, p. 100.

6. *Ibid.*, p. 52.

7. (New York, 1927), p. 236.

8. *Ibid.*, p. 240. Forster precedes this analysis by one of James's *The Ambassadors* as an example of "Pattern." Although he never states it overtly, Forster is simply demonstrating, in his contrast between James and Proust (Pattern and Rhythm), the difference between conscious and unconscious intention.

9. Mr. Cox uses these very terms in referring to *Tom Sawyer*; he does not indicate, however, whether or not he draws them from Forster.

10. Forster, *op. cit.*, p. 239.

11. We can see the same principle at work in the material that Twain decided not to use in the novel itself. Chapter III of *Life on the Mississippi*, for example, uses the device of Huck's overhearing conversations while hidden on a raft in the same way that he overhears the discussion of Bill and Packard on the *Walter Scott*.

12. De Voto, *op. cit.*, pp. 67-68.

13. It may be significant that the phrase "honest injun" occurs immediately following Jim's first interview with Huck too.

The Unity and Coherence of Huckleberry Finn

Richard P. Adams

Huckleberry Finn received very little critical attention of any kind before 1948. Students up to then were more interested in the life of Samuel Clemens than in the esthetic qualities of his work. It was generally felt that he was not an artist, and that any esthetic consideration of his writing would be a waste of time.

In 1948, however, Lionel Trilling published his brilliant introduction to the Rinehart edition.[1] His defense of the ending of the book, which had always been deplored, led to a controversy. T. S. Eliot, in another brilliant introduction, published in 1950, agreed with Trilling.[2] In 1953 Leo Marx dissented, attacking Trilling, Eliot, and the book.[3] Others, such as E. M. Branch, Gladys Bellamy, J. M. Cox, Lewis Leary, and Frank Baldanza, have approached the story from various esthetic points of view and offered various critical opinions.[4] Several theories and suggestions emerge concerning theme and structure, style and technique, and the esthetic value of the work. But no discussion has yet presented a formula that fully or systematically accounts for the greatness of *Huckleberry Finn* as a work of literary art.

Tom Sawyer has been more fortunate. In 1939 Walter Blair made an analysis of it which shows clearly and fairly completely the principles of construction and of unity that Clemens used in his better fiction. There are, Blair says, four "lines of action" in *Tom Sawyer*, all concerned with the boy's development toward

From *Tulane Studies in English*, 6 (1956), 87-103. Reprinted with permission.

manhood and moral maturity.

> Each one of these is initiated by a characteristic and typically boyish action. The love story begins with Tom's childishly fickle desertion of his fiancée, Amy Lawrence; the Potter narrative with the superstitious trip to the graveyard; the Jackson's Island episode with the adolescent revolt of the boy against Aunt Polly, and Tom's youthful ambition to be a pirate; the Injun Joe story with the juvenile search for buried treasure. Three of these narrative strands, however, are climaxed by a characteristic and mature sort of action, a sort of action, moreover, directly opposed to the initial action. Tom chivalrously takes Becky's punishment and faithfully helps her in the cave; he defies boyish superstition and courageously testifies for Muff Potter; he forgets a childish antipathy and shows mature concern for his aunt's uneasiness about him. The Injun Joe story, though it is the least useful of the four so far as showing Tom's maturing is concerned, by showing Huck conquering fear to rescue the widow, has a value as a repetition—with variations—of the motif of the book.[5]

The interweaving of these four lines of developing action, Blair feels, gives "reasons for believing that the theme, the main action, and the character portrayal in the novel are one—the developing of Tom's character in a series of crucial situations."[6] That is to say, quite correctly I think, that *Tom Sawyer*, for all its apparent casualness of construction, has a high degree of organic unity. Blair does not say that it has a coherent plot, nor would I, but the clear implication is that it does not need one. Its unity and coherence are thematic and symbolic—imaginative in the Coleridgean sense. Its elements are not related by the logic of cause and effect. Instead, they are fused in an organization of imagery that transcends any concept of plot or story line as a series of causally related events.

Huck Finn has a somewhat different structure, but the principle is the same or very similar. It has a symbolic pattern or organization of imagery, not a plot in the traditional sense. Critics who ignore Clemens's warning and come to it looking for a plot are likely to go astray, fall foul of Trilling and Eliot, and bog down in a fruitless effort to prove that the ending, or the whole book, is a failure. When a critic gets that far out on a limb it is not necessary to shoot him.

The most obvious element of structure in *Huck Finn*, and the one most often noticed, is the picaresque journey down the river, full of inconsequently interspersed and apparently aimless adventures. But it is dangerous to say that much and stop, for the inconsequence does not preclude a plan, and the aimlessness is only apparent. Trilling, in discussing the special qualities of the river as a road, points out some profitable directions for further inquiry. The important thing, he says, is that the river is a moving road,

> ...and the movement of the road in its own mysterious life transmutes the primitive simplicity of the form: the road itself is the greatest character in this novel of the road, and the hero's departures from the river and his returns to it compose a subtle and significant pattern. The linear simplicity of the picaresque novel is further modified by the story's having a clear dramatic organization: it has a beginning, a middle, and an end, and a mounting suspense of interest.[7]

Trilling perhaps oversimplifies the linear quality of the picaresque novel as Clemens knew it, but he does not overestimate the complexity of *Huck Finn*, and his observations on the "living" quality of the river and on the alternation of Huck's river and shore experiences are valuable clues.

Another clue, of perhaps even greater value, is furnished by James M. Cox's discussion of Huck's "initiation." According to Cox, the "fake murder" that Huck stages in order to get away from his father "is probably the most vital and crucial incident of the entire novel,"[8] and Cox's observations on this event come close to defining the basic structure of the novel. The basic structure, which expresses the theme of the boy's growth and which carries the weight of the incidents and the imagery throughout, is a pattern of symbolic death and rebirth. As Cox points out, the central action on the river begins with Huck's pretended death. It ends with his mistaken recognition as Tom by Aunt Sally Phelps, when he feels that "it was like being born again,I was so glas to find out who I was." This pattern is kept in the focus of the reader's attention, as Cox also observes, by repeated deaths and escapes occurring between, before, and after the main events.

The pattern of death and rebirth is reinforced by the pattern Trilling observes in Huck's departures from and returns to the river; only we need to reverse Trilling's terms, for it is Huck's departures from and returns to shore which are cognate and parallel to the pattern of death and rebirth. The same pattern provides the framework for the "clear dramatic organization" which Trilling notices, and it roughly determines the kind of beginning, middle, and end that the story has. Putting Cox and Trilling together, and oversimplifying for the sake of initial clarity, we can state a more nearly complete definition of the structure of *Huckleberry Finn*. The beginning is Huck's life on shore in and around the village of St. Petersburg with the Widow Douglas and Pap. The middle, initiated by Huck's fake death, is his withdrawal from the life of society and civilization to the river; this withdrawal is repeated after each of his adventures on land. The end is his equivocal rebirth, his qualified return, under a false identity and with many reservations, to civilized life at the Phelps plantation.

The pattern of death and rebirth is also intimately concerned in the "mounting suspense of interest" which Trilling notes. The theme of the book, as we have hinted, is the same as that of *Tom Sawyer:* the growth of a boy to manhood, and his final acceptance of adult moral responsibilities. In this connection the pattern of death and rebirth is more than a technical device. In the tradition of romantic literature, to which *Huck Finn* belongs, it is a form with a meaning. The growth of a boy to manhood is perhaps the most popular of all themes for romantic fiction, and the structure which best expresses it is that of the death-and-rebirth pattern. The reason for this association is based in romantic philosophy, according to which the individual human personality is conceived as an organism which cannot undergo a fundamental change of any kind without being totally reconstituted. Its old self "dies" and its new self, an unpredictably different organism, is "born." Huck's initiation, his transformation from boy to man, is such a change. It is a radical reconstitution of his moral attitude toward the society in which he lives. He grows, therefore, during the time of crucial change, by "dying" out of society, withdrawing into nature on the river, and then returning or being "reborn" into society with a new and different attitude toward it.

It should not have to be said that this return is by no means an uncritical acceptance of conventional social values. The process of Huck's moral growth is, in fact, most emphatically indicated by his decision, made on three separate but closely related occasions, to free Jim from slavery, which is an act of rebellion against society. In a superficial sense the three decisions are the same, but each means more than the one before, because Huck knows more about the society he is deciding to oppose and because he sees more fully and clearly the implications of the decision and its probable consequences.

The context, which becomes increasingly solid and massive as Huck's knowledge increases, is a complex interrelationship of social, cultural, political, and economic forces. We might skeletonize it by making three simple statements, which we can then elaborate. First, slavery is evil. Second, the pseudo-aristocratic society of the ante-bellum South which fosters and depends on slavery is also evil. Third, the sentimental culture veneer with which that society conceals its evil from itself, if not from others, is evil as well. These propositions apply with increasing cogency to Huck's three decisions, as he learns more about the character and workings, the concrete personal meanings and moral values, of Southern slave-holding aristocracy. The relations among these three intertwined thematic strands in *Huck Finn* are so complex and pervasive that a thorough explication of them would be longer than the book. I shall not try to exhaust them here, but rather to indicate their general character and, by exploring a few of them in some detail, to show how they work.

Huck's first decision to help Jim escape is made casually enough in the process of his own flight from civilization and from the domination of his father. When he comes across his fellow runaway on Jackson's Island, he is so glad to have his lonesomeness relieved by any sort of company that he hardly thinks of difficulties. "People would call me a lowdown Abolitionist and despise me for keeping mum," he admits to Jim, "but that don't make no difference. I ain't a-going to tell, and I ain't a-going back there, anyways." But even this first and easiest decision is preceded by a fairly substantial development of motives and of symbolic motifs. Huck has been introduced to respectable society at the Widow's, where gentility is manifested painfully to him in regular hours, formal meals, and stiff clothing. When Miss Watson tells him about the bad place, he says he wishes he were there. "She got mad then, but I didn't mean no harm. All I wanted was to go somewheres...." Later the same night, in harmony with the fake murder which is to come, he says, "I felt so lonesome I most wished I was dead." Then, in the planning and organization of Tom Sawyer's gang, we see Huck's indirect exposure to the culture of popular books and the sentimental proprieties of "hightoned" robbery and exploitation. Tom and the gang, of course, are completely unrealistic about the crimes they propose to commit, and blissfully unaware that crime, as gilded by the popular romances, is morally wrong. Farther on, Huck is regaled with Pap's reverse snobbishness on the subject of education and with his poor-white's groundless assertion of superiority over the much better educated "free nigger."

These lights and others like them are placed so as to reveal what Clemens considered to be the characteristic weaknesses, follies, and injustices of prewar Southern society. The essentially false and hypocritical gentility of the would-be aristocracy, the febrile and morally confusing sentimentalism of its favorite literature, and the crime of slavery which was the real basis of its economic and social system are continually brought home to Huck and the reader, in all kinds of dramatic, representative, and symbolic ways. The incidents are not haphazardly chosen or arranged. Each has its revealing gleam to contribute to Huck's unconsciously dawning awareness of the true values of the civilization to which he is being asked to belong. The result is that he runs away and, without any great misgivings at first, agrees to help Jim do the same.

The second decision is made necessary by a qualm of conscience. The fugitives are approaching Cairo, or think they are, and they both believe that Jim is almost free. Says Huck, "It hadn't ever come home to me before, what this thing was that I was doing. But now it did; and it stayed with me, and scorched me more and more." The point of difficulty is that freeing Jim involves robbing his owner, Miss Watson, of the eight hundred dollars he is worth on the market; and Jim makes the difficulty greater by threatening to have his children stolen, if necessary, by an Abolitionist. Huck is immediately and properly horrified. "It most froze me to hear such talk.... Here was this nigger, which I had as good as helped to run away, coming right out flat-footed and saying he would steal his children—children that belonged to a man I didn't even know; a man that hadn't ever done me no harm." The juxtaposition of "his" and "belonged" in this sentence, so carefully calculated to drive home the shocking injustice of property rights in human flesh, should not obscure the fact that there is a real moral issue. The great wrong of slavery does not make the lesser wrong of robbery right; a point which most pre-Civil War anti-slavery propagandists preferred to overlook. The issue is resolved by the fact that Huck finds himself unable to turn Jim in, for reasons which he does not fully understand but which the reader can surmise. To put it most simply, his human feelings are stronger than the commercial morality with which they are in conflict—as of course they should be. Unable to do entirely right, he chooses the lesser evil and goes on helping Jim.

When he repudiates his own conscience in this way, Huck takes a long step farther in his repudiation of Southern society, which has formed his conscience. He says to himself, in his usual innocent way, "what's the use you learning to do right when it's troublesome to do right and ain't no trouble to do wrong, and the wages is just the same?... So I reckoned I wouldn't bother no more about it, but after this always do whichever come handiest at the time." The innocence is of Huck, not Clemens, and it represents a remarkably keen penetration into the difficult question of personal or individual morality in relation to social conventions. Huck realizes in practice, though never in conscious theory, that the question is not one of a simple conflict between the individual and the mass, or the social institution, but that the two interpenetrate, and that the individual conscience is usually an ally of the social pressure for conformity.

Thoreau, in "Civil Disobedience," feels himself on solid ground when his conscience tells him to oppose the extension of slavery and the government that sanctions and promotes it. "If," he says, "the injustice...is of such a nature that it requires you to be the agent of injustice to another, then, I say, break the law." That seems comparatively easy; all that is needed is the courage to stand up against the government, which Southerners have always had in abundance. But, when the ante-bellum conscience is formed in Missouri instead of Massachusetts, the battle becomes intensely complicated. Its lines are drawn mostly inside the personality, which is then divided against itself. As Trilling remarks, it is the paradox in Huck's own thinking, by the terms of which he does right by doing what he thoroughly believes, in his conscious mind, to be wrong, that makes his character heroic and Clemens's satire brilliant.[9] His battle is desperate, his victory sublime. If it is fine to follow as Thoreau does the dictates of conscience over law, it is finer and much more difficult to follow those of the right over conscience and law combined.

It is fair to say, as it is for the first decision, that everything leading up to this second one contributes to Huck's preparation for making it as he does. We can examine the process most efficiently, perhaps, by focussing on one incident, and tracing its relations to see how they bear on the larger meanings of the action. Let us take, for example, the adventure of Huck and Jim with the murderers on the wrecked steamboat *Walter Scott.*

This event has a number of bearings, mostly ironic, on the related themes of aristocracy and sentimental literature. One of the antipathies which Clemens cherished most warmly and flourished most often was his detestation of Sir Walter Scott and all or almost all his works. In *Life on the Mississippi* Scott is blamed for having checked the "wave of progress" in the South with his propaganda for medieval feudalism, which, according to Clemens, "sets the world in love with dreams and phantoms; with decayed and swinish forms of religion; with decayed and degraded systems of government; with the sillinesses and emptinesses, sham grandeurs, sham gauds, and sham chivalries of a brainless and worthless long-vanished society." The reality behind these shams was, Clemens felt, a sordid and quite common crime. He remarked in a notebook entry, probably made in 1888, that the establishment of a monarchy "is the same sort of crime that surprise and seizure of a weak community's property by a robber gang, and the conversion of the community itself into slaves, is.... A monarchy is perpetuated piracy. In its escutcheon should always be the skull and crossbones."[10]

In these terms, the presence of three murderous robbers on a wrecked steamboat named *Walter Scott* is neatly satirical. It echoes, on a note of considerably greater seriousness, the earlier activities of Tom's gang, one of which is a seizure of doughnuts and jam from "a Sundayschool picnic, and only a primer class at that," which Tom insists is a rich caravan—as if that would make the act less shamefully cruel. The American function of Scott and others like him, Clemens implies, is to excuse and gloss over the exploitation of slaves and poor whites, and to glamorize the exploiters as Southern chivalry. The actual behavior of the slave-owning class, according to Clemens's double-edged suggestion, is on the one hand as evil as that of a gang of thieves and murderers, and on the other as silly as that of Tom's infatuated band.

Part of the loot of the *Walter Scott*, which the robbers unknowingly bequeath to Huck and Jim, is a number of appropriate books "about kings and dukes and earls and such, and how gaudy they dressed, and how much style they put on, and called each other your majesty, and your grace, and your lordship, and so on, 'stead of mister...." Huck's reading to Jim from these books leads to a good deal of talk about Solomon and his wisdom, which Jim rather shrewdly questions, and about Louis XVI and "the dolphin," which prepares for the later advent of the bogus king and duke. The whole incident, in all its ramifications, contributes to the satirical exploration in Huck's experience of the various meanings, pretended and real, false and true, of the aristocratic idea in the South.

This incident is balanced as well as followed by the much more important one of Huck's separation from Jim in the fog and his practical joke in making Jim think that it was a dream. In this event Huck is made to realize that Jim is a proud and sensitive human being, not livestock or chattel goods, and that the joke has been a cruel and humiliating betrayal of a friend's feelings. Corrupted by his life in a slave society and by the propaganda with which that society tries to justify the crime of slavery, Huck has never before considered that a slave might have feelings as worthy of respect as anyone else's. The speech in which Jim shows him his error, full of simple dignity and a pathos that beautifully consists with its righteous indignation, opens Huck's eyes in a way that is likely to stay in his memory. His reaction is worthy. "It was fifteen minutes," he says, "before I could work myself up to go and humble myself to a nigger; but I done it, and I warn't ever sorry for it afterward, neither. I didn't do him no more mean tricks, and I wouldn't done that one if I'd 'a' knowed it would make him feel that way." This realization, occurring shortly before the second decision to help Jim escape, makes any other decision practically impossible. With his indirect, unconscious realization of the falseness of aristocracy to balance his new awareness of the humanity of the slave, Huck would find it the meanest trick of all to betray Jim and send him back into the status of a piece of property to be exploited by the robber gang which is the reality behind the sham front of Southern aristocracy.

The third and final decision is led up to by a more personal and extensive experience of upperclass Southerners than before. Shortly after the second crisis, Huck and Jim realize that they have passed Cairo in the fog, but before they can do anything to get back, the raft is wrecked by a steamboat and they are separated again. Huck finds himself ashore, beginning a new phase of the story and of his education. His shore adventures alternate, from this point on, with repeated escapes to the river, until he comes to the Phelps plantation. These adventures bring him more dramatically than before into contact, and more often into conflict, with aristocrats of various kinds. The increase of experience, knowledge, and understanding which he gains in this phase leads convincingly to his ultimate decision to repudiate aristocratic society by freeing its victim Jim.

The first aristocrats he meets in person, leaving aside the Widow, Miss Watson, and Judge Thatcher, are the Grangerfords, by whom he is strongly impressed and who are genuinely impressive in many ways. They have the typical aristocratic vitures: they are dignified, hospitable, proud, handsome, cultured (after a fashion), courteous, devout, and kind to strangers and dependents. But the more Huck learns of them, the more uneasy he becomes about their character and behavior. Clemens, through Huck's observations and comments, gradually undercuts the value of their culture. The description of the house, which is parallel to the account of "The House Beautiful" in *Life on the Mississippi*, is a skillful piece of irony. Huck admires the place immensely, while Clemens mercilessly exposes the queer mixture of arrogant show and pathetic provincialism that it presents to even a moderately sophisticated eye. The description leads up to and is ludicrously topped off by Huck's account of Emmeline Grangerford's esthetic misdeeds in crayon and verse, of the graveyard school run wild and gone to seed. The cultural pretensions of the aristocracy are, by this report, sufficiently harmless in themselves but crude, anachronistic, and highly absurd from any civilized modern point of view.

The feud which is going on between the Grangerfords and the Shepherdsons is a much more serious matter, and it does not depend on the same kind of irony for its effect. It is as deeply horrifying to Huck as it could possibly be to Clemens. The brutal killing of the two boys makes Huck so sick that he cannot even tell about it in detail without getting sick again; and his admiration for the better qualities of the aristocrats is more than canceled by this result of their violence.

The incident is a direct expression of feeling on the part of its author. In *Life on the Mississippi* Clemens goes somewhat out of his way to comment on a published opinion that the South had "the highest type of civilization this continent has seen...." He demonstrates the hollowness of the brag in a footnote with "Illustrations of it thoughtlessly omitted by the advertiser," consisting of newspaper accounts of four fights in which five Southern gentlemen were killed and one injured, with the usual incidental damage to bystanders, reference also being made to four other murders and one nonfatal stabbing in previous engagements involving some of the same gentlemen. The people concerned were of the highest class that Southern civilization had produced, including a general and his son, a bank president, a college professor, and "two 'highly connected' young Virginians" who fought a duel with butcher knives. It is from this kind of violence that Huck escapes to the river again, wishing that he "hadn't ever come ashore that night to see such things. I ain't ever going to get shut of them—lots of times I dream about them." Clemens had often dreamed about some violent episodes he witnessed as a boy.

Huck's reaction leads to one of his most lyric descriptions of the freedom, comfort, and beauty of the river, and the loveliness of life on a raft. But evil comes into this world also, in the shape of the two confidence men who palm themselves off as "the rightful Duke of Bridgewater" and "the late Dauphin.... Looy the Seventeen, son of Looy the Sixteen and Marry Antonette," and who take over in the true aristocratic robber-gang fashion. The cream of the jest is that the duke's claim is accepted by the other rogue so that he may in turn make his higher claim. The cream of the cream is that the duke then has to admit the king's superior status and rights in order that both may exploit the plebeian members of the little commonwealth. But the richest layer of all is Huck's good-naturedly cynical accommodation to the whole arrangement. He sees immediately what frauds these are, but he is pleased when the duke knuckles under; "for what you want, above all things, on a raft, is for everybody to be satisfied, and feel right and kind towards the others."

Clemens's feeling about the kind of imposition practiced—or at least attempted—here is given in another notebook entry: "There are shams and shams; there are frauds and frauds, but the transparentest of all is the sceptered one. We see monarchs meet and go through solemn ceremonies, farces, with straight countenances; but it is not possible to imagine them meeting in private and not laughing in each other's faces."[11] The fraud practiced by the bogus king and duke is no different from the frauds put over by real kings and dukes, except that the latter are bigger. As Huck explains to Jim, after the confidence men have worked over their first town together, they are lucky not to have Henry VIII on their hands, for he was a really accomplished crook; "If we'd 'a' had him along 'stead of our kings he'd 'a' fooled that town a heap worse than ourn done. I don't say that ourn is lambs, because they ain't, when you come right down to the cold facts; but they ain't nothing to *that* old ram, anyway." This observation reinforces the point already made, implicitly, that the Grangerfords and Shepherdsons, by their more serious imitation of aristocratic ways, are only presenting a more pernicious version of something which at best is a sham and a fraud.

Perhaps the most emphatic impression of the ugly side of Southern chivalry is given by the incident in which Huck witnesses the cold-blooded murder of old Boggs by Colonel Sherburn. Boggs is a noisy but harmless fool, Sherburn a fine example of aristocratic pride—brave and intelligent in his own way, but narrow, selfish, inconsiderate, harsh, and brutal. It is, again, a sickening scene, and it is based on a murder that Clemens witnessed as a boy. But it may be that the importance of the incident for the satirical aspect of the book lies mainly in the character of the townspeople, who are by and large a degraded lot. "There couldn't anything wake them up all over," says Huck, "and make them happy all over, like a dog-fight—unless it might be putting turpentine on a stray dog and setting fire to him, or tying a tin pan to his tail and see him run himself to death." They try half-heartedly to get Boggs to stop his offensive yelling and go home, but they also perversely enjoy the shooting and the old man's death, the view of the body in the drug store window, and the re-enactment of the murder by one of the onlookers. When they go to Sherburn's house with the announced intention of lynching him, he lectures them contemptuously and drives them off with a shotgun, which he does not have to fire.

His contempt seems justified, on the face of things. These are the same people who, after hooting the Shakespearean efforts of the king and duke, prove ripe for the Royal Nonesuch hoax. The duke, in his estimate of them, agrees with Sherburn. He prints at the foot of his handbill "LADIES AND CHILDREN NOT ADMITTED," remarking, "There...if that line don't fetch them, I don't know Arkansaw!" It does. But the deeper point is not explicitly stated here, or anywhere else in *Huck Finn*, nor is it fully understood, we may suppose, by either Sherburn or the duke. They see well enough that the people are ignorant, cowardly, and gullible; they do not see that the reason for that fact is the apparently opposite fact that an aristocracy is in power. Clemens, however, was aware of it and well convinced that poverty, both of the flesh and of the spirit, is the mirror image of aristocratic splendor and that universal cruelty is inevitably characteristic of any society divided into rigid classes with hereditary inequalities of function, privilege, and status.

This principle is explained more clearly in *A Connecticut Yankee*. The Yankee is shocked at the way poor peasants in Arthurian England rush out, heedless of right or justice, and help each other hang their neighbors in their lord's behalf, apparently unable "to see anything horrible about it." His comment is almost a direct reference to the satire in *Huck Finn*.

> It reminded me of a time thirteen centuries away, when the "poor whites" of our South who were always despised and frequently insulted by the slave-lords around them, and who owed their base condition simply to the presence of slavery in their midst, were yet pusillanimously ready to side with the slave-lords in all political moves for the upholding and perpetuating of slavery, and did also finally shoulder their muskets and pour out their lives in an effort to prevent the destruction of that very institution which degraded them. And there was only one redeeming feature connected with that pitiful piece of history; and that was, that secretly the "poor white" did detest the slave-lord, and did feel his own shame.

The Yankee also remarks that "It is enough to make a body ashamed of his race to think of the sort of froth that has always occupied its thrones without shadow of right or reason," and what Clemens obviously means is that any respectable race would blow such froth to the moon before letting it settle into power.

Huck, whose background is about as purely poor-white as it could be, is given almost exactly the same words—"It was enough to make a body ashamed of the human race"—to describe his feelings about the next incident. The king and duke are having a fine run of initial success in playing their confidence game on the Wilks girls and most of their neighbors. It is a game that Huck perfectly understands, and he becomes so much ashamed of himself for being involved in it, though unwillingly, that he takes the risky measure of telling the truth in order to break it up. The most painful aspect of the affair applies directly to the theme of slavery, being the inhumanity of the fake aristocrats in the sale of the Wilks family slaves, "the two sons up the river to Memphis, and their mother down the river to Orleans." Huck says again that "it most made me down sick to see it.... I can't ever get it out of my memory, the sight of them poor miserable girls and niggers hanging around each other's necks and crying...." The reader is likely to recall, as Clemens must have done, that this is not something only fakers do; it is precisely what Miss Watson does in planning to sell Jim "down to Orleans"; the general truth is that, as the Connecticut Yankee remarks in another place, "a privileged class, an aristocracy, is but a band of slaveholders under another name." The function of the king and duke is to show this basic identity, and underscore its meaning. Are these two scoundrels the most absurd, unmitigated, bare-faced buffoons of wickedness imaginable? So, Clemens wishes us to feel and understand, are all aristocrats. Kings, dukes, pirates, robbers, confidence men, and slaveholders are the same, all sorry. Anyone who respects them is a fool, anyone who fears them is a coward, and anyone who supports them or submits to them is a slave himself.

Huck is none of these things, though he is almost infinitely good-natured and accommodating. He goes along with the king and duke as well and as long as he can, and he feels sorry for them when the mob escorts them out of town, in tar and feathers, on a rail. But he spoils their game with the Wilkses, and he leaves them when the king sells Jim into bondage again. For him, their function has been to complete his education in the social realities of slavocracy and to put the finishing touches on his preparation for the final decision he has to make. They have done the job effectively; he is ready now to see Jim through to freedom in spite of anything. Unconsciously, but with deep conviction, he understands the society to which by accident of birth he belongs, and refuses to submit to it.

On this last occasion, Huck sees his problem as being more difficult than it has ever seemed to him before, because it presents itself to him in terms of the religious sanction which the institution of slavery enjoyed in the prewar South. His conscience, unable to win the battle alone, now tells him, in accordance with the Sunday-school teaching he feels he should have had, "that people that acts as I'd been acting about the nigger goes to everlasting fire." Again, Huck is expressing one of his author's ideas. Clemens remarks of his mother in the *Autobiography* that,

> kind-hearted and compassionate as she was, I think she was not conscious that slavery was a bald, grotesque, and unwarrantable usurpation. She had never

heard it assailed in any pulpit, but had heard it defended and sanctified in a thousand; her ears were familiar with Bible texts that approved it, but if there were any that disapproved it they had not been quoted by her pastors; as far as her experience went, the wise and the good and the holy were unanimous in the conviction that slavery was right, righteous, sacred, the peculiar pet of the Deity, and a condition which the slave himself ought to be daily and nightly thankful for.[12]

Huck has easily won out over public opinion, less easily over public opinion reinforced by his own conscience. The addition of the Deity to the list of powers with which he has to contend raises his battle to its ultimate pitch of intensity.

His first maneuver is to pray for the improvement of his character, but he realizes at once that the plea is hypocritical. To make it good, he writes a letter to Miss Watson to tell her where Jim is, but he gets to thinking about Jim's goodness and loyalty and kindness, and all the times they have helped each other, and again he makes up his mind.

I was a-trembling, because I'd got to decide, forever, betwixt two things, and I knowed it. I studied a minute, sort of holding my breath, and then says to myself:

"All right, then, I'll *go* to hell"—and tore it up.

It was awful thoughts and awful words, but they was said. And I let them stay said; and never thought no more about reforming.

With this decision, the middle or river section comes to its conclusion, and the ending of the book begins.

Clemens obviously had difficulty handling the ending. The reason seems to be that once Huck's final decision is made there is no longer any important part for Jim to play. His function in relation to the theme has been to test, or to furnish occasions when events would test, Huck's growing moral strength and mature independence. When that has been done, to the last possible extreme, Jim needs simply to be got out of the book as quickly and as unobtrusively as possible. Instead, Clemens plays up Tom Sawyer's long, elaborate, and almost meaningless escape plot. The final solution to the problem, the disclosure that Miss Watson has died and freed Jim in her will, is all that is needed, and the less said about it the better. And yet the escape plot is not altogether irrelevant. It furthers and completes the satire on sentimental literature, from which Tom draws his inspirations. It caps the ridicule of aristocratic pretensions by identifying Jim, the imprisoned slave, with the noble persons on whose renowned adventures his liberation is modeled. It is an immense expression of contempt for adult society, so easily and so thoroughly hoodwinked by a pair of audacious children; and the more absurd Tom's antics become, the more the satire is built up. It is as much an attack on conventional respectability as Huck's discomforts at the Widow Douglas's, or his observations on the culture of the Grangerfords, or his rebellion against slavery itself.

Huck's attitude at the end is a mixture, full of ironies and reservations of many kinds. Having made the great decision to repudiate society, physically, morally, and spiritually, he can hardly return to it without equivocation. In a sense, his acceptance of the name and status of Tom Sawyer on the Phelps plantation is a return, but it is made on completely false premises. Also Huck is glad in a way to submit to Tom's leadership and direction. The burden of lonely responsibility has weighed long and heavily. But he is not fooled for a minute into thinking that there is any validity in Tom's adherence to bookish or aristocratic authority. "When I start in to steal a nigger," he says, "I ain't no ways particular how it's done so it's done. What I want is my nigger...and I don't give a dead rat what the authorities thinks about it nuther." He has arrived at maturity and self-sufficiency, and he is poised at the end in a delicate balance, ready at any moment "to light out for the territory" in order to escape Aunt Sally's threatened continuation of the civilizing process begun by the Widow Douglas.

This aspect of the conclusion is exactly right. It would have been wrong—impossible in fact—for Clemens to bring the story to a stop, as he might have tried to do by having Huck accept the moral values of society and return to it uncritically in a "happy ending." The whole process of his development runs counter to any such result. The impression that Clemens has to leave, and does leave, in the reader's mind and feelings is that Huck will continue to develop. He will escape again, as many times as he needs to, from society and any of its restrictions which would hamper or prevent his growth. He will die and be reborn whenever his character needs to break the mold that society would place upon it. Accordingly, the structure of the story is left open; the conclusion is deliberately inconclusive.

Frank Baldanza, who has made the most direct attack so far on the problem of structure in *Huck Finn*, believes that the basic principle can be defined as rhythmic repetition, with variation and development, of many thematic motifs, which have the effect of stitching the book together internally. He further suggests that each recurrence "was impulsive on Twain's part, and that any pattern we find in the repetitions is either unconsciously or accidentally ordained."[13] My analysis would seem to bear out the observation that rhythmic, varied, and developmental repetition is important. It is not basic to the structure, but it certainly does support it and supply it with a texture of rich and complex harmony. However, this effect is not and cannot possibly be accidental; it fits too well with the larger thematic repetition of Huck's decision. And I suspect very strongly too that Clemens must have been aware of it, in some way, as being appropriate to the pattern of the work he meant to make. A close examination will show that the motifs most often repeated are those most intimately concerned with the aristocracy-slavery-sentimentalism relationship. Moreover the variations add up to a steady intensification of Huck's and the reader's awareness of the injustice, the hypocrisy, and the general moral ugliness and weakness of Southern society before the war. This intensification provides the milieu and the measure of Huck's development through the death-and-rebirth pattern from irresponsible boyhood to moral maturity.

The total result of these thematic, structural, and symbolic workings is a novel which has a remarkably high degree of consistency, coherence, and unity. Its theme is the growth of an individual personality. Its crisis is the moral decision, repeated three times, to repudiate the conventions of society and do the individually, humanly right thing. Its rising interest is given by the sharply increasing complexity of the individual awareness of the implications of such an action. Its structure is defined by the extinction of the old childish organizaton of mind and feelings, the symbolic death of the individual as he was, his withdrawal from society into nature, and his reconstitution, or symbolic rebirth, on a higher and more mature level of organization, as a better, more capable person. The theme and structure are concretely embodied and related in the texture, which reinforces both with a rhythmically repeated and varied pattern of appropriate motifs and images. The functional, organic interrelations of all these factors must have something to do with the effect of unity which readers generally feel in *Huckleberry Finn,* but which we are now only beginning to understand and be able to explain.

Notes

1. Reprinted in *The Liberal Imagination* (New York: Viking Press, 1950), pp. 104-117.

2. *The Adventures of Huckleberry Finn* (London: The Cressett Press, 1950), pp. vii-xvi.

3. Leo Marx, "Mr. Eliot, Mr. Trilling, and *Huckleberry Finn*," *American Scholar*, 22 (Autumn 1953), 423-440.

4. Edgar M. Branch, *The Literary Apprenticeship of Mark Twain* (Urbana: University of Illinois Press, 1950), pp. 199-216; Gladys C. Bellamy, *Mark Twain as a Literary Artist* (Norman: University of Oklahoma Press, 1950), pp. 340-347; James M. Cox, "Remarks on the Sad Initiation of Huckleberry Finn," *Sewanee Review*, 62 (Summer 1954), 389-405; Lewis Leary, "Tom and Huck: Innocence on Trial," *Virginia Quarterly Review*, 30 (Summer 1954), 417-430; and Frank Baldanza, "The Structure of *Huckleberry Finn*," *American Literature*, 27 (November 1955), 347-355. All of these, except the last, more or less strongly disagree with Trilling and Eliot about the ending.

5. Walter Blair, "On the Structure of *Tom Sawyer*," *Modern Philology*, 37 (August 1939), 84-85.

6. *Ibid*, p. 86. Leary, pp. 419-423, in his discussion of *Tom Sawyer*, confirms Blair's theory, but he does not apply it to *Huck Finn*.

7. Trilling, p. 115.

8. Cox, p. 395.

9. Trilling, pp. 111-112.

10. *Mark Twain's Notebook*, ed. A. B. Paine (New York and London: Harper & Brothers, 1935), p. 197.

11. *Ibid*., p. 196. Clemens neglected this view when he later met some royal persons himself.

12. *Mark Twain's Autobiography*, ed. A. B. Paine (New York and London; Harper & Brothers, 1924), I, 123.

13. Baldanza, p. 353.

Mark Twain and Charlie Chaplin as Heroes of Popular Culture

Glauco Cambon

If Mark Twain had survived by just a few years the reappearance of Halley's comet, he would have seen the beginnings of Charlie Chaplin's comet-like career through the American galaxy of Hollywood; and it is easy to conjecture that the author of *A Tramp Abroad, Tom Sawyer* and *The Gilded Age* would have cheered the antics of Chaplin's *Pilgrim.* At the risk of incurring imaginary biography, that nasty temptation of biographers, I will say that I cannot conceive of a Samuel Langhorne Clemens who, given a new lease of life, had proved unresponsive to films like *Gold Rush, The Kid, City Lights*.... And since, metaphorically speaking, the news of his death remains "greatly exaggerated", my anachronistic fancy has no great chance of being resented by serious scholars. Historically conscious but not time-bound, the curious mind keeps arranging improbable parties where, for example, Charlie Chaplin can finally meet Twain or listen to one of his lectures with the delight that our great-grandparents knew and for which Hal Holbrook has given us posthumous generations the best available substitute. I haven't done any research into this particular matter, but it seems safe to guess that Chaplin knows and likes his Twain.

Should this ever prove untrue, it wouldn't make the slightest difference to me, for my purpose in bringing the two artists into

From *Minnesota Review*, 3 (Fall 1962),77-82. Reprinted with permission.

the same context is to show certain fundamental affinities between them as popular mythmakers. Both reached the largest audience an artist can hope to get, without sacrificing their standards. Leslie Fiedler has sociologically defined Faulkner "the highbrow's lowbrow", but of our two chosen worthies it can be said that they are "the lowbrow's highbrows" as well. Twain's popularity was not of the meretricious kind, and popularity failed to corrupt Chaplin, who in his pig-headed way (whatever the merits of the case) preferred ostracism to obeisance. A distinction must be drawn between the former's closeness to agrarian folklore (Southern, Negro and Western) and the latter's use of a commercial mass-medium like the movies to dramatize the hopeless anonymity of modern city-man; though that distinction itself will have to be qualified when we realize how the practice of journalism, that king of the mass-media, concurred with folk-speech to shape Twain's art, while Chaplin, in focusing his camera-eye on the uprooted masses of the industrial age, discovered whatever "folklore" they could be said to harbor at the potential or residual stage. He could do that because, stark realist as he was and is, he never suppressed his sense of fable, something to which the disinherited will always respond. Russian critics, anthologized by Sergei Eisenstein in what is perhaps the most impressive tribute to Chaplin's genius, predictably emphasized the social criticism that operates in his screen-fables, but they did so without pedantry, and they brought out the Shakespearian affinities of our new-fangled clown. And there is no need to point out how warmly received Mark Twain is in Soviet Russia. I doubt this can be reduced to a matter of propaganda distortion. Whatever the dogmatic interpretations to which the American writer and the London-born moviemaker may be amenable, it is their secret commerce with Queen Mab that endears them both to so many people across so many boundaries.

Her whispered counsels have certainly inspired Chaplin to become a redeemer of vulgarity rather than artistically succumb to "mass culture." That mass culture need not be kitsch has become increasingly hard to believe since the era of the dime novels, of the slick movies and of doctored advertising; Chaplin has made that belief possible with his singlehanded accomplishment as actor, scenarist, director and producer. Other users of the mass media for entertainment purposes have evaded the clichés of mass culture to shroud their artistic purity in sophistication; he instead faced them from the start and reconverted them into artistic assets. One readily thinks of Poe's, Dostoevsky's or Chesterton's use of the detective story, and, to be sure, of Twain's reliance on certain dime-novel narrative devices.

The main point of comparison between him and the screen actor who has indelibly colored the Twenties in the filmy perspective of nostalgia is their successful dramatization of the Tramp as mythical figure. As such, "Charlot" acquired a life of his own beyond the limits of each plot, to dominate a screen saga that did an awful lot to keep the imagination alive in the urban masses all over the globe, so much so that we must count it as one of the humanizing forces at work in our Brave New World. Charlot, the popular mask, became more real than Chaplin himself, and when Chaplin dropped this mask for other impersonations in his postwar movies, it came as a shock of historical recognition: the times had changed indeed! Something of the kind happened to Mark Twain, who kept up his public *persona* of the "tramp abroad," with a touch of Tom Sawyer and Huck Finn, as a world-acclaimed lecturer. And certainly, both Twain's and Chaplin's late productions are attempts to get behind their respective mythical masks, to converse with them, to explain or transform them... whatever the results. There is no doubt, anyway, that Charlot's pantomime and Huck's fluvial monologue reflect the unfailing theatrical instinct of their creators.

In pointing out the kinship between these two signal embodiments of the Tramp myth I do not lose sight of their differences; but the latter can be taken for granted once we admit the artistic individuality of each creation. Achieved uniqueness—the success of art—still leaves room for significant comparison. Charlot is an adult moving around in a crowded urban world, while Huck is a frontier boy ranging the exhilarating spaces of the Mississippi and surrounding area; but Huck's brushes with the shore settlements' folks clearly anticipate Charlot's pathetic entanglements with his city milieu, and Charlot had his fling with the American romance of the promising wilderness in *Gold Rush*. Moreover, Charlot is a very childlike adult, and Huck is a child who has to shift for himself, the only adult he can trust and accept being Nigger Jim—the member of a primitive race that seeks emancipation. Jim and Huck have become one of the archetypal pairs of world literature (for broader reasons than Leslie Fiedler seems to admit) much in the same way as Charlie Chaplin and

Jackie Coogan came to establish their linked images in the popular mind, through a more ephemeral medium.

Both pairs, in fact, represent homeless innocence in a brutal or at best stuffy world. Their intuitively grasped paradox is that, fleeing away from established society or trying to survive as aliens in its heartless midst, they set up a numerically and financially minimal society of their own in which love and not law sanctions any ties. The association is consequently precarious, despite its emotional value, and in neither case does it exhaust the imaginative dimensions of the Tramp, who keeps leaving experience, persons and towns behind. The classical ending of many a Chaplin movie in the Charlot cycle, featuring the unforgettable flatfoot in baggy pants, derby hat and pliant cane that plods away towards disappearance on the open road, may recall *Huckleberry Finn's* conclusion with the announced plan to "light out for the West."

Whether alone or in congenial company, the Tramp must rely on his cunning to escape the many traps of the Establishment (or, in some cases, of the Bad-Guy tramps, like the murderous goldseeker in *Gold Rush,* and the river pirates, the Duke and the Dauphin, or Pap himself, in Twain's novel). This cunning, being very elemental (like that of children, animals, savages and peasants), fits in with the endearing attributes of goodness, generosity, innocence and wonderment that go into the making of Huck's and Charlot's images as naive heroes. They are both imaginative tricksters, and they had better be, in a world "they never made".... Huck's disguises and lies are of a piece with Charlot's hilarious improvisations when he finds himself in a tight spot; their occasional lawlessness, inherent in the type, is likewise of the comical rather than the sinister kind: Charlot the intinerant glazier sending his Kid around to break windowpanes so he can stay in business reminds me of Huck when he confesses to "lifting" a chicken that "was roosting uncomfortable."

Laughter has often been a vehicle for social critique, and the comical note Twain and Chaplin strike can go very far in that direction, though satire is only one of its aspects, for Huck's verbal mimicry, conveyed through the rhythms of a colorful dialect, is delightful comedy for its own sake, too, like Chaplin's balletsteps and facial mobility. Besides, their social commentary, when it does not become too explicit (as it often does in the late work of both), acts just as well in the guise of pathos or tragi-comedy. The strike scene in *Modern Times,* with its climactic resolution—the dead man left alone in the deserted street after police have dispersed the rioters—reminds me somehow of the Grangerford-Shepherdson feud in Twain's story, particularly on account of its poignant ending: a bewildered Huck Finn taking leave of his murdered friend Buck. Aimed as they are at illustrating the urgency of the Depression crisis and, respectively, the tragic absurdity of Southern feudal mores, the two episodes make their point without preaching, and the result that much more effective. Their "message" is one and the same thing with their poetry.

Tragic pathos and rollicking fun thus constitute the two extremes between which Mark Twain's and Charlie Chaplin's art moves, with a marked tendency of the latter extreme to prevail; and in between there are the intermediate notes of elegy, lyricism, love poetry, which assert themselves very strongly, for instance, in Chaplin's postwar movie *Limelight.* The lyrical breath of Huck's description of a Mississippi dawn at the beginning of Chapter XIX, or of the Phelps farm in Chapter XXII, is an unsurpassed feat of literary style which Chaplin never tries to rival because, unlike Twain, he is interested in man to the exclusion of nature; but when Huck tries to help Mary Jane and then says goodbye to her for good, Charlot's clumsy chivalry to his harried blonde heroines comes to mind.

Being of the naive kind, Chaplin's imagination, like Twain's, is prone to sentimentality on the one hand and farce on the other. Chaplin's farce, however, is always redeemed by his virtuoso pantomime, and it does not spoil our pleasure, aesthetically speaking, because the natural focus of attention in his case is the character, Charlot as mythical figure, not the plot or the total structure of one movie in which he appears. Therefore, if I relate Tom, Huck and Jim in their ludicrous finale to Charlot's gags, it is only to emphasize certain temperamental affinities between the two humorists, for aesthetic performance is another matter. Chaplin's vaudeville is no breach of style, while Twain's concession to farcical minstrel-show stereotype mars the otherwise impressive achievement of a book that can recapture in its *naive Dichtung* the freshness of Homer and the depth of Cervantes. Homer did have a place for slapstick in his epic, but he took care not to let Thersites have the last word.

These formal flaws, for all we know, may even have aided Twain's masterpiece to gain its enormous popularity, and to that extent we can forgive them, thinking of the poetry they have smuggled into so many crude minds. Reliance on popular stereotypes isn't always treacherous, though, as Chaplin's repertory of utterly simple fables shows. His Tramp is always having trouble with the representatives of authority and power: the cop, the rich man, and the rich man's clientele. These are frankly popular clichés, but since everything in a Chaplin movie revolves around Charlot, they aren't obtrusive at all; besides, the fairytale atmosphere makes them acceptable as King, Princess, Ogre, Witch and Gnome are in a Grimm story. Charlot's comico-sentimental impersonation of the Blue Prince to a sighing Princess of the slums, Charlot's self-angelization in the surreal escape-dream of *The Kid*, and Charlot's difficult but finally successful treasure-hunt in *Gold Rush* are all deeply rooted motifs of the popular imagination, to be found in so many pre-industrial folktales, and in interpreting them for the modern masses Chaplin instinctively knew he increased his own art's chances of success.

Twain's authority symbols—Aunt Sally, Miss Watson, the Widow Douglas, Judge Thatcher, the perverted Pap—are less stereotypical, but the basic attitude is the same; and he too uses the treasure-hunt motif to give scope to his young heroes' adventures. In defining Twain's and Chaplin's art as "naive" I have in mind two different but related meanings, i.e., Schiller's conception of spontaneous art, having the traits of wholeness and immediacy, the more current use of the word to denote candor or crudity. Candor certainly radiates from everything our two artists do, and it explains their popular appeal along with their occasional lapses. It was a candid mind which could set the sentimentalized child-savior story of *Saint Joan* above the matchless impishness of *Huckleberry Finn;* it is a naive mind which has abruptly broken the unity of an initially promising film like *A King in New York* to employ a little child (Chaplin's own son) as a solemnly vociferous mouth-piece of the author's heartfelt pacifist beliefs.

The myth of the Tramp, which writer and actor have brought to life in their different media, is itself a naive archetype of romantic ancestry, having in its blood the genes of Wordsworth's Wanderer (and Seer Child), of Black's Innocent, of Scott's Outlaw-Knight, of Rousseau's Natural Man & Noble Savage. The anarchic dream expresses the recurrent longing of society for regeneration, along with the protest of the disinherited against entrenched privilege; but Twain's and Chaplin's naive idyll has nothing in it of the mystique which characterizes the primitivism of a Lawrence, a Faulkner, a Hamsun. Hart Crane, in a partly great poem, identified Charlot with Parsifal, and something of the Pure Fool forever seeking the unattainable Grail of happiness, love and goodness is to be sensed in Chaplin's filmic creature as well as in Twain's imaginary child.

Chaplin's radical ideas parallel Twain's social protest, but I don't know that the tireless moviemaker now living in Switzerland would be at home in a totalitarian Communist society, or meet with tolerance there. His is the naive yearning for a utopia of pure goodness, and the shattering blows this undying dream of man received in our century finally found their repercussion in the dark disenchantment of *Monsieur Verdoux*, Chaplin's first postwar movie in which the fable of Bluebeard serves to bring home the problem of evil as one our tainted society cannot face or solve. "What is evil?" Verdoux ask his judges in the gripping final scene, on his way to execution; and the question, indeed the whole tone of the movie seems to echo Mark Twain's Satan in *The Mysterious Stranger*, which could be called Twain's *Monsieur Verdoux*.

Our two pilgrims' progress from humor to disenchantment and horror is similar, and testifies to their basically naive thinking. In an age which exposes the masses to endless manipulation through political or commercial propaganda their work seems to fulfill, by aesthetically handling a central myth in the language everybody can understand, a countervailing function. As long as there are artists like these around, we have some hope to fight the brutality and stultification which assault us from every side. They have helped the uprooted man of megalopolis to retain or achieve a visage, an identity, a human consciousness. They have done this by collaborating with Queen Mab, Puck, and Ariel, whom they have smuggled back into our midst from where they seemed forever exiled. Charlot's assembly-line ballet in *Modern Times*, besides providing the unifying formal rhythm to his fable, gave us a cry of alarm we cannot easily forget. Since I don't believe in writing or doing anything "impersonal," I shall conclude by saying that my viewing the Charlot movies as a war-tried adult in the last few years detracted nothing from the spell they cast on me in the late Twenties, when I first watched them, eagerly waiting for the luminous message from the screen as a child "sitting in darkness."

"Tears and Flapdoodle": Point of View and Style in Adventures of Huckleberry Finn

Janet Holmgren McKay

Mark Twain's *The Adventures of Huckleberry Finn* is one of the most stylistically significant works in American literature. T. S. Eliot is not alone in his evaluation of Twain as "one of those writers, of whom there are not a great many in any literature, who have discovered a new way of writing."[1] Literary critics have praised Twain time and again for creating a narrative style in *Huck Finn* which uses vernacular or colloquial American English to revitalize the imaginative representation of reality. However, few critics have actually examined the way in which Twain fashioned a consistent literary style for an apparently nonliterary form of discourse.[2]

To say that Twain created Huck's voice by copying the speech patterns of a young boy is factually inadequate, as any student of language knows. Spoken and written modes of discourse can never be identical, particularly in literature where the language must be highly conscious and compactly organized. What Twain actually does in *Huck Finn* is to use certain strategically placed vernacular and colloquial features[3] to create the impression of an untutored narrator, while simultaneously developing a sophisticated, innovative literary style which uses a full range of standard English constructions and literary devices.

From *Style*, 10 (Winter 1976), 41-50. Reprinted with permission.

The success of this stylistic *tour de force* depends upon the consistency with which Twain maintains Huck's narrative point of view. If Huck's language convinces the reader of his innocence, his perceptions and actions must support this impression. This essential interdependence of form and content further requires that Huck's style be rigorously coherent. However, after bringing the reader to accept the illusion of naive narration, Twain is free to play with both language and the related point of view for imaginative effects.

To understand this complex interaction we need both the linguist's attention to language structure—his knowledge of the social and cultural implications of particular linguistic forms—and the literary critic's awareness of the artistic significance of language devices in the individual context. Above all, however, we need substantiation of our stylistic perceptions with actual textual analysis. What linguistic devices establish Huck's voice and simultaneously achieve poetic effects in a particular context? Are these devices apparent elsewhere in the work, and if so, what artistic variations within them are evident here? A wide-ranging analysis of individual passages can then lead to an examination of the relationship of the individual passage to the work as a whole and to the larger literary stylistic context. Only then can we make convincing claims for "simplicity," "innovativeness," and "consistency."

A passage from the central section of the novel offers some interesting insights into the complexity of Twain's *Huck Finn* style and into the subtle narrative irony that Twain creates through the style. In the course of their journey down the Mississippi River, Huck and the runaway slave Jim are set upon by two con men who claim to be dispossessed aristocracy. Although Huck resolves to get along with the King and the Duke as long as they are around, he becomes increasingly disgusted with their antics. His aversion reaches a peak in the Wilks family incident when the King and Duke contrive to rob three defenseless girls, hiding their deceit in the trappings of familial love and Christian fellowship. The moment when the King, posing as both preacher and grieving brother, bursts forth in his "soul-butter and hogwash" speech provides Huck with an opportunity to vent his anger. The description which follows is a stylistic masterpiece—a subtle blending of Huck's and the King's voices balanced for the maximum satiric effect.

Well, by and by the king he gets up and comes forward a little, and works himself up and slobbers out a speech, all full of tears and flapdoodle, about its being a sore trial for him and his poor brother to lose the diseased, and to miss seeing diseased alive after the long journey of four thousand mile, but it's a trial that's sweetened and sanctified to us by this dear sympathy and these holy tears, and so he thanks them out of his heart and out of his brother's heart, because out of their mouths they can't, words being too weak and cold, and all that kind of rot and slush, till it was just sickening; and then he blubbers out a pious goody-goody Amen, and turns himself loose and goes to crying fit to bust.[4]

A number of literary scholars have noted that in the original draft of this section Twain used direct quotation to present the King's speech, but in revision he shifted to indirect discourse.[5] In fact, however, the discourse here is only partially indirect—a fact masked by one of the hallmarks of Huck's style, the run-on sentence.

Huck frequently uses run-ons, like the one here which constitutes nearly the entire paragraph. Within them he employs few overt marks of subordination, although many of his coordinate major clauses function as subordinate clauses.[6] While the relationships among the parts of this sentence are not always clearly defined, the structure is essentially cumulative—to borrow a descriptive term from Francis Christensen. In a cumulative sentence the main clause, which Christensen numbers "one," establishes the topic and subsequent clauses and sentence modifiers elaborate it with increasing specificity. These elaborations have a narrower focus than the main clause and are therefore assigned a lower level of generality.[7] Both the cumulative structure and the loose coordination are typical of the conversational style in English.[8] Furthermore, they contribute to the reader's impression of Huck's naiveté and lack of linguistic sophistication.

In the compound/complex sentence of this paragraph, an important variation on the cumulative structure creates a narrative frame for the King's discourse. The sentence follows a pattern of decreasing levels of generality up to the absolute, "words being too weak and cold." In the next phrase, "and all that kind of rot and slush," Huck returns to the level of general description he used at the beginning of the sentence. Thus Twain begins with Huck's introduction, moves into Huck's rendition of the King's words ("its being a sore trial for him and his brother"), and finally, in the middle of the sentence, gives us the King himself speaking ("it's a trial that's sweetened and sanctified to us"). From this point on, we move gradually back to Huck's voice, passing once again through the intermediate stage of Huck's account of the King ("because out of their mouths they can't"). The sentence's structure can be represented roughly as follows:[9]

HUCK [2]Well, by and by (adv)
[1]the king he gets up and comes forward a little,
and works himself up and slobbers out a speech,
[2]all full of tears and flapdoodle, (reduced RC)
HUCK/KING [2]about its being a sore trial...(Abs as object of prep)
[3]after the long journey...(PP)
KING [3]but it's a trial that's sweetened and sanctified
to us...(Major C)
HUCK/KING [3]and so he thanks them out of his heart...
(Major C)
[4]because out of their mouths they can't,
(SC)
[5]words being too weak...(Abs)
HUCK [2]and all that kind of rot and slush,
[3]till it was just sickening; (SC)
[1]and then he blubbers out a pious goody-goody Amen....

Twain accomplishes the changes in narrative perspective by contrasting Huck's style to the bombastic posturings of the King, although he incorporates the latter into Huck's narration. The passage's lexicon reveals the major distinctions between Huck's narrative voice and his recounting of the King's speech. In the frame clauses at the beginning and the end of the sentence, an element of disdain marks Huck's key lexical choices and constitutes one thread of lexical cohesion. Thus the King "slobbers" and "blubbers"; his speech, which Huck finds "sickening," is "rot," "slush," and "flapdoodle." The verb phrases Huck uses to encompass the King's entire act—"works himself up," "turns himself loose"—also clearly reflect Huck's scorn for the King's histrionics in this fraudulent scene.

Phrasal verbs, which play a prominent role in Huck's casual style, are numerous in the frame elements—"gets up," "comes forward," "works up," "slobbers out," "blubbers out," "turns loose," "goes to"; however, none occur within his presentation of the King's discourse. Furthermore, most of Huck's vernacular syntactic constructions occur in the frame elements, where, in addition to the ambiguity of syntactic relations which we will examine below, we find tautology ("the king he," "all full of"). Finally, lexical choices and constructions which the reader has come to associate with Huck through constant repetition are prominent in the opening and closing. Two of Huck's favorite adjectives of disdain are "sickening" and "goody-goody." Structurally, "goody-goody" exemplifies a pattern in Huck's style of forming slang adjectives by adding a *-y* suffix to other adjectives and nouns.[10] Semantically, it reflects Huck's persistent skepticism about people who try to be good by "sivilized" standards.

When Huck records the King's speech, he adopts the King's ostentatiously pious vocabulary. The clichéd phrases, such as "sore trial," "poor brother," "sweetened and sanctified," and "holy tears," force the reader to focus on the pretense of genteel mourning. Tearfulness becomes a dominant theme, linking the paragraph to the surrounding descriptions where the King, the Duke, the Wilks sisters, and the townspeople carry on excessively. Huck's term "slush" effectively captures the mental and physical sogginess of the scene.

All of this "sobbing and swabbing" (p. 227) contrasts sharply with Huck's own understated emotional expressions. For instance, during the Shepherdson/Grangerford feud when Huck's friend Buck is killed, Huck says, "I cried a little when I was covering up Buck's face, for he was mighty good to me" (p. 160). The contrast resides in the language, and the reader's perception of Huck develops from the contrast. Huck's actions and the language he uses to describe them are Twain's most powerful indictment of the "pretended or misguided piety" (Smith, 118) and the maudlin sentimentality of the pre-Civil War South. However, in striving for the maximum satiric effect Twain was not content to rely on irony—a fact which accounts in part for his decision to shift from direct to indirect discourse in this passage. Huck's scathing denunciation becomes the angle from which we view the sham and adds to his moral authority. Outrage reinforces satire. Notice that with the adjective "pious"—a lexical choice not suitable to Huck's colloquial vocabulary and made unnecessary by Huck's own "goody-goody"—we sense Twain pushing beyond the limits of Huck's narration to make his point.

Another interesting example of authorial control occurs in the "diseased/deceased" pun. Throughout the Wilks episode, the King in the role of Harvey Wilks, noted English minister, attempts to introduce terms of learning and gentility into his speech—a linguistic impersonation which allows Twain to characterize the King while mocking the genteel values which the

King mimics. In the process the King comes up with some ludicrous malapropisms, like his confusion of "orgies" and "obsequies" (p. 233). In this passage, because Twain uses the frame of indirect discourse, it is not clear whether the King actually uses "diseased" for "deceased" or whether Huck mixes the two up. The error thus serves two purposes. The King's subsequent "orgies/obsequies" error makes it likely that this one is his, too. As such, it plays a part in Twain's satire, for it focuses on the King's ignorance and on the ignorance of those who hear him and still believe his ruse. However, Huck uses "diseased" again a few pages later ("Well, then pretty soon all hands got talking about the diseased again..." pp. 232-33.) As Huck's error, it adds to the ironic distance between Huck and the implied author. In both the "orgies/obsequies" and the "diseased/deceased" confusions Twain is playing on the macabre logic of the substitutions—a rhetorical manipulation that would be beyond Huck.

Although the changes in narrative perspective are indicated primarily by lexical devices, some important syntactic variations also play a part. Huck normally uses the active voice in his clauses and sentences, the majority of which follow the subject-verb-object pattern. The consistency with which Twain maintains this pattern makes variations on it all the more striking. Thus in this passage a single passive construction is strategically located in the clause wholly attributable to the King ("it's a trial that's sweetened and sanctified to us"). This one small shift has multiple functions. It adds a pompous note to the King's speech; it contrasts the King's evasiveness with Huck's habitually straight-forward style; and it permits Twain to play on the repetition of "it's a trial," with its sermon-like rhythm (reminding us of the King's ministerial impersonation). Finally, the passive construction makes the change from third person (him, his) to first person (us) pronouns less noticeable—an important linguistic function. Twain scrupulously avoids any features that might make Huck's style obstruct rather than support the reader's involvement with the story.[11] Thus, for instance, although many of Huck's sentences are run-on, their cumulative, right-branching construction makes then easily comprehensible. Here the pronoun shift might constitute a potential impediment, so it is subtly obscured.

Huck generally begins his sentences and clauses with their subjects, as I noted above, occasionally prefacing those that begin new paragraphs with a simple transition like the "well, by and by" we find here. One clause in this sentence, however, violates this pattern with its opening—"because out of their mouths." The variation heightens the satire by drawing the reader's attention to what *is* coming out of the King's mouth and by providing an ironic contrast to the maudlin repetition "out of his heart and out of his brother's heart."

Finally, Huck's phrase "and all that kind of rot and slush," which begins the closing frame element, has an ambiguous relationship to the sentence. Although it functions as a disdainful comment on what the King has said, structurally the phrase is either a coordinate object with "speech" or more likely another modifier of "speech." Thus it reminds the reader of the connection between this concluding part of the sentence and the opening. Ambiguity is a typical colloquial feature of Huck's style, but as with all of Huck's idiosyncratic features Twain rarely uses it without a larger structural purpose.

Other features of Huck's which have a rhetorical function include his usual conjunctions "and," "and then," "and so," which tend to move the passage along at a rapid pace, adding to what Ferguson calls the sense of "compression" (p. 222). Huck frequently uses his repetition and parallelism, and here these features are concentrated in the King's simulated sermon style—"to lose the diseased"/"to miss seeing diseased alive," "its being a sore trial"/"but it's a trial," "this dear sympathy"/"these holy tears," "out of his heart"/"out of his brother's heart"/"out of their mouths." Finally, Huck's narration constantly benefits from an apparently guileless alliteration and sound symbolism—part of his innate feeling for the play of language. Although not obtrusive, the plosives /p/, /b/ and the hard /g/, /k/ sounds pervade the frame elements while smoother sibilants /s/ highlight the King's speech.

While most of the linguistic features I have discussed thus far have tended to distinguish Huck's voice from his account of the King's speech, in one area Twain minimizes the distinction to capitalize on the dramatic potential of the scene. Throughout the passage Twain has Huck use what Martin Joos in *The English Verb* labels the narrative actual present tense.[12] As with the French, "historical present," to which Joos compares the English construction, the reader is aware that the event described took place in the past because of other contextual markers, like Huck's "by and by." However, the shift in tense is both a feature typical of conversation style and a means of showing the narrator's intense involvement. As Joos says, the narrative actual "has a firm basis in speech, where the use of actual tense for past events comes naturally to the lips of a man who gets himself involved in what he is talking about." In addition to characterizing Huck's attitude, the shift in tense here suggests direct discourse. To provide a smooth transition from the preceding paragraph which is in the past tense, Twain concludes that paragraph with two nonstandard preterits which have the same form as the standard present ("...and *give* the next woman a show. I never *see* anything so disgusting"). Twain's choice of a particular nonstandard feature for its rhetorical value is evident here, since Huck uses the nonstandard preterit "seen" elsewhere as in the fifth sentence of the novel—"I never seen anybody but lied one time or another..." (p. 1).

Thus in this paragraph Twain tailors the colloquial features to the literary situation, pulling the inherent opposition of the two into a taut, productive balance. This inquiry into the structure and function of a short passage only hints at the rich linguistic resources of *Huck Finn*. The finest work of an author dedicated to the power and versatility of language, the novel is an outstanding example of the role language plays in creating the reality of a fictional setting.

Through the consistent use of certain linguistic features Twain characterizes Huck and makes the reader believe in the reality of Huck's vision. Huck's style both because of its apparent simplicity and because of the way in which it contrasts with the hypocrisy of acceptable language use comes to represent honesty in a dishonest world. Ultimately, the reader distinguishes truth from falsity by the linguistic contrasts of the text. By putting the more "sivilized" constructions in the mouth of a scoundrel like the King, Twain insures their demise. They are buried by Huck's honest indignation, by Twain's satiric juxtaposition of "tears and flapdoodle."

Notes

1. T. S. Eliot, "American Literature and American Language," *To Criticize the Critic* (New York: Farrar, Straus & Giroux, 1965), p. 54.

2. Notable exceptions to this general tendency are Charles Clerc's article "Sunrise on the River: 'The Whole World' of Huckleberry Finn," *Modern Fiction Studies*, 14 (1968), 67-78, and Richard Bridgman's "Henry James and Mark Twain," chapter three in *The Colloquial Style in America* (New York: Oxford University Press, 1966).

3. Careful distribution of nonstandard and casual features characterizes all of Twain's composition. As Sydney J. Krause notes, "in order that it might *count*, he had to use dialect judiciously, and the same was true of his colloquial diction at large and his illiterate grammar." "Twain's Method and Theory of Composition," *Modern Philology*, 56 (1959), 176.

4. Samuel Langhorne Clemens, *The Adventures of Huckleberry Finn*, Vol. XIII of *The Writings of Mark Twain*, Author's National Edition (New York: Harper and Brothers, 1912), pp. 227-28. Subsequent page references to this work will appear in the text. No thoroughly accurate edition of *Huck Finn* is presently available; therefore, I have chosen this edition because it is the same as the Definitive Edition and much more readily accessible. The few punctuation differences in the 1885 American version as reproduced in the Norton Critical Edition (*Adventures of Huckleberry Finn: An Annotated Text*, ed. Sculley Bradley, Richmond Croom Beatty, E. Hudson Long [New York: W. W. Norton & Co., Inc., 1972]), are not significant for the analysis of this passage.

5. DeLancey Ferguson, *Mark Twain: Man and Legend* (New York: Russell & Russell, 1966), pp. 221-22; Henry Nash Smith, *Mark Twain: The Development of a Writer* (New York: Atheneum, 1967), p. 121.

6. David Crystal and Derek Davy in *Investigating English Style* (Bloomington: Indiana University Press, 1969) label such structures "dependent coordinate," a pattern in which "the coordinate component is functionally as much dependent on the preceding clause as a subordinate clause in the same position," p. 59, n. 9.

7. *Notes Toward a New Rhetoric* (New York: Harper & Row, 1967), pp. 5-9.

8. For a general analysis of conversational English see Crystal and Davy, chapter 4, "The Language of Conversation," particularly the discussion of sentence types, p. 110.

9. The numbering system within the diagram is based on Christensen's analytical model as are the grammatical labels for types of phrases and clauses. Christensen (p. 9) uses the following abbreviations of "free-modifiers"—sentence modifiers that are nonrestrictive: SC-subordinate clause; RC—relative clause; Abs—absolute; PP—prepositional phrase. I have added the two designations adverbial (adv) and major clause (Major C) to account for some typical patterns in Huck's sentences.

10. I use the designation "slang" based on the findings of Hans Marchand, *The Categories and Types of Present-Day English Word-Formation*, Alabama Linguistic and Philological Series, No. 13 (University of Alabama Press, 1966). Marchand notes that "beginning with the 18th c., the sf [suffix-*y*] has shown a tendency to form words of a colloquial, slangy character," p. 288.

11. Thus, for instance, Robert Lowenherz notes that Twain restricts "dialect

spelling to less than one percent of Huck's narrative speech...consistently throughout the novel." "The Beginning of 'Huckleberry Finn'," *American Speech*, 38 (1963), 197.

12. *The English Verb: Form & Meanings* (Madison: University of Wisconsin Press, 1968), p. 131.

Huck and the Games of the World

Bruce Michelson

The structure of *Huckleberry Finn* might seem a question worth putting to rest for a while, even if the secret of that structure still evades us. Because so much has been said about the form of this novel, and because we have learned so much already that makes sense, one needs strong reasons for raising the issue now. I do so only because I think we can begin to explain why so many *different* motifs have been turned up, how they can be reconciled with one another, and what really constitutes the novel's core: the way in which structure and moral concern connect with the personality of Mark Twain the man. We have always had trouble with this last matter: we have yet to explain what the inmost man and the essential forms of his fiction have to do with one another. Without pretending to offer some "bottom-line" solution to all of the mysteries of *Huckleberry Finn*, I do think we can make some headway if we pay closer attention to Mark Twain's enormous, lifelong obsession with play and games. Biographies of Mark Twain make much of this fascination, of Twain's delight in making up new games, in acting out children's fantasies, in poker and billiards, in wild costumes, cake-walks, impersonations, jokes, toys, pranks, puzzles, riddles—play and games of every imaginable kind.[1] With all this remembered, I suggest that we look at *Huckleberry Finn* as a novel about all that, about people who play games, who make games out of everything, including matters of moral consequence—and who run into trouble be-

From *American Literary Realism*, 13 (Spring 1980), 108-21. Reprinted with permission.

cause they do so. Nearly everyone in Huck's and Jim's world (including Huck, some of the time) takes play beyond the boundaries of childhood, safety, and common sense; the world of the novel is always at play in the wrong place and at the wrong time. If we are willing to read the book in this way, we will see that many of the major episodes and motifs will make better sense, resonate with one another, when we take them together. We will see that the constant play motif in the novel helps define Huck as a character, the evil that he faces, and everyone of importance that he meets on his journey. To read the book in this way, we need only accept a few basic ideas about the nature of play, ideas which would have appealed to the "horse sense" of both a play-loving Mark Twain and his clear-headed hero.

The reading will, in fact, stand or fall on the definitions and limits we can agree on for "play" and "game." There are some theorists on play who claim that virtually every human act, or for that matter every cosmic event, is a gesture in some sort of grand game;[2] but two widely accepted authorities, Johan Huizinga and Roger Caillois, both insist on play's separateness from "real life," and most people (including Samuel Clemens) seem to agree. For most of us a murder is a murder, not a game; and to say that this swindle or that feud, or a mob action or a street-shooting, or all life and all art are only forms of play is to say cleverly almost nothing at all. The question that needs to be raised is whether people involved in the desperate acts that litter *Huckleberry Finn* are led to them by a basic confusion about where play ends and the world of "not-play" reality begins.

The common definitions of play assume this much—that the play world is one physically and imaginatively distinct from everyday life, that in this separate world the rules of conduct and the consequences of it are other than what they are in the normal scheme of things. Play is a fictive act, requiring some kind of make-believe, tending to separate or isolate the players from the non-players; and play is pleasurable in and of itself, not simply for the "stakes," if stakes there are.[3] All real play is vulnerable. Illusions are brittle, and spoil-sports may ruin games for the committed players.[4] People can carry play to extremes too, and bring on events which expand well beyond the safe and bounded world of the game. Make-believe for its own sake might be innocent, but it is not by nature harmless. Huizinga and Caillois agree that play which outrages or injures or degrades outsiders is play that has turned corrupt; and, according to Huizinga, the worst, most insidious perversion of the play-impulse is what he calls "puerilism," destructive childishness, evasive mock-innocence which turns the celebrations of true play into the cruel, selfish, and pointless rituals which threaten social order and the best in the human spirit.[5] No evil is so frightening as that which pretends to innocence. No grown-up crime shocks so much as that which passes itself off as the sport of children. But then again, neither Huizinga nor any other student of play has even pretended that the distinctions between real and corrupt play, or play and *not*-play, are always clear. These principles have everything to do with the structure of *Huckleberry Finn*. The evil that lurks in Huck's world is at bottom an evil of childishness, wanton playfulness carried too far and too long; and it is this theme that makes one novel out of the games of children and the violence of their elders. Huck must make his way through the mock-play of an adult world—and in the process, he must face the cruel, thoughtless, and essentially lonely gamester, the Tom Sawyer, in himself.

In his sensitive reading of Mark Twain's major fiction, James M. Cox speaks often of Twain's and Huck's dedication to "pleasure" as something one must keep in mind in reading *Huckleberry Finn*. For Cox, however, the disruption of the pleasure is a disruption of form: he seems to hold that Twain loses grip on his novel when both Twain and his narrator stray from the safe world of pleasure into the realm of moral consequences. The problem of the book's structure (which Cox sees as rising up much earlier than the "Phelps Farm" chapters which most readers worry over) lies in Twain's failure to keep the hedonist away from the violence;[6] my own case differs not only in giving play some definition, but in holding that the passage out of play and into mayhem, unexpected danger, and moral confusion is so recurrent, so widespread, so deliberate, and so common not only to Huck's misadventures but to those of everyone he meets that it becomes a dominant informing principle of the book, a principle of great importance to plot coherence, to character development, to theme. When Twain is dealing with what the so-called grownup world does to child's play, he is truly in control as a novelist. It is only when he goes *back* to the play of the real children, at the end of the book, that we should wonder whether he has lost his grip on his fiction.

Huckleberry came and went, at his own free will. He slept on doorsteps in fine weather and in empty hogsheads in wet; he did not have to go to school or to church, or call any being master or obey anybody; he could go fishing or swimming when and where he chose, and stay as long as it suited him; nobody forbade him to fight; he could sit up as late as he pleased; he was always the first boy that went barefoot in the spring and the last to resume leather in the fall; he never had to wash, nor put on clean clothes; he could swear wonderfully. In a word, everything that goes to make life precious, that boy had. So thought every harassed, hampered, respectable boy in St. Petersburg.[7]

Thus Huck, as we first see him in *The Adventures of Tom Sawyer*. He begins here truly as "Tom Sawyer's Comrade," the boy whose daily life exemplifies, to Tom and every other "respectable" child in town, the total freedom and irresponsibility that they all yearn for. In fact, this is the way many readers remember Huck, readers who have not looked at either *Tom Sawyer* or *Huckleberry Finn* since childhood: Lucky Huck, whose life is one free and jolly time for ever and ever. The general impression only underscores the fundamental irony of Huck's life. When we move from *Tom Sawyer* to *Huckleberry Finn*, we find that Huck, in his own book, is of course *not* the happy, playful boy that everybody takes him for. He can enjoy freedom, and be powerfully imaginative when he has to; but he truly is the "perfect sap-head" when it comes to such play of make-believe as Tom leads him into; and the happy truancy that the whole town sees is really a struggle for survival. To Widow Douglas, Huck is a "poor lost lamb" because he has been having (she thinks) such a good time, beyond the reach of tight collars, scratchy trousers, and Christian self-discipline. To others, especially his peers, Huck's life is the stuff of fantasy. No one will see him clearly, for everyone wants to see free play where there is only rootlessness and loneliness and quite a bit of desperation. Sometimes, of course, Huck himself is fooled. Sometimes he sees himself as Tom Sawyer.

When we first meet Huck in his own book, we find him in some danger. We are not far into the novel before we sense the tension building: if the boy fails to change morally, the child will not mature, but deteriorate into a childish man. The heart may be sound; but in that Tom Sawyer play world—which Huck seeks to enter—sound hearts and good moral instincts are things to be hooted at. Playing Tom's game Tom's way requires moral compromises which can be uncomfortable to watch; but Huck does not seem to mind. The greatest threat which he faces is that fate that could befall him if nothing intercedes—as so much does—to change what the boy-man believes and what he does.[8] Pap is there precisely to suggest that fate. Of course Pap is a bigoted, villainous drunk whom we detest from the outset; but there are just enough gross resemblances between father and son to make us uneasy, and these resemblances are stressed in the narrative. The opening chapters set the parallels repeatedly: the boy's indolence and the man's dissipation, the boy's comic superstitiousness and the man's atavism, the boy's offhand bigotry and the man's vicious prejudice. In chapter II, Huck has had enough of respectability; he sneaks out an upstairs window to go play with Tom. Chapter V tells us of the father climbing out the same second story for his own after-hour fun. The old man wants whiskey; his son wants only a good time with another boy—but if nothing changes, how long will it be before the easy-living son takes to "forty-rod" for his own "good old time"? To worry about this is not to fall into Miss Watson's hysteria. The parallel actions of son and father are too many to be accidental. Huck spills salt at the breakfast table, and in a superstitious quiver, retreats to the yard—where he finds bootprints, recognizably Pap's by the mark of the father's own superstitions:

> They had come up from the quarry and stood around the stile a while, and then went on around the garden fence. It was funny they hadn't come in, after standing around so.... I was going to follow around, but I stooped down to look at the tracks first. I didn't notice anything at first, but next I did. There was a cross in the left boot-heel made with big nails, to keep off the devil.[9]

After he is abducted up-river by his father, Huck takes to life with Pap more than we would like him to; the boy enjoys everything about it except the "cowhide part." But the climax of the like-father, like-son arrangement comes on the last night that Huck sees Pap alive. Knowing how war can bring out appalling resemblances between enemies, Twain ends the father-son relationship with a melodramatic and revealing tableau. Pap, deliriously drunk, has been chasing his "satan" son around the cabin with a knife. Finally, exhausted, the old man collapses in the corner to "rest up" before killing the boy:

> So he dozed off, pretty soon. By-and-by I got the old split-bottom chair and clumb up, as easy as I could, not to make any noise, and got down the gun. I slipped the ramrod down it to make sure it was loaded, and then I laid it across

the turnip barrel, pointing towards pap, and set down behind it to wait for him to stir. And how slow and still the time did drag along. (p. 28)

The father asleep with the knife; facing him, the boy asleep with the gun. Huck's calm here is as frightening as Pap's savagery, and the mirroring of the boy to the man gives a final chill. The son is in a "tight place" indeed, for how easily could he sour into the father sprawled at the other side of the small room, blocking the boy's escape to a better future—were not an education in the nature of evil coming to Huck's rescue. It makes no sense and serves no purpose to call Pap a bad gamester or even a grotesque parody of a player; his kind of evil needs no other name. Pap is the abyss which his son somehow has to learn to avoid. The adventures which follow his escape, wild and humorous as we often find them, are at the same time a cogent sequence of sobering lessons in the way of adults, and specifically in the moral limits of play and games. These lessons come to Huck in a language that the boy can understand: the language of the Tom-Sawyer world he admires.

Huck's flight from Pap is straight into that world. The boy enters it even as he fakes his own murder in the cabin:

I took the axe and smashed in the door—I beat it and hacked it considerable, a-doing it. I fetched the pig in and took him back nearly to the table and hacked into his throat with the ax, and laid him down on the ground to bleed.... Well, next I took an old sack and put a lot of big rocks in it,—all I could drag—and I started it from the pig and dragged it to the door and through the woods down to the river and dumped it in, and down it sunk, out of sight. You could easy see that something had been dragged over the ground. I did wish Tom Sawyer was there, I knowed he would take an interest in this kind of business, and throw in the fancy touches. Nobody could spread himself like Tom Sawyer in such a thing as that. (p. 31)

Obviously Huck underrates his own skill. He throws in "fancy touches" enough; in fact, he loses sight of where fun ends and serious business begins, much as he has before under Tom's guidance. This sham murder is no game (somebody must be accused of it, and that somebody turns out to be Jim); but Huck, delighting in the make-believe, is blind to any consequences beyond the moment. Too fond of simulated mayhem, too unwary of the differences between play-violence and the real thing (much as young Sam Clemens was, as Twain portrays him in "The Private History of a Campaign that Failed"), Huck is ready for the first major scare of his river trip, his encounter with a real murder scene, in all its mad clutter and grim importance:

> There was heaps of old greasy cards scattered around over the floor, and old whiskey bottles, and a couple of masks made out of black cloth; and all over the walls was the ignorantest kind of words and pictures, made with charcoal. There was two old dirty calico dresses, and a sun-bonnet, and some women's under-clothes, hanging against the wall, and some men's clothing, too. We put the lot into the canoe; it might come good. There was a boy's old speckled straw hat on the floor; I took that too. And there was a bottle that had had milk in it and it had a rag stopper for a baby to suck. We would a took the bottle, but it was broke. (p. 45)

This matter of a real crime is both the first and the last lesson in the novel, for Huck does not know that the victim is Pap until Jim tells him so in the book's closing sentences. That is as it should be, for when he discovers the murder, Huck has not rid himself of his father, just as Huck has not rid himself of Tom. All the lessons about play and moral consequences have yet to be learned.

Huck learns those lessons slowly and painfully. In that section of the novel which Mark Twain finished before pigeonholing it in 1876, Huck is trying to be the impish gamester, modeling himself on Tom; but by the end of those sixteen chapters he has been cured of his heartless games and his practical jokes, or at least those which he starts himself. This part of the river journey, in fact, is a parade of bad jokes and ill-timed games of make-believe, each of which backfires on the playful Huck. Shortly after the episode of the murder scene, Huck hides a dead snake in Jim's blanket, hoping for "some fun when Jim found him there" (p. 46). Huck gets his fun: bitten by the live snake drawn to the body of the dead one, Jim suffers for four days. But when Jim recovers, so does Huck's misguided play-impulse. The next drifting wreck that happens along induces him to invoke Tom Sawyer again as a kind of patron genius of festivity, and to make ready for another ill-timed bit of child's play:

> "Stick a candle in your pocket; I can't rest, Jim, till we give her a rummaging. Do you reckon Tom Sawyer would ever go by this thing? Not for pie, he wouldn't. He'd call it an adventure—that's what he'd call it; and he'd land on that wreck if it was his last act. And wouldn't he throw style into it?—wouldn't he spread himself, or nothing? Why, you'd think it was Christopher C'lumbus discovering Kingdom-Come. I wish Tom Sawyer *was* here." (p. 57)

Once again Huck finds more than he wants to. There is no "respectable" gang of Tom Sawyer robbers on the *Walter Scott* (the name calls up Tom's own patron god of make-believe). There are only real robbers, resembling playful children only in their ignorance of the danger towards which they drift. By the time Jim leads Huck out of these amusements which Jim had begged to pass by, there is only one prank left in the boy. And when that practical joke is played, its failure brings Huck to the crisis moment in the novel, the experience which changes him most profoundly. When Jim knows the truth, that Huck has played games with human affections, Jim speaks with such dignity and sensitivity that he, Jim, by himself, guides Huck around the turning point of the boy's moral development. Huck's later decision to help Jim in his escape is born here, born hard in that silent quarter of an hour in which the boy learns the lesson of the black man's humanity.

> It was fifteen minutes before I could work myself up to go and humble myself to a nigger—but I done it, and I warn't ever sorry for it afterwards, neither. I didn't do him no more mean tricks, and I wouldn't done that one if I'd a knowed it would make him feel that way. (p. 72)

Everything depends on this moment of awakening, which is brought about by one more little game that has gone too far. After the incident, Huck has not only given up "mean tricks" of the Tom Sawyer style, he is done with his gamester's loneliness. He has given up the solitude of the player's world for the companionship of a real one. The end of the novel's first section is the end of Huck's adventures *as* a lonely Tom, and the beginning of his adventures in another's company, moving through a world of grown-ups who refuse to learn the lesson that the child already knows.

This is the essence of the grotesque in the world of Huck, that it is a world peopled with overgrown Toms, a world in which selfishness, murder and cruelty masquerade as games, as "fun," as child's play, as harmless practical joking. The Shepherdsons and the Grangerfords, whom he meets next, are not everyday bushwhackers; what pains us most about them is that they pretend their feud is a manly sport, something to teach like baseball to young children.[10] The feud has plenty of resemblances to a proper game: it has no purpose other than its own perpetuation; it has rules; it runs on illusions; it moves along at a measured pace, with time outs, regular moves and countermoves, like a game of checkers. In fact, Buck Grangerford describes the feud much as Tom might introduce Huck to some new game. And Buck meets with the same kind of incredulous questioning that makes Huck a "sap-head" player in Tom's eyes:

> "Well," says Buck, "a feud is this way. A man has a quarrel with another man, and kills him; then that other man's brother kills *him*; then the other brothers, on both sides, goes for one another; then the *cousins* chip in—and by-and-by everybody's killed off, and there ain't no more feud. But it's kind of slow, and takes a long time."
>
> "Has this one been going on long, Buck?"
>
> "Well I should *reckon*! it started thirty years ago, or som'ers along there. There was trouble 'bout something and then a lawsuit to settle it; and the suit went agin one of the men, so he up and shot the man that won the suit—which he would naturally do, of course. Anbody would."
>
> "What was the trouble about, Buck?—land?"
>
> "I reckon maybe—I don't know."
>
> "Well, who done the shooting?—was it a Grangerford or a Shepherdson?"
>
> "Laws, how do *I* know? it was so long ago."
>
> "Don't anybody know?"
>
> "Oh, yes, pa knows, I reckon, and some of the other old folks; but they don't know, now, what the row was about in the first place." (p. 89)

The gamelike shape of this bloodbath is exactly what makes it comic and frightening at the same time. There are rules, but no one believes them; there are time outs, which only underscore the pointlessness of it all; there are illusions, but they are used to exploit and even to murder children. The latest casualty has in fact been a child: another boy, exactly Huck's age, has been assassinated—unarmed—on a public road by a grown man. But when Huck damns the murderer as a coward, Buck will hear none of it. The killers must tell themselves and their children that all of this is a fair fight, and that everyone respectably follows a code of honor. What more terrible, more ironic delusion can a world teach its children than that ambush and murder are honorable ways of settling anything? We know that something is rotten here from the start: all these guns and dogs turned out upon Huck, a hungry boy out of the river; and Buck, Huck's replica down to his name, dragging a gun himself, rubbing sleep from his eyes, and asking:

"Ain't they no Shepherdsons around?"
They said, no, 'twas a false alarm.
'Well," he says, "if they'd a ben some, I reckon I'd a got one."
They all laughed, and Bob says:
'Why, Buck, they might have scalped us all, you've been so slow in coming."
"Well, nobody come after me, and it ain't right. I'm always kep' down; I don't get no show." (p. 81)

Everything we hear about the feud makes it seem like a mockery of respectable sport. Buck ambushes another boy, Harney Shepherdson, and barely escapes with his life. He returns home to get a chiding for not stepping out "into the road" (p. 88), but Huck sees the father's pride that the son is blossoming into an effective assassin. The regular Sunday truce further stresses the difference between what these people profess and what they really do. The famous interlude in which the Shepherdsons and Grangerfords gather in the same church to hear about brotherhood and forgiveness (their guns on their knees, all the while) parodies a "time out" in an honest game. And parody gives way to holocaust, of course, as Huck's unarmed surrogate is gunned down from ambush, with his brother, by a gang of Shepherdsons, who will no doubt ride home to tell more tales of victory in a fair fight.

Huck drifts out of the world of the manly duelists, and into the hands of the confidence men, after a respite of only one half of one chapter. The Duke and the King, of course, are no more engaged in the game of pure, joyful impersonation than the Grangerfords are in a true game; further, there is no point arguing whether the con artist is by nature a corrupt gamester, an artist *manqué*, or anything else. The point is that these two intruders on the raft *begin*, in our company, as practical jokers, pretenders such as we have seen before in Tom. It is easy to forget that these two rogues earn our hatred over time. When no harm is done, when the trick is performed with style, for incidental profit, and with no real hardship to the victim, then it seems that the confidence "game" might be worthy of its name. We do not really worry about the moral issue of the impersonations at the camp meeting, at which the citizens of Pokeville, with their childish love for exotic stories, get what they pay for from the King, posing as a reformed pirate who has wandered in from the South Seas. And we feel no qualms about seeing Huck help them "sell" the crude, vengeful people of Bricksville, the next town down river. But our opinions change—as do Huck's—when the con "games" no longer show anything of real play in them, when sport and spectacle and a good joke give way to ruthless venality. That change takes place in the long episode with the Wilks family. To Huck and the reader now, the schemes grow intolerable, and the King has no luck excusing them as of no more consequence than a prank:

> "Why, how you talk!" says the king. "We shan't rob 'em of nothing at all but jest this money. The people that *buys* the property is the suff'rers; because as soon's it's found out 'at we didn't own it—which won't be long after we've slid—the sale won't be valid, and it'll all go back to the estate. These-yer orphans 'll git their house back agin, and that's enough for *them*; they're young and spry, and k'n easy earn a livin'. *They* ain't agoing to suffer. Why, jest think—there's thous'n's and thous'n's that ain't nigh so well off. Bless you, *they* ain't got noth'n to complain of." (p. 141)

Too late: Huck already knows the difference between practical jokes and villainous fraud. The con men have stopped the harmless "selling" of people and have begun selling them for real: they auction off the longtime servants of the family, and eventually they sell Jim, "for forty dirty dollars" (p. 168), to Silas Phelps. Huck has *almost* been led too far in confounding fraud with practical joking; but now he makes another moral decision, and he brings the career of the con men to an end.

Just how they end is important too, for in dealing out justice the outraged citizens of the shore show just how much they resemble the drifters whom they tar and feather. What makes the punishment so "awful cruel," as Huck terms it (p. 182), is the festivity with which it is carried out. These villains have pretended that orphan-robbing is a harmless joke; the punishment they are dealt makes a holiday out of torment. It is not a case of punishment to fit the crime. It is another suggestion of how much the evil in Huck's world consists of a failure to keep play separate from serious moral action, and how the specific villains Huck meets are at home in the world of similar villainy. That truth is never so clear as it is in Bricksville, a town where childishness and cruel, grotesque games are the established custom of everyday life.

It is common knowledge that the key incident in the Bricksville episode, the shooting of old Boggs by Colonel Sherburn, comes from an incident of Mark Twain's youth, the murder of Sam

Smarr by a merchant named Owsley, not far from the Clemens doorstep in Hannibal. But how perfectly is that episode translated into fiction, for by giving it the right context, Twain gives it meaning and shape. The setting: the town Huck comes to consists of nothing but faceless, overgrown boys—grown-up versions, really, of Pap, of the man Huck might have grown up to be. They mock a child's escapism with ill-tempered vagrancy, a child's curiosity with their listless sadism, a child's taste for noise and spectacle with their ghoulish voyeurism. We remember that Tom, on occasion, takes pleasure in tormenting dogs and poisoning cats (we recall the pinchbug incident and the disposal of the "painkiller" in *Tom Sawyer*), but Tom has nothing on Bricksville, where such cruelty is Main Street entertainment:

> You'd see a muddy sow and a litter of pigs come lazying along the street and whollop herself down in the way, where folks had to walk around her.... And pretty soon you'd hear a loafer sing out, "Hi! *so* boy! sick him, Tige!" and away the sow would go, squealing most horrible, with a dog or two swinging to each ear, and three of four dozen more a-coming; and then you would see all the loafers get up and watch the thing out of sight, and laugh at the fun and look grateful for the noise. Then they'd settle back again till there was a dog-fight. There cound't anything wake them up all over, and make them happy all over, like a dog-fight—unless it might be putting turpentine on a stray dog and setting fire to him, or tying a tin pan to his tail and see him run himself to death. (p. 114)

The fun-seekers like nothing so well as a visit from Boggs, whenever that harmless old drunk has lost himself in his own favorite, dangerous brand of fun.[11] When Boggs comes, he comes as Tom Sawyer the Black Avenger, the great marauder returned to terrorize the homefolk. But while the boy has sense enough to confine such make-believe to the private play-world of children, the man does his pretending in the middle of town. And everyone but Sherburn encourages him—in Bricksville the play world and the real world are always dangerously mingled.

All it takes to ruin a game, no matter how large, is one good spoilsport. Too late, a few of the townspeople recognize that at one o'clock somebody is going to start "playing" for real:

> The crowd looked mighty sober; nobody stirred, and there warn't no more laughing. Boggs rode off blackguarding Sherburn as loud as he could yell, all down the street; and pretty soon back he comes and stops before the store, still keeping it up. Some men crowded around him and tried to get him to shut up, but he wouldn't; they told him it would be one o'clock in about fifteen minutes,

and so he *must* go home—he must go right away. But it didn't do no good. (p. 115)

There is no saying just why Sherburn decides to take Boggs seriously this time, or why he murders the old man after Boggs has shut his mouth and tried to get away. Sherburn is inscrutable. He is an instrument of those consequences that await any grown-up in this novel who lets his make-believe go too far. The killing is yet another parody of a fair fight: in this case, a duel according to the Code of Honor. Sherburn cuts a fine figure as a duelist—if we forget that Boggs is unarmed and begging for his life:

He was standing perfectly still, in the street, and had a pistol raised in his right hand—not aiming it, but holding it out with the barrel tilted up towards the sky.... Boggs and the men turned round, to see who called him, and when they see the pistol the men jumped to one side, and the pistol barrel come down slow and steady to a level—both barrels cocked. Boggs throws up both of his hands, and says, "O Lord, don't shoot!" Bang! goes the first shot, and he staggers back clawing at the air—bang! goes the second one, and he tumbles backwards onto the ground, heavy and solid, with his arms spread out. (p. 116)

Sherburn tosses the gun down in the street—a classic gesture of the duel, and at the same time a gesture of contempt for anyone who mistakes violence for a game, as Boggs has. Very soon after, armed with a shotgun, a weapon of indiscriminate violence, Sherburn repeats his lesson for a lynch mob, who have come ready for anything except the realty of what they say they intend to do.

For Bricksville learns nothing. Until it was too late, the villagers were blind to Boggs's danger; they are blind now to both the fact of the old man's death and the moral choice it brings. The murder itself, after a moment's shock, becomes one more municipal thrill:

The streets was full, and everybody was excited. Everybody that seen the shooting was telling how it happened, and there was a big crowd packed around each one of these fellows, stretching their necks and listening. One long lanky man, with long hair and a big white fur stove-pipe hat on the back of his head, and a crooked-handled cane, marked out the places on the ground where Boggs stood, and where Sherburn stood, and the people following him around from one place to t'other and watching everything he done, and bobbing their heads to show they understood, and stooping a little and resting their hands on their thighs to watch him mark the places on the ground with his cane; and then he stood up straight and still where Sherburn had stood, frowning and having his hat-brim down over his eyes, and sung out, "Boggs!" and then fetched his cane down slow to a level, and says "Bang!" staggered backwards, says "Bang!" again, and fell down flat on his back. The people that had seen the thing said he done it perfect; said it was just exactly the way it all happened. Then as much as a dozen people got out their bottles and treated him. (p. 117)

Having milked the fun out of the shooting, the townsfolk decide to play lynchmob. Really, there is no other way to describe what they do, for they have nothing of the vengeful resolve of a *real* mob. They impersonate the rage which they do *not* feel at the old man's murder. Everyone goes along for the same reason that Huck does, to see the spectacle of everybody else in violent action. And so, facing a hundred people now, Sherburn has no less advantage than he had facing just one man. He remains the classic spoilsport, facing down the fake mob simply by exposing them as pretenders, by ridiculing the difference between their make-believe and the ways of people brought together in deadly earnest:

"Your mistake is, that you didn't bring a man with you; that's one mistake, and the other is that you didn't come in the dark, and fetch your masks. You brought *part* of a man—Buck Harkness, there—and if you hadn't had him to start you, you'd a taken it out in blowing.

You didn't want to come. The average man don't like trouble and danger. *You* don't like trouble and danger. But if only *half* a man—like Buck Harkness, there—shouts "Lynch him, lynch him!' you're afraid to back down—afraid you'll be found out to be what you are—*cowards*—and so you raise a yell, and hang yourselves onto that half-a-man's coat tail, and come raging up here, swearing what big things you're going to do.... Now the thing for *you* to do, is to droop your tails and go home and crawl in a hole. If any real lynching's going to be done, it will be done in the dark, Southern fashion; and when they come they'll bring their masks, and fetch a man along." (p. 118-119)

Sherburn strikes home, and it is no wonder the crowd disperses. These townsmen are cowards, hiding in a comfortable, amoral playworld and refusing to recognize moral choices when they are faced with them. They are helpless to end their games where they should be ended, and to face the real urgencies when they must be faced. It is no wonder as well that Huck flees directly from this scene to a circus, for the Big Top nicely mirrors the permanent circus that Bricksville makes of life. Once more the boy finds a crowd of locals delighting in a cruel spectacle; this time, it is a Boggs-like drunkard, helpless (Huck thinks) on a strong wild horse. It turns out of course that everyone has been "sold" by this neat piece of acrobatics; but as we might expect, only Huck has learned to worry about drunks in trouble, to tell serious business from "fun," and to feel human compassion when it ought to be felt.

All of which brings us to the problem of the last thirteen chapters of the novel, which support a critical industry all by themselves. Many readers continue to sympathize, more or less, with Hemingway's always-quoted charge that Twain was "cheating" in his ending for the book.[12] Others accept, more or less, this or that ingenious argument for the coherence of the Phelps Farm episode with the rest of the novel. The case I am making here leads me to what might seem a paradoxical point of view. The book's Phelps Farm chapters do reflect and fulfill the pattern I have been tracing; but it is one thing to say so, and another to hold that these chapters work as they should. They go on and on, working to death a very few ideas, and there is no apologizing for that. But the charge that Twain is betraying Huck as a character is more serious, and needs to be answered.

Huck's passivity in these closing chapters, his reversion into Tom's helper and sidekick as Tom invents cruel games at Jim's expense, ought to trouble us. Tom, after all, is doing exactly what everybody else on the river has done: he is making a game out of a moral matter, and bringing into it not only a helpless slave but also some unwitting outsiders who can and will shoot real guns at these make-believe conspirators. But we must bear in mind that Huck's moral silence is the puzzlement of a child facing the most puzzling lesson of any in the book: that the games of his only playmate, his only child-friend, are as heartless, foolish and dangerous as the games of the grown-ups. The corrupt adult game is more grotesque and much easier for the child to recognize as monstrous than the bad games of another child: the childish man is always a more alien and repulsive thing than the childish boy. Huck can see through the corrupt games of the adults—but Tom he has always respected as the master of revels in the *child* world. Huck has always mistaken Tom's secondhand imaginings for true make-believe; he has always deferred to Tom, when it has come to games, and has always taken his judgments on play as law. The lessons he has endured on the river have all been lessons in the bad ways of the *adult* gamester, and it should not surprise us that he retreats now from that world of adult corruptions and consequences back into what he believes are the real games of children, overseen by the one child that he respects and trusts. It is one more powerful irony that Huck should put his faith in Tom at the last, that there are still serious limits to what he knows of right and wrong, that he is still fourteen years old and not the absolutely mature man that we might want him to be. Were Mark Twain to make him so, that would be "cheating" indeed. Huck has come as far on his moral journey as a plausible boy of that time could, he has come as far as the lessons about corrupt *adult* play will carry him. The book would certainly be tidier if Huck's boyishness were utterly gone at the end, and if he had learned the most subtle lessons about play and moral consequences—but Mark Twain did not sacrifice his best character for the sake of tidiness, and we should be thankful for that. The last third of the novel is too anti-climactic and too long to please, but in allowing Huck to flee back into the world of children, Twain keeps faith with Huck and with the essential theme of the novel as well.

To locate a theme is not necessarily to bring anyone closer to explaining a novel's power; but as it happens, knowing how play works in *Huckleberry Finn* does have some real use. It helps us to understand better how the novel, free and vulgar and enduringly funny as it is, maintains that tragic edge which so many readers have sensed in it. Much has been said already about the tragic overtones of *Huckleberry Finn,* and there has been some argument about whether this or that formal rule of tragedy is satisfied by something in the novel. I do not hold that *Huckleberry Finn* is a tragedy in any formal sense; but the overtones we sense in it, the revelation behind all the laughter, deserves a moment of discussion. Most definitions of tragedy count as essential the defeat of good by something evil which comes from *within,* an internal corruption which twists and preys upon the very essence of the good until its doom is assured. If we read *Huckleberry Finn* as a book about the childlike and the childish, about play and games and their difficult commerce with the reality around them, we can go some distance in explaining to ourselves the strains we hear, our sense of a tragedy involving something less clear but much larger than Huck himself. There are whisperings all through the novel of the perishability and the betrayal of that spirit which was so much a part of Mark Twain's personality, a spirit which he wrote about all through his life, as the good—perhaps the *only* good—in human nature.

Huckleberry Finn is about many things, but it is certainly about the play-impulse and the corruption it undergoes in the world of the adult. In the years before Mark Twain found Huck, the genuine play of children and truly childlike grown-ups found its place at the heart of *The Innocents Abroad, Roughing It, Life on the Mississippi, Tom Sawyer*; now, in *Huckleberry Finn,* true play is repeatedly parodied and tainted by adult laziness, adult stupidity, adult greed, in a world where villainy hides behind a child's ways and apes a child's innocent amusements. In such a world, Huck and all true children with him seem to be shadowed by a doom as sure as the flight of time and the coming of maturity. Huck has slipped past the fate which his father embodied; but by the time he decides to "light out for the Territory ahead of the rest" (p. 229), he has seen enough to know that he will never be far ahead of the rest, that the Shepherdsons, Grangerfords, Dukes, Dauphins, and Tom Sawyers will always be right behind him. And we have seen enough to know that Huck, for all that he has learned in such a short time, about the play, sports, spectacles, and "mean tricks" of children and grown-ups, will have to light out ahead of himself as well, keep ahead of a future which promises to turn a child's indolent pleasures into a man's vices, a child's games into a man's crimes, a child's fantasies into the schemings of those "one-horse men" among whom Twain counted a grown-up Tom Sawyer. This is a humorous novel, a celebration of freedom, simplicity, and sheer fun; but it is at the same time a novel about a boy and a world endangered by their own love of make-believe, by the finest thing Mark Twain could turn up in himself and in his otherwise damned human race. There may be many paradoxes in *Huckleberry Finn,* but there are few indeed which do so much both to organize the novel *and* show us the heart of one magnificent, fun-loving, childlike, troubled writer.

Notes

1. Numerous examples of these tastes can be found in Albert B. Paine, *Mark Twain: A Biography,* 3 vols. (New York: Harper, 1912); Paul Fatout, *Mark Twain in Virginia City* (Bloomington: Indiana Univ. Press, 1964); and William Dean Howells, *My Mark Twain,* ed. Marilyn Baldwin (Baton Rouge: Louisiana State Univ. Press, 1967). Edward Wagenknecht nicely summarizes Twain's play ob-

session in *Mark Twain: The Man And His Work* (Norman: Univ. of Oklahoma Press, 1967), pp. 82-83.

2. For example,

> ...children's games are one sort—and a prefiguration—of the games that grown up children play: men, marvelous and miserable beings, unsuccessful toys, even when they take themselves terribly seriously. The game is not only one of the fundamental forces, one of the prefigurations. It pervades them all, it incorporates them: all "are in" the game of someone or something. Behind the masks no one and nothing is hidden, other than the game of the world. Moreover, play should not be set in opposition to serious and profitable activities. It lifts the veil that covers difference and indifference in regard to unity, to difference, and to indifference. The whole man is both player and toy no matter what he does. (Kostas Axelos, "Planetary Interlude," trans. Sally Hess, *Yale French Studies*, 41 [1968], pp. 6-7.)

3. Johan Huizinga, *Homo Ludens* (Boston: Beacon, 1955), p. 132; Roger Caillois, *Man, Play, And Games*, trans. Meyer Barash (New York: Glencoe, 1961), pp. 9-10.

4. Huizinga, pp. 11-12; Caillois, pp. 8-9.

5. Huizinga on Puerilism:

> ...it is always possible to come upon phenomena which, to a superficial eye, have all the appearance of play and might be taken for permenant play-tenedencies, but are, in point of fact, nothing of the sort. Modern social life is being dominated to an ever-increasing extent by a quality that has something in common with play and yields the illusion of a strongly developed play-factor. This quality I have ventured to call by the name of Puerilism, as being the most appropriate appellation for that blend of adolescence and barbarity which has been rampant all over the world for the last two or three decades. (p. 205)

6. *Mark Twain, The Fate of Humor* (Princeton: Princeton Univ. Press, 1966), pp. 167-184.

7. *The Writings of Mark Twain*, Author's National Edition (New York: Harper, 1899-1911), XVII, 71.

8. Harold Simonson refers rightly to these moments, when Huck falls under Tom's spell at the expense of Huck's own better nature, as moments of Huck's moral "death." ("*Huckleberry Finn* as Tragedy," *The Yale Review*, 59 [Summer 1970], 534.)

9. *The Adventures of Huckleberry Finn*, 2nd ed., ed. Sculley Bradley, Richmond C. Beatty, E. Hudson Long, and Thomas Cooley (New York: Norton, 1977), p. 18. Subsequent references to this edition appear parenthetically in the text.

10. The most thorough discussion of violent agonistic play (duels, jousts, regulated chivalric warfare, and the like) is in Huizinga, pp. 89-104. See also Ruskin's eloquent defense of honorable, regulated war as a form of true play. (*The Works of John Ruskin*, ed. E. T. Cook and Alexander Wedderburn [London: George Allen, 1905], XVIII, 465-474.)

11. Kenneth Lynn was among the first to observe that Bricksville's major vice is that it "regards suffering as a circus." (*Mark Twain and Southwest Humor* [Boston: Little, Brown, 1959], p. 237.)

12. Ernest Hemingway, *The Green Hills of Africa* (New York: Scribner's 1935), p. 22.

Law and Nature in the Adventures of Huckleberry Finn

Catherine H. Zuckert

No one would write an article "Why Huckleberry Finn Is Not the Great American Novel," unless there were a considerable body of opinion to the contrary.[1] Yet the reasons why Twain's masterpiece should be regarded as the most essentially, most distinctively American novel have not been made altogether clear. Following Ernest Hemingway, most critics have pointed to the careful replication of various American dialects Twain himself stresses in his introductory explanatory note. Until very recently they have regarded the novel itself as flawed; like Hemingway, they have tended to believe that one should stop reading before the sale of Jim.[2]

Although Lionel Trilling and George C. Carrington have pointed out the extraordinary literary or structural coherence of the novel, most readers still tend to see Huck's return to slave society merely as a sign of defeat or denial of his earlier, nobler aspiration to help Jim to freedom.[3] Even critics like James M. Cox and David F. Burg, who defend the unity of the novel on substantive or thematic rather than merely literary or organizational grounds, do so primarily in terms of Twain's bitter irony or incipient despair.[4] I wish to argue, on the contrary, that Twain's novel has thematic as much as literary unity, i.e., that Huck's return to society is a necessary, even logical conclusion of his attempt to find

From: *Proteus*, 1 (Fall 1984), 27–35. Reprinted with permission.

freedom in nature. This return constitutes as important a part of Twain's realism as his careful presentation of the various dialects, because, as he shows, it is not possible to attain freedom through flight.[5]

Obviously the runaway slave Jim cannot secure his freedom simply by floating down the Mississippi (into slave territory) or passively letting nature take its course. But even the white orphan Huck proves unable to maintain his independence from the force-based domination of adults when the "duke" and the "dauphin" board his raft. Huck has to return to civil society, Twain shows, because the force and fraud that characterize relations among men in "the state of nature" make it impossible to secure anyone's right to life, liberty, property, or the pursuit of happiness outside the protection of the law. Jim does acquire his freedom at the end of the novel, but he does so through the operation of two forces Huck despises—religion (in the form of Miss Watson's conscience) and law (in the form of her will). Although the conclusion of the *Adventures of Huckleberry Finn* is sober, it is not completely cynical or despairing.

The *Adventures of Huckleberry Finn* clearly depicts the "hero's" withdrawal from society to seek freedom living in nature and his subsequent return. James Fenimore Cooper first created this, the "classic" American "myth" or motif in his tales of the Leatherstocking; and the significance not only of Huck's escape but also of his return may initially be seen, by comparing Huck's adventures with those of his literary predecessor, Natty Bumppo. Twain effectively destroyed Cooper's reputation as "the American Scott" or "*the* American novelist" through his famous enumeration of Cooper's "literary offenses."[6] Cooper's first and worst fault, according to Twain, lies in the faulty organization of his tales, which do not, in Aristotelian terms, have a clear beginning, middle, and end. The *Adventures of Huckleberry Finn* clearly does: it begins with Huck's withdrawal from civil society on the banks of the river, has its center and climax during his trip down the Mississippi, and concludes back in civil society on the banks at the Phelps farm.

Twain also clearly corrects the inauthenticity and inconsistency he complains of in Cooper's dialogues and dialects as well as the physical impossibilities in the relations suggested among streams, woods, and houseboats (or rafts). Most important, however, Twain "corrects" Cooper's unrealistic portrayal of the relations among human beings in "the state of nature," as well as the lack of consistency, as it were, between Cooper's political thought and his literary practice. Twain's critique of Cooper in practice, as it were, is even more thoroughly devastating than his critique in theory.

Where Cooper himself preached the need for law and order, especially with respect to property rights, his hero Natty consistently brings the legitimacy of those self-same laws into question by fleeing the settlements.[7] In *Huck Finn*, on the other hand, the law as represented by Judge Thatcher and the Widow Douglas initially appears to be a source of protection, at least potentially, of both person and property. Huck even seeks to use the law to secure his "found inheritance" from the machinations of his natural father, but Pap manages to steal his son away from his legal guardian and so to place him outside legal protection. The problem with the law does not appear to be the constraint it places on individual freedom so much as its ineffectiveness; it is too weak, it seems, to protect people from violence at the hands of others. Indeed, Twain's account of Huck's adventures brings to the fore the many forces that tend to undermine the rule of law in America.

Like Natty, Huck is clearly a representative of natural sentiment. He is, as he presents himself at the beginning of his story, an untutored orphan who has grown up in the back-alleys with little or no parental supervision; and he likes his freedom of movement. When the Widow Douglas tries to adopt and educate him in both manners and morals, Huck finds her regular hours dismal, starched and ironed shirts uncomfortable, school a bore, and prayers and Bible lessons almost unbearable. He decides, he tells us on the very first page of his narrative, "to light out." Like Natty, Huck seeks freedom by escaping the external constraints society imposes on his freedom of movement and action. But unlike Natty, Huck also tells us, he almost immediately returns. Tom Sawyer tells Huck that he cannot join his gang unless he returns to the Widow's, so Huck goes back. His social desires are even stronger, it seems, than his dislike of physical restraint.[8] By depicting his "natural man" as a boy, Twain not only supplies a more realistic locus of untouched nature but also changes the substance. For both Cooper and Twain, the natural man is a great innocent, but in Twain, he is definitely not self-sufficient.

Where Natty attributes both his freedom and his religion to his solitary existence[9], Huck all by himself feels "so lonesome I most wished I was dead" (p. 5). Huck is thus overjoyed when Tom calls him down from his room to have some midnight adventures. And in chapter two, Twain presents us with a comic version of the great contrast between the two friends that will re-appear so "blackly" at the end. For example, Tom begins by wanting to tie up Jim in his sleep, i.e., to make him a prisoner, but Huck persuades him into merely tricking Jim into thinking that the witches took his hat. Tom displays his curious mixture of conventional morality/immorality when he insists on leaving a nickel to pay for the candles they take from Jim's table, and then goes on to organize a gang of "murderers and robbers." Tom is not so concerned about acting dishonestly, we see, as he is about acting basely. "We ain't burglars," Tom explains to his cohort. "That ain't no sort of style .... We stop stages and carriages on the road, with masks on, and kill the people and take their watches and money .... I've seen it in books; and so of course that's what we've got to do" (p. 10). Neither the legal nor the religious injunctions against killing and stealing have much weight for Tom, but he does clearly recognize the force of authority—in the form of the romantic novels he has read. Tom wishes to achieve the glory of the heroes for himself; above all, he wants to be envied for his daring exploits.

Tom may be a natural leader, but he does not prove able to keep his gang together; having fewer ambitions and less imagination, they finally quit.[12] As Huck reports:

> We played robber now and then about a month, and then I resigned. All the boys did. We hadn't robbed nobody, hadn't killed any people, but only just pretended .... So then I judged that all that stuff was only just one of Tom Sawyer's lies. I reckoned he believed in the A-rabs and the elephants, but as for me I think different. It had all the marks of a Sunday-school (pp. 16–17).

As opposed to Tom, Huck is something of a pragmatic empiricist. As he tests Miss Watson's claims about God's help to those who pray by trying for fish hooks, so he rejects Tom's claim that there were di'monds, A-rabs, and elephants at the Sunday-school picnic the boys invade and disrupt. He did not see any; and he doesn't see any "profit" in pretense.[10]

Yet Huck is never able to resist Tom's influence entirely. Even on the river, Huck insists on boarding and investigating the sinking steamboat because Tom Sawyer would have. "He'd call it an adventure ... and he'd land on that wreck if it was his last act" (p. 65). Huck misses the danger and excitement Tom's search for style introduces into the lives of his associates. Nature, as represented by Huck, is by no means immune to the influence of convention, so strongly represented by his "respectable" friend Tom. Indeed, Huck admits, the longer he stays at the Widow's, the less uncomfortable he finds "sivilization." When he leaves his foster home, in fact, he does not do so by his own volition. His natural father steals him not only in order to put a claim to his son's fortune but also in order to prevent his son from learning to read and so become superior to his father.

Nevertheless, Huck easily returns to the irregular hours and dirty clothes of his previously "uncivilized" life with Pap.[11] Only when he finds himself confined to the cabin for days at a stretch, does Huck begin to be unhappy. As Pap's trips to town grow longer and the drunken beatings on his return get worse, Huck becomes lonely and restless. Finally, he decides to arrange his own escape. Faking evidence of his own murder, so that others will not seek to follow him, Huck loads a canoe with supplies from the cabin and escapes to an uninhabited island in the middle of the river. There he meets and takes up with the runaway slave Jim.

Rather than flee the confinement of family ties, Jim has run away from fear of separation from his loved ones. Overhearing Miss Watson consider selling him down river, Jim decides to escape, to find his way up the Ohio to a free state, to earn enough money to buy back his wife and children, and so to reunite them.[12]

Despite their somewhat different views of society, both Huck and Jim are glad to find company. Life in nature, it turns out, is not altogether pleasant. In the first place, the two friends cannot feed themselves without the assistance of civilization—the equipment in the form of the gun, fish hooks, and frying pan Huck has brought with him, the cornmeal and bacon Huck buys from the settlements, to say nothing of the melons and chickens he occasionally "borrows." Nature alone does not really support human life. Indeed, life in nature proves to be rather dangerous. There are rattlesnakes as well as strawberries on the island; and the two friends quickly learn that they have to keep moving. They have to leave the island and raft down the river, if they want to keep free of the control of other men.

Nature, as Twain paints it, is not kind. Jim's hopes of reaching liberty are first frustrated when separated in a fog the two friends float past Cairo. Flight from society to nature does not secure freedom, Twain shows, because human beings both desire and need to associate with each other in reaching their goals. Jim has no hope of obtaining freedom without Huck's assistance, and Huck wants company.

To be satisfying, moreover, that company has to be animated by mutual concern for the other's welfare. Huck first experiences the price of trying to prove his superiority by playing a Tom-like "joke" on Jim on Jackson's Island, when the mate of the dead snake Huck puts in Jim's bed joins its dead companion and its bite almost kills Huck's friend. Twain drives the point home, however, when Jim's expression of relief at finding Huck safe and alive after their separation in the fog shames Huck out of pretending he was on the raft with Jim all the time.

"It was fifteen minutes before I could work myself up to go and humble myself to a nigger; but I don it, and I warn't ever sorry for it afterward, neither. I didn't do him no' more mean tricks, and I wouldn't donehat one if i'd 'a' knowed it would make him feel that way" (p. 84).

Huck's feelings enable him to overcome conventional differences. They show that there is a natural basis for human society not only in mutual interest but also in mutual respect. Unfortunately, human beings often fail to recognize their common species as often as their common interest. As the conversation Huck and Jim have right before they are separated in the fog reveals, human beings often confuse nature and convention.[13]

Believing that human beings are all basically the same, Jim is amazed to learn that Frenchmen do not speak the same way he does, indeed, that he could not understand them at all. "Lookey here, Jim," Huck responds, "does a cat talk like we do? . . . Does a cow? . . . It's natural and right for them to talk different from each other, ain't it?" "Course," says Jim, but "is a cat a man, Huck?" Jim does not understand the way convention intervenes in the communication of feeling and meaning from one man to another. He thinks that men are basically all the same, related to one another, members of one big family. Huck, on the other hand, does not recognize the difference between conventional and natural distinctions. Where Jim sees only nature, Huck sees only convention.[14]

Twain brings the opposition between nature and convention to a climax shortly thereafter, when, discovering that he and Jim have floated past Cairo, Huck confronts the slave hunters. Torn between his "conscience" and his pleasure, Huck chooses the latter and lies in order to save Jim.

They went off and I got aboard the raft, feeling bad and low, because I knowed very well I had done wrong, and I see it warn't no use for me to try to learn to do right; . . . Then I thought a minute, and says to myself, hold on; s'pose you'd 'a' done right and give Jim up, would you felt better? . . . No, says I. . . . Well, then, . . . what's the use you learning to do right when it's troublesome to do right and ain't no trouble to do wrong and the wages is just the same?" (p. 89).

At the same time, Twain also brings out the difference between Huck's self-understanding and the reader's reaction to the narrator. Where Huck believes he has acted wrongly, we admire his nobility.[15] But how, we ought to ask, can such good natural sentiments be overtaken by evil and unnatural conventions like slavery? Twain provides an answer in Huck's subsequent "adventures."

Understanding humanity as one big family, Jim fails to see the way in which generational or family differences can create divisions among men. But, Twain ironically reminds us, both slavery and aristocracy are justified by claims about differences of birth, generation, and family. The family is a form of natural association, but the family can become tyrannical, as in Pap's treatment of Huck, or a source of warfare, as Twain subsequently shows in the Grangerford-Shepherdson feud. Natural attachments alone do not produce peace and harmony, because these same attachments lead men to prefer their own to the rights of others. The Grangerford-Shepherdson feud begins when the losing party in a court case refuses to accept the verdict, and his family backs him up. Men have to recognize a common authority, if they are to live in peace. The family itself has a legal foundation, Twain reminds his readers, by leaving only two survivors of the feud—Harley and Sophia who run off *to get married*. Jim's own family is sundered precisely because the law gives him and his no protection.[16]

But if Jim does not understand the way nature must be supplemented by convention, Huck does not understand the way in which nature can be used to question the legitimacy of unjust laws. When Jim objects to King Solomon's proposal to cut the baby in halves and divide them between the two women who claim to be the baby's mother, Huck ironically retorts that Jim does not see the "pint." The point, of course, is that Soloman tests the truth of the claims through an appeal to natural feelings. Yet we see throughout Twain's tale that Huck himself never recognizes how his own feelings and personal attachments may be used to test the truth of others' claims. Whatever Miss Watson and others, preeminently Tom Sawyer, tell him is right, Huck thinks, *is* right, respectable and religious.

Huck acts on the basis of his feelings, but when his own feelings or experience contradict socially approved norms, Huck simply concludes that he and his are bad. As a result, Huck never learns from his experience. Although he himself implicitly recognizes Jim's status as a fellow human being when he swallows his pride and apologizes to a "nigger," Huck continues to regard Jim as rightfully Miss Watson's property and himself as wrong to assist the slave to freedom. At the end of his "adventures," moreover, Huck is determined to light out again for the territories, where he surely will encounter more force and fraud.

As a natural man, Huck lacks self-consciousness. He does not recognize his own goodness, because recognition of the goodness of nature comes only in contrast to the pretensions of society. The contrast is evident to the reader, however. Huck's natural sociability repeatedly brings him into contact with other men on the banks of the river, and these "adventures" reveal both the goodness and the limitations of natural sentiment or compassion that Huck represents.

After Huck withdraws from the protection of the law, he repeatedly finds it necessary to appeal to the compassion of the inhabitants of the river banks. But as Huck's conversations, first with the ferryman and later with the slave hunters reveal, men have compassion only when they have no reason to fear for themselves. Compassion is counteracted, in fact, both by fear and by greed. It is also limited by convention. Human beings feel compassion only for creatures they believe are fundamentally like them. In the South, "niggers" do not count. Even Huck, when he arrives at the Phelps farm in the guise of Tom Sawyer, reports that no one was hurt in the supposed ferry crash. It only "killed a nigger" (p. 213), he says. Although Aunt Sally is kind, she does not demur.[17]

Compassion in itself does not discriminate sufficiently among its beneficiaries. Huck's plan to paddle Jim back up the river to Cairo and freedom is stymied when he takes two other fugitives from the law aboard the canoe and the raft. (Huck helps them because he regards all fugitives from the law, like Jim, to be his fellows.) As a result, we see, compassion alone proves wholly inadequate to protect the weak and vulnerable from the rapacity of the strong.

Even though Huck has no illusions about the fraudulent character of his new guests' claims to be a "duke" and even the lost French "dauphin," he acquiesces in their pretensions and allows them to rule on the raft. "If they wanted us to call them kings and dukes," Huck explains, "I hadn't no objections, 'long as it would keep peace in the family." Clearly Huck has no notion of the real basis of family life or natural association; how could he, having had a father like Pap? "If I never learnt nothing else out of Pap," Huck continues to reflect, "I learnt that the best way to get along with his kind of people is to let them have their own way" (p. 121). An isolated individual has little defense against the rule of force and fraud.

Utterly lacking concern for his own image in the eyes of others, Huck also fails to appreciate the character and dangerous consequences of the desire for distinction. He regards the fraudulent claims of the Duke and the Dauphin as harmless play-acting à la Tom Sawyer. Yet, as Twain shows, this desire for distinction is the source of the conventions that limit, if they do not altogether destroy compassion. The desire to be recognized as better than others leads people to forget or even deny their common humanity. Poor as he is, Pap curses the government that will let "niggers" vote and decides not to participate himself. The "aristocratic" Grangerfords show no mercy for their enemies the Shepherdsons. The "king" proves as willing to defraud the boy who has helped him as he is to steal from any other stranger. Most dramatically, at the end of the story, Tom Sawyer allows Jim to suffer unnecessarily; indeed, Tom wants to perpetuate Jim's incarceration indefinitely in order to gratify his own desire to perform glorious deeds after the fashion of the princely heroes of the novels he has read and to pass on the same opportunity to his sons.[18] Letting such people act out their desire for distinction simply serves to deceive and harm others.

Fearful that the "duke" or "dauphin" will turn Jim in for the reward, Huck feels powerless to resist. "It wouldn't 'a' done no good," he concludes, "and, besides, it was just as I said: you couldn't tell them from the real kind" (p. 150). Living outside the law himself, Huck cannot appeal to its protection. Moreover, he does not see the difference between law and force. Understanding freedom solely as the absence of externally imposed restraint, Huck is unable to distinguish legitimate from illegitimate rule.

Twain shows the ugly results of the open substitution of violence for legal justice in the dirty Arkansas town the party next visits. After a harmless old drunk accuses him of swindling, Colonel Sherburn shoots him down in the street in cold blood. When a mob gathers at his doorstep, Sherburn defies them to lynch him in broad daylight. There is no real "man" among you, he taunts, as the crowd gradually withdraws. Blacks are not the only people read out of the race, so to speak, in the South. Where violence rules, humanity appears to be mere weakness. "Men," as Sherburn understands them, enforce their will on others and so prove their right to rule. They are the true masters.[19] Perceiving their vulnerability as individuals, the others act only anonymously, masked, in a crowd, at night. As Sherburn points out, legal order dissolves. "Why don't you juries hang murderers," he asks and then answers, "because they're afraid the man's friends will shoot them in the back, in the dark—and that's just what they would do" (p. 141). There is no rule of law in the American South that Twain depicts, because the people themselves are not willing to obey it. They are in this respect just like Huckleberry Finn.

When the "duke" and "dauphin" swindle the inhabitants of this town with a brief, somewhat obscene performance of the None-such, no one in the audience suggets taking them to court. Rather, in order to protect their own reputations, the men in the audience decide to help the frauds take in the whole town, in order to take action against them later with rotten eggs and tomatoes as a mob. These people do not like conventional constraints any more than Huck does; they attend the performance in droves only after the "duke" adds one line to the advertisement: no women and children allowed. Huck's desire to escape the confines of law and morality is all-too-common, but in adults, it does not look quite so innocent.[20] In fact, it is not.

When the "duke" and "dauphin" next attempt to impersonate Peter Wilks's British brother and nephew in order to inherit the estate, we see how grief and compassion lead people to deceive themselves, almost willfully. An old friend of the Wilks' family and citizen of the town shouts out that the two imposters are frauds; the "king" has been giving the worst imitation of a British accent the doctor has ever heard. Both the daughters and townsmen want to believe the strangers, however. Only when the real relatives arrive and there is a lawyer-led investigation of the claims of both parties does the truth come out.

All of Huck's "adventures" on the banks of the river—his experience with the family feud, mob justice, the contest over the Wilks' will, and the final abortive attempt to free Jim—show that law is the only effective way to settle conflicts and end disputes. Yet in all four instances, we also see the law being undermined by a kind of natural aversion, represented by Huck, to any externally imposed restraints on the passions.

After the "duke" and the "dauphin" lose all their money in the attempt to defraud the Wilks' daughters, they turn Jim in for part of the reward. Torn between his "conscience," which prompts Huck to write Miss Watson a letter informing her of the location of her runaway nigger and his attachment to his friend, which leads him finally to tear up the letter, Huck resolved to be "damned" and to steal Jim in order to free him. Huck cannot believe his good fortune when the woman at the Phelps farm where they are holding Jim greets him by the name of "Tom Sawyer." What easier disguise for Huck to assume! He is even more amazed when the eminently respectable Tom agrees upon arrival to help him free a slave. It looks as if Huck's adventures will have a happy ending, after all. Because the Phelps are so trusting and kind, Jim is not very well chained or guarded. He will be very easy to steal.

Tom insists on creating difficulties, however, because he wants to engage in daring exploits. They have to steal sheets from Aunt Sally, make a rope ladder, and sneak it in to Jim, because prisoners always use such, even though he is being kept in a one-story cabin. Likewise Tom insists that Jim scratch out messages copied from several prisoners in stories on his plates and throw them out of the window. Huck draws a line when Tom suggests that Jim ought to saw off his own leg rather than lifting the bed and taking the leg-iron with him, and Jim refuses to keep rattlesnakes, as Tom suggests, as well as rats in his cell. Tom, nevertheless, succeeds in making the prisoner's escape truly dangerous, when he writes two anonymous notes warning the Phelps family that a band of brigands is coming to steal their runaway slave. The neighbors form a posse, and Tom gets a bullet in his leg as they flee. After the wound becomes infected, Tom falls unconscious, Jim insists that Huck go back to town for a doctor while the slave stays to tend the sick boy rather than run for his freedom as Huck suggests. Only when Tom regains consciousness in the midst of his family does he reveal the news he brought with him: Miss Watson has already freed Jim in her will!

Although Huck grieves for the pain and worry they caused Aunt Sally, Tom never expresses regret. He will continue to play prince and robber; he glories in the worried consternation his "daring" has provoked. At first glance, Huck and Tom thus appear to be almost totally opposite. Huck cares nothing for his reputation where Tom seeks glory. Huck is unconventional and pragmatic, where Tom seeks to follow his literary authorities in designing his exploits. Most fundamental, Huck seeks to free a friend, where Tom would keep a free man in jail indefinitely for the sake of his own and his children's amusement. Yet, at bottom, Huck and Tom represent the same very dangerous American tendency, the tendency to equate happiness and freedom with existence outside the law. There is a reason, after all, why they are such good friends. They have something important, but also very dangerous in common.

In the *Adventures of Huckleberry Finn*, Twain shows that there is no freedom without law and that the law has to rest on consent. Idealization of the return to nature and a confused vision of an aristocratic past undermine the respect for both men and their laws on which democracy depends. Unfortunately, most critics have not perceived the way in which the "black humor" at the end draws out the meaning of the entire plot.

Such critics have, it seems, remained too much within the spell of Huck's first person narrative; and Huck himself never learns. Twain separates himself from his narrator at the very beginning of the novel, however, by prefacing the story with both a "notice" and "explanatory" by "the author." Huck begins his own tale by noting the distinction between himself and "Mr. Mark Twain." And the story works gradually to separate the consciousness of the reader from the consciousness of the narrator. We see not only that Huck is good but also that he is young, weak, and vulnerable. Neither compassion nor family offer sufficient protection against greed and the desire for dominion. As Huck and Jim experience it, life in nature, outside the law, is dominated by force and fraud. As Huck should have learned at the Wilks, law is the only effective way to protect the innocent from the rapacious. But, Twain's story also shows, law alone will not suffice.

Laws are not always just, and men do not always obey them. To be just, the law must be based on a recognition of the natural equality of all human beings, the natural equality so dramatically realized in the friendship of Huck and Jim.[22] Unfortunately, Twain also shows, there are natural forces which work to undermine both the recognition of that natural equality and the laws based upon it.

Both the desire for distinction, which Tom embodies, and the desire for ease or the absence of external restraints, which characterizes Huck, undermine respect for the rights of others upon which republican government depends. The institution of slavery provides the most dramatic example of the problem, because it reminds us how convention, mixed with greed and the desire for distinction can lead some human beings to deny the very humanity of others. As the Sherburn incident at Bricksville shows, however, slavery is but one example of man's inhumanity to man.

At one level, Twain's novel would thus appear to reaffirm the "self-evident" truths proclaimed in the American Declaration of Independence. First and foremost, that all men are created equal. Jim's concern for the integrity of his family, his willingness to risk life and limb to live as a free man, and his devotion to his young white friends all demonstrate that the black slave is the equal, if not the better of any white depicted in the narrative. Slavery is clearly based on force and convention, contrary to nature, just plain wrong. All men may be endowed by their Creator with certain inalienable rights, the Declaration further teaches, but to secure those rights, they have to establish governments. Neither Jim nor Huck (nor the Wilks' heirs nor anyone else in the novel) can secure either life or property from the designs of others except through the agency of law. When these laws fail to secure life and liberty, men like Jim have a right "to alter and abolish them," i.e., to rebel. The rule of law is important, but uninformed by a sense of the natural goodness of human life Huck represents so powerfully, that law will be unjust.

On a second level, however, Twain clearly doubts that human beings like Huck will ever learn. In the *Adventures of Huckleberry Finn* he not only reminds us through Jim's enslavement that Americans have not lived up to their professed political principles, but he also indicates the reasons or causes of their failures. Their natural desires to be free of all external constraints or to be recognized as better than others are just too strong.

Twain's skepticism about the potential educability of human beings makes him explicitly anti-didactic. The prefatory "notice ... by order of the author, per G.G., Chief of Ordinance," announces:

> Persons attempting to find a motive in this narrative will be prosecuted; persons attempting to find a moral in it will be banished; persons attempting to find a plot in it will be shot.

The notice is obviously ironic, however; if nothing else, the *Adventures of Huckleberry Finn* has a clear story-line or "plot." We have seen, moreover, how ineffective Twain thinks "ordinances" can be. He perhaps puts his point more plainly in his *Autobiography*: "Humor must not professedly teach or professedly preach, but it must do both if it is to live forever."[23] Where Cooper had Natty somewhat awkwardly preach sermons on the glories of God's Creation, Twain lets his naive narrator reveal both the goodness and the failings of human nature without explicit commentary. The lesson is in the plot for the reader to see, if he will.

Notes

1. William O'Connor, "Why *Huckleberry Finn* is not the Great American Novel," *College English*, XVIII (October 1955), 6–10.

2. Philip Young, *Ernest Hemingway* (New York, 1952), pp. 181–212. Andrew Lang and Newton Arvin, *Mark Twain: Selected Criticism*, Arthur L. Scott, ed. (Dallas, 1955), pp. 40, 233, for early examples; Dixon Wecter, "Mark Twain," *Literary History of the United States*, ed. Robert Spiller, et al. (New York, 1948), II, p. 933, and Bernard De Voto, *Mark Twain in Eruption* (New York, 1968), p. 77; Leo Marx, "Mr. Eliot, Mr. Trilling, and *Huckleberry Finn*," *The American Scholar*, 22, No. 4 (Autumn 1953).

3. Lionel Trilling, "Huckleberry Finn," in *The Liberal Imagination* (New York, 1950), pp. 104–17, and George C. Carrington, *The Dramatic Unity of Huckleberry Finn* (Columbus, Ohio, 1976), pp. 153–59.

4. James M. Cox, *Mark Twain: The Fate of Humor* (Princeton, 1966), p. 178 f., and David F. Burg, "Another View of *Huckleberry Finn*," *Nineteenth Century Fiction*, 29, (December 1974), pp. 299–319.

5. The search for freedom theme is widely stressed in Twain scholarship. Henry Nash Smith, "A Sound Heart and a Deformed Conscience," in *Mark Twain: A Collection of Critical Essays* (Englewood Cliffs, NJ, 1963), pp. 84–86, emphasizes the necessary futility of the attempt as opposed to Leo Marx, *op. cit.;* Edgar M. Branch, *The Literary Apprenticeship of Mark Twain* (Urbana, Illinois, 1950), pp. 199–216; and Gladys Carmen Bellamy, *Mark Twain as Literary Artist* (Norman, Oklahoma, 1950), pp. 341–42, who all celebrate the flight to freedom.

6. Mark Twain, "Fenimore Cooper's Literary Offenses," *North American Review*, CCCCLXIV (July 1895), 1–12. Perry Miller. *Nature's Nation* (Cambridge, 1967, p. 282, points out the implicit criticism of Cooper in *Huck Finn*.

7. The "classic" commentator on Cooper's contradictory mind is Vernon Louis Parrington, *Main Currents in American Thought* (New York, 1927). II, pp. 214–16, 229. See *The Pioneers* for Natty as an opponent of the law of property; *The American Democrat* and *The Littlepage Trilogy* for Cooper's defense of property.

8. Campbell Tatum, "Dismal and Lonesome: A New Look at *Huckleberry Finn*," *Modern Fiction Studies*, 14 (Spring 1968), 47–55, goes too far when he suggests that

Huck's lonesomeness is "pathological." There is a long-standing tradition, stemming from Aristotle, which regards human beings as inherently and naturally social. By showing that Huck strongly desires the society of others, Twain provides a motive, somewhat lacking in Cooper, for his hero's befriending a man of another race in the generally lonesome state of nature.

9. James Fenimore Cooper, *The Prairie* (New York, 1964), p. 260.

10. Huck's skepticism about religion would also appear to make him more authentically natural than Natty. Surely religion is a social phenomenon. William R. Manierre, "Huck Finn, Empiricist Member of Society," *Modern Fiction Studies*, 14 (Spring 1968), 57–66, emphasizes the way Huck tests the claims of both society and religion in the early chapters.

11. Martha Banta, "Escape and Entry in *Huckleberry Finn, Modern Fiction Studies*, 14 (Spring 1968), 79–80, points out Huck's attachment to his ease and comfort. This is the "freedom" Huck, as opposed to Twain's readers, seeks.

12. When they argue that Miss Watson's change of heart at the end of the novel is incredible, neither H.N. Smith nor Leo Marx, *op. cit.*, pays attention to the fact that Jim runs before Miss Watson has entirely made up her mind. He tells Huck that "I here old missus tell de widder whe gwyne to seel me down to Orleans, *but she didn' want to*, but she could git eight hund'd dollars for me, en it wuz sich a big stack o' money she couldn' resis! De widder she try to git her to say she couldn't do it, but *I never waited to hear de res!* I lit out might quick . . . " (p. 43, emphasis added). Miss Watson's Christian morals, rigid and strict as we know from Huck, stand against materialism. We do not know that she actually decided to sell Jim over her sister's opposition. In any case, she definitely had an attack of conscience. Textual citations to the *Adventures of Huckleberry Finn* (New York, 1965).

13. Walter Blair, *Mark Twain and Huck Finn* (Berkeley, 1960), pp. 348–49, and William O'Connor, *op. cit.*, pp. 6–10).

14. See Jane Johnson Benardette, "Huckleberry Finn and the Nature of Fiction." *Massachusetts Review*, 9 (Spring 1968), 210–22.

15. James M. Cox, *Mark Twain: The Fate of Humor* (Princeton, 1966), p. 170 f., points out that the humor of the novel depends upon the inversion of values. "Thus what for Huck is his worst action—refusing to turn Jim in to Miss Watson—is for the reader his best."

16. The significance of the broken family in *Huck Finn* has received a good deal of critical attention. Eric Solomon, "Huck Finn Once More," *College English*, 22 (December 1960), 172–178, argues that the novel acquires its unity from Huck's search for family. Unfortunately for this argument, Huck consistently resists attempts by the Widow, Pap, and Aunt Sally to "adopt" him. Kenneth S. Lynn, "Huck and Jim," *Yale Review*, XLVIII (Spring 1958), 422, argues that Huck finds a father in Jim. Unfortunately, Jim is more dependent on Huck than vice versa.

17. Cf. Carson Gibb, "The Best Authorities," *College English*, 22 (December 1960), 179, reprinted in Richard Lettis, *et al.*, *Huck Finn and His Critics* (New York, 1962), p. 431, on this passage: "[C]ustom brutalizes."

18. See Daniel Hoffman, *Form and Fable in American Fiction* (New York, 1965), pp. 328–29, and Judith Fetterlay, "Disenchantment: Tom Sawyer in Huckleberry Finn," *PMLA*, LXXXVII (January 1972), 73, for connections between the Duke and the Dauphin, on the one hand, and Tom Sawyer, on the other.

19. Alexandre Kojeve, *Introduction a la Lecture de Hegel* (Paris, 1947), pp. 9–34, for a pertinent analysis of the master-slave relation.

20. Twain's letter to W.D. Howells on the subject of a "grown-up" Tom Sawyer is often quoted: "If I went on, now and took him to manhood, he would just be like all the one-horse men in literature and the reader would conceive a hearty contempt for him. . . . "

21. Kenneth S. Lynn, "Welcome back from the raft, Huck honey!" *American Scholar*, XLVI (Summer 1977), 338–47, is correct in protesting the reading of the novel simply as a celebration of the rebellion against "civilization" or convention. The Widow Douglas is presented as a decent alternative, as Lynn argues. Lynn goes too far when he argues that Huck merely wishes to return to St. Petersburg in one of Tom's plays, however. Once Jim is free, Huck does not need or desire Tom's play-acting anymore than he did at the beginning of the story when he resigned from Tom Sawyer's gang.

22. As Leslie A. Fiedler, "Come Back to the Raft Ag'in, Huck Honey!" in *An End to Innocence* (Boston, 1955), p. 143, points out: "[I]t is the social fact, our overt behavior toward the Negro, that must be modified to accord with our laws and the, at least official, morality they objectify."

23. Mark Twain, *Autobiography*, ed. Charles Nieder (New York: Washington Square Press, 1961), p. 298.

Huck, Jim, and American Racial Discourse

David L. Smith

They [blacks] are at least as brave, and more adventuresome [compared to whites]. But this may perhaps proceed from a want of fore-thought, which prevents their seeing a danger till it be present. . . . They are more ardent after their female: but love seems with them to be more an eager desire, than a tender delicate mixture of sentiment and sensation. Their griefs are transient. Those numberless afflictions, which render it doubtful whether heaven has given life to us in mercy or in wrath, are less felt, and sooner forgotten with them. In general, their existence appears to participate more of sensation than reflection. To this must be ascribed their disposition to sleep when abstracted from their diversions, and unemployed in labor.

—Thomas Jefferson, *Notes on the State of Virginia* (187–88)

Almost any Euro-American intellectual of the nineteenth century could have written the preceding words. The notion of Negro inferiority was so deeply pervasive among those heirs of "The Enlightment" that the categories and even the vocabulary of Negro inferiority were formalized into a tedious, unmodulated litany. This uniformity increased rather than diminished during the course of the century. As Leon Litwack and others have shown, even the Abolitionists, who actively opposed slavery, frequently regarded blacks as inherently inferior. This helps to explain the widespread popularity of colonization schemes among Abolitionists and other liberals.[1] As for Jefferson, it is not surprising that he held such ideas, but it is impressive that he formulated

From: *Mark Twain Journal*, 22.2 (Fall 1984), 4–12. Reprinted with permission.

so clearly at the end of the eighteenth century what would become the dominant view of the Negro in the nineteenth century. In many ways, this Father of American Democracy—and quite possibly of five mulatto children—was a man of his time and ahead of his time.[2]

In July of 1876, exactly one century after the American Declaration of Independence, Mark Twain began writing *Adventures of Huckleberry Finn*: a novel which illustrates trenchantly the social limitations which American "civilization" imposes on individual freedom. The book takes special note of ways in which racism impinges upon the lives of Afro-Americans, even when they are legally "free." It is therefore ironic that *Huckleberry Finn* has often been attacked and even censored as a racist work. I would argue, on the contrary, that except for Melville's work, *Huckleberry Finn* is without peers among major Euro-American novels for its explicitly anti-racist stance.[3] Those who brand the book "racist" generally do so without having considered the specific form of racial discourse to which the novel responds. Furthermore, *Huckleberry Finn* offers much more than the typical liberal defenses of "human dignity" and protests against cruelty. Though it contains some such elements, it is more fundamentally a critique of those socially constituted fictions—most notably romanticism, religion, and the concept of "the Negro"—which serve to justify and to disguise selfish, cruel, and exploitative behavior.

When I speak of "racial discourse," I mean more than simply attitudes about "race" or conventions of talking about "race." Most importantly, I mean that "race" itself is a discursive formation, which delimits social relations on the basis of alleged physical differences.[4] "Race" is a strategy for relegating a segment of the population to a permanent inferior status. It functions by insisting that each "race" has specific, definitive, inherent behavioral tendencies and capacities, which distinguish it from other "races." Though scientifically specious, "race" has been powerfully effective as an ideology and as a form of social definition, which serves the interests of Euro-American hegemony. In America, race has been deployed against numerous groups, including Native Americans, Jews, Asians, and even—for brief periods—an assortment of European immigrants.

For obvious reasons, however, the primary emphasis historically has been on defining "the Negro" as a deviant from Euro-

American norms. "Race" in America means white supremacy and black inferiority[5]; and "the Negro," a socially constituted fiction, is a generalized, one-dimensional surrogate for the historical reality of Afro-American people. It is this reified fiction which Twain attacks in *Huckleberry Finn*.

Twain adopts a strategy of subversion in his attack on race. That is, he focuses on a number of commonplaces associated with "the Negro," and then he systematically dramatizes their inadequacy. He uses the term "nigger," and he shows Jim engaging in superstitious behavior. Yet he portrays Jim as a compassionate, shrewd, thoughtful, self-sacrificing and even wise man. Indeed, his portrayal of Jim contradicts every claim presented in Jefferson's description of "the Negro." Jim is cautious, he gives excellent advice, he suffers persistent anguish over separation from his wife and child, and he even sacrifices his own sleep in order that Huck may rest. Jim, in short, exhibits all the qualities that "the Negro" supposedly lacks. Twain's conclusions do more than merely subvert the justifications of slavery, which was already long since abolished. Twain began this book during the final disintegration of Reconstruction, and his satire on antebellum Southern bigotry is also an implicit response to the Negrophobic climate of the post-Reconstruction era (Berkove; Gollin; Egan, esp. 66–102). It is troubling, therefore, that so many readers have completely misunderstood Twain's subtle attack on racism.

Twain's use of the word "nigger" has provoked some readers to reject the novel. (See Hentoff). As one of the most offensive words in our vocabulary, "nigger" remains heavily shrouded in taboo. A careful assessment of this term within the context of American racial discourse, however, will allow us to understand the particular way in which the author uses it. If we attend closely to Twain's use of the word, we may find in it not just a trigger to outrage, but more importantly, a means of understanding the precise nature of American racism and Mark Twain's attack on it.

Most obviously, Twain uses "nigger" throughout the book as a synonym for "slave." There is ample evidence from other sources that this corresponds to one usage common during the Antebellum period. We first encounter it in reference to "Miss Watson's big nigger, named Jim" (Ch. 2). This usage, like the term "nigger stealer," clearly designates the "nigger" as a piece of property: a commodity, a slave. This passage also provides the only apparent textual justification for the common critical practice of labelling Jim, "Nigger Jim," as if "nigger" were a part of his proper name. This loathsome habit goes back at least as far as Albert Bigelow Paine's biography of Twain (1912). In any case, "nigger" in this sense connotes an inferior, even subhuman, creature, who is properly owned by and subservient to Euro-Americans.

Both Huck and Jim use the word in this sense. For example, when Huck fabricates his tale about the riverboat accident, the following exchange occurs between him and Aunt Sally:

> 'Good gracious! anybody hurt?'
> 'No'm. Killed a nigger.'
> 'Well, it's lucky, because sometimes people do get hurt' (Ch. 32).

Huck has never met Aunt Sally prior to this scene, and in spinning a lie which this stranger will find unobjectionable, he correctly assumes that the common notion of Negro subhumanity will be appropriate. Huck's off-hand remark is intended to exploit Aunt Sally's attitudes, not to express Huck's own. A nigger, Aunt Sally confirms, is not a person. Yet this exchange is hilarious, precisely because we know that Huck is playing upon her glib and conventional bigotry. We know that Huck's relationship to Jim has already invalidated for him such obtuse racial notions. The conception of the "nigger" is a socially constituted and sanctioned fiction, and it is just as false and as absurd as Huck's explicit fabrication, which Aunt Sally also swallows whole.

In fact, the exchange between Huck and Aunt Sally reveals a great deal about how racial discourse operates. Its function is to promulgate a conception of "the Negro" as a subhuman and expendable creature, who is by definition feeble-minded, immoral, lazy, and superstitious. One crucial purpose of this social fiction is to justify the abuse and exploitation of Afro-American people by substituting the essentialist fiction of "Negro-ism" for the actual character of individual Afro-Americans. Hence, in racial discourse every Afro-American becomes just another instance of "the Negro"—just another "nigger." Twain recognizes this invidious tendency of race-thinking, however, and he takes every opportunity to expose the mismatch between racial abstractions and real human beings.

For example, when Pap drunkenly inveighs against the free mulatto from Ohio, he is outraged by what appears to him as a crime against natural laws. (Ch. 6). In the first place, a "free nigger" is, for Pap, a contradiction in terms. Indeed, the man's clothes, his demeanor, his education, his profession, and even his silver-headed cane bespeak a social status normally achieved by only a small elite of white men. He is, in other words, a "nigger" who refuses to behave like a "nigger." Pap's ludicrous protestations discredit both himself and other believers in "the Negro," as many critics have noted. But it has not been sufficiently stressed that Pap's racial views correspond very closely to those of most of his white Southern contemporaries, in substance if not in manner of expression. Such views were held not only by poor whites but by all "right-thinking" Southerners, regardless of their social class. Indeed, not even the traumas of the Civil War would cure Southerners of this folly. Furthermore, Pap's indignation at the Negro's right to vote is precisely analogous to the Southern backlash against the enfranchisement of Afro-Americans during Reconstruction. Finally, Pap's comments are rather mild compared to the anti-Negro diatribes which were beginning to emerge among politicians even as Twain was writing *Huckleberry Finn*. He began writing this novel during the final days of Reconstruction, and it seems more than reasonable to assume that the shameful white supremacist bluster of that epoch—exemplified by Pap's tirade—informed Twain's critique of racism in *Huckleberry Finn*. (See Pettit, *Mark Twain and the South*, 35–50).

Pap's final description of this Ohio gentleman as "a prowling, thieving, infernal, white-shirted free-nigger" (Ch. 6) almost totally contradicts his previous description of the man as a proud, elegant, dignified figure. Yet this contradiction is perfectly consistent with Pap's need to reassert "the Negro" in lieu of social reality. Despite the vulgarity of Pap's personal character, his thinking about race is highly conventional and, therefore, respectable. But most of us cannot respect Pap's views, and when we reject them, we reject the standard racial discourse of both 1840 and 1880.

A reader who objects to the word "nigger" might still insist that Twain could have avoided using it. But it is difficult to imagine how Twain could have debunked a discourse without using the specific terms of that discourse. Even when Twain was writing his book, "nigger" was universally recognized as an insulting, demeaning word. According to Stuart Berg Flexner, "Negro" was generally pronounced as "nigger" until about 1825, at which time Abolitionists began objecting to that term (57). They preferred "colored person" or "person of color." Hence, W.E.B. Du Bois reports that some black Abolitionists of the early 1830s declared themselves united "as men, . . . not as slaves; as 'people of color,' not as 'Negroes' " (245). Writing a generation later in *Army Life in a Black Regiment* (1869), Thomas Wentworth Higginson deplored the common use of "nigger" among freedmen, which he regarded as evidence of low self-esteem (28). The objections to "nigger," then, are not a consequence of the modern sensibility but had been common for a half century before *Huckleberry Finn* was published. The specific function of this term in the book, however, is neither to offend nor merely to provide linguistic authenticity. Much more importantly, it establishes a context against which Jim's specific virtues may emerge as explicit refutations of racist presuppositions.

Of course, the concept of the "nigger" entails far more than just the deployment of certain vocabulary. Most of the attacks on the book focus on its alleged perpetuation of racial stereotypes. Twain does indeed use racial stereotypes here. That practice could be excused as characteristic of the genre of humor within which Twain works. Frontier humor relies upon the use of stock types, and consequently, racial stereotypes are just one of many types present in *Huckleberry Finn*. Yet while valid, such an appeal to generic convention would be unsatisfactory, because it would deny Twain the credit which he deserves for the sophistication of his perceptions (see Ellison, Hansen, Lynn).

As a serious critic of American society, Twain recognized that racial discourse depends upon the deployment of a system of stereotypes which constitute "the Negro" as fundamentally different from and inferior to Euro-Americans. As with his handling of "nigger," Twain's strategy with racial stereotypes is to elaborate them in order to undermine them. To be sure, those critics are correct who have argued that Twain uses this narrative to reveal Jim's humanity. Jim, however, is just one individual. Much more importantly, Twain uses the narrative to expose the cruelty and hollowness of that racial discourse which exists only to obscure the humanity of all Afro-American people.

One aspect of *Huckleberry Finn* which has elicited copious critical commentary is Twain's use of superstition (see especially Hoffman, "Jim's Magic"). In nineteenth century racial discourse, "the Negro" was always defined as inherently superstitious.[6] Many critics, therefore, have cited Jim's superstitious behavior as an instance of negative stereotyping. One cannot deny that in this respect Jim closely resembles the entire tradition of comic darkies (see Woodard and MacCann), but to observe this similarity is a negligible feat. The issue is, does Twain merely reiterate clichés, or does he use these conventional patterns to make an unconventional point? A close examination will show that in virtually every instance, Twain uses Jim's superstition to make points which undermine rather than revalidate the dominant racial discourse.

The first incident of this superstitious behavior occurs in Chapter 2, as a result of one of Tom Sawyer's pranks. When Jim falls asleep under a tree, Tom hangs his hat on a branch. Subsequently, Jim concocts an elaborate tale about having been hexed and ridden by witches. The tale grows more grandiose with subsequent retellings, and eventually Jim becomes a local celebrity, sporting a five-cent piece on a string around his neck as a talisman. "Niggers would come miles to hear Jim tell about it, and he was more looked up to than any nigger in that country," the narrator reports. Jim's celebrity finally reaches the point that "Jim was most ruined, for a servant, because he got so stuck up on account of having seen the devil and been rode by witches." This is, no doubt, amusing. Yet whether Jim believes his own tale or not—and the "superstitious Negro" thesis requires us to assume that he does—the fact remains that Jim clearly benefits from becoming more a celebrity and less a "servant." It is his owner, not Jim, who suffers when Jim's uncompensated labor diminishes.[7]

This incident has often been interpreted as an example of risible Negro gullibility and ignorance, as exemplified by blackface minstrelsy. Such a reading has more than a little validity, but can only partially account for the implications of this scene. If not for the final sentence, such an account might seem wholly satisfactory, but the information that Jim becomes, through his own storytelling, unsuited for life as a slave, introduces unexpected complications. Is it likely that Jim has been deceived by his own creative prevarications—especially given what we learn about his character subsequently? Or has he cleverly exploited the conventions of "Negro superstition" in order to turn a silly boy's prank to his own advantage?

Regardless of whether we credit Jim with forethought in this matter, it is undeniable that he turns Tom's attempt to humiliate him into a major personal triumph. In other words, Tom gives him an inch, and he takes an ell. It is also obvious that he does so by exercising remarkable skills as a rhetorician. By constructing a fictitious narrative of his own experience, Jim elevates himself above his prescribed station in life. By becoming, in effect, an author, Jim writes himself a new destiny. Jim's triumph may appear to be dependent upon the gullibility of other "superstitious" Negroes, but since we have no direct encounter with them, we cannot know whether they are unwitting victims of Jim's ruse or not. A willing audience need not be a totally credulous one. In any case, it is intelligence, not stupidity, which facilitates Jim's triumph. Tom may have had his chuckle, but the last laugh, clearly, belongs to Jim.

In addressing Jim's character, we should keep in mind that forethought, creativity and shrewdness are qualities which racial discourse—see Thomas Jefferson—denies to "the Negro." In that sense, Jim's darky performance here subverts the fundamental definition of the darky. For "the Negro" is defined to be an object, not a subject. Yet does an object construct its own narrative? Viewed in this way, the fact of superstition, which traditionally connotes ignorance and unsophistication, becomes far less important than the ends to which superstition is put. This inference exposes, once again, the inadequacy of a positivist epistemology, which holds, for example, that "a rose is a rose is a rose." No one will deny the self-evidence of a tautology; but a rose derives whatever meaning it has from the context within which it is placed (including the context of traditional symbolism.) It is the contextualizing activity, not das *Ding-an-sich*, which generates meaning. Again and again, Twain attacks racial essentialism by directing our attention, instead, to the particularity of individual action. We find that Jim is not "the Negro." Jim is Jim, and we, like Huck, come to understand what Jim is by attending to what he does in specific situations.

In another instance of explicitly superstitious behavior, Jim uses a hairball to tell Huck's fortune. One may regard this scene as a comical example of Negro ignorance and credulity, acting in concert with the ignorance and credulity of a fourteen-year-old white boy. That reading would allow one an unambiguous laugh at Jim's expense. If one examines the scene carefully, however, the inadequacy of such a reductive reading becomes apparent. Even if Jim does believe in the supernatural powers of this hairball, the fact remains that most of the transaction depends upon Jim's quick wits. For example, the soothsaying aside, much of the exchange between Huck and Jim is an exercise in wily and understated economic bartering. In essence, Jim wants to be paid for his services, while Huck wants free advice. Jim insists that the hairball will not speak without being paid. Huck, who has a dollar, will only admit to having a counterfeit quarter. Jim responds by pretending to be in collusion with Huck. He explains how to doctor the "quarter" so that "anybody in town would take it in a minute, let alone a hair-ball" (Ch. 4). But obviously it is not the hair-ball who will benefit from acquiring and spending this counterfeit coin (cf. Weaver and Williams).

In this transaction, Jim serves his own interests while appearing to serve Huck's interests. He takes a slug which is worthless to Huck, and through the alchemy of his own cleverness, he contrives to make it worth twenty-five cents to himself. That, in antebellum America, is not a bad price for telling a fortune. But more importantly, Twain shows Jim self-consciously subverting the prescribed definition of "the Negro," even as he performs within the limitations of that role. He remains the conventional "Negro" by giving the white boy what he wants, at no real cost, and by consistently appearing to be passive and subservient to the desires of Huck and the hair-ball. But in fact, he serves his own interests all along. Such resourcefulness is hardly consistent with the familiar, one-dimensional concept of "the superstitious Negro."

And while Jim's reading is formulaic, it is hardly simple-minded. He sees the world as a kind of Manichean universe, in which forces of light and darkness—white and black—vie for dominance. Pap, he says, is uncertain what to do, torn between his white and black angels. Jim's advice, "to res' easy en let de ole man take his own way" (Ch. 4), turns out to be good advice, because Huck greatly enjoys life in the cabin, despite Pap's fits of drunken excess. This mixture of pleasure and pain is precisely what Jim predicts. Admittedly, Jim's conceptual framework is not original. Nonetheless, his reading carries considerable force, because it corresponds so neatly to the dominant thematic patterns in this book, and more broadly, to the sort of dualistic thinking which informs much of Twain's work. (To take an obvious example, consider the role reversals and character contrasts in *Pudd'n-head Wilson* or *The Prince and the Pauper*). And most immediately, Jim's comments here reflect tellingly upon his situation as a black slave in racist America. The slave's fate is always torn between his master's will and his own.

In this reading and other incidents, Jim emerges as an astute and sensitive observer of human behavior, both in his comments regarding Pap and in his subtle remarks to Huck. Jim clearly possesses a subtlety and intelligence which "the Negro" allegedly lacks. Twain makes this point more clearly in the debate scene in Chapter 15. True enough, most of this debate is, as several critics have noted, conventional minstrel show banter. Nevertheless, Jim demonstrates impressive reasoning abilities, despite his factual ignorance. For example, in their argument over "Poly-voo-franzy," Huck makes a category error by implying that the difference between languages is analogous to the difference between human language and cat language. While Jim's response—that man should talk like a man—betrays his ignorance of cultural diversity, his argument is perceptive and structurally sound. The humor in Huck's conclusion, "you can't learn a nigger how to argue," arises precisely from our recognition that Jim's argument is better than Huck's.

Throughout the novel, Twain presents Jim in ways which render ludicrous the conventional wisdom about "Negro character." As an intelligent, sensitive, wily and considerate individual, Jim demonstrates that one's race provides no useful index of one's character. While that point may seem obvious to many contemporary readers, it is a point rarely made by nineteenth-century Euro-American novelists. Indeed, except for Melville, J.W. De-Forest, Albion Tourgee, and George Washington Cable, white novelists virtually always portrayed Afro-American characters as exemplifications of "Negroness." In this regard, the twentieth century has been little better. By presenting us a series of glimpses which penetrate the "Negro" exterior and reveal the person beneath it, Twain debunks American racial discourse. For racial discourse maintains that the "Negro" exterior is all that a "Negro" really has.

This insight in itself is a notable accomplishment. Twain, however, did not view racism as an isolated phenomenon, and it was his effort to place racism within the context of other cultural traditions which produced the most problematic aspect of his novel. For it is in the final chapters—the Tom Sawyer section—which most critics consider the weakest part of the book, that Twain links his criticisms of slavery and Southern romanticism, condemning the cruelties which both of these traditions entail. (See Altenbernd). Critics have objected to these chapters on various grounds. Some of the most common are that Jim becomes reduced to a comic darky (e.g., Marx, Schmitz), that Tom's antics undermine the seriousness of the novel, and that these burlesque narrative developments destroy the structural integrity of the novel. Most critics see this conclusion as an evasion of the difficult issues which the novel has raised. There is no space here for a discussion of the structural issues, but it seems to me that as a critique of American racial discourse, these concluding chapters offer a harsh, coherent, and uncompromising indictment.

Tom Sawyer's absurd scheme to "rescue" Jim offends, because the section begins with Huck's justly celebrated crisis of conscience, which culminates in his resolve to free Jim, even if doing so condemns him to hell. The passage which leads to Huck's decision, as familiar as it is, merits reexamination:

> I'd see him standing my watch on top of his'n, stead of calling me, so I could go on sleeping; and see him how glad he was when I come back out of the fog; and when I come to him again in the swamp, up there where the feud was; and such like times; and would always call me honey, and pet me, and do everything he could think of for me, and how good he always was; and at last I struck the time I saved him by telling the men we had small-pox aboard, and he was so grateful, and said I was the best friend old Jim ever had in the world, and the *only* one he's got now; and then I happened to look around, and see that paper. . . . I studied a minute, sort of holding my breath, and then says to myself: 'All right, then, I'll *go* to hell"—and tore it up (Ch. 31).

The issue here is not just whether or not Huck should return a contraband[8]—an escaped slave—to its proper owner. More fundamentally, Huck must decide whether to accept the conventional wisdom, which defines "Negroes" as subhuman commodities, or the evidence of his own experience, which has shown Jim to be a good and kind man and a true friend.

Huck makes the obvious decision, but his doing so represents more than simply a liberal choice of conscience over social convention. Twain explicitly makes Huck's choice a sharp attack on the Southern church. Huck scolds himself: "Here was the Sunday school, you could a gone to it and if you'd done it they'd a learnt you, there, that people that acts as I'd been acting about that nigger goes to everlasting fire" (Ch. 31). Yet despite Huck's anxiety, his choice is obviously correct. Furthermore, by the time that Twain wrote these words, more than twenty years of national strife, including Civil War and Reconstruction, had established Huck's conclusion regarding slavery as a dominant national consensus. Not even reactionary Southerners advocated a reinstitution of slavery. Since the Southern church had taught that slavery was God's will, Huck's decision flatly repudiates the church's teachings regarding slavery. And implicitly, it also repudiates the church as an institution by suggesting that the church functions to undermine, not to encourage, a reliance on one's conscience. To define "Negroes" as subhuman removes them from moral consideration and therefore justifies the callous exploitation of them. This view of religion is consistent with the cynical iconoclasm which Twain expressed in *Letters from the Earth* and others of his "dark" works.[9]

In this context, Tom Sawyer appears to us as a superficially charming but fundamentally distasteful interloper. His actions are governed not by conscience but rather by romantic conventions and literary "authorities." Indeed, while Tom may appear to be a kind of renegade, he is in essence thoroughly conventional in his values and proclivities. Despite all his boyish pranks, Tom represents a kind of solid respectability—a younger version of the Southern gentleman, as exemplified by the Grangerfords and the Shepherdsons (see Hoffman, *Form and Fable*, 327–28). Hence, when Tom proposes to help Huck steal Jim, Huck laments that "Tom Sawyer fell, considerable, in my estimation. Only I couldn't believe it. Tom Sawyer a *nigger stealer!*" (Ch. 33). Such liberating activity is proper for Huck, who is not respectable, but not for Tom, who is. As with the previous example, however, this one implies a deep criticism of the status quo. Huck's act of conscience, which most of us would now endorse, is possible only for an outsider. This hardly speaks well for the moral integrity of Southern (or American) "civilization."

To examine Tom's role in the novel, let us begin at the end. Upon learning of the failed escape attempt and Jim's recapture, Tom cries out, self-righteously: "turn him loose! He ain't no slave; he's as free as any creature that walks this earth" (Ch. 42). Tom has known all along that his cruel and ludicrous scheme to rescue the captured "prisoner" was being enacted upon a free man; and indeed, only his silence regarding Jim's status allowed the scheme to proceed with Jim's cooperation. Certainly, neither Huck nor Jim would otherwise have indulged Tom's foolishness. Tom's gratuitous cruelty here in the pursuit of his own amusement corresponds to his less vicious prank against Jim in Chapter 2. And just as before, Twain converts Tom's callous mischief into a personal triumph for Jim.

Not only has Jim suffered patiently, which would in truth represent a doubtful virtue. (Jim is not Uncle Tom.) Jim demonstrates his moral superiority by surrendering himself in order to assist the doctor in treating his wounded tormentor. This is hardly the behavior which one would expect from a commodity, and it is *precisely* Jim's status—man or chattel—which has been fundamentally at issue throughout the novel. It may be true that Tom's lengthy juvenile antics subvert the tone of the novel, but they also provide the necessary backdrop for Jim's noble act. Up to this point, we have been able to admire Jim's good sense and to respond sentimentally to his good character. This, however, is the first time that we see him making a significant (and wholly admirable) moral decision. His act sets him apart from everyone else in the novel except Huck. And modestly (if not disingenuously), he claims to be behaving just as Tom Sawyer would. Always conscious of his role as a "Negro," Jim knows better than to claim personal credit for his good deed. Yet the contrast between Jim's behavior and Tom's is unmistakable. Huck declares that Jim is "white inside" (Ch. 40). He apparently intends this as a compliment, but Tom is fortunate that Jim does not behave like most of the whites in the novel.

Twain also contrasts Jim's self-sacrificing compassion with the cruel and mean-spirited behavior of his captors, emphasizing that white skin does not justify claims of superior virtue. They abuse Jim, verbally and physically, and some want to lynch him as an example to other slaves. The moderates among them, however, resist, pointing out that they could be made to pay for the destruction of private property. As Huck observes: "the people that's always the most anxious for to hang a nigger that hain't done just right, is always the very ones that ain't the most anxious to pay for him when they've got their satisfaction out of him" (Ch. 42). As if these enforcers of white supremacy did not appear contemptible enough already, Twain then has the doctor describe Jim as the best and most faithful nurse he has ever seen, despite Jim's "resking his freedom" and his obvious fatigue. These vigilantes do admit that Jim deserves to be rewarded, but their idea of a reward is to cease punching and cursing him. They are not even generous enough to remove Jim's heavy shackles.

Ultimately, *Huckleberry Finn* renders a harsh judgment on American society. Freedom from slavery, the novel implies, is not freedom from gratuitous cruelty; and racism, like romanticism, is finally just an elaborate justification which the adult counterparts of Tom Sawyer use to facilitate their exploitation and abuse of other human beings. Tom feels guilty, with good reason, for having exploited Jim, but his final gesture of paying Jim off is less an insult to Jim than it is Twain's commentary on Tom himself. Just as slaveholders believe that economic relations (ownership) can justify their privilege of mistreating other human beings, Tom apparently believes that an economic exchange can suffice as atonement for his misdeeds. Perhaps he finds a forty-dollar token more affordable than an apology. But then, just as Tom could only "set a free nigger free," considering, as Huck says, "his bringing-up" (Ch. 42), he similarly could hardly be expected to apologize for his pranks. Huck, by contrast, is equally rich, but he *has* apologized to Jim earlier in the novel. And this is the point of Huck's final remark, rejecting the prospect of civilization. To become civilized is not just to become like Aunt Sally. More immediately, it is to become like Tom Sawyer.

Jim is, indeed, "as free as any creature that walks this earth." In other words, he is a man, like all men, at the mercy of other men's arbitrary cruelties. In a sense, given Twain's view of freedom, to allow Jim to escape to the North or to have Tom announce Jim's manumission earlier would be an evasion of the novel's ethical insights. While one may escape from legal bondage, there is no escape from the cruelties of this "civilization." There is no promised land, where one may enjoy absolute personal freedom. An individual's freedom is always constrained by one's social relations to other people. Being legally free does not spare Jim from gratuitous humiliation and physical suffering in the final chapters, precisely because Jim is still regarded as a "nigger." Even if he were as accomplished as the mulatto from Ohio, he would not be exempt from mistreatment. Furthermore, since Tom represents the hegemonic values of his society, Jim's "freedom" amounts to little more than an obligation to live by his wits and to make the best of a bad situation.

Slavery and racism, then, are social evils which take their places alongside various others which the novel documents, such as the insane romanticism that inspires the Grangerfords and Shepherdsons blithely to murder each other, generation after generation. Twain rejects entirely the mystification of race and demonstrates that Jim is in most ways a better man than the men who regard him as their inferior. But he also shows how little correlation there may be between the treatment one deserves and the treatment one receives.

If this conclusion sounds uncontroversial from the perspective of 1984, we would do well to remember that it contradicts entirely the overwhelming and optimistic consensus of 1884. And no other nineteenth-century novel so effectively locates racial discourse within the context of a general critique of American institutions and traditions. Indeed, the novel suggests that real individual freedom, in this land of the free, cannot be found. "American civilization" enslaves and exploits rather than liberates. It is hardly an appealing message.

Given the subtlety of Mark Twain's approach, it is not surprising that most of his contemporaries misunderstood or simply ignored the novel's demystification of race. Despite their patriotic rhetoric, they, like Pap, were unprepared to take seriously the implications of "freedom, justice, and equality." They, after all, espoused an ideology and an explicit language of race which was virtually identical to Thomas Jefferson's. Yet racial discourse flatly contradicts and ultimately renders hypocritical the egalitarian claims of liberal democracy. The heart of Twain's message to us is that an honest person must reject one or the other. But hypocrisy, not honesty, is our norm. For too many of us continue to assert both racial distinction and liberal values, simultaneously. If we, a century later, continue to be confused about *Adventures of Huckleberry Finn*, perhaps it is because we remain more deeply committed to both racial discourse and a self-deluding optimism than we care to admit.[10]

Notes

1. The literature on the Abolition movement and on antebellum debates regarding the Negro is, of course, voluminous. George Fredrickson's excellent *The Black Image in the White Mind* is perhaps the best general work of its kind. Fredrickson's *The Inner Civil War* is also valuable, especially pp. 53–64. Leon Litwack closely examines the ambivalence of Abolitionists regarding racial intermingling (214–46). Benjamin Quarles presents the most detailed examination of black Abolitionists, though Vincent Harding offers a more vivid (and overtly polemical) account of their relationships to white Abolitionists (101–194).

2. The debate over Jefferson's relationship to Sally Hemings has raged for two centuries. The most thorough scholarly accounts are by Fawn Brodie, who suggests that Jefferson did have a prolonged involvement with Hemings, and by Virginius Dabney, who endeavors to exonerate Jefferson of such charges. Barbara Chase-Riboud presents a fictionalized version of this relationship in *Sally*

Hemings. The first Afro-American novel, *Clotel: Or the President's Daughter* (1853) by William Wells Brown, was also based on this alleged affair.

3. For dates of composition, see Blair. For a discussion of Melville's treatment of race, Carolyn Karchner's *Shadow Over the Promised Land* is especially valuable. Articles on *Benito Cereno* by Joyce Adler and Jean Yellin are also noteworthy. Rayford Logan and Lawrence J. Friedman provide detailed accounts of the racist climate in Post-Reconstruction America, emphasizing the literary manifestations of such attitudes. Friedman's discussion of George Washington Cable (99–118), the outspoken Southern liberal, is very informative. For a general historical overview of the period, C. Vann Woodward's work remains unsurpassed. John W. Cell offers a provocative reconsideration of Woodward's arguments, and Joel Williamson's new book documents the excessively violent tendencies of Southern racism at the end of the century.

4. My use of "racial discourse" has some affinities to Foucault's conception of "discourse." This is not, however, a strictly Foucaultian reading. While Foucault's definition of discursive practices provides one of the most sophisticated tools presently available for cultural analysis, his conception of power seems to me problematic. I prefer an account of power which allows for a consideration of interest and hegemony. Theorists such as Marshall Berman (34–35) and Catherine MacKinnon (526) have indicated similar reservations. Frank Lentriccia, however, has made a provocative attempt to modify Foucaultian analysis, drawing upon Gramsci's analysis of hegemony. See Foucault, *The Archaeology of Knowledge*, *Power/Knowledge* (esp. 92–108), and *The History of Sexuality*, (esp. 92–102).

5. This is not to discount the sufferings of other groups. But historically, the philosophical basis of Western racial discourse—which existed even before the European "discovery" of America—has been the equation of "good" and "evil" with light and darkness (or, white and black.) (See Derrida; Jordan, 1–40; and West, 47–65). Economically, the slave trade, chattel slavery, agricultural peonage, and color-coded wage differentials have made the exploitation of African-Americans the most profitable form of racism. Finally, Afro-Americans have long been the largest American "minority" group. Consequently, the primacy of "the Negro" in American racial discourse is, to use Althusser's term (87–126), "Overdetermined." The acknowledgment of primary status, however, is hardly a claim of privilege.

6. Even the allegedly scientific works on the Negro focused on superstition as a definitive trait. See, for example, W.D. Weatherford and Jerome Dowd. No one has commented more scathingly on Negro superstition than William H. Thomas, who was, by American definitions, a Negro himself.

7. Hoffman in Form and Fable (331) reveals an implicit understanding of Jim's creativity, but he does not pursue the point in detail.

8. This term became a part of the official military vocabulary during the Civil War, referring to a slave who had gone "AWOL."

9. A number of works comment on Twain's religious views and the relation between his critiques of religion and of racism. See Ensor; Pettit, "Mark Twain and the Negro"; and Gollin.

10. I would like to thank my colleagues, David Langston and Michael Bell, for the helpful suggestions which they offered to me regarding the essay.

Works Cited

Adler, Joyce. "Melville's *Benito Cereno*: Slavery and Violence in the Americas." *Science and Society*, 38 (1974), 19–48.

Altenbernd, Lynn. "Huck Finn, Emancipator." *Criticism*, 1 (1959), 298–307.

Althusser, Louis. *For Marx*. London: Verso Editions, 1979.

Berkove, Lawrence I. "The Free Man of Color in *The Grandissimes* and Works by Harris and Mark Twain." *The Southern Quarterly*, 18.4 (1981). 60–73.

Berman, Marshall. *All That Is Solid Melts into Air*. New York: Simon & Schuster, 1982.

Blair, Walter. "When Was *Huckleberry Finn* Written?" *American Literature*, 30 (March 1958), 1–25.

Brodie, Fawn. *Thomas Jefferson, an Intimate History*. New York: Norton, 1974.

Brown, William Wells. *Clotel: Or the President's Daughter*. New York: Arno Press, 1969.

Chase-Riboud, Barbara. *Sally Hemings*. New York: The Viking Press, 1979.

Cell, John W. *The Highest Stage of White Supremacy*. New York: Cambridge University Press, 1982.

Clemens, Samuel. *Adventures of Huckleberry Finn*. Eds. Scully Bradley, Richmond Croom Beatty, E. Hudson Long, and Thomas Cooley. 2nd ed. New York: Norton, 1977.

Dabney, Virginius. *The Jefferson Scandals*. New York: Dodd, Mead, 1981.

Derrida, Jacques. "White Mythology." *New Literary History*, 6 (1974), 5–74.

Dowd, Jerome. *Negro Races*. New York: Macmillan, 1907.

Du Bois, William E.B. *The Souls of Black Folk. Three Negro Classics*. Ed. John Hope Franklin. New York: Avon, 1965.

Ellison, Ralph. "Change the Joke and Slip the Yoke." *Shadow and Act*. New York: Vintage, 1964, 45–59.

Egan, Michael. *Mark Twain's Huckleberry Finn: Race, Class and Society*. Atlantic Highlands, NJ: Humanities Press, 1977.

Ensor, Allison. *Mark Twain and the Bible*. Lexington: The University of Kentucky Press, 1969.

Flexner, Stuart Berg. *I Hear America Talking*. New York: Van Nostrand Reinhold, 1976.

Foucault, Michel. *The History of Sexuality*. Vol. 1. New York: Vintage, 1980.

———. *Power/Knowledge*. Ed. Colin Gordon, New York: Pantheon, 1980.

Fredrickson, George M. *The Black Image in the White Mind*. New York: Harper Torchbooks, 1971.

———. *The Inner Civil War*. New York: Harper Torchbooks, 1971.

Friedman, Lawrence J. *The White Savage: Racial Fantasies in the Postbellum South*. Englewood Cliffs, NJ: Prentice-Hall, 1970.

Gollin, Richard and Rita. "*Huckleberry Finn* and the Time of the Evasion." *Modern Language Studies*, 9 (Spring 1979), 5–15.

Gramsci, Antonio. *Selections from the Prison Notebooks.* New York: International Publishers, 1971.

Hansen, Chadwick. "The Character of Jim and the Ending of *Huckleberry Finn.*" *Massachusetts Review*, 5 (Autumn 1963), 45–66.

Harding, Vincent. *There Is a River.* New York: Harcourt, Brace Jovanovich, 1981.

Hentoff, Nat. "Huck Finn Better Get Out of Town by Sundown." Column. *The Village Voice*, 27 (May 4, 1982).

———. Is Any Book Worth the Humiliation of Our Kids?" Column. *The Village Voice*, 27 (May 11, 1982).

———. "Huck Finn and the Shortchanging of Black Kids." Column. *The Village Voice*, 27 (May 18, 1982).

———. These Are Little Battles Fought in Remote Places." Column. *The Village Voice*, 27 (May 25, 1982).

Higginson, Thomas Wentworth. *Army Life in a Black Regiment.* Boston: Beacon Press, 1962.

Hoffman, Daniel. *Form and Fable in American Fiction.* New York: Oxford University Press, 1961.

———. "Jim's Magic: Black or White?" *American Literature*, 32 (March 1960), 47–54.

Jefferson, Thomas. *Notes on the State of Virginia. The Portable Thomas Jefferson.* Ed. Merrill D. Peterson. New York: Viking, 1975.

Jordan, Winthrop. *White Over Black.* New York: Norton, 1968.

Karchner, Carolyn. *Shadow Over the Promised Land.* Baton Rouge: Louisiana State University Press, 1980.

Lentricchia, Frank. "Reading Foucault (Punishment, Labor, Resistance)." *Raritan* 1.4: 5–32.

———. "Reading Foucault (Punishment, Labor, Resistance)." Part II. *Raritan* 2: 41.70.

Litwack, Leon F. *North of Slavery.* Chicago: The University of Chicago Press, 1961.

Logan, Rayford. *The Negro in American Life and Thought: The Nadir, 1877–1901.* New York: The Dial Press, 1954.

Lynn, Kenneth S. *Mark Twain and Southwestern Humor.* Boston: Little, Brown, 1959.

MacKinnon, Catherine A. "Feminism, Marxism, Method, and the State: An Agenda for Theory." *Signs*, 7:3 (1982), 515–544.

Marx, Leo. "Mr. Eliot, Mr. Trilling and *Huckleberry Finn.*" *The American Scholar*, 22 (Autumn 1953), 423–40.

Paine, Albert Bigelow. *Mark Twain, A Biography.* New York: Harper, 1912.

Pettit, Arthur G. "Mark Twain and the Negro, 1867–1869." *Journal of Negro History*, 56 (April 1971), 88–96.

———. *Mark Twain and the South.* Lexington: The University of Kentucky Press, 1974.

Quarles, Benjamin. *Black Abolitionists.* New York: Oxford University Press, 1969.

Schmitz, Neil. "Twain, *Huckleberry Finn*, and the Reconstruction." *American Studies*, 12 (Spring 1971), 59–67.

Thomas, William Hannibal. *The American Negro.* New York: The Negro Universities Press, 1969. Reprint of 1901 ed.

Weatherford, W.D. *Negro Life in the South.* New York: Young Men's Christian Association Press, 1910.

Weaver, Thomas and Williams, Merline. Mark Twain's Jim: Identity As An Index to Cultural Attitudes." *American Literary Realism*, 13 (Spring 1980): 19–30.

West, Cornel. *Prophesy Deliverance.* Philadelphia: Westminster Press, 1982.

Williamson, Joel. *The Crucible of Race.* New York: Oxford University Press, 1984.

Woodard, Fredrick and MacCann, Donnarae. "*Huckleberry Finn* and the Traditions of Blackface Minstrelsy." *Interracial Books for Children Bulletin*, 15:1–2 (1984), 4–13.

Woodward, C. Vann. *Origins of the New South.* Baton Rouge: Louisiana State University Press, 1971.

________. *The Strange Career of Jim Crow.* Third Edition. New York: Oxford University Press, 1974.

Yellin, Jean Fagan. "Black Masks: Melville's 'Benito Cereno.' " *American Quarterly*, 22 (Fall 1970), 678–89.

APPENDIX

The Pictorial Huck Finn: *Mark Twain and His Illustrator, E. W. Kemble*

Beverly R. David

Thanksgiving Day 1884, three full months before official publication, New York and Chicago newspapers were already proclaiming *Huckleberry Finn* indecent.[1] It was not Mark Twain's prose that was offensive, however, it was one of the illustrations. Three thousand advance sales copies of the book had left the printers and were in salesmen's hands with an illustration showing Uncle Silas in a flagrant act of indecent exposure (Fig. 1). Someone at the printers had mischievously altered the engraving plate, producing an obscene addition never intended by Twain or the illustrator. Twain immediately recalled all available copies of the book. The offending page was torn out and replaced by tipping in a retouched drawing (Fig. 2). The mystery of the infamous page 283 echoed through scholarly articles during the thirties and was only completely solved in 1960.[2]

Curiously enough, no one has ever wondered about any other effect of the 174 illustrations. Is only an "indecent" illustration capable of stimulating response from a reader? Novels of the 19th century were loaded with pictures; was there no impact on the reader's imagination? Mark Twain, as we shall see, thought illustrations were not only important to his work but that they

---

From *American Quarterly*, 26 (October 1974), 331-351. Reprinted with permission. Revised by the author.

had a major influential effect on his readers. He "decided his novel (*Huck Finn)* would be illustrated after his own ideas"[3] evidently to make certain that readers would be affected by consideration of both text and illustration. A penurious businessman, he nevertheless spent thousands of dollars on the drawings. Though anxious for an early publishing date and busy with writ-

*Figure 1**

*Figure 1 by permission of *American Book Collector*, 10 (June 1960), 31-34. Figures 2 through 19 by permission of the University of Michigan Rare Book Room Collection.

ing and a Southern lecture tour, he spent valuable time checking, editing and approving each sketch. Twain as skillful writer and editor was perfectly aware that what his "genteel" audience saw in the illustrations would shape their reading of the story and that the illustrations would manipulate the responses of his readers.

"WHO DO YOU RECKON IT IS?"

Figure 2

HUCKLEBERRY FINN.

Figure 3

Huckleberry Finn entered American fiction in *The Adventures of Tom Sawyer* swinging a cat by the tail (Fig. 3). Yet it is a drastically changed Huck who became the hero of his own novel in *Adventures of Huckleberry Finn* (Fig. 4). What happened to the romantic outcast dressed in the castoff clothes of a full-grown man? The widow Douglas "allowed she would sivilize"[4] Huck, but who altered his size and shape, freckled his face, designed his clothes and changed his age? The obvious answer is Mark Twain; however, that is too easy, and *wrong*. Many of the changes in Huck were not the author's doing.

Mark Twain, always interested in the illustrations of his books, had never before had control over the selection of an artist. Now, however, since he had set up his nephew, Charles Webster, in a publishing house to produce *Huck Finn*, one of his major concerns was the illustrator. Mark Twain wanted an illustrator who would follow his ideas in the drawings and, to make sure his ideas were followed, he demanded editorial control of every sketch. Webster, on Mark Twain's advice, tried prelimi-

HUCKLEBERRY FINN.

Figure 4

JIM.

Figure 5

nary drawings from Kemble. Mark Twain had remembered Kemble's work from the pages of *Life* and told Webster "*That* is the man I want to try."[5] Webster also approved, Kemble won the commission, the contract was signed and E. W. Kemble became Huck Finn's illustrator. He was 23, had been drawing professionally only two years, had no formal artistic training and had never been out of New York.

This was early April 1884, and the publishing rush was on. Chatto and Windus, Mark Twain's English publisher, wanted proofs immediately, to start early canvassing. The only existing manuscript had been forwarded from Mark Twain to Howells for editing. Howells helpfully arranged for a typist to make two copies but his editing was sloppy and Mark Twain had to re-edit most of the work. This made a complete manuscript unavailable to Kemble and put him at a disadvantage. He worked from both edited and unedited chapters and often had no manuscript at all.

OUT OF BONDAGE.

Figure 6

In May he pleaded with Webster to "send me the manuscript from XIII Chapter on....as there are illustrations here which are described minutely and I'm afraid to touch them without the reading matter to refer to."[6] His fear was well founded. The unavailable text had caused him to incorrectly put "Texas" on the pilothouse of the steamboat. The error did not escape the watchful eye of Mark Twain. He reproved Kemble with "That word had better be removed from that pilot house—that is where a boat's *name* is put, & that particular boat's name was, Walter Scott."[7]

This confused shuffling of manuscript chapters and drawings from Kemble to Webster to Mark Twain caused not only factual errors but also problems of consistency in Kemble's drawings. Nigger Jim, seen as a grown man in the early chapters (Fig. 5), bears faint resemblance to the tall boy Jim portrayed later in the novel (Fig. 6). And in none of the many drawings of Jim is there a hint of his legendary "hairy arms and breast" (p. 60) which he proudly insisted prophesied his eventual wealth. Though Jim's hairiness can be dismissed as an oversight on the part of Kemble as a New York illustrator unaware of Negro characteristics, it is a strange error for Mark Twain not to catch if hairiness was his intention for Jim. After all, he knew Negro characteristics well and realized that hair or lack of it would make his Nigger Jim different from the usual Negro.

Most of these problems developed because of the difficult and hectic deadlines imposed by Mark Twain and were compounded by the unavailability of the manuscript. Kemble's pictures of Jim in early chapters were sent through Webster to Mark Twain in "batches of half dozen or more."[8] If the drawings pleased him he sent them on to the printer, Kemble never seeing them again. Months later, when Kemble was drawing Jim again for a late chapter, he sketched what was described in the available text: two young boys on a raft. In this instance, Kemble had to modify the literal facts of the text. Huck and Jim, according to most of what Mark Twain narrated in the raft episodes, are "always naked, day and night (p. 159)." Mark Twain, whose constant worry was that he might offend his reader, required Kemble to put clothes on Huck and Jim. Kemble, therefore, provided socially acceptable images for Mark Twain's characters despite the sense of the story.

Added confusion for Kemble's work of illustration came from his eccentric working habits. Elated at his first big commission, he decided to be a true professional and hire a model for his sketches. He described his method in a *Colophon* article many years later:

> The story called for a variety of characters, old and young, male and female. In the neighborhood I came across a youngster, Cort Morris by name, who tallied with my idea of Huck. He was a bit tall for the ideal boy, but I could jam him down a few pegs in my drawings and use him for the other characters...I used my young model for every character in the story—man, woman and child.[9]

Kemble's Cort, "grinning, and one side of his cheek well padded with a sour ball"[10] posed for the first drawing, the cover design for *Huck Finn* (Fig. 7). Writing his hesitant approval of the design, Mark Twain commented: "All right & good, & will answer; although the boy's mouth is a trifle more Irishy than neces-

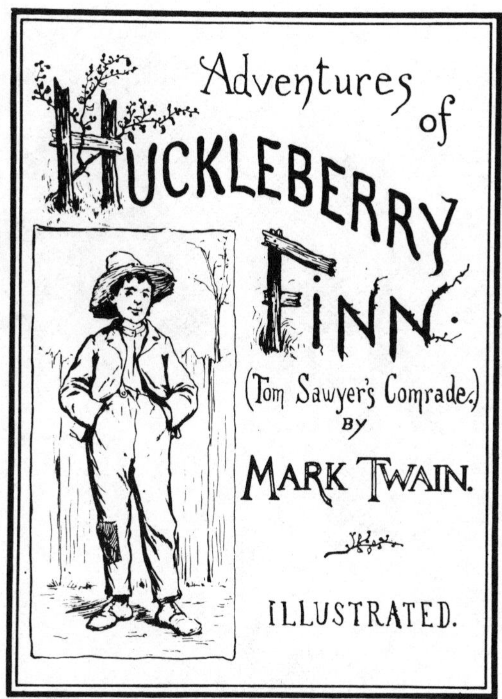

Cover of the first American edition of *Adventures of Huckleberry Finn*, 1885.

Figure 7

sary."[11] It is no wonder Mark Twain was dubious, considering Kemble's methods; however, the writer's "own ideas" of the visual image of Huck did not rest on the model problems but on an Irish heritage. Probably, Mark Twain's "ideas" contained the seeds of both ethnic and financial judgment. His pique at the drawing is understandable within the context of his consuming passion for sales figures. Realizing that contemporary local-colorists had limited their audience and therefore their monetary gain by geographically and ethnically restricting their subject matter, Mark Twain directed his editing toward a larger audience, a wider terrain and heavier sales. There would be little sense, in his mind, to limiting the appeal of Huck Finn to the increasing but unpopular urban Irish when the novel and its hero had a potentially limitless audience. The "Irishness" needed control, less prominence, especially in so promotionally visible a place as the cover design.

JUDGE THATCHER SURPRISED.

THINKING.

SOLID COMFORT.

Figure 8

Mid-May saw batches of drawings being sent from New York to Twain in Hartford. Kemble's frontispiece (see Fig. 4), which has become universally famous, drew another curious response from Mark Twain: "The frontispiece has the usual blemish—an ugly, ill-drawn face. Huck Finn is an exceedingly good-hearted boy, & should carry a good & good-looking face... The pictures will *do*—they will just barely do—& that is the best I can say for them."[12] Could Huck's freckle-faced grin be called ugly? How good-looking did Huck seem to Mark Twain? These critical comments on the boy-hero's appearance and character are important points in ascertaining Mark Twain's theory of illustrating. Since the first-person narrative of *Huckleberry Finn* prevented the author from adequately describing Huck except for his clothing and habits, the right picture was a way of creating a character for the reader. In fact, it was the only way of establishing a definite physical appearance. Just as he had been critical of the cover, Twain wanted an accurate image throughout to control the reader's image of Huck. Kemble's Huck, therefore, became a near dandy compared to the dirty hobo who began life as Tom's comrade (see Fig. 3). Kemble adopted very little from the original Huck of *Tom Sawyer*—the swinging cat became a dead rabbit and there is a pop gun to show a harmless, not malicious intent. The tramp attire (battered felt hat, too large, baggy pants) was transformed into a typical boy's clothing: straw hat, white shirt, close-fitting pants and shoes. Huck would have gagged but Kemble made the reader of Mark Twain's novel feel comfortable (Fig. 8).

Mark Twain's editorial policy was not limited to the character of Huck. A group of seventeen drawings, all sketched from the Cort Morris model, if we can believe Kemble, also disturbed Mark Twain because: "The faces are generally ugly, & wrenched into over-expression amounting sometimes to distortion. As a rule, (though not always) the people in these pictures are forbidding and repulsive. Reduction will modify them, no doubt, but it can hardly make them pleasant folk to look at. An artist shouldn't follow a book too literally, perhaps—if this is the necessary result."[13]

Mark Twain's story describes such charming people as the drunkard pap with his long and greasy hair and his fish-belly white skin; the equally inebriated murderers, Bill and Jake Packard; the nigger-hunting cowards in the smallpox episode; two seedy con men, the Duke and the Dauphin; and the delightful

"COURTING ON THE SLY."

Figure 9

plug-chewing inhabitants of Brickville. Obviously, for Mark Twain, the purpose of the illustrations was to diminish the reality of his characters and not to represent their personality. Illustration, for Mark Twain, became a persuasive way of suppressing the dirty, brutal and cowardly elements of his people. Pleasant drawings might convince the reader they were pleasant folk.

These seventeen drawings were sent back to Kemble for modification. When they were reworked, Webster commented to Mark Twain that, "Kemble has fixed the last lot so that they will be all right."[14] "I shall not relax my efforts to get better work out of Kemble."[15] Better meant less literal and more pleasant. Most of the critical haggling between Mark Twain and Kemble stopped after this group of drawings was approved. The illustrations of the people in the novel became more pleasing to the eye and Mark Twain's comments are full of "rattling good" and "They please me exceedingly."[16]

Some of the text, however, even Mark Twain realized could

"A PIRATE FOR THIRTY YEARS."

Figure 10

never be rendered acceptable in illustration. One drawing submitted by Kemble for Chapter 20 depicting "the lecherous old rascal kissing the girl at the campmeeting" was deleted by Mark Twain in a letter explaining: "It is powerful good, but it mustn't go in...Let's not make *any* pictures of the campmeeting. The subject won't *bear* illustrating. It is a disgusting thing, & pictures are sure to tell the truth about it too plainly."[17]

The answer for Mark Twain when a subject was too disgusting or delicate for illustration was to avoid the issue completely. Of Kemble's drawings approved for this chapter, only one relates to the incidents at the meetings, an innocent and bashful rendition of two lovers "Courting on the Sly" (Fig. 9). The other chapter drawing is a marvelously funny handling of the imagined adventure of the King in his pirate escapade (Fig. 10). Mark Twain thereby had omitted all visual references to the King as a lecherous old roué and emphasized the ridiculous side of his character. The line "and some of them he hugged and kissed as many as

TRAGEDY.

Figure 11

five or six times" (p. 174) reads, after seeing this image, like an old buffoon's innocent clowning. How could a reader imagine harm from a crazy old fool dressed as a bowlegged pirate? Though Mark Twain notes in his letter that he personally enjoyed the robust humor of the original drawing, his editorial good sense cautioned him to control carefully incidents involving sex, religion and the church. The truth of the lines might slip by the casual reader without offending, but it seemed reckless to awaken the "genteel" audience to the whole truth of the campmeeting situation by adding a picture of the proceedings.

The sexuality of the King's escapades is, in fact, constantly played down both in Mark Twain's narrative and in the Kemble drawings. One episode, similar in tone to the campmeeting scene but without the troublesome church-religion connotations, occurs in the Royal Nonesuch performance. "The King come a-prancing out on all fours, naked, and he was painted all

THE DEATH OF BOGGS.

Figure 12

over, ring-streaked-and-striped, all sorts of colors, as splendid as a rainbow, and never mind the rest of his outfit" (p. 196). Mark Twain shows his skill here in handling a potentially explosive subject. By diverting the reader quickly from the word naked to a dazzling description of a rainbow and then flatly suppressing further details, the possibly offensive "naked" is diverted and much of the potential suggestiveness becomes ambiguous. Kemble's illustration for the performance uses the same technique. Hilariously funny, the drawing ignores the nakedness and focuses on the ludicrous. Even the caption adds to the comedy—"Tragedy" indeed. The sexual connotations are implied by the writer and the illustrator but the truth is left to the fertile imagination of the reader (Fig. 11).

Kemble's illustrations, under Mark Twain's guiding editorial hand, worked therefore in a number of interesting ways. When referring to a delicate or disgusting subject the drawings would

JIM SEES A DEAD MAN.

Figure 13

tone down the ugly or brutal aspects, making them appear pleasantly humorous. Other times, with particularly offensive material, the drawings would substitute a comically irrelevant topic. These techniques, obviously more Mark Twain's than Kemble's according to the correspondence, also were used to make the violence of the novel acceptable.

Mark Twain's dissatisfaction with some drawings was expressed in such a declaration as, "if he (Kemble) would only modify his violences."[18] In an adventure full of drunkenness; deaths by murder, fall, feuds; mob scenes showing lynching, nigger-hunting, tar-and-feathering; and the funeral practices billed as "orgies," it seems ludicrous to cry foul when the drawings show violence. Yet Kemble obviously followed Mark Twain's advice. Of the 174 illustrations, *none* can be considered visually violent. Even in those drawings specifically portraying murder the emotional shift is away from horror toward the analytical.

For example, look at the murder scene in the Sherburn-Boggs

OLD HANK BUNKER.

Figure 14

section (Fig. 12). The text has Colonel Sherburn, a well-dressed man of 55, standing in the street with a pistol pointed at the sky, ready to shoot. Boggs comes reeling across the street, bareheaded, with a friend on either side holding his arms. Boggs' daughter is, at the same second, coming on the run. "Boggs and the men turned round, to see who called him, and when they see the pistol the men jumped to one side, and the pistol barrel come down slow and steady to a level—both barrels cocked. Boggs throws up both of his hands, and says, 'O Lord, don't shoot!' Bang! goes the first shot, and he staggers back clawing at the air" (p. 186).

The drawing depicts the cold-blodded facts of the murder but the savage spirit is softened by omissions and a subjective point of view. A much younger Sherburn is shown impassively shooting Boggs. There are no friends, no daughters and only a hint of a crowd. Boggs is seen from the rear, the angle preventing a view of what must have been terror in the old man's face as he shouts, "O Lord, don't shoot!" The body, leaning forward in an almost

"PLEASE DON'T, BILL"

Figure 15

crucifixion pose, appears strangely calm. The caption—though most captions for the drawings use lines directly from the text[19]—reads simply, "The Death of Boggs." The effect is stark and unmoving rather than terrifying. Mark Twain's direction to Kemble to modify the violence transforms this episode of a merciless murder into a cold statement of death.

The other deaths in *Huck Finn*—murderous, accidental or natural— are all depicted as humorous incidents or de-emphasized by omitting illustration. Avoidance or comedy are the major ways of dealing with death. The drawing of the naked dead man (who by the last chapters is revealed as pap), shot in the back of the head in a grisly scene in the "House of Death" chapter, avoids the corpse and shows a picture "of Jim peering into the dark window of the submerged house" (Fig. 13). The only drawings of Hank Bunker, the drunkard who fell off "the shot tower and spread himself out so that he was just a kind of layer" (p.81) on the ground, shows him alive and well, fearless in looking over his left shoulder at the new moon—the reason given by Huck for his untimely death (Fig. 14). There are two drawings of the at-

"IT AIN'T GOOD MORALS."

Figure 16

THE WRECK.

Figure 17

"THEY GOT HIM OUT AND EMPTIED HIM."

Figure 18

tempted murder of Jim Turner aboard the steamboat *Walter Scott:* one of Jake and Bill tantalizing the helpless Jim (Fig. 15); and one of the two culprits arguing over the "Morality" of the killing (Fig. 16). The final deaths of all three due to natural causes—a sudden storm that prevented Huck from rescuing the beleaguered trio before the ship breaks up and they are presumably drowned—are pictured with as much ambiguity as the prose: a shadowy picture of the listing wreck devoid of human life (Fig. 17).

In the most violent portion of the novel, the Shepherdson-Grangerford feud, nothing of the yearly slaughter is shown, not even the final killing "of Buck and his youthful cousin." Of the stacks of corpses—three from Huck's imagined family; poor, poetic Emmeline's pining away; the uncounted shootings due to the senseless feud; and finally Buck and his cousin—the only death illustrated is that of Stephen Dowling Bots (Fig. 18). In the most viciously destructive section of *Huck Finn,* this trivial, al-

"HE HAD A RAT!"

Figure 19

most comic, death is visualized. Mark Twain's editorial intentions are apparent. If the language describing Emmeline's poetic practices does not give the reader sufficient clue to the overtones of pathetic humor in the poem and scene, the accompanying illustration graphically describes Mark Twain's intention.

Despite the many bodies strewn across the pages of *Huck Finn,* Kemble's drawings show no coffins, no graveyard and only one funeral. And that ceremony for Peter Wilks is truly, in the King's words, "an orgie." The drawing for the Wilks funeral focuses not on the flowers or bier, not on the minister's sermon, not on the grieving family, but on the comical antics of the undertaker and the sleeping congregation. His "*He had a rat*!" (p. 233) (Fig. 19) in prose and picture turns a possibly solemn occasion into another hilariously funny incident. A reader has little chance for prolonged sympathy with either the living or the dead.

Mark Twain's frequent comments on *Huck Finn's* being not

strictly a boy's book are understandable given its stark realities and mayhem. The accompanying Kemble illustrations, however, either dismiss these themes entirely or render them comical. The drawings are not offensive, are nonviolent, and for the most part are funny. From the visual viewpoint, Mark Twain's story is definitely in the genre of the boy's novel.

Mark Twain's "ideas" on the usefulness of the illustrations reduced the impact of the major elements of the novel. Because one of his main concerns was the manipulation and control of a mass audience, illustration became a tool that converted the cruelty and sexuality of the story into a series of humorous boyish adventures. *Huck Finn* was a pictorially pleasant book about a good-looking boy that would amuse an easily offended, always apprehensive, "genteel" 19th century audience. Mark Twain's editorial ideas were proved right. *Adventures of Huckleberry Finn* became one of the most successful novels in American fiction, in part because of the writer's understanding of his audience and in part because Kemble served Mark Twain's purposes so well.

Notes

1. *New York World*, Nov. 27, 1884, p. 1; *New York Tribune*, Nov. 29, 1884, p. 3; *Chicago Tribune*, Nov. 30, 1884, p. 23.

2. A history of the many articles produced about the first edition problems and a copy of the defaced plate were finally handled in an article by Franklin J. Meine, "Some Notes on the First Editions of *Huck Finn*," *American Book Collector*, 10 (June 1960), 31-34.

3. Albert Bigelow Paine, *Mark Twain, A Biography* (New York: Harper Bros., 1912), 2:772.

4. Mark Twain, *Adventures of Huckleberry Finn* (New York: Charles Webster and Company, 1885), p. 17. All further textual references will be to this edition and will be included in the text.

5. Samuel Webster, *Mark Twain: Business Man* (Boston: Little, Brown, 1946), p. 246.

6. E. W. Kemble to Charles Webster, 2 June, 1884, Mark Twain Papers, University of California Library, Berkeley, California.

7. *Business Man*, p. 262.

8. *Business Man*, p. 250.

9. E. W. Kemble, "Illustrating Huckleberry Finn," *Colophon* (Feb. 1930), Pt. 1.

10. Kemble, *Colophon*, Pt. 1.

11. *Business Man*, p. 253.

12. *Business Man*, p. 255.

13. Ibid.

14. *Mark Twain's Letters to his Publishers*, ed. Hamlin Hill (Berkeley: Univ. of California Press, 1967), pp. 174ff.

15. *Letters to his Publishers*, p. 174.

16. *Business Man*, p. 260.

17. Ibid.

18. Ibid.

19. In Allison Ensor's, "The Contributions of Charles Webster and Albert Bigelow Paine to *Huckleberry Finn*," *American Literature*, 40 (May 1968), 222-27, there is proof that Mark Twain wrote neither captions nor running heads for the first-edition illustrations.

Adventures of Huckleberry Finn on Film

Perry Frank

Adventures of Huckleberry Finn, Mark Twain's American epic, has been produced as a theatrical film five times in America (1920, 1931, 1939, 1960, and 1974). In addition, a Russian version of the novel was filmed in 1973. It has also been made as a television movie at least twice (1975, 1978). Besides the full-length treatments, Encyclopedia Britannica Films produced a three-part educational film which included dramatizations from the novel in 1965.

Treatments of *Huckleberry Finn* have varied in quality, with all the versions departing from the novel to a significant degree. Regardless of merit, the screen treatments have received mixed reviews, reflecting perhaps the public ambivalence toward the novel itself. Productions have followed several times within a year of *Tom Sawyer,* and some of the tone of the earlier book often has been carried over into the *Huckleberry Finn* project. Bowdlerizations of the latter into a saccharine adventure story have disappointed lovers of the novel.

Twain was filmed within the first decade of commercial filmmaking in America. Robert Irwin, writing in the summer 1967 issue of the *Mark Twain Journal,* refers to a 1900 version of *The Adventures of Tom Sawyer.* A second silent *Tom Sawyer* was produced in 1917 by Paramount and directed by William Desmond Taylor; a sequel featuring the same cast, *Huck and Tom,* was made later the same year.

Eager to recapture a waning juvenile audience, Paramount followed up with the first screen treatment of *Huckleberry Finn* in 1920. Also directed by the gifted Taylor the film featured unknown Lewis Sargent as Huck. The rest of the cast included Orral Humphrey as the Duke, Tom D. Bates as the King, George Reed as Jim, Martha Mattox as Miss Watson, Edythe Chapman as Aunt Polly, and Frank Lanning as Pap. With relatively strong players and extensive location shooting, the film had many merits and received good notices. The *Variety* review dated February 27, 1920 praises Lewis Sargent. The *New York Times* review of February 23, 1920 is generally favorable, but notes that some episodes are omitted, and complains about the intrusion of a romantic interest between Huck and Mary Jane Wilks. The review also notes the violence done to the ending by making Huck return to the Widow's rather than heading out for the territory, as in the novel.

Despite the distortions of the screenplay, scholar William K. Everson praises it in *American Silent Film*, calling it "possibly still the best screen adaptation of Mark Twain." He ascribes the flaws in the script, as well as shortcomings in the editing, to Paramount's cautious policy at the time and the studio's reluctance to tamper with a formula which had produced box office success with the earlier *Tom Sawyer* production. Unfortunately, this version is now out of distribution.

Hollywood waited a decade before tackling Twain again, but in 1930 Paramount came out with the first sound version of *The Adventures of Tom Sawyer*. Directed by John Cromwell and featuring famous child-stars Jackie Coogan (Tom) and Junior Durkin (Huck), the film scored another commercial success. The following year, again attempting to ride Tom Sawyer's coattails, the same cast was brought together in a 73-minute remake of *Huckleberry Finn*. Norman Taurog, who began his acting career with the sound era and specialized in light, workmanlike fare, directed the heavily revised screenplay by Grover Jones and William McNutt.

According to Mordaunt Hall's August 1931 *New York Times* review, this version features Becky Thatcher (played by Mitzi Green) and incorporates other material from Tom Sawyer; apparently this treatment, like the 1920 film, relies heavily on a romantic interest to carry the story. The action begins in Hannibal, where Huck is made fun of in school by insensitive classmates.

After being dragged to a deserted cabin by his Pap (played by Warner Richmond), Huck and Tom run away to become "pirates" and travel down the river together, encountering many adventures along the way. The boys pick up the fraudulent King and Duke, who have been put ashore by a steamer; the pair tries to swindle the bereft Wilks girls, and are exposed by Huck and Tom. The end of the film finds Tom ready to reconcile with Becky Thatcher and Huck enamoured of Mary Jane Wilks. Although the noted black actor Clarence Muse played Jim, the *New York Times* review gives no indication of how, or if, he figures in the plot of this much-adulterated *Huckleberry Finn.*

The film on the whole was well received. Mordaunt Hall praised the principals, and noted that Junior Durkin as Huck resembled his illustrations. The August 9, 1931 *Film Daily* also gave the picture high marks, asserting that "everyone who enjoyed Tom Sawyer will get just about as much refreshing entertainment out of this second picture...." The August 11, 1931 *Variety* review praises the supporting performances of Clarence Muse and Jane Darwell (the Widow Douglas), and describes the direction as balanced and smooth. Richard Dana Skinner, in the August 26, 1931 issue of *Commonweal,* admitted that the story had undergone vast modifications but said it "remains an epic of boyhood on the edge of adolescence." The only dissenting voice located was the review in the August 26, 1931 issue of *Outlook* which complained that the story "had been changed almost beyond recognition," and said further that "those who know Mark Twain will be furious, and those who do not will see a passably entertaining story about children called Huck and Tom."

MGM released the third feature-length *Adventures of Huckleberry Finn* in 1939, about a year after David Selznick produced a very successful, and apparently faithful adaptation of *Tom Sawyer* for United Artists. Produced by Joseph Mankeiwicz and directed by Richard Thorpe, this 91-minute black and white release featured child star Mickey Rooney as Huck and the gifted black actor Rex Ingram as Jim. In contrast to the *Tom Sawyer* of the previous year, the screenplay by Hugo Butler departs significantly from the original, omitting the Grangerford episode as well as the Phelps segment which includes Tom Sawyer and comprises the last fifth of the novel. In this version, which was filmed on the Sacramento River, Jim is turned in to the authorities by Captain Brandy (Minor Watson), a friend of Mary Jane and Susan Wilks (played by Lynn Carver and Jo Ann Sayers), after the King and Duke (Walter Connolly and William Frawley) are routed. Captain Brandy, who expresses abolitionist sentiments, takes Huck up the river to free Jim as a lynch mob closes in. The film concludes with Jim headed north on the River Queen after being freed by the Widow at Huck's behest. Huck, safely back at the Widow Douglas's, waves goodbye from the dock. The final cut shows a corncob pipe in his back pocket and his shoes on the dock—our reminder that Huck will not be "sivilized."

Reviews were fairly negative, with the February 2, 1939 *Variety* asserting that "the film fails to catch the rare and sparkling humor and sincerity of the author's original." The April 26, 1939 *New Republic* praised Rooney, but scored Walter Connolly and William Frawley as resembling "end men from some insolvent minstrel show." *Film Daily* of February 17, 1939 blamed Twain for the film's failure, inexplicably stating that the "close parallel to the printed word only serves to emphasize how outdated Mark Twain has really become." The same review criticized the direction for creating characters which lacked the subtlety and humor of Twain's originals. "Huck Finn ... becomes a rough homespun version of Mickey Rooney trying to forget that he is a sophisticate of the Hardy Family and pretend he is just a child of the backwoods. ...The bald incidents of the immortal story with this treatment become very flat and mechnical and uninteresting." The *New York Times* review of March 3, 1939 perhaps comes closest to the heart of the problem. Bosley Crowther described the film as "an average, workmanlike piece of cinematic hokum ...(which) affords little, if any insight into the realistic boyhood world of which old Mark wrote with such imperishable humor." Crowther continues to note that the slight importance attached to the world of adult authority reduces the rebellion of the "outlaws" to school-boy antics and buffoonery.

From the vantage point of 1984, Thorpe's *Huck* looks uninspired. Rooney projects a self-conscious cuteness which is counter to the Twain character. One startling departure from the novel is Huck's metamorphosis into an abolitionist who convinces the Widow Douglas to free Jim in a speech allowing as "it ain't right for one human being to own another." The moral complexity of Huck's ambivalence and choice is therefore lost in this version.

The King and Duke, who are the major supporting figures in

this treatment, seem too slick for their parts and do not convey the seediness which makes them believable in the novel. The Widow (Elizabeth Risdon) and Miss Watson (Clara Blandick) become humorous parodies of stuffy gentility, with no suggestion of the intrinsic goodness which, as Crowther suggests, gives them significance. Rex Ingram as Jim gives the best performance of the film, although his part is simplified and abbreviated, and his mannerisms have an Uncle Tom quality which will offend some contemporary viewers. The cinematography and sets are competent without being creative in any way. All in all, the treatment seems aimed for a juvenile audience without attaching too much importance to the underlying meaning of the novel or the potential for richer cinematic approaches.

A generation passed before Hollywood attempted another *Huckleberry Finn;* possibly the glut of war pictures during the forties and the conservative atmosphere of the fifties did not favor a return of the classic, in however modified a form. In 1960 MGM brought out its second *Adventures of Huckleberry Finn*, with noted child actor Eddie Hodges as Huck and former boxing champion Archie Moore as Jim. The film was produced by Samuel Goldwyn, Jr., and directed by Michael Curtiz.

While not one of Curtiz's masterpieces, the 107-minute color production goes beyond appeal to the juvenile audience and attempts to capture some of the flavor of the novel. As in earlier productions, the screenplay departs markedly from the original, cutting out major portions and incorporating new material. This version begins in Hannibal with the arrival of a great river boat, which Huck views with wonder and awe. Huck is abducted by Pap Finn, played convincingly by Neville Brand, and ends up on Jackson's Island with Jim as in the novel. A brief encounter with the Grangerfords and Shepherdsons, which looks as though it might have been edited from longer sequences, is all that remains of that episode; the balance of the film revolves around adventures with the King and Duke (Tony Randall and Mickey Shaughnessy), who unsuccessfully attempt to defraud Mary Jane and Joanna Wilks (Sherry Jackson and Patty McCormick), and are exposed by Huck. Huck, who is afraid that Mary Jane Wilks will "sivilize" him like the Widow, leaves with Jim. The pair board a river boat, but unfortunately the King and Duke are also on board, and Jim and Huck have to jump ship.

Landing in a river town, Huck joins a circus and bills Jim as an

African king in order to get a ride across the river to free territory. The King and Duke catch up with them and expose their ruse; Huck escapes, but Jim is branded as a runaway slave and locked up. Huck springs him by dressing up as a girl and pretending to have been sent to fetch him; the two are pursued by dogs through the woods, and Jim reaches the river and swims for freedom while Huck decoys the hounds. The final cut shows Jim on shore alone, a river boat in the background.

The film received relatively favorable reviews, with high marks from Bosley Crowther (*New York Times*, August 4, 1960) on the location setting (the Sacramento River again), and the photography (by Ted McCord). Both Crowther and Robert C. Roman, in the June/July 1960 issue of *Films in Review*, commented on the inadequacy of Eddie Hodges as Huck, and felt the appeal of the film was hurt by this crucial miscasting. Crowther describes Hodges as "cute," but points out that this characteristic misses the essence of Huck as many see him. On the other hand, Archie Moore, in his debut as an actor, was praised for his characterization of Jim. The river boat and circus sequences which were added to the narrative may have been developed to give him more exposure.

Produced in an era of heightened consciousness of race relations, this version focuses on the relationship between Huck and Jim. Huck begins with reservations about helping Jim escape, but the slave's warmth, courage, and humanity create a strong bond between them which culminates in Huck's decision to defy the authorities (and risk his soul). Some of the great dialogue is preserved, as when Jim confides in Huck about his family. The problem is that the moral lesson seems grafted on to an otherwise fast-paced adventure story; the profound spiritual dilemma is reduced to a homily for school children.

Curtiz has taken some care in developing the secondary characters. The King and the Duke are foils for each other, with the King's clever aggressiveness played off against the doltish Duke. The Wilks sisters, Mary Jane and Joanna, also are a nice contrast—the glamorous but credulous Mary Jane sets off tomboyish, commonsensical Joanna in an interesting way. Neville Brand as Pap and Finlay Currie as Captain Sellers (from the River Boat sequence which is drawn loosely from *Life on the Mississippi*) give very competent although not complex performances. While the continuity leaves something to be desired, editing of individual scenes is polished, and Ted McCord's color photography (now badly faded) must have added to the appeal of the film when it was released.

Cinematic treatment of Twain took an unlikely turn in 1973-1974 with the independently produced musical versions of *The Adventures of Tom Sawyer* and *Adventures of Huckleberry Finn*. Funded by Reader's Digest and released through United Artists, this 118-minute color *Huck* was directed by J. Lee Thompson, who died before completion of the film; the production was finished under the supervision of Robert F. Blumofe. Jeff East starred as Huck and Paul Winfield played Jim. The screenplay and score were written by Robert B. Sherman and Richard M. Sherman. Laszlo Kovacs photographed the film in color on location in Illinois and Mississippi.

In this treatment, Jeff East plays a somewhat anemic Huck to a young, idealized Jim, who is shown with his lovely wife (Odessa Cleveland) in a slave setting. As in the novel, Pap Finn (Gary Merrill) unexpectedly appears to demand money from Miss Watson (Ruby Leftwich) and the Widow Douglas (Lucille Benson). Huck is abducted by Pap, and Jim takes leave of his family, to bursts of song ("Freedom," sung by Roberta Flack). Meanwhile, Huck escapes from Pap's shack and arranges things to appear that he has been murdered. The two wind up on Jackson's Island, and in a reversal from the novel, Huck is bitten by a snake and nursed back to health by Jim. The pair strike out by raft for Cairo, and enroute Huck learns that he has supposedly been murdered by Jim; he witnesses a senseless and bloody feud between the Grangerford's and the Shepherdson's and saves Jim from being caught by slave-hunters.

Jim and Huck pick up the King and Duke (played by Harvey Korman and David Wayne) as they are put off a river boat in disgrace. Huck is caught up in their ventures in order to avoid their turning Jim in as a runaway, and participates in the charade in which the King and Duke attempt to defraud Mary Jane and Susan Wilks (Kim O'Brien and Jean Fay) of their inheritance. Huck exposes the con and gives the king a hotfoot as he is preparing to auction off the Wilk's estate. Taking leave of Mary Jane, with whom he has developed a romantic interest, Huck finds Jim in a clearing shackled to a tree. Huck's wiles prevail, and he frees Jim, who runs for the river. The finale shows Jim telling Huck that Pap is dead, thus making it possible for Huck to return to the

Widow, clear Jim of the murder, and buy freedom for Jim's wife and child. The final cut shows Huck on the river bank watching Jim push off for freedom.

Reviews indicate that the Reader's Digest version of *Tom Sawyer* produced in 1973 (and directed by Don Taylor) had some vitality and that the musical numbers were integrated into the dramatic structure. The same cannot be said for the 1974 production of *Huckleberry Finn,* which received a uniformly bad press. The tone was off, according to Tom Milne, writing in *Monthly Film Bulletin,* June 1974. Not only were the characters crude and sketchily played, the songs pallid echoes of those in Tom Sawyer, but Thompson's jump-cut technique was wrong for a landscape that cried out for long takes. Dorothy Some in the June/July 1974 issue of *Films in Review* characterized the film as "a depressing musical based on Mark Twain's great story." Although Lawrence Van Gelder, reviewing the film for the *New York Times* of May 25, 1974, credits Paul Winfield with a strong, dignified performance as Jim, and thought Korman and Wayne outstandingly funny as the King and Duke, his final judgment is that the film is "a lavish bore." A tongue-in-cheek Alexander Stuart in the August 1974 issue of *Films and Filming* observed, "Trouble is, ev'ryone in this flicker looks like they never eat'n anythin' but traditional, home-baked apple pie." The April 13, 1974 clip from *Variety* sums it up: "An improbable operetta treatment, predictable right down to the music cues, combined with a script that is almost patronizing when it isn't paternalistic, makes the late Arthur P. Jacobs' valedictory production slightly embarrassing."

Interestingly, Sherman and Sherman's screenplay, which took such a beating in critiques of the film, in some respects follows the novel more closely than other versions. The beginning and ending are markedly different, of course: Jim is initially shown with a family in slave quarters, and the closing action drops the Phelps sequence and distorts the finale of the novel by leaving the viewer with the impression that Huck will return to the Widow Douglas. In between, the incidents of the abandoned houseboat, the Sarah Williams episode, the narrow escape from slave hunters, the Grangerford sequence, the Shakespearean show fiasco, and the Wilks chapters are all included.

As several reviewers noted, however, the film is off in tone. Perhaps the novel cannot lend itself to a musical treatment. The score certainly seems pedestrian and intrusive, with the possible exceptions of the theme song, "Freedom," and "Royalty," sung by Korman and Wayne. The Twain dialect, or even dialogue, are attempted only in a few places, and interest is sustained by broad overacting on the parts of the supporting characters. Jeff East looks more like Huck than Rooney or Hodges; his performance is passable, although a little pale. Without the dynamics and dialogue from Twain, the role can be insipid. Paul Winfield's performance, praised for its "dignity," passes into an idealization which does not serve the production. Jim becomes significant because of his humanity, not his nobility. Laszlo Kovacs's photography is good and the effort to film the production in Illinois and Mississippi is commendable.

Two made-for-television movies have also been based on *Huckleberrry Finn*. The 1975 video film was produced for ABC by Steven North and directed by Robert Totten. The teleplay was prepared by Jean Holloway. Royal Dano impersonated Mark Twain as narrator, Ron Howard starred as Huck, and Antonio Fargas played Jim.

In this 78-minute color treatment, Jim and Huck set off down the river after Huck escapes from his Pap and discovers Jim hiding out on Jackson's Island. There is much stage business involving Huck's trick on his father, Jim and Huck on the island, and the search party looking for Huck's body. Further time is taken up with Twain's "narration" and the intercutting of stills with freeze frames from key scenes. The result is a drastic abbreviation of the action, which for this *Huck* includes mainly the episodes with the King and the Duke (played by Jack Elam and Merle Haggard). After the pair are exposed as frauds, Huck learns that Jim has been captured and is being held prisoner by the Phelps family.

The remaining sequences deal with Huck's impersonation of Tom when he encounters Aunt Sally, the boys' tribulations in freeing Jim (which culminate in Tom's being shot), and the final discovery that Miss Watson has died, freeing Jim. Twain appears in the final cut to offer a homily on the river and friendship, backed by the theme song, "Said the River, I'm Your Friend" (sung by Roy Clark).

As the April 2, 1975 review in *Variety* noted, the film is slow, with stills and freeze frames, the Twain narration, long takes, padded dialogue, and much stage business diluting the dramatic impact of the action. Ron Howard and Donny Most (who plays

Tom), seem more like good ol' boys than the mercurial characters Twain envisioned. The King and Duke are predictably overplayed, and Mary Jane Wilks (Patty Weaver) seems excessively glamorized. Antonio Fargos is a thin, mean-faced Jim who does not fit the character. The moral impact of the film is diffused by making the relationship between Huck and Jim one of good pals. The photography (by Andrew Jackson) and the California locations are satisfactory, and the total effect might appeal to preteen audiences who have no acquaintance with the novel.

A second television *Adventures of Huckleberry Finn* was made in 1978 for Schick-Sunn Classics, Inc. This 97-minute color feature was produced by Bill Cornford and directed by Jack B. Hively from a teleplay by Tom Chapman. Kurt Ida stars as Huck, Brock Peters plays Jim, and Dan Monahan is Tom.

This treatment begins prior to the action of the novel, in sequences lifted from *Tom Sawyer*. A cemetary scene leads to the discovery of the money which is placed in trust for Huck by Judge Thatcher (Jack Kruschen). The boys pledge friendship with a young, slick, obliging Jim, who warns Huck that Miss Watson is planning to send him to school back east. Later, Huck admonishes Miss Watson that it is wrong for one human being to own another. Huck returns to his room to find Pap Finn (played by Cliff Osmond) who demands his money and takes Huck to his shack. Huck escapes and fakes his own murder, Jim is accused, and both end up on Jackson's Island.

In hiding, Jim tells Huck of his plan to flee to a free state, and the two prepare a raft for the journey. Huck dresses up as a girl and goes back to town to find out what is happening; he learns that a search party is headed for the island, and the two shove off on the Mississippi. Next, Huck throws slave hunters off Jim's trail by pretending his folks have small pox. Later, the raft is splintered by a river boat, and Huck washes ashore on a sandbar where he is accosted and tied up by a man identified as a Grangerford; Jim rescues him, and some children who help the two remind him of the family he has left behind.

Huck and Jim come upon the King and the Duke, who are being pursued by an angry crowd and beg to be taken aboard the raft. A large, grey-haired Duke (Forrest Tucker) and a short, dark King with bangs (Larry Storch) involve Huck and Jim in their antics which include building a church congregation and putting on a rum theatrical performance. Huck and Jim dash from the theater ahead of an angry mob; when Huck reaches the raft, Jim is not there, but he finds a muddy wanted poster. Huck sets out to find Jim, and learns that he is being held prisoner in the town where Tom Sawyer is expected for a visit to Aunt Sally.

Huck impersonates Tom at Aunt Sally's and intercepts Tom to fill him in on the ruse; the boys find Jim in a barn and pry him loose. While being pursued through the woods, Huck is wounded. The final sequence shows him at Aunt Sally's begging for Jim's freedom; the denouement occurs when it is revealed that Miss Watson has already freed Jim, as a result of Huck's previous moralizing. Jim and Huck shake hands, and Huck promises to loan him the money to buy his family's freedom. The final cut shows Huck and Tom planning a new adventure.

While preserving some of the episodes from the novel, this version of *Huckleberry Finn* is not especially interesting. Miscasting is a problem, with a big, strapping Huck projecting the image of an all-American 1970s teenager whose most serious conflict with his father involves use of the family car. Tom is also too old and large for his part. Jim in this treatment is a jiving buddy, completely missing the simplicity and dignity of the original. The intrusion of antislave sentiments on the part of Huck early in the narrative subverts the moral dilemma which carries so much of the dramatic impact of the story. Deletion of the Wilks episode, which is important in the novel and other film versions, also weakens the narrative.

In addition to the seven American productions, a Russian *Huckleberry Finn* was made in 1973. The film was released by Mosfilm Studios in Moscow, and directed by Georgi N. Daneliya, a gifted film artist with a penchant for Twain. Daneliya also wrote the screenplay. Eleven-year-old fourth grader Roma Madyanov starred as Huck, and Felix Immokuede, a Nigerian geology student at Moscow's Patrice Lumumba University, played Jim. The Duke was acted by Georgian Vakhtang Kikabidze, a singer, and Yevgeny Leonov, a popular Moscow character actor, played the King. Vladimir P. Basov, a well-known director in his own right, played Pap. The production was filmed on the Dneiper River; other segments were shot in the Baltic region of Lithuania, where some river towns resemble those along the Mississippi. The film was photographed by Vadim I. Yusov.

Besides the feature-length treatments of *Huckleberry Finn*, in 1965 Encyclopedia Britannica, Inc., produced a three-part educational series intended to illuminate the novel. The films were written and narrated by Clifton Fadiman, and included dramatized segments from the story.

Part I, *What Does Huckleberry Finn Say?*, defines the novel as a tale of adventure, a picture of a world, and a drama of moral conflict. Concentrating on the last two themes, Fadiman comments on excerpts which include Huck and his Pap, Huck with the Grangerford family, and the Boggs-Sherburn incident. Fadiman makes the point that as Huck tries to escape from civilization, he encounters it at every turn, and that evil exists at both the bottom and top of the social scale. The moral conflict of the novel is rendered in scenes where Jim chastizes Huck for playing him as a fool, and where Huck writes, and then tears up, his letter to Miss Watson informing on Jim.

In Part II, *The Art of Huckleberry Finn*, Fadiman points out formal structures which tie the novel together. These include language, the river, point of view, and the motifs of money and appearance versus reality. The Sarah Williams episode and excerpts from the Phelps sequences are shown, as well as some scenes centering on money. Part III, *Huck Finn and the American Experience*, shows how the novel differs from other classics, both ancient and modern. Instead of using idealization as a mode of thematic development, Twain celebrates the commonplace, using the vernacular, poking fun at both real and pretended erudition, and incorporating humor as a major dramatic device. Dramatized episodes include Huck's improvisation when he impersonates Tom to Aunt Sally, and the argument between Huck and Jim over King Solomon.

Fadiman's commentary probably does not go beyond what most college instructors can bring to the text. The most interesting aspects of the series are the dramatizations, which could be effective in involving secondary and college students in the novel. The treatments differ strikingly from all the other versions of *Huckleberry Finn* in one important respect: the dialogue, and even the dialect, is taken verbatim from Twain's text. Without name actors or elaborate sets, and even with the difficulties—sometimes apparent—of rendering the language, the scenes are nevertheless powerful and engrossing. The dramatizations were directed by Larry Yust. Scott McCarter starred as Huck, James Edwards played Jim, and Mark Twain was impersonated by Jamie Forster. Other members of the cast included Jim Boles as Pap;

Jane Ellis, Miss Watson; Lillian Bronson, the Widow Douglas; Bill Benedict, the King; Joe Haworth, the Duke; and Duane Chase as Tom.

Despite the periodic efforts to film *Huckleberry Finn*, the results have been less than satisfactory. The first two versions (1920, 1931) received reasonably favorable reviews and did good box office business, but were not considered major film achievements. Attempts seem to have gone down hill since then, with the 1939, 1960, 1974, and the two video versions getting fair to poor receptions.

No doubt the continuing interest in filming *Huckleberry Finn* relates to the novel's central role in the canon of American literature—a role which has taken on increased dimensions with the passing years. Considered by many to be the first—and perhaps the greatest—modern American novel, its humor, cinematic setting, and adventurous plot make it an obvious film subject. At the same time, its complex moral vision, social criticism which centers on the race issue, and the difficult dialect coupled with a first person point-of-view, present problems for filmmakers if they are interested in rendering a faithful adaptation. The upshot is that Hollywood, like the larger society, has been uncertain about whether to treat *Huckleberry Finn* as a major adult work, or as a children's tale.

As noted above, *Huckleberry Finn* was produced several times shortly after *Tom Sawyer*, in an apparent attempt to capitalize on the appeal of the latter to the juvenile audience (1920, 1931, 1939, 1974). This orientation has led to major revisions of the original, as screenwriters have deleted or softened elements of child abuse, alcoholism, racial oppression, decadence and cruelty which are contained in the novel. The first two film versions brought Tom Sawyer into the early part of the adventure, and a romantic interest was added to both. The Sherburn-Boggs and Grangerford-Shepherdson episodes, which include violence unsuitable for audiences of children, have been deleted from nearly all treatments, and new material has been substituted to move the story along.

Likewise, the racial theme, which is central to Huck's moral development in the novel is minimized in the 1920 and 1931 treatments. Later versions put more emphasis on the relationship between Huck and Jim, with the focus shifting to reflect changing societal attitudes. Michael Curtiz's 1960 film comes closest to dealing with the issue in Twain's terms, but the moral lesson seems grafted on to the adventure story. In the 1970s versions, Huck is made the facile spokesman for the forces of good, an approach which diffuses the issue and subverts the crisis of conscience which lends weight to the original.

Aside from the difficulties of producing a compelling script, the novel presents some other problems for filmmakers. Casting is crucial, and it has not been possible to find juvenile leads who can do justice to the part of Huck, and, to a lesser extent, Tom. Child stars of the past—Eddie Hodges, Mickey Rooney—have projected a "cuteness" which is out of sync with the scruffy, unselfconscious Huck that many envision. Later versions have tended to insensitive, rather stolid characterizations. Jim has also proved a problem, with early treatments embodying an "Uncle Tom" quality, and later films producing an unbelievable "buddy" or companion which is jarring to audiences who know the novel. In keeping with the dependence on farce to carry *Huckleberry Finn* as it has been produced, supporting characters have tended to be overdrawn, with Mark Twain in whiskers appearing as narrator several times. In addition to casting, the attempts at location shooting have fallen short of their potential to convey the grandeur of the Mississippi, and the score has been notably weak in some versions, especially those of 1960 and 1974.

While the measure of a film is not the degree to which it is faithful to its sources, in this case adaptations of the original material have not served the productions. Not surprisingly, Hollywood scriptwriters have come up with a less compelling story than Mark Twain; *Huckleberry Finn* on celluloid has neither been the powerful vision of America and moral allegory of the novel, nor an engrossing children's film on its own terms. The approach of Hollywood perhaps reflects the ambivalence of the larger society toward the novel and its themes. In 1984, *Adventures of Huckleberry Finn* is overdue for a serious film treatment worthy of the original.

Notes

1. Robert Irwin, "The Failure of Tom Sawyer and Huckleberry Finn on Film," *Mark Twain Journal*, 13 (Summer 1976), 9-11

2. William K. Everson, *American Silent Film* (New York: Oxford University Press, 1978), pp. 150-151.

3. Robert C. Roman, "The Adventures of Huckleberry Finn," *Films in Review,* 11 (June/July 1960), 364-66.

4. Tom Milne, "Huckleberry Finn," *Monthly Film Bulletin,* 41 (June 1974), 127-28.

5. Dorothy Some, "Huckleberry Finn," *Films in Review,* 25 (June/July 1974), 374-75.

6. Alexander Stuart, "Huckleberry Finn," *Films and Filming,* 20 (August 1974), 374-75.

Sources

Books and Articles

Everson, William K. *American Silent Film.* New York: Oxford University Press, 1978.

Feature Films in 8mm, 16mm, and Videotape. 7th ed. Comp. and ed. by James L. Limbacher. New York and London: R. R. Bowker, 1982.

Irwin, Robert. "The Failure of Tom Sawyer and Huckleberry Finn on Film." *Mark Twain Journal,* 13 (Summer 1967), 9-11.

Milne, Tom. "Huckleberry Finn." *Monthly Film Bulletin,* 41 (June 1974), 127-28.

Roman, Robert C. "The Adventures of Huckleberry Finn." *Films in Review,* 11 (June/July 1960), 364-66.

Shabad, Theodore. "'Huck Finn' Put on Film in Soviet." *New York Times,* November 29, 1972, p. 32.

Some, Dorothy. "Huckleberry Finn." *Films in Review,* 25 (June/July 1974), 374-75.

Stuart, Alexander. "Huckleberry Finn." *Films and Filming,* 20 (August 1974), 48-9.

TV Feature Film Source Book. Syosset, N.Y.: Broadcast Information Bureau, Inc., 1983.

Reviews

Commonweal. Review of *Huckleberry Finn*. By Richard Dana Skinner. August 26, 1931, p. 406

Film Daily. "Tom Sawyer." November 23, 1930, p. 10.

__________ . "Huckleberry Finn." August 9, 1931, p. 10.

__________ . "Huckleberry Finn." February 17, 1939, p. 6.

Newsweek. "Review of *Huckleberry Finn*." February 27, 1931, p.24.

The New Republic. Review of *Huckleberry Finn*. April 26, 1939, p. 336.

New York Times. "'Tom Sawyer' in Movies." December 31, 1917, p. 13:4.

New York Times. Review of *Huckleberry Finn*. February 23, 1920, p. 17:2.

__________. "Jackie Coogan's Return." By Mordaunt Hall. December 20, 1930, p. 6.

__________. "Another Mark Twain Classic." By Mordaunt Hall. August 1931.

__________. "The Adventures of Tom Sawyer." By Bosley Crowther. February 17, 1938, p. 17:2.

__________. "Huckleberry Finn." By Bosley Crowther. March 3, 1939, p. 21:2.

__________. "The Adventures of Huckleberry Finn." By Bosley Crowther. August 4, 1960, p. 17:1.

__________. "Screen: A Vapid Huckleberry Finn." By Lawrence Van Gelder. May 25, 1974, p. 16:1.

Variety. Review of *Huckleberry Finn*. February 27, 1920, p. 46.

__________. Review of *Tom Sawyer*. February 16, 1938, p. 15.

__________. "Huckleberry Finn." February 2, 1939, p. 12.

__________. "Huckleberry Finn." April 3, 1974, p. 14.

__________. "Huckleberry Finn." April 2, 1975, p. 57.

Filmography

Huckleberry Finn

Paramount
1920
Silent, black and white

Director: William Desmond Taylor
Scenario: Julia Crawford

Huck: Lewis Sargent
Jim: George Reed
Tom: Gordon Griffith
Pap: Frank Lanning
King: Tom D. Bates
Duke: Orral Humphrey
Miss Watson: Martha Mattox
Aunt Polly: Edythe Chapman

Huckleberry Finn

Paramount
1931

73 minutes, black and white

Director: Norman Taurog
Adaptors: Grover Jones, William McNutt
Camerman: David Abel
Recording Engineer: Gene Merritt

Huck: Junior Durkin
Jim: Clarence Muse
Tom: Jackie Coogan
Pap: Warner Richmond
Becky Thatcher: Mitzi Green
Junior: Eugene Pallette
Sid Sawyer: Jackie Searl
Widow Douglas: Jane Darwell
Senior: Oscar Apfel
Mary Jane: Charlotte V. Henry
Miss Watson: Lillian Harmer
Judge Thatcher: Guy Oliver
Aunt Polly: Clara Blandick
Ella: Doris Short
Mrs. Thatcher: Cecil Weston
Abigail Prentice: Aileen Manning
Teacher: Frank McGlynn

The Adventures of Huckleberry Finn

MGM
1939
98 minutes, black and white

Producer: Joseph L. Maniewicz
Director: Richard Thorpe
Screenplay: Hugo Butler
Photography: John Seitz
Editor: Frank E. Hull

Huck: Mickey Rooney
Jim: Rex Ingram
King: Walter Connolly
Duke: William Frawley
Mary Jane: Lynne Carver
Susan: Jo Ann Sayers
Captain Brandy: Minor Watson

Widow Douglas: Elizabeth Risdon
Pap: Victor Killian
Miss Watson: Clara Blandick

The Adventures of Huckleberry Finn

MGM
1960
107 minutes, color

Producer: Samuel Goldwyn, Jr.
Director: Michael Curtiz
Script: James Lee
Photography: Ted McCord
Art Directors: George W. Davis, McClure Capps
Set Directors: Henry Grace, Robert Priestly
Score: Jerome Moross

Huck: Eddie Hodges
Jim: Archie Moore
King: Tony Randall
Duke: Mickey Shaughnessy
Pap: Neville Brand
Mary Jane: Sherry Jackson
Joanna: Patty McCormick
Sheriff's wife: Judy Canova
Mr. Carmody: Andy Devine
Lion Tamer: Buster Keaton
Captain Sellers: Finlay Currie
Widow Douglas: Josephine Hutchinson
Grangerford Man: Parley Baer
Slave Catcher: John Carradine
Sheriff: Royal Dano
Riverboat Singer: Dolores Hawkins
Barber: Sterling Holloway
Slave Catcher: Dean Stanton

The Adventures of Huckleberry Finn

United Artists-Reader's Digest
1974
117 minutes, color

Producer: Arthur P. Jacobs

Director: J. Lee Thompson (completed by Robert F. Blumofe)
Screenplay: Robert B. Sherman, Richard M. Sherman
Music and Lyrics: Robert B. Sherman, Richard M. Sherman
Photography: Laszlo Kovacs
Editor: Michael Anderson
Music Supervision: Fred Warner
Production Design: Philip Jefferies
Set Decoration: Robert DeVestel
Sound: Larry Jost, Jim Pilcher

Huck: Jeff East
Jim: Paul Winfield
Duke: David Wayne
King: Harvey Korman
Col. Grangerford: Arthur O'Connell
Pap: Gary Merrill
Mrs. Loftus: Natalie Trundy
Widow Douglas: Lucille Benson
Miss Watson: Ruby Leftwich
Mary Jane: Kim O'Brien
Susan: Jean Fay
Jim's Wife: Odessa Cleveland
Jason: Joe Boris
Kyle: Danny Lantrip
Wayne: Van Bennett
Mrs. Grangerford: Linda Watkins
Miss Emmeline: Jean Combs
Miss Charlotte: Frances Fawcett
Miss Maryanne: Suzanne Prystup
Horatio: H. L. Rowley
Marybelle: Doris Owens
Buck: Frank Mills
Miss Sophia: Sherree Sinquefield

Songs:
"Freedom," sung by Roberta Flack
"Some Day, Honey Darling," sung by Paul Winfield
"Rotten Luck," sung by Gary Merrill
"Cairo, Illinois," sung by Jeff East, Paul Winfield
"A Rose in a Bible," sung by Jean Combs, Suzanne Prystup
"Royalty," sung by Harvey Korman, David Wayne
"Royal Nonesuch," sung by Harvey Korman

"Into His Hands," sung by Harvey Korman, mourners
"What's Right, What's Wrong," sung by Jeff East
"Huckleberry Finn," sung by chorus

Huckleberry Finn

ABC
1975
90 minutes, color

Producer: Steven North
Director: Robert Totten
Teleplay: Jean Holloway
Photography: Andrew Jackson
Music: Earl Robinson
Illustrator: Robert David Totten

Huck: Ron Howard
Jim: Antonio Fargas
Tom: Donny Most
Mark Twain: Royal Dano
Pap: Range Howard
King: Jack Elam
Duke: Merle Haggard
Widow Douglas: Jean Howard
Aunt Sally: Dee Carroll
Silas Phelps: James Almanzar
Aunt Polly: Sarah Selby
Mary Jane: Patty Weaver

Song: "Said the River I'm Your Friend," sung by Roy Clark

Adventures of Huckleberry Finn

Schick-Sunn Classics
1978
97 minutes, color

Producer: Bill Cornford
Director: Jack Hively
Teleplay: Tom Chapman

Huck: Kurt Ida
Jim: Brock Peters
Tom: Dan Monahan
Pap: Cliff Osmond

King: Larry Storch
Duke: Forrest Tucker
Judge Thatcher: Jack Kruschen
Widow Douglas: Helen Kleeb
Miss Watson: Lurene Tuttle

The Adventures of Huckleberry Finn

Mosfilm Studios
1973

Director: Georgi N. Daneliya
Screenplay: Georgi N. Daneliya, Viktoriya Tokareve
Cinematography: Vadim I. Yusov

Huck: Roma Madyanov
Jim: Felix Immokuede
Pap: Vladimir P. Basov
King: Yevgeny Leonov
Duke: Vakhtang Kikabidze

What Does Huckleberry Finn Say?
The Art of Huckleberry Finn
Huckleberry Finn and the American Experience

Encyclopedia Britannica Films, Inc.
1965
78 minutes, color

Commentary: Clifton Fadiman
Director: Larry Yust

Huck: Scott McCarter
Jim: James Edwards
Mark Twain: Jamie Forster
Pap: Jim Boles
Widow Douglas: Lillian Forster
Miss Watson: June Ellis
Tom: Duane Chase
King: Bill Benedict
Duke: Joe Haworth

A Mark Twain Chronology

1835 Samuel Langhorne Clemens born November 30 in Florida, Missouri, third of five children of John Marshall Clemens of Virginia ancestry and Jane Lampton of Kentucky stock.

1839 Family moved to river town of Hannibal, Missouri, where he had irregular schooling.

1847 Father died.

1848 Apprenticed as printer.

1851 Contributed to brother's newspaper.

1853 Worked as journeyman printer and journalist in St. Louis, New York, Philadelphia, Keokuk, and Cincinnati, and contributed humorous sketches to newspapers until 1856, when he apprenticed as a steamboat pilot under Horace Bixby.

1857 Worked as a pilot on the Mississippi River until 1861.

1861 Left for Nevada with his brother Orion, who had been appointed secretary to the territorial governor by President Lincoln.

1862 Began working in Nevada and California as miner, printer, and reporter.

1865 Published "Jim Smiley and His Jumping Frog" in New York *Saturday Press* on November 18 under his adopted pseudonym Mark Twain, and it was widely reprinted. Began an association with Bret Harte and Artemus Ward.

1866 Delivered first lecture in San Francisco on October 2 and initiated a platform career that would last until 1906.

1867 Published his first book, *The Celebrated Jumping Frog of Calaveras County, and Other Sketches*. Visited Europe, the Mediterranean, and Palestine to write reports for the *Alta California* and New York *Tribune* newspapers.

1869 *The Innocents Abroad*, based on his travel reports.

1870 Married Olivia Langdon of Elmira, New York, and bought part ownership of Buffalo *Express* newspaper.

1872 *Roughing It*.

1873 Moved to Hartford, Connecticut.

1873 *The Gilded Age* in collaboration with Charles Dudley Warner.

1875 *Sketches, New and Old.*
1876 *The Adventures of Tom Sawyer.*
1880 *A Tramp Abroad.*
1882 *The Prince and the Pauper.*
1883 *Life on the Mississippi.*
1884 *Adventures of Huckleberry Finn.*
1888 Honorary Master of Arts degree conferred by Yale University.
1889 *A Connecticut Yankee in King Arthur's Court.*
1891 Extensive travel abroad through 1900. Closely associated with William Dean Howells until his death.
1892 *The American Claimant.*
1893 Bankrupted in panic of 1893 because of heavy investments in Paige typesetting machine.
1894 *Pudd'nhead Wilson* and *Tom Sawyer Abroad.*
1896 *Personal Recollections of Joan of Arc.*
1897 *Following the Equator.*
1899 "The Man That Corrupted Hadleyburg."
1900 Moved to New York City.
1904 Wife died.
1906 *What is Man*? Began writing what would be published in 1924 as his *Autobiography.*
1907 Honorary Doctor of Letters degree conferred by Oxford University.
1908 Moved to Redding, Connecticut.
1910 Died at Stormfield, his house in Redding, on April 21.

An Annotated Checklist of Criticism on Adventures of Huckleberry Finn, *1884–1984*

Thomas A. Tenney

Huckleberry Finn appears in many different perspectives in the nearly 600 articles and books which are listed here. It has been praised as a gem of our national literature and faulted for having an awkward ending. It has been attacked by early critics as a disreputable account of a boy and a black man on a raft, and by some more recent ones as insensitive on racial issues. Perhaps the questions are still open; in any case, I have tried to give as complete a picture as possible of the way the public and the critics have responded to *Huckleberry Finn* over the years.

Most of these bibliographic entries and abstracts appeared previously in my *Mark Twain: A Reference Guide* (Boston: G. K. Hall, 1977) and annual supplements in *American Literary Realism;* they are reproduced here with the kind permission of G. K. Hall and *American Literary Realism*. I would recommend these sources, and others listed below, for a fuller account of Mark Twain's life and work.

Before the main body of this bibliography there are sections on editions of *Huckleberry Finn*, guides for further study of Mark Twain, and lists of some essay collections which reprint articles otherwise difficult to obtain; a number of articles listed in the main bibliography are cross-referenced to these reprintings.

I have tried to use abbreviations, sparingly, limiting them to

Mark Twain's major works and to standard bibliographic sources. For the latter I abbreviate *Abstracts of English Studies* as *AES*, and cite the annual bibliographies of the Modern Humanities Research Association and the Modern Language Association as MHRA and MLA, respectively. The abbreviation MT should be self-explanatory, as should most abbreviations for his works: *AC, The American Claimant* (1892); *CY, A Connecticut Yankee in King Arthur's Court* (1889); *FE, Following the Equator* (1897); *GA, The Gilded Age* (1873, with Charles Dudley Warner); *HF, Adventures of Huckleberry Finn* (First British edition 1884, first American edition 1885 — purists do not precede it with the article "*The*," as the first edition did not); *IA, The Innocents Abroad* (1869); *JA, Personal Recollections of Joan of Arc* (1896; not "*The*" *Personal Recollections*, as it is a friend who is recollecting her); *LOM, Life on the Mississippi* (1883); *MS, The Mysterious Stranger* (1916, also, the manuscripts from which it was assembled after MT's death); *P&P,The Prince and the Pauper* (1882); *PW, Pudd'nhead Wilson,* (1894); *RI, Roughing It* (1872); *TS, The Adventures of Tom Sawyer* (1876).

1. Editions of *Huckleberry Finn*

Walter Blair and Victor Fischer are editing the first scholarly edition of *Huckleberry Finn* for publication in 1985. Professor Blair has devoted a lifetime of study to Mark Twain, and his *Mark Twain & Huck Finn* (1960) and *Mark Twain's Hannibal, Huck & Tom* (1969) are particularly important and influential works. A member of the staff at the Mark Twain Project (Berkeley), Mr. Fischer has been working on *Huckleberry Finn* for five years. In addition to his own considerable expertise, he has the benefit of daily contact with other Twain editors and the resources of the Mark Twain Papers. The community of Mark Twain scholars look forward with confidence to a *Huckleberry Finn* which should remain the standard edition for many years to come. Following established practice, the University of California Press will also issue a reader's edition, with the authoritative text established by Mr. Fischer but without the extensive textual apparatus.

Up to the present time the edition preferred for scholarly citation has been the first American edition (New York: Charles L. Webster and Company, 1885). Excellent copies are scarce and valuable, but copies in poorer condition are relatively common in libraries and private collections. Furthermore, Chandler Press (San Francisco) reprinted this edition of *Huckleberry Finn* in facsimile (1962), once with introductory material by Hamlin Hill, and again as *The Art of Huckleberry Finn,* edited by Hill and Walter Blair and expanded to include a number of useful critical essays.

As for other editions of *Huckleberry Finn* there is little to be said. The best of them merely reproduce the text of the first American edition but do not improve on it. Two other editions, however, deserve further comment.

The first of these is the "Mississippi Writings" volume in the *Library of America* series containing the texts of *Tom Sawyer, Life on the Mississippi, Huckleberry Finn,* and *Pudd'nhead Wilson.* This is part of a series funded by grants of nearly two million dollars from the Ford Foundation and the National Endowment for the Humanities and represents the fulfillment of Edmund Wilson's dream of a standard edition of American authors. The Twain volume is well printed on permanent, acid-free paper, but the text of *Huckleberry Finn* is merely that of the first American edition, and will soon be superseded.

Something of a curiosity is *The Annotated "Huckleberry Finn,"* (New York: Clarkson H. Potter, 1981). It is edited by Michael Patrick Hearn, whose previous books include *The Annotated "Wizard of Oz," The Annotated "Christmas Carol,"* and *The Art of the Broadway Poster.* Mr. Hearn has added interesting marginal illustrations and comments (some of them incorrect and some taken from other editions of *Huckleberry Finn* without attribution), but this edition is to be faulted mainly for its text, which is that of the first British edition (preceding the first American edition by a few weeks). No reason is given for supposing that differences between this and the first American edition represent Mark Twain's own preferences. Hearn has silently changed spellings without indicating where he has done so, and he has overlooked such British forms as "armour" and "jewellery" in this story of a boy on the Mississippi River.

In sharp contrast to these two editions is a beautiful facsimile of the *Huckleberry Finn* manuscript from the Buffalo and Erie County Public Library, published by the Gale Research Company (Detroit, 1982). Approximately three-fifths of the text survives: half of Chapter 12, Chapters 13, 14, and 22 to the end. This is a priceless asset, the more so because Fischer's forthcoming California edition will list departures from the manuscript, line by line. The 12-page introduction by Louis J. Budd not only provides the solid historical and textual background we would expect from a highly respected scholar, but also raises provocative questions about ways in which Twain's revisions reveal his intentions in the novel.

2. Bibliographies

The largest and most complete bibliography of writings about Mark Twain and his works is my own *Mark Twain: A Reference Guide* (Boston: G. K. Hall, 1977). This is updated and extended by annual supplements which have been appearing in the journal *American Literary Realism* since 1977.

A pioneering bibliography of Mark Twain scholarship is Roger Asselineau's *The Literary Reputation of Mark Twain from 1910 to 1950: A Critical Essay and a Bibliography* (Paris: Marcel Didier, 1954). The introductory essay is a sound and valuable survey of criticism for the years 1910-1950, and is followed by what was at the time the fullest annotated bibliography of writings about Mark Twain ever compiled. Although I have examined most of the works Asselineau lists and written my own annotations, for a few items his book is still my only source.

E. Hudson Long's *Mark Twain Handbook* (New York: Hendricks House, 1957) provides a good survey of biographical and critical studies, with extensive discussion of Twain's life and works, and an annotated bibliography.

Maurice Beebe and John Feaster's "Criticism of Mark Twain: A Selected Checklist" in *Modern Fiction Studies*, 14 (Spring 1968), 93-139 is a listing of American scholarship, with the useful feature that it lists almost sixty general works with page references for discussions of *Huckleberry Finn;* these listings would be helpful for extending the present bibliography.

Alan Gribben brought the survey of major studies up to date in 1980, with "Removing Mark Twain's Mask: A Decade of Criticism and Scholarship," in *ESQ: A Journal of the American Renaissance*, 26 (2nd Quarter), 100-108; (3rd Quarter), 149-171. In addition to assessing the influence of individual scholars and what he considers seminal works, he points to future directions in Twain scholarship and areas in which investigation might be particularly fruitful. We are further indebted to Professor Gribben for his *Mark Twain's Library: A Reconstruction* (Boston: G. K. Hall, 1980, 2 vols.) which lists nearly 5,000 books, articles, poems, plays, magazines, etc. with which Twain was familiar.

In addition to the *Reference Guide* supplements appearing in *American Literary Realism*, there are several other guides which list books and articles on Twain, often before they appear there. The most valuable of these is the "Mark Twain" bibliographic essay of approximately twenty pages each year, appearing in James Woodress, ed., *American Literary Scholarship: An Annual* (Durham, NC: Duke University Press). Authors of these surveys have been John C. Gerber (for 1963-1968 articles), Hamlin Hill (for articles 1969-1976), and Louis J. Budd (1977—). Coverage is more selective than in my own *Reference Guide* supplements, and annotations are briefer, but they are valuable in that they reflect the judgments of experienced Twain scholars.

Finally, because all bibliographies are incomplete and quickly out of date, the reader should consult the annual bibliographies of the Modern Language Association and the Modern Humanities Research Association (each contains a number of items not listed in the other), as well as *Abstracts of English Studies, America: History and Life, American Literature, Essay and General Literature Index, Humanities Index, MidAmerica* (Michigan State University), *The Reader's Guide to Periodical Literature, Western American Literature,* and *The Year's Work in English Studies.*

3. Essay Collections

The following books are useful sources of articles on *Huckleberry Finn,* and, more broadly, on Mark Twain and his works. Of these the most easily obtainable is the Norton Critical Edition of *Huckleberry Finn* (ed. Bradley and others, 1962, revised ed. 1977). A number of listings in the main section of this bibliography note reprintings in the following collections.

Anderson, Frederick, ed. With the assistance of Kenneth M. Sanderson. *Mark Twain: The Critical Heritage.* London: Routledge & Kegan Paul, and New York: Barnes & Noble, 1971.

Reprints reviews of MT's books and evaluations of his writing, in his lifetime and for the period immediately after his death, in chronological order, with an extensive introduction.

Bowen, James K., and Richard Van DerBeets, eds. *Adventures of Huckleberry Finn. With Abstracts of Twenty Years of Criticism.* Glenview, Illinois: Scott, Foresman and Company, 1970.

Includes a brief, cogent summary of recent work, noting the dramatic growth of serious interest, in Edgar M. Branch, "Mark Twain Scholarship: Two Decades," followed by 40 abstracts of articles on *HF* (all but three by the original authors). These are so extensive (averaging approximately 400 words) that they might be called condensations rather than abstracts. The editors note that these "treat...a variety of important critical considerations: the structure of the novel... its ending in particular... characterization... themes and motifs... language and style...historical contexts... and folklore... among others."

Bradley, Sculley, Richmond Croom Beatty, and E. Hudson Long, eds. *Samuel Langhorne Clemens, Adventures of Huckleberry Finn. An Annotated Text. Backgrounds and Sources. Essays in Criticism.* New York: W. W. Norton, 1962.

A classroom casebook, with text of *HF* (including the "Raftsmen Passage" from *LOM* — see Beidler, 1968 and Manierre, 1968), plus significant background and source material and excerpts from MT's autobiography, the Paine biography, etc. Also contains a valuable set of reprinted critical essays from periodicals and excerpts from books. A 1977 revision edited by Bradley, Beatty, Long, and Thomas Cooley contains a significantly different collection of critical essays, making it desirable for libraries to have both editions on their shelves.

Budd, Louis J., ed. *Critical Essays on Mark Twain, 1867-1910.* Boston: G. K. Hall, 1982.

These 64 general estimates, poems, obituaries, news stories, interviews, and reviews of MT's lectures and books (all reprinted in full) provide a more complete and sharply focused portrait of MT in his own time than appears in other essay collections. Long involved in a study of the way MT appeared in the popular press, Budd argues persuasively that estimates appearing in magazines attract more scholarly attention than those in newspapers because they are now more accessible, but newspaper accounts were often fully as penetrating, and closer to the mass readership MT sought as his public. Such accounts comprise nearly half of this collection, chosen as "reactions most illuminating for Twain's critical reputation at the time."

Cardwell, Guy A. *Discussions of Mark Twain*. Boston: D.C. Heath, 1963.

A collection of critical essays from periodicals and excerpts from books.

Cohen, Ralph, ed. *The Adventures of Huckleberry Finn*. New York: Bantam Books, 1964.

Added matter for the student includes a critical discussion, "Games and Growing Up: A Key to Understanding *Huckleberry Finn*"; "Is *Huckleberry Finn* a Great Novel? Opinions, Reviews, and Comments;" "*Huckleberry Finn* and *The Catcher in the Rye*; "Mark Twain: A Biographical Sketch."

Gerber, John C., ed. *Studies in "Huckleberry Finn."* Columbus, Ohio: Charles E. Merrill, 1971.

Contains early reviews, excerpts from various sources concerning "The Fracas Created by the Concord Public Library" in 1885, and articles and excerpts from books by nine critics since MT's death.

Hill, Hamlin, and Walter Blair, eds. *The Art of Huckleberry Finn: Text, Sources, Criticisms*. San Francisco: Chandler, 1962.

The text is a facsimile of the first edition. The biographical and literary source material includes excerpts from writings by Dixon Wecter, John Marshall Clemens (MT's father), William Wright, Charles Dickens, Thomas Carlyle, Julia A. Moore, Johnston J. Hooper, Richard M. Johnston, and W. E. H. Lecky; the criticism is less extensive. There is also useful classroom material on the writing of *HF*, with suggestions for use of sources and criticisms, and a short bibliography; this is an excellent teaching text.

Kesterson, David B., ed. *Critics on Mark Twain: Readings in Literary Criticism*. Coral Gables, Florida: University of Miami Press, 1973.

"Critics on Mark Twain: 1882-1940" (pp. 13-36) and "Critics on Mark Twain Since 1940" (pp. 37-50) consist largely of very brief excerpts from 31 sources. There are also longer or complete reprintings of critical material in the remainder of the book.

Leary, Lewis., ed. *A Casebook on Mark Twain's Wound*. New York: Thomas Y. Crowell, 1962.

A collection of critical essays from periodicals and excerpts from books, tracing the Brooks-DeVoto controversy over the supposedly harmful effect of his friends and environment on MT; opens with a summary of the debate in an essay, "Standing with Reluctant Feet"; reprinted in his *Southern Excursions: Essays on Mark Twain and Others* (1971).

Lettis, Richard, Robert F. McDonnell, and William E. Morris., eds. *Huck Finn and His Critics*. New York: Macmillan, 1962.

A casebook for students, consisting of the text of *HF* (including the "Raftsmen Passage" published in *LOM*—see Beidler, 1968 and Manierre, 1968), and a generous assortment of critical articles from periodicals and excerpts from books. Includes questions for students, topics and suggestions for research, "Notes on the Critics," and a bibliography which lists a number of studies of J.D. Salinger's *The Catcher in the Rye.*

Lynn, Kenneth S., ed. *"Huckleberry Finn": Text, Sources and Criticism.* New York: Harcourt, Brace & World, 1961.

A casebook, similar to those compiled by Bradley and Lettis.

Marks, Barry R., ed. *Mark Twain's Huckleberry Finn* (Problems in American Civilization). Boston: D. C. Heath and Company, 1959.

A collection of critical essays on *HF.*

Schmitter, Dean Morgan, ed. *Mark Twain: A Collection of Critical Essays.* New York: McGraw-Hill, 1974.

Essays from journals and excerpts from books. The material is in two sections, the first on MT's life, literary career, and the themes of humor and pessimism, and the second devoted to criticism of major works.

Scott, Arthur L. ed. *Mark Twain: Selected Criticism.* Dallas, Texas: Southern Methodist University Press, 1955.

Reprints a number of useful critical articles and excerpts from books, 1867-1951; a revised edition appeared in 1967.

Simpson, Claude M., ed. *Twentieth Century Interpretations of "Adventures of Huckleberry Finn": A Collection of Critical Essays.* Englewood Cliffs, New Jersey: Prentice-Hall, 1968.

Discussions of *HF* by major authors and critics; includes some articles not readily obtained elsewhere.

Smith, Henry Nash, ed. *Mark Twain: A Collection of Critical Essays.* Englewood Cliffs, New Jersey: Prentice-Hall, 1963.

Contains essays by critics over a period of years, from periodicals and excerpted from books, dealing broadly with MT's life and several of his works.

4. Checklist of Criticism

Adams, Richard P. "The Unity and Coherence of *Huckleberry Finn.*" *Tulane Studies in English,* 6 (1956), 87-103.

After summarizing much of the debate over the structure of *HF,* concentrates on Huck's moral growth in a context of the evil of slavery itself, of "the pseudo-aristocratic society which fosters and depends on slavery," and "the sentimental culture veneer with which that society conceals that evil from itself, if not from others." A happy ending in which Huck is reconciled to the values of his society is clearly impossible, but in terms of

Huck's maturation and of the portrayal of a society there is "a remarkably high degree of consistency, coherence, and unity." Reprinted in Marks (1959); Bradley (1962); Lettis (1962); Simpson (1968).

Agarwal, B. B. "Educational Ideas in *Huckleberry Finn.*" *Mark Twain Journal*, 21 (Fall 1983), 2-4.

"Huck's educational training conforms with modern pedagogy. He learns by activity and experience, self-imposed discipline, appeal to the senses and development of moral character from within rather than from without, by indoctrination.... Huck is the symbol of the life-long learner and explorer of new territories not only in the world of river but also in the heart of man."

Allen, Margot. "*Huck Finn*: Two Generations of Pain." *Interracial Books for Children Bulletin*, 15, No. 5 (1984), 9–13.

At the age of thirteen, the only black student in a ninth-grade class in Oregon, the writer was extremely uncomfortable with *HF*; three years ago, her son, the only black student in a ninth-grade class in Pennsylvania, went through the same discomfort when the teacher asked him to read the part of Jim aloud because he had "the perfect voice for it." Mrs. Allen and her husband complained first to the school and then to the Pennsylvania Human Relations Commission and to the Pennsylvania NAACP, and she participated in a panel on teaching *HF* (See Chambers, 1984). She argues that there is a cost to both black and white students in reading *HF*, and it should not be taught before the upper grades of high school, at the earliest.

Allen, Michael. "Idiomatic Language in Two Novels by Saul Bellow." *Journal of American Studies, 1 (October), 275-280.*

"In *The Adventures of Augie March* and *Henderson the Rain King* Bellow is, of course, using a fictional convention invented by Mark Twain" in *HF*, but "none of the modern inheritors of this convention, not even Faulkner, can generate gratuitous exuberance and dense meaningfulness as Twain does in this one book: Hemingway, Salinger and Bellow alike carefully conserve their rather limited vitality for more diluted stylistic effects." The excitement in reading *HF* "is a response to a tension of style, involving the counter-pointing of the rhythms and incorrectnesses of a South-Western small town idiom against Victorian literary and subliterary language."

Allen, Walter. "Introduction," *The Adventures of Huckleberry Finn*. London: Paul Elek, (Camden Classsics) 1948. Pp. 9-16.

Depicts MT's background and personality as "fully documented in Mr. Brooks's *The Ordeal of Mark Twain*, which may be taken as the case for the prosecution." *HF* "is, of course, a dreambook, a dream of freedom," and MT's return—"not a realistic return"—to Hannibal boyhood. Huck represents a freedom MT never had, without ties or consciousness of sin; but he now "excites pity in the reader; he is a pathetic character."

———. *The Urgent West: The American Dream and Modern Man*. New York: Dutton, 1969. Pp. 168-79 and passim.

Calls *HF* "the classic of boyhood everywhere. It dramatizes every man's dream of freedom" (p. 172). "Huck's sweetness of mind and common sense, which is the product of seeing truly, irradiate the book. He is, in fact, that rarest of characters in fiction, the human being who convinces us as being positively good" (p. 177).

Altenbernd, Lynn. "Huck Finn, Emancipator," *Criticism*, 1 (Fall, 1959), 298-307.

"The purpose of this article is to show that the final episode is the thematic climax of the novel because the rescue of Jim from the cabin is an allegory representing the Civil War": although the South could have freed the slaves voluntarily, romantic nonsense (represented by that of Tom Sawyer) interfered. "What actually frees Jim, and what will actually free the nominally emancipated slave, is a voluntary act of human love," first from Huck, then from Miss Watson, who gives him his freedom in her will.

Alter, Robert. *Rogue's Progress: Studies in the Picaresque Novel*. Cambridge, Mass.: Harvard University Press, 1964, Pp. 117-21.

Places Huck in a tradition of picaroons, with compassion but also with a sufficiently "thick skin to prevent experience from paralyzing him or torturing him excessively," while rejecting society's hypocrisies. *HF* is superior to the traditional picaresque novels in its language, which reflects Huck's moral position.

Andersen, David M. "Basque Wine, Arkansas Chawin' Tobacco: Landscape and Ritual in Ernest Hemingway and Mark Twain," *Mark Twain Journal*, 16 (Winter 1971-1972), 3-7.

The social ritual at Berguete of sharing wine, described in *The Sun Also Rises*, has its parallel in the dispute over chewing tobacco in *HF*: "Reciprocity, beginning even with such material symbols as wine and tobacco, is not just essential to civilization, it *is* civilization."

Andrews. William L. "Mark Twain and James W. C. Pennington: Huckleberry Finn's Smallpox Lie." *Studies in American Fiction*, 9 (Spring 1981), 103-12.

MT drew on Charles Ball's *Slavery in the United States* as a source for *HF*, and with his interest in the genre it is possible that he also read *The Fugitive Blacksmith; or, Events in the History of James C. Pennington, Pastor of a Presbyterian Church, New York, Formerly a Slave in the State of Maryland, United States* (1849). Like Huck, Pennington deceived some slave-catchers with a lie about smallpox, and both *HF* and Pennington's book employ "the lies of a runaway [as] a useful pretext for social criticism and moral reflection." While there is no proof that MT had read Pennington's book, the ex-slave was quite prominent in New York when MT was there in 1853, and MT also would have heard of Pennington through the praise of him in the conclusion of *Uncle Tom's Cabin*.

Anon. "*The Bear* and *Huckleberry Finn*: Heroic Quests for Moral Liberation." *Mark Twain Journal*, 12 (Spring 1963), 12-13, 21.

Ike McCaslin and Huck lack parents and find substitute fathers in older Negroes; they undergo initiations in isolation, and both novels end on an affirmative note: "Both boys have transformed their knowledge and ability into charity and humility, and both are now guided by a moral vision."

Anon. "The Boy and the River." *Times Literary Supplement* (10 November 1950), 708.

A review of the Cresset Press edition of *HF* with a ten-page introduction by T.S. Eliot. Sees Eliot as being at a disadvantage, having read *TS* and *HF* only as an adult and consequently unable to assess MT's achievements, including "his ability to write, simultaneously and in the same book, both as the boy of 30 or 40 years ago and as the mature man looking back on the same event."

Anon. "Bright Debut of an Old Pro. Boxing Champ Archie Moore opens film career in '*Huckleberry Finn*.'" *Life*, 48 (20 July 1960), 113-14.

Includes three photographs of Moore, only one of them from the film. "Toe-the-mark Twain purists and Huck Fin-niks will object to the film which has lost almost all the Twain bite. At best, with Eddie Hodges playing Huck it is a pleasant enough adventure for the family and kids, with Archie easily the best thing in it."

Anon. "Huck, Dorothy and the Vigilantes." *America*, 146 (24 April 1982), 312–13.

The recent attack on *HF* in Fairfax County, Virginia re-opens the issue of censorship. Books have been banned elsewhere, among them *The Wizard of Oz* ("Dorothy and Toto as countercultural radicals?"), *Mary Poppins*, and *The Grapes of Wrath*. Still, there have been overstatements: *HF* was never actually banned in the Virginia school, some printed material (not *HF*) is unsuitable for young students, and often censorship is merely a way for interest groups "to show muscle in a community." Limiting access to books is a last resort: "Even on the primary and secondary levels, exposure to a variety of ideas—presented with sensitivity to a student's ability to absorb and criticize them—is a basic principle of democracy."

Anon. "Huck Finn Tabooed by Denver Library." *Harper's Weekly*, 46 (6 September 1902), 1253.

A brief note, concluding: "It all sounds like a practical joke on the Denver library; but it is an offence against our national common-sense which ought to be quickly removed."

Anon. "'A Little Kind of Low Chuckle.'" New York *Times* (16 April 1982), 26.

An editorial; in part: "Not content with describing 'The Adventures of Huckleberry Finn' as 'racist trash,' John Wallace, an administrator at the

Mark Twain Intermediate School in Fairfax, Va., added that anyone who taught the book was racist too. Speaking for the school's Human Relations Committee, he asked that it be removed from the curriculum.... Fortunately, Mr. Wallace and his colleagues have been overruled by the area school superintendent, Doris Torrice. So the children at the Mark Twain Intermediate School, and their teachers, can all get back on the raft with Huck and Jim and travel into one of the greatest of all American novels."

Anon. "Mark Twain's Huck Finn Gets His Mouth Washed Out with Revisions." *Washington Post* (September 8, 1983), C5.

An interview with John H. Wallace, a former administrator at the Mark Twain Intermediate School and the Henry David Thoreau Intermediate School. He has moved to Chicago, founded the John H. Wallace and Sons Publishing Company, and this week is bringing out the first edition of 10,000 copies of the *Adventures of Huckleberry Finn Adapted*. Wallace says he spent two summers working on his version of *HF*, improving what has "become a classic because it does ridicule black people by calling [Jim] a nigger ... My book is so much better." But he anticipates the question: "What has this jerk done with an American classic?"

Anon. "Selling Huck Down the River." Washington *Post* (9 April 1982), A18.

An editorial on the banning of *HF* in the Mark Twain Intermediate School (Fairfax County,Va.): in years gone by, *HF*"offended all those illiberal and small-minded values that most richly deserved to the offended," and now it is attacked as racist. "But in fact, the novel *satirizes* the racist attitudes of the time, and if, as one of its opponents says, it is asinine to expect seventh-graders to understand satire," then what are teachers for? Surely they are there to help kids understand things in their context, to appreciate them."

Anon. "Think Back, Too." *New York Times* (1 January 1984), E-12.

An editorial, prompted by the beginning of the Orwellian year 1984. *HF* was criticized as coarse and vulgar when it appeared, and now it is criticized as racist, which it is not. "What's a culture to do about its past? That's what all the theorizing about 1984 is about. The difficulties of freedom were plain long before George Orwell added his classic. To blot out 1884 by purging or purifying Twain is to rob life, and the passage of time, of all meaning."

Anon. [Banning of *HF* by the Concord Public Library.] Boston *Transcript* (17 March 1885).

[Source: Long passage reprinted in Marks (1959), p. xi.] The committee does not call the book actually immoral, but it "contains but little humor, and that of a very coarse type"; it is "the veriest trash ... rough, coarse and inelegant, dealing with a series of experiences not elevating, the whole book being more suited to the slums than to intelligent, respectable people." Also excerpted in Gerber (1971), Kesterson (1973), and Bradley (1977).

Anon. [Banning of *HF* by Concord Public Library.] Springfield, Mass. *Republican*, as quoted in *The Critic*, 6 (28 March 1885), 155.

[Source: Reprinted in Gerber (1971)] "Mr. Clemens is a genuine and powerful humorist, with a bitter vein of satire on the weaknesses of humanity which is sometimes wholesome, sometimes only grotesque, but in certain of his works degenerates into a grotesque trifling with every fine feeling. The trouble with Mr. Clemens is that he has no reliable sense of propriety. His notorious speech at an *Atlantic* dinner, marshalling Longfellow and Emerson and Whittier in vulgar parodies in a Western miner's cabin, illustrated this, but not in much more relief than the *Adventures of Tom Sawyer* did, or these Huckleberry Finn stories, do...." Also reprinted in Bradley (1977).

Anon. [Brief comment on *HF*.] *Fair Play* (Valley Falls, Kansas; 11 August 1888), 1.

Huck was right to flee the smothering, regulated goodness of "the Widder": "The widow was good—good as *she* could be, but she had no right to expect others to abide by her notions of the fitness of things. In the sum of her excesses and defects the widow's conduct may, or may not, have been more nearly correct than that of average people. We only know that taking human nature as it is, her life would have been intolerable to most."

Anon. [Brief Review: *HF*.] *Athenaeum*, No. 2983 (27 December 1884), 855.

Laudatory and descriptive. "For some time Mr. Clemens has been carried away by the ambition of seriousness and fine writing. In *Huckleberry Finn* he returns to his right mind and is again the Mark Twain of old time.... Jim and Huckleberry are real creations, and the worthy peers of the illustrious Tom Sawyer." Reprinted in Anderson (1971), with a suggestion that the reviewer may be William Ernest Henley.

Anon. [Reprinted item from *The Summary*, "A weekly journal published in the interests of the New York State Reformatory."] *Critic*, 6 (20 May 1885), 264.

"The Reformatory Library also procured *Huckleberry Finn*," was impressed with it as irreligious, as the Concord library had been, "and the fact came under the notice of Professor Sanborn, who was visiting us." He wrote the Superintendent: "I have read 'Huckleberry Finn,' and I do not see any reason why it should not go into your Reference Library, at least, and form the subject of a debate in your Practical Morality Class. I am serious in this." Reprinted in Gerber (1971), 9-10.

Anon. [Review: *HF*.] *British Quarterly Review*, 81 (January-April 1885), 465-66.

Although MT "is sometimes a little coarse, sometimes a little irreverent, and inclined to poke fun at the Old Testament," his humor redeems him and "Huckleberry Finn's adventures are told with a prevailing dryness and sense of reality which do much to compensate for offences against taste." The book is discussed as a successful sequel to *TS*, with no reference to the events after Huck escaped from his father's cabin.

Anon. [Review: *HF*.] *The Congregationalist* (London: Hodder and Stoughton), 14 (March 1883), 251-52.

"A new book from the pen of Mark Twain hardly needs an introduction from the pen of any reviewer. It carries its own recommendation with it in the name of its author, who never writes without furnishing us with as abundant material for serious thought as for merry laughter. *Huckleberry Finn* has all the characteristic qualities of its author: his quaint humor, his abundant common sense, his genial sympathy, his felicitous skill in hitting off the peculiarities both of classes and individuals."

Anon. [Review: *HF*.] *Westminster Review* n.s., 67 (April 1885), 596.

"'The Adventures of Huckleberry Finn' are good even for Mark Twain.... There is abundance of American humour of the best sort; plenty of incident, sometimes thrilling, at others, extravagantly burlesque; charming descriptions of scenery, and admirable sketches of character."

Archer, William. *America Today: Observations and Reflections*. New York: Scribner's, 1899.

On MT, pp. 212-13: "If any work of incontestable genius, and plainly predestined to immortality, has been issued in the English language in the past quarter century, it is that brilliant romance of the Great Rivers, *The Adventures of Huckleberry Finn*. Intensely American though he be, 'Mark Twain' is one of the greatest living masters of the English language." (This may have appeared previously in *Pall Mall Gazette* or *Pall Mall Magazine*, according to a note on p. vii.)

Arikawa, Shoji. "On *The Adventures of Huckleberry Finn*." *Kyushu American Literature*, No. 22 (May 1981), 82–84.

(Follows Nishimura's article in a section headed: "Synopses of the Reports of the Symposium concerning *The Adventures of Huckleberry Finn* at the 33rd Annual Convention of the English Literary Society of Kyushu, Held at Kagoshima University on October 26, 1980.") "Huck Finn is human, innocent and generous. But Huck seems to have at the bottom of his heart a dark, mysterious and instinctive inclination to death," and alludes to death or wishes for it repeatedly. Other major characters use similar words at their critical moments: Laura in *GA*, Hank in *CY*, Roxana in *PW*, Joan in *JA*, and Richards in "Hadleyburg"; *MS* "is just full of dark images like those in Huck in the condensed and intensified form. In other words, Huck essentially is typical of almost all major characters of Mark Twain's work in terms of an inclination to death and in this sense, he represents Mark Twain himself who condemns the human race and runs away from civilization." The disputed ending is "the author's satire on what is called an adventure."

———. "Huck and Death." *Kyushu American Literature*, No. 8 (1965), 19–24. [Source: MHRA *Annual Bibliography* (1965), No. 6956.]

———. "Huckleberry Finn in Japan." *The English Record* 21 (February

1971), 20-26.

A general discussion of *HF* and the response of Arikawa's students, nineteen-year-old girls, over a five-year period; there is no specifically Japanese perspective applied to such topics as race, the river, and the character of Huck.

Arner, Robert D. "Acts Seventeen and *Huckleberry Finn*: A Note on Silas Phelps' Sermon." *Mark Twain Journal*, 16 (Summer 1972), 12.

Allison Ensor's note on Chapter 37 of *HF* in *Explicator* (1967) should be expanded: not only does the Biblical chapter refer to the brotherhood of all men in verse 26, but in verse 29 it cautions against the worship of Mammon, "the chief reason the Southerners...continue to hold slaves"; moreover, "the fact that one of the preachers mentioned in Acts Seventeen, the man who accompanies Paul to Athens, is named Silas seems further evidence that this is no casual allusion on Twain's part."

Ashmead, John. "A Possible Hannibal Source for Mark Twain's Dauphin." *American Literature*, 34 (March 1962), 105-07.

Reprints "A Visit from our Bourbon" from the Hannibal *Journal* for 12 May 1853; this hard-drinking pretender visiting a newspaper office may explain why MT's notes describe the Duke and Dauphin in *HF* as "printers."

Atherton James S. "To Give Down the Banks and Hark from the Tomb!" *James Joyce Quarterly*, 4 (Winter 1967), 75-83.

On quotations from *HF* incorporated in *Finnegans Wake*.

Auden, W. H. "Huck and Oliver." *Listener*, 50 (1 October 1953), 540-41.

Contrasts attitudes toward nature in *HF* and *Oliver Twist*; observes Huck's stoicism and calls his decision to free Jim "an act of moral improvisation." There is in the book "a kind of sadness, as if freedom and love were incompatible." (From a BBC Third Programme broadcast.) Reprinted in Smith (1963).

Bailey, Roger B. "Twain's *Huckleberry Finn*, Chapters 1 and 2." *Explicator* 26 (September 1967), Item 2.

The fact that Huck trips over a root but Tom Sawyer steps on and snaps a dry twig (like a Fenimore Cooper character) reveals the contrast between between Huck's realism and Tom's romancing.

Baker, Carlos. "Two Rivers: Mark Twain and Hemingway." *Mark Twain Journal*, 11 (Summer 1962), 2.

Shows similarities in descriptions of rivers by Huck (Chapter 19) and by Frederick Henry in *A Farewell to Arms* (Chapter 31). Many more such parallels could be drawn, though not as evidence of direct influence; the two writers share a directness and appearance of simplicity.

Baker, Russell. "The Only Gentleman." *New York Times* (14 April 1982), A23.

On the banning of *HF* in Mark Twain Intermediate School. In Baker's own school years "schoolteachers seemed determined to persuade me that 'classic' was a synonym for 'narcotic,'" and now he waggishly suggests that they all be reserved for adults who can appreciate them—Shakespeare, Dickens, and Melville along with *HF*. Black and white students "might misread Twain as outrageously as Mr. Wallace [Robert T. Wallace—see below] has in thinking the book is about the dishonesty, dumbness and inhumanity of blacks. This is the kind of risk you invite when you assign books of some subtlety to youngsters mentally unprepared to enjoy them." One must be mature to understand irony such as that of *HF*, "full of pessimism about the human race and particularly its white American members." Those Huck and Jim encounter are fools at best, and "the one of honor...is black Jim, the runaway slave. 'Nigger Jim,' as Twain called him [actually, Twain didn't—T.A.T.] to emphasize the irony of a society in which the only true gentleman was held beneath contempt." But, since the racial issue has been raised, "the only sensible thing for the Mark Twain Intermediate School to do is tackle the matter head-on, put aside some other things and conduct a school-wide teach-in to help its students understand what Huck and Jim are really saying about their world."

Baldanza, Frank. "The Structure of *Huckleberry Finn*." *American Literature*, 27 (November 1955), 347-55.

"I propose to show that without advanced planning, and spurred by momentary impulses—in all probability unconsciously—Mark Twain constructed whole passages of *Huckleberry Finn* on an aesthetic principle of repetition and variation." Reprinted in Marks (1959) and Lettis (1962).

Banfield, Beryle. "More on the Study ... " *Interracial Books for Children Bulletin*, 15, No. 5 (1984), 10–11.

A study to determine the effect of reading *HF* on the racial attitudes of ninth-graders is seriously flawed and should not be used to justify continued teaching of the novel. (See Chambers, 1984.)

Banta, Martha. "Escape and Entry in *Huckleberry Finn*." *Modern Fiction Studies*, 14 (Spring 1968), 79-91.

Huck's flight to the river and his failure to escape thereby from society must be explained, not by the reader's moral preconceptions, but by Huck's "loose-hung code that is beholden only to what provides the free, the easy, and the comfortable." Huck's experiences reflect MT's own discovery that there can be no escape from the consequences of heredity and environment: novelty may offer man a free choice of new routes, "or may simply show him driven by yet one more compulsive thrust into predetermined paths of action."

———. "Rebirth or Revenge: The Endings of *Huckleberry Finn* and *The American*". *Modern Fiction Studies*, 15 (Summer 1969), 191-207.

"Huck Finn and Christopher Newman meet head-on with the forces of conscience well past mid-way in their quests," and neither heaven nor

Claire de Cintré is a real loss; both heroes make the decisions that result in personal satisfaction.

Barchilon, Jose, and Joel S. Kovel. "*Huckleberry Finn*: A Psychoanalytic Study." *Journal of the American Psychoanalytic Association*, 14 (October 1966), 775-814.

Deliberately limited to evidence in *HF*, excluding biographical data and evidence from MT's other works. "The essential feature of the method is that we treat the novels as if they were the life histories of real people." Subsections are "The Structure of Huck's Personality"; "The Wish to be Dead: Reunion with the Dead Mother"; "The Wish to Kill the Mother and Its Resolution through Passivity"; "The Theme of Moses and the Wish to Live: The Nile and the Mississippi"; "Jim's Character"; "Sexuality in *Huckleberry Finn*"; "Tom Sawyer's Character"; "Huck's Growth through the Relationship with Jim"; "Children's Games: The Three Orphans Reborn as Siblings"; "The Wish to Have a Negro Mother?"; "The Relationship of the Moses Myth to the Story of Huck"; "A Wanderer on the American Frontier"; and a "Postcript" on "Method" and "Goals." Reprinted (in part: pp. 799-808) in Gerber (1971).

Barksdale, Richard K. "History, Slavery, and Thematic Irony in *Huckleberry Finn*." *Mark Twain Journal*, 22 (Fall 1984), 17–20.

The times of slavery are an unhappy memory for Americans, and particularly for blacks, who would like to shield their children from the ignominy and the continuing racial divisiveness. An encounter with the world MT depicts is painful for black children, the more so because few teachers are fully prepared to place *HF* in its historical and psychological setting. This might seem to justify demands that *HF* be taken off required reading lists and made an optional selection, the more so because irony is difficult to teach; but "although Jim's roots lie deep in the soil of slavery and American racism and although his is an honest and forthright portrayal of a slave runaway and although young black teenagers are traumatized by reading about the Jims of slavery-time, the great difficulty with *Adventures of Huckleberry Finn* is that it is one of America's best pieces of ironic fiction. To a nation that was and is sharply divided on matters of race, Twain's novel suggests that friendships between black and white can best be forged by the least of us and then only under the worst of circumstances. Undoubtedly, only a reading audience of some maturity and perceptive insight ... can grasp the far-reaching implications of a white Huck and a black Jim floating down the river of American life."

Barnes, Daniel R. "Twain's *The Adventures of Huckleberry Finn*, Chapter I." *Explicator*, 23 (April 1965), Item 62.

Biblical prototypes cast light on the portrayal of the lives of the major characters, as in the parallel between Huck and Moses in the "bullrushers."

Barnett, Louise K. "Huck Finn: Picaro as Linguistic Outsider." *College Literature*, 6 (Fall 1979), 221-31.

Huck faces a "public language" which supports group values and attitudes; its support is authority, but not necessarily understanding, as is seen in Tom's defense of "ransom" and Buck's of "feud." As Huck gradually recognizes Jim's full humanity, "we can almost see him ticking off aspects of being a man," such as the capacity to be hurt, the dignity that gives him the right to an apology, and existence as a person rather than mere property. In the end Huck must withdraw from "a society of fools and knaves and ... that language which serves their purposes."

Bassett, John Earl. "*Huckleberry Finn*: The End Lies in the Beginning." *American Literary Realism*, 17 (Spring 1984), 91–98.

Despite the linear sequence of events on the river, the course of *HF* is circular. Tom begins and ends by playing tricks on Jim, and in between he "is actually the most important absent presence in the book," whether as Huck's touchstone for how an escape should have been done in style or as a counterpart of the King and Duke. Huck, on the other hand, is individual and non-conformist (the other great such figure in our literature is Thoreau), but passive, literal: "paradoxically, Twain creates his greatest 'stretcher' by means of a voice that denies fiction, that insists on limiting cognition to empirical perceptions and values to pragmatic consequences."

Beaver, Harold. "Run, Nigger, Run: *Adventures of Huckleberry Finn* as a Fugitive Slave Narrative." *Journal of American Studies*, 8 (December 1974), 339-61.

Jim is an adult and a slave, and his situation is not Huck's: "If young Huck is taken in by that river-born camaraderie between black and white on a Mississippi raft, it does not follow that his friend (and victim) was equally taken in."

Beck, Warren. "Huck Finn at Phelps Farm: An Essay in Defense of the Form of Mark Twain's Novel." *Archives des Lettres Modernes*, Nos. 13-15 (Juin-Septembre 1958), 1-31.

"What makes the Phelps farm episode conclusively relevant, therefore, in spite of its juvenile flavor, is the constant presence of the realistic and increasingly responsible Huck, and his repeated interpolations as the half-detached and more than half-skeptical foil to Tom's fancifulness and enslavement to tradition" (p. 22). [32-page pamphlet, with an abstract in French on p. 32.]

———. "*Huckleberry Finn* versus *The Cash Boy*." *Education*, 49 (September 1928), 1-13.

Compares *HF* to the turgid, shallow boy stories of Horatio Alger, Jr.: Huck is notable for his warmth, integrity, and wisdom, and he could grow with a college education as the Alger hero could not.

Beidler, Peter G. "The Raft Episode in *Huckleberry Finn*." *Modern Fiction Studies*, 14 (Spring 1968), 11-20.

MT dropped the episode, which had already appeared in *LOM*, on the advice of his publisher, Charles Webster; the intention was to make the book shorter, as a companion volume to *TS*. In the excision MT lost a passage important technically as the explanation of how Huck learned that the raft had passed Cairo, and psychologically for revealing his "generally morbid outlook on life, his repeated identification with dead and suffering human beings." Huck's lies add to the psychological portrait, since "in many of them Huck casts himself in the role of a boy who is alone in the world and whose family is dead, sick, or in grave danger." Reprinted in Bradley (1977).

Belden, H. M. "Scyld Scefing and Huck Finn." *Modern Language Notes*, 33 (May 1918), 315.

Seeking a body with a floating loaf of bread was anticipated in "divination by shield, sheaf, and candle."

Bell, Millicent. "*Huckleberry Finn*: Journey without End." *Virginia Quarterly Review*, 58 (Spring 1982), 253-67.

Huck's trip down the river does not bring his or Jim's liberation, and even the projected flight for the territory would only have been "for a couple of weeks or so." Huck becomes content to drift, and may best be seen as the instrument of MT's own "liberation of style [such] as he had never achieved before, the attainment of a voice not only perfectly suited to its fictional function but deeply expressive of his own deepest resources of insight." *HF* "is far more the history of a consciousness receiving experience and altering as a consequence than it is objective social realism. It is a novel of the inward self and that self, as so frequently is the case in the first-person novel, was a projection of the writer's own."

Bellman, Samuel I. "Peripheral (?) Characters in *Huckleberry Finn* and *Catcher in the Rye*." *Mark Twain Journal*, 19 (Winter 1977-1978), 4-6.

In Emmeline Grangerford and Jim's daughter 'Lizabeth "Twain suggested a timeless realm of pathetic suffering or dead children, a domain more enduring, more engaging to the sensitive reader" than is the "macabre circus" of *HF* as a whole. Huck longs for the Territory and Holden Caulfield for an imaginary rye-field, places of safety for "helpless and/or wronged children."

Belov, S.B., ed. *The Adventures of Huckleberry Finn: Text and Criticism*. Moscow: Raduga Publishers, 1984.

A critical edition somewhat similar to the Norton (ed. Bradley et al.), this has merits of its own and if available would be useful to American undergraduates. The English-language text of *HF* is like what would be found in an ordinary American edition, and on pp. 231–311 there are 33 excerpts in English from criticism including an unsigned review in *Athenaeum* (27 Dec. 1884) and statements by Brander Matthews, Robert Bridges, Thomas Sergeant Perry, Andrew Lang, Frank R. Stockton, Walter Besant, Barrett Wendell, William Dean Howells, Archibald Henderson, Reuben Post Hallek, Albert Bigelow Paine, John Macy, H.L. Mencken, Waldo Frank, Van Wyck Brooks, Stuart P. Sherman, Vernon Louis Parrington, Stephen Leacock, V.F.

Calverton, Bernard DeVoto, Theodore Dreiser, Sterling Brown, James T. Farrell, Ralph Ellison, Dixon Wecter, T.S. Eliot, W.H. Auden, Wright Morris, Philip Foner, Walter Blair, Henry Nash Smith, and Maxwell Geismar. The remainder of the book is in Russian. G.P. Zlobin's preface surveys MT criticism by the authors listed above and also Upton Sinclair, Sinclair Lewis, Robert Spiller, Leo Marx, Ernest Hemingway, and Leslie Fiedler, showing little sympathy for any sort of psychological analysis and much sympathy for criticism which supports a view of MT as radical in his treatment of American capitalism (pp. 5–22). Zlobin also wrote explanatory notes on the criticism (pp. 351–363). The explanatory notes and glossary for *HF* are by A.I. Poltoratsky (pp. 315–50).

Belson, Joel Jay. "The Nature and Consequences of the Loneliness of Huckleberry Finn." *Arizona Quarterly*, 26 (Autumn 1970), 243-48.

Huck is an outcast from a society which "by denying the rightness of every truly humane impulse he seeks to express ... by convincing him of his own intellectual and moral inadequacy and by providing no approval or positive satisfactions ... isolates him finally and absolutely as nature, as Twain presents it, does not do." He is a fugitive, victim, and observer, and his chief protection is concealment from an unintelligible and hostile world.

__________. "The Argument of the Final Chapters of *Huckleberry Finn*." *Mark Twain Journal*, 21 (Spring 1983), 11-12.

"The ending is realistic, not romantic or heroic." It is consistent with the previous chapters, which show that any freedom is possible "only in the process of running itself, and each pause ... brings us back to a place similar to the one we left."

Benardete, Jane Johnson. "*Huckleberry Finn* and the Nature of Fiction." *Massachusetts Review*, 9 (Spring 1968), 209-26.

"It is the thesis of this essay that *Huckleberry Finn* is a book about the nature of fiction (which epitomizes the deceptive power of language, for fiction is told or written and heard or read although it is known to be untrue): that each episode illustrates some quality of fiction; that the major theme of Huck's development is his increasing preference for fiction over fact; and that the novel itself is deliberately devised to exemplify fiction's power to distort life."

Bennett, James R. "The Adventures of Huck Finn in Chapter One." *Iowa English Yearbook*, 12 (1967), 68-72.

"The opening chapter suggests all the major motifs of the novel—freedom, the slave society, religion, money, illusion, and the family, superstition, loneliness, death, and moral growth. Chapter One presents a series of concise scenes which epitomize the book."

Bennett, Jonathan. "The Conscience of Huckleberry Finn." *Philosophy: The Journal of the Royal Institute of Philosophy*, 49 (April 1974), 123-34.

"I shall use Heinrich Himmler, Jonathan Edwards and Huckleberry

Finn to illustrate different aspects of a single theme, namely the relationship between *sympathy* on one hand and *bad morality* on the other." In Huck's case, sympathy wins out over bad morality, as in Himmler's it does not; and the morality of Edwards "was worse than Himmler's," in that he approved of the eternal torment of the damned as good in itself. [For further discussion, see Harris, 1977.]

Bercovitch, Sacvan. "Huckleberry Bumppo: A Comparison of *Tom Sawyer* and *The Pioneers*." *Mark Twain Journal*, 14 (Summer 1968), 1-14.

Despite MT's ridicule of Cooper, the two books are similar in structure and in such characters as the town patriarchs Judge Thatcher and Judge Temple, who stand at opposite poles from Huck and Natty; other parallels are evident as well, but there are also significant differences in the treatment of the frontier myth and the Indian.

Berger, Arthur Asa. "Huck Finn as an Existential Hero: Making Sense of Absurdity." *Mark Twain Journal*, 18 (Summer 1976), 12-17.

Central to our national literature for its humor and use of the vernacular, *HF* is marked by its realism and by "absurdity and alienation and other existential concerns."

Berkove, Lawrence I. "The 'Poor Players' of *Huckleberry Finn*." *Papers of the Michigan Academy of Science, Arts, and Letters*, 53 (1968), 291-310.

"*Huckleberry Finn* is best read as a novel which denies to all of its characters the possibility of any meaningful measure of freedom and, in moving to this end, is consistently unified in both theme and structure." The concluding chapters underscore the lesson that "all men are poor players in a drama without significance. Through an examination of one recurring literary device, impersonation, and two recurring themes, romanticism and fate, I will attempt to demonstrate how Twain drives inexorably to this conclusion." [Also summarized in Gerber (1968), p. 78.]

Bernstein, Melvin H. "Silas Phelps' Unwritten Sermon." *Religious Education*, 53 (March-April 1953), 257-61.

In Chapter 37 of *HF* Uncle Silas Phelps was reading Acts 17, which contains Paul's affirmation of the brotherhood of all mankind—an important message to such a world as MT drew in *HF*.

Bidewell, George Ivan. "Mark Twain's Florida Years." *Missouri Historical Review*, 40 (January 1946), 159-73.

On the influence of life in Florida, Missouri, before the Clemens family moved to Hannibal and during the summers of 1840-1846 which the boy spent there on the farm of his uncle John A. Quarles. Through parallel passages from the Paine biography and *HF*, argues that the Quarles farm was the model for the Silas Phelps farm in *HF*.

Bier, Jesse. "'Bless You, Chile': Fiedler and 'Huck Honey' a Generation Later." *Mississippi Quarterly*, 34 (Fall 1981), 456-62.

On Fiedler's essay arguing a homosexual element in *HF* (1948) "Fiedler is an old friend and former colleague of mine, and now that the critical dust has almost settled again, he may not mind a demurral from me as much as from downright hostile quarters." Bier suggests that Jim's relation to Huck is like that of a father, replacing Pap Finn, and he "almost always has his children on his mind." He accuses Fiedler of using evidence very selectively, calling him "always more the critic, even the polemicist, than the scholar."

———. *The Rise and Fall of American Humor*. New York: Holt, Rinehart and Winston, 1968.

On MT, pp. 117-61, with a valuable discussion of *HF* and the reasons why it is "inaccessible" to foreigners.

Billingsley, Dale B. "'Standard Authors' in *Huckleberry Finn*." *The Journal of Narrative Technique*, 9 (Spring 1979), 126-31.

Seemingly unrelated episodes on shore are linked by "a complex set of literary motifs that are repeated and transformed to bind the novel together." For example, *Pilgrim's Progress* is mentioned twice, and the revival in Chapter 20 is a kind of Vanity Fair for knaves and fools; there are also structural allusions to the Bible, Shakespeare, and Sir Walter Scott.

Birchfield, James. "Jim's Coat of Arms." *Mark Twain Journal*, 14 (Summer 1969), 15-16.

MT's criticism of romantic foolishness appears often in *HF*, where the wrecked steamboat is named the *Walter Scott*, and Tom and Huck both display "unlikely bits of historical and antiquarian book learning." Tom Sawyer's confused description of a coat of arms shows him "possessed by the aristocratic delusions which infect the South ... fascinated by the ceremony, the trappings and externalities of the chivalric code"; Huck, on the other hand, thinks of the old nobility as "regular rapscallions."

Bixler, Phyllis. "Idealization of the Child and Childhood in Frances Hodgson Burnett's *Little Lord Fauntleroy* and Mark Twain's *Tom Sawyer*." Selma K. Richardson, ed., *Research About Nineteenth-Century Children and Books*. Urbana-Champaign: University of Illinois Graduate School of Library Sciences, 1980. Pp. 85-96.

This discussion of childhood stories with a pastoral setting treats *Fauntleroy* as *georgic*, and a symbolic statement of innocence rather than a literal account. *TS* is *bucolic*: the freedom from work or responsibilities is *otium* (as opposed to *negotium*, or "duty"—the terms were originally military), and defined by a negation of adult restrictions; thus, the bucolic play depends on these restrictions and is not a true rebellion. In *HF* "the games become real," Huck "is on a collision course against society, and Mark Twain has a real hero, not a mock hero, on his hands. His idyll of childhood is turning into a nightmare." The conclusion puts Huck "back in Tom's bucolic childhood world where heroism is only imaginary and battles with adults and society are only a game."

Black, Linda. "Louisa May Alcott's 'Huckleberry Finn.'" *Mark Twain Journal*, 21 (Summer 1982), 15-17.

About the character Dan Kean, in *Little Men* and in *Jo's Boys*; there is a brief comparison of Dan to Huck, and a statement that Louisa May Alcott was one of the critics expressing disapproval of *HF* when it appeared.

Blackburn, Alexander. "Confidence Men in *Huckleberry Finn*." *The Myth of the Picaro: Continuity and Transformation of the Picaresque Novel, 1554-1954.* Chapel Hill: University of North Carolina Press, 1979. Pp. 177-187; also passim (indexed).

The King and the Duke "symbolize a deformed part of Huck that is in conflict with his natural goodness," and he does not fully overcome that part: he forgets Jim during the Grangerford episode, and later joins Tom's heartless fooling. "What we are loath to admit about Huck is his failed humanity, so we would like to believe that he escapes into freedom even at the sacrifice of love. The truth is that *Huckleberry Finn* has neither real freedom nor lasting love for our comfort. It is almost a nihilistic book. It is certainly a very sad book."

Blair, Walter. "The French Revolution and *Huckleberry Finn*." *Modern Philology*, 55 (August 1957), 21-35.

In addition to *A Tale of Two Cities*, of which the influence on *HF* has been previously noted (and is here discussed), MT was familiar with a number of other books dealing with the French Revolution; of these, Thomas Carlyle's seems particularly influential, not only for its depiction of royalty and as a source for elements of the burlesque escape of Jim, but also for its portrait of the cruelty and the cowardice of mobs.

__________ . *Mark Twain & Huck Finn*. Berkeley and Los Angeles: University of California Press, 1960.

Blair calls this his "attempt to define the forces which gave *Adventures of Huckleberry Finn* its substance and its form." While considering the importance of MT's boyhood and piloting on the river, he feels that the way they were transmuted into fiction is more important; "therefore I discuss in greater detail the forces shaping such modifications—the man's life, his reading, his thinking, and his writing between 1874 and 1884" (p.vii). This definitive study concludes with a discussion of *HF*'s popularity abroad in translation, and there is an appendix titled "First New York Edition, First Issue," discussing the bibliographical points and the damaged plate on p. 283 (pp. 385-87; see Sioui, 1962). Chapter 5 ("Tom and Huck"), pp. 71-76 is reprinted in Bradley (1962, 1977); pp. 131, 134-44 are reprinted in Simpson (1968); "Raft and Shore: Wish and Belief," pp. 334-46, in Gerber (1971).

__________ . "Mark Twain, Hank, and Huck." *Horse Sense in American Humor from Benjamin Franklin to Ogden Nash*. Chicago: The University of Chicago Press, 1942. Pp. 195-217 (and passim).

On the alternation of the fool and the wise narrator, as Twain and Clemens. Hank Morgan is decent but an ignoramus, and *CY* attacks MT's

America as well as Arthur's England. Tom Sawyer is the dupe of books and Huck and Jim follow him despite their common-sense reservations, both in *HF* and in *TS Abroad*, which contains "a whole series of dialogues which equal or surpass the dialogues in the earlier book" and a further probing of the mentality of St. Petersburg.

————. *Mark Twain's Hannibal, Huck & Tom.* Berkeley and Los Angeles: University of California Press, 1969.

A volume of the CEAA edition of MT's works, consisting of unpublished material on Hannibal and the villagers, and manuscript material dealing with Huck and Tom; includes the texts of *Huck Finn and Tom Sawyer Among the Indians*, and *Tom Sawyer: A Play*.

————. "Was *Huckleberry Finn* Written?" *Mark Twain Journal*, 19 (Summer 1979), 1-3.

HF is marked by inconsistencies that do not detract from MT's art or the reader's enjoyment: the action takes place at some time between 1835 and 1845, yet Huck summarizes *TS* (1876) and refers to the "Mark Twain" name (first used in 1863); moreover, Huck's vocabulary and spelling belie his supposedly limited education, and dialect is rendered inaccurately. Finally, Huck would have been too busy having adventures to write them down. Such objections are not valid: MT was writing in an established convention of first-person narration, he understood that the impression of vernacular style is more important than literal rendition, and Huck is effective both as a narrator and as a character.

————. "When Was *Huckleberry Finn* Written?" *American Literature*, 30 (March 1958),1-25.

Contends that Paine is nearer the truth in giving periods of composition as 1876, 1880, and 1883 than is DeVoto in giving only 1876 and 1883. "Furthermore, I believe that both, with most other students of Twain, overestimate the influence of Clemens's Mississippi River trip of 1882 on the novel. If my beliefs prove to be well founded, significant revisions of the story of the genesis of the book will be necessary." The evidence includes letters and recorded conversations, MT's notes, notebooks, and the surviving manuscript material.

————. "Why Huck and Jim Went Downstream." *College English*, 18 (November 1956), 106-07.

William Van O'Connor has criticized as a flaw the trip on the raft, since free territory lay across the river in Illinois; the objection has been made before, by DeVoto and by Dixon Wecter, but takes no account of the activity of slave-catchers there, or the fact that Huck's father had got money from Judge Thatcher "to hunt for the nigger all over Illinois with."

Blassingame, Wyatt. "The Use of the Lie in *Huckleberry Finn* as a Technical Device." *Mark Twain Quarterly*, 9 (Winter 1953), 11-12.

There are twenty-nine lies told by seven liars before Tom shows up at his Aunt Sally's, with little artistic justification.

Bluefarb, Sam. "*Huckleberry Finn*: Escape from Conscience and the Discovery of the Heart." *The Escape Motif in the American Novel: Mark Twain to Richard Wright*. Columbus: Ohio State University Press, 1972. Pp. 12-24.

HF is "the first modern American novel in which the theme is dominant," anticipating later novels in the genre in "violence, the difference between the uses of rhetoric and the contrasting realities, conscious and unconscious hypocrisy, gratuitous cruelty ... but in amounts that may seem immodest or overplayed when we compare the work with the novels that follow it."

Blues, Thomas. *Mark Twain & and the Community*. Lexington: The University Press of Kentucky, 1970.

In *GA*, *TS*, *P&P*, and *HF* the protagonists are committed to the community although MT repudiates its values and stability; he was "deeply distrustful of the character and fearful for the fate of the individual who attempts to triumph over the community." *CY* fails because MT could no longer use this commitment as a structural device.

________. "The Strategy of Compromise in Mark Twain's 'Boy Books.'" *Modern Fiction Studies*, 14 (Spring 1968), 21-31.

"The heroes of *Tom Sawyer, The Prince and the Pauper*, and *Huckleberry Finn* harbor aggressive designs against the community," but each hero achieved his victory in a way that left the community's stability intact, through "a compromise solution that had the important value of permitting triumph without isolation."

Boggan, J.R. "That Slap, Huck, Did It Hurt?" *English Language Notes*, 1 (March 1954), 212-15.

Huck's concern over "the plain hand of Providence slapping me in the face and letting me know my wickedness was being watched all the while from up there in heaven" has been exaggerated by the critics: his statements elsewhere show that "hell has no emotional meaning for Huck ... the force of his exclamation is much diminished ... Twain's attempt to win an added Christian sympathy for his good 'bad boy' is unconvincing."

Boland, Sally. "The Seven Dialects in *Huckleberry Finn*." *North Dakota Quarterly*, 36 (Summer 1968), 30-40.

MT's use of dialect is not an end in itself, but a literary tool to delineate characters. The speech of the Negro and backwoodsman is represented phonetically, in a conspicuous "eye-dialect," but there is no such representation of the pronunciation of more educated persons. The dialects are used to represent regional and social differences in the characters, and there is also "a childhood lingo that cuts across all other distinctions." "The study was limited to the text of the novel ... no conclusions were drawn as to the relation of the novel to linguistic realities."

Booth, Wayne C. *The Rhetoric of Fiction*. Chicago and London: The University of

Chicago Press, 1961.

Very brief comments on Huck Finn as a narrator, passim (indexed).

Borges, Jorge Luis. "Una Vindicación de Mark Twain." *Sur*, 5 (Noviembre 1935), 40-46.

Supports DeVoto's view of MT as vigorously American, in opposition to "la depresiva tesis de Brooks." "Mark Twain (importa repetirlo) ha escrito *Huckleberry Finn*, libro que basta para la gloria. Libro ni burlesco ni trágico, libro solamente feliz."

Bosha, Francis J. "Mark Twain in Japan: A Checklist of Translations, 1899-1978." *Mark Twain Journal*, 19 (Summer 1979), 8-13.

This "working checklist ... compiles most of the Japanese translations of Twain's stories and novels, published in book form," excluding excerpts translated for textbooks and translations published in newspapers and magazines.

Bowden, Edwin T. *The Dungeon of the Heart: Human Isolation and the American Novel*. New York: Macmillan, 1961. Pp. 30-43 and passim.

Huck is detached, but sympathetic, and has a deep sense of ethics (p. 35). He gradually comes to form a commitment to Jim.

Bradbury, Malcolm. "*Huckleberry Finn*: An Epic of Self-Discovery." *UNESCO Courier*, 35 (June 1982), 15–17.

HF has "moral dignity" in Huck's maturation, and transcends other boys' books in that it is an exploration of society rather than merely an adventure. "Like Holden Caulfield, in J.D. Salinger's *The Catcher in the Rye* (a book that clearly owes much to *Huckleberry Finn*), Huck protects enough of childhood to keep his innocence and seeks enough of adulthood to acquire judgment." Illustrations include two stills from "a Soviet TV production of the *Adventures of Tom Sawyer* which is astonishingly faithful to the spirit and detail of Mark Twain's novel. The three-hour film, directed by Stanislav Gorovukhin, was shot on location with the banks of the Dnieper taking the place of the Mississippi valley."

Branch, Edgar Marquess. *The Literary Apprenticeship of Mark Twain. With Selections from His Apprentice Writing*. Urbana: University of Illinois Press, 1950.

Primarily concerned with MT's literary career from the beginnings to the *Quaker City* excursion (1867), but concluding with "Apprentice and Artist: *Huckleberry Finn*" (pp. 195-216).

———. "Mark Twain and J. D. Salinger: A Study in Literary Continuity." *American Quarterly*, 9 (Summer 1957), 144-58.

Without attempting to show influence or "to compare the 'then' and 'now' of American society through the illustrative use" of *HF* and *The Catcher in the Rye*, Branch reveals parallels in "narrative pattern and style, characterization and critical import.... Independently and in his own right each author has probed beneath surface facts—so dramatically contrasted in Huck's and Holden's environments—to the experiential continuity of American life."

———. "The Two Providences: Thematic Form in 'Huckleberry Finn.'" *College English*, 11 (January 1950), 188-95.

Miss Watson and the Widow Douglas offer contrasting conceptions of heavenly providence. From these, there follows a choice between conventional morality and humanitarian idealism; the duality is implicit in the style of the novel, providing thematic unity. Reprinted in Gerber (1971).

Branch, Watson. "Hard-Hearted Huck: 'No Time to Be Sentimentering.'" *Studies in American Fiction*, 6 (Autumn 1978), 212-18.

The opening third of the article summarizes the critical debate over Huck's apparent indifference to the deaths of other characters in *HF*, which Branch attributes to his dual role as character and the narrator writing after the events and the feelings of the time: Huck tries to control his present emotions and is limited in his ability to express his past ones, but he is honest, sympathetic, and humane.

Brauer, Arlette. "Life is Still Perilous for HUCK FINN." *MD* [a non-technical magazine for the medical profession], 28 (June 1984), 117–20, 125, 128, 133.

This is a substantially researched and workmanlike article directed at a sophisticated audience whose specialization is not in American literature. Scholars will not be greatly troubled by a few minor errors concerning MT's life and works, and in the extensive treatment of the critical reputation of *HF* there is much of interest on the reaction of black parents and educators of the present time. Ms. Brauer reproduces in facsimile most of an unsigned interview with John H. Wallace in the *Washington Post* for 8 Sept. 1983 (which see), on which is superimposed the front cover of Wallace's adaptation of *HF* with the language made inoffensive. In conclusion, Ms. Brauer cites a complaint to Pennsylvania's Human Rights Commission over the teaching of *HF*, and the response by "a group from Pennsylvania State University, which includes the Forum of Black Affairs, . . . studying the effect of the book on 300 white ninth-graders in the district. The study's report: 'Reading *Huckleberry Finn* and discussing it in class actually enhanced the racial attitudes of whites toward blacks.' The district has made the reading of the book optional 'pending further study.' "

Briden, Earl F. "Huck's Great Escape: Magic and Ritual." *Mark Twain Journal*, 21 (Spring 1983), 17-18.

Drawing chiefly on Hoffman (1961), DeVoto (1932), and Lynn (1959), argues that the escape from Pap's cabin combines slave superstitions about the compulsive behavior of witches (who will count the spilled corn meal grain by grain) and the Mosaic themes of the Passover (smeared blood--see Exodus 12:23) and despoiling the place Huck left (see Exodus 11:2, 12:36).

———. "Huck's Island Adventure and the Selkirk Legend." *Mark Twain Journal*, 18 (Winter 1976-1977), 12-14.

MT read and appreciated *Robinson Crusoe* and other writings of Defoe, but may also have found inspiration in William Cowper's "Verses Supposed to be Written by Alexander Selkirk, During His Solitary Abode in the Island of Juan Fernandez," which contains "ideas not expressly treated in Crusoe's tale yet strikingly echoed in Huck's."

Bridgman, Richard. "Henry James and Mark Twain." *The Colloquial Style in America*, New York: Oxford University Press, 1966. Pp. 78-130; also passim.

The chief difference between the two is in subject-matter: "Huck and the other characters in his book talk about things, whereas the Jamesian characters discuss states of being" (p. 78). Quotes Alice B. Toklas as saying that MT was Gertrude Stein's favorite American writer—whom "she was continuously reading," but recognizes possible hyperbole: this was in a letter to MT's biographer Miss Jerry Allen, and transcribed in a copy of her book given to Miss Isabel Lyon (MT's secretary).

Brogunier, Joseph. "An Incident in *The Great Gatsby* and *Huckleberry Finn.*" *Mark Twain Journal*, 16 (Summer 1972), 1-3.

Compares the killings of Myrtle Wilson and Boggs, noting the reactions by Nick and Huck and by the morbidly curious neighbors. Fitzgerald admired MT and expressed his indebtedness to the influence of *HF* in a letter of August 9, 1939.

Brooks, Cleanth. "The Teaching of the Novel: *Huckleberry Finn.*" *Reports and Speeches of the First Yale Conference on the Teaching of English, April 1 and 2, 1955*. New Haven: Master of Arts in Teaching Program, Yale University. [Information by kindness of Patricia L. Bodak, Yale University Library.] Reprinted in Edward J. Gordon and Edward S. Noyes, eds., *Essays on the Teaching of English: Reports of the Yale Conferences on the Teaching of English*, New York: Appleton-Century Crofts, 1960. Pp. 203-215. This was also combined with a discussion of teaching stories by Faulkner and Joyce but with few other changes, as "The Criticism of Fiction: The Role of Close Analysis" as a lecture at Georgetown University in 1959 and published in Paul R. Sullivan, ed., *The Critical Matrix*, Washington, D.C.: Georgetown University, 1961; on *HF*, pp. 77-90 (reprinted in Brooks, *A Shaping Joy: Studies in the Writer's Craft*, New York: Harcourt Brace Jovanovich, 1971; on *HF*, pp. 152-165).

Emphasizes teaching: *HF* does "have the requisite closeness of grain, the fineness of texture, the attention to the detail of the pattern that go with the arrangement of more subtle effects" and justify intensive reading. Brooks stresses the importance of Huck as narrator, "a lens that organizes the picture, giving it a certain depth and focus." Huck's "gaze is in its innocence cleansing, but also fortifying," and his moral development is a central theme. Brooks warns that Trilling's reference to Huck and Jim on the raft as "a community of saints" (1948) may "distort" *HF* and "confuse the student."

Brooks, Van Wyck. "The Genesis of Huck Finn." *Freeman*, 1 (31 March 1920), 59-63.

HF succeeds because MT through Huck "was licensed to let himself go.... Huck's illiteracy, Huck's disreputableness and general outrageousness are so many shields behind which Mark Twain can let all the cats out of the bag with impunity." Eastern respectability had controlled MT but not changed his instincts: "You see what happens with Mark Twain when the lion-tamer turns his back."

__________. *The Times of Melville and Whitman*. New York: Dutton, 1947. Passim on MT (indexed).

"Mark Twain in the West" (pp. 283-300) argues that "Mark Twain with his fathomless naivity prepared the ground, as Whitman did, for a new and unique American art of letters, in a negative way with the *The Innocents Abroad*, in a positive way with the Western writings in which he contributed to establish and foster this art." *TS, HF*, and the first half of *LOM* "were germs of a new American literature with a broader base in the national mind than the writers of New England had possessed, fine as they were." On pp. 448-64, "Mark Twain in the East" shows MT as "the greatest American folkwriter of the time," who did not understand or respect his craft: "He seemed all but indifferent to *Huckleberry Finn* when he was at work on this best of his best," and squandered his energies on ill-conceived projects. "Even Mark Twain's great books, with their brilliant beginnings, ended badly"; but some of his works "were destined to live with the best in America." Excerpted in Gerber (1971).

__________. [Introduction.] Sherwood Anderson, "Letters to Van Wyck Brooks." *Story: The Magazine of the Short Story*, 19 (September-October 1941), 42-62.

Anderson comments frequently on MT in these letters, written 1918-1938, coming to his defence at the time Brooks was working on *The Ordeal of Mark Twain:* "Of course your book cannot be written in a cheerful spirit. In facing Twain's life you face a tragedy. How could the man mean what he does to us if it were not a tragedy. Had the man succeeded in breaking through he would not have been a part of us. Why can't you take it that way?" In his introduction to the letters Brooks says that when the book was published, Anderson "showed me clearly where my study had fallen short. I had failed to write the most important chapter, in which I should have praised *Huckleberry Finn*. I was too much concerned with the psychological problem, and the psychologist inhibited the poet in me. I regretted this as much as Sherwood, who loved Mark Twain above all writers."

Brown, Clarence A. "*Huckleberry Finn:* A Study in Structure and Point of View." *Mark Twain Journal*, 12 (Spring 1964), 10-15, 5.

The novel "must be read as a 'pastoral,' albeit one on which a nightmare world of human injustice and brutality constantly impinges"; thus, "the concluding episode in the novel is simply Huck's return to the world of Tom Sawyer." The core of the narrative is not Jim's flight to freedom, "but, quite simply, the adventures of Huckleberry Finn." Too much can be made of his moral growth—at the Phelps farm he returns to the world from which he set out. "While Huck functions as a sensitive center of consciousness, he does not function as a direct voice for Twain," and MT's style, through unlike that of Henry James, is equally effective in conveying to the reader the consciousness of the central character.

Brown, Deming. *Soviet Attitudes toward American Writing*. Princeton, New Jersey: Princeton University Press, 1962.

This is a general study in which most of the references to MT are in lists of American authors long popular with Russian readers. There is an account of more interest describing Communist reaction when *HF* was removed from New York City schools in 1958, after Negro protests. Clearly, said *Inostrannaya Literatura*, in this day of Little Rock and McCarthy MT was removed because he fought for racial equality (p. 197). Yel. Romanovna was even more misled in describing the Mark Twain Society as having long operated "under the aegis of Truman, Churchill, and DeGaulle"—and now there were plans for an affiliate of the society in Western Germany, with a membership of 50,000! (p. 165).

Brown, Robert B. "One Hundred Years of Huck Finn. It was a difficult birth, but it looks as if the child will live forever." *American Heritage*, 35 (June/July 1984), 81–85.

A brief popular account of the writing, publication, and vicissitudes of reputation of *HF*, with a list of 52 years in the period 1883–1983 in which events of greater or lesser interest occurred (sometimes a banning, sometimes only the publication of a translation into yet another foreign language). Somewhat squeamishly and vaguely describes the mutilation of the picture of Uncle Silas Phelps [someone added a penis on the printing plate], and briefly describes the objections of black readers to the depiction of Jim and the use of That Word. Illustrations of Huck from Dutch, French, German, Norwegian, and Russian editions are reproduced.

Brown, Spencer. "*Huckleberry Finn* for Our Time: A Re-Reading of the Concluding Chapters." *Michigan Quarterly Review*, 6 (Winter 1967), 41-46.

The "uneasy amusement" and "irritation" intelligent readers feel over the ending are "the reactions Mark Twain deliberately provoked" in an attack on slavery through showing its effect on ordinary, kind people, and most of all, its effect on Huck and Jim: "Thus slavery has corrupted and rendered selfish the best character in the novel" and reduced the manly Jim to a clown.

Brown, Sterling. *The Negro in American Fiction*. Washington, D.C.: The Associates in Negro Folk Education, 1935; rpt. New York: Argosy-Antiquarian Ltd., 1969.

On pp. 67-69, depicts MT as sympathetic, tracing his portrayal of Negroes from the "largely traditional" picture in *GA*, and the "bitter memory of cruelty and separation" in "A True Story," to *HF*, where "Jim is the best example in nineteenth century fiction of the average Negro slave (not the tragic mulatto or the noble savage), illiterate, superstitious, yet clinging to his hope for freedom, to his love for his own. And he is completely believable." *PW* is a decline "from the great tenderness and truth of this portrait" and would have been the better for a fuller development of Roxy.

Browne, Ray B. "Huck's Final Triumph." *Ball State Teachers College Forum*, 6 (Winter 1965), 3-12.

After summarizing the debate over the ending of *HF*, argues that the book's theme is "Huck's search for personal liberation," for the maturity that will allow him to proclaim that he is his own master. The novel's theme develops in three strands as Huck outgrows Tom, Jim and Pap, and in the end he can be true to himself rather than to society.

Brownell, Frances V. "The Role of Jim in *Huckleberry Finn*." *Boston University Studies in English*, 1 (Spring-Summer 1955), 74-83.

Jim is passive or absent in most of the episodes involving physical action, and his main role is that of "moral catalyst ... it is my thesis that Jim's primary function is to further the characterization of Huckleberry Finn: by his presence, his personality, his actions, his words, to call forth from Huckleberry Finn a depth of tenderness and moral strength that could not otherwise have been fully and convincingly revealed to the reader."

Budd, Louis J. "Southward Currents under Huck Finn's Raft." *Mississippi Valley Historical Review*, 46 (September 1959), 222-37.

"Perhaps no analysis of *Huckleberry Finn* can fix its proportions of escape, abstract moralizing, basic human warmth, nostalgia, clowning, and social commentary. The debate over the course of the New South, however, was an important factor in the novel's genesis," and it "was revised and finished between 1880 and 1883, when Twain was an active and sometimes angry commentator on the southerner's way of life and his peculiar institutions."

Burg, David F. "Another View of *Huckleberry Finn*." *Nineteenth-Century Fiction*, 29 (December 1974), 299-319.

The ending of *HF* is not the failure described in "largely moralistic interpretations which argue its shortcomings"; on the contrary, "it constitutes both a valid formal completion of the novel and an emphatic declaration of the author's metaphysics." *HF* "is, in fact, a revolutionary novel. It dispels the conventional morality and the conventional wisdom of its own time and ours. And in its joining of a vision of life's absurdity with a circular structure, *Huckleberry Finn* comprehends and manifests the essence of literary modernity." Huck "is the first absurd hero in our literature, and his story is the prototype of the American novel of black humor."

Burns, Graham. "Time and Pastoral: *The Adventures of Huckleberry Finn*." *Critical Review* (Melbourne), No. 15 (1972), 52-63.

Extends the approach of Leo Marx in *The Machine in the Garden* (1964);

but where Marx "concentrates almost exclusively on the technological subversion of the pastoral ideal.... I want to argue, myself, that the lyrical river journey in *Huckleberry Finn,* while splendidly realized as a naturalistic recreation, it is also felt, as we experience it, as a kind of analogue for life itself; and that the characteristic pacing of Twain's writing in the central lyrical episodes creates a sense of timelessness central to its pastoral qualities."

Buxbaum, Katherine. "Mark Twain and *American Dialect.*" *American Speech,* 2 (February 1927), 233-36.

"The inconsistencies of Huck's speech can hardly be attributed to anything but carelessness," although there may be a counterpart in the alternation between correct and incorrect usage by actual persons. Nonetheless, MT's "admirable use of phonetic spelling" is superior to that of Lowell and others, and even his inconsistency adds to the book's unstudied charm.

Byers, John R., Jr. "Mark Twain's Mary Jane Wilks: Shamed or Shammed?" *Mark Twain Journal,* 17 (Winter 1973-1974), 13-14.

Huck writes in Chapter 27 of "them devils laying right there under her own roof, shaming her and robbing her"; the word "shaming" is probably misspelled.

———. "Miss Emmeline Grangerford's Hymn Book." *American Literature,* 43 (May 1971), 259-63.

The "Ode to Stephen Dowling Bots, Dec'd" from *HF* and Isaac Watts's "Alas! and did my Saviour Bleed!" are printed in parallel columns to show a possible derivation; particularly significant are parallels in the first and second lines, the common bathos, and similar structure of questions and answers concerning death.

Cady, Edwin H. "Huckleberry Finn by Common Day." *The Light of Common Day: Realism in American Fiction.* Bloomington and London: Indiana University Press, 1976. Pp. 88-119.

In *HF* morality is based on the value of the individual (p. 32); Cady notes an element of the mock-heroic (pp. 65-66). On *HF* as picaresque and anti-romantic, pp. 88-119. Pp. 88-89, 101-19 reprinted in Bradley (1977).

Callan, Richard J. "The Burden of Innocence in Melville and Twain." *Renascence,* 17 (Summer 1965), 191-94.

A comparison of *Billy Budd* and *HF,* whose authors were skeptics about man and "in the matter of religiosity...shook and shocked us into attention. Finally, the leading characters of those fictions and some of their predicaments have a surprising similarity."

Cambon, Glauco. "What Maisie and Huck Knew." *Studi Americani,* 6 (1960), 203-20.

MT and James both faced problems of showing reality through the eyes of a child, although Maisie's world is that of society while for Huck freedom can only be achieved by escape. Both characters are saved by experience rather than coarsened by it. In a postscript Cambon points out that MT's "imaginative withdrawal is a simpler solution than James's."

Canora, Vivien Ordoña. "The Initiation-Disaffiliation Theme in *The Adventures of Huckleberry Finn* and the *Nick Adams* Stories." *CETA Journal* (College English Teachers Association—Visayas and Mindanao), 2 (May 1973), 138-45.

Essentially two parallel but separate studies, consisting largely of description and summary; demonstrates that Hemingway's character and Huck meet the world's brutalities and "end rebelling against their respective societies by disaffiliation" and flight, Huck to the Territory and Nick to foreign lands.

Carkeet, David. "The Dialects in *Huckleberry Finn.*" *American Literature,* 51 (November 1979), 315-32.

MT respected the antebellum humorists and Joel Chandler Harris, and profited by their example. He took pains with the details of dialect, making hundreds of changes between his original manuscript and the final published version. There are some inconsistencies (partly owing to the composition of *HF* over seven years), and MT meant his "Explanatory" preface seriously. Rather than the six white dialects MT mentions there, Carkeet has found nine.

Carrington, George C., Jr. *The Dramatic Unity of "Huckleberry Finn."* Columbus: Ohio State University Press, 1976.

Carrington concludes his preface with a statement of his aims: "First I will try to define what kind of world Twainian man finds himself in and how he reacts to his sense of that world. Then I will define the mechanism, which I call 'drama,' by which man tries to give his world stability and patterns, that is, to structure it, to give it meaning.... Then I will try to show that the whole novel, including the ending, 'speaks' that method, and is a structure of episodes that lack surface connections but are intimately connected on the level of deep structure—that is, are similar in basic elements and are generated one from another by consistent rules...the qualities of *Huckleberry Finn* are inevitable, and the ending is necessary and right."

Carstensen, Broder. "*The Adventures of Huckleberry Finn:* Die Problematik des Schlusses." *Neueren Sprachen,* 12 (Dezember 1961), 541-51. Reprinted in Franz H. Link, ed., *Amerika, Vision und Wirklichkeit: Beitrage deutscher Forschung zur amerikanischen Literaturgeschichte.* Frankfurt am Main, Bonn: Athenäum Verlag, 1968. Pp. 199-210.

Explains the weak ending of *HF* in terms of MT's use of his unfinished novel, *The Mysterious Stranger,* also dealing with a prisoner. Concludes: "Huckleberry Finn is no Ulysses, Faust, Don Quixote, Don Juan and no Hamlet, and *Huckleberry Finn* does not belong in the library of great books of world literature." [In German.]

Carter, Everett. "The Meaning of, and in, Realism." *Antioch Review,* 12 (March 1952), 78-94.

"There never was a less metaphysical man, at least before the hopelessness of determinism closed down upon him;" MT's "aim was to be authentic, and...to find his rewards in the market-place." *Huckleberry Finn* is significant for its sustained irony, but it was written before 1890, when a realist could still write for Americans who believed in a happy ending.

Carter, Paul J. "Mark Twain: 'Moralist in Disguise.'" *University of Colorado Studies, Series in Language and Literature,* No. 6 (1957), 65-78.

"Twain's morality, like Huck's, was emotive, intuitive, and uncertain. It was a morality which could be both militant and tolerant. It prompted his sharpest satiric judgments and his most trivial diatribes....he could seldom see life without raging or moralizing, and the detachment necessary to art was lost.... This innate conflict was the price he paid for his sensitivity."

Casey, Daniel J. "Huckleberry in Finland: A Comparison of Twain and Kivi." *Moderna Språk,* 62 (Dececember 1968), 385-94.

MT's universal appeal is attested by the ease with which Casey was able to introduce *HF* to students in the United States, Italy, and Finland; moreover, *HF* is much like the book portraying the Finnish national character, Kivi's *Seven Brothers,* in that both books concern the independence, self-reliance, and compassion of outcast characters.

———. "Universality in *Huckleberry Finn:* A Comparison of Twain and Kivi." *Mark Twain Journal,* 14 (Winter 1967-1968), 13-18.

Argues the case for the book's universal appeal by comparing it to Aleksis Kivi's *Seven Brothers,* which portrays the Finnish national character; does not suggest influence.

Cecil, L. Moffitt. "The Historical Ending of *Adventures of Huckleberry Finn:* How Nigger Jim Was Set Free." *American Literary Realism,* 13 (Autumn 1980), 280-83.

Huck's simple plan would have worked, but "Mark Twain chose Tom's plan because it travesties so scathingly the botched way our nation's freeing of the slaves was actually accomplished." Both emancipations were marked by delay, gratuitous cruelty, and a bloody conflict which could have been avoided.

Chamberlain, Bobby J. "Frontier Humor in *Huckleberry Finn* and Carvalho's *O Coronel e o Lobisomem.*" [*The Colonel and the Werewolf*] *Comparative Literature Studies,* 21 (Summer 1984), 201–15.

The Brazilian frontier is still vast, and its humor, like that of the 19th-century American frontier, is based on backlands folk tradition. Chamberlain takes the two novels as representative, noting such common qualities as a deadpan narrator, trickery, and non-standard language (including coined words); however, his description of Carvalho's novel suggests that it has less in common with *HF* than with the work of such authors as Johnson Jones Hooper, Thomas Bangs Thorpe, and George Washington Harris.

Chambers, Bradford. "Scholars and *Huck Finn*: A New Look." *Interracial Books for Children Bulletin*, 15, No. 4 (1984), 12–13.

On issues of racism brought up at a conference at Pennsylvania State University (26–28 April 1984). Participants in some of the 16 panels [most of them concerned with *HF* on the college or graduate level] seemed unconcerned or insensitive, but the black panel (subtitled "Humor—At Whose Expense?") drew more than half the participants at the conference. "In his opening remarks James Stewart said that the issue was not banning *Huck Finn*, but when and how to teach it." Margot Allen described her pain and her son's pain on reading *HF* in school, a generation apart. Jane Madsden attacked a study purportedly demonstrating that ninth-graders are not negatively affected by reading *HF*, and Terrell Jones, author of the study, responded that his findings were only tentative, but he had urged that *HF* not be taught below grade 11 or 12, and that area schools undertake a racism-awareness program. "Twain's effective use of irony to satirize social evils was acknowledged by everyone, but the dialog raised a second question: What is the age level at which children can understand the irony? By the end of the discussion, there was considerable agreement that the humor in *Huck Finn* was too sophisticated for use in elementary school, but several participants wondered if high school students are any better equipped." Chambers "met the following day with representatives of the Penn State College of Education and the Black Studies Program. We agreed to jointly develop a set of lesson plans that teachers might use with *Huck Finn*."

Chander, Jagdish, and Narindar S. Pradhan, eds. *Studies in American Literature: Essays in Honour of William Mulder*. Delhi: Oxford University Press, 1976.

On pp. 4-7 of his "Psychoanalysis and Modern American Criticism," Darshan Singh Maini briefly summarizes treatments of MT by Fiedler, Brooks, Kaplan, and Geismar, and on pp. 23, 27 n. 18 of "Leslie A. Fiedler: Critic as Mythographer" Neila Seshachari argues that Fiedler's "Come Back to the Raft Ag'in, Huck Honey!" (1948) records "a genuine archetypal myth." Chander's own "American Novel—a Voyage of Self-Discovery" summarizes *HF* as told from the perspective of the dispossessed.

Chase, Richard. "Mark Twain and the Novel." *The American Novel and Its Tradition*. Garden City, New York: Doubleday Anchor Books, 1957. Pp. 138-56.

On *HF* (pp. 138-49), praises the language and Huck's clear vision, noting the mythic quality previously mentioned by DeVoto—it takes the forms of initiation and the ritual of exorcism; discusses the attack on romantic falsifications. Only in *HF* and first part on *LOM* is there anything really first rate by MT, and Fiedler and Leavis over-praise *PW*. Pp. 138-49 (on *HF*) reprinted in Lettis (1962).

Christopher, J. R. On the *Adventures of Huckleberry Finn* as a Comic Myth." *Cim-*

arron Review, No. 18 (January 1972), 18-27.

Northrop Frye's *Anatomy of Criticism* (1957) mentions *HF* three times; "The purpose of this essay is simply to investigate the ways in which Northrop Frye's Theory of Myths is applicable to this Twain fiction."

Clark, Marden J. "No Time to Be Sentimentering." *Mark Twain Journal*, 21 (Spring 1983), 21-23.

Though little explored, the contrast between sentimentality and genuine emotion in *HF* is "one of the more fascinating sources of interest and thematic energy. Emmeline Grangerford's verse is comic, but the Grangerfords and Shepherdsons show both warmth and courage and a false sense of honor that brings death. There are contrasts elsewhere, as in the sentimentalized religion of Miss Watson and the genuine religion of the Widow Douglas, and the playing on the sentimentality of others by Huck and by the King and Duke. The ending remains a critical problem, but *HF* "as a whole develops and dramatizes one of the most persuasive arguments in literature against the cheap and shallow and sentimental and in favor of the genuine, the deep, the earned emotion."

Clemens, Cyril. "The Model for *Huckleberry Finn*." *Hobbies—the Magazine for Collectors*, 59 (February 1955), 106-9.

"Not long before his death," Courtland P. Morris told Cyril Clemens about posing as model for all the characters in *HF* in the illustrations by Edward Windsor Kemble.

Clerc, Charles. "Sunrise on the River: The 'Whole World' of *Huckleberry Finn*." *Modern Fiction Studies*, 14 (Spring 1968), 67-78.

A rhetorical analysis of a 400-word paragraph at the beginning of Chapter 19. Its strength lies not in mere accurate imitation of an uneducated boy's speech, but in a sophisticated art: "Any suggestion of sloppiness in the passage may be dispelled...by a consideration of the wide variety of rhetorical forms and grammatical techniques used to achieve vividness and vivacity."

Coard, Robert L. "Huck Finn and Mr. Mark Twain Rhyme." *Midwest Quarterly*, 10 (July 1969), 317-29.

"A study of Huck Finn's rhymes, placed in the larger context of Mark Twain's rhymes in his other prose, should shed considerable light on the exuberant word-play that, perhaps as much as any unified theme, helped to shape an American masterpiece."

__________. "Huck Finn and Two Sixteenth Century Lads." *Midwest Quarterly*, 23 (Summer 1982), 437-46.

On the interrelationship of *HF* and *P&P*. The two overlap in their periods of composition, and Coard argues a number of parallels, among them brutal fathers, protective father-substitutes and "a similar pattern involving separation and reunion and heroic altruism by the guardian adult" (Miles Hendon and Jim), even "major plot services" by the minor characters Miss Watson and Father Andrew. A major difference is the fresh language of *HF*, in contrast to "the often blowsy rhetoric" of *P&P*.

Coffee, Jessie A. "Mark Twain's Use of 'Hain't' in *Huckleberry Finn*." *American Speech*, 37 (October 1962), 234-36.

The form *ain't*, used 305 times, commonly represents the present *am not*, *is not*, and *are not*; the form *hain't* is used 74 times, where the word *have* or *has* is indicated, as in the present perfect, or in the expression *he has not got*.

Collins, Billy G. "Huckleberry Finn: A Mississippi Moses." *Journal of Narrative Technique*, 5 (May 1975), 86-104.

Draws numerous parallels between *HF* and the story of Moses in *Exodus*. *HF* has a three-part structure, and the debated ending is "thematically and technically necessary to balance the first section of the novel and conclude the Moses analogy. Warnings are delivered to the Egyptians, (comic) plagues are visited upon enslaved and enslavers alike, and the tale concludes with the achievement of freedom by the enslaved and the plan to depart for the territories, which corresponds to the Israelites' escape into the 'wilderness.'" MT "succeeded in demonstrating the evils of slavery, but no one, apparently, observed the biblical parallel. It may be partly for this reason that Twain published in 1894, nine years after *Huckleberry Finn*, a sequel called *Tom Sawyer Abroad*."

Colwell, James L. "Huckleberries and Humans: On the Naming of Huckleberry Finn." *Publications of the Modern Language Association*, 86 (January 1971), 70-76.

MT did not see huckleberries until he went to Hartford in 1868; the name suggests rusticity and wildness. "Finn" came from a Hannibal drunkard, like the father of Tom Blankenship, the boy on whom Huck was modeled. Moreover, "To the nonpsychologically trained ear, 'Huck' is to 'Mark' about as 'Finn' is to 'Twain,' and the resemblance seems both striking and deliberate."

Coveney, Peter. "Mark Twain and Richard Jefferies." *Poor Monkey: The Child in Literature*. London: Rockcliff, 1957; on MT, pp. 169-184. Rpt. Harmondsworth, Middlesex, and Baltimore, MD.: Penguin Books, 1967, with new volume title, *The Image of Childhood/The Individual and Society: A Study of the Theme in English Literature*; on MT, pp. 215-32.

On *TS*, *HF*, and—following Van Wyck Brooks—MT's inner torment. "By alluding to the man...we see how much *Huckleberry Finn* is a remarkable distillate of the various and complex factors which went to the production of Mark Twain's extraordinary sensibility." The creation of Tom's character reveals "the factors making for weakness. In the creation of Huckleberry Finn we see no less the triumph of Mark Twain the artist over his regressing and weakening impulses. In that one novel of childhood, the personal nostalgia and unbalance of the man expands in an astonishing way into a commentary on American society, and finally on civilization itself."

Cowie, Alexander. "Mark Twain Controls Himself." *American Literature*, 10 (January 1939), 488-91.

A reply to DeLancey Ferguson ("Huck Finn Aborning," 1938): MT "did like to write a more robust style than was agreeable to his late Victorian public," but tempered what he said. "Whether Olivia or Howells or Mark Twain was the censor does not much matter."

Cox, James M. *Mark Twain: The Fate of Humor*. Princeton, New Jersey: Princeton University Press, 1966.

On the role of humor in shaping MT's literary identity as it appears in his major works. "Southwestern Vernacular" (pp. 167-84, on *HF*) reprinted in Simpson (1968); pp. 172-84 reprinted in Bradley (1977).

———. "Mark Twain, the Height of Humor." Louis D. Rubin, Jr., ed., *The Comic Imagination in American Literature*. New Brunswick, New Jersey: Rutgers University Press, 1973. Pp. 139-48.

A rebel against the Union and a deserter from Confederate forces, MT remained a troublemaker when he went to Nevada. As a humorist he dealt with a less reputable genre, but learned a balance between affront to his audience and a bland predictability; thus, we can laugh at the townspeople duped by the "Royal Nonesuch" in *HF*, where "the image of a naked King which reduces us to a wail of pain in *King Lear*, finally reduces us to helpless laughter." (See Whiting, 1944, and Graves, 1968.)

———. "Remarks on the Sad Initiation of Huckleberry Finn." *Sewanee Review*, 62 (July-September 1954), 389-405.

On Tom and Huck's antithetical values, and MT's fascination with Tom. Reprinted in Marks (1959).

———. "Toward Vernacular Humor." *Virginia Quarterly Review*, 46 (Spring 1970), 311-330.

A discussion chiefly in terms of MT's *HF*, and of Ring Lardner and J. D. Salinger.

———. "Walt Whitman, Mark Twain, and the Civil War." *Sewanee Review*, 69 (Spring 1961), 185-204.

"Mark Twain's Civil War was never the historical Civil War but an emotional equivalent of that war in which Mark Twain was perpetually involved as he created for himself and for his nation an image of the past which could contain the war instead of being destroyed by it." For MT the cost "was ultimately to be overtaken by the chaos of the inner war that all the stratagems and evasions of humor, burlesque, and parody could not resolve." He was the novelist—or poet—of Reconstruction, "for in *Huckleberry Finn* he brought not the old south but an entirely new south back into the Union."

Cox, John E. "On the Naming of Huckleberry Finn." *Publications of the Modern Language Association*, 86 (October 1971), 1038.

A brief letter to the editor in response to Colwell (1971): "The boy was a 'hick' who loved to have 'fun,' or a 'fun hick.' The transposition of letters would not have been all that difficult."

Coyle, William. "Never the Twain." *CEA Critic*, 26 (November 1963), 1, 3.

On school adaptations of *HF*, some American and some British, which he saw on sale in Brazil when he was a Fulbright lecturer there. Simplified classics have their value to foreign students, but *HF* is a poor choice, with the language destroyed and with it the characterization. "Little remains but the plot, which some have defended but few have praised."

Crichton, Andrew B. "Rolling Along with Huck and Jim down the Mighty Mississippi a Hundred Years Later." *Proteus*, 1:2 (1984), 15–18.

The head of a highschool English department, Crichton has been using *HF* to show his composition students how a professional goes about his work. He contrasts Greg Matthews' *The Further Adventures of Huckleberry Finn* with the authentic voice in *HF*, and concludes with praise for Huck's direct and forthright control of language.

Cross, Randy K. "*Huckleberry Finn*: The Sacred and the Profane." *Mark Twain Journal*, 21 (Spring 1983), 27-28.

In *HF*, MT satirizes religion and denies the divinity of Christ; he ridicules the power of prayer and satirizes the hypocrisy of church-goers. Chapter 33 is a parody of the Resurrection, with Huck as Christ and Tom as Thomas, who doubted.

Crowe, Charles. "Mark Twain's *Huckleberry Finn* and the American Journey." *Archiv für das Studium der neuren Sprachen und Literaturen*, 199 (1962), 145-58.

Summarizes critical views of the book; argues that it must be recognized as "a great comic novel and a boy's tale," with Huck as "the single authentic American folk hero and...the voyage down the river as a mythic representation of the fundamental national experience."

Cude, Wilfred. "'False as Harlots' Oaths': Dunny Ramsey Looks at Huck Finn." *Studies in Canadian Literature*, 2 (Summer 1977), 164-87.

The character in *Fifth Business* (1970) by Robertson Davies is older and more sophisticated, but in his own way a fugitive, and ambivalent in his view of his North American world. The character Dunny calls Huck "a charming, knowing little fellow, possessed of insights and perceptions beyond his years," but cannot acknowledge that he himself is an old innocent. At length, Cude treats parallels between Huck and Dunny, with *HF* and *Fifth Business* as complementary novels.

Cummings, Sherwood. "What's in Huckleberry Finn?" *English Journal*, 50 (January 1961), 1-8.

An analysis geared to teaching in high school. Students are accustomed to television dramas in which the moral values are clear and nothing is left to inference; but MT tells the story through Huck, who himself is unaware of what MT is implying. The two major themes are Huck's rejection of society and his struggle with his conscience.

Currie, H. MacL. "Aristophanes and Mark Twain." *Notes and Queries* (London), 203, n.s. 5 (April 1958), 165-68.

Compares the attitude of the two as revealed in the latter part of the *Thesmophoriazusae* and in Chapters 36-39 of *HF*. They were "not dissimilar in spirit," and if there is no evidence that MT had read Aristophanes, he did read widely and the plays were readily available in the Bohn classical series.

Da Ponte, Durant. "*Life* Reviews *Huckleberry Finn*." *American Literature*, 31 (March 1959), 78-81.

The unsigned review, "Mark Twain's Blood-Curdling Humor," appeared in the old comic magazine, *Life*, 5 (26 February 1885), 119; it was probably written by Robert Bridges. One month later *Life* expressed satisfaction at the news that the Concord (MA) Library Committee had banned the book. The mention of "a polite version of the 'Gyascutus'" story indicates that an analogue of "The Royal Nonesuch" was familiar to Bridges and some of his readers (*See* Whiting, 1944, and Graves, 1968).

David, Beverly R. "Mark Twain and the Legends for *Huckleberry Finn*." *American Literary Realism*, 15 (Autumn 1982), 155-65.

Edward Windsor Kemble's letters and his original drawings for *HF* (in the McKinney Collection at Vassar College) indicate that he wrote captions for the illustrations in the first edition, rather than Charles Webster as was previously thought. MT edited and sometimes completely rewrote what "Kemble obviously considered...only working captions" to fit them better with the text. [The attribution of running heads in the first edition to Albert Bigelow Paine is a misreading of Ensor's 1968 *American Literature* article.]

———. "The Pictorial *Huck Finn*: Mark Twain and His Illustrator, E. W. Kemble." *American Quarterly*, 26 (October 1974), 331-51.

Reprints 20 illustrations from *HF*, including the mutilated p. 283 cut and the replacement that was tipped in (*See* Sioui, 1962). Concerned with potential sales, MT was attentive to the book's illustration, making it "a tool that converted the cruelty and sexuality of the story into a series of boyish adventures."

Davis, Thadious M. "Foreword." *Mark Twain Journal*, 22 (Fall), 2–3.

Professor Davis is Guest Editor of this special issue, "Black Writers on *Adventures of Huckleberry Finn*, One Hundred Years Later." Here, she discusses the continuing controversy over racial issues in *HF* as taught in the schools, and MT's inability to depict the black experience "with the same veracity and intensity accorded that of a Huck Finn or a Tom Sawyer." One must turn to black writers "for the rendering of those other experiences and realities, especially the interior ones which proceed from an assumption that Huck never comes to know: the free territory lies *within* as well as without." There are various concerns, some overlapping, in the essays in this issue by Richard K. Barksdale, Rhett S. Jones, Julius Lester, Charles H. Nichols, Charles H. Nilon, Arnold Rampersad, David L. Smith, and Kenny J. Williams.

Delaney, Paul. "You Can't Go Back to the Raft Ag'in Huck Honey!: Mark Twain's Western Sequel to *Huckleberry Finn*." *Western American Literature*, 11 (Fall 1976), 215-29.

On MT's unfinished "Huck Finn and Tom Sawyer Among the Indians," which with *TS* and *HF* would have formed a trilogy of boyhood, culminating in loss of innocence. Huck's flight to the Territory "results not in idyllic independence but in horrifying loneliness," and there is no longer a raft to which he can flee from the horrors he encounters. "Huck can witness such evils as murder, grave-robbing, graft, fraud, hypocrisy—but they do not affect him because he is in no way part of them. But to a fourteen- or fifteen-year-old boy a knowledge of sexual evil is fundamentally different. Perception of such an evil involves a recognition of the inter-relationedness of one's own desires with a universal experience which can somehow result in the horror of Peggy Mills being ravished between four stakes." Boyish innocence is no longer possible, and Huck "begins a transformation which leads eventually to the metamorphosis of the Twainian hero from the innocent to the transcendent figure."

DeMenil, Alexander Nicholas. "Samuel L. Clemens." *The Literature of the Louisiana Territory*. St. Louis: St. Louis News, 1904. Pp. 197-202.

MT's literary career was "a puzzle to me. It had always seemed to me impossible that a writer who violated nearly all the canons of literary art, and whose themes were so thoroughly commonplace, should become so extensively known and so widely popular as Mr. Clemens has become. Of course, his fame is only of to-day, but it is wonderful that it is so widespread and hearty, even if it is merely ephemeral." MT "deals of the everyday and commonplace—he is often coarse" [as in *HF*]; he is "irreverant, if not blasphemous" [as in *IA*]; and he is "unnatural and straining after effect" [as in *TS*]. "As a humorist, he paints no typical characters," and "as a novelist, what could possibly be more wretchedly untrue to history and human nature than his *Personal Recollections of Joan of Arc*—a twentieth-century Joan, labelled fifteenth century? Mark Twain lacks the education absolutely necessary to a great writer; he lacks the refinement which would render it impossible for him to create such coarse characters as Huckleberry Finn." He is popular because he makes people laugh.

Dendinger, Lloyd N. "Mark Twain, Samuel L. Clemens." Frank N. Magill, ed. *Critical Survey of Long Fiction* (English Language Series). Englewood Cliffs, NJ: Salem Press, 1983. Vol. 7, 2660–2670.

One of a series of introductory discussions of authors and their works, this follows a standard format including "Achievements," "Biography," and "Analysis." The discussion of MT's works is chiefly on *TS* and *HF*, and the boys "who embody that mythic America, midway between the wilderness and the frontier super-state." MT's work is "dualistic," in the pairing of "characters, situations, states of being, ideas, and values."

Dennis, Larry R. "Mark Twain and the Dark Angel." *Midwest Quarterly*, 8 (January 1967), 181-97.

On the varied perspectives toward death in *HF*; they are all denied to Edwards in *The Great Dark*.

Desai, S. K. "Time in *Huckleberry Finn*." M. K. Naik, S. K. Desai, and S. Mokashi-Punekar, eds., *Indian Studies in American Fiction*. Dharwar: Karnatak University, and Madras: Macmillan India, 1974. Pp. 68-76.

Auden (1953) associated Huck's stoicism in part with an acceptance of the immediate present for itself without assuming the future will be the same or that it will be influenced in the same ways as it was before. Following Auden, Desai will "examine various aspects of the novel, thematic, structural and stylistic, with particular reference to the attitude to time that underlies the novel."

Desmond, John F. "*Huckleberrry Finn* and the Failure of Anamnesis." *Mark Twain Journal*, 21 (Fall 1983), 8-10.

The major incidents in *HF* follow a three-fold development of exposition, confrontation with evil, and—most important—assessment through recollection. Together they regulate Huck's moral development, but the process breaks down in the final chapters; there Huck becomes a mere narrator of events, no longer assessing them.

DeVoto, Bernard. "Introduction." *Adventures of Huckleberry Finn (Tom Sawyer's Companion)*. New York: The Limited Editions Club, 1942. Pp. ix-1xx.

In three successive sections DeVoto describes his own textual editing of *HF*, the history of its composition, and, in "Noon and the Dark" (liii-lxx), discusses *HF* critically. In "A Note by the Illustrator" (lxxi-1xxvi) Thomas Hart Benton discusses his own efforts to achieve authenticity and praises Edward Windsor Kemble, the original illustrator. DeVoto re-used his introduction in *Mark Twain at Work* (1942).

__________. *Mark Twain at Work*. Cambridge, Mass. Harvard University Press; London: Humphrey Milford, Oxford University Press, 1941.

Working from the manuscripts, DeVoto says "something about the actual writing" of *TS* and *HF* "for the first time by any critic. What is said-...does outline the nature of his talent, its abundance, and its hiatuses." A concluding essay, "The Symbols of Despair," is based "on a vast accumulation of data which Mr. Paine ignored and Mr. Brooks never heard about. The present essay indicates the true ordeal of Mark Twain. Anyone who is familiar with Mr. Brooks's book will see at once that my interpretation of it differs altogether from his" (pp. vii-ix). Contains text of "the Great Dark" and early manuscript material for *TS* and *HF*, including "Boy's Manuscript." "The Symbols of Despair" is reprinted in Smith (1963), and material on *TS* in Scott (1955, 1967), and Marks (1959); there is also an excerpt in Cardwell (1963).

Dickinson, Asa Don. "Huckleberry Finn is Fifty Years Old—Yes; But Is He Respectable?" *Wilson Bulletin for Librarians*, 10 (November 1935), 180-85.

A general discussion of *HF*, followed by an account of the difficulty of getting the book into the children's section at the Brooklyn Public Library. Dickinson wrote MT, whose reply (December 21, 1905) is reproduced in facsimile; there is also a page of photographs showing MT's grave, and several of his homes, including the one on Fifth Avenue, New York City.

Donaldson, Scott. "Pap Finn's Boy." *South Atlantic Bulletin*, 36 (May 1971), 32-37.

Although Huck matures he remains a loner like his Pap, but rejects society rather than being rejected by it. In matters of religion, as in those of race, Huck maintains a view like his father's—little more than a set of superstitions.

Dorris, Ronald. "Paternal Relationships in *Huckleberry Finn*." *Proteus*, 1:2 (1984), 57–60.

"The father/son theme stays in the forefront of *Huckleberry Finn*. This is a theme which requires examination not only for the spiritual and material coming of age for a boy, but also the material and spiritual coming of age of a nation." Father figures include Pap Finn, Jim, the King, and Louis XIV (cited as Jim's father in one of the inscriptions in the "evasion" section). Jim recognizes his own mistake as a father when he struck his deaf daughter, and he criticizes Solomon's judgement as that of a man with so many children to spare that he does not properly value one baby. "Yet, Jim is not bitter. He realizes that if ever there is to be responsibility between fathers and sons in any nation, someone responsible must assume the role of father."

Dos Passos, John, and Alan Tate. "The Situation in American Writing." *Partisan Review*, 6 (Summer 1939), 26-92.

Dos Passos and Tate were among those answering a questionnaire question concerning figures in a "usable past." Dos Passos says "the best immediate ancestor (in Auden's sense) for today's American writing is a dark star somewhere in the constellation containing Mark Twain, Melville, Thoreau and Whitman." Tate: "I place Mark Twain nearer to Augustus Longstreet than to Walt Whitman; he was a regional writer in *Huckleberry Finn*, and he mastered a subtly modulated style; compare this with the vulgarity of *The Gilded Age*, written when Mark Twain had accepted the nationalist myth. At his best Twain was regional and universal; toward the end of his life he became national and parochial."

Doughty, Nanelia S. "Realistic Negro Characterization in Postbellum Fiction." *Negro American Literature Forum*, 3 (Summer 1969), 57-62, 68.

Defends MT against the accusation that his Negroes are ridiculed as stereotypes: in *HF* "Like all Clemens' blacks, Jim is a *pre-war* slave. His submissiveness is the necessary bearing of the wholly-owned chattel—*not* a synthetic attitude decreed by the author." In *GA*, Uncle Dan'l may resemble the comic stereotype, but he is in fact a kindly, devout Negro from before the War. In *PW*, Roxy's courage and gaiety are emphasized, but her color is not: "So Clemens ignored mere color as a causative factor. He also discards heredity. The crucial element in the development of 'Tom's character is environment.

Doyno, Victor A. "Over Twain's Shoulder: The Composition and Structure of *Huckleberry Finn.*" *Modern Fiction Studies*, 14 (Spring 1968), 3-9.

"Twain created in *Huckleberry Finn* three parallel sequential patterns of action. Each pattern involves first the meeting of Huck with someone who thinks him dead, the formation or renewal of a partnership to free the slave which ends in failure, and finally, the exchange of forty dollars." This pattern extends through "the natural world [of] the Mississippi...the picaresque adventures and deceptions of the King and Duke; and, finally, the burlesque romanticism of Tom's plot on the Phelps's farm. This pattern, and the ultimate impossibility of winning the slave's freedom," become increasingly evident: "for Huck freedom exists, if at all, in the process of seeking freedom." The disputed ending is an appropriate framing element.

Drake, Robert Y., Jr. "Huck Among the Doctors." *National Review*, 9 (19 November 1960), 320-22.

Critics have often misread *HF*, either because of Freudian preconceptions (as in the case of Leslie Fiedler) or through an inability to understand the Southwestern "intuitive apprehensions that paradox inevitably lies at the heart of reality," as in the "paradox of slavery in the midst of a people so historically committed to the quest for freedom." Huck himself is always concerned "with the *individual*...never with *society* and *institutions*, which, all too often, degenerate into a mob. (Unlike the sociologist or the 'enlightened' legislator, he is not concerned with class or race as such.)"

Dwivedi, A. N. *Mark Twain's "The Adventures of Huckleberry Finn" (Critical Study)*. Bareilly, India: Prakash Book Depot, 1973.

A general study of MT and *HF* on the introductory level, discussing such topics as style, humor, themes, and language. Dwivedi draws heavily on the familiar scholarship; his own chapter titles are often taken with little or no change from the titles of familiar critical articles.

Dyson, A. E. "Huckleberry Finn and the Whole Truth." *Critical Quarterly*, 3 (Spring 1961), 29-40; reprinted in *The Crazy Fabric: Exercises in Irony* (New York: St. Martin's Press, 1965), 96-111.

Argues against simplistic readings: for example, there is not a simple contrast between corrupt society and virtuous outsiders, since "the Duke, the King, and Huck's father...are all far further away from the 'respectable' folk than Huck himself is," and they "are all failures, who stand outside society...simply because they are lazy, vicious, and by nature parasitic." In contrast, the respectable people do not wholly lack the virtues embodied in Huck and Jim. The disputed ending of the story is consistent with "the logic and texture of the whole book," in that "actual human progress does come about...through muddled insights, muddled kindliness, muddled actions as much as from the straightforward vindication of ideals." Article reprinted from the 1965 book in Schmitter (1974).

Edwards, June. "Morality and *Huckleberry Finn.*" *Humanist*, 44 (March–April 1984), 35–36.

"It's a terrible book to give to a child—if one believes in absolute values and admits no hierarchy of moral reasoning." Censors of the right oppose a supposed undermining of traditional values and fail to see that Huck respects sincerity and has "much natural wisdom." Others object to the portrayal of blacks and the use of the word "nigger," missing MT's ironic point.

Egan, Michael. *Mark Twain's "Huckleberry Finn": Race, Class and Society*. London: Published for Sussex University Press by Chatto & Windus, Ltd., 1977.

"Twain's novel is one of the very best histories of its period because it details and concretises...the full experience of an entire way of life" (p. 134). Grim in its concerns, "its intellectual somberness is supported by images of gloom and midnight so persistent they must be accounted deliberate and thematic" (p. 10). Egan's topics include (in chapter titles) "Dialectic of Form and Structure"; "Twain's Fiction and the Reading Public"; "Racism, Slavery and Freedom'; and "The Religion of Violence."

Eliot, T. S. [Introduction.] *The Adventures of Huckleberry Finn*. New York: Chanticleer Press, 1950.

"In the writing of *Huckleberry Finn* Mark Twain had two elements which, when treated with his sensibility and his experience, formed a great book: these two are the Boy and the River.... We come to understand the River by seeing it through the eyes of the Boy; but the Boy is also the spirit of the River." Also praises the colloquial ease of Huck's diction. Reprinted in Bradley (1962, 1977), Simpson (1968, condensed), and Kesterson (1973). Translated into Swedish by Sven Barthel in *Bonniers Litterara Magasin*, 20 (December 1951), 751-56.

———. *American Literature and the American Language*. An Address delivered at Washington University on June 9, 1953. *Washington University Studies*. New Series. Language and Literature, No. 23 (1953). Reprinted in *Sewanee Review*, 74 (January-March 1966), 1-20.

In *HF*, MT "reveals himself to be one of those writers, of whom there are not a great many in any literature, who have discovered a new way of writing, valid not only for themselves but for others. I should place him, in this respect, even with Dryden and Swift, as one of those rare writers who have brought their language up to date, and in so doing, 'purified the dialect of the tribe.' In this respect I should put him above Hawthorne: though no finer a stylist, and in obvious ways a less profound explorer of the soul." MT's Mississippi is "the universal river of human life—more universal, indeed, than the Congo of Joseph Conrad.... There is in Twain, I think, a great unconscious depth, which gives to *Huckleberry Finn* this symbolic value: a symbolism all the more powerful for being uncalculated and unconscious" (pp. 16-17).

Ellis, Allan B. "The Computer and Character Analysis." *English Journal*, 53 (October 1964), 522-27.

A computer analysis of Huck Finn's language revealed "a character who describes his surroundings in great detail but does not talk about things which we would label *Status*, or *Culture*, or *Societal Institutions*. We were, by computer, able to get up to that point a vague glimpse at Huck Finn, a feeling—ever so weak—about what he is like." Further analysis revealed changes in vocabulary with changes in theme, and a portrait of Huck much like that from traditional readings. (*See* reply by Glen A. Love, below.)

———, and F. André Favat. "From Computer to Criticism: An Application of Automatic Content Analysis to the Study of Literature." Philip J. Stone, Dexter C. Dunphy, Marshall S. Smith, and Daniel M. Ogilvie, eds., *The General Inquirer: A Computer Approach to Content Analysis*. Cambridge, Mass.: M.I.T. Press, 1961. Pp. 628–38.

By way of example, applies "General Inquirer" procedures to *HF*, examining Huck in his relation to death. All sentences "spoken" by Huck (narration and dialogue, excluding only statements made by other characters) were submitted to the tagging routine of the Psychosociological Dictionary. "Retrieving on the DEATH tag, which includes such words as autumn, cry, dark, end, mourn, rest, separation, and still" turned up sentences in every chapter of *HF*; then the researchers obtained tag tally graphs for "contexts in which DEATH retrievals occurred, and found that among the categories in these sentences, those of NATURAL-WORLD, SELF, OTHER, MALE-ROLE, FEMALE-ROLE, and FAMILY seemed to predominate." The function of the computer in automatic content analysis of this sort is clerical, examining and organizing data to facilitate the "reasoning, evaluating, and judging" of the literary critic.

Ellison, Ralph. "Change the Joke and Slip the Yoke." *Partisan Review*, 25 (Spring 1958), 45-59. 212-22; reprinted in *Shadow and Act* (1964).

An answer to an essay by Stanley Edgar Hyman on Negro American literature and folklore (immediately preceding). On *HF*, Ellison argues that "Twain fitted Jim into the outlines of the minstrel tradition, and it is from behind this stereotype mask that we see Jim's dignity and human capacity—and Twain's complexity—emerge." MT was still too close to the Reconstruction to escape "the white dictum that Negro males must be treated either as boys or 'uncles'—never as men. Jim's friendship for Huck comes across as that of a boy for another boy rather than as the friendship of an adult for a junior; thus there is implicit in it not only a violation of the manners sanctioned by society for relations between Negroes and whites, there is a violation of our concept of adult maleness." Ellison suggests that it was concern over this question that led Leslie Fiedler to argue a homosexual relationship in "Come Back to the Raft Ag'in, Huck Honey!" Fiedler was "so profoundly disturbed by the manner in which the deep dichotomies symbolized by blackness and whiteness are resolved that, forgetting to look at the specific form of the novel, he leaped squarely into the middle of that tangle of symbolism which he is dedicated to unsnarling and yelled out his most terrifying name for chaos." Excerpted in Bradley (1977).

———. *Shadow and Act*. New York: Random House, 1964.

Includes "The Seer and the Seen" (1946; published in *Confluence*, December, 1953), pp. 24-44; "Change the Joke and Slip the Yoke" (*Partisan Re-

view, Spring, 1958), pp. 45-59; "The Art of Fiction: An Interview" (*Paris Review*, Spring, 1955), pp. 167-83; "Some Questions and Some Answers" (*Preuves*, May, 1958), pp. 261-72. On Huck who, "like Prometheus...embraces the evil implicit in his act in order to affirm his belief in humanity," and the recognition of Jim's humanity (and on "Hemingway's blindness to the moral values of *Huckleberry Finn* despite his sensitivity to its technical aspects"), pp. 29-36. On MT's failure to represent Jim as an adult, pp. 50-51; again on the central moral question in *HF*, pp. 182-83. On language, Ellison speaks of "having inherited the language of Shakespeare and Melville, Mark Twain and Lincoln and no other," although American Negro speech has been important to our language (pp. 266-67). Pp 58-59, on Ellison's own use of folklore, and his ability to imagine himself as Huck Finn more readily than as Jim, reprinted in Simpson (1968), pp. 112-13.

Elsbree, Langdon. "Huck Finn on the Nile." *South Atlantic Quarterly*, 69 (Autumn 1970), 504-10.

On his experiences and observations as a Fulbright teacher of American literature in Cairo, 1966-67. He felt that although the Nile was not the Mississippi, Huck "might have stopped earlier and hoped to grow up in a community that was not too far from home."

Ensor, Allison. "The Location of the Phelps Farm in *Huckleberry Finn*." *South Atlantic Bulletin*, 34 (May 1969), 7.

After summarizing guesses by various scholars, concludes "that Pikesville and the Phelps farm are located in the extreme southeastern part of Arkansas," citing MT's *Autobiography* and *TS, Detective*.

__________. " 'Norman Rockwell Sentimentality': The Rockwell Illustrations for *Tom Sawyer* and *Huckleberry Finn*," Sara deSaussure Davis and Philip D. Beidler, eds. *The Mythologizing of Mark Twain*. University, AL: University of Alabama Press, 1984. Pp. 15–36 (also passim on *HF* in other articles in this volume; indexed).

What Henry Nash Smith said figuratively (in praising Alan Gribben's monumental *Mark Twain's Library* as a corrective) is more literally true of the sixteen color illustrations Rockwell made for editions of *TS* and *HF* published by the Heritage Press in 1936 and 1940 (there were also ninety-one black-and-white drawings Ensor says are of less interest and are not discussed here). Rockwell went to Hannibal, as previous illustrators had not, and took pride in his more faithful rendering of certain local scenes. However, as Ensor points out, there were errors and inconsistencies with the texts, and the facile cheerfulness of Rockwell's illustrations has had an unfortunate influence on the way the public sees *TS* and *HF*. '"One can only regret that, by their narrow focus, they have masked the incisive satire of *Huckleberry Finn* and those darker, more terrifying moments in *Tom Sawyer*."

__________. "Twain's *The Adventures of Huckleberry Finn*, Chapter 37." *Explicator*, 26 (November 1967), Item 20.

MT had already quoted in *IA* from Acts XVII, and would have known Paul's statement that God "hath made of one blood all nations of men for to dwell on all the face of the earth"; thus, the fact that Uncle Silas Phelps was preparing next week's sermon from the same chapter may be an ironic thrust at his dual role as minister and slaveowner.

Erskine, John. "The First and Best Story of Main Street: John Erskine Tells Why *Huckleberry Finn* has won a place among the Immortals." *Delineator*, 110 (February 1927), 10, 94, 97.

TS is "built up with anecdotes, each one complete in itself, and none developed beyond the point of the joke"; in MT's better-constructed book, Huck "tells us far more than he knows; through his naive confessions we see the panorama of his world and become sophisticated. We are really studying ourselves." Reprinted in Erskine's *The Delight of Great Books* (1928); also reprinted in Lettis (1962).

Fadiman, Clifton. "An Afterword." *The Adventures of Huckleberry Finn*. New York: Macmillan, 1966. Pp. 317–18.

Appreciative, for young readers: "There are three wonderful creations in this book. Two of them are people, and their names are Huck and Jim. The third is a river, a river that somehow binds us as a people."

Farrell, James T. "Mark Twain's *Huckleberry Finn* and *Tom Sawyer*." *The League of Frightened Philistines and Other Papers*. New York: Vanguard, 1945. Pp. 25-30.

MT has been misunderstood, particularly by Lewis Mumford (in *The Golden Day*) and Van Wyck Brooks. He had a healthy sense of justice despite his cynicism. Tom and Huck can rise above MT's discouragement because they are boys, and Huck is "an ideal expression of the positive side of Mark Twain." Today the boys "stand as a test not only of ourselves but of the whole of American society," asking why the promise has not been realized. Reprinted in Lettis (1962).

———. "Twain's *Huckleberry Finn* and the Era He Lived In." *New York Times Book Review* (12 December 1943), 6, 37.

"Mark Twain was both a democrat and a cynic"; he was disillusioned, but "through his two unspoiled boys Twain forcefully emphasized his own attitudes and values.... Tom and Huck are symbols of the possibilities in human beings."

Ferguson, Delancey. "Clemens' ... *Huckleberry Finn*." *Explicator*, 4 (April 1946), Item 42.

A reply to a query by P.B.A. in *Explicator*, 4 (November 1945), Q. 7 (In *Mark Twain at Work*, p. 54, DeVoto says MT disregards the fact that Jim could have reached free soil by crossing the river to Illinois; can any reader comment?). Ferguson explains: Jim could not escape directly across the river into Illinois, because he would be quickly captured for a reward; his chances would be better if he entered free territory some distance from where he had escaped.

———. "Huck Finn Aborning." *Colophon*, n.s., 3 (Spring 1938), 171–80.

Textual changes in the manuscript of *HF* show, not submission to censorship, but improvements in tone, language more suitable for Huck, and clarification of details. Reprinted in Bradley (1962, 1977) and Scott (1955, 1967).

Fertel, R.J. " 'Free and Easy'? Spontaneity and the Quest for Maturity in the *Adventures of Huckleberry Finn.*" *Modern Language Quarterly*, 44 (June 1983), 157–77.

Since the 1950s, criticism of *HF* "has in large part centered upon themes associated historically with the Romantic movement: spontaneity, primitivism, unmediated experience and vision, and the attack upon artifice and conventionality," and in some respects rightly so; but Fertel argues that beginning with the "well-formed Ciceronian balance" of clauses in the introductory "Notice" and the opposition in the first chapters "between innocent spontaneity and untutored naturalness, and the value of care, craft, and thought," MT is at best ambivalent in his treatment of primitivism. *HF* "is about an attractive boy's failure to mature, and makes perfectly clear what prevented his growth": his passivity and failure to take responsibility for his actions.

Fetterley, Judith. "Disenchantment: Tom Sawyer in *Huckleberry Finn.*" *Publications of the Modern Language Association*, 87 (January 1972), 69-74.

In *TS* Tom was a leader, but in *HF* he has nothing to offer, is pointlessly cruel in his jokes, and becomes a minor tyrant. He has counterparts throughout *HF*, as in his sharing with Miss Watson "the syndrome of moralism, aggression, and hypocrisy"; the Grangerford-Shepherdson feud reveals a false code of honor when "Southern chivalry is exposed as sneaking up behind a couple of kids and shooting them in the back. But the exposure of that cruelty is not so important as the exposure of the connection between that cruelty and the language of honor. What Mark Twain is recording in *Huckleberry Finn*, through the Grangerfords, through Miss Watson, and through Tom Sawyer, is his sense of the inevitable connection between moralism, the language of right and wrong with its inevitable concomitant of self-righteousness, and the fact, the act, of aggression." Reprinted in Bradley (1977). (*See* reply by Anna Mary Wells, 1972,)

Fiedler, Leslie A. "As Free as Any Cretur...." *New Republic*, 133 (15 August 1955), 17-18; (22 August), 16-18.

"*Pudd'nhead Wilson* is, after all, a fantastically good book, better than Mark Twain knew or his critics have deserved. Morally, it is one of the most honest books, in our literature, superior in this one respect to *Huckleberry Finn*; for here Twain permits himself no sentimental relenting, but accepts for once the logic of his own premises." When the real Tom Driscoll is freed at the end there is an ironic echo of Tom Sawyer's declaration that Jim was "as free as any cretur that walks this earth," and the indictment of the community's racism becomes "a local instance of some universal guilt and doom." Reprinted in Smith (1963).

————. "Boys Will be Boys!" *New Leader*, 41 (28 April 1958), 23-26.

HF conformed to the 19th century taboo on any intimations of sex in books about children, although MT faced violence frankly; however, in *TS* Tom takes both the punishment and the blame for Becky's damaging the schoolmaster's book: "It is as necessary to him that Becky retain her mythical Goodness as it is for her that he retain his equally mythical Badness." Reprinted in *No! In Thunder* (1960), and *The Collected Essays of Leslie Fiedler* (1971).

————. "Come Back to the Raft Ag'in, Huck Honey!" *Partisan Review*, 15 (June 1948), 664-71.

A general discussion of the Negro and homosexuality in American culture and literature, and only treating *HF* in passing; the title is not a quotation from *HF*. Reprinted in Fiedler's *An End to Innocence* (Boston: Beacon Press, 1952), pp. 142-51; *The Collected Essays of Leslie Fiedler* (New York: Stein and Day, 1971, 2 vols.), I, 142-51; Cardwell (1963).

————. "Duplicitious Mark Twain." *Commentary*, 29 (March 1960), 239-48.

"*Love and Death in the American Novel*, from which the essay has been adapted, will be published this month." "The *persona* called Mark Twain...is, first of all, a funny man, but more particularly, one who is funny at the expense of culture: an antiliterary writer, whose best books are travesties of others." Nevertheless, "he is not an open rebel," but "at worst a genteel Noble Savage, the friend of enlightened clergymen." "He was a man fitfully intelligent when he did not know he was thinking, a spottily skillful stylist when he was not aware he was writing artistically." "To make of Twain a cult or a case...is...to lose the sense of him as a poet, the possessor of deep and special mythopoetic power, whose childhood was contemporaneous with a nation's." If we consider *TS* and *HF* "not as sequels but as alternative versions of the same themes, these themes will reveal themselves in their mythic significance...dreamed twice over, the second time as nightmare."

————. "Good Good Girl and Good Bad Boy." *New Leader*, 41 (14 April 1958), 22-25.

On the literary Cult of the Child: the portrayal of the boy must reject the aristocratic "little gentleman," like Sid Sawyer. *HF* exists on a superficially comic and a deeper tragic level; it is "an astonishingly complicated novel, containing not one image of the boy-child as a symbol of the good life of impulse, but a series of interlocking ones: boys within boys." Reprinted in *No! In Thunder* (1960) and *The Collected Essays of Leslie Fiedler* (1971).

————. "*Huckleberry Finn*: The Book We Love to Hate." *Proteus*, 1:2 (1984), 1-8.

HF is currently under fire for supposed racism, but over the years has been condemned as immature, unstructured, coarse, and immoral, a poor model for children. "It was therefore predictable from the start that scarcely a year would pass during the century since its publication that has not seen Twain's book forbidden somewhere in the United States.... What is surprising ... is that even as *Huckleberry Finn* has remained a banned book, it has also become a *required* one ... " Its "persistent popularity ... has in fact always troubled members of any elite, esthetic, moral, or political, whose members feel they know better than the unredeemed masses what is good for them."

__________. *Love and Death in the American Novel*. New York: Criterion Books, 1960.

[Source: 1966 revised edition, New York: Stein and Day.] On MT, pp. 269-90, 402-08, 456-68, and passim (partly accessible through the index). Places heavy emphasis on *HF* and *PW*, on themes of the child, sexuality, race, and Gothic traditions. Includes material which appeared as "Duplicitous Mark Twain" in *Commentary* (1960). Pp. 553-74 of the 1960 edition reprinted in Leary (1962), pp. 277-300 as "Faust in The Eden of Childhood." "Accommodation and Transcendence" (pp. 575-91, on *HF*) reprinted in Gerber (1971).

Fields, Howard. "The First Amendment. Principal in Fairfax County, Va. Recommends Restriction of 'Huckleberry Finn.' " *Publishers Weekly*, 221 (17 April 1982), 18.

A short news story on the controversy over *HF* at Mark Twain Intermediate School; for additional details see the entries in the preceding bibliography for two anonymous newspaper editorials, and articles by Russell Baker, Dorothy Gilliam, and John Wallace.

Fischer, Victor. "Huck Finn Reviewed: The Reception of *Huckleberry Finn* in the United States, 1885-1897." *American Literary Realism*, 16 (Spring 1983), 1-57.

Despite a failure of major journals to review it (in part because of MT's own interference with sending out review copies), *Adventures of Huckleberry Finn* was not ignored by American critics...to the extent supposed (See Vogelback, 1939), nor were the reviews as uniformly unfavorable or as ignorant of what Mark Twain achieved as has been thought." Fischer lists 14 reviews of the chapters of *HF* as they appeared in the *Century*, 33 reviews of the book 1884-1885, 30 later reviews 1886-1910, 58 articles and editorial comments on the banning of *HF* by the Concord Public Library (many supported MT), 4 news items on the illustration which had been mutilated to make it obscene (*See* Sioui, 1962), 4 comments on the bust by Karl Gerhardt used as a frontispiece, and 23 news stories on the suit against Estes and Lauriat (the Boston booksellers that had advertised *HF* for sale at a price below that charged by subscription agents).

Fishkin, Shelley Fisher. "Twain, in '85." *New York Times* (18 February 1985), A17.

An "Op-Ed" page defense of *HF* against charges of racism: the book itself is an attack on racism through an irony some readers fail to recognize. When MT attacked mistreatment of the Chinese in a story for a San Francisco paper in the 1860s, his editor bowed to the prejudices of readers and refused to publish it. In 1870 he treated the theme ironically in "Disgraceful Persecution of a Boy"—a boy arrested for stoning Chinese, when everything he had learned from his elders taught him that it was "a high and holy thing" to abuse them.

Flory, Claude R. "Huck, Sam and the Small-Pox." *Mark Twain Journal*, 12 (Winter 1964-1965), 1-2, 8.

MT was well acquainted with Harriet Beecher Stowe, and—as Walter Blair has pointed out—there are parallels between *Uncle Tom's Cabin* and *HF*. There is a further parallel in Mrs. Stowe's *Sam Lawson's Oldtown Fireside Stories* (1871), in which pretended smallpox is used to frighten away a man who came to collect a debt, just as Huck evaded the slave-catchers in Chapter 16.

Fluck, Winfried. *Ästhetische Theorie und Lieraturwissenschaftliche Methode: eine Untersuchung ihres Zusammenhangs am Beispiel der amerikanischen Huck Finn-Kritik.* Stuttgart: J. B. Metzlersche Verlagsbuchhandlung, 1975.

Analyzes the critical reception of *HF* as a model of the various movements in American literary criticism, and attempts to discover the premises underlying the different views of the book; Fluck denies that *HF* is an organic whole unified by themes, patterns, cultural conflicts, etc., arguing that it is episodic, reflecting MT's spontaneous composition. [In German.]

Fox, Maynard. "Two Primitives: Huck Finn and Tom Outland." *Western American Literature*, 1 (Spring 1966), 26-33.

The character in Willa Cather's *The Professor's House* (1925) followed Huck in a tradition in which nature is not necessarily benevolent; but both boys "found independence, spontaneity, freedom, and an energizing vitality in their retreats from the center of population."

Frank, Waldo. "The Land of the Pioneer." *Our America*. New York: Boni & Liveright, 1919. Pp. 37-44.

"Out of the bitter wreckage of his long life one great work emerges by whose contrasting fire we can observe the darkness. This work is *Huckleberry Finn*. It must go down in history, not as the expression of a rich natural culture like the books of Chaucer, Rabelais, Cervantes, but as the voice of American chaos, the voice of a pre-cultural epoch.... Huckleberry Finn is the American epic hero. Greece had Ulysses. America must be content with an illiterate lad. He expresses our germinal past. He expresses the movement of the American soul through all the sultry climaxes of the Nineteenth Century." Frank describes MT as "a man of genius.... The soul of Mark Twain was great," but anticipates Van Wyck Brooks (1920) in arguing that the frontier life followed by Eastern respectability destroyed the artist MT might have been: apart from *HF*, "the balance of his literary life, before and after, went mostly to the wastage of half-baked, half-believed, half-clownish labor." *What Is Man?* is the work of MT's last years, "the profane utterance of a defeated soul bent upon degrading the world to the low level where it was forced to live." Reprinted in Scott (1955, 1967).

Frantz, Ray W., Jr. "The Role of Folklore in *Huckleberry Finn*." *American Literature*, 28 (November 1956), 314-27.

For Huck, folklore is the equivalent of a religion governing his actions, values and virtues; in the book folklore supports much of the thematic development and serves as a device for foreshadowing events.

Fraser, John. "In Defense of Culture: *Huckleberry Finn*." *Oxford Review*, No. 6 (Michaelmas 1967), 5-22.

Summarizing and answering a number of critics' statements on *HF*, argues that in many ways the book is "soothing," and "Huck's progress through the ostensible dangers of the trip downstream is largely that of the kind of superboy of Tom Sawyer's imaginings. The depiction of slavery is not a central theme, but consists of set-pieces; in general the treatment of the Negro is validated rather than attacked. Huck is not a coherent and developing character, just as Gulliver is not, because, like Swift, MT was concentrating on the local and the immediate.

Freedman, Samuel N. "The First Edition of *Huckleberry Finn*: An Overview." *Proteus*, 1:2 (1984), 36–40.

A thin and derivative account, somewhat inaccurate (as in explaining MT's books were sold by subscription because "bookshops were very limited in scope and were generally part of a stationery store"). This appears to be drawn largely from the familiar sources, but makes no mention of "Tak Sioui" [John Hacac], *Huckleberry Finn: More Molecules* (1962); Franklin J. Meine, "Some Notes on the First Editions of 'Huck Finn,' " *American Book Collector*, 10 (June 1960), 31–34; or Jacob Blanck, "In Re *Huckleberry Finn*," *New Colophon*, 3 (1950), 153–59, which attacks the two Irving S. Underhill articles Freedman did use as bad work which the old *Colophon* ought never to have accepted: "the bibliographical problem of *Huckleberry Finn* was rendered an appalling disservice by their publication."

Freese, Peter. " 'Adventures of Huckleberry Finn' and 'The Catcher in the Rye': Zur examplarischen Deutung der Romananfänge." *Die Neueren Sprachen* [new series] 22 (December 1973), 658–68.

Analysis of the first 108 words of *HF* and the first 128 words of J.D. Salinger's novel will give students abundant introduction to the meaning and aid in their understanding of the two books. [In German.]

__________. "Jerome David Salinger: *The Catcher in the Rye*." *Literature in Wissenschaft and Uterricht*, Band I, Heft 2 (1968), 123–152.

On pp. 130-34, "Huckleberry Finn in *The Waste Land*," a summary of studies comparing *The Catcher in the Rye* and *HF*. [In German.]

Fussell, Edwin. "Hemingway and Mark Twain." *Accent*, 14 (Summer 1954), 199-206.

Noting Philip Young's essay in comparative biography and psychology in the "Adventures of Huckleberry Finn" chapter of his *Ernest Hemingway* (1952), Fussell says that "Young's view of the Mark Twain-Hemingway connection and mine are not really contradictory; they are more like Marvell's lovers, so parallel they never meet." Fussell discusses the treatment of emotional, imaginative, and literary integrity in *Huckleberry Finn*, and Hemingway's concern with these matters in *In Our Time*, *The Sun Also Rises*, and other works.

Gaffney, W. G. "Mark Twain's 'Duke' and 'Dauphin.'" *Names: Journal of the American Dialect Society*, 14 (September 1966), 175-78.

After the embarrassment over having used the name of a real Eschol Sellers in *GA*, MT was careful in naming characters; he could call a rascal in *HF* the Duke of Bridgewater because the actual Dukedom was extinct: Francis Egerton, third Duke of Bridgewater, had been one of the wealthiest men in the world, and his son, from whom MT's character claimed descent, died a bachelor and without issue. The Dauphin could not claim descent from English or other active European thrones, because they were all occupied. "Literally the only way to outrank the Duke of Bridgewater was to be the (equally disinherited) rightful King of France."

Galligan, Edward L. *The Comic Vision in Literature*. Athens: University of Georgia Press, 1984. Passim on MT (indexed). Pages 56–63 appeared in 1978 in *Sewanee Review* as "True Comedians and False: *Don Quixote* and *Huckleberry Finn*."

__________. "True Comedians and False. *Don Quixote* and *Huckleberry Finn*." *Sewanee Review*, 86 (Winter 1978), 66–83.

Huck and Jim are true comedians, as are Quixote and Sancho, but there is "savage criticism in the portrait of Tom Sawyer," who, like the Duke and King, is a false comedian. "True comedians are blessed fools while false comedians are damned fools."

Gardner, Joseph H. "Gaffer Hexam and Huck Finn." *Modern Philology*, 66 (November 1968), 155-56.

Although *A Tale of Two Cities* has often been suggested as a source for Pap's attack on Huck for learning to read and write, there is a closer analogue in *Our Mutual Friend*; Gardner documents MT's familiarity with Dickens' work.

Gargano, James W. "Disguises in *Huckleberry Finn*." *University of Kansas City Review*, 26 (March 1960), 175-78.

"The 'disguises' in Huckleberry Finn...are the vehicle of Twain's indictment of human dissimulation and gullibility." Huck and Jim use disguises as protection, the King and Duke as "predator's tools in their ceaseless battle to gull and exploit mankind." "Perhaps it is as a disguise that the author's much-discussed prefatory 'notice' can best be understood. Only too aware of the Swiftian implications of *Huckleberry Finn*, he attempted to disarm his readers by insisting that his literary intentions were altogether innocent."

Gaston, Georg Meri-Akri. "The Function of Tom Sawyer in *Huckleberry Finn*." *Mississippi Quarterly*, 27 (Winter 1973), 33-39.

"Tom, a true child of his society, is capable of terrible selfishness and cruelty," and serves as a foil in the portrayal of Huck's moral development.

Gaylin, Willard. "Two Routes to Unselfish Behavior. From Twain to Freud: An Examination of Conscience." *Hastings Center Report* (Institute of Society, Ethics, and the Life Sciences), 6 (August 1976), 5-8.

Chiefly on the broader topic of conscience, but opens with an example from *HF*, when Huck sees the King and Duke ridden on a rail. "The words that Twain uses in an attempt to dissect the emotions of conscience are enormously sophisticated and not redundant. They are the words that only a student of conscience, or an intuitive genius, would have used: 'ornery,' 'humble,' and 'to blame.'"

Gerber, Helmut E. "Twain's *Huckleberry Finn*." *Explicator*, 12 (March 1954), Item 28.

There is geographical, chronological, and thematic unity, and also a five-part "structural unity based on the pattern or rhythm of the alternating settings," but "organically asymmetrical or irregular." Huck has solved a problem and is changed by it.

Gerber, John C. "Practical Editions: Mark Twain's *The Adventures of Tom Sawyer* and *The Adventures of Huckleberry Finn*." *Proof*, 2 (1972), 285-92.

MT's concern with precise degrees of emphasis in his writing is revealed by his attention to both conventional punctuation and liberal use of dashes, parentheses, brackets, italics, and exclamation points, and his linking by hyphens words not customarily joined; "as a result, the exact accidental in one of his novels can be almost as crucial for meaning as the right word." Unfortunately, there is no single text of *TS* that can be used as printer's copy for a new edition, and even *HF* presents problems because the manuscript used by the printer is lost. School and college texts of both books introduce large numbers of variants and "are unsatisfactory, in some instances dramatically so. At best, our students are reading approximations of what Mark Twain wanted them to read."

__________. "The Relation between Point of View and Style in the Works of Mark Twain." *Style in Prose Fiction, English Institute Essays*, 1958; New York: Columbia University Press, 1959. Pp. 142-71.

"Twain's style is so intimately dependent upon his point of view that it flourishes only to the extent that the point of view is detached and sharply restricted," providing psychological distance and "forcing him to focus upon a specific and concrete situation" (p. 143). This accounts for the superiority of *HF* to *TS* and *CY*. Reprinted in Lettis (1962).

Gerstenberger, Donna. "*Huckleberry Finn* and the World's Illusions." *Western Humanities Review*, 14 (Autumn 1960), 401-06.

The consistent metaphor of disguise and pretense may reveal "a significance for the novel not unlike that which an examination of the dramatic metaphor in *Hamlet* has provided." Huck (who can join society only through one disguise or another, but never as himself) gradually learns that "it is the elaborate illusion that the world insists is reality which causes man's moral confusion."

Gibb, Carson. "The Best Authorities." *College English*, 22 (December 1960), 178-83.

Tom and Huck "believe niggers and people are two different things," but MT is not ending *HF* "with a burst of spleen" aimed at "two likable youngsters"; his target is the culture which has shaped their attitudes. Reprinted in Lettis (1962).

Gibson, Donald B. "Mark Twain's Jim in the Classroom." *English Journal* 57 (February 1968), 196-99, 202.

On the twentieth-century problems arising from the stereotyped portrayal of Jim in *HF*, and from MT's ambivalent attitude toward him.

Gilliam, Dorothy. "Banning Huck." Washington *Post* (12 Aprii 1982), B1.

Argues that *HF* is not actually banned at the Mark Twain Intermediate School (Fairfax County, VA), just removed from the required reading list. Still, the subject is sensitive, and "if 'Huck Finn' is going to be discusssed, it should be taken up under the guidance of a teacher or a librarian who is trained to discuss the historical context of the book and the author. This is the way we develop the sensibilities that will eliminate the banning of books once and for all. 'Huckleberry Finn' is a classic. But the messages it carries for both black and white children are at best mixed, and it cries out for careful interpretation. That is what the school wants to give it."

Glazier, Lyle. "Huckleberry Finn: The 'Uncreated Conscience.'" *Decadence and Rebirth: Hacettepe Lectures in American Literature*. Ankara: Hacettepe University Press, 1971. Pp. 53-63.

What MT says in *HF* is filtered through Huck's intuition, and even the Colonel Sherburn episode is in character, as Huck struggles between sympathy for Boggs and his daughter, and admiration for the stately Colonel—who "in his vanity is a grown up equivalent of the romantic adolescent Tom Sawyer." In the end Huck confronts a two-fold evil: "His public conscience damns him for his loving kindness toward Jim; his private conscience damns him for participating in the values of the Establishment." The Territory is no refuge, and "there is rebirth only in humor."

Gloster, Hugh. *Negro Voices in American Fiction*. (Chapel Hill, 1948), 106-7. [Not seen; quoted in Haslam (1969).]

Gloster contends "that 'the foundations' of the present tendency to depict Negroes as human beings in literature 'were laid in the last quarter of the nineteenth century in the works of such writers as Albion Tourgee, G. W. Cable, and Mark Twain.'"

Goldstein, Wallace L. "Mark Twain's Use of Diction in *The Adventures of Huckleberry Finn*." *The English Record*, 31 (Winter 1980), 11-13.

"*Huckleberry Finn* serves as an excellent study of Twain's vernacular and the author's belief in the resiliency of American English. He employs his unusual word formations, illiteracies, distortions, misspellings, and innovations to make the language more vivid and appropriate. This use of language helps to make the novel such an artistic masterpiece."

Gollin, Richard, and Rita Gollin. "*Huckleberry Finn* and the Time of the Evasion." *Modern Language Studies*, 9 (Spring 1979), 5-15.

The authors suggest reading the final chapters "as an Aesopian satire on enlightened white attitudes toward the freed black men, not in the 1840's, when the story is set, but in the 1880's, when the chapters were written."

Gooder, R. D. "One of Today's Best Little Writers?" *Cambridge Quarterly*, 1 (Winter 1965), 81-90.

On J. D. Salinger; contrasts *Catcher in the Rye* and *HF*, observing that Holden "calls the tune, and proves himself morally and spiritually superior to everyone except his little sister... Holden judges all, but is not judged... Where do we ever find Holden in a position of admitted moral inferiority, as we find Huck when he admits he has played a mean trick on Jim? Where does Holden have to make the difficult choice between what he has been taught and what he knows in himself is right, as Huck has to do when he decides to shield Jim?"

Goodyear, Russell H. "Huck Finn's Anachronistic Double Eagles." *American Notes and Queries* 10 (November 1971), 39.

Although *HF* was published in 1885 and the preface says "Time: forty to fifty years ago," Chapters 16 and 22 mention twenty-dollar gold pieces—which were first minted in 1849.

Gordon, Edward J. "What's Happened to Humor?" *English Journal*, 47 (March 1958), 127-33.

Huck Finn sees through the self-deceptions of others; he is contrasted with John Marquand's character George Apley, who deceives himself.

Goto, Akio. "Seijuku no Kyozetsu—Mark Twain no Amerikateki Seikaku" ["Rejection of Maturity—Mark Twain's American Character"]. *Eigo Seinen [The Rising Generation] (Tokyo)*, 115 (1 May 1979), 286-87.

Huckleberry Finn, as far as he insisted on being a child of nature, had to reject society and man. After all, Mark Twain was a product of the Gilded Age. [In Japanese; abstract by Yasuo Hashiguchi.]

Gottfried, Leon. "The Odyssean Form: An Exploratory Essay." Peter Uwe Hohendahl, Herbert Lindenberger, and Egon Schwartz, eds., *Essays on European Literature in Honor of Liselotte Dieckmann*. St. Louis: Washington University Press, 1972. Pp. 19-43, passim.

On the *Odyssey*, *Don Quixote*, *Joseph Andrews*, and *HF*. In each there is a contrast of "home" and "road," with problems in the final homecoming (p. 29), a "pattern of flight and return," and "a symbolic death" for the hero; and "at some point he is rescued naked or nearly so from pit, ditch, river, or sea. In each work, finally, there is an initiation, that is, a significant transmission of values from an older, wiser, or higher ranking central figure to his junior" (p. 33). *HF* "is the least hopeful" of the four books, because MT "found (or presented) no social reality of any sort that he could affirm as being worthy of his heroes."

Graves, Wallace. "Mark Twain's 'Burning Shame'." *Nineteenth-Century Fiction*,

23 (June 1968), 93-98.

The "Royal Nonesuch" of *HF* appears in the typescript as "The Burning Shame." Graves repeats a Swedish version as he heard it told in the thirties. "Interesting for its sustained drama as well as its obscenity," the story involves two destitute actors who performed for an audience from which women and children were excluded. One actor appeared on hands and knees, naked, while his partner introduced the act: "'And now, gentlemen, you are about to see The Tragedy of the Burning Shame.' He inserted a candle in the naked man's posterior, and lit it. When nothing further happened, the audience shouted for something more; the man said the performance was over....'have you ever seen a better example of a "Burning Shame"?'" And the actors fled with the receipts. [Also see Whiting (1944).]

Gray, Richard. "Kingdom and Exile: Mark Twain's Hannibal Books," in *American Fiction: New Readings*. London: Vision; Totowa, NJ: Barnes & Noble, 1983. Pp. 80–99.

MT's language in *LOM* and *TS* was inadequate to establish his double vision of romance and reality, the personal and the public, although even in *TS* Huck begins to emerge with "his own voice, ... his own, profoundly anti-social values." Although MT began *HF* as a mere sequel to *TS*, during a time while it was set aside he read widely in southwest humor (working on an anthology) and returned to the manuscript with a changed attitude and readiness to explore the conflict between the individual and the expectations of society. The Grangerfords are one mixture of the real and the romantic, Huck a different and perhaps more hopeful one, a focus for MT's own nostalgia; the attention in his language to empirical detail gives it color and immediacy. Huck is "both an expression of Twain's belief in perfectability and a gathering-point for all his deepest feelings about childhood." *CY* is more like *LOM* than like *HF*, despite the vernacular hero, and MT's feelings toward Hank's "lost land" are as ambiguous as they are to the worlds of *TS* and *LOM*. *PW* once more shows a community ambiguously viewed, and with some affection, but there is no Adamic figure like Huck to weave past, present, and future together. His river books comprise a spiritual autobiography of MT.

Green, Martin. "Twain and Whitman: The Problem of 'American' Literature." *Reappraisals: Some Commonsense Readings in American Literature*. London: Hugh Evelyn, 1963.

Gregory, Stanford W., Jr., and Jerry M. Lewis. "Huck Finn and the Game Model Gloss." *Qualitative Sociology*, 3 (Summer 1980), 136-51.

"This paper uses Mark Twain's last chapters of *The Adventures of Huckleberry Finn* to explicate how the game model can be used as a gloss. The game model gloss then is a unique combination of sociological conceptualizations presented through the medium of a lively literary allegory. We feel this paper extends the concept of glossing and furthers the understanding of the game metaphor in sociological theory."

Considers MT as an entertainer and *HF* "a charming children's book, with some beautiful passages," but not a major novel (pp. 142-43). However, "in ways that transcend the limits of humour, Twain was a fine lyric poet, a master of spoken language in print, and a beautiful ironist. The first two talents are best exemplified in *Huckleberry Finn*, but the third becomes major in *A Connecticut Yankee*; and this book represents Twain's true achievement perhaps better than the more famous one.... The important part of the book is the friendly, uncritical but lively irony it directs at the Yankee himself and what he stands for."

Grenander, M. E. "*Benito Cereno* and Legal Oppression: A Szaszian Interpretation." *Libertarian Studies* (New York, Oxford: Pergamon Press), 2 (1978), 337-42.

Applies the insights of the psychiatric scholar Thomas S. Szasz in interpreting Ken Kesey's *One Flew Over the Cuckoo's Nest* to Melville's novella; *HF* here is chiefly a basis of comparison, having been written safely after the Civil War when slavery was no longer an issue. Grenander insists that Huck's decision to help Jim in his escape is indeed a crime by the laws of the day, and also the sin of theft, but Huck "does not question the morality of the law; he simply decides to break it. Moreover, his opinion of the very conventional Tom falls when he thinks that Tom has also decided to break the law in helping a slave escape.... Huck makes a completely individual decision to break the law in one instance; it never occurs to him to challenge the moral foundation of the law itself. Tom Sawyer, however, does not break the law even in the single instance involving Jim; he merely pretends to do so." Melville's *Benito Cereno* attacked slavery well before The War, and "in effect turns the institution upside down, and portrays whites as the slaves of a band of African Negroes."

Griska, Joseph M., Jr. "Two New Joel Chandler Harris Reviews of Mark Twain." *American Literature*, 48 (January 1977), 584-89.

After a one-page introduction on the acquaintance of MT and Harris, their extant correspondence, and the Harris review of *P&P*, reprints "Two New Books" and "'Huckleberry Finn' and His Critics" from the Atlanta *Constitution* of 11 June 1882 and 26 May 1885. The first of these, on *The Stolen White Elephant*, is interesting for comment on MT's artistry and "habit of looking keenly after his interests" in his dealings with publishers. The *HF* review lambastes the critics who have taken their cue from the action of the Concord Public Library (which banned the book) and unjustly called *HF* coarse and inartistic; Harris praises *HF* for the artistry and the example of "manliness and self-sacrifice."

Gross, Seymour L. "Sherwood Anderson's Debt to *Huckleberry Finn*." *Mark Twain Journal*, 11 (Summer 1960), 3-5, 24.

Places particular emphasis on "I Want to Know Why," which Anderson said was popular because it was "a story of immaturity...much like Mark Twain at his best." Gross adds that "both boys are morally finer than the adult world which they are describing," but distrust their own judgments. There are similarities in irony, criticism of society, and use of the Negro as "a kind of moral center."

Grover, Guru Dayal. *Mark Twain: The Adventures of Huckleberry Finn (A Critical Study)*. Delhi: Doaba House, 1970.

A very general treatment, with no specifically Indian perspectives. "My method has been to arrive at an eclectic synthesis of several approaches to the novel, and to concentrate on a close reading of the text, and to assess whatever contributions the text itself demands from folklore, myth, ritual, biograpical, and literary antecedents."

Gullason, Thomas Arthur. "The 'Fatal' Ending of *Huckleberry Finn*." *American Literature*, 29 (March 1957), 86-91.

The concluding episode, "based on Tom's lie, cannot be considered fatal because Huck settles conflicts presented earlier in the novel. Important themes, which are repeated and varied, furnish the key." In the last chapters Huck rejects "Tom's romantic irresponsibility...and society's cruel nature...understands Jim's true worth." Huck's honest and humble facing and resolving of the conflicts shows his developing strength of character (p. 91). Reprinted in Bradley (1962).

Gupa, Rameshwar. "The Central Theme in *The Adventures of Huckleberry Finn*," in M. K. Naik, S. K. Desai, and S. Mokashi-Punekar, eds. *Indian Studies in American Fiction*. Dharwar: Karnatak University, and Madras: Macmillan India, 1974, Pp. 55-67.

The theme is escape, "from, as I take it, the predicament of existence; release, rather, from tension—the existential tension." "What is being enacted in the book is the existential predicament. There is an unconscious search for *existence clarification*. Great books do nothing else." There is extensive citation of other critics' notions as to what constitutes the central theme.

Gwynn, Frederick L., and Joseph L. Blotner, eds. *Faulkner in the University: Class Conferences at the University of Virginia 1957-1958*. Charlottesville: The University of Virginia Press, 1959. Passim on MT (indexed).

Faulkner places MT among "the masters from whom we learned our craft" (p. 243), and calls him "all of our grandfather" (p. 281). He ranks *Moby-Dick* above *HF* because "*Huckleberry Finn* is a completely controlled effort and *Moby-Dick* was still an attempt that didn't quite come off, it was more than one human being could do" (p. 243). Discussing *Catcher in the Rye* as a novel of the youth who "must someday be a man, more intelligent than some, more sensitive than most," he says Holden's "tragedy was that when he attempted to enter the human race, there was no human race there." In contrast is "Huck Finn, another youth already father to what will some day soon be a man. But in Huck's case all he had to combat was his small size, which time would cure for him...and even as it was, all the adult world could do to harm him was to skin his nose a little; humanity, the human race, would and was accepting him already; all he needed so do was just to grow up in it."

Hamblen, Abigail Ann. "The Best-Known Teenager: Huck Finn." *Mark Twain Journal*, 13 (Winter 1966-1967), 15-19.

"Huck Finn's is a sensitive imaginative mind," though practical rather than philosophical; he matures in the book but still cannot accept the shackles of civilization.

__________ . "Uncle Tom and 'Nigger Jim': A Study in Contrasts and Similarities." *Mark Twain Journal*, 11 (Fall 1961), 13-17.

"Because of lack of opportunity for development, Jim's mentality and his moral nature cannot be matched with those of Uncle Tom," but the two slaves are similar in loyalty and in the loyalty and love they inspire in the white people around them.

Hansen, Chadwick. "The Character of Jim and the Ending of *Huckleberry Finn*." *Massachusetts Review* 5 (Autumn 1963), 45-66.

Jim was Huck's "moral burden," in that "by his constant presence, and his constant decency, and his constant humanity he forces Huck to do something more than drift with the river. He forces Huck to come to grips with that part of himself which belongs to society." In the ending Huck and Jim both allow themselves to be drawn into Tom's romantic schemes, but not without reservations. The closing sentences represent "for Huck an emotional, if not an intellectual rejection of civilization," and an escape both for Huck and for Jim.

Hapgood, Norman. "My Feeling about Mark Twain." *Mark Twain Quarterly*, 2 (Winter 1937-1938), 15.

Brief comments on having found MT appreciated everywhere. "Some years ago, I was having a private chat with Sir James Barrie, and in the course of it I spoke of Hawthorne with *The Scarlet Letter* and *The House of the Seven Gables*, and Mark Twain, with *Tom Sawyer* and *Huckleberry Finn*, as at the top of American fiction. The author of *Peter Pan* agreed, but added that also those books are up near the top of English fiction."

Harkey, Joseph H. "When Huck Finn Smouched that Spoon." *Mark Twain Journal* 15 (Summer 1970), 14.

About a class discussion of the word "smouch," which a freshman looked up in the *Oxford English Dictionary*; he reported meanings of "Jew" and "filch." There is no evidence that MT's use of the term was anti-Semitic, however.

Harris, Joel Chandler. [Letter to the editor.] *Critic*, 7 (28 November 1885), 253.

Praises MT and singles out *HF*; "There is not in our fictive literature a more wholesome book." Harris letter reprinted in Gerber (1971); excerpted in Kesterson (1973).

Harris, John. "Principles, Sympathy and Doing What's Right." *Philosophy: The Journal of the Royal Institute of Philosophy*, 52 (January 1977), 96-99.

Bennett errs in "The Conscience of Huckleberry Finn" (1974), because Huck has no organized moral principles of his own. "To represent Huck as facing a dilemma is misleading, for Huck does not *decide* to give way to the pressure of his conscience, he just collapses under it."

Harris, Susan K. "'This Peace, This Deep Contentment': Images of Temporal Freedom in the Writings of Mark Twain." *Essays in Literature*, 7 (Fall 1980), 210-12.

"Over the years Mark Twain constructed an entire landscape comprised of places and figures which allow him to move both his characters and himself outside of concrete time" (i.e., "history...the human experience of irreversible change"). Huck found such escape on the raft, and MT in the tranquility of ocean travel; later, water and space became interchangeable among his "preferred images." Composing "No. 44, The Mysterious Stranger," MT recognized "that the problem he was trying to clarify concerned temporal as well as spatial freedom."

Harrison, James G. "A Note on the Duke in 'Huck Finn': The Journeyman Printer as Picaro." *Mark Twain Quarterly*, 8 (Winter 1947), 1-2.

The Duke belongs to a literary type that had appeared earlier in American literature, and MT referred elsewhere to the improvidence and recklessness of journeyman printers.

Hart, John E. "Heroes and Houses: The Progress of Huck Finn." *Modern Fiction Studies*, 14 (Spring 1968), 39-46.

Identifies the term "house" broadly, to include "sheds and rafts, huts and mansions," and even steamboats. A view of Huck's journey as a progression from house to house gives the story unity; "in one way or another, the house stands for civilization, a container of ambiguities: of freedom and bondage, of mystery and insight, of good and evil, of life and death."

Harter, Hugh A. "Mark Twain y la tradición picaresca." Manuel Criado de Val, ed. *La picaresca: Origenes, textos y estructuras*. Madrid: Fundación Universitaria Española, 1979. Pp. 1161–66.

Don Quixote influenced *TS* and *HF*, and in *LOM* MT praised Cervantes as a counterbalance to the pernicious effects of Sir Walter Scott's books. Familiar with *Lazarillo de Tormes* and the writings of LeSage, MT portrayed the figure of the trickster (as in the fence-painting episode in *TS*) and the cruelty of society (as in the tar-and-feathering of the King and Duke in *HF*). But Huck differs from the traditional picaro in that he has a heart and a conscience, and in his loyalty to Jim. [In Spanish.]

Harwood, C. Edwin. "Twain's *Huckleberry Finn*, Chapter XIV." *Explicator*, 28 (December 1969), Item 36.

The debate between Huck and Jim on why a Frenchman speaks French is "no digression at all but an ingenious statement of a main theme of the book...the brotherhood of man." The insight revealing the point was that of Miss Laura Helton, while writing an examination.

Haslam, Gerald W. "*Huckleberry Finn*: Why Read the Phelps Farm Episode?" *Research Studies* (Washington State University), 35 (September 1969), 189-97.

Although the ending of *HF* is weakened by stylistic excesses, and defenses based on form are unsatisfactory, it can be justified "as a logical extension of the often-emphasized moral texture of the novel.... the dissonance one senses in the final episodes of the novel is largely a product of Twain's fictional projection of the seminal moral dilemma of a slave-holding society: human beings viewed as commodity."

Haupt, Garry. "The Tragi-Comedy of the Unreal in Ralph Ellison's *Invisible Man* and Mark Twain's *Adventures of Huckleberry Finn*." *Interpretations* (Memphis State University), 4 (1972), 1-12.

Emphasis is on Ellison and his novel, and on *HF* only to explore parallels and influence. "Ellison found his American literary roots in the nineteenth-century novel because he felt it presented a rounded picture of the Negro, saw the Negro as symbolic of general American problems, and communicated a strong sense of social responsibility. All of these factors bind Ellison to Twain, as he himself has pointed out." In *Invisible Man* an overdependence on the outside world causes loss of self, while for Huck his moral development puts his instinctive self in conflict with a false self. "The moral conflict is a pseudo-conflict, because the norms of society as they exist in Huck's mind are unreal."

Hayashi, Sachiko. "The Role of Humor in *The Adventures of Huckleberry Finn*." *Shonan English Language and Literature*, 13 (March 1983), 1-14.

Looking for elements of pure humor, as opposed to satire, the author begins by examining the "cheerful," or "mere" humor of MT's early works, elements of which continue into the first sixteen chapters of *HF*. Mrs. Hayashi argues that the next part, written later, follows a general shift in MT's humor to a darker conception in the 1880s. The foolery of the last chapters is a return to the "relaxed approach toward humor" which marked the beginning, a return to "humor for amusement" after the "humor as a weapon" of the middle chapters of the book. "Aggressive humor is intense and leaves a strong impression on us, but is indifferent and detached. On the other hand, 'mere' humor for amusement can convey sympathy and include the readers in the work itself, and so never diminishes the value of the work." *HF* blended the two, at a time when MT's popularity was at its zenith.

Hayashi, Tetsumaro. "Mark Twain's *The Adventures of Huckleberry Finn*: Hope for Mankind." *Lumina*, No. 3 (1960).

[Source: Kamei, Shunsuke, "Mark Twain in Japan," *Mark Twain Journal*, 12 (Spring 1963), 20.]

__________ . "'The Style Is the Man Himself': A Review Article on Hiroshige Yoshida's *Huckleberry Finn Studies: Research Notes, Style, and Glossary* (q.v., 1980). *Kyushu American Literature, No*. 22 (May 1981), 88-90.

Often a foreigner is more inquisitive about an author's language than a native scholar, and Dr. Yoshida has explored areas of *HF* that are long neglected yet especially interesting to the Japanese. "He takes up, for instance, the curious tension in Mark Twain's literature both between subject matter and style and between the theme of violence and Twain's perfectly controlled prose. Twain uniquely developed a style in control of his subject matter, for Twain's style became the objective representation of the moral attitude of the author toward his material. Dr. Yoshida, believing in the importance of this intricate relationship between style and content, penetratingly treats Mark Twain's stylistic features, especially his use of dialect, wholly unique in *Huckleberry Finn*." Apparently this is for the general student at the beginning level, including useful and basic bibliography, glossary, and interpretation. "Although the first four chapters as critiques of the novel are very perceptive and enlightening essays on *Huckleberry Finn* and Mark Twain as a conscious artist, the highlight of this meticulous scholarly book is found in Dr. Yoshida's study of Mark Twain's style and use of dialect in *Huckleberry Finn*, because these chapters were written by an experienced scholar aware of the crucial need of linguistic background for Japanese scholars of Mark Twain in particular and those of American literature in general."

Hearn, Michael Patrick. "Expelling *Huck Finn*." *The Nation*, 235 (7–14 August 1982), 117.

HF has been under fire as a racist book at schools around the country, most conspicuously at Mark Twain Intermediate School, in Fairfax County, Virginia. Hearn defends *HF* and concludes: "Because of the recent public outcry, Fairfax County has ruled that *Huckleberry Finn* may be taught, but only with 'appropriate planning.' One wonders how it must have been presented before this ruling. The problem is the teaching, not the novel. How could anyone assign the book and not place it within its proper historical context? Should any class fail to discuss the humanity of Mark Twain's novel, then the school board should keep *Huckleberry Finn* and chuck the teacher."

————. "Mark Twain, E.W. Kemble, and *Huckleberry Finn*." *American Book Collector*, n.s. 2 (November–December 1981), 14–19.

On Kemble's illustrations for *HF* and MT's view of his work. A popular treatment of the subject, acknowledging a debt to earlier studies but not replacing them. Hearn adds usefully by citing additional *HF* illustrations made by Kemble for later editions and for a special MT cartoon Sunday supplement of the New York *World* (10 December 1899).

Hemingway, Ernest. *Green Hills of Africa*. New York: Scribner's, 1935. On MT, pp. 22-23 only.

"All modern American literature comes from one book by Mark Twain called *Huckleberry Finn*. If you read it you must stop where Nigger Jim is stolen from the boys. That is the real end. The rest is just cheating. But it's the best book we've had. There was nothing before. There has been nothing as good since." MT and Henry James "both lived to be old men but they did not get any wiser as they got older. You see we make our writers into something very strange." Hemingway cites pressures that include the demands of an expensive standard of living, and the effect of the critics on an author who heeds them.

Hentoff, Nat. *The Day They Came to Arrest the Book*. New York: Delacorte Press, 1982.

A novel about censorship in a high school, with particular focus on the furor over an attempt to remove *HF* from a reading list and the library as racist, sexist, and immoral. The presentation is balanced: except for the school principal there are no fools or villains, but only honest and well-meaning persons whose convictions collide. The issue for Hentoff is not racism, sexism, or immorality; it is the free and open exchange of ideas.

_________. "Huck Finn Better Get Out of Town by Sundown." *Village Voice*, 27 (4 May 1982), 8.

Begins a four-part series on current efforts by black parents and professional censor John Wallace to remove *HF* from the schools. *HF* has met opposition from the beginning, though until recently on the grounds of irreverance and emphasis on the lower classes. Hentoff describes his own young adult novel, *The Day They Came to Arrest the Book* (1982), on the banning of *HF* in a school: the principal is the only unsympathetic character in it.

________. "Is Any Book Worth the Humiliation of Our Kids?" *Ibid*. (11 May 1982), 8.

A sensitive exploration of the various motives of censors and book-banners, some sincere and some politicized. Hentoff has talked with black parents who object to *HF* and Jewish parents who object to *The Merchant of Venice*. "I think they're wrong in wanting to throw out or hide these works, but they do raise questions about how to teach certain books. Questions that go even more deeply into the nature of teaching itself."

________. "Huck Finn and the Shortchanging of Black Kids." *Ibid* (18 May 1982), 8.

In Warrington, Pa. a black eighth-grader allegedly was "harassed verbally and physically" after his class read *HF*. Details are uncertain, but the school removed *HF* from the junior high reading list. Hentoff argues that *HF* is not difficult to understand, but a major novel, and that any conflicts over the themes treated provide a teaching opportunity.

________. "These Are Little Battles Fought in Remote Places." *Ibid*. (25 May 1982), 4.

On his conversation with an official in an unnamed school district who is fighting to keep *HF* as required reading for ninth-graders: it is told by an adolescent, it is simple in its form, and it ties in well with nineteenth-century American history. Moreover, it is about Huck's own maturing. The official recognizes the sensitivity of black parents: "I can assure them we teach it sensitively, and they'll say, 'It still hurts my child.' And I'll say the child can choose another book. But what book can replace *Huckleberry Finn?*"

———. "Romeo, Romeo, I Can Hardly Hear You." *Washington Post* (23 November 1984), A27.

On censorship of books in the schools. Three young adult novels by Judy Blume have been removed from school libraries in Peoria despite high recommendation for them by the American Library Association, and a school edition of *Romeo and Juliet* published by Scott, Foresman is bowdlerized, despite false statements to the contrary in the accompanying teacher's guide. And Huck Finn is in trouble again, not only in America (in Waukegan, Illinois this time), but also in England: "The Inner London Education Authority is currently ordering all of its employees, including non-teachers, to take 'race consciousness' courses. In one of those courses, certain books are condemned for their infectious racism. One of them is 'Huckleberry Finn.' Well, Huck never did think he and 'sivilization' had much in common."

Herreshoff, David. "Teaching Mark Twain in the 1960s, 1970s, and 1980s." *Monthly Review* [NY: "An Independent Socialist Magazine"], 36 (June 1984), 38–45.

Herreshoff's students at Wayne State University are largely from a working-class background. In the 1960s they could understand the parallel he drew between the more privileged students at the University of Michigan and their chapter of the radical Students for a Democratic Society, and the respectability of Tom Sawyer's Gang in *HF*. The 1970s were a period of liberal retreat, but the 1980s may be a time of new insurgency during which MT's attacks on imperalism (as in "To the Person Sitting in Darkness") and racism will gain new relevance. Herreshoff draws a parallel between the "Evasion" chapters at the end of *HF* and the assault on black freedoms in America during the years when *HF* was being written.

Higgins, William. "I Try To Do It Another Way and Am Sorry." *Ball State Teachers College Forum* 3 (Winter 1962), 13-14.

In the manner of Chapter 14 of *HF*, a dialogue in which Huck tries to explain symbolism, myth, and structure in the book to Jim, but fails in the attempt: "I never saw a nigger so down on critics. Anyway, maybe Jim was right and they are all like that fellow Percrusty Aunt Polly told me about.... But making a book over is harder than the first time, so I guess I won't tackle it."

Highfill, Philip H., Jr. "Incident in *Huckleberry Finn*." *Mark Twain Journal*, 11 (Fall 1961), 6.

When Huck was revealed as a boy in girl's clothes when he clapped his knees together to catch a lump of lead (Chapter 11), MT could have been following an English source "in the grab-bag of scholarly argument, ana, and country custom called *Literary Anecdotes...Of Professor Porson and Others; from the Manuscript Papers of the Late E. H. Baker*...London, 1852 (Anecdote No. CCXXXIV The Two Thieves, p. 282)."

Hill, Hamlin. "*Huckleberry Finn's* Humor Today." M. Thomas Inge, ed. *Huck Finn Among the Critics: A Centennial Selection 1884–1984*. Washington: United States Information Agency, Division for the Study of the United States, 1984. Pp. 231–44. [This edition is for overseas distribution only. American publication of Hill's essay will be in Robert Sattelmeyer and J. Donald Crowley, eds., *One Hundred Years of Huckleberry Finn: The Boy, His Book, and American Culture*, University of Missouri Press, 1985.]

HF changes for readers as the world changes. At the end of the 19th century commentators praised the book in impressionistic terms, "neglecting [the] ... complexity, moral paradox, or ironic subtlety ... " Later critics took *HF* more seriously, discussing the structure, irony, and unreliable narrator. Hill now applies James E. Miller's description of ingredients in modern American novels to *HF*: since World War II, the fictional world has been "sick, hostile, or treacherous, and ... the recurring stance of the hero has reflected some mixture of horror, bewilderment, and sardonic humor ... The nightmare world, alienation and nausea, the quest for identity, and the comic doomsday vision—these are the four elements that characterize recent American fiction" (*Quests Surd and Absurd*, Univ. of Chicago Press, 1967). Hill's telling examples demonstrate how these qualities keep *HF* fresh today while works by MT's contemporaries seem dated. To call the bleak vision of *HF* "comic" is to observe the sardonic ironies: Jim becomes merely "as free as any cretur that walks on this earth," and the heroic words "hell, Providence, 'Sivilization,' and freedom" are comic and trival in *HF*. MT makes the reader his "prey," and works "to strip away ... idealistic delusions and replace them with a soberer notion of Huck's and the reader's own imperfectability."

Hill, John S. "Huck Finn's Reaffirmation of Rejection." *Mark Twain Journal*, 13 (Summer 1967), 16-17.

The concluding episode exploits both Jim and Huck, reflecting "the view that a white person of a lower class may also be duped, be used for sport." Huck has already gone through successive stages under the rule of the South, as a rebel, and again under the rule of the South, and in the end he rebels once more against the old order and Tom Sawyer, its symbol.

Hiner, James. "Mark Twain: Ambivalence Not Disjunction." *American Quarterly*, 16 (Winter 1964), 620-21.

The conflicts in *HF* between raft and shore, the real and the romantic, have been misread by critics who seek in MT an allegiance to either side. "Head and heart are not merely opposed...but self contradictory. The heart goes toward suicide, and the head to madness. Those are the ultimate conditions of each drive."

Hinz, John. "Huck and Pluck: 'Bad' Boys in American Fiction." *South Atlantic Quarterly*, 51 (January 1952), 120-29.

Tom and Huck belong to a literary tradition reacting against the "model" boy; unfortunately, because of pressure for adjustment and conformity, "perhaps the real boy is lost forever."

Hiscoe, David W. "The 'Abbreviated Ejaculation' in *Huckleberry Finn.*" *Studies in American Humor*, n.s. 1 (February 1983), 191–97.

The quoted words are Pascal Covici's, referring to the point in Ch. 33 where Tom starts to blurt out that Jim is already free, but stops himself: "What! Why Jim is----" There are earlier "mirror scenes" in Ch. 11, where Huck almost tells Mrs. Judith Loftus something about Jim (he stops with "Why *he*----" and allows her to give him information that spoils her husband's chances at the reward for Jim), and Ch. 31, where the Duke starts to tell Huck that Jim is with "a farmer by the name of Silas Ph---" Thus, Tom's words before the elaborate freeing of the free Jim are a warning that someone is about to be duped; but readers looking for sensationalism overlook the warning, as Huck does.

Hoffman, Daniel G. "Jim's Magic: Black or White?" *American Literature*, 32 (March 1960), 45-54.

Jim's "superstitions are used structurally to indicate his slavery while a slave and his spiritual freedom with Huck"; freed from credulity with his escape from bondage, "he becomes a magician able to read the mysterious signs of nature."

———————. "Mark Twain." *Form and Fable in American Fiction*. London and New York: Oxford University Press, 1961.

On pp. 317-42, "Black Magic—and White—in *Huckleberry Finn*," showing three attitudes toward life, indicated in supernatural terms: both "the conventional piety of the villagers" and "the irrelevant escape of the romantic imagination" are "morally inadequate." "The third—which pays homage to the river god—gives dignity to human life" through the world of supernatural omens understood by Jim; Jim, too, undergoes growth in the story. This article is a complete revision of "Jim's Magic: Black or White?" (1960). This 1961 revision is reprinted in part in Bradley (1962, 1977), Leary (1962), and Smith (1963). On pp. 343-50, "Huckleberry Finn: His Masquerade," on his disguises, his several identities, and his problem of preserving his essential self. In the end, as in the beginning, Huck's only safety lies in flight.

Hoffman, Frederick J., and Roy Harvey Pearce. "Notes on Reading *The Adventures of Huckleberry Finn.*" *The Growth of American Literature*. New York: American Book Company, 1956. Pp. 856-861.

Directed toward the student, provides a useful discussion of the way MT dramatically evokes the past. The anticlimactic ending of *HF* is appropriate: "Twain's intuition that he must return Huck to boy-life and the world of Tom Sawyer was right. He had strained the metaphysical and tragic implications of his form far enough."

Hoffman, Michael J. "Huck's Ironic Circle." *Georgia Review*, 23 (Fall 1969), 307-22.

HF "is not a novel about a boy's moral awakening, nor a polemic against slavery, nor a book about how good instincts are stronger than an evil society. We have always overestimated Huck Finn and have likewise underestimated his creator.... The dynamic theme that runs throughout *Huckleberry Finn* is an unresolved dialectic between the moral responsibility of the individual and the morality of the society in which he moves and against which he must function." Huck does not share the perceptiveness of MT and the reader; he never truly learns to regard Jim as an equal, but believes in property rights and the institution of slavery, and he follows the leadership of Tom Sawyer. The ending is consistent with this unimaginative Huck: "The irony of the book has now come full circle in that Huck has not rejected society's standards at all. He just feels personally inconvenienced by things like school, and clothes. But he still believes just as strongly that society is right." Reprinted (revised) in *The Subversive Vision/American Romanticism in Literature*. Port Washington, NY: Kennikat, 1973. Pp. 102-17.

Holland, Jeffrey R. "Soul-Butter and Hog Wash: Mark Twain and Frontier Religion." *"Soul-Butter and Hog Wash" and Other Essays on the American West.* Provo, UT: Brigham Young University Press, 1978. Pp. 5-32.

Page 5 is an abstract which begins: "In this essay, Jeffrey R. Holland, formerly dean of religious instruction at Brigham Young University and now LDS Church Commissioner of Education, argues persuasively that Mark Twain's work from *Roughing It* through *Huckleberry Finn* can be viewed as the journey of a seeker looking for a satisfactory religious philosophy. In the end, Twain concluded that the simplicity and basic Christianity of sincere frontier religion offered the only satisfactory answer to his search." Holland finds a less cynical "and somewhat more reflective Twain" than is commonly accepted, and in the following essay reveals his thorough, sympathetic familiarity with MT's published writings.

Holland, Laurence B. "A 'Raft of Trouble': Word and Deed in *Huckleberry Finn*." *Glyph* (Johns Hopkins Textual Studies), 5 (1979), 69-87.

"What *Huckleberry Finn* is about is the process, with its attendant absurdities, of setting a free man free." Jim is rescued repeatedly, but futilely, "and Twain it was, though with more complex motives than Tom's, who thought up the crude sport that is condemned in Tom, the 'adventure' as Tom calls it to which Twain devoted so much of *The Adventures of Huckleberry Finn*. Twain's conscience is therefore stirred not only as a Tom Sawyerish, fish-belly white citizen who never freed a slave in his life, but by the lie he perpetrated in the very act of forming his fiction" on what MT called elsewhere a "lie of silent assertion." Reprinted in Eric J. Sundquist, ed., *American Realism: New Essays*. Baltimore, London: The Johns Hopkins University Press, 1982. Pp. 66-81.

Hood, Robert E. "Mark Twain's Huck Finn." *Scouting* [published eight times a year by Boy Scouts of America for adult leaders]. 62 (March-April 1974), 28-31, 68.

A popular account, largely descriptive, praising the book for its humor. Illustrated by Mary Ellen Mark's color photographs made during the filming of the current musical treatment (the cover illustration is also from the filming).

Howe, Irving. "Anarchy and Authority in American Literature." *Denver Quarterly*, 2 (Autumn 1967), 5-30.

On the raft, "itself so wonderful a symbol of the isolation, purity and helplessness on which the anarchist vision rests," Huck and Jim "create a community of equals," but the idyllic existence is constantly threatened by the world and it cannot last (pp. 22-25).

Howell, Elmo. "Huckleberry Finn in Mississippi." *Louisiana Studies*, 7 (Summer 1968), 167-72.

On the locations in Mississippi of some of the incidents in *HF*, in which MT's "purpose is to give a kindly rendering of a country and a civilization" he loved.

———. "Uncle John Quarles' Watermelon Patch." *Midwest Quarterly*, 9 (April 1968), 271-82.

On the tender recollections in *HF* of MT's own boyhood days on his uncle's farm: "He had been in Eden and he knew whereof he spoke." (Documentation is from familiar works on MT).

———. "Uncle Silas Phelps: A Note on Mark Twain's Characterization." *Mark Twain Journal*, 14 (Summer 1968), 8-12.

"Mark Twain was a friend of the Negro...and he never failed to speak out against the injustice he suffered, particularly in the South," but he "also loved those Valley people who enslaved Jim.... Thus *Huckleberry Finn* is built around a paradox": the Phelps family "are among Mark Twain's favorite people, and Uncle Silas Phelps is his finest portrait of a good man," kindly and decent rather than clever.

Hoy, James F. "The Grangerford-Shepherdson Feud in *Huckleberry Finn*." *Mark Twain Journal*, 18 (Winter 1975-1976), 19-20.

Stresses the importance of the names, which represent "wandering herders versus settled gardeners."

Hughes, John B. "*Lazarillo de Tormes y Huckleberry Finn*." Manuel Criado de Val, ed. *La picaresca: Origenes, textos y estructuras*. Madrid: Fundación Universitaria Española, 1979. Pp. 1167–1172.

Close reading and comparison of the two works may reveal aspects not apparent in other context. Hughes does not propose to treat the major problem of picaresque influences such as Cervantes, but to concentrate on the voices and perspectives of the two narrator-protagonists. Both Huck and Lazarillo are totally independent, alienated, and in each book the constant presence of the first-person narrator is the basic fact which determines all the rest. [In Spanish.]

Hunting, Robert. "Mark Twain's Arkansaw Yahoos." *Modern Language Notes*, 73 (April 1958), 264-68.

Chapters 21-22 ("An Arkansaw Difficulty" and "Why the Lynching Bee Failed") "in point of view and in tone...stand apart from the rest of the novel....the mask slips and...the reporter in these two chapters looks suspiciously like Mark Twain himself," lacking in Huck's compassion. (See reply by E. Arthur Robinson, 1960).

Ignatieff, Leonid. "American Literature in the Soviet Union." *Dalhousie Review*, 25 (Spring 1955), 55-66.

"10,000,000 copies of the works of Jack London and 3,000,000 copies of the works of Mark Twain circulated in the USSR between the early twenties and 1940, these two authors being consistently the favourite American writers in that country." Although Soviet critics have tried to exploit the social criticism of these authors, "Jack London...was too inconsistent to be of much help. Mark Twain offered greater promise.... Unfortunately for them, it was not the later works at all, but *Tom Sawyer, The Prince and the Pauper*, and *Huckleberry Finn* that interested the Soviet public."

Inge, M. Thomas. "Huckleberry Finn, symbol of freedom, turns 100." *The Virginian-Pilot/The Ledger-Star* (Norfolk) (9 December 1984), C1-C2. Reprinted in *Randolph-Macon College Bulletin*, 56 (Winter 1985), 24–26.

Huck is a living figure like Falstaff, Hamlet and Don Quixote, and *HF* is probably the most widely reprinted, translated, and read of our novels, a leading candidate for the title of the "Great American Novel." *HF* has been criticized as coarse, flawed in its structure, and, more recently, as racist, but has won praise from perceptive readers. Telling "his own story in his own language," Huck speaks for "the national spirit." Moreover, "The novel strikes at the very heart of a political dilemma of the modern world, and that is the proper balance between personal liberty and social responsibility."

Irwin, Robert. "The Failure of *Tom Sawyer* and *Huckleberry Finn* on Film." *Mark Twain Journal*, 13 (Summer 1967), 9-11.

The reluctance of producers to give offence has resulted in false interpretations, despite pains taken to achieve authenticity in casting, costumes, and scenery. A number of film versions are discussed, and there is a bibliography of reviews.

James, Stuart B. "The Politics of Personal Salvation: The American Literary Record." *Denver Quarterly*, 4 (Autumn 1969), 19-45.

Huck Finn is "another Tocquevillean democrat...yet another American fictional character at odds with and fleeing from the culture in which he grew up. But when we ask the question, What are his responsibilities to this culture, we hit a snag," because of its nature as a brutalizing, slaveholding society. There is a danger, however, that such portraits of society by MT and others will breed in the young contempt for all laws and encourage the "very idealistic and self-righteous role of the Holy Revolutionary." Huck's answer was to escape, deserting Jim (pp. 34-39).

Jeffersen, Douglas W. "Mark Twain: *Adventures of Huckleberry Finn*." Hans-Joachim Lang, ed. *Der amerikanische Roman von den Anfängen bis zur Gegenwart*. Düsseldorf: August Bagel Verlag, 1972. Pp. 142–167 (notes 394–96).

Praises MT's descriptive power and evocation of the river. The narrative voice of the uneducated Huck sets *HF* apart from previous classical American novels, although his part in the action varies through the book. Following Ellison, Lynn, and Hoffman, sees Jim as somewhat idealized though still reflecting established stereotypes. The ending of the book is a falling-off, but preferable to a moralized sentimental conclusion. [In German.]

Jenkins, William D. "From a Hugglebeddy Fann." *James Joyce Quarterly*, 6 (Fall 1968), 89–91.

Extends James S. Atherton's account (1967) of verbal borrowings and adaptations from *HF* in *Finnegans Wake*.

John, George. "A Note on the Ending of *Huckleberry Finn*." *Literary Criterion* (University of Mysore, India), 8 (Winter 1967), 56-61.

Huck's interest is in the freeing of Jim, and "by his submission to rules, he is in a sense coming to terms with society. Huck is all along characterized as a person with horse-sense." His submission parallels the implementation of the Emancipation Proclamation: "The attempt to translate this democratic ideal into social reality, involved innumerable legalities. Especially so, in the Southern states. These legal rituals seem inhuman, and yet the realist has to accept them."

Johnson, James William. "The Adolescent Hero: A Trend in Modern Fiction." *Twentieth Century Literature*, 5 (April 1959), 3-11.

Compares *HF* and *Catcher in the Rye* (p. 5) as illustrating "the difference between the nineteenth- and twentieth-century use of the adolescent," in that *HF* is external in its emphasis: Huck looks at the world and it is Huck's world that Twain is concerned with." Moreover, Huck's choices are determined by his character, which shows compassion, candor, honesty, and humor from the first: "His is an adult intelligence masquerading as an adolescent."

Jones, Horace P. "Twain's *Adventures of Huckleberry Finn*." *The Explicator*, 43 (Fall 1984), 43.

Hemingway's statement has become a classic: "All modern American literature comes from one book by Mark Twain called *Huckleberry Finn*. If you read it, you must stop where the Nigger Jim is stolen from the boys. That is the real end. The rest is just cheating.... " (*Green Hills of Africa*, 1932, p. 210). But this is misleading: "Jim is never 'stolen from the boys,' " since his legal owner is Miss Watson, not somebody on the raft. Furthermore, the king and duke are too old to be called "boys."

Jones, Joseph. "The Duke's Tooth-Powder Racket: A Note on *Huckleberry Finn*." *Modern Language Notes*, 61 (November 1946), 468-69.

According to a New York paper, there really were scoundrels who sold a dentrifice that removed the enamel with the tartar. (*See HF*, Chapter 19).

Jones, Rhett S. "Nigger and Knowledge: White Double-Consciousness in *Adventures of Huckleberry Finn.*" *Mark Twain Journal*, 22 (Fall 1984), 28–37.

The point of departure is an oft-cited passage in *The Souls of Black Folk* in which W.E.B. Du Bois contends that black people see themselves through their own eyes and through those of whites. By the same token whites alternately see the humanity of blacks and, when it is advantageous to do so, close their eyes to that humanity. "Huck manifests white double consciousness as he shifts back and forth between his own regard for Jim as a person and the kind of person the society tells him Jim must be," he is more perceptive than Tom, but in the end he submits to Tom's view of Jim. "Huck is not interested in the fate of Jim—much less that of his family—nor is Tom, nor was Twain." Black readers feel betrayed by MT's willingness to diminish Huck and return to conventional white public fictions in the end, but it would be a mistake to ban *HF* on this account: "Twain deserves a careful reading as a white person who almost, but not quite, publicly emancipated himself from racism. He and his books cry out for reflective careful study, not angry attempts to prohibit the readings of his work."

Kamei, Shunsuke. "*Huckleberry Finn No Boken* no kaishaku ni tsuite" ["On Interpretations of *The Adventures of Huckleberry Finn*"] *Hikaku Bungaku Hikaku Bunka [Comparative Literature and Comparative Culture*]. Tokyo: Kobundo, 1961. Pp. 243-259.

Myth criticism, symbolistic criticism and socio-political criticism do not adequately interpret *Huckleberry Finn* including the controversial ending. *Huckleberry Finn* is a story without order, and a key to interpreting such a story is Whitman's "Do I contradict myself?/Very well then I contradict myself./(I am large. I contain multitudes.)" [In Japanese; abstract by Yasuo Hashiguchi.]

Kanapa, Jean. [Preface.] *Les Aventures d'Huckleberry Finn*, traduit de l'américain par Suzanne Nétillard. Paris: Éditions d'Hier et d'Aujourd'hui, 1948.

[Source: Asselineu (1954), No. 1145, describing Kanapa's preface as "a communist interpretation of Mark Twain" which charges his bolder works are suppressed in America but that in Russia he is very popular and known for anti-imperialist views.]

Kaplan, Charles. "Holden and Huck: The Odysseys of Youth." *College English*, 18 (November 1956), 76-80.

"In addition to being comic masterpieces and superb portrayals of perplexed, sensitive adolescence," *The Catcher in the Rye* and *HF* "deal obliquely and poetically with a major theme in American life, past and present—the right of the nonconformist to assert his nonconformity." In a concluding note, Kaplan says that his article was accepted for publication before the appearance of Arthur Heiserman and James E. Miller, Jr., "Some Crazy Cliff," in *Western Humanities Review*, (Spring, 1955), 129-184, and "the numerous parallels between the two can be attributed only to coincidental simultaneous generation."

Kaplan, Harold. "*Huckleberry Finn*: What It Means to Be Civilized." *Democratic Humanism and American Literature*. Chicago and London: University of Chicago Press, 1972. Pp. 225-52.

"Huck is demonstrably a frontier Thoreau, who has a ritualistic need for isolation, and whose escape from his social role is dramatized by his false death and funeral" (p. 237). "For Huck this isolation won't sustain itself" and he needs Jim (p. 238). "Huck and Jim continually face the community on shore, and thereby discover the primary values that might redeem its existence" (p. 242). As in Melville's *The Confidence Man*, "the issue...remains the question of whom to trust" (p. 251). In the end Huck has been civilized: he "lives in the civilized imagination of his society."

Kapoor, S. D. "Tradition and Innovation in *Huckleberry Finn*." *Modern Review*, No. 762 (June 1970), 409-13.

[Source: Abstract in *AES*, 17 (1973-1974), 1806.] Treats American identity, confrontation with reality, and speech, as revealed in MT's portrayal of social reality against a historical background.

Karl, Frederick R. "Joseph Conrad and *Huckleberry Finn*." *Mark Twain Journal*, 11 (Summer 1960), 21-22.

MT matured between *TS* and *HF* as Conrad did between *Youth* and *Heart of Darkness;* there are similar treatments of river and shore in the two mature works, which "as studies in human degradation surrounded by the possibilities of regeneration...symbolize an era."

Kaul, A. N. "*Huckleberry Finn*: A Southwestern Statement." *The American Vision: Actual and Ideal Society in Nineteenth-Century American Fiction*. New Haven and London: Yale University Press, 1963. Pp. 280-304.

On the community of the raft.

Kazin, Alfred. "Almost Perfect." *Library Journal*, 87 (15 November 1962), 4243-5 (also numbered as Children's Section, 23-25).

Although *HF* deteriorates in the horseplay of the last chapters, the ending is a way of returning the action to *TS*, where it began. Modern critics are more conscious of such blemishes than was MT, who did not necessarily notice—or care: *HF* "is the product of a mind whose lapses were virtually necessary to his imaginative strength. For he had above all to feel easy to write at all, and if he had had to check himself every time he was in danger of displeasing the unnaturally severe taste of our time he wouldn't have found himself in the unexpected depths of *Huckleberry Finn*."

———. "The Scholar Cornered: A Progression of Children" [From *A Critics Notebook*]. *American Scholar*, 32 (Spring 1964), 171-83.

On *TS* and *HF*, pp. 176-77, 180-81; notes "the indulgent, arch, patronizing tone that Mark Twain adopts in *Tom Sawyer*" as typical of boy stories until Crane's *Whilomville Stories* of 1900 and Tarkington's *Penrod* of 1914. "Only once, actually, did Mark Twain break through this all-too-twinkly, chuckly softness": in *HF*, where the boy's "experience is *not* middle-class, not comfortable, not an exclusive concern with fun and games."

Keetch, Brent. "Mark Twain's Literary Sport." *Mark Twain Journal*, 18 (Summer 1976), 7-10.

"The purpose of this paper is to advance the view that *Huck Finn* has a fully logical structure that enhances the theme of a boy's quest for freedom." The title of this essay is derived from a misreading of Henry Nash Smith (1965); Smith calls *HF*, "a literary sport," in the sense that it does not belong to any literary tradition, has "no connections with the past, no history." Misunderstanding the sense in which Smith used the word, Keetch refers to "the literary sport played by Twain" (p. 7) and concludes: "Such sport as this evokes the laughter of the gods" (p. 10).

Kelley, Karol. "*Huckleberry Finn* as a Popular Novel." *Proteus*, 1:2 (1984), 19–26.

A statistical analysis comparing *HF* to other best-selling novels of the period 1870–1899 reveals that MT "employed a great many of the ideas that were current in his lifetime. His work was full of patterns that would be familiar to readers of popular novels." Kelley prepared a questionnaire for the central characters in 105 novels over the periods 1850–1869, 1870–1899, and 1900–1919, then "coded the answers to my questions and using these data, created an SPSS (Statistical Package for the Social Sciences) system file." *HF* differs from other best-selling novels by men in that only 40% showed fraternal love, as MT did, and 75% showed romantic love, as he did not, except as leading to violence; moreover, MT "appeared to associate family love with pain and guilt." Huck is coded as having many of the common traits that promote social inter-action, and Tom and Jim compensate where he is somewhat deficient: "Still, if Huck was not usually cheerful or decisive, Jim was. If the boy was not usually self-assertive or self-disciplined, Tom was." Coding Huck in the category of "morality" creates a "problem in logic," in that his behavior is inconsistent; the result is only "a ranking of medium in morality"—shocking the readers of the time.

Kellner, Robert Scott. "Mark Twain and the Mental Cripple: The Challenge of Myth." *Mark Twain Journal*, 21 (Fall 1983), 18–20.

Defending *HF* against recent accusations of racism, argues that MT is actually satirizing those who accept the stereotypes: "Twain's language and imagery about the blacks in his stories work together as a mirror in which bigoted readers ultimately see themselves."

Kelly, James J. "They're Trying to Kill *Huckleberry Finn*." *Mark Twain Journal*, 13 (Winter 1965-1966), 13-14.

On the removal of *HF* from New York schools as racially offensive, and (briefly) on past bannings of the book. Kelly defends the portrayal of Jim and the representation of Negro speech, using arguments that would themselves now be considered racially offensive.

Kemble, E. W. "Illustrating Huck Finn." *Colophon*, Part I (February 1930); pages not numbered.

Kemble was 23 when he illustrated *HF*, and was paid $2,000 for the job. He used one model, a boy named Cort Morris, for all the characters—including Huck, Jim, and all the men and women. When *HF* was filmed, the director, William Desmond Taylor, made the characters fit the drawings.

Kendall, Lyle H., Jr. "The *Walter Scott* Episode in Huckleberry Finn." *Nineteenth-Century Fiction*, 16 (December 1961), 279-81.

The organization of *HF* is based on "Huck's emancipation, from Pap Finn, from the King and the Duke, and from Tom Sawyer's darkly humorous influence." In the cabin Pap had called Huck the "Angel of Death," and this is "precisely what Huck becomes on board the *Walter Scott* six chapters later." Kendall identifies Pap Finn with "Old Hatfield," murdered by Jim Turner, and "ironically, Pap Finn's evil existence is to be closed out by Huck's exacting retribution for his father's murder" when Huck strands the robbers on the wrecked steamboat.

Kerr, Howard. "'Sperits Couldn't A Done Better': Mark Twain and Spiritualism." *Mediums, and Spirit-Rappers, and Roaring Radicals: Spiritualism in American Literature, 1850-1900*. Urbana, Chicago, London: University of Illinois Press, 1972. Pp. 155-89.

A thorough treatment of spiritualism in MT's life and works. Includes his visits to mediums in San Francisco, seances in the Nook Farm colony, and visiting mediums in London with Olivia after Susan's death—although he was not a believer. Kerr relies principally on the familiar published material about MT, but has discovered interesting parallels between the tricks of Tom and Huck at the Phelps farm and the activities of a spirit at the home of the Reverend Eliakim Phelps in 1850: in each case there were straw-stuffed dummies, anonymous letters, mysterious writings in unknown symbols, and wandering sheets, spoons, nails, and candlesticks. Details of the Eliakim Phelps haunting were available to MT (pp. 173-80).

Kiernan, Brian. "Motives in the Narrative: Some Remarks on *Huckleberry Finn*." *Sydney Studies in English*, 8 (1982–1983), 70–79. [Not seen. Source: 1983 MLA Bibliography, No. 6845.]

Kim, Wook-Dong. "*Huckleberry Finn*: Mark Twain and Early American Humorists." *English Language and Literature* (English Literary Society of Korea), 69 (Spring 1979), 109-24.

"This essay is an attempt to point out Twain's indebtedness in his *Adventures of Huckleberry Finn* to the early American humorists, especially to the Old Southwestern humorists, and to show how he reshaped this raw material so that it fitted into the novel." Starting his investigation with Blair, DeVoto, Henry Nash Smith, and other writers on the subject but not Kenneth S. Lynn's *Mark Twain and Southwestern Humor* (1959), Kim adds his own critical comment praising MT for transcending his sources.

King, Bruce. "*Huckleberry Finn*." *Ariel: A Review of International English Literature*, (University of Calgary), 2 (October 1971), 69-77.

The "absolute internalization of moral values is peculiarly American," and "*Huckleberry Finn* is a spiritual autobiography. Its main themes are the development of Huck's acceptance of Jim as an equal...and his willingness to be rejected by society and risk damnation so that Jim may escape." The trip down the river has as its archetype "the traditional allegory of the soul's pilgrimage through this world." It is a radical book, though not in the sense that it would substitute populism: consider Pap Finn. "Huck, isolated, uncorrupted, true to himself, could never be assimilated into any society." Reprinted in Schmitter (1974).

Kinghorn, Norton D. "E. W. Kemble's Misplaced Modifier: A Note on the Illustrations for *Huckleberry Finn*." *Mark Twain Journal*, 16 (Summer 1973), 9-11.

On MT's reactions to the *HF* illustrations by Kemble. On p. 322 his illustration of Uncle Silas Phelps with a brass warming pan that "belonged to one of his ancestors with a long wooden handle" showed a wooden handle on the pan and on the ancestor, a wooden leg—which might have been called a "handle" in contemporary slang.

Kirkham, E. Bruce. "Huck and Hamlet: An Examination of Twain's Use of Shakespeare." *Mark Twain Journal*, 14 (Summer 1969), 17-19.

The Duke's speech in Chapter 21 combines garbled lines from *Hamlet* and *Macbeth*, in which "indecision...prevents Hamlet from acting when he should and keeps Macbeth from acting when he shouldn't," and from *Richard III*, in which Richard acts without regard for moral questions. As a confidence man, the Duke "is required to have the ability to shift ground on a moment's notice and channel his activities in another vein," and he is a man of action, in contrast to the passive Huck. "It is ironic that a man with his moral character on the raft should give the very moral advice that Huck, the innocent aboard, most needs." "After Huck has heard and memorized the speech on action from '*Hamlet*' after he has seen the Duke operate on the Wilkses and Jim sold into slavery again, he...rebels against his environment...and says he will 'go to work and steal Jim out of slavery again.'"

Klaus, Rosemarie. "Mark Twain und die Negerfrage [Negro Question]—*Huckleberry Finn*." *Zeitschrift für Anglistik und Amerikanistik*, 5 (1957), 166–81. (An excerpt from her 1955 Berlin typescript dissertation, *Mark Twain, der Kritiker seiner Zeit* [*the Critic of his Time*].)

On MT's sympathy toward blacks, drawing on familiar works by and about him. The treatment of *HF* is conventional, arguing the interdependence of Huck and Jim, and Huck's growing recognition of Jim's humanity. [In German.]

Knight, Grant C. "Mark Twain." *American Literature and Culture*. New York: Ray Long and Richard R. Smith, 1932. Pp. 358-67.

MT is important as an American voice for independence from Europe and for recording social history, as in *TS*, *HF*, and *LOM*. MT is remembered as humorist, rather than as a novelist or essayist. Knight praises *CY* as "a masterpiece in irony," which exposes evils of the past and shows the advantages of living in a later time. *HF* "does not strike the bottom of human experience. All its events are seen through immature eyes," and it is not outstanding in dignity, humor, tragedy, or weight and power.

Kohli, Raj K. "Huck Finn and Isabel Archer: Two Responses to the Fruit of Knowledge." *Banasthali Patrika* (Rajasthan), 11 (July 1968), 73-82. Special Number on American Literature, ed. by Rameshwar Gupta. [Proceedings of the Seminar on American Literature, 2-3 March 1968 at Banasthali Vidyapath.]

[Source: *MLA Bibliography* (1968), Nos. 78, 10284.]

Kolb, Harold H., Jr. "Mark Twain, Huck Finn, and Jacob Blivens: Gilt-Edged, Tree-Calf Morality in *The Adventures of Huckleberry Finn*." *Virginia Quarterly Review*, 55 (Autumn 1979), 653-69.

HF shows patterns in which Huck gradually learns of Jim's humanity, but also reveals that he has not fully learned his lesson; furthermore, other passages suggest that Huck "has an instinctive compassion for Jim from the beginning.... These three patterns—moral development, moral backsliding, moral stasis—complicate but do not contradict the lesson of honesty, justice, and mercy first recognized by Joel Chandler Harris." Despite Huck's rough exterior, "the glow of his inner virtue makes him a bed-fellow—however incongruously gritty and uncombed—with Ilbrahim, little Eva, Baby Rue, and Elsie Dinsmore." He therefore shares qualities with pious fools in MT's works, such as "Mamie Grant, the Child Missionary," and Jacob Blivens, "The Good Little Boy Who Did Not Prosper." *HF* ends in Tom Sawyer-ish burlesque because "Tom is the rightful hero of Mississippi Valley society; Jim's debasement and Huck's suppression are precisely what the whole novel is about....even though Mark Twain created a spotless moral hero he was reluctant to let his hero triumph." He never wrote another *HF* because "it became impossible for him to believe in his hero."

Kotsilibas-Davis, James. *Great Times, Good Times: The Odyssey of Maurice Barrymore*. Garden City, NY: Doubleday, 1977. Brief mentions of MT passim (indexed).

On p. 271, Lionel Barrymore's account of an evening in New York (late February, or early March, 1888—he was nine, and had run away from boarding school) when a Mr. Clemens stopped to talk to Lionel and his father Maurice Barrymore as they dined at the Hoffman House. Lionel was unimpressed until he realized it was MT, whereupon he excitedly began quoting whole paragraphs of *HF*: "My father moved to fetch me a kick under the table and tried to stop me from this impertinence of reciting Mark Twain's own story back to him, but Mr. Clemens laid a hand on his arm and gave me his whole attention. At the end of my recital there were tears in his eyes."

Kraus, W. Keith. "*Huckleberry Finn*: A Final Irony." *Mark Twain Journal*, 14 (Winter 1967-1968), 18-19.

The supposedly genuine Wilks heirs are a second set of frauds, who probably "met the same young man, or someone as equally well informed about the Wilks' family, as the King and Duke." The "lost" luggage and William's broken arm are clever ruses, but suspicion is raised by their lack of grief at Peter's death, by Harvey's "poor grammar and lapses into colloquial speech," and by the vagueness of his description of the tattoo on Peter's chest.

Krause, Sidney. "Huck's First Moral Crisis." *Mississippi Quarterly*, 18 (Spring 1965), 69-73.

Huck's moral awareness of Jim does not come in the fog episode in Chapter 15 (as Lionel Trilling suggests), since his reponse there is psychological rather than moral; apologizing to Jim and recognizing him as a person prepares Huck for the following chapters, in which he "saves Jim by dint of courage and wit" from slave hunters.

__________. "Twain and Scott: Experience versus Adventures." *Modern Philology*, 62 (February 1965), 227-36.

MT "felt that unsound social views yielded an unsound literature and that bad writing sprang from a stultification of experience. Both situations he regarded as excesses of romanticism, and he tried to combat them by injecting critical analogues of romantic fiction into his books. In *Adventures of Huckleberry Finn* there is a group of such analogues that implicate Sir Walter Scott's representation of history as adventures."

Krauss, Jennifer. "Playing Double in *Adventures of Huckleberry Finn*." *Mark Twain Journal*, 21 (Fall 1983), 22-24.

In his prefatory disclaimer of motive, moral, and plot, MT dictates the reader's response. "This mandate, which comes before the body of the work, seems to suggest an overall interpretation of *Adventures of Huckleberry Finn* as an examination of American literary form." Telling *HF* through the independent voice of Huck, MT reveals a national schizophrenia and a need to break free of European traditions.

Krauth, Leland. "Mark Twain, Alice Walker, and the Aesthetics of Joy." *Proteus*, 1:2 (1984), 9–14.

In *HF* and *The Color Purple* "a dark universe of human inhumanity becomes the precondition of the joy that eventually dominates each work." For Jim, for example, the famous "trash" episode which leads Huck to apologize is "a claiming of self," as Celie's is when *Mr.* _______ tells her she is poor, black, ugly, a woman, "Goddam . . . you nothing at all," and then she asserts herself. "In each case, the agency of joy—a surprising release of the self from the world of pain—involves nothing less than the novel's controlling moral vision." Walker's characters change dramatically for the better, and in *HF* bad characters are replaced by better ones as the novel progresses: "As Pap is replaced by Jim, Emmeline Grangerford by Mary Jane Wilks, Judge Thatcher by Lawyer Levi Bell, the Grangerfords and Shepherdsons by Silas and Sally Phelps (and perhaps even the Duke and the King by Tom and Huck), we witness the reality of human goodness."

__________ . "Mark Twain in Japan." *Mark Twain Journal*, 12 (Spring 1963), 10-11, 20.

On MT's reputation in Japan, and translations of his works. His reputation as a funny man, and the Japanese emphasis on British culture and lack of a frontier tradition have reduced his literary influence, despite his wide popularity. Cites Masajiro Hamada's *Mark Twain: His Character and Works* (1955) as the only "notable book on Mark Twain" he knows, "and of recent works on Twain I can cite only two articles: Tetsumaro Hayashi's 'Mark Twain's *The Adventures of Huckleberry Finn*: Hope for Mankind' in *Lumina* No. 3 (1960) and Shunsuke Kamei's 'On Interpretations of *The Adventures of Huckleberry Finn*' in *Comparative Literature and Comparative Culture* (1961)."

Kravec, Maureen T. "Huckleberry Finn's Aristocratic Ancestry." *Mark Twain Journal*, 18 (Summer 1976), 19-20.

"One of the most subtle instruments of semantic irony concerns Huck's surname," which may be linked with the Fin MacCool of James MacPherson's "Ossian" forgeries; the root "fiona" means "white" or "fair." MT has shown "the pernicious effect of a culturally-imposed notion of nobility upon natural mankind," though Pap is evidence that Huck's natural nobility was not hereditary. Furthermore, the Ossian poems were fabrications.

Kruse, Horst H. "Annie and Huck: A Note on *The Adventures of Huckleberry Finn*." *American Literature*, 39 (May 1967), 207-14.

MT's "A Complaint About Correspondents" (written in late 1865 or early 1866) contains what purports to be a letter from his niece Annie. "It is ... safe to conclude that in writing Annie's letter Mark Twain realized what could be done with the combination of the first-person narrator and the child perspective," a forerunner of Huck, who is "perfectly suited for his purposes both as a humorist and as a social and moral critic."

Krutch, Joseph Wood. "Speaking of Books." *New York Times Book Review* (23 May 1953), 2.

HF "conclusively...proves that a great work of fiction does not need to be what is called a 'good novel' or, indeed, a merely 'good' anything else." It is melodramatic and badly structured, "a botched job," but "uniquely delightful" in the same way as is the last quarter of *LOM*. *HF* has epic "largeness of plan ...and there are ways in which an epic is better than even a 'good' novel." Reprinted in Bradley (1962).

LaHood, Marvin I. "Huck Finn's Search for Identity." *Mark Twain Journal*, 13 (Winter 1966), 11-14.

"Huck Finn is one of a handful of classic American frontier heroes-...who are able to find their identity only in opposition to the society that threatens their freedom. All are essentially anarchic, and must 'light out for the territory ahead of the rest." Huck sees through the hypocrisy of those around him, including Tom and the Phelpses, and seeks "a society with a heart as good as his."

Lane, Lauriat, Jr. "Letters to the Editor." *College English,* 18 (November 1956), 108-9.

A reply to Gilbert M. Rubenstein's criticism of his article on *Huckleberry Finn;* Lane calls Rubenstein's approach "both 'moral' in the wrong sense and unduly sentimental," and briefly answers his objections. There are also a letter by William Van O'Connor (1956), and a concluding word by the editor.

__________. "*Why Huckleberry Finn* is a Great World Novel." *College English,* 17 (October 1955), 1-5.

It is authentic, with real human figures, a real society, genuine moral and ethical problems, with a generally direct and realistic treatment; it transcends national limitations, is epical in form, and contains the allegory of Huck's journey "through the world of spirit, ever working out a pattern of increasing involvement with the world of reality and with his own self, both cast aside at the beginning of the journey." Reprinted in Marks (1959), and Bradley, (1962).

Lang, Andrew. "The Art of Mark Twain." *Illustrated London News,* 98 (14 February 1891), 222.

A general defense of MT as a serious writer in addition to being a gifted humorist. "I have abstained from reading his work on an American at the Court of King Arthur, because here Mark Twain is not, and cannot be, at the proper point of view. He has not the knowledge which would enable him to be a sound critic of the Middle Ages." But in *TS* and *HF* he reveals himself as "one among the greatest contemporary makers of fiction" and *HF* is "a masterpiece." Reprinted in *The Critic* (London), 18 (7 March), 130; 19 (25 July), 45-46 (as "Mr. Lang on the Art of Mark Twain," mistakenly attributed to *Illustrated News of the World).* Reprinted in Anderson (1971): "This article is apparently Lang's response to Clemens' request for support in the face of adverse criticism." Also reprinted in Scott (1955, 1967).

Langman, Fred. "Landscapes and Identity in the American Novel." *American Studies International,* 16 (Summer 1978), 34-47.

On *HF,* pp. 42-43: while Cooper's descriptions are static, and Hawthorne's dynamic, in *HF* description has become the expression of a sensibility. What Huck sees, the way he sees it, is what Huck is."

Leary, Lewis. "Tom and Huck: Innocence on Trial." *Virginia Quarterly Review,* 30 (Summer 1954), 417-30.

The structure and theme of *TS* express "a deeply underlying principle which haunted Mark Twain." In three sections, *TS* shows that adventure "leads innocently to knowledge of evil .. wins out over prosaic adult methods of doing things," and, "compounded in part of the spirit of make-believe, imagination, illusion—that adventure, not common sense, leads to the wiping out of evil." In *HF,* Huck's response to evil was fear, repulsion, a desire to escape, but Tom's imaginative actions at the end, like Huck's attempt to flee, fail to end the evil. *HF* is the finer book, in which "the contrived innocence of Tom fails," while "the questing spirit of Huck, who would be impatient at our even raising the spirit of innocence, lives on."

Leavis, F.R. "The Americanness of American Literature: A British Demurrer to Van Wyck Brooks." *Commentary*, 14 (November 1952), 466-74.

On MT, pp. 471-72: "It wasn't Huck who wrote *Huckleberry Finn;* the mind that conceived *him* was mature, subtle, and sophisticated." MT, "though so unmistakably and profoundly American, writes out of a full continuity with the European past."

__________. "Mark Twain's Neglected Classic: The Moral Astringency of *Pudd'nhead Wilson*," *Commentary*, 21 (February 1956), 128-36.

"The present essay appears as an introduction to a new edition of *Pudd'nhead Wilson* that Grove Press is bringing out this month" (editor's note, p. 128). "A classic in its own right...for all the unlikeness, it bears a very close relation to *Huckleberry Finn;* a relation of such a kind that to appreciate the lesser work is to have a surer perception of the workings of the greater." There is power in the central irony of the exchange of the babies and their lives, although the book is not faultless. Article reprinted in Cardwell (19633) and in Kesterson (1973). Excerpt from the 1955 printing as introduction to *PW* (London: Chatto & Windus) in Simpson (1968) (noting that the article was also reprinted in Leavis, *Anna Karenina and Other Essays*, London: Chatto & Windus, 1967).

Lee, Mary K. "The Overt, Unreliable, Naive Narrator in the Tall Tale and *Huckleberry Finn*." *Mark Twain Journal*, 21 (Spring 1983), 39.

Applies the insights of Lynn (1959) and other critics to support the thesis that the form creates dramatic tension through an open hoax recognized by the audience able to distinguish between author and narrator.

Lemon, Richard. "Huckleberry Finn. His *Adventures* was published 100 years ago this week, and it changed forever the face America saw in the mirror." *People*, 23 (25 February 1985), 67–70, 73.

A good account for the general reader, based on research in the standard sources; illustrations are posed photographs. Lemon says Huck's virtues are his candor, simplicity, and love of freedom. As we enjoy the American wild we can remember *HF*: "We been there before."

Lester, Julius. "Morality and *Adventures of Huckleberry Finn*." *Mark Twain Journal*, 22 (Fall 1984), 43–46.

No motel in town could find a room for Lester when he drove through Hannibal in 1973, and this article is more an angry response to American racism than to his recent reading of *HF*. "I am grateful that among the many indignities inflicted on me in childhood, I escaped *Huckleberry Finn*. As a black parent, however, I sympathize with those who want the book banned, or at least removed from required reading lists in schools. I know that my children's education will be enhanced by not reading *Huckleberry Finn*." In his anger, Lester finds MT's racism the answer to such questions as why Jim did not know he could simply cross the river into Illinois to be free, and says Jim's dehumanization "is emphasized by the fact that Miss Watson's will frees Jim but makes no mention of his wife and children." [She was not their owner—see *HF*, Ch. 16.] Apart from the racial issue, Lester calls *HF* harmfully seductive in its escapism: "Twain's notion of freedom is the simplistic one of freedom from restraint and responsibility."

Levidoya, I. M. *Mark Tven Bibliograficheski Ukazatel' Russkih Perevodoy I Kritiches-kol Literatury Na Russkom Yazke 1867-1972 [Mark Twain / A Bibliography of Translation into Russian and of Criticism in Russian 1867-1972]*. Moscow: Izdatelstvo Kniga, 1974.

An extensive list of 1606 items (only lightly annotated), plus appendices and 41 pages of index.

Levy, Alfred J. "The Dramatic Integrity of Huck Finn." *Ball State University Forum*, 20 (Spring 1979), 28-37.

Underlying attacks on the ending "is the notion that the sole moral and dramatic center of *Huckleberry Finn* is the scene in which Huck tears up the letter and consigns himself to hell. A close corollary is the notion that this action is a climax to a reasonably consistent learning process that unfolds during the deepening relationship between Huck and Jim on the river." Levy argues that Huck's character and point of view are consistent, and MT "refuses to sentimentalize the final chapters." Throughout, Huck is practical, unphilosophical, though innately kind. He accepts his position in society and regards Tom as his social and intellectual superior. MT and his contemporaries did not see the ending as flawed in the sense that recent critics have, and in fact MT often read selections from the Phelps Farm segment on his lecture tours.

Levy, Leo B. "Society and Conscience in *Huckleberry Finn*." *Nineteenth-Century Fiction*, 18 (March 1964), 383-91.

The critical view that equates what Huck calls "conscience" with the views of the society in which he lives are basically correct, but "criticism of the novel has suffered from too much insistence upon its schematic or doctrinal aspects. "Natural man is not necessarily innocent—*vide* the degraded Pap—and the growing closeness of Huck and Jim is "the recognition and fullfillment of mutual needs so strong that they can transcend racial barriers"; hence, Huck's decision to help Jim escape may be, not "rebellious and isolating," but "a socializing decision through which he begins to discover a deeper bond with society than any he has known."

Lewis, Stuart. "Twain's Huckleberry Finn, Chapter XIV." *Explicator*, 30 (March 1972), Item 61.

While Huck takes the traditional view of Solomon's wisdom in proposing to divide a baby, "Jim realizes the terror of one man's holding absolute power over another.... The test is too close for comfort."

Light, James F. "Paradox, Form, and Despair in *Huckleberry Finn*." *Mark Twain Journal*, 21 (Fall 1983), 24-25.

Divides *HF* into three sections, dominated by Tom, by Huck and Jim, and again by Tom. The great affirmation of Huck's decision to help Jim escape would have been a climax, but it is followed by a return to "civilized" denials of human worth, truth, and decency. No longer a slave under the law, Jim enters a larger slavery in a world of lies. Both Huck and Jim are controlled ultimately by forces outside themselves.

Light, Martin. "Sweeping out Chivalric Silliness: The Example of Huck Finn and *The Sun Also Rises.*" *Mark Twain Journal*, 17 (Winter 1974-1975), 18-20.

Tom Sawyer and Robert Cohn are romantic and Quixotic, and Huck Finn and Jake Barnes, "linked by their adherence to common sense and the lessons of experience, bear a likeness to Sancho Panza." Hemingway follows MT in the attack on romantic folly once swept away by Cervantes but restored by Sir Walter Scott.

Lindberg, Gary. *The Confidence Man in American Literature.* New York and Oxford: Oxford University Press, 1982. On MT, pp. 183-202, 226-28, and passim (indexed).

By MT's time "the question is how one can hold onto one's inner being in a field of competitive and soul-less con men. The soured public world is reflected in P. T. Barnum, Tom Sawyer, the Robber Barons, and the Snopeses. In Huck Finn and V. K. Ratliff, Mark Twain and William Faulkner fashion the rogue-as-survivor, a special version of the con man" (pp. 11-12). Tom Sawyer's appeal is dual, as the boyish trickster and the enterprising "young man who will go Far and Make Something of Himself" (p. 188); his role in *HF* "becomes much clearer when it is seen not as a follow-up but as a reconsideration of Tom Sawyer" (p. 187). Though "one of the great shape-shifters in our literature" (p. 196), Huck retains his inner self. In the buffoonery of the last fifth of *HF* "there is something terrifying about Tom's emptiness and about the social habits that encourage it. Tom becomes the secret agent of a society of fictions, and his mission is to convert Huck's and Jim's problems into an extended joke, and thus to evacuate Huck's major affirmations of all their radical content" (p. 198).

Lindberg, John. "*The Adventures of Huckleberry Finn* as Moral Monologue." *Proteus*, 1:2 (1984), 41–49.

As a narrator Huck follows the models set out in "The Celebrated Jumping Frog of Calaveras County" and "How to Tell a Story": his narration is deadpan, his vision innocent, and the reader must recognize the ironies for himself. "Huck's tale is the same as the authorial voice of the book. It is wholly consistent and it continually relates all diverse events to its own moral preoccupation, saving Jim." Lindberg suggests a succession of sections, each with its own climax developing out of Huck's increasing anxiety: "Introduction," "Initiation," "Boetia and Arcadia," "Distant Voices," "The Madding Crowd," "Chivalry," "Honor," "Confirmation," and "Alienation." Combining MT's love for the monologuist with his love for children, *HF* flows along with no motive other than that of life to survive, no moral other than that of human bonds, "no plot, other than the inconsequent delays of the humorous monologuist seeming to lose his way but always dropping hints of shared pleasure, like the river creating paradisal islands on its way to the sea."

Linneman, William R. "*Punch* and *Huckleberry Finn.*' *English Language Notes,* 2 (June 1965), 293-94.

The weekly "Roundabout Readings" column for January 4, 1896, tells of the author's eleven-year-old nephew's "keen and appreciative enjoyment" of *HF* and adds his own praise of "this Homeric book—for Homeric it is in the true sense, as no other English book is, that I know of."

Little, Gail B. "Three Novels for Comparative Study in the Twelfth Grade." *English Journal,* 52 (October 1963), 501-5.

On examining narrative technique, the three protagonists, and literary achievement in *HF, The Catcher in the Rye,* and *Intruder in the Dust.*

Lloyd, James B. "The Nature of Twain's Attack on Sentimentality in *The Adventures of Huckleberry Finn.*" *University of Mississippi Studies in English,* 13 (1972),59-63.

Characters cry a total of 71 times in *HF,* for the right reason, or sentimentally, or hypocritically; this crying is one of MT's ways of demonstrating a proper balance of head and heart.

Logan, Rayford W. *The Negro in American Life and Thought : The Nadir, 1877-1901.* New York: Dial, 1954.

Describes MT as "both a traditionalist and a non-conformist" in his attitude toward Negroes, and quotes Sterling Brown's praise for the depiction of Jim in *HF.*

Long, E. Hudson. "Tom Sawyer's 'Pitchiola.'" *Twainian,* 20 (September-October 1961), 4.

When the captive Jim was urged in Chapter 37 of *HF* to raise a flower, MT's source was *Picciola, the Prisoner of Fenestrella, or Captivity Captive,* by Joseph Xavier Saintine (pseudonym for Boniface), 1798-1865.

Long, William J. *American Literature: A Study of the Men and the Books that in the Earlier and Later Times Reflect the American Spirit.* Boston and New York: Ginn, 1913.

Criticizes MT's crudity in *IA, CY,* but also in *TS,* with its "dime-novel sensationalism," its emphasis on "the lawless, barbarous side of boy-life...its self-assertion without its instinctive respect for authority" (pp. 466-67). *HF* "ends not with a moral climax," but in Jim's rescue "by the most approved dime-novel methods. The portrayal of all these astonishing scenes is vivid and intensely dramatic; one needs hardly to add that it is a portrayal, not of the great onward current of American life, but only of its flotsam and jetsam." Still, MT portrayed character and scene vividly, and "was at heart a reformer" (pp. 467-68). Some critics believe his "more dignified works," such as *P&P* and *JA,* will last longer (p. 466).

Loomis, C. C., Jr. "Twain's *Huckleberry Finn.*" *Explicator,* 18 (January 1960), Item 27.

Tom Sawyer "lacks Huck's realism, toughness, and moral sensitivity," but his romanticism offers a means of seeing the often brutal world as adventure.

Loomis, Edward W. "Three Notes on Plot." *Spectrum,* 4 (Spring-Summer 1960), 94-99.

The absurd ending of *HF* follows the absurdity of the novel's prose. (Also on plot in James Gould Cozzens and as described in *The Notebooks of Henry James.)* [Source: *AES,* 3 (1960), 1610.]

Lorch, Fred W. "A Note on Tom Blankenship (Huckleberry Finn)." *American Literature,* 12 (November 1940), 351-3.

Quotes reports in the Hannibal *Daily Messenger* in 1861 that Tom was sentenced to thirty days in the county jail for stealing turkeys (21 April); and suspected of stealing onions (4 June); and two horses, a wash tub of clothes, and a quantity of bacon, butter, molasses, and sugar, in addition to robbing a chicken house (12 June).

Love, Glen A. [Letter to the Editor.] *English Journal,* 54 (January 1965), 61-62. A reply to Allan B. Ellis, "The Computer and Character Analysis" (1964).

It is not necessarily true that "the things a character says reflect his state of mind." A case in point is Huck's lying and "blubbering" to deceive the slave-hunters with hints of smallpox on the raft. For applications such as this, "computer analysis...must develop far more sophisticated means than are suggested by Professor Ellis for dealing with evasion, ambiguity and irony, before its techniques will be of real use to the scholar."

Lowe, William J. "The Mountain Shakes." *College English,* 23 (October 1961), 62-63.

Eric Solomon (1960) and Carson Gibb (1960) in their investigations of *HF* "are trying to bolster the weak ending of a fine novel with materials drawn from today's frame of reference"—MT was tired when he wrote it, and modern psychology and portraits of Tom as a modern playboy are inappropriate to a novel of an earlier age. In a brief rebuttal, Carson Gibb says that Lowe's premise would reduce literature of the past to mere relics.

Lowenherz, Robert J. "The Beginning of *Huckleberry Finn.*" *American Speech,* 38 (October 1963), 196-210.

In the opening 108 words, "Mark Twain firmly establishes the vernacular speech of his narrator, Huck, characterizes him, enunciates one of the major themes of the story [truth and falsehood], provides a frame of reference for the action, and even works in some free advertisement for his earlier novel *The Adventures of Tom Sawyer.*" Here, as in the rest of *HF,* MT used phonetic spelling of dialect "sparingly" and "functionally."

Lowery, Captain Robert E. "The Grangerford-Shepherdson Episode: Another of Mark Twain's Indictments of the Damned Human Race." *Mark Twain Journal*, 15 (Winter 1970), 19-21.

The names of the feuding families in *HF* allegorically represent the roots of the conflict: *grange* suggests a farmer, "particularly a gentlemen farmer with large holdings," and a "'ford'—a river crossing or a port—implies settlement, stability, and permanence in a specific area." The Shepherdsons, by contrast, represent nomads, and, significantly, "are always on horseback." Other details, such as the artificial fruit with which the Grangerfords decorate their home, reveal them as "only imitations of the noble and cultured society which established itself in the South."

Lycette, Ronald. "Mark Twain Mapping His Territory." *ETC: A Review of General Semantics*, 29 (June 1972), 155-64.

MT's "works reveal a persistent effort to understand the process that enables a man to grow emotionally and intellectually," as is revealed in *Old Times on the Mississippi* and *HF*.

Lynn, Kenneth S. "Huck and Jim." *Yale Review*, 47 (March 1958), 421-31.

MT's early interest in Joan of Arc grew from reading about her in her prison cell, and "in a sense Twain spent all his life-time writing about Joan; the tension between the nightmare of being locked up and forgotten and the dream of liberation is in all his best work." In *HF* there is a succession of Biblical themes, especially that of Moses—and a parallel in that when Moses led the Israelites toward freedom he moved toward death, and the movement carrying Jim to freedom will separate the two friends. Huck undergoes rebirths in a cycle of initiations culminating in deaths, and Jim passes through successive bondages. Reprinted in Kaplan (1967). Also reprinted in *Visions of America/Eleven Literary Historical Essays*. Contributions in American Studies, Number 6. Westport, CT., and London: Greenwood Press, 1973.

__________. *Mark Twain and Southwestern Humor*. Boston and Toronto: Little, Brown, 1959.

Many readers have misunderstood MT's mask of innocence, and more have confused the Southwestern humorists with the backwoods mind they described. "My belief, however, is that Mark Twain was conscious and deliberate creator, and one of the purposes of this book is to treat him as such....As with Mark Twain, my primary assumption about the humorous tradition behind him is that it is a self-conscious art, and not an expression of American mindlessness." Portions on *HF* reprinted in Bradley (1962, 1977).

__________. "Welcome Back from the Raft, Huck Honey!" *American Scholar*, 46 (Summer 1977), 338-47.

Attacks the "dropoutsville interpretation" of HF, which takes Huck's concluding statement that he will "light out for the Territory" at face value, as an indictment of the society Huck had seen; in fact, MT, at the end of *HF* "not only tried to tell us that Huck was planning to return to St. Petersburg, but he showed signs of feeling ashamed of himself for relegating the strong and admirable Widow Douglas to a minor role in her own household." Teachers from junior high to graduate school tend to misrepresent *HF*, reflecting the bias in postwar America against the family and its restraints on pleasure seeking.

MacInnes, Colin. "Everything on Our Raft." *New Statesman*, 65 (21 June 1953), 933-34.

On MT's portrayal of his times, and his language and his controlled balance of the tragic and the idyllic. "*Huckleberry Finn* is one of those stories, rare even among masterpieces, on which grace has descended absolutely; and this is because the narrative, so charming and arresting in itself, is constantly and effortlessly sustained by underlying theme and symbol." For example, "the raft is a birth-life symbol, and therein lies its fascination."

MacKethan, Lucinda H. "Huck Finn and the Slave Narratives: Lighting Out as Design." *The Southern Review*, 20 (April 1984), 247–64.

The slave narratives were a popular genre in the 1840s and 1850s, and MT knew, borrowed from, or showed parallels to books by Charles Ball, William Wells Brown, Frederick Douglass, James Pennington, and others. There are similarities between Brown's narrative both in tone and in the point of view of a young boy, written down by an older man. MacKethan argues convincingly that excising the "raftmen's passage" from Ch. 16 brings *HF* closer to the conventions of slave narratives. Jim's failure in his first escape attempt means little: Douglass and Brown also failed the first time.

Magistrale, Tony. "Protecting the Children: Huck Finn, E.T., and the Politics of Censorship." *Childhood Education*, 61 (September–October 1984), 9–12.

Spielberg's movie *E.T.: The Extra-Terrestrial* was banned in the Scandinavian countries to children under twelve for its negative depiction of the adult world as hostile toward children. There are parallels between the boy Elliott and Huck, in that each has a friend who must be hidden and protected from adult society, each grows in empathy with his friend and in a heightened sense of life, and "both children choose to reject the most important foundations on which their societies are grounded—slavery and science." Moreover, "Huck Finn and Elliott represent indictments of society that span generations of families, decades of history." Censoring a book or a movie shows a lack of the courage to confront complex problems, and "both movie and book inform us that we have not been adequate parents, educators or human beings."

Mailer, Norman. "Huckleberry Finn, Alive at 100." *New York Times Book Review* (9 December 1984), 1, 36–37.

First reviews of great novels are often wrong-headed, and *Anna Karenina* and *Moby Dick* drew harsher criticism than *HF*. Mailer makes the customary bow to Hemingway's dictum that "all modern American literature comes from" *HF*, then reviews *HF* as if it were a glorious first novel of 1984, marred only by similarities to the work of several twentieth-century authors, including Hemingway himself: "The mark of how good 'Huckleberry Finn' has to be is that one can compare it to a number of our best modern American novels and it stands up page for page, awkward here, sensational there—absolutely the equal of one of those rare incredible first novels that come along once or twice in a decade. So I have spoken of it as kin to a first novel because it is so young and so fresh and so all-out silly in some of the chances it takes and even wins. A wiser older novelist would never play that far out when the work was already well along and so neatly in hand. But Twain does." But for all its freshness *HF* is a work of its own day, "luminous" with the central image of the river, the comradeship of Huck and Jim. Mailer notes the depiction of slavery, but errs in insisting that "his name is not Jim but Nigger Jim" [the latter form appears nowhere in *HF*].

Malhotra, M. L. *Bridges of Literature: 23 Critical Essays in Literature.* Mayur Colony, Ajmer (India): Sunanda Publications, 1971.

"Notes on Mark Twain's Humour" (pp. 25-37) considers MT as frontiersman and newspaperman, primarily a humorist, though conceding that he was more. In *HF* emphasizes the humorous aspects of Pap, and the King and Duke. The essay ends by noting that Hal Holbrook, "who physically resembles him a great deal in every detail," has shown the durability of MT's humor by "making huge money" out of stage appearances. ["Read at the All-Rajasthan Universities Seminar on American Literature, sponsored by the USEFI, at Government College, AJMER (1968)."]

"Is *Huckleberry Finn* a Flawed Work?" (pp. 45-54) argues that "the book fails to tell how [Huck's] non-conformism is a pragmatic approach to life"; Huck's decision to run away at the end and the "evasion of the issues" illustrate this failure. The book survives because of its vitality and humor. ["Read at the Regional Seminar on American Literature held at Nainital (1969)."]

__________. "The Question of Unity in *Huckleberry Finn.*" *The Banasthali Patrika* (Rajasthan), No. 11 (July 1968), 69-72.

[Source: MHRA *Annual Bibliography* (1968), 7753. Additional publication facts in MLA Bibliography (1969), Nos. 78, 10288.]

Malin, Irving. "Mark Twain: The Boy as Artist." *Literature and Psychology,* 11 (Summer 1961), 78-84.

MT's "fiction is boyish and incomplete" because "he does not face squarely the emotional patterns which are involved" in his treatment of "authoritarianism and rebellion in the family and outside." Bixby and Brown in *LOM,* and Jim and Pap in *HF,* represent good and bad fathers, and an ambivalent view on MT's part. In *CY* the Boss is "a good, powerful father-image for the dark ages." *PW,* like *CY,* "is a cruel book written by an immature author," and in *Hadleyburg* and in *MS* "we enter a new world, where we meet the triumphant bad father." As Americans we have made MT, with his hatred and love of power, "a national father after all. Perhaps some day we will grow up."

Manierre, William R. "Contemporary Relevance of *Huckleberry Finn.*" Pp. 77-94 in Klaus Lanzinger, ed., *Americana Austriaca*. Beitrage zur Amerikakunde. Band 3. Wien und Stuttgart: Braumüller, 1974.

[Source: *MLA Bibliography* (1974), Nos. 102, 9629.]

__________. "Huck Finn, Empiricist Member of Society." *Modern Fiction Studies*, 14 (Spring 1968), 57-66.

The opening chapters do not represent Tom's point of view, or that of society; rather, the first three prepare for the story and define "the moral standards which give it meaning. The values of St. Petersburg—money, church, 'aristocracy,' to name only the most important—are equated with untruth, Tom Sawyer's 'lies,' and, for the moment at least, are rejected"; the fourth chapter introduces Pap and gives portents of future troubles. These first four chapters juxtapose opposing concepts, and Huck pragmatically tests and either accepts or rejects various ways of dealing with experience; in the end his pragmatism has become "merely verbal."

__________. "'No Money for to Buy the Outfit': *Huckleberry Finn* Again." *Modern Fiction Studies*, 10 (Winter 1964), 341-48.

The pragmatic Huck is "a natural born joiner. He 'joins' Tom's gang; he 'joins' Jim; later, he 'joins' the Grangerfords; later still he 'joins' Mary Jane Wilks and her cause; finally, he 'joins' society, presumably for good.... Huck's 'moral growth' has, I believe, been vastly overestimated."

__________."On Keeping the Raftsmen's Passage in *Huckleberry Finn*."*English Language Notes*, 6 (December 1968), 118-22.

Removal of the passage to serve as padding for *LOM* damages *HF* structually by obscuring Huck's responses to Jim's imminent freedom; the passage should be restored. (See Beidler, 1968.)

__________. "Parallel Scenes in *Tom Sawyer* and *Huck Finn*." *CEA Critic*, 30 (November 1967), 1,4,6-7.

Carries further Walter Blair's discussion in *Mark Twain & Huck Finn* (Chapter 5), to show that *TS* contains "rehearsals" of three scenes in *HF* dealing with Huck's inner debate.

Marks, Barry A. "The Huck Finn Swindle." *Western American Literature*, 14 (Summer 1979), 115-32.

Defines the tall tale as a deception revealing inadequacies in the victim, then interprets *HF* as belonging to this genre, not only in the many deceptions practiced by the characters (some good-naturedly and without malice), but also in the very form and the fact that Huck and Jim fled deeper into slave territory, with no reason for their flight, since Pap was dead and Jim was free.

__________. "The Making of a Humorist: The Narrative Structure of *Huckleberry Finn*." *The Journal of Narrative Technique*, 12 (Spring 1982), 139–45.

Told in the first person, *HF* is two-tiered: it has a "narrative past" when the events took place and a "narrative present" when the narrator sits down to write about his completed experience. At that point, Mark argues, "each of his two closest friends has told Huck a critically important lie": Tom in withholding the information that Jim is already free and Jim in withholding the information that Pap is dead. Thus, the flight down the river, Huck's agonizing over whether to betray Jim to Miss Watson, and the humiliating "evasion" at the end were needless, as Huck knows when he writes about them. Having been deceived himself, Huck in turn withholds information and deceives the reader.

Marshall, Archibald. "Last Century's Literary Favorites: I, *Huckleberry Finn*." *Literary Digest International Book Review*, 2 (January 1924), 104, 106.

Appreciative: a masterpiece, though the ending is weak.

Marshall, Gregory. "Blood Ties as Structural Motif in *Huckleberry Finn*." *Mark Twain Journal*, 21 (Spring 1983), 44-46.

Huck instinctively invents families when necessary, as when talking to Mrs. Judith Loftus, the ferryman, the slave hunters, the Grangerfords, and the Duke and Dauphin. These ruses never succeed for long, and the episodes are marked by a progression in each from the invention or acceptance of false blood ties to a return to true ones.

Martin, Jay. "The Broken Speech: Mark Twain and Henry Miller." Marta Sienicka, ed., *Procedings of a Symposium on American Literature, Czechnica* [Poland] 29 *August-7 September 1979*. Poznan: Universitet w Poznaniu, 1979. Pp. 213-24.

A failure, Miller was free "to divulge what for others had remained concealed," and he even sought "some way to express what was unsayable." By contrast, Martin understands "Mark Twain as concealing his treasured being, refusing to divulge in public what he knew in private about himself." At odds with his father, he identified with the black slaves his father whipped and sold, and MT "supported two black students at Yale, as if these were his own secret children." "The most common story in *Huckleberry Finn* is the death of a father," and Huck even "symbolizes in the killing of a hog the desire to slay his father, who had identified with hogs, slept with hogs in the tanyard, and referred to his hand as 'the hand of a hog.'" MT sought to be authentic, and began to be by "exposing his true self...to kill his conscience, to rid himself of his deformed relation to his father and to redefine himself as a son.... If he could succeed in doing so at all, it was only by learning the language of the unspeakable."

__________. "The Unspeakable and the Unsayable: The Psychology of Language in Mark Twain and Henry Miller." *Gradiva* (State University of New York, Stony Brook), 2 (Fall 1979), 1-8.

A variant of "The Broken Speech: Mark Twain and Henry Miller," (above). The argument is the same, but there are differences in wording; for example in the first two paragraphs here are the words "despair" and the "dark," which in the other version were "bad dream" and "bad dreams."

Martin, Terence. "The Negative Character in American Fiction." Louis J. Budd, Edwin H. Cady, and Carl L. Anderson, eds., *Toward A New American Liter-*

ary History: Essays in Honor of Arlin Turner. Durham, NC: Duke University Press, 1980. Pp. 230-43.

A national identity can be defined in terms of what America does *not* have: kings, aristocrats, oppression. On *HF*, pp. 237-38, 241-43: Huck chafes at the Widow's rules, and must flee Pap. On the raft "he can enjoy the presocial world which is the dream of the negative character," but he needs society to give him an identity, and when alone he is lonesome.

Elsewhere in this volume, Robert E. Spiller notes that "it was Mark Twain finally who forced the opposites of the genteel East and the raw barbarism of the open West into a still somewhat crude new American mould in which humor triumphed over violence and the comic spirit (mixed with tragedy) again created a major literature" (p. 14). Lewis P. Simpson argues that in deciding to "go to hell" rather than betray Jim, Huck is doing "just what his role in the historical society tells him to do," in contrast to Tom, who "keeps history open to the imagination by falsifying history and degrading the imagination" (pp. 32-33).

Marx, Leo. *The Machine in the Garden: Technology and the Pastoral Ideal in America*. New York and London: Oxford University Press, 1964. Pp. 319-40 and passim.

In *HF* the pastoral mode "for the first time...is wholly assimilated to a native idiom." The motif of the intruding machine "has as much to do with the defects as with the merits of the work," and MT's "ingenious efforts to contrive an affirmation virtually break his masterpiece in two" (p. 319). In between the perspective of the innocent traveler who sees only beauty and that of the pilot to whom lovely details stand for hidden dangers stands Huck, with a "willingness to accept the world as he finds it, without anxiously forcing meanings on it" (p. 334).

———. "Mr. Eliot, Mr. Trilling, and *Huckleberry Finn*." *American Scholar*, 22 (Autumn 1953), 423-40.

Replying to their defense of the ending, Marx argues that "it jeopardizes the significance of the entire novel. To take seriously what happens at the Phelps farm is to take lightly the entire downstream journey." When Huck says to Jim on Jackson's Island "They're after us!" he identifies himself with Jim's flight from slavery; yet in the end, although Jim is free, it was not the journey that took him to freedom. The symmetry of structure that some critics see is imposed on the novel from outside; in fact, the journey was doomed to failure, but "Clemens did not acknowledge the truth his novel contained," the inevitability of a partial defeat. Reprinted in Marks (1959), Bradley (1962, 1977), Lettis (1962), Cardwell (1963), and Simpson (1968).

———. "The Pilot and the Passenger: Landscape Conventions and the Style of *Huckleberry Finn*." *American Literature*, 28 (May 1956), 129-46.

As in *TS* and *LOM*, MT uses landscape as "a primary source of unity and meaning." The superiority of *HF* lies in its style, and "the distinguishing mark of style is language." It is in Huck that MT can strike a balance between the extremes of elevated description common in travel literature, on the one hand, and too harsh a reality on the other: "It does not occur to Huck to choose between beauty and utility." Reprinted in Smith (1963).

__________. "Two Kingdoms of Force." *Massachusetts Review*, 1 (October 1959), 62-95.

On *HF* and the destruction of the raft, pp. 69-71. "Clemens provides his hero with an Arcadian landscape, a profound sense of unity with nature, and then he causes sudden, menacing intrusion of the machine." [Revised, this essay became a part of Marx's *The Machine in the Garden* (1964).]

Matthews, Brander. "Of Mark Twain's Best Story." *Books and Play-Books: Essays on Literature and the Drama*. London: Osgood, McIlvaine, 1895. Pp. 184-92.

On the truth and vitality of *HF*. On pp. 160-61, writing of Robert Louis Stevenson, he recalls Stevenson's "hearty praise of Mark Twain's *Huckleberry Finn*, and his cordial belief that it was a great book, riper in art and ethnically richer than the *Tom Sawyer* of which it is the sequel."

__________. [Review: *HF*.] *Saturday Review* (London), 59 (31 January 1885), 153-54.

HF is superior to *TS*, because of the skill and self-restraint with which MT tells the story through Huck, this is the work of "a literary artist of a very high order." [Unsigned, the review is attributed to Matthews by Walter Blair in *Mark Twain and Huck Finn* (1960), p. 5, and by Anderson and Sanderson in *Critical Heritage* (1971), where it is reprinted. Also reprinted in Bradley (1962, 1977) and Gerber (1971).

Matthews, Greg. *The Further Adventures of Huckleberry Finn*. New York: Crown Publishers, 1983.

A sequel to *HF*. Huck's father is alive, and murders Judge Thatcher, but Huck is accused. He flees toward California with Jim (whose wife and children were bought out of slavery by Huck but then died in the fire at the Widow Douglas'), pursued by the man-hunter Chauncey Thermopylae Bartlett. They journey with emigrants, Indians, and even for a time with a traveling brothel known as "The McSween Heavenly Angels Choir." That Word is pervasive once more, though Huck reproves one white man who calls Jim a "nigger" (p. 302). Huck tells black slaves in California they are free, and when necessary Jim strikes white men. There are the "boundless suspense, thrills, and cliff-hangers" promised on the dust jacket, but not quite the "unerring reproduction of Twain's distinctive style."

Maugham, W. Somerset. "The Classic Books of America." *Saturday Evening Post*, 212 (6 January 1940), 64-66.

HF "stands head and shoulders above the rest of [MT's] work. It is an authentic masterpiece," and MT "now is, I think, universally recognized as one of the greatest American authors." His writing in "a literary manner," as in *LOM*, is "but indifferent journalese"; but in *HF* he "produced a model of the vernacular style which has served as a foundation for some of the best and most characteristic writers of the present day. He showed them that a living manner of writing is not to be sought in the seventeenth and eighteenth century writers of England, but in the literary language of their own people." Huck's language is a literary artifice, but if MT "had not had the unfortunate notion of bringing in that boring little muttonhead, Tom Sawyer, to ruin the last chapters, [*HF*] would have been faultless."

Mavor, James. *My Windows on the Street of the World*. London and Toronto: J. M. Dent, 1923.

William Morris read aloud from *HF* until past two in the morning, then stayed up until five to finish it (1: 197).

Maxwell, D. E. S. "Twain as Satirist." *American Fiction: The Intellectual Background*. New York: Columbia University Press; London: Routledge and Kegan Paul, 1965, Pp. 192-235; also, p. 292 on *HF*.

A major study, beginning with eighteenth-century conceptions of satire, then treating MT's satire as an assault on the failure of institutions as seen in *HF* and other works.

May, Charles E. "Literary Masters and Masturbators: Sexuality, Fantasy, and Reality in *Huckleberry Finn*." *Literature and Psychology*, 28:2 (1978), 85-92.

Links "the conflict between Tom Sawyer frame of the book and its Huckleberry Finn center" to MT's own ambiguous views toward sexual bawdry, adding that "what little sexuality there is in the book lies latently concealed in the ...Tom Sawyer frame. Finally, and most importantly, I suggest that Twain's conflict between sexuality and purity manifests itself in *Huckleberry Finn* as a conflict between fantasy and reality." The indelicate "1601" and "Some Thoughts on the Science of Onanism" furnish "clues to Twain's association of locker room sexuality with storytelling itself"; and MT in constructing the fantasy that is *HF* is more like Tom than like Huck.

Mayberry, George. "Huckleberry Finn Enriched."*Nation*, 207(26 August 1968), 154- 57.

Discusses in some detail several of the more than twenty paperbound editions of *HF* intended for classroom use. Most of those here considered contain useful introductions, and several include biographical summaries, critical essays, and, in some cases, materials for class study. *The Norton Critical Edition* and the *Harbrace Sourcebook* contain a wealth of supplementary material, as does *The Art of Huckleberry Finn* (Chandler), in which the text is a facsimile of the first American edition, with the original Kemble illustrations. The Viking, Bobbs-Merrill, Riverside, and Rinehart editions range from good to superb, and a simple Chandler edition using a facsimile of the first edition (with the Kemble illustrations) and an introduction and bibliography by Hamlin Hill is "my favorite among paperback editions and...possibly the 'best buy.'" Editions published by Pocket Books, Bantam, Dell, and Signet reveal small concern by their editors for MT's material. The poorest of these is the Reader's Enrichment edition (Pocket Books, Washington Square Press), in which the background material is "barely adequate" and "the sections on writing skills, vocabulary development and spelling include the fascinating suggestion to study such words as 'ingots,' 'nabob,' and 'reticule,' 'because they are popular with good writers and speakers.'" The Bantam, Dell, and Signet editions are considerably better, and some of the supplementary material is quite good.

__________ . "Reading and Writing." *New Republic*, 110 (1 May 1944), 608.

The language in the circus episode in *HF* typifies "a kind of writing no means exclusively American, but marked in modern American writing at its best. Its apparent artlessness, emphasized by Huck's grammatical lapses and broad boy's dialect, conceals a structure that, if of a somewhat simpler order, is as consciously controlled as the grandiloquent prose architecture of the eighteenth century. It is prose that superbly fulfills its function." Hemingway and Sherwood Anderson have acknowledged their debt to MT, and the functional prose is also evident in Fitzgerald, Dos Passos, Faulkner, and Caldwell.

McAleer, John J. "Noble Innocence in *Huckleberry Finn*." *Ball State Teachers College Forum*, 3 (Winter 1962), 9-12.

On the use of nakedness to reveal both innocence and a gross exploitation of it, taking examples from MT, Sherwood Anderson, Hemingway, and Swift; also shows parallels between Anderson and MT in depicting the destructive power of the machine.

McCullough, Joseph B. "Uses of the Bible in *Huckleberry Finn*." *Mark Twain Journal*, 19 (Winter 1978-1979), 2-3.

"Although critics have been quick to point out that Mark Twain makes frequent use of the Bible for striking ironic effect, little attempt has been made to identify specific Biblical allusions for the purpose of analyzing them in the light of the story in which they appear." In *HF* there are loaves cast on the water, Jim's hairiness (comparable to that of Esau), the story of Balaam, and Miss Watson taking Huck into the closet to pray. Barnes (1965) has explored the parallel between the situations of Huck and Moses but there is "a more subtle equation of Huck and Moses in Huck's giving Jim a roasted snake to eat as an antidote for its poison, "a parody of a Biblical story" of the brazen serpent; MT "repeats the brazen serpent motif" in Chapter 20 with the story of the King at the camp-meeting.

McDowell, Edwin. "From Twain, a Letter on Debt to the Blacks." *New York Times* (14 March 1985). Pp. 1, 16.

A letter of 24 December 1885 to Francis Wayland, dean of the Yale Law School, blunts recent accusations that *HF* reflects racism on the part of the author. MT inquires about helping with the expenses of a black student. He would be less willing to do so for a white, "but I do not feel so about the other color. We have ground the manhood out of them, & the shame is ours, not theirs, & we should pay for it." The student, Warner T. McGuinn, was commencement orator at his graduation in 1887, and became a lawyer in Baltimore, where he was twice elected to the city council; Supreme Court

Justice Thurgood Marshall called him "one of the greatest lawyers who ever lived." The letter was authenticated by Shelley Fisher Fishkin of Yale; collectors Richard and Nancy Stiner made it available after reading her article (see Fishkin, 1985) contending that *HF* ironically attacked racist attitudes. Fishkin adds that MT planned to aid another black Yale law student, and did pay the tuition of A.W. Jones at Lincoln University; he also supported the European apprenticeship of Charles Ethan Porter, a black sculptor, and interceded with President Garfield to prevent the dismissal of Frederick A Douglass as marshal of the District of Columbia. History professor Sterling Stuckey of Northwestern University called MT's letter "a clear condemnation of the larger society for what it had done and was doing to black people. It couldn't be a clearer, more categorical condemnation of racism in American life and I'm not at all surprised to find that it came from Twain." As for complaints that *HF* is racist, Stuckey says: "My sense of the criticism is that it comes mainly from the nonacademic side of the black community, not from black intellectuals. In my judgment, 'Huck Finn' is one of the most devastating attacks on racism ever written."

McIntyre, James P. "Three Practical Jokes: A Key to Huck's Changing Attitude Toward Jim." *Modern Fiction Studies*, 14 (Spring 1968), 33-37.

Beginning with Chadwick Hansen's 1963 study, traces Huck's growing awareness of Jim's humanity: first Tom hung Jim's hat on a tree, then Huck nearly killed him in a joke involving a rattlesnake skin, but it was only through offending Jim's human dignity in the "trash" episode that Huck fully recognized his companion as an individual rather than a type. McIntyre's interpretation contrasts with Hansen's picture of Jim as developing from a minor figure to a symbol of man.

McKay, Janet Holmgren. *Narration and Discourse in American Realistic Fiction*. Philadelphia: University of Pennsylvania Press, 1982.

An introductory chapter lays a foundation in current critical theory for successive chapters examining *The Bostonians*, *The Rise of Silas Lapham*, and *HF* as novels in which the authors "sought to limit authorial involvement in the story" (p. 29). Discusses *HF* as a novel of "sophisticated naïveté," arguing that "in many ways, *Huck Finn* is a book about language. Huck's language is his vision, and his vision is both profound and unique" (p. 140).

———. "'Tears and Flapdoodle': Point of View and Style in *The Adventures of Huckleberry Finn*." *Style*, 10 (Winter 1972), 41-50.

HF "is one of the most stylistically significant works in American literature"; in it MT uses "certain strategically placed vernacular and colloquial features to create the impression of an untutored narrator, while simultaneously developing a sophisticated, innovative literary style which uses a full range of standard English constructions and literary devices." An analysis of the King's "soul-butter and hog-wash" speech shows MT satirizing social and religious hypocrisy by a contrast of the King's style and that in which Huck reports his words.

McMahan, Elizabeth E. "The Money Motif: Economic Implications in *Huckleberry Finn*." *Mark Twain Journal*, 15 (Summer 1971), 5-10.

Money provides plot motivations and is a means of characterization; it also "serves to focus the reader's attention on the central theme: the indictment of human greed and hypocrisy in a corrupt, profit-oriented society."

McNamara, Eugene. "*Adventures of Huckleberry Finn*: Chapter One as Microcosm." *Mark Twain Journal*, 18 (Summer 1977), 17-18.

"Huck makes his way thematically in this brief chapter, between civilization and freedom, between hypocritical and sentimentalized Calvinism and the supernatural signs of mysterious and powerful nature, between individualism and conformity."

__________. "Huck Lights Out for the Territory: Mark Twain's Unpublished Sequel." *University of Windsor Review*, 2 (Fall 1966), 68-74.

Huck's concluding statement has received undue attention from critics who ignore Tom Sawyer's suggestion, noted "a scant nine paragraphs before it," that the boys go off for an adventure in the territory among the Indians; MT's intention was simply to leave the way open for a sequel, such as the unfinished *Huck Finn and Tom Sawyer Among the Indians*, here discussed.

Mehar, Surjit S. *Mark Twain: The Adventures of Huckleberry Finn* (A Critical Study). New Delhi: Rama Brothers Educational Publishers, 1970.

A general study, aiming "to introduce an American classic to the new generation of readers, and to invite them to share its rich experience." Approximately one third of the text (pp. 53-101) is a chapter-by-chapter summary of the plot.

Meier, Susan Roberts. "Huck, Holden, and the Experiment That Didn't Blow Up the Lab." *English Journal*, 72 (November 1983), 32–34.

Despite the title this has very little to do with *HF* or *Catcher in the Rye*: the author describes having a high school class draw pictures of *reality*.

Melnikov, I. "Raskoldovannoe Leto" ["Disenchanted Summer"; on *HF*.] *Detskaya Literatura*, 7 (1968), 41-43.

[Source: *MHRA Bibliography* (1968), No. 7760].

Mencken, H. L. *Happy Days, 1880-1892*. New York: Knopf, 1940. Pp. 166-70.

As a boy, he took *HF* off the shelf at home: "I had not gone further than the first incomparable chapter before I realized, child though I was, that I had entered a domain of new and gorgeous wonders"; his father saw what he was reading and reacted with "a kind of shy rejoicing." Mencken continued to reread *HF* annually, "and only a few months ago I hauled it out and read it once more—and found it as magnificent as ever." He also read the rest of MT's books after *HF*, but found them heavier going.

Meriwether, James B., and Michael Millgate, eds. *Lion in the Garden: Interviews with William Faulkner*. New York: Random House, 1968. Passim on MT (indexed).

Faulkner notes *HF* is "too loose" to be called a novel, "just a series of events" (p. 56). Hawthorne and James were not strictly American authors, as MT, Whitman, and Sandburg were (pp. 167-68).

Metzger, Charles R. "The Adventures of Huckleberry Finn as Picaresque." *Midwest Quarterly*, 5 (April 1964), 249-56.

Unlike the romantic Tom Sawyer, "Huck...is doomed to play the picaresque role, as are possibly all picaros, because he is an essentially honest person living in a dishonest world." MT knew about the picaresque literary character Gil Blas de Santillana, and Huck embodies attributes of the picaro.

Michaelson, L.W. "Four Emmeline Grangerfords." *Mark Twain Journal*, 11 (Fall 1961), 10-12.

Possible literary models for the "Ode to Stephen Dowling Bots, Dec'd" In chapter 17 of *Huckleberry Finn* are in the poetry of Julia A. Moore, Bloodgood H. Cutter, William McGonagall (1830-189?), and Seba Smith.

Michelson, Bruce. "Huck and the Games of the World." *American Literary Realism*, 13 (Spring 1980), 108-21.

Accounts for the structure of *HF* and "why so many *different* motifs have been turned up, how they can be reconciled with one another, and what really constitutes the novel's core: the way in which structure and moral concern connect with the personality of Mark Twain the man....I do think we can make some headway if we pay closer attention to Mark Twain's enormous, lifelong obsession with play and games." Many crucial incidents parody their real-life counterparts.

Miller, Bruce E. "*Huckleberry Finn:* the Kierkegaardian Dimension." *Illinois Quarterly*, 34 (September 1971), 55-64.

In *TS*, MT portrays boyish egotism and pursuit of excitement and pleasure. "In *Huckleberry Finn* he examines another side—the tentative reaching towards companionship, the sorting out of responsibilities, and the troubled investigation of oneself and one's surroundings," and "Huck's final move to the Indian Territory, like Abraham's pilgrimage to Mount Moriah in Sören Kierkegaard's account expresses a unique spiritual adjustment which replaces the norms of social intercourse with a transcendent and terrifyingly immediate acquaintance with supernatural force."

Miller, J. Hillis. "Three Problems of Fictional Form: First-Person Narration in *David Copperfield* and *Huckleberry Finn*." Roy Harvey Pearce, ed., *Experience in the Novel: Selected Papers from the English Institute*. New York and London: Columbia University Press, 1968. Pp. 21-48.

Miller, Michael G. "Geography and Structure in *Huckleberry Finn*." *Studies in the Novel*, 12 (Fall 1980), 192-209.

Miller argues a geographical accuracy through chapter 18, using river reports and similar sources to support his thesis and carefully reckoning the speed of the raft and the safe hours of running in the darkness. In his precision MT drew on a trained pilot's memory—which, he conceded in *LOM*, was a mixed blessing in that it took the romance from the river.

Chapter 19 marks a change in the kind of journey, as Henry Nash Smith notes (1958) from a linear movement toward the goal of freedom, to a drifting characterized by the contrast of life on the raft and on shore. At this point, Miller shows, MT dropped his geographical precision.

Miller, Perry. "An American Language." *Nature's Nation*. Cambridge: Harvard University Press, 1967. Pp. 208-40.

The third and final section, "Huckleberry Finn," calls *HF* "the originating point for modern American literature because of its mastery of language," in a tradition of simplicity like that of early New England Puritan writers; Miller compares the eloquence of Huck's plain style to that of Thomas Hooker's prose. There is strength, too, in the refusal to moralize; and in speaking through Huck MT was able to "respect the reticences which had originally been calculated devices of plain discourse." On the question of MT's intellect, Miller asks what Americans would take themselves to be, if it had not been for *HF*: "How without that book, would even those of us who have never seen the Mississippi River know who we are?" The portion on *HF* originally appeared as "Mark Twain and His Successors" in *The Alumni Bulletin* of Bangor Theological Seminary, 33 (April 1958), 12-21.

__________. "The Romance and the Novel." *Nature's Nation* (see above). Pp. 240-78.

On MT, pp. 262-263, 267-275; from *IA* through *TS, LOM, HF*, to *MS*, "we are subjected to one sustained, unremitting forensic attack on the Romance." MT's assault on the Romance amounted to this: "that it is inherently dishonest because everywhere it is a lie told by the respectable and civilized in order to glorify and delude themselves." The three essays which comprise this chapter were delivered as the Jacob Ziskind Lectures at Smith College in 1956.

Miller, Robert Keith. "An American Odyssey: *The Adventures of Huckleberry Finn*." *Mark Twain*. New York: Frederick Ungar Publishing Company, 1983. Pp. 85–111.

After five pages of plot-summary, the remainder of this essay surveys a small part of the *HF* scholarship (the five most recently published works cited appeared in 1960, 1961, 1962, and 1974) and makes pedestrian critical judgments.

Millichap, Joseph R. "Calvinistic Attitudes and Pauline Imagery in *The Adventures of Huckleberry Finn*." *Mark Twain Journal*, 16 (Winter 1971-1972), 8-9.

Presbyterianism has been predominant as subject matter and ideological influence in Southern literature (although Baptist and Methodist churches are more common), because it insists on human limitations. St. Paul's influence on the thinking of John Calvin is reflected in *HF*, especially in the treatment of Huck's father, a figure of the "fallen Adam in the New World." This role is underscored by Huck's references to him as "the old man," who became drunk and "raised Cain...A body would a thought he was Adam—he was just all mud," and by the illusory snakes and devils of his *delirium tremens*.

Mills, Nicolaus. "Charles Dickens and Mark Twain." *American and English Fiction in the Nineteenth Century: An Antigenre Critique and Comparison*. Bloomington and London: Indiana University Press, 1973.

Compares *Great Expectations* and *HF* in their division into three sections dealing with childhood and the home, with society as a whole, and with psychological and moral decisions. (Incorporates parts of "Social and Moral Vision in *Great Expectations* and *Huckleberry Finn*" (1970).

__________. "The Crowd in the Classic American Novel." *The Centennial Review*, 26 (Winter 1982), 61–85.

On MT, and especially *HF*, pp. 77–85. Like Cooper, Hawthorne, and Melville, he "was not prepared to separate his belief in democratic man from his fear of democratic man." The ultimate bastion of slavery was the lynch mob, the brutality and cowardice of which MT condemns not only in *HF*, but also in *P&P* and, more forcefully yet, in *CY*.

__________. "Prison and Society in Nineteenth-Century American Fiction." *Western Humanities Review*, 24 (Autumn 1970), 325-31.

Cooper, Hawthorne, Melville, and MT all found the structure of society imprisoning. "Throughout *Huckleberry Finn* slavery is seen imprisoning whites as well as blacks," and *CY* shows that MT "saw exploitation characteristic of society as a whole, not merely the antebellum South."

__________. "Social and Moral Vision in *Great Expectations* and *Huckleberry Finn*." *Journal of American Studies*, 4 (July 1970), 61-72.

A meticulously detailed and documented comparison of the two books, noting the boys' "outward allegiance to a society whose values they instinctively oppose," in which home is dominated by women, the values are those of an oppressive economic and legal system, and religion has been reduced to a defence of the corrupted society. The boys face similar psychological and moral decisions, and there is even a parallel in final betrayal by the River: "At the moment when it should lead to freedom it leads to the capture of Magwitch and Jim."

Mizener, Arthur. "Mark Twain: *Huckleberry Finn*." *Twelve Great American Novels*. New York: New American Library, 1967. Pp. 37-48.

Mizener's preface describes his book as being intended "for the reader who...does not feel entirely at home with novels when he tries to read them seriously." The discusssion of *HF* is sensible but breaks no new ground.

Monteiro, George. "Innocence and Experience: The Adolescent Child in the Works of Mark Twain, Henry James, and Ernest Hemingway." *Estudos Anglo-Americanos*, No. 1 (1977), 39-57.

On *HF*, pp. 43-46: reversing the 18th-century view of the child as merely a future adult, the Romantic poets regarded growing up not as the way to a desirable maturity, but as the tragedy attending a loss of poetic vision. *HF*, however, departs from 19th-century American nostalgia to treat the child as a victim who can nonetheless "still cut through the shams and deceits of his society." To "oversimplify...but only by a little...the child is the only bearer of those values espoused (if not practiced) by his society: honesty of perception and expression, and loyalty to one's friends."

Moore, Olin Harris. "Mark Twain and Don Quixote." *Publications of the Modern Language Association*, 37 (June 1922), 324-46.

"The purpose of this paper is to trace the influence of Cervantes upon Mark Twain, with particular attention to the supposedly autobiographical tales *Huckleberry Finn* and *Tom Sawyer*." The humor of both authors "lies to a great extent in the contrast between imaginative and unimaginative characters," and MT, more widely read than is generally recognized, parodied literary sources and created characters misled by their reading.

Morioka, Sakae. "*Huck Finn* and *A Farewell to Arms*." *Kyushu American Literature*, 5 (April 1962), 27-35.

Compares the two as moral pilgrimages, in worlds "essentially *without women*" embodying water symbolism, and similar in style. The styles of both are masculine, simple, and direct, abundant in their use of monosyllables; to illustrate this last point, contrasts syllable-counts for sample pages from *HF* and *A Farewell to Arms* to those for pages in Fitzgerald's *The Great Gatsby* and Faulkner's *A Fable*, both of which tend more toward polysyllables. Morioka suggests that "apparently, Twain's style is natural, informal and casual, while on the other hand Hemingway's is staccato, clean-cut and generally very formal and artificial," but in fact Hemingway's is more natural and informal than it appears, while MT's is "actually artificial and made-up." To heighten his comparison, Morioka makes comparatively minor changes in a passage from each author's work, making it strikingly reminiscent of the other author's style.

Morley, Christopher. "Hunting Mark Twain's Remainders." *Saturday Review of Literature*, 13 (2 November 1935), 15-16.

Praises *HF* for its humor and beauty, and suggests that except for *HF* and *TS* "the other books are fast fading out." Takes issue with MT's more solemn critics, and quotes with satisfaction a passage from Don Marquis's *Chapters for the Orthodox* in which God tells a reporter that MT has been given his own river in Heaven and once ran a steamboat race through Hell. Satan once asked to borrow MT and his river, and MT was willing, but "his wife and William Dean Howells wouldn't let him."

Morris, Courtland P. "The Model for Huck Finn." *Mark Twain Quarterly*, 2 (Summer-Fall 1938), 22-23.

Memories by the boy who posed for the *HF* illustrations by E. W. Kemble, from May 1-October 1, 1884; he was paid four dollars per week.

Morsberger, Robert E. "Pap Finn and the Bishop's Candlesticks: Victor Hugo in Hannibal." *CEA Critic*, 31 (April 1969), 17.

Jim's troublesome escape at the end of *HF* includes several elements borrowed from Dumas: from *The Man in the Iron Mask, The Count of Monte Cristo,* and *Twenty Years After*. Less evident is the conversion and downfall of Pap Finn, patterned on the conversion of Jean Valjean in *Les Miserables*. These incidents in *HF* parody their romantic models.

Moses, W.R. "Mark Twain's Best Satire of Cooper." *Mark Twain Journal*, 21 (Fall 1983), 25–27.

Treatment of class distinctions in the King-Duke sequence in *HF* makes stronger comment than in MT's two famous essays on Cooper: "In general shape or outline, the adventures and the social relationships on which they depend are equivalent. Yet if Cooper uses his romances to make one kind of statement about human nature and right relationships, Twain uses his novel to make a quite different statement; and the second has the effect of undercutting and ridiculing the first."

———. "The Pattern of Evil in *Adventures of Huckleberry Finn*." *Georgia Review*, 13 (Summer 1959), 161–66.

There is a progression of types of evil, similar to that of Dante's *Inferno*, from Pap's incontinence to the violence of the feuding Shepherdsons, and finally to the fraud of the King and Duke. A comic ending is needed because MT could not leave Huck in Hell or raise him to a Purgatory (unless one chooses so to interpret Aunt Sally's threat to adopt and civilize him).

Mulqueen, James E. "Huck Finn, Imagist Poet." *CEA Critic*, 37 (March 1975), 14-15.

HF "contains passages which anticipate most of the requirements laid down by the imagists: to use the language of common speech; to employ the exact word; to create new rhythms; to render particulars and not deal in vague generalities; to produce poetry that is hard and clear, never blurred nor indefinite." Both MT and the imagists rebelled against artificially-elevated diction. Huck's description of dawn on the river (Chapter 19) is reproduced, first set as prose and then in short lines and stanzaic groups as though it were written as a poem, and discussed in terms of its poetic qualities.

Nagel, James. "*Huck Finn* and *The Bear*; the Wilderness and Moral Freedom." *English Studies in Africa*, 13 (March 1969), 59-63.

Both MT and Faulkner saw the South as cursed by its history of slavery, with the Negro a continuing reminder; the old order, founded on injustice and maintained by brutality, could not endure. In *HF* and *The Bear* a white boy too young to share the cultural guilt is paired with a Negro male, a victim of the old order, with a good heart and simple but practical mind. Most probably the pairing is not homoerotic, as Fiedler suggests (1948), but rather an attempt to reduce race relations to basic human relations. In both stories physical isolation produces "a social vacuum in which basic human essence floats freely." Both stories "appeal to a latent wish for moral freedom" and "parallel on several levels the experience of each man as he grows up."

Nasu, Yorimasa. "Mark Twain's 'Horseshoe Pattern' and *Huckleberry Finn*." *Jimbungaku (Studies in Humanities*, Doshisha University), 93 (January 1967), 70-84. [In Japanese; abstract in English by Nasu, 91-92.]

Here and in other essays Nasu argues that most of MT's novels and short stories follow a pattern described in the *Autobiography* (1924, 1, 237), where MT likened a narrative to "a brook that never goes straight for a minute, but *goes*, and goes briskly, sometimes ungrammatically, and sometimes fetching a horseshoe three-quarters of a mile around, and at the end of the circuit flowing within a yard of the path it traversed an hour before...." *HF* in its three parts (Chapters 1-7, 8-31, 32-43) "traces the 'horseshoe pattern' of Tom's heroic world—Huck's anti-heroic world—the world of Tom's frivolousness and Huck's awakening."

Nichols, Charles H. " 'A True Book—With Some Stretchers': *Huck Finn* Today." *Mark Twain Journal*, 22 (Fall 1984), 13–16.

HF reflects the conflicts within MT, who had a strong sense of justice yet never quite freed himself of the prejudices of his time, and the book dramatizes the contradictions within a society which professes high ideals but condones mindless feuding, abuse of children, robbing the weak, and the enslavement of black people. "It is my contention that *Huckleberry Finn* is an indispensable part of the education of both black and white youth. It is indispensable because (1) it unmasks the violence, hypocrisy and pretense of nineteenth-century America; (2) it re-affirms the values of our democratic faith, our celebration of the worthiness of the individual, however poor, ignorant, or despised; (3) it gives us a vision of the possibility of love and harmony in our multi-ethnic society; (4) it dramatizes the truth that justice and freedom are always in jeopardy.... *Huck Finn* is instinct with life. We can all profit by wrestling with the issues the book raises."

Nichols, Charles S. "Color, Conscience, and Crucifixion: A Study of Racial Attitudes in American Literature and Criticism." *Jahrbuch für Amerikastudien*, 6 (1961), 37-47.

Chiefly on the Negro as seen from without by Melville, MT, and Faulkner, and as seen from within by Richard Wright, Ralph Ellison, and J. Saunders Redding. "*Pudd'nhead Wilson* is essentially an anti-Negro book...a most superficial and contrived work." In *HF*, "Nigger Jim is a more stereotyped portrait of the black man than we find in Melville, yet more alive than Tom or Roxy. Here again it is well to be reminded that the point of view is that of the boy, Huck, who is trying to realize himself in a society whose hypocrisy the author is criticizing." Nichols argues, however, that "in writing on the character of Jim, American critics have again, by and large, assumed that Negro character represents evil"; his examples, however, deal with superstition and with Fiedler's assumption that the relationship of Huck and Jim is homosexual.

Nielsen, Veneta. "The Savage Prophet or Who's Afraid of Samuel Twain?" *Proceedings of the Utah Academy of Sciences, Arts, and Letters*, 43:2 (1966), pp.1-7.

A broad religious discussion, drawing on Jonathan Edwards, Jean Jacques Rousseau, Fyodor Dostoevsky, Leo Tolstoy, Voltaire, Edward Albee, and others. "The primary purpose of this paper is to speak of one brief episode in the novel *Huckleberry Finn*, an episode which establishes with superb subtlety the positive religion of Samuel Clemens.... Clemens draws heavily upon his contemporary Titans and the Old Testament, and does this by the method of parable or allegory. This episode is the parable of the feud between the tribes of Saul, Colonel Grangerford, and Shepherdson. The argument of these comments depends a little on the assumption that the name Shepherdson refers to the biblical shepherd's son. It is possible, but not entirely relevant that the young Sophia, who loved and escaped with Shepherdson, is wisdom incarnate. To stretch this point is not necessary, however. Clemens was a prophet, ironically, of love."

*Nigro, August J. "The Undiscovered Country in *Huckleberry Finn*." *The Diagonal Line: Separation and Reparation in American Literature*. Selinsgrove, PA: Susquehanna University Press, 1984. Pp. 88–97. [Not seen.]

Nilon, Charles H. "The Ending of *Huckleberry Finn*: 'Freeing the Free Negro.' " *Mark Twain Journal*, 22 (Fall 1984), 21–27.

"As Twain develops the story of Jim's freedom in the last twelve chapters, he describes metaphorically the way black people were being 'freed' in the South at the time he was finishing the novel," exploited by whites who pursued ends of their own while pretending to work for the freedom of the blacks as Tom pretended to work for the freedom of Jim. Figuratively MT shows that George Wasington Cable and the black writers William Wells Brown and Paul Laurence Dunbar had shown directly: that the black people freed by law were in fact less than they had been as slaves. "Twain suggests that, like Jim, people in the post-Reconstruction South were losing a sense of selfhood, and often were forced to see themselves as inferior."

Nishimura, Masami. "Huckleberry Finn as a Character." *Kyushu American Literature*, No. 22 (May 1981), 82. [See Arikawa, 1981.]

"Huck is...more 'a son of society' than 'a child of nature,' and ignorance, not innocence, is his trademark." Although his heart is sound, his behavior is "utilitarian," and he "is temperamentally after what is 'free and easy and comfortable.'"

N[ock], S. A. "Editorial Comment." *College and University*, 33 (Winter 1958), 202-203.

A lengthy discussion of MT's portrayal of Negroes, and white attitudes toward them, in *HF*, which has just been removed from New York City schools: "Anyway, a whole big cityful of youngsters may no longer, it seems, discover for themselves the magnanimity of Jim, and may no longer see for themselves how magnanimity encourages gentleness and thoughtfulness in others. What is probably the most powerful defense of the Negro ever written is now banned."

———. "The Essential Farce." *Phylon Quarterly*, 20 (Winter 1959), 358-63.

Defends the ending of HF by arguing that the foolery at the Phelps Farm is a necessary cover for the use of Tom Sawyer as a *deus ex machina* who intercedes at a time when the existing arrangements for freeing Jim are doomed to ultimate failure. The farce, moreover, is artistically essential, and successful: "The farce is good farce. It is funny. There are those who consider it too long, but there are also those who do not. It brings the novel to a bright and cheerful conclusion: the grief and the nightmares are past, and the little boy is home."

O'Connor, William Van. "Why *Huckleberry Finn* Is Not the Great American Novel." *College English*, 17 (October 1955), 6-10.

"The critical acumen of Eliot and Trilling notwithstanding, there are a number of flaws in *Huckleberry Finn*, some of them attributable to Twain's refusal to respect the 'work of art' and others attributable to his imperfect sense of tone." Twain is hardly the "Lincoln of our literature" that Howells called him: "If Lincoln had written novels, he would, without doubt, have been a greater novelist than Twain. His virtues include Twain's and surpass them." Huck's appeal is through an immature sort of innocence, and thus of limited usefulness as a symbol; "If we refuse to over-value him as a symbol, we may be less inclined to over-value the novel, or to over-value the language in which it is written." Reprinted in Marks (1959).

__________ . [Letter to the Editor.] *College English*, 18 (November 1956), 108.

Stands firmly on the ground he took when he "tried to relate the Huck cult to our American desire to live in a state of innocence," and adds as a postscript: "I have discovered that criticizing Twain is apparently as irreverent and sacrilegious as criticizing Mother's Day." The letter is in answer to the strictures of Gilbert M. Rubenstein (1956) and Walter Blair (1956) and is followed by a letter by Lauriat Lane, Jr. in answer to Rubenstein, and concluding remarks by the editor concerning the flight down the river.

Oehlschlaeger, Fritz H. "Huck Finn and the Meaning of Shame." *Mark Twain Journal*, 20 (Summer 1981), 13-14.

Huck wrote in Chapter 28 of "them devils laying right there under [Mary Jane Wilks's] own roof, shaming her and robbing her." John R. Byers, Jr., has suggested the word "shaming" is misspelled and MT must have meant "shamming" (1973). Oehlschlaeger takes issue: "The idea of shame figures centrally in two of the most significant moments in Huck's moral awakening": Jim's reproachful "trash is what people is dat puts dirt on de head er dey fren's en makes 'em ashamed" (Chapter 15) and Mary Jane's caution to her sister that "you oughtn't to say a thing to another person that will make *them* feel ashamed" (Chapter 26).

Ohashi, Eizo. *The Adventures of Huckleberry Finn, with Introduction and Notes*. Tokyo: Kenkyusha, 1923.

This is the oldest and still one of the best editions of *HF* with notes for Japanese students. The author's introduction gives a brief bibliographic discussion and comments on MT's works. The 173 pages of notes include elaborate and minute explanations; there is also a 20-page glossary. [In Japanese; abstract by Sachiko Hayashi.]

Okamoto, Katsumi. "Tragedy of Mark Twain, the Man and Artist." *Geibun* (Kinki University), 3 (August 1962), 1-32.

On MT's seriousness, his deterministic philosophy, and his literary style, with particular attention to *HF* and Huck's development.

Olan, Levi A. "The Voice of the Lonesome: Alienation from Huck Finn to Holden Caulfield." *Southwest Review*, 48 (Spring 1963), 143-50.

Begins with the Brooks thesis, chiefly on the destructive influence of surroundings on MT, though warning that his "posing and childish self-adulation" and the probability that "the major part of his literary productivity is of a low grade" should not blind the reader to the merits of *HF*, in which "he responded to the human situation as a total being, an artist who apprehends by a mysterious talent and creates uninhibited by either logic or purpose," anticipating the theme of alienation in modern literature.

Opdahl, Keith M. "'You'll Be Sorry When I'm Dead': Child-Adult Relations in *Huck Finn*." *Modern Fiction Studies*, 25 (Winter 1979-1980), 613-14.

Justifies the recent turn toward psychological probing: *HF* "is dream-like...a dream from first to last" in events and characters. The relation of defenseless Huck to adults typically goes through three stages: fear, a discovery that "the adult proves not to be the enemy he'd seen"; and then (except for Jim) "the adults turn ugly indeed, becoming a real threat." At the center of *HF* is an "emotional nightmare": all the adult males are father-figures, and Huck is the suffering child, thrown off balance by each adventure. In turn he injures many adults, and "has a darker, unconscious side of which not even Twain was aware." In accepting Jim's humanity Huck surmounts not only racism but also a "deeply felt resentment toward fathers."

Oriard, Michael. "From *Tom Sawyer* to *Huckleberry Finn*: Toward Godly Play." *Studies in American Fiction*, 8 (Autumn 1980), 183-202.

"From *Tom Sawyer* to *The Mysterious Stranger* the moral vision of each of Twain's major novels is based somehow on ideas of legitimate and illegitimate games, of authentic and inauthentic playing. To write fiction, of course, is to 'play' with words and ideas, and some writers are more explicitly playful than others. Twain is not just one of these playful artists, but one who uses specific games and modes of playing in his novels to define character and even to express a basic vision of life." In *TS* and *HF*, MT "established the norms by which play can be judged in his other novels as well, and in so doing he created in Huck Finn the most fully autonomous and self-sustaining character in all his fiction, the genuine 'godly player.'"

Ornstein, Robert. "The Ending of *Huckleberry Finn*." *Modern Language Notes*, 74 (December 1959), 698-702.

Miss Watson's freeing of Jim in her will is not a sacrifice, but "perhaps the crowning act of selfishness and pious greed: the desire to make the best of all possible worlds." Tom's childish intervention can be explained in personal terms: he could free a slave, as MT could attack slavery, when it had become safe to do so.

Ostrom, Alan. "Huck Finn and the Modern Ethos." *Centennial Review*, 16 (Spring 1972), 162-79.

It is a misreading to see *HF* in terms of our day, as "a socially liberal/radical *Bildungsroman*": the novel's structure reveals a denial of the perfectability of man, and Huck, no Noble Savage, is merely "trying his best, a man of good will trapped in a world he never made."

Parr, Susan Resneck. "*Adventures of Huckleberry Finn (Tom Sawyer's Comrade)*, (1885), by Mark Twain." *The Moral of the Story: Literature, Values, and American Education*. New York, London: Teachers College Press [Columbia University], 1982. Pp. 39–52.

The volume concerns teaching ethical values and moral choice, with chapters on a number of authors including Hawthorne, Tolstoy, James, Conrad, Chopin, Kafka, Ralph Ellison, Toni Morrison, and others; typical chapter format includes a series of questions as a guide to reading, and discussion questions for class, papers, or exams. "Essentially, Huckleberry Finn explores the influence of social, political, and religious values on individual choice. In this regard, much of the novel's brilliance lies in Huck's continued innocence."

Passon, Richard H. "Twain and Eighteenth-Century Satire: The Ingénue Narrator in *Huckleberry Finn*." *Mark Twain Journal*, 21 (Fall 1983), 33-36.

Well-read in eighteenth-century satire, MT drew Huck on the models of Gulliver and the narrator of Goldsmith's *Citizen of the World*. An innocent narrator strengthens the irony because the reader does not take everything at face value, is an objective observer because he is an outsider, and achieves a twofold satire through the contrast of what he sees and his own simple, common sense. MT adds a further dimension in that Huck changes and matures.

*Past, Ray. "Huck's Luck," in Roberto Bravo-Villaroel, Robert J. Morris, Harley D. Oberhelman, and William T. Patterson, eds. *Homage to Faye LaVerne Bumpass*. Lubbock: Texas Tech University, Department of Classical and Romance Languages, and Latin American Area Studies Program, 1981. Pp. 61–67. [Not seen. Source: 1981 MLA Bibliography, No. 6379, with annotation: "On Spanish language translation by Amando Lázaro Ros."]

Patterson, Robert G. "Death on the Mississippi: Mark Twain's *Huckleberry Finn*." *Psychological Perspectives*, 7 (Spring 1976), 9-22.

Traces archetypal parallels, especially in Huck's faked death and Buck's real one. A number of authorities are cited on the significance of the use of an axe, killing of a pig (Demeter's sacrificial animal), putting the pig in water, sleeping in the canoe (a parallel to the cradle of Iacchus in the procession at Eleusis), and the spilling of grain. Huck's putting his own hair on the bloody axe is symbolic sacrifice, and here "three vital elements—the body of the initiate, the body of the sacrificial animal, and the instrument of fertility and rebirth—unite with an archetypal consistency which cannot be dismissed as mere coincidence." The literal death of Buck Grangerford in the river also follows archetypal patterns, here traced in less detail. Broadly, the life-death motif helps account for the wide appeal of *HF*, as well as providing thematic consistency and structural coherence. Even the apparent failure of Huck to mature is appropriate to "an Iacchus-figure, the 'eternal youth.'"

Paul, Angus. "Huck and Jim Begin Their Next 100 Years of Rafting Through the American Psyche." *The Chronicle of Higher Education*, 29 (13 February 1985), 5-6.

For a readership of academics, provides an overview of the current reputation of *HF*, controversies surrounding it in the past and today, and forthcoming editions. In the opinion of both Henry Nash Smith and Louis Budd, there has been too much scholarly attention paid to *HF*—obscuring the book itself and distracting attention from other important works such as *IA*, *CY*, and some of the shorter writings. In a box at the top of p. 6 Paul lists forthcoming events scheduled for 1985 honoring MT on the 150th anniversary of his birth, the 75th of his death, and the centennial of the American publication of *HF*.

Pauly, Thomas H. "Directed Readings: The Contents Tables in *Huckleberry Finn*." *Proof*, 3 (1973), 63-68.

Critical discussions of *HF* have often quoted and been influenced by one of two tables of contents; they are presumably the work of Charles L. Webster and Albert Bigelow Paine, but in any event not by MT.

Pearce, Roy Harvey. "'The End. Yours Truly, Huck Finn': Postscript." *Modern Language Quarterly*, 24 (September 1963), 253-56.

The territory for which Huck was going to "light out" was Indian Territory (now Oklahoma); although he sought to escape civilization, he would be only "one step ahead of the rest: boomers, dukes and dauphins, Aunt Sallies, Colonel Sherburns, and Wilkses—civilizers all." Reprinted in Bradley (1977).

————. "Huck Finn in His History." *Études Anglaises*, 24 (Juillet-Septembre 1971), 283-91.

Hawthorne's Hester Prynne and Melville's Ishmael will ultimately come to terms with their society, but Huck by his nature cannot: "His function, it turns out, is to demonstrate the absolute incompatability of the sort of self he is and the sort of world in which he tries so hard to live. He gains no sense of his own history and has no future.... He exists not to judge his world but to furnish us the means of judging it—and also our own world as it develops out of his."

Pearson, E[dmund] L[ester]. "The Children's Librarian versus Huckleberry Finn: A Brief for the Defense." *Library Journal*, 32 (July 1907), 312-14.

"Extreme Respectability" in the children's departments of public libraries is excluding *TS* and *HF*, which Pearson defends for honest portrayal: "Not Henty's wooden heroes, nor golden-curled, lace-collared Fauntleroys; but real boys." Reprinted in *The Library and the Librarian*. Woodstock, VT: Elm Tree Press, 1910. Pp. 26-32.

Pease, Ralph. "Huckleberry Finn Talks about what Mr. Twain Did to His Story." *Mark Twain Journal*, 21 (Spring 1983), 48-49.

Written in a voice resembling Huck's, repeats what "this college fellow...Mr. Pease" explained about the story as amplified by MT from what Huck had told him. MT shifted the emphasis to show that people are selfish, wish to be superior to others, and "like killing too much." Moreover, MT attacked the social patterns of the time, and demonstrated the falsity of values held by respectable society.

Peck, Richard E. "A Mark Twain 'Literary Offense.'" *Mark Twain Journal*, 14 (Winter 1968), 7-9.

In *HF*, MT commits literary offences of which he accused Fenimore Cooper, particularly in violation of rules on the relevancy of incidents to the development of the plot, and on the use of language appropriate to the characters.

Pederson, Lee A. "Negro Speech in *The Adventures of Huckleberry Finn*." *Mark Twain Journal*, 13 (Winter 1965-1966), 1-4.

An expanded version of a paper read to the American Dialect Society at the 1964 meeting of the Modern Language Association, this "preliminary report on a projected study of all the literary dialects in the novel" is a "brief account...limited to phonology," revealing close correspondence between the speech in *HF* and that still in use.

Perry, Thomas Sergeant. "Mark Twain." *Century*, 30 (May 1885), 171-72.

A review of *HF*. The use of Huck as narrator lends unity and truthfulness; the ending seems contrived. Perry applies terms of humor to questions now taken differently, as in Huck's "mixed feelings about rescuing Jim, the negro, from slavery. His perverted views about the unholiness of his actions are most instructive and amusing." Reprinted in Lettis (1962), Anderson (1971), Gerber (1971), and Bradley (1977).

Piacentino, Edward J. "The Significance of Pap's Drunken Diatribe against the Government in *Huckleberry Finn*." *Mark Twain Journal*, 19 (Summer 1976), 19-21.

No mere digression, the passage introduces the ironic method MT used throughout *HF*, "establishes as a recurring motif the pattern of hypocritical behavior exhibited in the actions of many of the characters Huck encounters," and "initiates Huck's as well as the reader's education into the inhuman, pretentious ways of antebellum southern white society."

__________. "The Ubiquitous Tom Sawyer: Another View of the Conclusion of *Huckleberry Finn*." *Cimarron Review*, 37 (October 1979), 34-43.

"The concluding section of *Huckleberry Finn*...as I have attempted to demonstrate, was presumably used by Mark Twain not only to restore the initial tone of romantic levity, which he had deviated from in the middle section, but also to affirm his preference for the state of childhood innocence. In veering from his original purpose, as expressed in the prefatory notice at the outset of the novel, Twain, in the satirical middle section, encountered the problem of how to make the events work out so that his comical purpose would not be obscured." The burlesque ending is his clumsy way of doing so.

Pinsker, Sanford. "Huckleberry Finn, Modernist Poet." *Midwest Quarterly*, 24 (Spring 1983), 261-73.

Huck is briefly compared to Emmeline Grangerford and James Joyce's Stephen Daedalus, but the topic is Huck's dark, honest vision in a "death-haunted novel" in which "he is simultaneously, a realist and a mystic." The romancing Tom Sawyer will "prevail," and carrying "much of the baggage of his adolescence into adulthood,...find that it is a very marketable commodity." This is a familiar side of MT, but "his fascination with Huck Finn whispered darker truths about the world modernists would learn to call 'alienating.'" For Huck himself there is a brief respite when he takes on the identity of Tom Sawyer in the final chapters, "because parental figures will love him...and because rehearsed responses replace that lonely clarity that had been his fate as Huck Finn."

__________. "The Urban Tall Tale: Frontier Humor in a Contemporary Key." Sarah Blacher Cohen, ed., *Comic Relief: Humor in Contemporary American Culture*. Urbana: Univ. of Illinois Press, 1978. Pp. 249-62.

On MT, pp. 251-55: in *HF* "'lies' turn inexplicably into dark truths." "Ironically...at the point when Huck seems to have learned what mythic journeys of initiation would teach, Twain introduces a highly disturbing snapper. In this sense, the episode at the circus is emblematic of those larger vacillations between illusion and reality which characterize life on the Phelps plantation. Good cheer—rather than grim recognition—is the note on which Jim is sadistically 'rescued' and the novel itself is resolved."

Piper, Henry Dan. "Fitzgerald, Mark Twain and Thomas Hardy." *Fitzgerald Newsletter*, No. 8 (Winter 1960), 1-2.

Fitzgerald admired MT, and called the Paine biography "excellent." A member of the International Mark Twain Society, he sent a note to the 1935 banquet: "*Huckleberry Finn* took the first journey *back*. He was the first to look *back* at the republic from the perspective of the West. His eyes were the first eyes that ever looked at us objectively that were not eyes from overseas." (Hardy is not mentioned in connection with MT; in a letter he expressed admiration for Fitzgerald.) Fitzgerald's tribute is reprinted in Simpson (1968).

Pizer, Donald. "Late Nineteenth-Century Realism: An Essay in Definition." *Nineteenth-Century Fiction*, 16 (December 1961), 263-69.

The realism discussed is diverse in subject matter and "ethically idealistic. Three texts will illustrate my thesis: Howells' *The Rise of Silas Lapham* (1885), Twain's *Adventures of Huckleberry Finn* (1884), and James's *What*

Maisie Knew (1897)." In the first two books "the social world is the embodiment of evil," and the latter two "juxtapose a child and an evil world.... The three writers...dramatize a vision of experience in which individuals achieve that which is still a goal for mankind at large."

__________. *Realism and Naturalism in Nineteenth-Century American Literature.* Carbondale and Edwardsville: Southern Illinois University Press; London and Amsterdam: Feffer & Simons, Inc., 1966.

Uses *HF*, *The Rise of Silas Lapham*, and *What Maisie Knew* to illustrate his thesis that late nineteenth-century American realism does not always stress the representative, and it is subjective and ethically idealistic (pp. 3-10); briefly comments on statements by Leo Marx on the destruction of the raft in *HF* as illustrating MT's hostility toward the coming of the machine, and W. F. Taylor on MT's stated approval of the machine.

Plessner, Monika. "Huckleberry Finns wirkliches Ende." *Frankfurter Hefte*, 24 (1969), 441-46.

[Source: *MLA Bibliography* (1969), No. 6486.]

Podhoretz, Norman. "The Literary Adventures of Huck Finn." *New York Times Book Review*, (6 December 1959), 5, 34.

Seventy-five years after the publication of *HF*, surveys its reputation among critics and argues that MT "was asserting through the image of life on the raft that the State of Nature is a reality, and he was asserting through the character of Huck that the distinction between the individual and society is a true distinction and a necessary one."

Poirier, Richard. "*Huckleberry Finn*: Attitudes toward Tricks and Adventure." *Exercise Exchange* (Holt, Rinehart and Winston), 10 (November 1962), 23-24.

A series of questions for college freshmen, first for reading Chapters 1-16 and 32 through "Chapter the Last," and then writing an essay of no more than four pages on the significance of the attitudes of Tom, Huck, and MT.

__________. "Mark Twain, Jane Austen, and the Imagination of Society." Reuben A. Brower and Richard Poirier, eds., *In Defense of Reading: A Reader's Approach to Literary Criticism*. New York: E. P. Dutton, 1963. Pp. 282-309.

Criticisms of Jane Austen by Emerson, Henry James, and MT "reveal a significantly American dissatisfaction with the novel of manners." MT's fantasy of *PW* and *MS* moves "toward a saturnalia of repudiation," but *HF*, "more complicated than anything in James before *The Bostonians*," has MT's "affection for a character whose longings are a curious and inseparable blend of Isabel Archer's dream of 'freedom' with some of Mark Twain's own nostalgic desire for community."

__________. "Transatlantic Configurations: Mark Twain and Jane Austen." *A World Elsewhere: The Place of Style in American Literature*. New York: Oxford University Press, pp. 144-207; also passim on MT.

"An enlarged and considerably revised version of an essay first printed in *In Defense of Reading*." Pp. 183-95. Reprinted, abridged as "Huck Finn and the Metaphors of Society," in Simpson (1968).

Poli, Bernard. "Mark Twain's Gods and Tormentors: the Treasure, the River, the Nigger and the Twain Brother," in Marcus Cunliffe, ed., *American Literature to 1900*. London: Barrie & Jenkins (in association with Sphere Books Ltd.) *History of Literature in the English Language*, 8 (1973). Pp. 334-53.

Emphasizes a central pattern of duality and ambivalences which "will now make us aware of innumerable binary systems on which Mark Twain bases his variations when he spins out the thread of his stories: characters presented in pairs who reveal two sides of the author's personality such as Sid/Tom, Tom/Huck, Huck/Jim... landscapes described in contrasted terms: mountain/water—river/shore—island/cave; and details of literary compositions in which the author unwittingly betrays his method and perhaps also the secret topography of his psyche." Thus, MT could dream of riches, but also portray the dream as the way to destruction, he could see the non-white races symbolically as the noble Negro and the cruel Indian, and he depicted a river of Edenic tranquility and exploding steamboats. The essay as a whole is characterized by a neatness and ingenuity which some may find provocative and others excessive. For example, Poli finds in "The £1,000,000 Bank-Note" and "The Esquimau Maiden's Romance" [both written in 1893] opposing views by MT of his marriage to a wealthy woman, and Poli calls it " a remarkable 'coincidence'" that the friend MT nursed in *RI* (thereby failing to develop his mining claim, and losing it) was Captain John Nye—and Olivia Clemens' friend Emma Nye came to visit, fell ill, and died.

Power, William. "Huck Finn's Father." *University of Kansas City Review*, 28 (Winter 1961), 83-94.

"Mark Twain minimizes, even conceals, the force of Huck's animus against his father," who "is responsible for Huck's moral development"; "Huck's strength, finally, is Finn's."

Pritchett, V. S. "Books in General." *New Statesman and Nation*, 113 (2 August 1941), 113. Reprinted as "The American Puritan" in his *In My Good Books*, pp. 175-82.

A review briefly discussing *PW* but chiefly on *HF*: "although it is one of the funniest books in all literature and really astonishing in the variety of its farce and character, we are more moved than we are amused by it" because "the particular character of American nostalgia is that it is not only harking back to something lost in the past, but suggests also the tragedy of a lost future." Reprinted, slightly abridged, as "*Huckleberry Finn* and the Cruelty of American Humor" in Bradley (1962), and as "Cruelty in *The Adventures of Huckleberry Finn*' in Lettis (1962).

Quirk, Tom. "The Legend of Noah and the Voyage of Huckleberry Finn." *Mark Twain Journal*, 21 (Summer 1982), 21-22.

In Chapter 9 Huck and Jim on the island move to a cave up the hill on

Jim's insistence because he can tell from "the birds that deliver a message" that it will rain. The island floods and the stranded animals become tame, Huck and Jim go through the floating house, and Jim covers the naked corpse of Huck's drunkard father as Shem had covered the nakedness of the drunken Noah. This last incident, which led to Noah's cursing of Ham and his descendents, had been often cited as a theological defense of slavery, but "it is Jim, a slave, who demonstrates his humanity, even moral superiority, by performing the act of Shem."

Raban, Jonathan. *Mark Twain: "Huckleberry Finn."* London: Edward Arnold, 1968. Studies in English Literature No. 36.

One of a series of studies intended for "the advanced sixth-former and the university student." The study concludes: "*Huckleberry Finn* is a masterpiece of equivocation: its humour suddenly switches into tragic realism; its two languages, vernacular and rhetoric, are perpetually opposed; its characters, so important for brief periods, fade into the passing blur of the crowd. It tells two truths, and they will not be reconciled" (pp. 59-60).

Raffel, Burton. "Mark Twain's View of *Huckleberry Finn*." *Ball State University Forum*, 24 (Summer 1983), 28–37.

MT began *HF* with no clear plan, and the appearance of Pap Finn was a narrative opportunity which he seized and developed. The progress of *HF* is largely improvisational, but the greater part of it succeeds because to MT "it was in important ways—not exclusively, but importantly—a book about a nexus of issues wound round in human slavery and freedom, in social hypocrisy and religious pretension. It is in those issues, particularly as centered in Jim as a runaway slave, that the book finds itself, finds its narrative way, and rolls through episode after episode that likewise revolve around these same issues." The improvisation breaks down in the final chapters, as is illustrated in the inconsistency toward the end of Ch. 35 where Tom, though aware Jim has been freed by Miss Watson's will, tells Huck they can't spend as much time digging Jim out as he would like because when Uncle Silas learns Jim is not from New Orleans "his next move will be to advertise Jim, or something like that."

Rampersad, Arnold. "*Adventures of Huckleberry Finn* and Afro-American Literature." *Mark Twain Journal*, 22 (Fall 1984), 47–52.

Rampersad takes as his point of departure Hemingway's dictum that "all modern American literature comes from" *HF* and asks whether this holds true for the work of black writers; considering this question may add to our understanding of their work, as well as of *HF*. "And, although it is not my concern here at all, the attempt may also cast some light on the ongoing controversy about the suitability of the book for use by young black readers." Relating *HF* to the work of 32 black American writers, Rampersad finds differences in the use of dialect, entrusting the narration to an unsophisticated child, the depiction of slavery, the male bonding and "twinning" of a black character and a white one, the relation of Nature to humanity, and "the propriety of comedy in a fiction about race." *HF* "clearly anticipated eventual trends in black fiction, even if, for much of black literary history, its example went largely ignored. Moreover, "whatever the limitations in his depiction of Jim (and they are considerable), Mark Twain made it clear that Jim was good, deeply human, loving, and anxious for freedom. It is a reflection on American culture that such an approach should be historic." MT "went further than any black writer of the nineteenth century," with the possible exception of Martin R. Delany, in ridiculing white claims to a superior civilization. Most importantly, *HF* anticipates later black fiction in showing the moral dilemma in American society, and Huck's alienation; perhaps the major compromise in *HF* is not the clumsy ending, but MT's failure to "suggest that Jim can catch Huck's dangerous virus." MT "flinched before the potentially dangerous confrontation of these two major aspects of his work—its democratic folk and racial features, and its depiction of the alienation and moral disorder endemic to Southern and even American culture"; the two elements would come together in the work of William Faulkner and Richard Wright.

Rao, B. Ramachandra. "Structural Devices in *The Adventures of Huckleberry Finn*." *Banasthali Patrika*, 14 (1970), 23-29.

[Source: *MLA Bibliography* (1971), No. 8001.]

Rao, Chitra. "Mark Twain. *Huckleberry Finn:* Alienation and the Search for Identity." *ALPH* (Jaipur: University of Rajasthan, Department of English) (1968-1969), 1-4.

A sound but conventional critical discussion. Contains no bibliography or notes.

Reardon, John D. " 'Shakespearean Revival!!! ': Satire of American Elizabethans." *Mark Twain Journal*, 21 (Fall 1983), 36–38.

The Duke's soliloquy (*HF*, Ch. 21) parodies "the rip and rave acting technique which characterized the American theatre" of the early nineteenth century. Common borrowings from Shakespeare included "plot elements, scene devices and a host of slant plagiarisms as well as actual duplications of poetry.'

Reilly, Charlie. "An Interview with John Barth." *Contemporary Literature*, 22 (Winter 1981), 1-23.

On p. 23: "There are images in fiction that haunt my imagination, so much so that I even keep a little list of them. Foremost of them are: Odysseus trying to get home; Scheherazade telling her stories; Don Quixote riding with Sancho across LaMancha; and Huckleberry Finn floating down that river. I would love one day, without aspiring to include myself in that biggest of leagues, to come up with a similar image, one that was as much larger than the book in which it appeared as those images are larger than those stories in which they appear. I love language, and I really believe that Huck's language, Huck's voice, is as much a substance in that novel as the image of Huck and Jim drifting down the Mississippi."

Reinfield, George. "Huckleberry Finn, Candidate for Greatness." *Mark Twain Journal*, 10 (Fall-Winter 1979), 12-14

The book is a great novel, which reveals "the barefaced duplicity of fortune tellers," the cowardice of lynch mobs, and "the growth of character of Huck and Jim as they entrust each other with their freedom and form a fast friendship"; in the portrayal of the King and Duke "royalty comes in for a sound thrashing."

Remes, Carol. "The Heart of Huckleberry Finn." *Masses & Mainstream,* 8 (November 1955), 8-16.

A popular account, not obtrusively Marxist, in a Marxist journal. "One does not think of Huck as a boy. He seems to be the embodiment of the conscience of a decent humanity confronted with the evils in society and wanting to right them."

Rexroth, Kenneth. "Classics Revisited—XLVI: *Huckleberry Finn.*" *Saturday Review,* 50 (13 May 1967), 14-15.

An anti-Odyssey: "It would have been quite impossible for Mark Twain not to have had Homer constantly in mind, as he must also have had *Robinson Crusoe,* the travels of Peter and Paul, *Pilgrim's Progress,* and dozens of others, not the least Marco Polo. He carefully contradicts them all." The raft carries Huck and Jim "through a universe of moral chaos," but in the controversial ending "the social lie wins again against the brotherhood of man." Reprinted in *Classics Revisited*. New York: Avon Books, 1969. Pp. 280-85.

Reyes, Pedro A., Jr. "A Difference of Grammar." *Diliman Review* (University of the Philippines, Quezon City), 9 (Jananuary 1961), 117-23.

Comparing *HF* with Joyce's *A Portrait of the Artist as a Young Man,* finds "the statement of revolt in different grammars," with Huck's "WE" contrasted to Stephen's inward-turning "I".

Ridland, J. M. "Huck, Pip, and Plot." *Nineteenth-Century Fiction,* 20 (December 1965), 286-90.

Huck struggles with his conscience, and his decision to help Jim parallels that of Pip in *Great Expectations* to help the escaped convict Magwitch; Pip has learned morality from a "tall and bony" older sister comparable to Miss Watson, and in each book there is a collision with a steamboat on a river.

Roberts, Bette B. "Huck Finn and Ed Gentry: The River Revisited." *Iowa English Bulletin,* 30 (Fall 1980), 14,16.

On pedagogical questions: "Considered together, Mark Twain's *Huckleberry Finn* and James Dickey's *Deliverance* provide a strong base for the comparison and contrast of ideas and style which can lead to significant perception of literature.... Understanding these books may indeed be synonomous with understanding almost a hundred years of social history."

Roberts, Thomas. "*Huckleberry Finn:* Understanding Comic Devices." *Exercise Exchange* (Holt, Rinehart and Winston, Inc.), 10 (November 1962), 22-23.

A freshman exercise: as preparation for reading *HF* students are asked to rewrite Josh Billings' "Essa on the Muel" once to correct comic misspellings and a second time to remove dialectal forms and vocabulary errors, then write an essay on the comic appeal of "Essa on the Muel."

Robinson, E. Arthur. "The Two 'Voices' in *Huckleberry Finn*." *Modern Language Notes*, 75 (March 1960), 204-08.

The authorial intrusion in *HF* is not limited to Chapters 21-22 (discussed by Robert Hunting, 1958). Rather, "not infrequently, Huck seems oblivious of implications which are clear to the reader," as in the passage where Jim talks of stealing his wife and children out of slavery: "the thoughts are Huckleberry Finn's but the significance is Mark Twain's." As Huck matures, he becomes more able to carry the irony himself.

Robinson, Forrest G. "The Silences in *Huckleberry Finn*." *Nineteenth-Century Fiction*, 37 (June 1982), 50-74.

Often in MT's fiction and even in his autobiographical writings, thoughts of death can grow out of reverie and stillness; those thoughts can be comforting, and the ghosts evoked, companionable, as when MT's thoughts in the empty Hartford house turn back to Susan, Livy, George and Henry Robinson, and Charles Dudley Warner. In *CY*, *JA*, and "The Chronicle of Young Satan," in the silences a character may grow lonely, weary of life, perhaps imagining ghosts. So, too, in *HF*: Huck becomes lonely in the solitudes, and "*Huckleberry Finn* is not a very happy book. This is so because Huck is not a very happy person."

Rodnon, Stewart. "*The Adventures of Huckleberry Finn* and *Invisible Man:* Thematic and Structural Comparisons." *Negro American Literature Forum*, 4 (July 1970), 45-51.

There are similarities in "the journey concept, the education motif, and the essential theme," as well as something deeper than "a satiric examination of...American society" and a "basic-goodness-of-the-heart theme." "The novels are stylistically alike in at least four areas: language, folklore, humor, and narrator point-of-view." In *Shadow and Act* (1964), Ellison has commented on Jim's role as a symbol of humanity for Huck, whose decision to help him escape represents MT's acceptance of a personal responsibility.

Rollins, Ronald G. "Huckleberry Finn and Christie Mahon: *The Playboy of the Western World*." *Mark Twain Journal*, 13 (Summer 1966), 16-19.

MT's novel and Synge's play show parallels in that the fathers are "cruel, arbitrary and despotic tyrants," and when Huck and Christy escape "both flights are similar in that they involve fake or symbolic murders," after which the boys hide their true identities or personalities and later are reborn to new maturity.

Rose, Alan Henry. *Demonic Vision: Racial Fantasy and Southern Fiction*. Hamden, CT: Archon Books (Shoe String Press), 1976.

Includes "*Tom Sawyer*: The Making of a Safe World" (pp. 72-85) and

"'A Prisoner of Style': The Uses of Art in *Huckleberry Finn* and *Pudd'nhead Wilson*" (pp. 86-100); also passim on MT (indexed). These chapters, and the book as a whole, emphasize the mingled scorn and fear in portrayal of the Negro (and Indian) as fool and as devil; they are heavily indebted to the familiar scholarship, quotations from which constitute a significant portion of the text of this slim book.

Rose, Danis. "More on Huck Finn." *A Wake Newsletter*, 17 (April 1980), 19–20.

An extension of previous work by Rose on Joyce's use of *HF* in *Finnegans Wake*.

Rosenberg, Jerome H. "Cultural Symbolism in *Robbery Under Arms*." *World Literature Written in English*, 17 (November 1978), 488–504.

On the 1888 novel by Australian popular novelist, Rolf Boldrewood (pseud. for Thomas Alexander Browne). Despite comparisons of the outlaws' hideout in the Terrible Hollow to the river in *HF* as a retreat, and parallels of "death and rebirth symbolically depicted," the frequent references to *HF* here are only used to illuminate the Australian novel and there is no attempt to demonstrate that *HF* was an influence.

Royot, Daniel. "Éléments Phonologiques du Dialect Noir dans Huckleberry Finn.'" *Languages Modernes*, 66:1 (1972), 79-83.

This examination of Negro dialect in *Huckleberry Finn* consists chiefly of three lists: "Graphonologie: Système Vocalique" (on the pronunciation of specific phonemes); "Phonétique et Morphologie" (on the structure of words, as in the adding or dropping of sounds); "Valeur de la Transcription" (notes that Jim's speech is a synthesis of "Low Colloquial," "Southern Speech," and Negro dialect).

Rubenstein, Gilbert M. "The Moral Structure of *Huckleberry Finn*." *College English*, 18 (November 1956), 72-76.

Lauriat Lane, Jr. and William Van O'Connor (in the October, 1955 *College English)* obscure or deny the greatness of the book; Lane extends the moral realism "into fantastic patterns of allegory and symbolism" and O'Connor "commits the graver fault of misreading the realities of the book entirely." What the book is actually about is "nothing that the ordinary reader—not given to supersubtle speculations and distortions, but possessed only of common sense and a responsive ear—would fail to understand and appreciate": clear, direct insight, and "the humorous but sharp exposure of human failings on the one hand and the warm faith in human goodness and equality on the other." Reprinted in Bradley (1962).

Rubin, Louis D., Jr. "Mark Twain Tonight." *The Teller in the Tale*. Seattle and London: University of Washington Press, 1967. Pp. 52-82. Also see "Concerning Cide Hamete Benengeli and Others," pp. 17-21 on *HF*.

The book is concerned with the authorial presence in the novel. Rubin notes different uses of MT's presence when Huck decided to risk his soul for Jim and later on, at Phelps Farm (pp. 17-21), and takes up the matter at greater length in "Mark Twain Tonight" (which is not a review of Hal Holbrook's stage impersonation of MT).

__________. "Mark Twain's South: Tom and Huck" in Louis D. Rubin, Jr., ed., *The American South: Portrait of a Culture.* Baton Rouge: Louisiana State University Press, 1980. Pp. 190-205.

Although Tom and Huck are instantly recognizable as mythic figures of an idyllic South, the adult MT understood the fakery, the violence, the injustice of slavery; *TS* has a strength missing from other boys' books because it recognizes the underlying dread. But Tom, like the cub-pilot of *Old Times on The Mississippi,* was too close to the established society to criticize it: "Rather, Huck represents the views and sensibilities of the *adult* Mark Twain. His role in *Huckleberry Finn* is to search out the moral dimensions of the community of Sam Clemens' rearing." MT's questioning "is why he was, as Allen Tate has said, the first modern Southern writer. His was the first important literary inner duel with his own memory and conscience...."

__________. "Southern Local Color and the Black Man." *Southern Review,* n.s. 6 (October 1970), 1011-30; on *HF*, 1026-30.

Huck provides a voice, and Jim a basis for evaluating "the moral worth of the town and the countryside along the river." MT may not have recognized the importance of his theme of Jim's yearning for freedom; Ralph Ellison has argued that Jim's character could be more fully rounded, though he is a triumph of characterization and understanding, a symbol of humanity.

Rulon, Curt M. "Geographical Limitation of the Dialect Areas in *The Adventures of Huckleberry Finn.*" *Mark Twain Journal,* 14 (Winter 1967-1968), 9-12.

Internal evidence suggests that "the Phelps farm is probably located well south of Memphis rather than above Memphis as Stowell would have it but still in southern Arkansas rather than in northern Louisana as Marx maintains." "What is important for the linguistic geographer is that the general location is in the proximity of the Mississippi River below Cairo, Illinois, which point is the heel of an overturned boot configuration delimiting known contemporary dialect areas: Midland and Southern, respectively."

Sage, Howard. "An Interview with Ralph Ellison: Visible Man." *Pulp,* 2 (Summer 1976), 12, 10-11.

In a general discussion of American authors and the American experience, and the search for a national literature, notes the central position of the race problem as a moral concern, the literary importance of oral lore as seen in MT, and the significance in *HF* of "Afro-American speech, superstition, humanity." Like other American writers of the nineteenth century, MT was non-academic, and he knew both the black and white oral traditions and folklore of the Mississippi River and elsewhere, and used what he could of the available traditions and conventions. There is a concern for a national voice in the novel, and "how to get a particular ethnic accent on the page. Even Mark Twain manages to caricature the speech of Jim in the book, not because he meant to do so, but because the tradition, the convention out of which he worked, was that of the minstrel show and Afro-American speech was considered implicitly funny in those days."

Samuels, Thomas Charles. "Mr. Trilling, Mr. Warren, and *An American Tragedy*." *Yale Review*, 53 (Summer 1964).

Pp. 637-39 concern Leo Marx and the debate over *HF*: "Since he had demonstrated that the ending is a cruel travesty of the book's human, unillusioned attack on hypocrisy and discrimination, Marx neatly proves that Trilling and Eliot had stressed form and ignored morality. He then shrewdly speculates that so egregious a blunder in critics so eminent could only result from an indifference to the book's moral point."

Sapper, Neil G. "'I Been There Before': Huck Finn as Tocquevillian Individual." *Mississippi Quarterly*, 24 (Winter 1970), 35-45.

Tocqueville used the terms of individualism and conformity to denote prevalent American qualities. Huck had a strong sense of the community of the raft, but he rejected the civilization on shore and thereby "demonstrated finally and conclusively that he was a Tocquevillian individual. Perhaps he was the only one that we have had."

Sattelmeyer, Robert, and J. Donald Crowley, eds. *One Hundred Years of Huckleberry Finn: The Boy, His Book, and American Culture*. Columbia: University of Missouri Press, 1985.

The following essays are included: Millicent Bell, "*Huckleberry Finn* and the Sleights of the Imagination"; Stanley Brodwin, "Mark Twain in the Pulpit: The Theological Comedy of *Huckleberry Finn*"; Louis J. Budd, "A Nobler Roman Aspect of *Adventures of Huckleberry Finn*"; George C. Carrington, Jr., "Farce and *Huckleberry Finn*"; James M. Cox, "A Hard Book to Take"; Victor Doyno, "*Adventures of Huckleberry Finn*: The Growth from Manuscript to Novel"; Allison R. Ensor, "The Illustrating of *Huckleberry Finn*: A Centennial Perspective"; John C. Gerber, "The Continuing *Adventures of Huckleberry Finn*"; Stephen Gilman, "*Adventures of Huckleberry Finn*: Experience of Samuel Clemens"; Jan M. Gordon, "Fan-Tods 'wid' de Samurai: *Huckleberry Finn* in Japan"; Alan Gribben, "I Did Wish Tom Sawyer Was There: Boy-Book Elements in *Tom Sawyer* and *Huckleberry Finn*"; Hamlin Hill, "*Huck Finn*'s Humor Today"; William E. Lenz, "Confidence and Convention in *Huckleberry Finn*"; Jay Martin, "The Genie in the Bottle: *Huckleberry Finn* in Mark Twain's Life"; Fritz Oehlschlaeger, "Gwyne to Git Hung: The Conclusion of *Huckleberry Finn*"; Roy Harvey Pearce, "Yours Truly, Huck Finn"; Tom Quirk, "Life Imitating Art: *Huckleberry Finn* and Twain's Autobiographical Writings"; Robert Regan, "Huck Finn in the Wake of the *Quaker City*"; Robert Sattelmeyer, "Interesting but Tough: *Huckleberry Finn* and the Problem of Tradition"; David R. Sewell, "We Aren't All Trying to Talk Alike: Varieties of Language in *Huckleberry Finn*"; Robert Shulman, "Fathers, Brothers and the Diseased: The Family, Individualism, and American Society in *Huck Finn*"; Eric Solomon, "My *Huckleberry Finn*: Thirty Years in the Classroom with Huck and Jim"; Jeffrey Steinbrink, "Who Wrote *Huckleberry Finn*? Mark Twain's Control of the Early Manuscript"; Paul Taylor, "*Huckleberry Finn*: The Education of a Young Capitalist"; Nancy Walker, "Reformers and Young Maidens: Women and Virtue in the *Adventures of Huckleberry Finn.*"

Sawey, Orlan. "The Consistency of the Character of Nigger Jim in *Huckleberry Finn.*" *TAIUS: Texas A & I University Studies,* 4 (September 1971), 35-41.

Argues that "Jim is shown, not as an inconsistently portayed type, but as a real person reacting consistently to his varying environments."

Scanlon, Lawrence E. "'They're After Us' Again." *Mark Twain Journal,* 13 (Summer 1966) 20-21.

In "Mr. Eliot, Mr. Trilling, and *Huckleberry Finn,*" Leo Marx puts undue stress on Huck's words to Jim; in fact he is as much a fugitive as Jim is, but has not yet come to identify his own flight with Jim's.

———. "Unheroic Huck," *East-West Review* (Doshisha University, Kyoto, Japan), 2 (Winter 1965), 99-114.

Huck is a passive character, "happiest when allowing himself to drift with the river," and the freedom he wishes "is the freedom to do nothing." In *TS* and *HF* the womb images of hogshead, canoe, cave, and wigwam represent not a rebirth, but rather a death wish.

Schacht, Paul. "The Lonesomeness of *Huckleberry Finn.*" *American Literature,* 53 (May 1981), 189-201.

Following Huck's own meanings without projecting outside implications on his words reveals "that 'lonesomeness' has less to do with society or neurosis than with Nature; that it has a significant though perhaps recondite relation to a play by Shakespeare; and that it can help us to a new understanding of another important word in *Huckleberry Finn:* 'freedom.'" Sometimes, "lonesome" denotes "not a state of mind but a quality of Nature" for Huck, who is hardly alone while on the raft with Jim. Nature can be benign, or, as in *King Lear,* terrible; but its very fury can be beautiful, as Huck recognizes. And, as in *Lear,* true freedom comes in love and companionship.

Schieck, William J. "The Spunk of a Rabbit: An Allusion in *Huckleberry Finn.*" *Mark Twain Journal,* 15 (Summer 1971), 14-16.

Shortly before saving Jim from the slave-hunters, Huck wrote, he couldn't speak up because he lacked courage, "the spunk of a rabbit"; but he drove them away by pleading with them to come on the raft to help his father, ill with small-pox. Asking for the opposite of what he wants repeats a device in *Uncle Remus, His Songs and Sayings* (1880), where Brer Rabbit begs Brer Fox not to throw him in the briar patch.

Schmitz, Neil. "On American Humor." *Partisan Review,* 47:4 (1980), 559-77.

"What occurs in nineteenth-century American humor as it variously imagines [the] illiterate, [the] *other* who stands on the periphery of writing, is a gradual crystallization of the humorous style into a single metaphor, Huckspeech, an antimetaphorical metaphor that is turned against metaphorical thinking, against the complicated thought that makes treaties, bills of indenture, and literature." Schmitz variously considers Philip Roth, Gertrude Stein, and 19th-century humorists, but apart from contrasting the values of Tom and Huck, and using the term "Huckspeech" throughout, says relatively little about MT.

__________. *Of Huck and Alice*. Minneapolis: University of Minnesota Press, 1983.

Passim on MT and on *TS*, *LOM*, and other works, and, especially, *HF* (indexed). Ranging from Jacksonian dialect humor to the present, Schmitz takes *HF* and the development of "Huckspeech" as a turning point. The "Alice" of the title is Gertrude Stein's companion, Alice B. Toklas; she and Huck allow Stein and MT to escape the confines of conventional writing, and like the cartoon figure Krazy Kat (who also appears here *passim*), satirize cruel authority. Apart from the treatment of language, Schmitz comments usefully on themes and situations in MT (as in giving a fresh view of the interdependence of Huck and Jim). His exploration of humor in American literature treats an array of authors as diverse as George Washington Harris, Ralph Ellison, Ishmael Reed, and David Ross Locke ("Petroleum V. Nasby").

__________. "The Paradox of Liberation in *Huckleberry Finn*," *Texas Studies in Literature and Language*, 13 (Spring 1971), 125-36.

"The freedom Huck strives to attain is his right to be a child, not an impertinent manikin like Tom Sawyer, but the unregenerate poetic child alive in his body and sensitive to the mystery of being in the world." For Jim, however, the question is one of his manly independence, and he shows his recognition of a slave's position in his attack on Solomon's proposal to divide the child—he has seen "black families dismembered on the [auction] block." The ending throws away the character Jim "after he has served as a 'moral burden.'" The emancipations of Huck and Jim were different and conflicting in nature.

__________. "Twain, *Huckleberry Finn*, and the Reconstruction." *American Studies* (Kansas; formerly *Midcontinent American Studies Journal)*, 12 (Spring 1971), 59-67.

"Jim's situation at the end of *Huckleberry Finn* reflects that of the Negro in the Reconstruction, free at last and thoroughly impotent, the object of devious schemes and a hapless victim of constant brutality."

Schönemann, Friedrich. "'Mark Twains' 'Huckleberry Finn' (Zum 70. Geburtstag, 1885-1955)." *Archiv für das Studium der neueren Sprachen*, 192 (1956), 273-89.

Discusses the book's realism, structure, and portrayal of character; the secondary sources cited are chiefly book-length general studies of MT. [In German.]

Schonhorn, Manuel. "Mark Twain's Jim: Solomon on the Mississippi." *Mark Twain Journal*, 14 (Winter 1968-1969), 9-11.

Defending the portrayal of Jim in Chapter 14 against the contention of Daniel Hoffman (1951, p. 321) and Chadwick Hansen (1963), that he is shown as a minstrel-show comic, argues that in the passage discussing Solomon's wisdom Jim and Huck are taking the roles previously given to Huck and the romantic Tom Sawyer; subsequently, when the lost raft is found by the Grangerford slaves, Jim amicably settles the question of its ownership with an ease and grace that contrast with the bloody feud over a trifling lawsuit thirty years in the past.

Schubert, Karl. "Mark Twain: *Adventures of Huckleberry Finn*." Edgar Lohner, ed., *Der amerikanische Roman im 19. und 20. Jahrhundert*. Berlin: Erich Schmidt Verlag, 1974. Pp. 70-91.

A general discussion for readers who must be provided the necessary background in American literature; draws on other MT works and the more important *HF* scholarship, stressing the importance of language, Huck's role as narrator, and the importance of his character (innocent, unsophisticated, humorless, and compassionate). [In German.]

Schultz, Lucille M. "Parlor Talk in Mark Twain: The Grangerford Parlor and the House Beautiful." *Mark Twain Journal*, 19 (Summer 1979), 14-19.

MT's descriptions of a pretentious house in a river town in Chapter 33 of *LOM* and of the Grangerford parlor in Chapter 17 of *HF* reveal "the sham and sentimentality of the Sir Walter Scott South," and are parallel in many details; but Huck's naive admiration makes the latter more successful in its humor.

Schwartz, Edward. "Huckleberry Finn: The Inward Thoughts of a Generation." *Mark Twain Quarterly*, 9 (Winter 1952), 11-16, 23-24.

A general critical article, conventionally documented, on *Huckleberry Finn* as "a concrete expression of the life and values of the people of the Mississippi Valley of pre-Civil War days," and the frontier and institutional moralities.

Scott, Arthur L. "The *Century Magazine* Edits *Huckleberry Finn*, 1884-1885." *American Literature*, 27 (November 1955), 356-62.

Describes alterations made in the interest of genteel taste by Richard Watson Gilder in publishing more than a quarter of the novel in the *Century*.

Sears, Robert R. "Episodic and Content Analysis of Mark Twain's Novels: A Longitudinal Study of Separation Anxiety." Joseph P. Strelka, ed., *Yearbook of Comparative Critizism, 7: Literary Criticism and Psychology*. University Park and London: Pennsylvania State University Press, 1976. Pp. 198-206.

In collaboration with Deborah Lapidus and Christine Cozens, Sears divided nine of MT's novels written in the period 1868-1900 into episodes constituting discrete units, each with thematic unity. In *GA* (MT's share), *TS, HF, PW, P&P, JA, CY, Hadleyburg, Captain Stormfield's Visit to Heaven*, and *The Chronicle of Young Satan* there are 599 such episodes, in eighteen sets. Because MT was a premature infant and because of his early childhood life and the nature of his marriage he "had a high potential for responding with anxiety to the threat of the loss of love," and he "was a highly apprehensive man who responded to the birth of his children as significant threats to his relationship with his wife." The theme of "loss of love" appears most strongly in episodes written at the three peak points: in 1874 (in the three months surrounding the birth of his second daughter); in the winter of 1879-1880 (when it became evident that Mrs. Clemens was "unexpectedly and unwantedly pregnant again"), and during the tragic period 1897-1900, when MT was writing *The Chronicle of Young Satan*. According to the notes, Sears and Lapidus described their method in "Episodic Analysis of Novels" (1973); "a more detailed report of these findings is being prepared in collaboration with Deborah Lapidus, who participated in development of the episodic and content analysis of the novels, and Christine Cozzens, who helped in the elaboration of the system to permit its use for scoring Mark Twain's letters."

__________, and Deborah Lapidus. "Episodic Analysis of Novels." *Journal of Psychology*, 85 (1973), 267-76.

Among the novels analyzed are *Captain Stormfield's Visit to Heaven, TS, HF, CY, PW, MS, IA*, and *P&P*. Episodes are used as a basis for investigation of the growth of MT's personality.

Seelye, John. "The Craft of Laughter: Abominable Showmanship and *Huckleberry Finn*." *Thalia: Studies in Literary Humor*, 4 (Spring/Summer 1981), 19–25.

The conclusion "recommends itself to us precisely because it *is* bad ... like the greatest of literary problems, Hamlet's hesitation, it is essential to an understanding of art as entertainment." Resenting his position as popular entertainer, MT played a practical joke on the reader. Deceptions and trickery pervade *HF*, and in the end we learn that Jim has been free for weeks, Pap dead, the flight down the river unnecessary; Huck of course would have known all this as he began his narration.

__________. "'De Ole True Huck': An Introduction." *Tri-Quarterly*, 16 (Autumn 1969), 5–19.

The introduction and the final chapters of Seelye's *The True Adventures of Huckleberry Finn*. In the introduction Seelye summarizes objections to MT's *HF* by librarians, pressure groups, and critics; his version will retell the story as the "crickits" would have it.

__________. *The True Adventures of Huckleberry Finn*. Evanston, Illinois: Northwestern University Press, 1970.

A rewriting of *HF* to give the critics a version that answers their objections.

Seib, Kenneth. "Moses and the Bulrushers: A Note on *Huckleberry Finn*." *Mark Twain Journal*, 18 (Summer 1977), 13-14.

In Chapter 1 the story of Moses (which "would have appealed to the Widow Douglas because of its sentimentality") foreshadows later events in HF and represents a success story and themes of birth and death, slavery and freedom. Buck's conundrum in Chapter 17 about where Moses was when the candle went out is not gratuitous: Huck, too, is "in the dark," and this and the succeeding chapters are the "darkest" in the book.

Shaw, Patrick W. "Huck's Children: The Contemporary American Picaro." *Mark Twain Journal*, 21 (Fall 1983), 42-43.

Examines Salinger's *The Catcher in the Rye*, Ellison's *Invisible Man*, Bellow's *The Adventures of Augie March*, Kerouac's *On the Road*, Donleavy's *Ginger Man*, and Purdy's *Malcolm* as literary offspring of *HF*. Unlike the heroes of these works, Huck resembles such ancestors as Tom Jones and Roderick Random in that he is an outcast from his society rather than a rebel, and acts from a sense of "right" rather than social consciousness.

Shear, Walter. "Games People Play in *Huckleberry Finn*." *Midwest Quarterly*, 20 (Summer 1979), 378-93.

A behavioral approach: "*Huckleberry Finn* demonstrates how games allow role-players to display their command of social situations to one another. The accent they put on supposedly civilized or superior values, however, invariably reveals the inadequacies of their purely personal performances.... As master improvisator, on the other hand, Huck is the ideal player."

Shockley, Martin Staples. "The Structure of *Huckleberry Finn*." *South-Central Bulletin*, 20 (Winter 1960), 3-10.

"I propose that *Huckleberry Finn* is thematically coherent and structurally unified. I propose a logical, ordered, five-part structure, with introduction, rising action, climax, falling action, conclusion. I propose proportion and balance among these parts, achieving a total aesthetic harmony." Thus, the Phelps farm chapters, though unsatisfactory as a conclusion, may be interpreted as falling action; the true conclusion is the brief "Chapter the Last: Nothing More to Write," in which Huck, having repudiated the civilization he has seen, "is ready to live by innate morality, a free man."

Shukla, Sheo Bhushan. "The Quest for a Better Civilization: A Study of *Huckleberry Finn*." *The Uttar Pradesh Studies in English* (The Official Organ of the Uttar Pradesh Association for English Studies), 2 (1982), 77-83.

"In the Romantic tradition of Wordsworth and Shelley, to which Mark Twain is considered to be an heir, the antithesis of civilization is nature and noble 'savage.' Mark Twain admires nature and believes in the healing instincts of an individual." However, nature is not always benign, and MT "does not believe in the noble savagery of man." "A man born in civilization cannot be free from it by running away from it. He must struggle with it to overcome it. Huck Finn does struggle with it and is able to overcome it." Furthermore, it is the civilization of the South that MT attacks: "It is a well-known fact that he admired the civilization of the North, its efficiency and speed, its progressivism and egalitarianism. At the same time he was shrewd enough to see that it lacked that creative vitality which he could discern in 'the boy-life out on the Mississippi' and which alone is the abiding principle of genuine growth and evolution." He would like to see a superior civilization based on "'sound heart' or instinctive love for one's fellow human beings," freedom and integrity. "The whole novel is a quest for a new kind of civilization in artistic terms."

Sidgwick, Arthur, and Eleanor Mildred Sidgwick. *Henry Sidgwick: A Memoir by A.S. and E.M.S.* London and New York: Macmillan, 1906.

Quotes the Cambridge professor's journal (29 March 1885), praising *HF*: "Huck Finn is a kind of boyish, semi-savage Gil Blas, of low—the lowest—Transatlantic life, living by his wits on the Mississippi. The novelty of the scene heightens the romantic *imprévu* of his adventures: and the comic *imprévu* of his reflections is—about once every three times—irresistably laughable" (p. 406).

Sidnell, M. J. "Huck Finn and Jim: Their Abortive Freedom Ride." *Cambridge Quarterly*, 2 (Summer 1976), 203-11.

MT was more perceptive than his critics who view the ending of *HF* as flawed: "Life on the raft has offered a beautiful vision of what might be the relationship of negro and white, but the vision is not, and cannot be, a representation of America as it really is." Huck "must return to the trivially vicious world of Tom Sawyer's America," at the end "utterly changed not in itself but in our perception of it."

Simonson, Harold R. "*Huckleberry Finn* as Tragedy." *Yale Review*, 59 (Summer 1970), 532-48; reprinted (revised) in *The Closed Frontier: Studies in American Literary Tragedy*. New York: Holt, Rinehart and Winston. Pp. 57-76.

The concluding section is "a dramatic travesty of this rebirth, of Huck's becoming Tom. The tragedy rests in the irony that only as Tom can Huck survive" (p. 60).

Simpson, Claude M., Jr. "Huck Finn after *Huck Finn*." O. M. Brack, Jr., ed., *American Humor / Essays Presented to John C. Gerber*. Scottsdale, AZ: Arete Publications, 1977. Pp. 59-72.

On the published and unpublished sequels to *HF*. Although MT "never ceased to see the value of Huck as an outsider and foil, he was primarily concerned with Huck's narrative voice rather than the full range of the youth's personality. By not creating opportunities for Huck to continue to reveal himself in all his narrative depths, Twain misjudged the essence of his greatest book and sacrificed opportunities he may never have been aware of."

Sioui, Tak. "*Huckleberry Finn*": *More Molecules*. N.p.: privately printed, 1962. [Copyright by John Hakac.]

Attributes the mutilation of the illustration on p. 283 of the first edition of *Huckleberry Finn* to E. W. Kemble, the illustrator. Two states of the offending engraving are reproduced, with the portrayal of Uncle Silas (saying, "Who do you reckon it is?") made more clearly indecent after a first alteration which could have been considered accidental. [The engraving plate was scratched to put an erect penis on the figure of Uncle Silas.] It is also argued that the illustration on p. 290 ("A Pretty Long Blessing") is also indecent: "If one is hesitant about deciding on the artist's intention, he should try blotting out the false leg-line in the table cloth with a finger in order to simplify the view" (p. 25). *MLA Bibliography* (1964) No. 6286, gives place of publication as Tucson, Arizona.

Skerry, Philip J. "*The Adventures of Huckleberry Finn* and *Intruder in the Dust*: Two Conflicting Myths of the American Experience." *Ball State University Forum*, 13 (Winter 1972), 4-13.

Compares MT's and Faulkner's novels on "the basic narrative level, the psychological level, the sociological level, and the symbolic level," with opposing interpretations of the American experience and the American hero.

Slater, Joseph. "Music at Colonel Grangerford's: A Footnote to *Huckleberry Finn*." *American Literature*, 21 (March 1949), 108-11.

Huck's reference in Chapter 17 to the piano "that had tin pans in it" is not comic exaggeration: there were such pianos at the time. "When the Last Link Is Broken" and "The Battle of Prague" would have been appropriate selections to play.

Sloane, David E. E. *Mark Twain as a Literary Comedian*. Baton Rouge: Louisiana State University Press, 1979.

MT's humor reflects an egalitarian vision sharing less with the undemocratic outlook of the southwestern local colorists than with that of the literary comedians of the 1850s and the Civil War years, many of them northern. "Literary comedy does provide a sense of the origin of his ethics and the centrality of his jokes in developing his ethical viewpoints"; the tradition appears in "the vulgar pose, ironic showmanship, pragmatic valuing of the individual over bureaucracy," and it illuminates MT's "vision of corporate society as essentially corrupt." Sloan argues the influence of northeastern humorists (devoting a chapter to Artemus Ward), and traces humor, social criticism, and literary comedy through *GA*, *P&P*, *HF*, *CY*, *AC*, and *PW*.

Smith, David L. "Huck, Jim, and American Racial Discourse." *Mark Twain Journal*, 22 (Fall 1984), 4–12.

The notion of "race" as delimiting behavior and capacities is an instrument of repression, and one which MT attacks in *HF*. "The book takes special note of ways in which racism impinges upon the lives of Afro-Americans, even when they are legally 'free.' It is therefore ironic that *Huckleberry Finn* has been attacked and even censored as a racist work. I would argue, on the contrary, that except for Melville's work *Huckleberry Finn* is without peers among major Euro-American novels for its explicitly anti-racist stance." In subverting "race," MT "focuses on a number of commonplaces associated with 'the Negro,' and then he systematically dramatizes their inadequacy. He uses the term 'nigger,' and he shows Jim engaging in superstitious behavior [often to his own advantage]. Yet he portrays Jim as a compassionate, shrewd, thoughtful, self-sacrificing and even wise man.... Jim, in short, exhibits all the qualities that 'the Negro' supposedly lacks." Attention to the pervasive use of the word "nigger" reveals "not just a trigger to outrage, but more importantly, a means of understanding the precise nature of American racism and Mark Twain's attack on it"; nowhere does he use it in *HF* as though it were a part of Jim's proper name.

Smith, Henry Nash. "Mark Twain, *The Adventures of Huckleberry Finn*." Wallace Stegner, ed., *The American Novel from James Fenimore Cooper to William Faulkner*. New York and London: Basic Books, 1965. Pp. 61-72.

"Huck's habit of moral improvisation, his antinominian attitude toward established authorities and institutions, his tolerance of a wide disparity between theory and practice" stem from what MT called his "sound heart and a deformed conscience." The book's structure reveals basic American attitudes, from near farce at the start to a growing richness in the quest for freedom, and then a "tragic realization that freedom cannot be attained in this or any world," and MT apparently "taking refuge from tragedy in a joke."

__________. *Mark Twain: The Development of a Writer*. Cambridge, MA: The Belknap Press of Harvard University Press, 1962.

"This book considers first the problems of style and structure Mark Twain faced at the outset of his career, and then traces his handling of these problems in nine of his principal works [*TS, HF, CY, IA, LOM, Hadleyburg, MS, PW, RI*]. Since questions of technique necessarily involve questions of meaning, I have dealt also with his ethical ideas. The inquiry leads ultimately to the consideration of how his writing reveals a conflict between the dominant culture of his day and an emergent attitude associated with the vernacular language of the native American humorists." The concluding chapter previously appeared in *Massachusetts Review* (1962). The chapter titled "A Sound Heart and a Deformed Conscience" is reprinted, more or less completely, in Smith (1963), Simpson (1968), Gerber (1971), Kesterson (1973), and Bradley (1977).

__________. "Mark Twain's Image of Hannibal: From St. Petersburg to Eseldorf." *Texas Studies in English*, 37 (1958), 3-23.

"Villagers of 1840-3," part of MT's memories which Smith collectively terms the "Matter of Hannibal," "embraced the glory of boyhood but it also embraced the terror and the guilt." From the idyllic portrayal of the small town in *TS* there is a decline in the image through *HF, CY, PW* and other works. "Mark Twain came nearer registering in fiction the death of nineteenth-century culture than did such contemporaries as Howells...or James." Unable from the 1890s to ignore his insights into the corruption of democracy by money and into war as a natural human condition, he was also unable to embody them successfully into his work. Nonetheless, "as we have slowly become aware, the development of twentieth-century American literature, its dominant themes and above all its language, began on the day in 1876 when Mark Twain conceived the idea of treating the Matter of Hannibal from the viewpoint of the outcast, Huckleberry Finn." Reprinted in Bradley (1962) and Cardwell (1963).

__________. "The Publication of Huckleberry Finn: A Centennial Retrospect." *Bulletin of the American Academy of Arts and Sciences*, 37 (February 1984), 18–40.

On the relation of *HF* to American society when it was published in 1885, drawing heavily on Fischer's "Huck Finn Reviewed" in the Spring, 1983 *ALR* (which see in above checklist): "I shall use contemporary critical reactions to the book as a point of departure for an inquiry into the intellectual and cultural ambience within which Mark Twain worked." *HF* was initially not well received for a variety of reasons, including the low regard in which popular humorists and books published by subscription were held, MT's lawsuit against the booksellers Estes & Lauriat for offering *HF* for sale below the subscription price, the banning of *HF* by the Concord Public Library, and the haphazard way in which review copies had been sent out. Nonetheless, there were many favorable responses to *HF*, although the lack of applicable critical theory made them somewhat unfocused, and there was little recognition of the importance of the language and narrative art of *HF*. Local-color writing had a mixed reputation at the time, and dialect was often the means of emphasizing class distinctions before Huck's speech appeared as an instrument of irony and assault on the prevailing high culture. Thomas Sergeant Perry is here discussed at length (pp. 35–37) for his insight, virtually unique at the time (in Smith's words), "that no character or event can be described without viewing it from some perspective or other (not only physical, but also moral and intellectual)." Henry James shared this insight, but lacked the breadth of taste to distinguish between MT and the ordinary humorists and local colorists. *HF* helped end "the decadent Romanticism" of the time and made the pleasure and energy of vernacular language available for a later age.

Snyder, John. "James's Girl Huck: What Maisie Knew." *American Literary Realism*, 11 (Spring 1978), 109-23.

On p. 109, briefly compares Maisie and Huck as narrators: although Maisie is sensitive as Huck is not, they share a "freedom to expand beyond the confines of convention, to create on their own new values which are as humane and lovely as the older generation's are selfish and crude."

Solomon, Andrew. "Jim and Huck: Magnificent Misfits." *Mark Twain Journal*, 16 (Winter 1972), 17-24.

Despite the damage done to the ending by MT's amateurishness, *HF* is "a brilliantly warm and comic portrait of two human beings, one white and one black, who fall outside of and above their society."

Solomon, Eric. "*Huckleberry Finn Once More.*" *College English*, 22 (December 1960), 172-78.

Both critics and defenders of the thematic unity of *HF* assume that MT's intention "was either to show Huck's growth to maturity, to hail the joys of freedom on the river, or to depict the escape from civilization and slavery." Judged under this assumption, the ending is a failure; but the book may also be viewed in terms of the major theme of a search for security, as exemplified by Huck's invention of various family patterns for himself. Reprinted in Bradley (1962); in Lettis (1962).

Solomon, Jack. "Huckleberry Finn and the Tradition of the *Odyssey*." *South Atlantic Bulletin*, 33 (March 1968), 11-13.

In the debated ending of *HF*, Tom's and Huck's use of disguises is in the tradition of the homecoming of Odysseus; there are other parallels, among them the journey, Huck's imprisonment in the hut, the destruction of the raft, and even—in Huck's faking his own death and later hiding gold in a coffin—a sort of descent into a world of the dead.

Sommers, Jeffrey. "'I Never Knowed How Clothes Could Change a Body Before': The Dual Function of Clothing in *Huckleberry Finn*." *Mark Twain Journal*, 20 (Summer 1981), 19-21.

"In the novel clothing functions in two important ways as a narrative device, both symbolizing the constriction of 'sivilization' and functioning ironically in the constant tension between appearance and reality."

Spacks, Barry B. "The Thematic Function of the 'Rescue' in *Huckleberry Finn*. *Mark Twain Journal*, 11 (Summer 1959), 8-9.

Unlike Odysseus, Huck is alienated, fleeing from home. The ending represents a seduction back to "Tom's frame of reference, into the culture of Miss Watson and Aunt Sally," but despite the fraud "Huck emerges from it still resisting the false gods of sentiment and complacency."

Spengemann, William C. *Mark Twain and the Backwoods Angel: The Matter of Innocence in the Works of Samuel L. Clemens*. Kent, OH: Kent State University Press, 1966.

"As Clemens presents it, the myth of American innocence entails three distinguishable but obviously related problems": "the moral drama" of the innocent hero confronting evil; "the conflict between agrarian and urban, industrial values"; and an examination of the reliability of MT's faith "by putting it to the imaginative test of setting, character, and action.... This tension between faith and fact engenders the conflict which makes his best work more than a mere reflection of popular sentiment and raises *Huckleberry Finn* to the level of prophecy" (pp. xi-xii).

Spilka, Mark. "Victorian Keys to the Early Hemingway: Part II—*Fauntleroy* and *Finn*." *Journal of Modern Literature*, 10 (June 1983), 289-310. ["Part I—*John Halifax, Gentleman*" in the March issue does not concern MT.]

Emphasis is on the shaping of Hemingway in his childhood, and only incidentally on the novels by MT and Frances Hodgson Burnett. However, Spilka notes provocatively that *HF* "gives full and serious attention to distinctly adult interests and to that extent belongs in a class with *War and Peace*," and so, in a modest way, does the slighter *Little Lord Fauntleroy*. There are overlapping affirmations—Mrs. Burnett's paragon is strong, fearless, tender—but MT's and Hemingway's heroes characteristically are most tender and manly away from women. Spilka convincingly argues both the strength and courage of Mrs. Burnett in her own life and the merits of the genteel tradition against which MT and Hemingway rebelled.

Stallman, R. W. "Huck Finn Again." *College English*, 18 (May 1957), 425-26.

"Everything in the novel goes by pairs. Doubleness is the dominant leitmotif, notably in the two Hucks," torn between conscience and conformity. "The structure of *Huckleberry Finn*, as I see it, consists of a recurrent counterpointing of the real or true event with the juxtaposed parody of it. Nothing is not parodied." The journey southward on the raft, masking the true intention to go northward, is "justifiable both at the literal and the thematic level.... Everything in the novel goes masked, even Moses in the bulrushes; that's what saved him." The article is followed by: "Note: This letter ends the discussion of *Huckleberry Finn* begun by Professor O'Connor's attack two years ago.—*Ed*." Reprinted as "Reality and Parody in *Huckleberry Finn*," in Bradley (1962).

Stanek, Lou Willett. "Huck Finn: 100 Years of Durn Fool Problems." *School Library Journal*, 31 (February 1985), 19–22.

For a general audience, describes Huck's troubles, beginning in 1885 when *HF* was new and banned by the Concord Public Library as "trash and suitable only for the slums"; in our own time *HF* has been criticized as racist. But others have criticized the critics in turn as prissy and insensitive to the book's power, and have defended the message of *HF* as strongly anti-racist.

Starke, Catherine Juanita. *Black Portraiture in American Fiction / Stock Characters, Archetypes, and Individuals*. New York and London: Basic Books, 1971.

On *HF*, pp. 175-180: "Mark Twain is an early, major novelist to give qualities of an individual to a Negro in our literature; because he gives him characteristics of a submissive slave and end-man comedian also, Jim's is a transitional image of a Negro as an individual." A trend had been established by 1884, when *HF* appeared in England, and "since then, other, more fully realized images of slaves who are also individuals have appeared in literature."

Stein, Allen F. "Return to Phelps Farm: *Huckleberry Finn* and the Old Southwestern Framing Device." *Mississippi Quarterly*, 24 (Spring 1971), 111-16.

"The events at Phelps Farm combine with the opening of the novel at St. Petersburg to enclose the account of the trip down the river in a frame which works in much the same way as did the framing device traditionally used by writers in this school of humor," but MT "subtly adds to the functions of the frame, thus enhancing the effectiveness of the novel."

Stein, Jean. "The Art of Fiction XIII: William Faulkner." *Paris Review*, 12 (Spring 1956), 28-52.

An interview: "This conversation took place in New York City, midwinter, early 1956." On Sherwood Anderson, p. 46: "He was the father of my generation of American writers and the tradition of American writing which our successors will carry on.... Dreiser is his older brother and Mark Twain the father of them both." On favorite characters in literature (p. 47): "Huck Finn, of course, and Jim. Tom Sawyer I never liked much—an awful prig."

Stein, Regina, and Robert Lidston. "The Mother Figure in Twain's Mississippi Novels." *Mark Twain Journal*, 21 (Spring, 1983), 57-58.

Takes MT's mother, Jane Clemens (as described by Albert Bigelow Paine and MT) as a model: she is prematurely old, outspoken, sometimes severe, but big-hearted. This model is applied with similar results to Aunt Polly in *TS*, to Roxy in *PW*, and to Mrs. Loftus, Mrs. Grangerford, and Aunt Sally Phelps in *HF*.

Stein, Ruth. "The ABC's of Counterfeit Classics: Adapted, Bowdlerized, and Condensed." *English Journal*, 55 (December 1966), 1160-63. Also, condensed as "Counterfeit Classics." *Education Digest*, 32 (April 1967), 39-41.

Uses school editions of *HF* as an example of the disservice done the reader when vocabulary is altered to fit word lists, passages are trimmed or toned down, and episodes are removed. "Transmission of our cultural heritage is accomplished partially through the teaching of the classics. Those that survive have an intrinsic merit of their own. It should not be snuffed out of existence by precautionary or hygienic measures....it is a foolish waste of money, time, and effort to settle for any of the inferior revisions."

Sten, Christopher. "'When the Candle Went Out': The Nighttime World of Huck Finn." *Studies in American Fiction*, 9 (Spring 1981), 47-64.

"The nocturnal and diurnal phases of the setting...merit examination, particularly the former, for it is vital to the book's prevailing mood of comic apprehension and provides a key to Mark Twain's view of its chief moral, social and psychological themes." The dark is important in four ways: as a cover for flight; for the Gothic and mock-Gothic moods of the story; for MT's sociology and metaphysics of evil; and, in conjunction with the daylight, to convey the Manicheanism, the ambivalence, of MT's mind.

Stephens, George D. "*Huckleberry Finn* as a Journey." *Mark Twain Journal*, 13 (Summer 1966), 11-15.

MT himself was an inveterate traveler and "at one time or another Twain read LeSage, Rabelais, Fielding, and Smollett. *Don Quixote* was an early and lasting favorite. He read and admired the work of Dickens." *HF* follows some of the traditions of the picaresque novel in the journal and adventures, and in the use of an anti-hero as the central character.

Stevenson, E. Burleson. "Mark Twain's Attitude toward the Negro." *The Quarterly Review of Higher Education Among Negroes*, 13 (October 1945), 326-64.

Argues that MT's attitude toward the Negro was "affectionate and friendly," as exemplified in *TS, HF, GA, PW*, and *LOM*. His attitude was sometimes mistaken, and MT failed to take "what might seem to us the manly stand on issues pertaining to the Negro. It is, however, an attitude that can be followed in building up strong racial ties." Documentation is from familiar sources and this article will be most useful on the introductory level.

Stewart, Randall. "Dreiser and the Naturalistic Heresy." *Virginia Quarterly Review*, 34 (Winter 1958), 100-116.

On *HF*: despite *What Is Man?* MT does not belong among the naturalists, "if for no other reason than the fact that Huck Finn is one of the most responsible of fictional mortals." Reprinted in *American Literature & Christian Doctrine* (1958), 120-21.

Stoehr, Taylor. "Tone and Voice." *College English*, 30 (November 1968), 150-61.

On pp. 157-61, "Sam Clemens and Mark Twain: Finding a Voice," discusses his gradual development of a persona, most successfully in *HF*.

Stone, Albert E., Jr. *The Innocent Eye: Childhood in Mark Twain's Imagination*. New Haven: Yale University Press, 1961.

[Source: 1970 reprinting "in an unaltered and unabridged edition," Hamden, Connecticut: Archon Books.] Placing MT in a context of the developing interest in childhood as a theme after the Civil War reveals his fascination with immaturity. Treats the portrayal of childhood in *TS*, *HF*, *JA*, and other works, distinguishing in the discussion of *CY* between the kind of innocence that is laudable and the kind that is merely a limitation. Pp. 153-58, dealing with *HF*, reprinted in Bradley (1962).

Stowell, Robert F. "Notes on Geography in *Huckleberry Finn*." *Mark Twain Journal*, 13 (Summer 1967), front and back covers.

Stowell's map on the front cover shows Huck and Jim's route, with state boundaries and approximate distances.

Strickland, Carol Colclough. "Emmeline Grangerford, Mark Twain's Folk Artist." *Bulletin of the New York Public Library*, 79 (Winter 1976), 225-233.

The mourning pictures described in Chapter XVII of HF belong to a well-established genre of "family mortuary grounds," four examples of which are here reproduced. Of the pictures by Emmeline Grangerford, the first "description is so thoroughly accurate in its details that it would appear either that Mark Twain was thoroughly familiar with the conventional elements of the mourning picture genre or that he was actually describing a particular mourning picture.... All the stock elements are there: the weeping willow, tombstone, and pensive mourner leaning on the monument." MT then burlesques the genre with Huck's descriptions of a young lady with a dead bird and one weeping over a letter.

———. "Of Love and Loneliness, Society and Self in *Huckleberry Finn*." *Mark Twain Journal*, 21 (Fall 1983), 50-52.

Nowhere at home, Huck finds respect and affection on the raft with Jim, but at a price: he must assume false roles when he goes ashore, and the raft itself will be invaded by the King and the Duke. In the end he rejects the security offered by the Phelpses.

Strong, William F. "Mark Twain's Oral Version of *Huckleberry Finn* and Its Effect on His Career as a Professional Oral Interpreter." *Texas Speech Communication Journal*, 7 (1982), 37–41.

Devotes relatively little space to *HF*. During his 1884–1885 lecture tour with G.W. Cable, MT found that simply reading from the pages of *HF* was less effective with audiences than was a different sort of performance he learned to give in which he reworked his material, dropping parts more appropriate to the printed page and changing emphasis (Strong notes that distances were increased in the lecture versions of his writing). MT developed an appearance of spontaneity through memorizing his material, cultivating the seemingly artless pause, and pretending his actual lecture was a digression from prepared texts. Strong draws usefully on Paul Fatout's and Fred Lorch's studies of MT's lecturing, MT's own comments on oral delivery, and on unpublished recollections of MT's secretary, Isabel Van Kleek Lyon.

Sühnel, Rudolph. "*Huckleberry Finn*," Karl Brunner, ed. *Anglo-Americana: Festschrift zum 70. Geburtstag von Professor Dr. Leo Hibler. Wiener Beiträge zur Englischen Philologie*, 62 (1955), 150–56.

HF is still insufficiently appreciated as a major work for adult readers. It was banned in many libraries in the nineteenth century as a bad moral influence, and the lesson took too well: even today there is no full translation on the market for the cultured German reader. But MT is a moralist (who does not moralize), and he has given Huck a fine sensibility, alert intelligence, and an intact inner scale of values, as a means of social comedy; moreover, *HF* is a comedy of manners. [In German.]

Sweets, Henry A. "*Huck Finn* at the Movies." *The Fence Painter* (Hannibal, MO), 4 (Late Fall 1984), 3.

Very briefly describes six American and two foreign film adaptations, the earliest in 1920.

________. "Publishing *Huckleberry Finn*." *Ibid*., p. 4.

A brief account based on the books by Walter Blair and Merle Johnson.

________. "Writing *Huckleberry Finn*." A very brief popular account of the writing and early reception.

Sykes, Robert H. "A Source for Mark Twain's Feud." *West Virginia History*, 28 (April 1967), 191-98.

The Shepherdson-Grangerford feud in *HF* is probably not based on a Darnell-Watson feud (described in *LOM* but not mentioned elsewhere); however, there are "ten significant points of similarity" to the actual feud of the Hatfields and McCoys.

Talbott, Linda Hood. "Huck Finn: Mark Twain at Midstream." *Nassau Review*, 1 (Spring 1969), 44-60.

HF was the work of MT in mid-career, between his early comedy and later disillusionment; this article focuses on "the developing characterization of Huck as a means of examining the struggle which Twain saw between the individual and society."

Tanaka, Teruo. "Huck Finn as Narrator." *Kyushu American Literature*, No. 24 (1983), 72–75. One of a series of "Synopses of the Reports of the Annual Seminar 1982. General Subject: First-Person Narrators in American Literature."

Relating *HF* to MT's "Private History of the 'Jumping Frog' Story" and "How to Tell a Story," Tanaka concludes: "What makes *Huck Finn* so great and memorable and what is missing in *Tom Sawyer* is not only the first-person narrator, but a successful use of one narrator, the boy Huck, with his rich and natural idiom, and his sustained point of view. Mark Twain's control in this respect must be regarded as marvelous, and it is certainly responsible for making the book a great one, a triumph."

Tanner, Tony. "The Literary Children of James and Clemens." *Nineteenth-Century Fiction*, 16 (December 1961), 205-18.

MT used a boy, a first-person vernacular narrator, whose own bewilderment produced moral clarity, but James used girls as protagonists, maintained his omniscience and ironic detachment, and "worked out a literary style...as far removed from the vernacular as possible"; there is "an increasing moral ambiguity in his work." James found innocence endearing, but to be outgrown, while MT "saw no dividend in the exchange of innocence for maturity."

————. "Mark Twain." *The Reign of Wonder: Naivety and Reality in American Literature*. Cambridge, England: Cambridge University Press, 1965. Pp. 97-183.

Beginning with the Simon Suggs and Sut Lovingood perspective, Tanner examines "the way in which the vernacular supplanted the official rhetoric in Clemens's writing," then turns to "examine some of the details of this important stylistic shift" (p. 127). In MT's inversion of oratory and of the pastoral situation, "the low uneducated figure is in fact wiser than the educated tourist, and he speaks more tellingly." His early works show him looking for appropriate speakers (p. 129). He found such a speaker in Huck Finn, and "The young vernacular rebel is alone with his wonder, his candour, and his sound heart" (p. 154); he stands in contrast to Tom Sawyer, who accepts the rules and outlook of society (Chapter 10, passim). "The Pond of Youth" is reprinted in Schmitter (1974).

Tarkington, Booth. "Introduction." *The Adventures of Huckleberry Finn*. New York: The Limited Editions Club, 1933. Pp. 5–11.

A chatty, appreciative discussion; in passing raps the Freudian critics (not mentioning Van Wyck Brooks by name) who consider MT a pessimist. Tarkington praises "Mr. Albert Begelow Paine's superb biography."

Tate, Allen. "Faulkner's *Sanctuary* and the Southern Myth." *Virginia Quarterly Review*, 44 (Summer 1968), 418-27.

[Apparently this was the introduction to an edition of *Sanctuary*.] Links *HF* with Augustus Baldwin Longstreet's *Georgia Scenes* as "a second crucial novel"; *HF* is "the first Southern novel in which the action is generated inside the characters. It is not perhaps the masterpiece that the academic Mark Twain 'industry' has made it out to be; yet for the reason I have indicated, it is a work of great originality and historical importance. These two works are the beginning of modern Southern literature; they are also important for American literature as a whole."

__________. "A Southern Mode of the Imagination." *Essays of Four Decades*. Chicago: Swallow Press, 1968. Pp. 577-92.

On *HF*, pp. 591-92, calling it "the first modern novel by a Southerner," with the mode of progression no longer that of rhetoric but with the action "generated inside the characters... Mark Twain seems not to have been wholly conscious of what he had done; for he never did it again." He was "a forerunner who set an example which was not necessarily an influence"; "the shift from the rhetorical mode to the dialectical mode had to be rediscovered by the twentieth-century novelists of the South." (The date "1959" appears at the end, but there is no indication of where this was previously published.)

Tatham, Campbell. "'Dismal and Lonesome': A New Look at *Huckleberry Finn*." *Modern Fiction Studies*, 14 (Spring 1968), 47-55.

"The Huck Finn who takes part in the events at the Phelps farm is a logical projection of the Huck Finn who at three crucial moments based his actions on his pathological fear of loneliness and his personal need for acceptance and comfort. The book ends where it began because that is what the book is all about. Twain simply did not have the confidence in man's ability to effect a moral progression to pose Huck as a conventional hero"; this reflects the outlook MT expressed in *What Is Man?*

Taylor, Nancy Dew. "The River of Faulkner and Mark Twain." *Mississippi Quarterly*, 16 (Fall 1963), 191-99.

Parallels in character suggest that Faulkner had *HF* in mind as he wrote *The Old Man*, and his tall convict may be "a composite of the outstanding characteristics of Huck, Jim, and Tom." There are also parallels in theme and in symbolic use of the river.

Thomas, Brook. "Language and Identity in the *Adventures of Huckleberry Finn*." *Mark Twain Journal*, 20 (Winter 1980-1981), 17-21. Reprinted, *ibid.*, 21 (Summer 1982), 7-10.

Lying is a major topic introduced on the first page of *HF*. Finding the language of society false and alien to him, Huck would prefer silence and flight, but he, too, must lie to survive in a world where assertion, speech, clothes, and documents are no proof of identity. Tom Sawyer is at home in this world, "for him stylization is primary," and his readiness to invent complications in freeing Jim parallels society, with its artificial laws, codes, and regulations. Huck would flee all this, but ironically he lives on in a work of fiction.

Tidwell, James Nathan. "Mark Twain's Representation of Negro Speech." *American Speech*, 17 (October 1942), 174-76.

Analysis of the pronunciations in *HF* reveals "honest and sincere" representation: "His failure to systematize his spelling allowed him to write each word as it would sound in a given sentence, and thus he could represent in full detail the nuances of Jim's pronunciation."

Tirumalai, C. K. "Father-Son Relationships in *Huckleberry Finn*." *Exercise Exchange* (Holt, Rinehart and Winston), 12 (November 1964), 22-23.

"The true father-son relationship that develops between Huck and Jim is contrasted not only with the relationship between Huck and his father, but also with the perverted and false father-son relationship between the duke and the king."

Toebasch, Wim. "Der Neger in de Amerikaanse Literatuur" [The Negro in American Literature]. *Vlaamse Gids*, 69 (September 1965), 602-15.

[Source: Abstract in *AES* (1965), 2825.] Notes the important character Jim in *HF*. [In Flemish.]

Torchiana, Donald T. "Will Huck Hang? The Individual and Society in *Huckleberry Finn*." *Mark Twain Journal*, 10 (Winter 1956), 5-8.

After examining the hairball oracle, Jim warns Huck to avoid water and all risks, "'kase it's down in de bills dat you's swyne to git hung"; MT "seldom fails to exploit a lie, a sign, or a conversation as a means of shepherding his flow of narrative." Huck avoids neither water nor risks, and a possible death by hanging is consistent with the book's theme of death and violence. His evasion of social rules and his plans to "light out for the territory" may make him a victim of "the lynch law of the West."

Towers, Tom H. "Love and Power in *Huckleberry Finn*." *Tulane Studies in English*, 23 (1978), 17-37.

Not a romantic idealist, Huck is like MT's other heroes in seeking "a freedom defined not by detachment from the world but by control over it." Like them, he equates freedom with power, but the available forms of power diminish his sense of self and he discovers an alternative in love: "Indeed, I would propose that the essential conflict in the novel is not between Huck and society, but between Huck's own antagonistic urges to power and to love."

Trachtenberg, Alan. "The Form of Freedom in *Adventures of Huckleberry Finn*." *Southern Review*, n.s. 6 (October 1970), 954-71.

"*Huckleberry Finn* became a cultural object of special intensity" as a view of freedom, "the precise negation of all the forces felt as oppressive in the 1950s.... Huck's freedom...requires that he achieve a conscious moral identity," but his role as narrator helps to define him; in any case MT "seriously doubted the possibilities of personal freedom within a social setting." The cost of Huck's freedom and survival is high: "he pays with his chance to grow up."

Trent, W. P., and John Erskine. "Mark Twain and Bret Harte." *Great Writers of America*. (Home University Library of Modern Knowledge), 1912. Pp. 232-50; on MT pp. 243-50.

Harte has greater delicacy, but MT has greater force; MT's honor led him to a lecture tour to repay his debts, while Harte "disappointed his countrymen"; also notes "the tragic decline of Bret Harte's character." MT's humor may be forgotten as tastes change, but *TS* revealed him as "a novelist of the first rank." There is a "tragic contrast between the boy's simple point of view and the things he saw but did not understand"; in *HF* "this note of elemental tragedy is increased until certain passages...would be hard to overmatch in any literature."

Trilling, Lionel. "Introduction." *The Adventures of Huckleberry Finn*. New York: Rinehart, 1948. Pp. v-xviii.

"In form and style *Huckleberry Finn* is an almost perfect work"; even the ending, though weak and too long, is important as a way of returning Huck to his anonymity (pp. xv-xvi). Trilling takes from Eliot's "The Dry Salvages" (in *Four Quartets*) the notion of the river as a god: "Huck himself is the servant of the river-god," this "power which seems to have a mind and will of its own, and...appears to embody a great moral idea" (p. vii). Reprinted in Bradley (1962, 1977), Cardwell (1963), Lettis (1962), and Marks (1959). Trilling published a revised version in *The Liberal Imagination: Essays on Literature and Society*. New York: Viking 1950; reprinted in Scott (1955, 1967).

__________. Ray B. West, and Lyman Bryson. "Mark Twain: *The Adventures of Huckleberry Finn*." George D. Crothers, ed., *Invitation to Learning: English & American Novels*. New York and London: Basic Books, 1966. Pp. 242-51.

One of a series of radio conversations on great novels; laudatory and somewhat general. Notes the terror in the book, and the significance of Huck's Pap. There are four kinds of authority: convention, nature, the supernatural, and (what counts with Huck) affection. There is brief comment on the importance of the language, and a concluding word on Huck's rejection of both convention and of romance: Tom does his rebelling in conventional terms, Huck does not.

Tulip, James. "Huck Finn—The Picaresque Saint." *Balcony/The Syndey Review*, No. 2 (Winter 1965), 13-18.

A broad and provocative criticism of *HF*. "I been there before," the concluding sentence, dramatically involves both Huck and MT, whose "deepest response is, then, to the past even at the moment when he appears to be sending his hero off into a hopeful future....Huck's run for the future is really a race from the past," and his "most vital image" is the lies he tells. They "have a saving effect, but their cause and their content imply a world that is damned: his family are dead, the farm has been sold up, there's smallpox on the raft." It is "the effervescence of the picaresque" that "establishes a moral order in the narrative," but one "which in its very quality of continual moments of release from the past is in no sense a triumph over that past." MT's "imagination is reaching out to a reality far beyond the capacity of Huck's imagination," and "the most dramatic writing in the book is to be found in those passages where Twain 'takes over' from Huck the role of hero-cum-narrator."

Tuttleton, James W. "Twain's Use of Theatrical Traditions in the Old Southwest." *College Language Association Journal*, 8 (December 1964), 190-97.

On the dramatic declaration and the camp meeting, as seen in *HF*. [Source: MHRA *Annual Bibliography* (1964), No. 6589; Abstract in *AES*, 10 (1967), 416.]

Umphlett, Wiley Lee. "The Social Focus of Mark Twain's Photographic Eye in *Huckleberry Finn*." *Proteus*, 1:2 (1984), 50–56.

MT was keenly aware of the literal realism of the photograph, commented on a number of occasions on scenes depicted as precisely as they could have been by the camera, and in *HF* achieved a similar realism both in visual descriptions (stationary and moving) and in catching the authentic voice of his different character types.

Underhill, Irving S. "An Inquiry into Mark Twain's Latest Book! *The Adventures of Huckelberry [sic] Finn*." *Colophon*, Part 6, (1931); 10 pp. (including facsimiles; pages not numbered).

About the copies of the first edition of *HF* shipped to California, and there altered to replace the offensive cut on p. 283. [*See* Sioui, 1962.]

Vales, Robert T. "Thief and Theft in *Huckleberry Finn*." *American Literature*, 37 (January 1966), 420-29.

"Huck has decided to steal Jim, and it is theft and its related synonyms which united all aspects of the novel. It is also through theft that we learn about the nature of man and society."

Vedder, Henry C. *American Writers of To-Day*. New York, Boston, Chicago: Silver, Burdett, 1894. Pp. 94, 124-40.

Vedder's article in the New York *Examiner* for 6 April 1893, here titled "Mark Twain" and augmented by a sketchy biographical introduction (pp. 124-29). Scott reprints the article without the added material in *Selected Criticism* (1955, 1967).

Also see Vedder's "Charles Dudley Warner" (pp. 87-103): "Mr. Samuel L. Clemens has published certain books in serious literature, without in the least persuading the public to take him seriously. Many read *The Prince and the Pauper* through with misgiving, lest a huge jest might after all be concealed beneath the apparently sober tale. They failed to enjoy the story, because they were continually and nervously looking for some hidden snare. It is only when, as 'Mark Twain,' he writes some such trash as *The Adventures of Huckleberry Finn* that this really capable writer can make sure of an appreciative hearing" (p. 94).

Vogelback, Arthur Lawrence. "The Publication and Reception of *Huckleberry Finn* in America." *American Literature*, 11 (November 1939), 260-72.

Chiefly on the chorus of complaint that the book was "vulgar," "coarse," and "inelegant"; also tells of the mutilated cut in the first state. [*See* Sioui, 1962; also see Fischer (1983).]

von Frank, Albert J. "Huck Finn and the Flight From Maturity." *Studies in American Fiction*, 7 (Spring 1979), 1-15.

Huck begins as "a mature man in a little boy's body": he smokes, swears, has his own money, and has been used to coming and going as he pleases; like many adults he is commonsensical and unimaginative. As in Hawthorne's "My Kinsman, Major Molineux," civilization is the place of hypocrisy and evil; but, unlike Robin's, Huck's moral lesson is a discovery of the good, as in finding a good father figure in Jim, and he can grow more child-like and gentle. The much-debated ending contrasts the theme of escape with that of irresponsible evasion, and the slapstick element avoids a tone of gloomy disillusionment. Huck has escaped into "an innocence and a childhood that historically had vanished from a general growing up of America."

Wagenknecht, Edward. "Huckleberry Finn as the Devil's Disciple." *Boston University Studies*, 18 (Spring 1970), 20-24.

On Huck's decision to go to Hell for Jim's freedom: "What he knows as God is only a cruel caricature of God. If this were what God is like, He would deserve no obedience." Religious history is filled with examples of defiance of church and state by "those who truly love God...The Devil's Disciple becomes God's own child" (p. 23).

Wagner, Jeanie. "*Huckleberry Finn* and the History Game." *Mark Twain Journal*, 20 (Winter 1979-1980), 5-10.

Attributes the inappropriateness of the concluding chapters of *HF* to MT's consuming interest during the summer of 1883 in developing a game for teaching historical dates: the conclusion "shows Mark Twain as brilliant but temporarily distracted."

Walcutt, Charles Child. "Freedom Afloat—and Adrift." *Man's Changing Mask: Modes and Methods of Characterization in Fiction*. Minneapolis: University of Minnesota Press, 1966. Pp. 31-34.

"There is no firm theme to be *realized* in the plot; hence the action must turn into melodrama and the characters, having no firm beginnings, do not develop in great problems and decisions but recede into deeper obscurity as the melodramatic conclusion takes over."

Waldhorn, Arthur. "Twain: *The Adventures of Huckleberry Finn*." J. Sherwood Weber, Jules Alan Wein, Arthur Waldhorn, and Arthur Zeiger, eds., *From Homer to Joyce: A Study Guide to Thirty-Six Great Books*. New York: Holt, Rinehart and Winston, 1959. Pp. 244-52.

Includes a survey of the book's critical reputation, "Questions for Study and Discussion," and a short annotated bibliography of critical discussions of MT.

Waldinger, Albert. "Interpreting the Passover Dream: Jim in Traditional Hebrew." *American Notes & Queries*, 22 (November/December 1983), 43–46.

Yehuda Karni's Hebrew translation of *HF* (*Hameorot Huklberi Fin*, Tel Aviv: Omanut, 1928?) draws on traditional Hebrew imagery of oppression and the quest for freedom; among the useful parallels are Jim's gift for prophecy, a fog in Ch. 15 equivalent to the "clouds and thick darkness" that wrapped Mt. Horeb (Sinai) in Deut. 4:11, and the rivers of Near Eastern history. "The source of Jim's journey is . . . ultimately the miracle of theophany far above Miss Watson's Hannibal."

Wallace, John H. "Huckleberry Finn Is Offensive." Washington *Post* (11 April 1982), p. B8.

An administrator at the Mark Twain Intermediate School, Fairfax County (VA) defends banning the book: "'Huckleberry Finn' uses the pejorative term 'nigger' profusely. It speaks of black Americans with implications that they are not honest, they are not as intelligent as whites and they are not human. All this, of course, is meant to be satirical. It is. But at the same time it ridicules blacks. This kind of ridicule is extremely difficult for black youngsters to handle. I maintain that it constitutes mental cruelty, harassment and downright racial intimidation to force black students to sit in a classroom to read this kind of literature about themselves. I read 'Huck Finn' when I was in high school—and I can remember feeling betrayed by the teacher. I felt humiliated and embarrassed. Ten years ago, my oldest son went through the same experience in high school, until I went to talk to the teachers about it; and he lost all interest in English classes." However, Wallace has no objections to having *HF* in a school library and "it's perfectly all right for college class use, especially at the graduate level."

Walsh, William. *The Use of Imagination: Educational Thought and the Literary Mind*. London: Chatto & Windus, 1959.

Huck is a voice of sanity and integrity, in contrast to Tom Sawyer and to the people he meets along the river; the river "represents life unconstrained by artifice, and value uncomplicated by pretence" (p. 145).

Warner, Deane M. "Huck and Holden." *CEA Critic*, 27 (March 1965), 4a-4b.

"I propose to show, through a discussion of *Huckleberry Finn*, *The Red Badge of Courage*, and *The Catcher in the Rye*, the evolution of American reaction to initiation, and how the perspective of pre-initiation innocence is an indication, and even an indictment, of contemporary attitudes."

Warren, Robert Penn. "Bearers of Bad Tidings: Writers and the American Dream." *New York Review of Books*, 22 (20 March 1975), 12-19.

On pp. 12-14 discusses MT's deep embodiment of the tensions of his age and his pessimistic ambivalences, as revealed in *HF*, *CY*, and elsewhere.

———. "Mark Twain." *Southern Review*, n.s. 8 (July 1972), 459-92.

A study of MT's incoherent character and his major works, with particular emphasis on *HF*.

Wasiolek, Edward. "The Structure of Make-Believe: *Huckleberry Finn*." *University of Kansas City Review*, 23 (October 1957), 97-101.

"The river, and life on the river, is fluid, sinuous, unpredictable. The shore, and life on the shore, is still rigid, and predictable," as in the Arkansas crowd's watching the daily spectacle of Boggs's drunkenness and in the feud whose origins are forgotten and which has become ritual; Huck can predict Tom Sawyer's actions and feelings because "Tom's behavior is a regulated show." The controversial ending is consistent with his world and one of grownups: "Both worlds are indifferent to real human situations; both are entranced with the rules of their play-acting."

Watanabe, Toshio. "*The Adventures of Huckleberry Finn* by Mark Twain." *Eigo Seinen* [*The Rising Generation*], 127 (December 1981), 574–75.

Looking through more than ten Japanese translations of *HF*, Mr. Watanabe concludes that it is one of the most difficult works to translate into Japanese. The main difficulties are how to translate first-person colloquial narration, how to show the sense of time going slowly like the Mississippi, and how to translate the word "sivilize." [In Japanese; abstract by Sachiko Hayashi.]

________. "Reading Mark Twain." *Amerika Bungaku Tokuhan* [*American Literature Reader*]. Yuhikaku, 1982. Pp. 92–108.

"One of the greatest characteristics of MT's work is a viewpoint with multiple eyes." He seems to accept the American common sense of the time, but shows the corrupted world. For example, *HF* has three viewpoints: one shows the negative features of the Southern world, one is that of a boy confronting the evils of society, and one is that of innocent nature which tries to unite everything. [In Japanese; abstract by Sachiko Hayashi.]

________. "A Seminar in Mark Twain." *Eigo Seinen* [*The Rising Generation*], 129 (1983): 24–26, 77–79, 131–33, 180–82.

In each of four parts, treats *HF* from a different perspective. (1) Loneliness: The basis is the loneliness of Huck and of nature, of the Mississippi, as well. The key words are "lonesome" and "lonesomeness." Huck is so lonely he is even afraid of the unknown world. (2) Conscience: Huck's conscience does not lead him to the moral life, but forces the common values of the outer world on him. In judging, Huck relies not on this conscience, but on his intuition or feeling. Mr. Watanabe says this judgment through one's feeling is a characteristic of American literature. (3) Ending: after examining various criticisms of the ending of *HF*, he picks up John Seelye's *The True Adventures of Huckleberry Finn* and suggests that we should not confine ourselves to criticism of a specific part. (4) After Mark Twain: about Sherwood Anderson. [In Japanese; abstract by Sachiko Hayashi.]

Weaver, Thomas, and Merline A. Williams. "Mark Twain's Jim: Identity as an Index to Cultural Attitudes." *American Literary Realism*, 13 (Spring, 1980), 19-29.

A sociological study, tracing Jim's successive portrayal by the critics as "a kind, simple, child-like being," a Noble Savage, the product of social circumstances, a family man, a Christ figure, etc. Here, Jim is depicted as "far from the innocent victim...." He has "an active impulse to chicanery which parallels the artful subterfuge of Huck Finn, Tom Sawyer, or any of the other notorious tricksters and confidence men appearing throughout Twain's fiction."

Webb, Howard W., Jr. "Mark Twain and Ring Lardner." *Mark Twain Journal*, 11 (Summer 1960), 13-15.

A comparison between the two, showing no evidence of influence or other contact except for Lardner's statement in the *New York Times Magazine* (25 March 1917, p. 44) that he felt George Ade had superseded MT as our national humorist and Booth Tarkington's *Penrod* had replaced *Huckleberry Finn*: "I've known Booth Tarkington's boys, and I've not known those of Mark Twain. Mark Twain's boys are tough and poverty-stricken and they belong to a period very different from that of our own boys."

Wecter, Dixon. [Introduction.] *The Adventures of Huckleberry Finn*. New York: Harper's, 1948.

[Source: Asselineau (1954), No. 1143; quotes Wecter's statement that "its real hero is Nigger Jim"—a striking realization for a later generation becoming aware of racial injustice.]

Welland, Dennis S. R. "Mark Twain the Great Victorian." *Chicago Review*, 9 (Fall 1955), 101-09.

"In *Huckleberry Finn* Mark Twain did something that Arnold never achieved with equal success: he fused, for once, art and morality in such a way that the morality is the inevitable outcome of the characters and situations of the story." Also treats *CY*, *IA*, and MT's views of the Byron scandal.

Wells, Anna Mary. "Huck Finn, Tom Sawyer, and Samuel Clemens." *Publications of the Modern Language Association*, 87 (October 1972), 1130-31.

A reply to Judith Fetterley's article in the January *PMLA*: Huck Finn is not Mark Twain or Samuel Clemens; what he "finally sees in Tom is unendurable, and if the function of art is to make us endure the unendurable, it is still hard to do it in a book for boys." Huck's decision to abandon civilization was not that of Clemens, who in his letters to Howells "was clearly identifying with Tom."

Wells, Arvin R. "Huck Finn and Holden Caulfield: The Situation of the Hero." *Ohio University Review*, 2 (1960), 31-42.

Examines in the books by MT and Salinger "the marked dissimilarities as contributory to the ultimately very different effects produced by these two novels," to reveal "the essential qualities and fundamental attitudes found in each" and emphasize "the fact that these novels are, after all, the products of two unique creative imaginations responding to quite different milieux."

Wells, David M. "More on the Geography of *Huckleberry Finn*." *South Atlantic Bulletin*, 38 (November 1973), 82-86.

Suggests localities for "the ferry landing near the steamboat wreck"; "the Grangerford estate, site of the feud"; "the creek where the duke and the king appear"; "Pokeville, site of the camp meeting"; "Bricksville, site of the Royal Nonesuch"; "the Wilkses' village and Pikesville." At times MT was careless in representing distances. P. 83 is a map of the river from "St. Petersburg" to "Pikesville."

Wendell, Barrett. *A Literary History of America*. New York: Scribner's, and London: T. Fisher Unwin, 1901.

Comparatively little on MT, but only because the book emphasizes authors no longer living. Compares MT to Franklin and Irving, despite lesser grace, for his sober confusion of fact and nonsense (pp. 101, 173, 508), and says that his power "would have been exceptional anywhere" (p. 513). *HF*, with its dialect, is a "masterpiece, that amazing Odyssey of the Mississippi," the product of "an artistic conscience as strenuous as Irving's, or Poe's, or Hawthorne's" (p. 477); it is "a book which in certain moods one is disposed for all its eccentricity to call the most admirable work of literary art as yet produced on this continent" (p. 503).

Werge, Thomas. "Huck, Jim and Forty Dollars." *Mark Twain Journal*, 13 (Winter 1965-1966), 15-16.

The generosity of the slave-hunters who give Huck forty dollars, which he promptly shares with Jim (Chapter 16) underscores Huck's sense of guilt in not betraying Jim; it contrasts with the action of the King, who sells Jim for forty dollars and keeps the money for himself. The concluding episode repeats the theme, when Tom Sawyer gives Jim forty dollars for his trouble as a prisoner. "This forty dollars is freely given and freely accepted, and this act of generosity recalls and reaffirms Huck's values while denying those predatory hunters whose lust for money is surpassed only by their absolute moral corruption."

Wermuth, Paul C. "Santayana and *Huckleberry Finn*." *New England Quarterly*, 36 (March 1963), 79-82.

Summarizes Santayana's "Tom Sawyer and Don Quixote" (*Mark Twain Quarterly*, 9 [Winter 1952], 1-3), observing that from all other evidence "Santayana seems to have been monumentally uninterested in Twain." Having been given a copy of *HF* by Cyril Clemens, he dutifully read it; but "in his wonderfully polite and subtle way," Santayana seems to be saying between the lines: "Well, here I am, an old man; I have taken my precious time to read this man's books because everybody said I should; and all I found was that I was right in the first place not to have read them years ago."

Wexelblatt, Robert. "The Unintelligible Hero." *Denver Quarterly*, 14 (Fall 1979), 49-65.

Among five types of unintelligible heroes, very briefly mentions Huck (pp. 59-60) as an example of "the hero who tries to be unintelligible...a poseur."

Wexman, Virginia. "The Role of Structure in *Tom Sawyer* and *Huckleberry Finn*." *American Literary Realism*, 6 (Winter 1973), 1-11.

In the dual world of *TS*, comic incidents involving boyish innocence prepare the way for incidents of a more somber kind, as in Tom's playing *Robin* Hood with *Joe* Harper before the murder of Dr. *Robin*son by Injun *Joe*, the search for treasure by Tom and Huck in a haunted house soon found by Injun Joe and a companion, and Huck's following the two villains through a maze of streets reminiscent of the cave in which the village children had been playing. The alternation of light and dark scenes "helps to preserve our sense of the comic in this book" and permits a conclusion which, "in true comic spirit, reaffirms social unity." *HF* takes a different course, as Huck's imagination is educated by experience, and his "creativity cannot be harmless as Tom's had been for he finds himself in a world where innocence is immoral rather than merely premoral." Again, MT parallels incidents from the dark and light worlds, but here the effect is to heighten the portraits of human depravity.

White, Ray Lewis, ed. *Sherwood Anderson's Memoirs: A Critical Edition*. Chapel Hill: The University of North Carolina Press, 1969.

Passim on MT (indexed), whom Anderson admired; on p. 342, Anderson calls *HF* "that amazingly beautiful book."

Whiting, B. J. "Guyuscutus, Royal Nonesuch and Other Hoaxes." *Southern Folklore Quarterly*, 8 (December 1944), 251-74.

A general discussion of practical jokes in the old Southwest, with some space devoted to several "Guyuscutus" monster hoaxes and a brief discussion of the connection to "The Royal Nonesuch" in *HF*. [*See* Graves, 1960.]

Will, George F. "Huck at a Hundred." *Newsweek*, 105 (18 February 1985), 92.

"Huck's story resonates in America's heart because it is about freedom understood in a distinctively American way, as the absence of social restraints, and obedience to the promptings of a pure heart." Will praises MT's language, and dismisses those who find *HF* racially offensive as "ninnies." He draws on the perspectives of T.S. Eliot and Leo Marx, and compares Huck to Jay Gatsby, whose "story, like Huck's, is about integrity of personality."

Williams, Kenny J. "*Adventures of Huckleberry Finn*; or, Mark Twain's Racial Ambiguity." *Mark Twain Journal*, 22 (Fall 1984), 38–42.

MT recognized and depicted the racism of his time but did not wholly rid himself of it; for all the merits of *HF* there is also much to deplore in the sometimes condescending view taken toward black people and the pervasive use of the word "nigger." *HF* has often been banned in schools and libraries, formerly because it might corrupt the young and now on the ground that it is "racist and degrading." But in fact *HF* reflects existing attitudes and rightly suggests "that the fates and fortunes of the races are so closely intertwined that one cannot exist without the other. Either consciously or unconsciously, Twain produced a classic statement that weighs the nation in the balance. He described an America that was his and an America that is ours. To ban the novel is to condemn the messenger for the message."

Williams, Philip. "Huckleberry Finn and the Dialectic of History." *Essays and Studies in English Language and Literature* (Tohoku Gakuin University, Sendai, Japan), 51-52 (1967), 59-98.

[Source *MLA Bibliography* (1971), No. 8016.]

Williams, Stanley T. "Introduction." *The Adventures of Huckleberry Finn*. New York: Dodd, Mead, 1953 (unpaged).

Despite its faults *HF* depicts its age and is a vital and serious book. The reader must beware too abstract a reading, and "we must not forget the distrust of Mark Twain, with his simple, earthy tastes in reading, of all symbolism."

Wilson, James D. "*Adventures of Huckleberry Finn:* From Abstraction to Humanity." *Southern Review*, 10 (January 1974), 80-94.

"The pragmatic Huck encounters a series of ideal codes of behavior" of the Widow Douglas, Tom Sawyer, his father, the Grangerfords, and Sherburn, "before discovering each one inadequate to meet the demands of his intuitive moral nature, his environment, and his companions." Ironically, in his personal life MT could put abstract intellectual concepts ahead of human needs, as in the painful destruction of his wife's religious faith.

Wolfe, George H., ed. *Faulkner: Fifty Years After "The Marble Faun."* University, AL: The University of Alabama Press, 1976. Passim on MT (indexed).

A collection of papers delivered at a Faulkner symposium; a few of Faulkner's statements on MT, published elsewhere, are quoted here. Includes his 1922 criticism of MT as "a hack writer who would not have been considered fourth rate in Europe, who tricked out a few of the old proven 'sure fire' literary skeletons with sufficient local color to intrigue the superficial and the lazy" (*The Mississippian*, 17 March). Faulkner later raised his estimate of MT, ranking *HF* as a competitor with *Moby Dick* as "the greatest single book in American Literature"; he preferred *Moby Dick* only because "*Huckleberry Finn* is a complete controlled effort and *Moby Dick* was still an attempt that didn't quite come off, it was bigger than one human being could do" (quoting from Gwynn and Blotner, eds., *Faulkner in the University*, Charlottesville, 1959, p. 15).

Wood, Clement. *More Adventures of Huckleberry Finn*. Cleveland and New York: World Publishing Company, 1940.

Depicts the growing Huck as taller, and matured in character and leadership. He and Tom go into the Indian Territory to rescue Tom's cousins Tillie and Marcia from the Pawnees.

Wood, Grant. "My Debt to Mark Twain." *Mark Twain Quarterly*, 2 (Fall 1937), 6, 14, 24.

TS and *HF* were boyhood favorites he reread until they were tattered;

Wood liked the adventure and the sense of fairness. "My favorite was *Huckleberry Finn*; probably, I realize now, because of its richness in sense impressions of the type that made my own boyhood so vivid."

Woodward, Robert H. "Teaching *Huckleberry Finn* to Foreign Students." *Mark Twain Journal*, 13 (Winter 1966-1967), 5-7.

Students from the Republic of Mali, West Africa, responded well to selections from *HF* in a class at San Jose State College.

Woolf, Leonard. "Mark Twain," *Nation and Athenaeum*, 36 (26 September 1925), 765.

A review of *The Florida Edition of Mark Twain* (Chatto & Windus); makes estimates of *TA* ("first-rate journalism"), *P&P* (betrays "a commonness and tawdriness, a lack of sensitiveness, which do not matter to the impetuous appetite of youth, but which cannot be ignored by the more discriminating and exacting taste of middle-age"), and *HF*; this, "in humour as in everything else, is far the best thing Mark Twain wrote. Its freshness, gusto, exuberant vitality are astonishing," especially under the influence of the river; there is a falling-off after the King and Duke come aboard. Woolf feels that MT's humor is losing its old charm, and ranks it below that of "Mr. Dooley" (Finley Peter Dunne).

Wouk, Herman. "America's Voice Is Mark Twain's." San Francisco *Chronicle* (5 August 1956), "This World" section, p. 20.

MT, "the archetype of American writers," is an exact observer whose novels are "extravagant romances." In *HF* he "established at a stroke the colloquial style which has swept American literature, and indeed spilled over into world literature." *HF* is "a jerky, uneven, patchwork tale...jerry-built....yet it is the crown of our literature." The modern writers "are hardly conceivable except coming after Twain." Reprinted in *Twainian*, 20 (November-December 1961), 4; 21 (January-February 1962), 4.

Wyatt, Bryant N. "*Huckleberry Finn* and the Art of Ernest Hemingway." *Mark Twain Journal*, 13 (Summer 1967), 1-8.

"Aside from the purely stylistic affinities between *Finn* and the writings of Hemingway, there are certain affinities of subject-matter," among them the opposition of reality and illusion, the loss of illusion, the use of superstition, the symbolic use of rivers, and self-realization through experience.

Yagi, Toshio. "*The Adventures of Huckleberry Finn* by Mark Twain." *America No Bungaku* [*American Literature*]. Nanundo, 1983. Pp. 156–63.

Tom's imagination is false and Huck's adventure is genuine. *HF* is the story of a boy's escape to nature from civilization, life in town, and Tom Sawyer. [In Japanese; abstract by Sachiko Hayashi.]

Yates, Norris W. "The 'Counter-Conversion' of Huckleberry Finn." *American Literature*, 32 (March 1960), 1-10.

On the phenomenon of conversion to and away from religion—in Huck's case to "wickedness" as an alternative to betrayal of Jim.

Yoshida, Hiroshige. *"Huckleberry Finn" Kenkyu—Kenkyu Note, Style, Glossary [A Study on "Huckleberry Finn"—Notes, Style, and Glossary]*. Tokyo: Shinozaki Shorin, 1980.

Instead of a thematic approach, the author discusses the genesis of *Huckleberry Finn* chronologically. (The novel was not written at a stretch.) Then he discusses stylistic traits and dialectal elements. Glossary is 93 pages. With index. (In Japanese; abstract by Yasuo Hashiguchi.)

__________. *"Huckleberry Finn Ko*—Phelps Farm Episode Ni Kansuru Ichi Kaishaku" ("Remarks on *Huckleberry Finn*—an interpretation of the Phelps Farm Episode"). *Eigo Seinen [The Rising Generation]* (Tokyo), 114 (1 February 1968), 84-86.

In the face of the gap between the Mississippi as it had been and as it was, MT had no other choice but to make a burlesque out of the Phelps farm episode, just as he had the Mysterious Stranger say, "For your race...has unquestionably one really effective weapon—laughter." (In Japanese; abstract by Yasuo Hashiguchi.)

Young, Philip. "Adventures of Huckleberry Finn." *Ernest Hemingway*. New York and Toronto: Rinehart, 1952. Pp. 181-212.

Compares Huck with Nick Adams, another outsider who cannot accept the values the world has presented him; both are honest and sensitive, lacking in humor and intensely serious (p. 202). Hemingway grew up as a young Huck Finn. [Unfortunately, Young draws somewhat trustingly on MT's *Autobiography* as a source of much of his biographical information.]

__________. *Ernest Hemingway: A Reconsideration*. University Park: Pennsylvania State University Press, 1966.

[Source: pp. 228-29, on *HF*, reprinted in Simpson (1968), pp. 113-114.] Describes Huck as hurt by his experiences, and not amused even by such nominally funny encounters as that with the Duke and Dauphin: "But Huck is not amused; they disgust him with mankind in general. He is wounded, and bitter, and suffering from both insomnia and nightmare, and he finally rebels." Faced with a decision on whether to betray Jim, "off on his own, exposed to the violence and evil of society as a whole, he renounces it....If it is good, he is wicked. And if it aims for heaven, he will go elsewhere."

__________. "*Huckleberry Finn*: The Little Lower Layer." *Three Bags Full: Essays in American Fiction*. New York: Harcourt Brace Jovanovich, 1972. Pp. 136-153.

HF represents a national dream of escape, but Huck is wounded by his experience on shore and has grown up out of MT's control; it is for this reason that the story is turned over to Tom Sawyer.

Yu, Beongcheon. "The Ending of *The Adventures of Huckleberry Finn*." *Phoenix* (The English Literature Society, Korea University, Seoul), 2 (Spring 1967), 23-30.

The conclusion must be read in conjunction with the episodes of the King and Duke, who "lie deliberately for money while Tom and Huck lie for anything but money." There is a thematic balance, and "the last extravaganza is an account of the retaliation children are capable of in the adult world."

Ziegler, Edward. "Huck Finn at 100." *Reader's Digest*, 126 (February 1985), 97–101.

A useful, accurate account for the general reader, noting early objections to *HF* as unrefined, more recent ones charging racism—which Ziegler denies. In addition to his own praise for the book and a very brief plot-summary, he cites the critical adulation *HF* has received from Hemingway and others.

Zimmer, Giles. "Grangerford and Cory: Similar Creations." *Mark Twain Journal*, 21 (Spring 1983), 59-60.

Compares the characters described in Chapter 18 of *HF* and Edwin Arlington Robinson's "Richard Cory": there are strong (though probably coincidental) similarities in the elegance which initially strikes the observer, their eventual failure, and the language and imagery used in describing them.

Zuckert, Catherine H. "Law and Nature in *The Adventures of Huckleberry Finn.*" *Proteus*, 1:2 (1984), 27–35.

HF "has thematic as much as literary unity ... Huck's return to society is a necessary, even logical conclusion of his attempt to find freedom in nature. This return constitutes as important a part of Twain's realism as his careful presentation of the various dialects, because, as he shows, it is not possible to attain freedom through flight." Unlike a Cooper novel, *HF* has a clear structure and does not misrepresent the state of nature. Huck and Jim depend on civilization for their equipment and some of their food, Huck tries to protect his property from Pap through the law, and in the end it is through law and religion that Jim is freed. Tom and Huck are dangerously mistaken to "equate happiness and freedom with existence outside the law." Lawlessness is ugly, whether in the swindles of the King and the Duke, the murderous feud of the Grangerfords and Shepherdsons, or the cold-blooded shooting of old Boggs by Colonel Sherburn. Having withdrawn from the protection of law Huck repeatedly appeals to the compassion of others, but such compassion is limited by fear, greed, convention, and the desire for distinction. It is only through law that life or property can be secure, but MT "clearly doubts that people like Huck will ever learn."

[Television adaptation of *Huckleberry Finn*, forthcoming on Public Broadcasting Service.]

The Great Amwell Company, which previously filmed *LOM*, "The Campaign that Failed," *MS*, *IA*, and *PW* for Public Broadcasting, has produced an adaptation of *HF* in four one-hour segments. Care was taken to capture the full meaning of *HF*, not just the highlights. Writer Guy Gallo had the advice of such respected MT scholars as Walter Blair and Hamlin Hill for his teleplay exploring the more adult themes; material such as the "raftsmen's episode" has not been filmed before. Producers are William Perry and Jane Iredale; Peter H. Hunt directed; the cast includes Jim Dale, Frederick

Forrest, Lillian Gish, Bernard Hughes, Richard Kiley, Butterfly McQueen, Geraldine Page, and Sada Thompson. Huck and Jim are played by Patrick Day and actor-playwright Samm-Art Williams, respectively. Advance views of certain scenes shown at the Washington meeting of the Modern Language Association (1984) show that this adaptation is visually magnificent, and in its attitude toward *HF* it is far different from the saccharine treatments of the past. It will appear on Public Broadcasting in 1986, and will be shown in countries around the world.

[Television Debate.] "Freeman Reports," Cable News Network (14 March 1985).

Shelley Fisher Fishkin of Yale has recently authenticated an 1885 MT letter to the dean of Yale Law School on paying the expenses of a black student (for text see McDowell, 1985). Here she talks with John H. Wallace, who has been trying since 1972 to ban *HF* from highschool classrooms; Sandi Freeman moderates. Calling himself "the greatest black authority in the country," Wallaces dismisses blacks with opposing views as subservient to white money (as in the case of an NAACP official) or "brainwashed" (as in the case of a black highschool student who telephoned the program from Richmond, CA to say that she had recently read *HF* in an advanced English class, felt she had learned an important moral lesson, and did not feel inferior or injured). Wallace repeats essentially what he has said elsewhere, dismissing *HF* as "racist trash," although he would be willing to see it kept in the schools for optional outside reading and "I really have no problem with this book being used at the college level." He contends that too many teachers are inept or racist. Professor Fishkin argues that both MT and *HF* are anti-racist, that good teaching and informed debate are essential, and that children must learn the lessons of history; for her own children the painful history is that of the Holocaust, in which two of their great-aunts died. She makes a strong case for encouraging a diversity of opinion and more sophisticated discussion.

[Television Debate on *HF*.] "Nightline," ABC-TV, 4 February 1985. [Transcripts $2.00 from Journal Graphics, Box 234, Ansonia Station, New York, NY 10023.]

Jeff Greenfield in Chicago and Ted Koppel in New York interviewed Meshach Taylor, who was currently playing Jim in a stage *HF* at Chicago's Goldman Theater; Nat Hentoff, who had written a number of times in defense of *HF* against those who would ban it; and John H. Wallace, "researcher for the Chicago School Board who has been fighting to ban *Huckleberry Finn* from schools since 1972" [including the Mark Twain Intermediate School, Fairfax, VA]. Wallace condemns *HF* as "racist trash" harmful to black children, but Taylor says he has played the part of Jim in performances abroad and all over the U.S., and many times before school groups, and has found students capable of learning to understand what he says he himself found "one of the best indictments against racism that I had ever read." Hentoff has visited classes over the years, and has observed *HF* being taught: it is difficult at first, "and the kids will say, 'yeah, when I started that ... it was pretty awful,' but then they begin to read the book, and see what's happening, and what happens to them then is what is called education."